AF148124

Lecture Notes of the Institute for Computer Sciences, Social Informatics and Telecommunications Engineering   605

The LNICST series publishes ICST's conferences, symposia and workshops.
LNICST reports state-of-the-art results in areas related to the scope of the Institute.
The type of material published includes

- Proceedings (published in time for the respective event)
- Other edited monographs (such as project reports or invited volumes)

LNICST topics span the following areas:

- General Computer Science
- E-Economy
- E-Medicine
- Knowledge Management
- Multimedia
- Operations, Management and Policy
- Social Informatics
- Systems

Hsiao-Hwa Chen · Weixiao Meng
Editors

Wireless and Satellite Systems

14th EAI International Conference, WiSATS 2024
Harbin, China, August 23–25, 2024
Proceedings, Part I

 Springer

Editors
Hsiao-Hwa Chen ⓘ
National Cheng Kung University
Tainan, Taiwan

Weixiao Meng ⓘ
Harbin Institute of Technology
Harbin, China

ISSN 1867-8211 ISSN 1867-822X (electronic)
Lecture Notes of the Institute for Computer Sciences, Social Informatics
and Telecommunications Engineering
ISBN 978-3-031-86195-6 ISBN 978-3-031-86196-3 (eBook)
https://doi.org/10.1007/978-3-031-86196-3

Preface

We are delighted to introduce the proceedings of the 14th European Alliance for Innovation International Conference on Wireless and Satellite Systems (EAI WiSATS 2024). This conference brought together researchers, developers and practitioners around the world who explore the latest advancements in wireless and satellite communication systems. The theme of EAI WiSATS 2024 was "The means of using the wireless and satellite services directly to the user for personal communications, multimedia and location identification".

The technical program of EAI WiSATS 2024 consisted of 42 full papers and 20 short papers in oral presentation sessions at the main conference tracks. The papers were selected from 182 submissions following a single-blind review process where reviewers were responsible for 2 papers each on average. The conference tracks were: Track 1 – Wireless Communication; Track 2 – Satellite Communications. Aside from the high-quality technical paper presentations, the technical program also featured three keynote speeches and two technical workshops. The three keynote speakers were Nei Kato from Tohoku University, Japan, Shiwen Mao from Auburn University, USA, and Tony Q.S. Quek from Singapore University of Technology and Design, Singapore. The two workshops organized were AI for Network and Network for AI (AIN&NAI) and AI in Future Satellite Communications (AIFSatCom). The AIN&NAI workshop aimed to introduce the use of AI to optimize and enhance network performance and the use of network infrastructure to support and improve AI applications. The AIFSatCom workshop aimed to gain insights into key challenges and design criteria for employing AI technologies to develop and implement future satellite-related services and applications.

Coordination with the steering chair, Imrich Chlamtac, was essential for the success of the conference. We sincerely appreciate his constant support and guidance. It was also a great pleasure to work with such an excellent organizing committee team for their hard work in organizing and supporting the conference. In particular, the Technical Program Committee, led by our TPC Co-Chairs Min Sheng, Peter Han Joo Chong and Shuyi Chen, completed the peer-review process of technical papers and made a high-quality technical program. We are also grateful to Conference Manager Lenka Vatrtová for her support and to all the authors who submitted their papers to the EAI WiSATS 2024 conference and workshops.

We strongly believe that the EAI WiSATS conference provides a good forum for all researchers, developers and practitioners to discuss all science and technology aspects that are relevant to wireless and satellite communication systems. We also expect that future EAI WiSATS conferences will be as successful and stimulating, as indicated by the contributions presented in this volume.

Hsiao-Hwa Chen
Weixiao Meng

Organization

Steering Committee

Imrich Chlamtac   University of Trento, Italy
Weixiao Meng   Harbin Institute of Technology, China

Organizing Committee

General Co-chairs

Hsiao-Hwa Chen   National Cheng Kung University, Taiwan
Weixiao Meng   Harbin Institute of Technology, China

TPC Chairs and Co-chairs

Min Sheng   Xidian University, China
Peter Han Joo Chong   Auckland University of Technology, New Zealand
Shuyi Chen   Harbin Institute of Technology, China

Local Chairs

Chenguang He   Harbin Institute of Technology, China
Shuai Han   Harbin Institute of Technology, China
Liang Ye   Harbin Institute of Technology, China
Lin Ma   Harbin Institute of Technology, China
Chengzhao Shan   Harbin Institute of Technology, China

Workshops Chair

Chenxiao Jiang   University of Science and Technology of China, China

Publicity and Social Media Chairs

Ce Zheng   Télécom Paris, France
Yifan Qin   Harbin Engineering University, China

Publications Chair

Qian Chen   University of Hong Kong, Hong Kong SAR,
                                   China

Web Chairs

Zhiqiang Li   Harbin Institute of Technology, China
Xianye Ben   Shandong University, China

Technical Program Committee

Ruofei Ma   Harbin Institute of Technology, China
Deyue Zou   Dalian University of Technology, China
Sai Xu   Northwestern Polytechnical University, China
Yiliang Liu   Xi´an Jiaotong University, China
Xiqing Liu   Beijing University of Posts and
                                   Telecommunications, China
Guodong Li   Harbin University of Science and Technology,
                                   China
Yang Qiu   Zhuhai College of Science and Technology, China
Xuewen Luo   Harbin Institute of Technology, China
Tianyu Zhao   Harbin Institute of Technology, China
Yang Li   Harbin Institute of Technology, China
Wenbin Sun   Northwestern Polytechnical University, China
Jichong Guo   Suzhou University of Science and Technology,
                                   China
Chunpeng Liu   Harbin Engineering University, China

Contents – Part I

Physical Layer

Contents – Part II

Satellite Communications

A Beam Hopping Algorithm Based on Multi-objective Optimization in LEO Satellite Systems

Weizhong Zhang, Dezhi Li, Zhenyong Wang$^{(\boxtimes)}$, and Qing Guo

School of Electronics and Information, Songjiang Laboratory, Harbin Institute of Technology, Harbin 150001, China
ZYWang@hit.edu.cn

Abstract. The limited onboard beam resources bring great challenges to low earth orbit (LEO) satellite communication systems. In addition, there are lots of difficulties in satisfying the nonuniform traffic requirements. At present, multi-beam satellite systems have the ability to solve the problem through utilizing beam hopping (BH) technology, which increases the system throughput by effectively scheduling beam resources. This paper proposes a BH algorithm based on multi-objective optimization, which takes into account metrics including traffic distribution, frequency multiplexing distance, time slot allocation and so on when designing BH patterns. Simulation results illustrate that the proposed algorithm performs well in throughput and average delay.

Keywords: Satellite Communication · Beam Hopping · Resource Allocation

1 Introduction

Low earth orbit (LEO) satellite communication systems are becoming more and more important in the 6th generation (6G) [1]. Due to the characteristic of seamless coverage and low construction cost, a number of commercial companies have constructed their own LEO constellations, such as SpaceX, OneWeb and so on [2]. However, the nonuniformity spatial and temporal distributions of traffic requirements cause challenges to make full use of the limited onboard resources [3]. On this condition, beam hopping (BH) technology has been proposed to effectively utilize the resources by time division multiplexing. Therefore, it is necessary to optimize the BH technology in LEO multibeam satellite (MBS) communication systems [4].

Reference [5] proposed a BH scheme based on genetic algorithm to improve the capacity of LEO systems, and simulation results illustrate the superior performance when comparing to systems without BH. Similarly, reference [6] and [7] also reveal the advantages of applying the BH technology to LEO systems. In addition, cochannel interference (CCI) could be suppressed to a certain extent by certain BH schemes. More specifically, reference [8] combined BH with precoding technology to mitigate

© ICST Institute for Computer Sciences, Social Informatics and Telecommunications Engineering 2025
Published by Springer Nature Switzerland AG 2025. All Rights Reserved
H.-H. Chen and W. Meng (Eds.): WiSATS 2024, LNICST 605, pp. 3–12, 2025.
https://doi.org/10.1007/978-3-031-86196-3_1

CCI caused by too short cochannel multiplexing distance. And frequency reuse scheme was considered in [9] when applying BH technology, however, although CCI could be eliminated through spatial isolation, the overall capacity of the system decreased because of lower resource utilization rate. A joint optimization of spectrum and power resources BH strategy was proposed in [10], and this scheme could not only increase the system throughput, but also satisfy the traffic demands of users as much as possible.

Currently, the resource allocation of LEO systems is almost based on terrestrial traffic requests, where the single-objective optimization of a certain resource will be carried out. However, an effective BH scheme should allocate multidimensional resources at the same time, which means it is necessary to consider various optimization objectives and constraints when designing BH algorithms. Therefore, this paper proposes a beam hopping algorithm based on multi objective optimization (MOBH) for LEO satellite systems, in which communication resources are divided into three dimensions including time, frequency, and beam. And the performances on throughput ratio and average delay are analyzed at the end of this article.

The rest of this paper is organized as follows. Section 2 describes the system model of LEO satellite systems with BH. Section 3 formulates the BH optimization problem and elaborates the solutions. The performance evaluation is presented in Sect. 4. Section 5 presents the conclusions.

2   System Model

This section presents a LEO satellite communication scenario with beam hopping and describes the traffic distribution statistics.

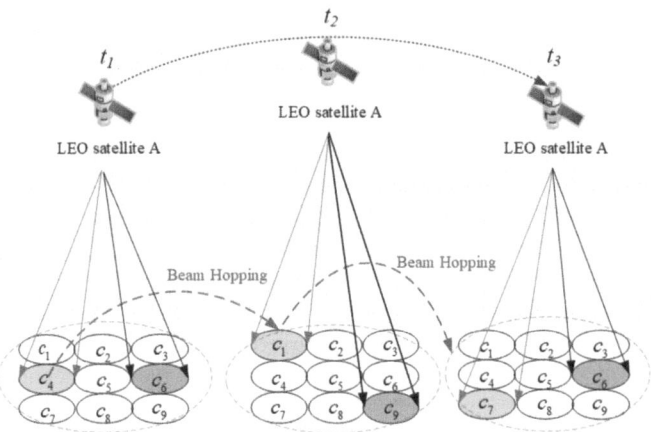

Fig. 1. LEO beam hopping satellite communication scenario

2.1   System Scenario

The system scenario is shown in Fig. 1, where every user can get service by accessing the nearest satellite. The LEO satellite can generate L_{max} beams simultaneously and allocate them to the user region which is divided into N cells. Assuming that b_i and c_i represent beam i and cell i respectively, and user j in c_i is defined as u_{ij}.

2.2 Traffic Distribution

The nonuniform traffic distribution characteristic of the proposed communication scenario is mainly caused by the random location distribution of users. Denoting the coordinate of u_{ij} is represented as a vector (x_{ij}, y_{ij}), and assuming it follows the two dimension normal distribution, then the probability density function can be expressed as follows.

$$f(x_{ij}, y_{ij}) = \frac{1}{2\pi\sigma_1\sigma_2} \exp\left\{-\frac{1}{2}\left[\frac{(x_{ij} - \mu_1)^2}{\sigma_1^2} + \frac{(y_{ij} - \mu_2)^2}{\sigma_2^2}\right]\right\} \tag{1}$$

where μ_1 and μ_2 represent expectation while σ_1 and σ_2 stand for variance.

The traffic demands of u_{ij} and c_i can be expressed as R_{ij} and R_i respectively, and both of them are functions of (x_{ij}, y_{ij}). We define T_i as the total throughput that c_i can obtain from the system, and it is related to the bandwidth W and transmission power P of the LEO satellite.

3 MOBH Algorithm

3.1 Frequency Multiplexing Distance Calculation

To improve spectral efficiency, full frequency reuse strategy should be applied in the proposed system. However, when beams owning the same frequency provide service for nearby cells, it is obvious that significant interference will be generated. Therefore, frequency multiplexing distance should be controlled properly to improve the signal to interference plus noise (SINR). The cochannel interference between LEO satellite beams is shown in Fig. 2.

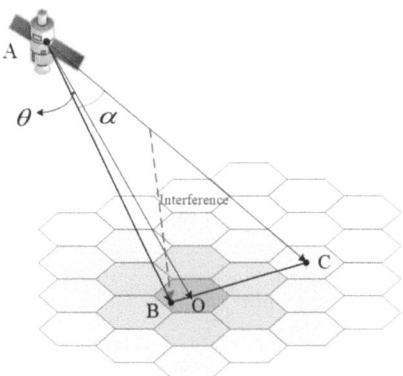

Fig. 2. Co-channel interference between LEO satellite beams

The antenna gain of the satellite is expressed as

$$G = G_0 \left[\frac{J_1(\mu)}{2\mu} + 36 \frac{J_3(\mu)}{\mu^3} \right]^2 \tag{2}$$

where $\mu = 2.07123\sin\theta/\sin(\theta_{3dB})$, and θ is the angle between AB and AO. θ_{3dB} is the half beam angle. G_0 represents the maximum gain when the off axis angle is zero. $J_1(\mu)$ and $J_3(\mu)$ are the first order Bessel function and the third order Bessel function respectively. Considering the interference from beam C, SINR of users located in cell O is derived as

$$\gamma_O = \frac{EIRP_t G_t(\alpha) G_r(0)(\lambda/4\pi r)^2}{N + EIRP_t G_t(\theta) G_r(0)(\lambda/4\pi r)^2} \tag{3}$$

where γ_O represents the maximum SINR of users in cell O and $EIRP_t$ is the equivlent isotropically radiated power of the satellite. $G_t(\alpha)$ and $G_t(\theta)$ is the useful antenna gain and interference antenna gain respectively. Simulation can be executed according to the parameters given in table 1.

Table 1. Antenna parameters of the LEO satellite

Parameters	Notation	Value
Beam radius of satellite	r	12 km
Height of satellite	H	550 km
Antenna efficiency	η	0.55
Half beam angle	θ_{3dB}	3.5°
Antenna aperture	D	0.1 m

The relationship between SINR and multiplexing distance are shown in Fig. 3.

Figure 3 illustrates that with the increase of multiplexing distance, SINR shows an upward trend. When the distance goes up to $3r$, SINR reaches a plateau and maintains the same level at 21 dB, which is close to SNR. Therefore, the distance between two different beams should be larger than $3r$ during the same time slot.

3.2 Time Slot Allocation

By allocating time slots to different beams of the satellite, traffic requirements of users should be satisfied as much as possible. The optimization problem is proposed as follow.

$$
\begin{aligned}
P_1 : & \min \sum_{i=1}^{N} |R_i - T_i|^2 \\
& s.t. \, C_1 : T_i \leq R_i \\
& C_2 : \sum_{i=1}^{N} M_i \leq L_{\max} Z \\
& C_3 : M_i \geq 0
\end{aligned} \tag{4}
$$

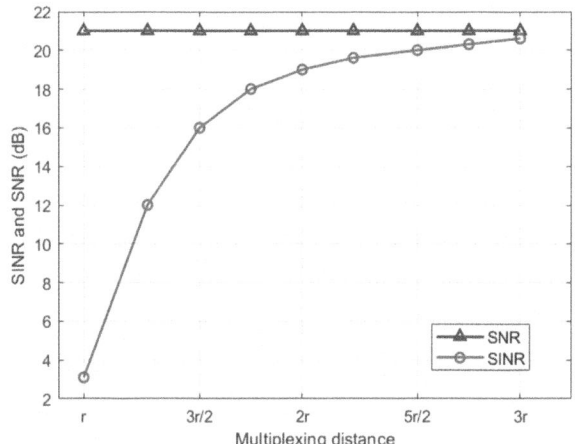

Fig. 3. Evaluation on frequency multiplexing distance

where M_i represents the number of time slots allocated to c_i, and $L_{\max}$ is the max numbers that beams are able to operate simultaneously in a single time slot. Z is the amount of time slots during a beam hopping period. The relationship between T_i and Z is $T_i = M_i \times \frac{W \times \eta_i}{L_{\max} \times Z}$, where η_i represents spectrum efficiency.

The goal of the optimization object P_1 is to satisfy the traffic needs and maximize the system throughput. C_1 is the constraint that communication resources are not able to be allocated to users whose traffic requirements are satisfied. C_2 represents that the number of beams working in the same time slots should be less than Z.

Actually, P_1 a convex optimization problem, which can be solved by leading in antithetic variables $\lambda_1, \lambda_2, \lambda_3$. According to Karush-Kuhn-Tucker (KKT) conditions, the Lagrangian function of this problem is expressed as

$$L(M_i, \lambda_1, \lambda_2, \lambda_3) = \sum_{i=1}^{N} |R_i - T_i|^2 + \lambda_1 (\sum_{i=1}^{N} M_i - L_{\max} Z) + \lambda_2 (T_i - R_i) + \lambda_3 M_i \quad (5)$$

Obviously, traffic allocation T_i and traffic request R_i cannot always be equal, so Eq. 5 should satisfy the following boundary conditions.

$$\lambda_2 = \lambda_3 = 0 \quad (6)$$

$$\sum_{i=1}^{m \times n} M_i - L_{\max} Z = 0 \quad (7)$$

Then, after taking the derivative of the Lagrangian function, we can get

$$\frac{\partial L(M_i)}{\partial M_i} = 2N_i \left(\frac{W \eta_i}{L_{\max} Z} \right)^2 - 2R_i \cdot \frac{W \eta_i}{L_{\max} Z} + \lambda_1 = 0 \quad (8)$$

By solving Eq. 8, M_i is expressed as

$$M_i = R_i \times \left(\frac{L_{\max} Z}{W \eta_i} \right) - \frac{\lambda_1}{2} \left(\frac{L_{\max} Z}{W \eta_i} \right)^2 \qquad (9)$$

Substituting the inequality boundary conditions, we can obtain

$$\lambda_1 = \frac{2}{N} \left(\frac{\sum\limits_{i=1}^{m \times n} R_i W \eta_i - W^2 \eta_i^2}{L_{\max} Z} \right) \qquad (10)$$

$$M_i = \frac{L_{\max} Z}{W \eta_i} (R_i - \frac{1}{N} \sum_{i=1}^{N} R_i) + \frac{L_{\max} Z}{N} \qquad (11)$$

3.3 Beam Hopping Pattern Design

During a beam hopping period, according to traffic distribution, cells are divided into hot spot areas and common areas. The beam hopping pattern design strategy should follow three criteria. Firstly, pre-allocation. A time slot is reserved for all cells even if there are no service demands. Secondly, priority allocation to high traffic regions. According to the number of time slots calculated by the previous sections, the cells which require more services are assigned slots in advance. Thirdly, interference avoidance. Frequency multiplexing distance must be satisfied when designing beam hopping patterns, and interference can be avoided by spatial isolation. A detailed description of designing beam hopping pattern is illustrated in Algorithm 1.

Algorithm 1: Beam Hopping Pattern Design

Input: The traffic demands matrix R , the total throughput T , the frequency multiplexing distance d_{th} .

Initialize: The allocated throughput matrix $A = \min\{R, T\}$.

1 : **For** $t = 0, 1, \cdots, Z$ **do**

2 : $\alpha_t \Leftarrow$ vectorize$\{A(x, y, t)\}$.

3 :   Sort the traffic request matrix: $index \Leftarrow \arg\max_s (\alpha_t)$.

4 :   **For** $i = 0, 1, \cdots, S$ **do**

5 :   **If** $d > d_{th}$ **then**

6 : $E\left(\left[\frac{index[i]}{N} \right], index[i] \left[\frac{index[i]}{N} \right] M, t \right)$ 1 .

7 :   **End If**

8 :   **End For**

9 : **End For**

Output: Beam hopping pattern matrix B .

---

4 Performance Evaluation

In this section, simulation experiments are presented to evaluate the performance of MOBH. Table 2 summarizes the simulation parameters.

Table 2. Simulation Parameters

Parameters	Notation	Value
Total capacity of a satellite	T_{sum}	1 Gbps
Capacity of every beam	T_{beam}	100 Mbps
Length of a single time slot	t_s	10 ms
The number of beams in a slot	L_{max}	10
The number of cells	N	37
Packet size	P_s	100 kb

In this paper, three different BH schemes are compared with MOBH. First, the fixed beam hopping (F-BH), which allocates a fixed number of time slots to each cell. Second, the random beam hopping (R-BH), which means that each satellite selects cells for service at each time slot randomly. The last one is the genetic algorithm beam hopping (GA-BH) [11], where every satellite calculates its own beam hopping pattern through a greedy strategy.

4.1 Throughput Ratio

Throughput ratio [12] is proposed to measure the utilization rate of the total capacity of a satellite, which has the form as

$$\eta = \frac{\sum_{i=1}^{N} T_i}{T_{sum}} \tag{12}$$

where η represents throughput ratio, and the total throughput provided by a satellite equals $\sum_{i=1}^{N} T_i$. The capacity of a satellite is T_{sum}.

The value of η is between 0 and 1, which is an intuitive reflection of the system throughput performance. When η equals 1, the satellite resource utilization reaches the maximum. Figure 4 describes the throughput ratio performance in detail.

Figure 4 reveals that with the increase of traffic requirements, for F-BH and R-BH, the throughput ratio shows an upward trend in the beginning, and then remains stable at about 50% and 60% respectively. For GA-BH and MOBH, the throughput ratio rises significantly at first and fluctuates around 90% in the end. When the value of traffic demands is less than 400 Mbps, the four BH schemes perform similarly. While when total user demands are larger than 600 Mbps, the performance of MOBH is ahead of the other three algorithms, especially when the requirements are more than 800Mbps. Although GA-BH takes the second place whose performance is close to MOBH, there is still a gap between 5% and 10%.

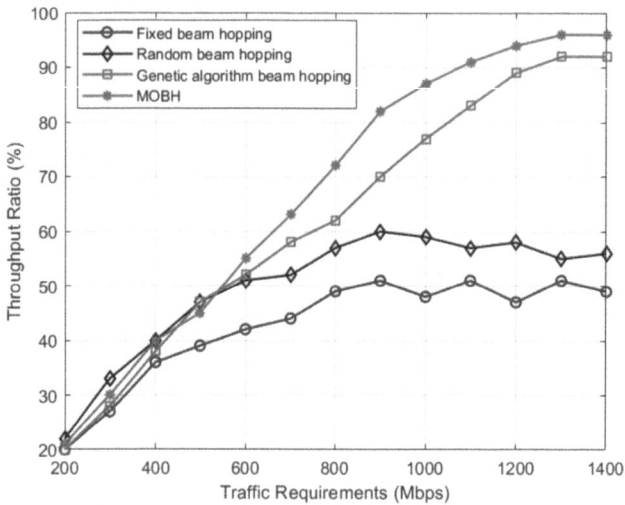

Fig. 4. The performance of throughput ratio among different BH schemes

4.2   Average Delay

In addition to throughput ratio, the performance of average delay is also important in beam hopping systems. The total delay is mainly composed of transmission delay, data processing delay and queuing delay. And we only consider the queuing delay in this paper because it is the most major metric. The average delay is defined as the mean value of the queuing delay, and the performance is shown in Fig. 5.

The graph illustrates that the average delay of R-BH stays constant at 550 ms and GA-BH hovers around 300ms. Both F-BH and MOBH show an upward trend but the former is more dramatically. When the traffic requirements less than 700Mbps, MOBH performs better than GA-BH and R-BH but worse than F-BH. However, it can be clearly seen in this figure that the average delay of F-BH increases to more than 800ms when traffic demands are heavy. Therefore, MOBH performs well in both low and high traffic requirements.

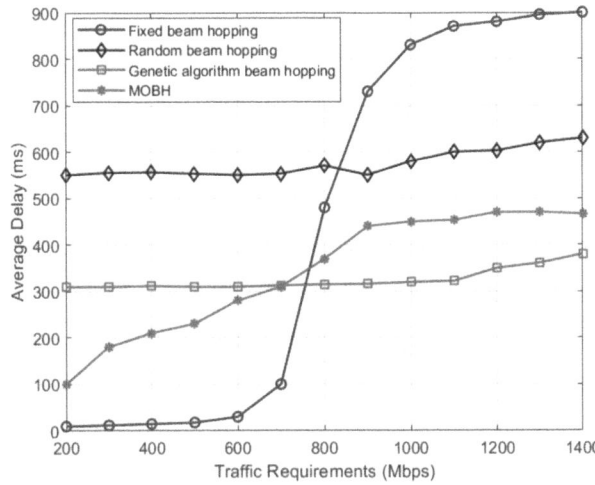

Fig. 5. The performance of average delay among different BH schemes

5 Conclusions

This study set out to find an effective resource allocation scheme for LEO multibeam satellite systems, and the MOBH algorithm is proposed to satisfy the nonuniformly distributed business requirements. At first, a beam hopping application scenario is established and the corresponding traffic distribution characteristic is expressed. Next, an optimization problem is proposed to maximize the traffic demands rate as much as possible. When designing the BH pattern, we take into account not only the cochannel interference caused by full frequency reuse, but also the dynamic equilibrium relationship between system throughput and user satisfaction. Finally, simulation results verifies that the proposed algorithm has excellent performance in terms of throughput ratio and average delay.

Acknowledgements. This paper is supported by the research project fund of Songjiang Laboratory (No. SL20230104).

References

1. Saad, W., Bennis, M., Chen, M.: A vision of 6G wireless systems: applications, trends, technologies, and open research problems. IEEE Network **34**(3), 134–142 (2019)
2. Del Portillo, I.: A technical comparison of three low earth orbit satellite constellation systems to provide global broadband. Acta Astronaut. **159**, 123–135 (2019)
3. Lei, J.: Multibeam satellite frequency/time duality study and capacity optimization. J. Commun. Netw. **13**(5), 472–480 (2011)
4. Tang, J., Bian, D., Li, G.: Optimization method of dynamic beam position for LEO beam-hopping satellite communication systems. IEEE Access **9**, 57578–57588 (2021)

5. Anzalchi, J., Couchman, A., Gabellini, P.: Beam hopping in multi-beam broadband satellite systems: system simulation and performance comparison with non-hopped systems. In: 2010 5th Advanced Satellite Multimedia Systems Conference and the 11th Signal Processing for Space Communications Workshop, pp. 248–255. IEEE (2010)
6. Tian, F., Huang, L., Liang, G., Jiang, X., Sun, S., Ma, J.: An efficient resource allocation mechanism for beam-hopping based LEO satellite communication system. In: 2019 IEEE International Symposium on Broadband Multimedia Systems and Broadcasting (BMSB), pp. 1–5. IEEE (2019)
7. Zhang, T., Zhang, L., Shi, D.: Resource allocation in beam hopping communication system. In: 2018 IEEE/AIAA 37th Digital Avionics Systems Conference (DASC), pp. 1–5. IEEE (2018)
8. Ginesi, A., Re, E.: Joint beam hopping and precoding in HTS systems. In: Prashant P., Kandeepan S. (Eds.): WiSATS 2017, LNICST, vol. 231, pp. 43–51, Springer, UK (2017)
9. Wang, Y., Bian, D., Hu, J., Tang, J., Wang, C.: A flexible resource allocation algorithm in full bandwidth beam hopping satellite systems. In: 2019 IEEE 3rd Advanced Information Management, Communicates, Electronic and Automation Control Conference (IMCEC), pp. 920–927. IEEE (2019)
10. Shi, S., Li, G., Li, Z., Zhu, H., Gao, B.: Joint power and bandwidth allocation for beam hopping user downlinks in smart gateway multibeam satellite systems. Int. J. Distrib. Sens. Netw. **13**(5), 1550147717709461 (2017)
11. Zhang, C., Yang, J., Zhang, Y., Liu, Z., Zhang, G.: Dynamic beam hopping time slots allocation based on genetic algorithm of satellite communication under time-varying rain attenuation. Electronics **10**(23), 2909 (2021)
12. Hu, X., Zhang, Y., Liao, X., Liu, Z., Wang, W., Ghannouchi, F.M.: Dynamic beam hopping method based on multi-objective deep reinforcement learning for next generation satellite broadband systems. IEEE Trans. Broadcast. **66**(3), 630–646 (2020)

A DQN-Based Routing Algorithm for Load Balancing in LEO Satellite Networks

Ziqi Sun[1], Jing Meng[2], Ruofei Ma[1(✉)], Gongliang Liu[1(✉)], Xiaoling Che[3], and Guodong Kang[4]

[1] Harbin Institute of Technology, Weihai 264200, Shandong, China
{maruofei,liugl}@hit.edu.cn
[2] Qian Xuesen Laboratory, CAST, Beijing 100094, China
[3] DFH Satellite Computer, LTD, Beijing 100094, China
[4] China National Space Administration Earth Observation and Data Center, Beijing 100101, China

Abstract. With the rapid development and popularization of low orbit satellite networks, their importance in global communication coverage and data transmission continues to be highlighted. However, due to the particularity of LEO(Low Earth Orbit) satellite networks, such as highspeed operation, limited channel capacity, and large latency, poses challenges to network load balancing and routing scheduling. The current routing algorithms for low orbit satellite networks mostly use traditional methods such as Dijkstra's shortest path, which lack real-time adaptability and intelligence to the high mobility of the network. Therefore, based on the deep reinforcement learning intelligent routing algorithm of DQN(Deep Q Network) has become a new approach to solve this problem. By combining the multidimensional information of LEO satellite networks and the advantages of DQN, this study proposes a new load balancing intelligent routing algorithm that comprehensively considers inter satellite link connectivity and link load conditions, and jointly optimizes multiple objectives. The aim is to improve network performance, reduce latency, and provide technical support and solutions for the future development of low orbit satellite networks.

Keywords: LEO Network · Routing Algorithm · Load Balancing · DQN

1 Introduction

Due to the lack of real-time adaptability and intelligence to network dynamic changes in traditional satellite routing algorithms, more scholars are focusing on novel satellite routing algorithms to cope with the challenges brought by future complex network structures and the increasing amount of data in satellite communication. The routing algorithm for LEO satellite networks is mainly used to solve the problem of efficient and reliable end to end data transmission in LEO satellite networks. Routing algorithms need to plan the optimal path in satellite networks by moving data packets from the source satellite to the destination satellite in this problem. The measurement of the optimal path

© ICST Institute for Computer Sciences, Social Informatics and Telecommunications Engineering 2025
Published by Springer Nature Switzerland AG 2025. All Rights Reserved
H.-H. Chen and W. Meng (Eds.): WiSATS 2024, LNICST 605, pp. 13–25, 2025.
https://doi.org/10.1007/978-3-031-86196-3_2

can be based on various indicators, such as latency, link bandwidth, link stability, link state, satellite load, hop count, etc. Considering the high mobility in satellite network topology, traditional routing techniques have the following drawbacks: (1) They cannot fundamentally avoid link and connection switching, as well as a series of switching control and rerouting calculation problems caused by them. (2) The computational cost is relatively high and it is difficult to implement on satellite, usually requiring the assistance of ground systems for calculation. (3) To achieve integration with ground IP networks, a series of intermediate processes such as protocol conversion and data format conversion are required, which will bring additional time and processing costs, making the system implementation more complex. Therefore, current research on low orbit satellite routing protocols mainly focuses on non-connected routing algorithms.

Some scholars have proposed some novel routing algorithms from different perspectives. A novel routing algorithm was proposed in reference [1], which takes into account the mobility and periodicity of satellite constellations. The algorithm predicts the network topology structure based on ephemeris, and transforms dynamic topology into static topology within multiple time slots. Based on this, consider the current state information of the channel, perceive global network information, and calculate routing tables. Reference [2] analyzed the characteristics of ground based ad hoc networks and proposed a routing algorithm suitable for satellite networks, improving the stability of satellite networks. Global network information is collected to calculate a routing table and make routing decisions based on it.

In recent years, software defined networking(SDN) [3] technology has been developing rapidly. Some scholars believe that this technology can be used to achieve unified control and scheduling of satellite nodes. The prominent advantage of SDN architecture is the separation of data forwarding and control nodes, which reduces the computational pressure on satellite nodes. The control node obtains global network information and makes routing decisions by regularly collecting information from forwarding nodes. Bertaux [4] elaborated on the advantages of satellite networks based on SDN architecture. Papa [5] proposed a mathematical framework to quantify the migration and reconstruction costs of satellite networks based on SDN architecture. Hu [6] optimized the network structure of traditional constellations for multicast routing in large multilayer satellite networks. The algorithm combines relevant ideas from graph theory to propose a new multicast routing strategy.

In recent years, machine learning has gradually entered people's field of vision. Artificial intelligence provides a new research direction for satellite network routing algorithms due to its outstanding performance in algorithm performance. In research on satellite routing, Bominmao [7, 8] advanced an efficient routing strategy using deep learning to quantify network information and enhance network intelligence. Utilizing deep belief networks to extract features from multidimensional network information and achieve routing decisions between source and destination nodes. Zuo [9] proposed an intelligent routing strategy with delay as the optimization objective, and LEO satellites make routing decisions through DQN networks. Liu [10] proposed an energy aware distributed routing strategy to address the node energy issue in satellite networks. Link status and energy information are transmitted between connected nodes. The algorithm optimizes for transmission latency and node energy, and uses deep reinforcement learning for routing selection. Wang [11] proposed using convolutional neural network (CNN) models to learn historical traffic data in satellite networks, and adjusting its output results based on the QoS of business data, which has better traffic control performance and routing flexibility.

Machine learning brings new opportunities for network routing. Combining SDN technology with machine learning can achieve unified control of satellite networks and adapt to its dynamic characteristics. Using machine learning for network routing optimization can adapt to the dynamics of large-scale networks, capture real-time network state information (such as latency and congestion state), and predict the impact of real-time routing on the network. Therefore, this article considers small low orbit satellite constellations and proposes an intelligent routing strategy for LEO satellite network load balancing based on DQN. It comprehensively considers the dynamics of inter satellite links and link load conditions, optimizes network performance, reduces latency, and improves network throughput, providing new solutions for the future development of low orbit satellite networks. By comparing with traditional algorithms, the method proposed in this paper has significant performance improvements.

2 System Model

2.1 LEO Satellite Network Model

The model scenario currently considers small low orbit satellite constellations and deploys an 8x8 single layer mesh constellation. The high mobility of nodes in low Earth orbit satellite networks is widely present. The network topology will change over time, and the connectivity and distance between satellites will also constantly change. Therefore, using the time slicing method, it is assumed that a satellite network in a time slot can be considered as a static topology, while the mesh structure assumes that each satellite node can have at most two same orbit links and two adjacent orbit links. Based on this, the influence of polar regions and dynamic topology on the connectivity between newer satellites is considered. Consider routing decisions within different time slots here and set a duration to update the network topology. Data packets are selected from the source node through each hop routing to reach the destination satellite node. During the process, each satellite node can obtain the link connection status and distance to each node in that time slot. The system model is displayed in Fig. 1.

2.2 Satellite Communication Model

The communication channel between low Earth orbit satellites can be considered as an additive Gaussian white noise channel, which is a linearly increasing broadband noise with a constant spectral density and amplitude of Gaussian distribution. The main consideration in this channel is free space path loss. When a data packet is transmitted between various nodes, this loss can be expressed as.

$$L = \left(\frac{c}{4\pi D_e f} \right)^2 \tag{1}$$

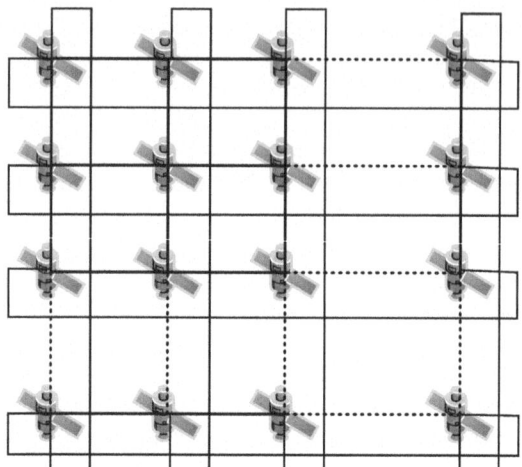

Fig. 1. Model diagram of LEO satellite network

Among them, f is the signal frequency, D_e represents the distance between satellite nodes, and c represents light speed. Signal to noise ratio is an effective parameter for measuring the channel state. In this communication model, this parameter is usually calculated using the following formula.

$$SNR = \frac{P_t G_t G_r}{k_B TBL} \tag{2}$$

where k_B is a constant value representing the Boltzmann constant. T_e means the equivalent noise temperature. And B represents the channel bandwidth. P_t represents the transmitting power. G_t and G_r represent the gain of the transmitting antenna and the receiving antenna. The channel capacity of links between satellite nodes is usually calculated according to Shannon formula.

$$C = B \log_2(1 + SNR) \tag{3}$$

In this communication model, the latency is considered from three parts, mainly including data transmission delay, signal propagation delay, and queuing delay. In this communication model, time delay is considered from three parts, mainly including data transmission delay, signal propagation delay, and queue waiting delay. The calculation method is as follows.

$$t_{total} = \sum_{e \in E} t_{prop} + \sum_{n \in N} t_{tran} + t_{queue} \tag{4}$$

Among them, t_{prop} represents the propagation delay which is only related to the distance between nodes. t_{tran} represents data transmission latency, which is related to the amount of data and transmission rate. t_{queue} Indicates queue waiting delay, which is related to queue size and transmission rate. The busier the network, the longer the waiting time in the queue. The packet loss rate of the data stream during the entire transmission process is obtained using the following formula.

$$loss = 1 - pac/n_{total} \qquad (5)$$

Among them, pac indicates successfully received data packets. And n_{total} represents the total forwarding volume of data packets during transmission.

2.3 Constraints of Satellite Networks

Bandwidth constraint. To ensure the normal transmission of data in the link, it is required that the required bandwidth for the task does not exceed the minimum value of the available bandwidth for all links on the path:

$$B_P \leq \min(B_{ij}, B_{jk}, \cdots, B_{pq}) \qquad (6)$$

Among them, B_P represents the required bandwidth for the task, and the bandwidth of each sub link is represented by B_{ij}.

Link Connectivity Constraints. The satellite network in a time slot can be considered as a static topology, and the connection status of links can be determined based on the duration of the links. To ensure that the links remain connected during data transmission, it is required that the minimum duration of all links on the path is not less than the set time slot length:

$$\min(c_{ij}, c_{jk}, \cdots, c_{pq}) \geq T \qquad (7)$$

Among them, T is the time slot, and the bandwidth of each sub link is represented by c_{ij}.

Transmission Rate Constraint. The task transfer rate must not exceed the set maximum transfer rate:

$$R_p \leq R_m \qquad (8)$$

Among them, R_p represents the task transmission rate, and R_m represents the set maximum transmission rate.

2.4 DQN Satellite Routing Model

Deep Q network is currently a popular deep reinforcement learning algorithm. And it is usually described as a Markov model. It can be represented as a quadruple(s, a, s', r), where s means the state space, a means the action space, r indicates the reward obtained after performing action a, and s' represents the new state reached after performing action *a*. The Q function maps actions and states to Q values, and chooses the appropriate action corresponding to the maximum probability in the Q function. Due to their expertise in modeling high-dimensional complex functions, neural networks can be used as function approximators to estimate this Q function. Combining DQN with routing algorithms can provide new ideas for solving high-dimensional multi objective optimization problems. In the routing model of the LEO satellite network in this paper, the controller collects link states and node information of the network at regular intervals as the state space for training routing strategies. The controller uses this routing strategy to output the optimal next hop node, and ultimately completes the routing process throughout the entire transmission process.

The action value function (Q function) represents the expected reward calculated by taking action *a* based on state *s* under the guidance of strategy π. Strategy π represents the mapping from state to behavior, equivalent to the decision-making strategy of an intelligent agent, and selects different behaviors based on different states, i.e. $a = \pi(s)$. Under the guidance of strategy π, the Q function of the robot is expressed as follows:

$$Q(s, a) = E_\pi [G_t | S_t = s, A_t = a] \tag{9}$$

where G_t represents discount reward, defined as follows:

$$G_t = R_{t+1} + \gamma R_{t+2} + \cdots = \sum_{k=t}^{T} \gamma^{k-t} R(s_k, a_k) \tag{10}$$

Among them, γ is the discount factor, which refers to the value ratio of future expected rewards at the current moment. Fγ^t decreases iteratively during the training process, and a smaller γ^t indicates a smaller impact of future rewards on the current reward. The calculation formula of the Q function is represented as follows:

$$Q_\pi(s_t, a_t) = E[R(s_t, a_t) + \gamma E_{a_{t+1} \sim \pi} Q_\pi(s_{t+1}, a_{t+1})] \tag{11}$$

Among them, $R(s_t, a_t)$ indicates the immediate reward corresponding to the action taken. The formula for solving the optimal behavior strategy by selecting the action corresponding to maximum Q value is as follows:

$$a = \arg\max_{a \in A} Q(s, a) \tag{12}$$

The DQN algorithm constructs labels for algorithm training through reward values of behavior, and the experience replay and target network effectively reduce the connections between datasets and improve the sparsity of data. The schematic diagram of the DQN algorithm is as follows (Fig. 2).

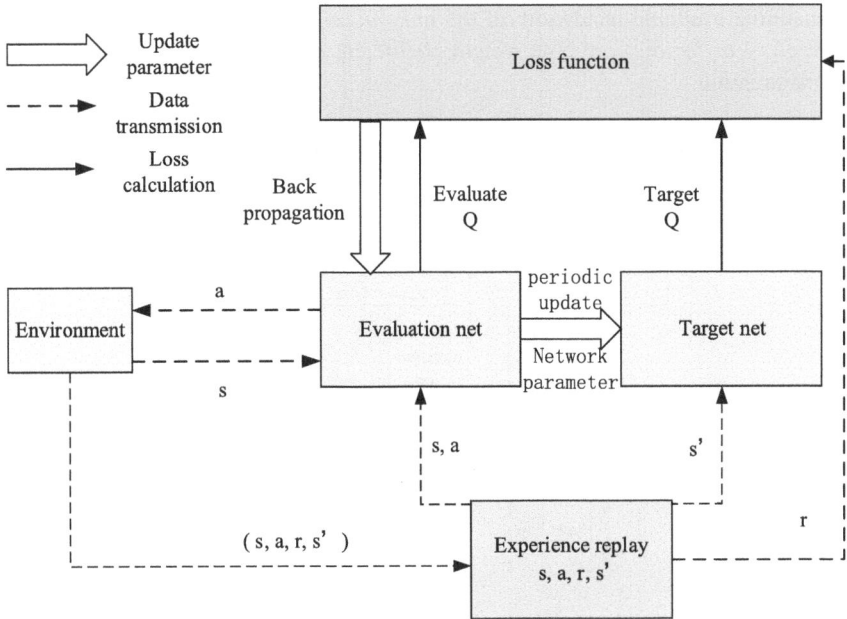

Fig. 2. Schematic diagram of DQN structure

3 Load Balanced Routing Algorithm Based on DQN

Figure 3 is the flowchart of the LEO satellite load balancing routing strategy based on DQN proposed in this article. To transform the satellite routing problem into a Markov decision process, it's important to define the state space, action, and reward in DQN reasonably, and optimize and compress the spatial dimension to improve network training efficiency. (1) State space: In this network model, the state space consists of link states and node information, mainly including the satellite node where the data packet is currently located, the load situation of adjacent satellite links, and the connectivity and distance between each satellite node. It is divided into three state matrices: position relationship matrix, load matrix, and distance matrix, which are merged into one state. (2) Action space: Actions represent next hop node selection. Considering the satellite network in this paper, each node is connected to four adjacent nodes, representing four output directions and four actions. Meanwhile, real-time connectivity of the four links is considered for judgment, and different output values are given. (3) Reward function: The reward function contains the objective we want to optimize. In this algorithm, the reward is defined as a function of distance, congestion level, and remaining available bandwidth, as shown in the following equation:

$$reward = -\omega_1 * d_n - \omega_2 * C_n + \omega_3 * B_n \tag{13}$$

Among them, *reward* represents the reward. And d_n represents the distance to the destination node. $_FC_n$ represents congestion levels of node n, $C_n = q_n/Q_m$. $_Fq_n$ represents the current queue length, and Q_m indicates the maximum queue length. $_FB_n$ represents the remaining available bandwidth of the link, ω_1, ω_2, ω_3 represents the weight coefficient, $\omega_1 + \omega_2 + \omega_3 = 1$. The weight coefficient can be adjusted according to the network situation.

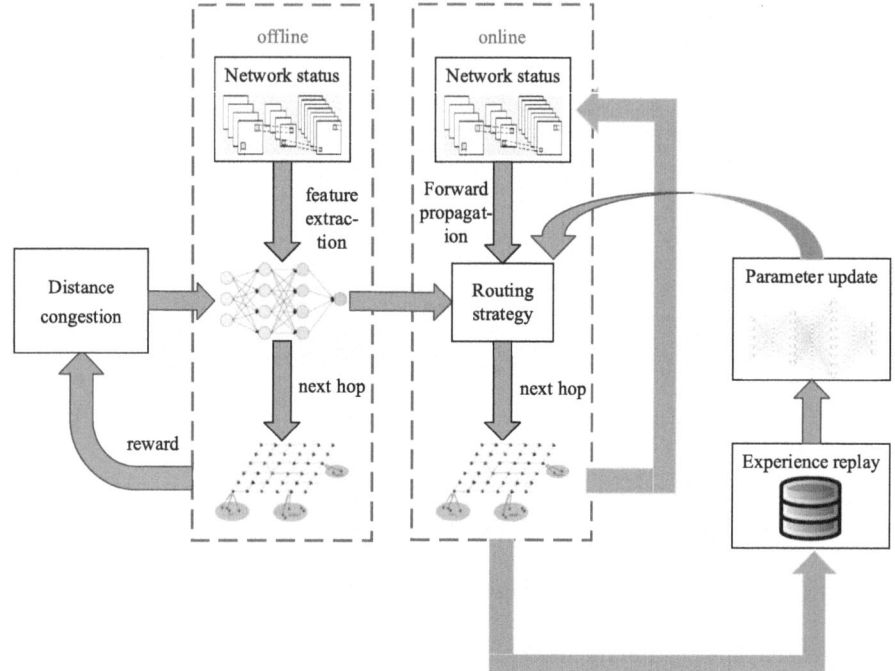

Fig. 3. DQN load balanced routing algorithm model

The algorithm mainly include two processes: offline learning and online decision making. The offline stage of the DQN routing model mainly utilizes historical traffic data and simulated data for learning. Firstly, preprocess the data, then select each hop action based on the reward function, store each hop action and its pre and post state, which includes multidimensional matrices such as connectivity, node congestion, link load, etc. Finally, use multi-channel convolutional neural network(CNN) for learning. In the online phase, the connection and distance between nodes in the satellite network are first calculated within the time slot, and network topology information is transmitted to each satellite node. The number and size of data packets are set, and the state of each node is initialized and initial loads following a Poisson distribution are allocated. Then, each node sends requests to each other and establishes connections, then shares network status and node information. Based on the link load and distance, the objective function value is calculated, and the optimal value is choosed as the next hop. Continuously repeat the above operation until the data transmission is completed, and update the network topology information, state matrix, store current state actions and other information when entering the next time slot to continue learning. Experience replay and network parameter updates will be conducted, and routing decisions will continue to be optimized to adapt to the new network state. The specific algorithm process can be found in Algorithm 1.

Algorithm 1: DQN based routing algorithm

Offline stage: initialize the environment, set source node S and destination node D; Train neural network, find and set appropriate hyperparameters, and send routing strategies to satellite nodes.

Online stage: Set the topology update duration T, timer t, and number of packets n; Calculate network topology information;

for packet $i = 1$ to n do:

    While the current node is D:

        Send requests to neighboring nodes to obtain link load information and distance information;

        Calculate the objective function value *reward* based on the trained routing strategy, and select the node that maximizes it as the next hop;

        Update node and link status, set the next hop as the current node;

        if $t > T$:

            Update link connection status and distance relationship;

            Reset timer;

        end if

        Store the action a, state s s', reward r and perform experience replay and network parameter updates;

    end while

end for

---

4 Simulation and Analysis

Generate a single-layer LEO constellation of 64 satellites using STK, with a total of 8 orbits, each with 8 satellites. The orbit altitude is 895.5km and the inclination angle is 86.4°. Use STK's corresponding functions to calculate the connection status and distance between satellite nodes, and generate a link matrix and a distance matrix. Due to the need to consider the multidimensional information of the network, multiple channels can be used to express the network state as a multidimensional matrix trained in neural networks. The neural network in the DQN model uses CNN to better utilize its matrix computing power for processing multidimensional resources and extracting features. The CNN model contains two convolutional layers with 16 and 32 convolutional kernels respectively. Related simulation parameters are listed in Table 1. The link channel capacity is set to 100 Mb/s, and the maximum data transmission rate for each task is 2 Mb/s. The initial load of each node follows a Poisson distribution, and the packet size is set to 512bit. The source and destination nodes are set for the task.

We use two traditional routing algorithms as comparative algorithms to highlight the performance advantages of the algorithm proposed in this paper. Dijkstra's shortest path is currently one of the most common routing algorithms, which provides the optimal routing decision for distance. Maximum flow algorithm considers maximizing traffic flows, which has good performance in throughput. Figure 4 shows the performance

Table 1. Simulation parameters

Parameters	Values
Height of LEO track	895.5 km
Number of LEO satellites	8 × 8
Orbit inclination angle	86.4°
Channel capacity	100 Mb/s
Maximum data rate	2 Mb/s
Size of packets	512 bit
Maximum queue length	100
Patch size	200
Learning rate	0.01
Soft update network weight	0.3
Action exploration attenuation	0.998
Minimum exploration rate	0.1
Reward attenuation	0.9

differences of the three algorithms in total end to end latency. From the simulation graph, it can be concluded that DQN based algorithm has a lower end to end latency. When the network is idle, the delay performance of three algorithms is not significantly different because the congestion situation in the network is not severe at this time, mainly focusing on propagation and transmission delay. As the number of packets increases, the congestion situation of the shortest path algorithm becomes more apparent, the queuing delay in nodes gradually increases, leading to a significant increase in total latency. Although the maximum flow algorithm can choose alternative paths to appropriately alleviate congestion, some routes are selected at the cost of sacrificing distance and latency, which increases propagation delay and overall delay slightly better than the shortest path algorithm. DQN based load balancing routing algorithm performs better in terms of end to end latency.

The simulation comparison of network throughput performance is shown in Fig. 5. From the simulation graph, it's not difficult to see the proposed algorithm performs the highest network throughput. When the network is idle, the difference in throughput performance between algorithms is not significant because the network load is low and there is no congestion when transmitting packets. When the traffic becomes busy, the congestion situation of the shortest path algorithm becomes more obvious due to link capacity limitations, reaching and maintaining the maximum value first, and the network throughput is the lowest. The maximum flow algorithm has a higher network throughput due to its ability to find an optimal traffic allocation scheme in the network, which maximizes the total traffic in the network. However, due to its high latency, its peak network throughput is slightly lower than the proposed algorithm. This algorithm continuously searches for nodes with lower congestion levels based on changes in network load, expands alternative paths, averages network load to more nodes, reduces single node reuse times, and alleviates network pressure. It follows that the load balancing routing algorithm based on DQN also has good performance in terms of network throughput.

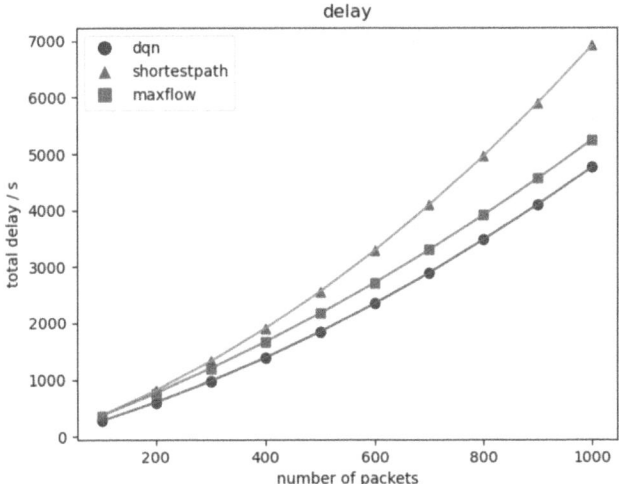

Fig. 4. Comparison of end to end latency performance

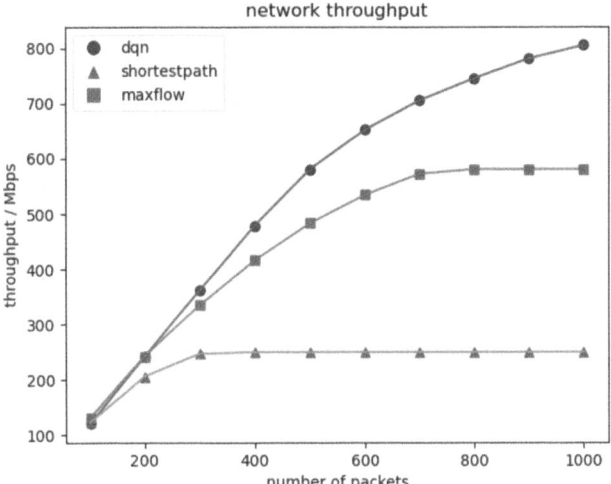

Fig. 5. Comparison of network throughput performance

Figure 6 displays the difference in the number of participating satellites among the three algorithms, which mainly reflects the performance of the algorithms in load balancing. The more satellites participate in forwarding, the fewer times each satellite node is reused, and more satellite nodes and routing paths are discovered to share network pressure and achieve load balancing. It is not difficult to see in the simulation diagram that DQN algorithm involves a larger number of satellites in forwarding. And as the number of data packets increases, new nodes will continue to expand, reducing the reuse frequency of old nodes and alleviating network congestion. The shortest path algorithm only considers the shortest path. So the satellites participating in forwarding only include the nodes on that path, resulting in link congestion and plenty of data packet backlog, which results in high transmission and queuing delays. The maximum flow algorithm is limited by network traffic. When the current flow in the link reaches its maximum capacity, the path containing that edge cannot be used as an augmenting path to expand new satellite nodes. As the amount of data continues to increase, the traffic near the destination node in the network approaches saturation, and the maximum flow algorithm no longer has new nodes participating in forwarding. From this, it is obvious to find that DQN based load balancing routing algorithm proposed in this paper involves a larger number of satellites in forwarding, and has a stronger ability for load balancing.

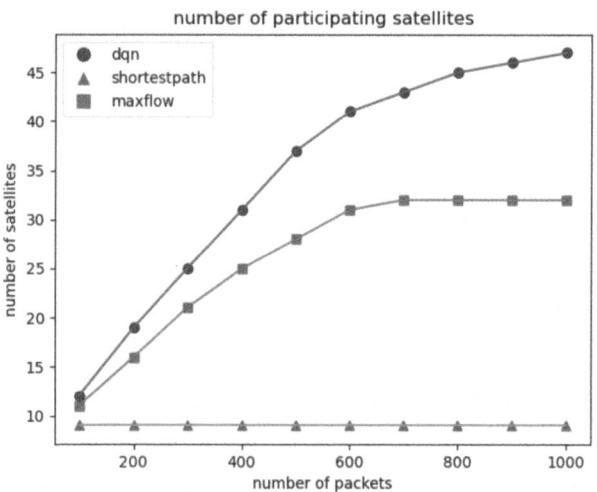

Fig. 6. Comparison of satellites participating in forwarding

5 Conclusion

This paper considers the high dynamism, large latency, and uneven network load characteristics of low orbit satellite networks. It analyzes the limitations of traditional satellite routing algorithms, which lack real-time adaptability and intelligence to network mobility, leading to a decrease performance and significant overhead. The idea of deep reinforcement learning is introduced in the routing scheduling strategy in the paper. By combining the features of LEO satellite networks and the advantages of DQN, an intelligent routing algorithm based on DQN which can effectively balance network load is proposed for low orbit satellite networks. This algorithm adopts the method of time slicing to learn the node connection relationship and load situation in the static topology of each time slot. It jointly optimizes multiple objectives such as the distance between target satellites, node congestion, and available link bandwidth, and provides an optimized next hop selection strategy for each node. Update the link connectivity matrix for different time slots and continue training to update network parameters. By comparing with traditional satellite network routing algorithms, it is obvious to find that the proposed algorithm has greater advantages in latency and network throughput, reduces the reuse of satellite nodes, alleviates the problem of uneven load in the network, and improves network performance.

References

1. Liu, Y., Liu, C.: Distributed dynamic routing algorithm for satellite constellation. In: Conference 2018 10th International Conference on Communication Software and Networks (ICCSN), pp. 300–304. IEEE (2018)
2. Liu, Z., Li, J., Chen, S., et al.: HGL: a hybrid global-local load balancing routing scheme for the Internet of Things through satellite networks. J. Int. J. Distrib. Sens. Netw. 13(3), 161–169 (2017)
3. Nunes, B., Mendonca, M., Nguyen, X., et al.: A survey of software-defined networking: past, present, and future of programmable network. J. IEEE Commun. Surv. Tutorials 16(3), 1617–1634 (2014)
4. Bertaux, L., Medjiah, S., Berthou, P., et al.: Software defined networking and virtualization for broadband satellite networks. J. IEEE Commun. Mag. 53(3), 54–60 (2015)
5. Papa, A., De, C., Vizarreta, P., et al.: Design and evaluation of reconfigurable SDN LEO constellations. J. IEEE Trans. Network Serv. Manage. 17(3), 1432–1445 (2020)
6. Hu, M., Li, J., Cai, C., et al.: Software defined multicast for large-scale multi-layer LEO satellite networks. J. IEEE Trans. Network Serv. Manage. 19(3), 2119–2130 (2022)
7. Mao, B., Fadlullah, Z., Tang, F., et al.: A tensor based deep learning technique for intelligent packet routing. In; Conference Globecom 2017–2017 IEEE Global. Communications Conference, pp. 1–6. IEEE (2017)
8. Mao, B., Fadlullah, Z., Tang, F., et al.: Routing or computing? The paradigm shift towards intelligent computer network packet transmission based on deep learning. J. IEEE Trans. Comput. 66(11), 1946–1960 (2017)
9. Zuo, P., Wang, C., Yao, Z., Hou, S., Jiang, H.: An intelligent routing algorithm for LEO satellites based on deep reinforcement learning. In: Conference in IEEE Vehicular Technology Conference (VTC-Fall), pp. 1–5 (2021)
10. Liu, J., Zhao, B., Xin, Q., Su, J., Ou, W.: DRL-ER: an intelligent energy-aware routing protocol with guaranteed delay bounds in satellite mega-constellations. J. IEEE Trans. Netw. Sci. Eng. 8(4), 2872–2884 (2021)
11. Wang, F., Jiang, D., Wang, Z., Lv, Z., Mumtaz, S.: Fuzzy-CNN Based Multi-Task Routing for Integrated Satellite-Terrestrial Networks. J. IEEE Trans. Vehicular Technol. 71(2), 1913–1926 (2022)

Design of Satellite Network Simulation Platform Supporting Distributed Controller

Haoxuan Lu[1,2], Dezhi Li[1,2], and Zhenyong Wang[1,2](✉)

[1] School of Electronics and Information, Harbin Institute of Technology, Harbin, China
ZYWang@hit.edu.cn
[2] Songjiang Laboratory, Harbin Institute of Technology, Harbin 150001, China

Abstract. Satellite networks, integral to future communication, benefit from SDN's advantages. Combining SDN with satellite networks, especially leveraging distributed controllers, shows promise. To facilitate research, we propose a simulation platform. Integrating STK, Containernet, Docker, and ONOS, it supports scenario and topology simulation and distributed control. Python scripts drive STK for scenario creation, Containernet for SDN network setup, and ONOS for controller functionality. Tests validate platform efficacy, showcasing ONOS's robustness and Docker node compatibility. This platform fosters satellite network research with scalability and practical applicability.

Keywords: Network simulation platform · Satellite network · Software Defined networking · Distributed controller

1 Introduction

In recent years, the booming telecommunications sector, driven by the rapid development and deployment of 4G and 5G technologies, has significantly transformed our lives and societal dynamics. As we transition into the era of B5G and 6G, satellite communication has reemerged as a focal point of research, with projects like SpaceX's Starlink and Amazon's Project Kuiper showcasing the feasibility and value of large-scale low Earth orbit (LEO) satellite constellations. Satellite communication, once overshadowed by terrestrial mobile communication, is now regaining attention due to its potential to complement and enhance existing networks. With advancements in satellite technology enabling higher on-board processing capabilities and mature inter-satellite links, large-scale LEO satellite networks offer broad coverage, resilience against natural disasters, high-speed communication, and massive user capacity [1]. Moreover, the flexibility of Software Defined Network presents promising applications in satellite networks, simplifying device management, enhancing reliability, and facilitating upgrades and adjustments [2]. However, the deployment of SDN in satellite networks faces challenges [3], particularly concerning the reliability and scalability of centralized controllers [4]. In response, there is a growing need for distributed SDN controllers to ensure reliability [5],

H.-H. Chen and W. Meng (Eds.): WiSATS 2024, LNICST 605, pp. 26–41, 2025.
https://doi.org/10.1007/978-3-031-86196-3_3

scalability, fault tolerance, and load balancing in large-scale satellite networks. Furthermore, the high cost, maintenance challenges, and industry secrecy associated with satellite networks underscore the importance of developing simulation platforms to reduce costs, accelerate development, and facilitate testing. Designing a satellite network simulation platform that supports distributed control is thus crucial for advancing research and development in this field. In summary, the development of satellite communication, coupled with the integration of SDN and the need for distributed control, underscores the significance of designing and implementing a satellite network simulation platform to support research.

The paper proposes a satellite network simulation platform with distributed control, integrating STK, Containernet, Docker, and ONOS. It consists of three main components: scenario simulation using STK for constellation scenarios, topology simulation with Containernet, and a distributed ONOS controller cluster for network management. The platform facilitates research on constellation design, network performance, routing, and distributed control functionalities, with scalability to simulate virtualized Docker node connections. Functional verification and performance testing confirm the platform's effectiveness in simulating large-scale LEO satellite networks and supporting Docker nodes.

2 The Design of Simulation Platform

2.1 Overall Framework of Simulation Platforms

The overall design framework of the simulation platform is illustrated in Fig. 1, consisting of three main components. The Satellite Network Scenario Simulation component is responsible for creating satellite network constellations, calculating link parameters, and generating satellite network topologies. It is primarily based on the STK simulation tool and Python scripts. The Network Topology Simulation component constructs the satellite network topology, runs host and switch nodes, and conducts network simulation tests. It mainly relies on Containernet, Docker, and Python scripts. The SDN Distributed Controller component is tasked with building a controller cluster, obtaining network topology views, and performing control functions such as routing calculations. It is primarily based on ONOS.

The simulation platform described above enables simulation from satellite network constellation construction to network topology testing. It supports distributed controllers and can facilitate research in areas such as satellite network constellation design, satellite network performance simulation testing, satellite network routing, and distributed controllers. It is capable of simulating network layers and can simulate both virtualized Docker satellite function nodes and physical nodes, demonstrating good scalability. This platform holds significant research significance and practical value.

2.2 The Satellite Network Scenario Simulation Component

Using Python scripts to invoke the STK engine, the Satellite Network Scenario Simulation component creates satellite network constellations and conducts simulation calculations for ISL (Inter-Satellite Link) parameters. The obtained information regarding

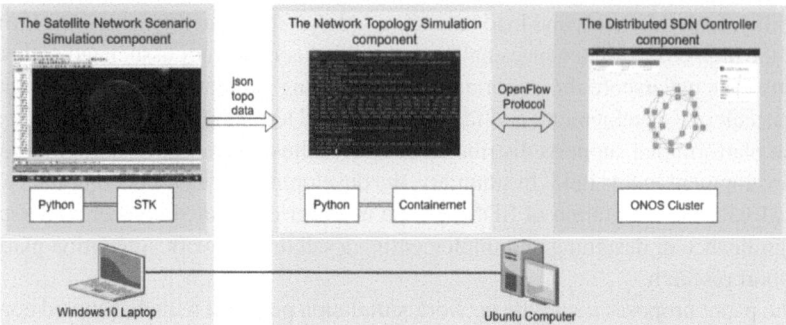

Fig. 1. The overall design framework of the simulation platform

satellite constellations and link parameters is utilized to generate a satellite network topology, which is then saved as JSON topology data and transmitted to the Network Topology Simulation component via Flask.

Using Python scripts to invoke STK for scenario simulation. Starting from version 11, STK introduced the capability to connect with Python, offering a new option alongside Matlab. It provides a rich Python API interface, enabling direct access to the STK Engine for scenario simulation and parameter calculations. Python also boasts abundant module resources, leading to higher development efficiency. In comparison to joint simulation with Matlab, although there are fewer reference documents due to its later introduction, it requires more in-depth research and investment, resulting in a higher learning curve. However, using Python scripts to call STK in satellite network simulation platforms offers greater flexibility, allows for programming language unification, facilitates platform integration, and avoids the limitations of Matlab.

2.3   The Network Topology Simulation Component

Using Python scripts, the satellite network topology JSON data is transformed into an SDN architecture network topology. This operates within the Containernet simulation tool based on Mininet, generating a simulated network environment consisting of satellite switches and nodes. These nodes can run Mininet hosts, virtualized Docker satellite function nodes, or physical nodes, and network performance testing is conducted using tools such as iperf or sflow. The network topology is connected to the SDN distributed controller component, which can retrieve the topology view of the simulated network and perform control actions.

To simulate the SDN satellite network, the satellite network simulation platform has chosen Containernet, a simulation tool based on Mininet. Containernet is a fork of Mininet, which is the most widely used simulation tool in SDN research. It offers more comprehensive support for SDN compared to other network simulation software and has the advantage of being able to connect with real devices. Containernet further enhances this capability by adding support for Docker, allowing containers to run as host nodes. This enables highly customizable node functionalities while improving operational and simulation efficiency.

To simulate satellite switching functionality within the SDN satellite network, the satellite network simulation platform has chosen to deploy OpenvSwitch virtual switches. OpenvSwitch is currently the most comprehensive multi-layer virtual SDN switch, boasting excellent scalability and programmability. It can be extensively deployed on Containernet through virtualization techniques, as illustrated in Fig. 2.

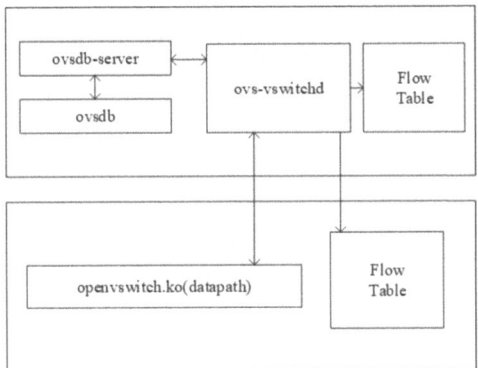

Fig. 2. OpenvSwitch structure

The SDN satellite network topology is created within Containernet using Python scripts. Upon receiving satellite network topology JSON data from the satellite network scenario simulation component, it generates the SDN satellite network topology. It creates satellite OpenvSwitch switch nodes and host nodes, then initiates the simulation network by invoking the APIs provided by Containernet and Mininet. Various network tests can be conducted within the simulation network. It is connected to the SDN distributed controller component, receiving control commands from the distributed controller.

With the Containernet tool, the design of the satellite network simulation platform supports the deployment of Docker nodes, enabling the simulation of Docker applications. Compared to ordinary host nodes, Docker nodes can implement a wider range of network functionalities, offering high flexibility to meet various research needs. This allows for the implementation of custom networks or protocol stacks.

2.4 The SDN Distributed Controller Component

Through comparison with other distributed SDN controllers like OpenDaylight, the design of the satellite network simulation platform has opted for the ONOS controller due to its excellent scalability and ease of development for research purposes. Being a project with collaborations from companies like Google, Amazon, and Microsoft, ONOS enjoys high recognition and practicality. Its modular structure facilitates customization and allows for the addition and removal of functionalities.

The architecture of the ONOS controller, as depicted in Fig. 3, interfaces with the southbound layer and connects to the simulation network running on Containernet using the OpenFlow 1.3 protocol. It communicates with the OpenvSwitch virtual switches, retrieves the overall topology view of the simulation network, and issues network control commands, performing tasks such as route computation and flow table installation.

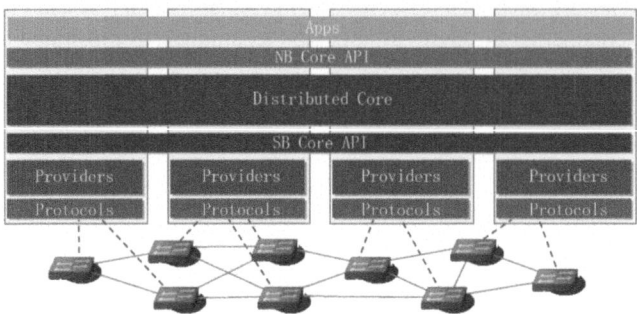

Fig. 3. ONOS structure

ONOS has undergone a series of version updates and has now iterated to version 2.7.0. Significant functional differences exist between versions, necessitating careful consideration based on specific needs. Regarding build tools, prior to version 1.7, ONOS controller compilation utilized Maven. In version 1.7, Buck was introduced as a compilation tool, while Bazel, adopted as the latest version's compilation method, replaced Buck in version 1.14. Differences in compilation tools affect the implementation of custom controller app functionalities, requiring the use of the corresponding version's compilation tool for construction. Developed by Google, Bazel boasts excellent scalability and robust functionality, with abundant reference materials available for research. Additionally, it has been the ONOS compilation tool of choice for a considerable period, thus selecting the ONOS controller based on Bazel compilation from version 1.14 onwards.

The current implementation of final consistency in the ONOS controller is achieved through Gossip, while strong consistency relies on Raft. Atomix, a distributed framework developed within the ONOS project, employs the Raft algorithm, offering better performance and higher availability compared to earlier versions which utilized Zookeeper and Hazelcast.

Regarding cluster deployment methods, starting from version 1.14, ONOS has transitioned to deploying controller clusters through independent Atomix clusters, as illustrated in the diagram. In contrast to the previous built-in approach, the data architecture of the distributed controller is now implemented through external Atomix, with ONOS internally retaining only replication protocol functionality, thereby achieving improved consistency and reliability.

3 Implementation of the Simulation Platform

3.1 The Simulation Process of the Platform

Based on the design proposed in the previous chapter, the implementation of a satellite network simulation platform supporting distributed control was conducted. The simulation process of the simulation platform, as illustrated in Fig. 4, consists of three parts: satellite network scenario simulation, network topology simulation, and the ONOS distributed controller.

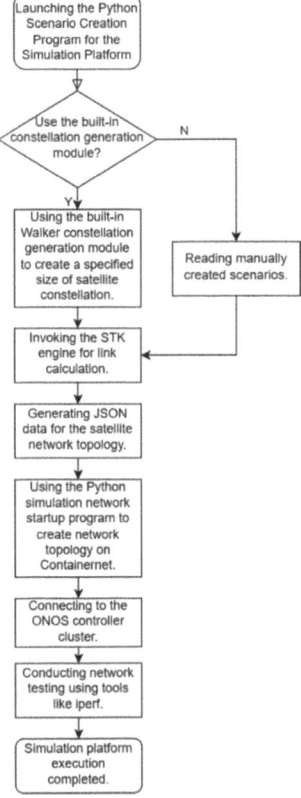

Fig. 4. The simulation process of the platform

The satellite network scenario simulation section utilizes Python programs to invoke the STK engine for the creation of satellite constellations. It completes the simulation calculation of ISL (Inter-Satellite Link) parameters and generates the satellite network topology based on the obtained satellite constellation and link parameter information. The resulting topology is saved as JSON topology data and transmitted to the network topology simulation section via Flask.

In the network topology simulation section, Python programs convert the satellite network topology JSON data into an SDN (Software Defined Network) architecture network topology. This runs on the Containernet simulation tool based on Mininet, generating a simulated network environment consisting of satellite switches and nodes. Nodes can run Mininet hosts, Docker virtualized satellite function nodes, or physical nodes. Network performance testing is conducted using tools such as iperf or sflow. The network topology is then connected to the SDN distributed controller section.

The ONOS distributed controller creates a controller cluster through Atomix, retrieves the switch and host node views generated by the network topology simulation section, and performs network management and control.

The satellite network scenario simulation section runs on a Windows 10 host to facilitate the use of the STK tool. The network topology simulation section and the ONOS distributed controller section run on Ubuntu 20.04 hosts or virtual machines. Virtual machines are used for development and testing, and Ubuntu hosts are utilized for higher simulation performance, thus enhancing simulation efficiency.

3.2 Implementation of Satellite Network Scene Simulation Module

The satellite network scenario simulation section is implemented through Python programming, comprising four modules: STK connection and scenario reading, Walker constellation creation, link calculation, and topology data generation. It invokes the STK engine to simulate satellite scenarios, generates network topology JSON data after link calculation, and transfers it to the network topology simulation section via Flask.

Two scenario options are provided: using the built-in Walker constellation creation module in Python programming or reading manually created satellite constellation scenarios with TLE data imported in the GUI. The number of ISLs (Inter-Satellite Links) supported ranges from 0 to 4, enabling connections between adjacent satellites in the Walker constellation.

Since version 11, the STK tool has supported integration with Python. Considering both stability and the richness of available references, version 11.6 was selected for implementing the simulation platform. The necessary library functions and modules, such as the Comtypes module for calling COM components, were configured through Anaconda. Following this, initialization Python scripts were used in the PyCharm environment to configure the connection with STK, importing the required STK modules into Python to ensure subsequent access to the corresponding API interfaces.

The built-in Walker constellation creation module in Python can generate a Walker constellation with specified parameters including orbit altitude, inclination, number of orbital planes, and number of satellites per orbital plane. Initially, within a newly created satellite scenario, a constellation is established. Satellites are then added to each orbital plane of the constellation following the Walker constellation pattern. The satellites are configured with Twobody propulsion and their initial states are set using classical orbital parameters, specifically the six orbital elements: semi-major axis, orbit altitude, eccentricity, inclination, right ascension of ascending node, and true anomaly. Once the constellation is established, the Propagate interface is invoked to compute the satellite orbits.

After creating or reading satellite constellation scenes using the built-in Walker module in Python, the link calculation module adds 0 to 4 inter-satellite links between satellite nodes and sets the link parameters. It then calls the STK engine to compute the status of the links, obtaining information such as distance, delay, energy, and error rate, which are saved in a dictionary and added one by one to a data list.

The topology data generation module saves the satellite network constellation and the obtained link information data in JSON format for the network topology simulation part to generate the simulation network. Using the Flask module, the JSON data is sent to Ubuntu virtual machines or hosts running the network topology simulation part and the ONOS distributed controller part. In the Ubuntu virtual machines or hosts, the Flask module receives the data and reads it using the JSON module for generating the simulation network topology.

3.3 The Implementation of the Network Topology Simulation Section and ONOS Controller Section

The network topology JSON data generated by the satellite network scene simulation section includes information about satellite nodes and their connections. The network topology simulation section converts this data into an SDN network topology consisting of switches and hosts through a Python program, which is then run on Containernet.

The program utilizes Containernet's Topo class to transform the network topology. It employs the 'addSwitch' method to create OpenvSwitch virtual switches corresponding to satellite nodes and uses either the 'addHost' method or the 'addDocker' method to create host nodes for each satellite node, simulating users or ground gateway stations.

Once the topology creation is complete, the Containernet tool is invoked to start the simulation network topology, enabling network simulation tests to be conducted and connecting to the ONOS controller cluster.

In Python programs, the Containernet is invoked and the satellite network topology is constructed using the Topo class through the Python API interface inherited from Mininet. The Containernet method is then used to start the Containernet simulation network. This method theoretically can achieve all the functionalities of the 'mn' command start mode, but it requires calling interfaces provided in modules like the node class on your own. There is limited reference material available, and the official API documentation does not provide detailed explanations, so research and experimentation are needed to determine the usage method.

To start the network topology and establish connection with the controller in the upper Docker, the key aspects are the utilization of the RemoteController class and the addSwitch method. By specifying the RemoteController class and setting the address and port number of the ONOS controller node in Docker, normal controller connection can be achieved. By specifying the call to the OVSSwitch class and setting the OpenFlow protocol version to 1.3, correct deployment of OpenvSwitch is achieved.

During the implementation process, three methods of deploying the ONOS controller were attempted, including running it natively on the host machine, within a virtual machine, and inside Docker containers. Running the controller natively on the host machine proved inconvenient for creating a controller cluster, so it was not adopted. Running it within a virtual machine allowed for the formation of a cluster with multiple controllers, but the overhead of virtual machines was significant and severely impacted the performance of the simulation platform. Running it inside Docker containers allowed for rapid creation and configuration of the controller cluster, while incurring much lower performance overhead compared to virtual machines, thus enhancing the performance of the simulation platform.

Multiple versions of ONOS, ranging from 2.7.0 to 1.14.0, were attempted during the deployment process. Incompatibilities were encountered with versions like 2.7.0, leading to the final selection of ONOS versions 2.1.0 and 2.2.2, which were able to fulfill the required functionalities while demonstrating good stability.

Within the deployed ONOS controllers, the openflow module is responsible for establishing connections with OpenvSwitch switches in the simulation network according to the OpenFlow 1.3 protocol. The fwd module handles routing decisions based on the obtained topology view, calculating and installing flow rules on the switches. The path visualization module combines the calculated routing paths with a classic GUI, presenting them within the topology view.

4 Platform Simulation Testing

After completing the implementation of the satellite network simulation platform supporting distributed control, the functionality and performance overhead were first tested. Subsequently, large-scale low earth orbit satellite network simulation tests were conducted to compare different scales of satellite networks. Following this, high availability testing was performed on the ONOS distributed controller cluster, and finally, testing was conducted on the deployment of Docker nodes.

Test Environment: The satellite network scenario simulation runs on a Windows 10 laptop with a 10th generation Intel Core i5 1065G4 processor (4 cores, 8 threads) and 16 GB of RAM. The network topology simulation and ONOS distributed controller components run on a Ubuntu host with an AMD Ryzen 5950X processor (16 cores, 32 threads) and 32 GB of RAM.

4.1 Functional Validation of the Simulation Platform

First, functional validation was conducted on the satellite network scenario simulation component. Through testing, it was determined that to ensure the visibility of inter-satellite links, the simulation platform requires a minimum number of orbital planes, set at 8. Additionally, a minimum of 8 satellites per orbital plane is required. Attempting to use parameters below these thresholds would result in errors in the link parameter calculation module. Testing involved creating a Walker constellation composed of 18 orbital planes, each containing 11 satellites, with an orbit altitude of 550 km and an inclination angle of 53°. The resulting satellite constellation scene is illustrated in Fig. 5.

After successfully creating the satellite constellation scene, the link calculation and topology generation modules were able to generate satellite network topology JSON data. The network topology simulation could convert the JSON data into an SDN satellite network topology and successfully initiate the simulation network on Containernet. The ONOS distributed controller component successfully started a controller cluster comprising three controller nodes. The network topology view obtained after connecting to the simulation network is illustrated in Fig. 6.

In Containernet, the 'pingallfull' command was used to conduct network connectivity tests and round-trip time tests between hosts, verifying the connectivity and link status of the simulated network. Simultaneously, tests were conducted on the routing calculation functionality of the ONOS distributed controller cluster. Results indicated that

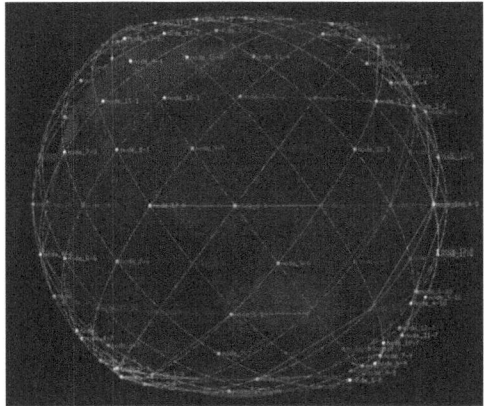

Fig. 5. Satellite constellation scene

Fig. 6. ONOS topology view

all host nodes could communicate normally, the ONOS controller could perform routing calculations using the minimum path algorithm based on the acquired global view, and it successfully installed flow tables for OpenvSwitch switches. Graphical comparisons were made using the obtained data. Due to the symmetry of the network topology, analysis of the data from one node to other nodes was sufficient. The round-trip time curve graph, as depicted in Fig. 7, illustrated the differences in delay between nodes at different distances, confirming the authenticity of the network topology. The round-trip time between nodes and other hosts exhibited significant differences based on varying distances, aligning with the characteristics of a global low earth orbit satellite network.

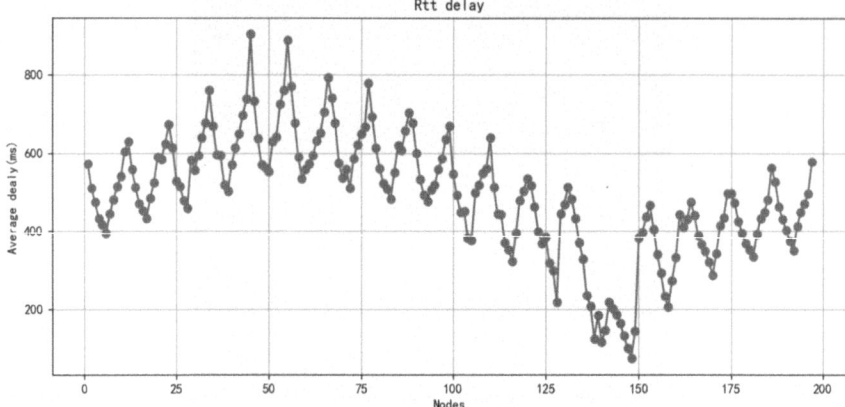

Fig. 7. The delay between nodes

To further ascertain the status of the links, the bandwidth of the links between hosts was tested using the iperf tool. Similarly considering the symmetry of the network topology, the results of analyzing and comparing the transmission bandwidth data from one node to other nodes are shown in Fig. 8. The data results confirm that parameters for all links have been correctly configured.

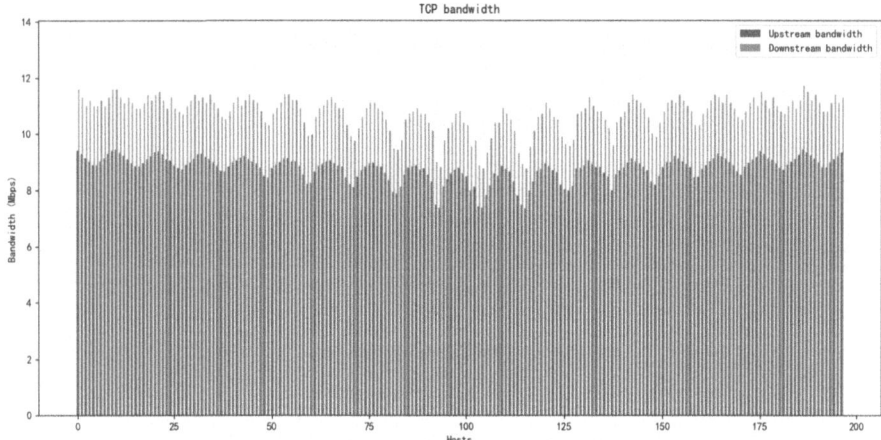

Fig. 8. TCP bandwidth

4.2 Analysis of System Error Characteristics

To validate the practicality of the simulation platform, performance overhead testing was conducted on simulation platforms of varying satellite constellation sizes, ranging from 8 × 8, 18 × 11, 18 × 22, 36 × 22 to 72 × 22 constellations.

Firstly, the CPU and memory usage during platform operation were tested. The CPU usage results are illustrated in Fig. 9.

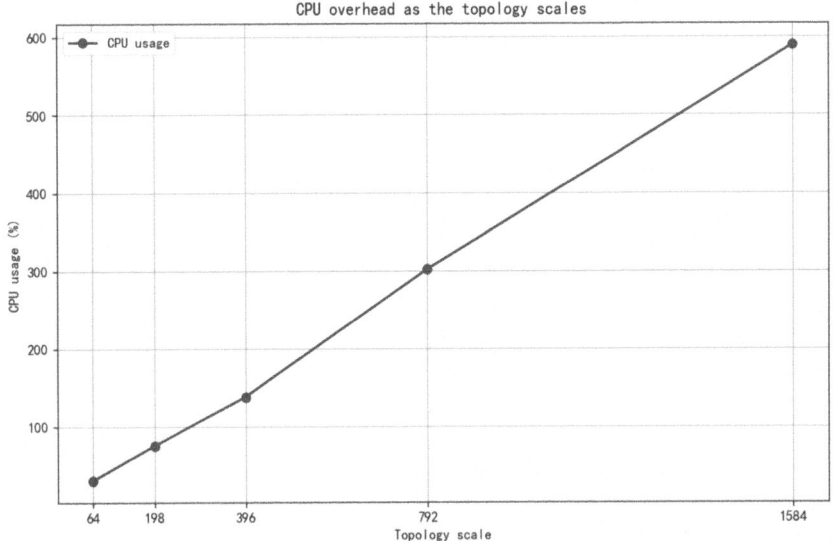

Fig. 9. CPU overhead as the topology scales

In the Ubuntu system, CPU utilization for each logical processor is calculated separately, thus for the test environment's host, the maximum CPU resource is 3200%, not 100%. Memory usage results are depicted in Figure Fig. 10.

CPU and memory usage include the performance overhead of OpenvSwitch switches, Containernet, and ONOS. Before the 36x22 topology, the Ubuntu simulation host ran smoothly without noticeable lag. Occasional lags were observed when simulating the 72 × 22 scale network topology, but simulation operations continued normally. Hence, on an Ubuntu host configured with a 5950X processor and 32 GB of RAM, it was possible to simulate a network topology with 1584 satellite nodes. For larger scale simulations, it is advisable to use more powerful hosts or implement optimizations.

Next, the time overhead of generating and launching the simulated network on Containernet was tested, with the results shown in Fig. 11. It was quickly completed when the scale was relatively small, but it took considerably longer for the 72 × 22 topology.

4.3 Comparison of Performance Tests for Different Scales of Satellite Constellations

The Starlink deployment process involves launching satellites one orbital plane at a time, gradually increasing the number of orbital planes. Additionally, different satellite constellations utilize various sizes and scales. Therefore, the simulation platform was utilized to conduct network performance tests on satellite constellations of different

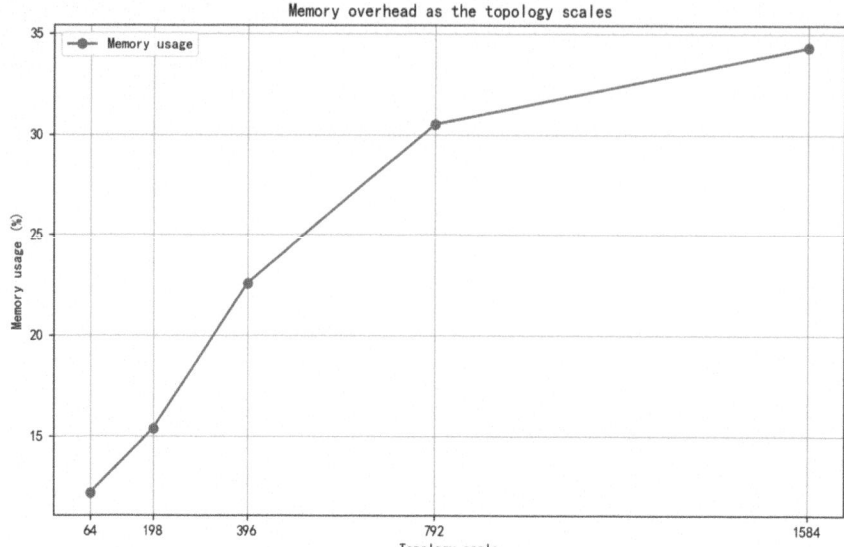

Fig. 10. Memory overhead as the topology scales

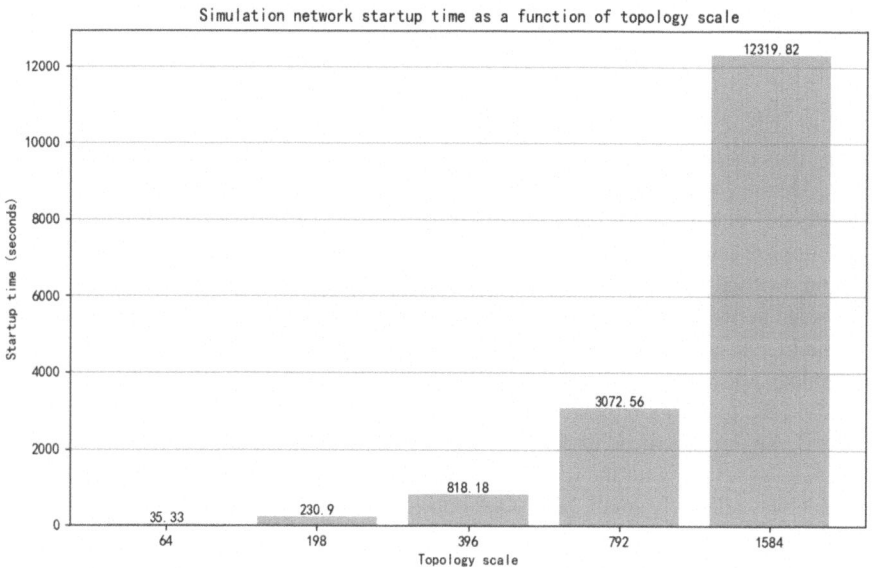

Fig. 11. Simulation network startup time as a function of topology scale

scales, including 8 × 8, 18 × 11, 18 × 22, 36 × 22, and 72 × 22 constellations, to facilitate simulation testing for deployment processes and different constellations.

The round-trip delay data obtained using the 'pingallfull' command on Containernet for constellations of different scales is illustrated in Fig. 12. It can be observed that as the constellation scale increases, there is a noticeable increase in maximum delay. This is because with a larger scale, more satellite nodes imply the possibility of traversing more hops, resulting in increased delay at remote ends. However, this does not necessarily indicate a decrease in performance, as smaller satellite constellations have poorer coverage capabilities and cannot provide continuous service.

The transmission bandwidth data obtained through the use of the 'iperf' tool for different constellations on Containernet is depicted in Fig. 13.

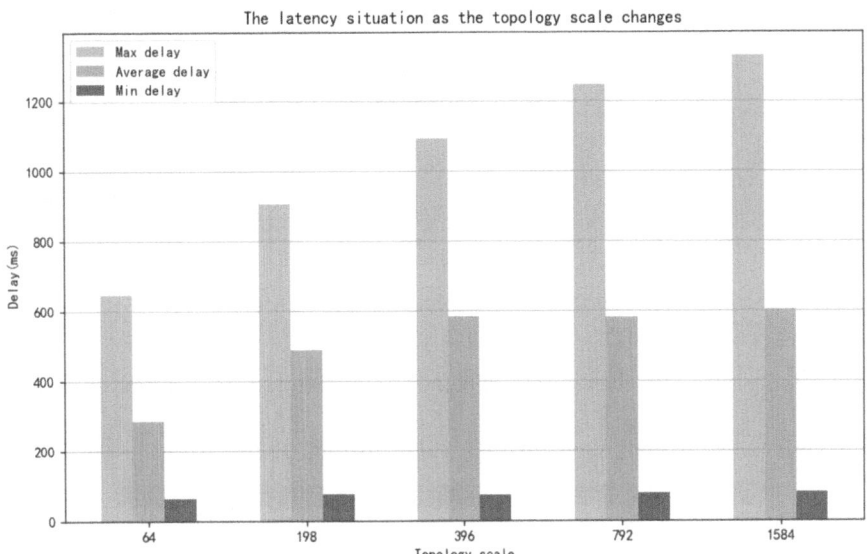

Fig. 12. The latency situation as the topology scale changes

It can be observed that there is no variation with the increase in satellite constellation scale. This is because the network topology tested only involved Container hosts and OpenvSwitch switches, without conducting tests involving the entire protocol stack or incorporating Docker nodes to enable additional network functionalities. Additionally, the number of hosts was relatively small, and congestion did not occur, resulting in consistent transmission bandwidth data.

4.4 High Availability Testing of ONOS Controller Clusters

The ONOS controller cluster is capable of providing backup functionality between controller nodes. Each switch maintains a standby list of backup controllers to connect to when connecting to the primary controller. In the event of a primary controller failure, the standby controller will take over the switches it was controlling, thus preventing network paralysis and ensuring continuous and stable service delivery to achieve high availability. Using a 72 × 22 topology, controller node backup takeover tests were conducted. Simulating the failure of the third ONOS controller, once it was taken offline,

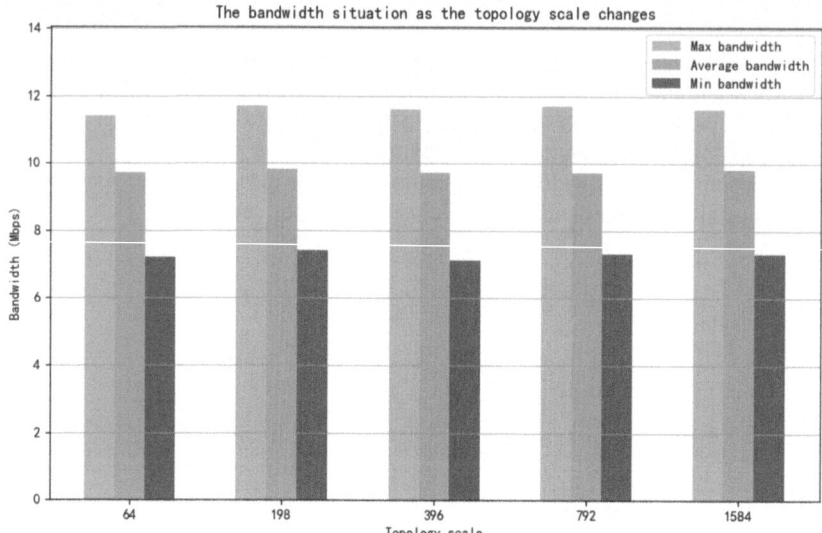

Fig. 13. The bandwidth situation as the topology scale changes

the remaining two controllers successfully took over control of the switches, as depicted in Fig. 14.

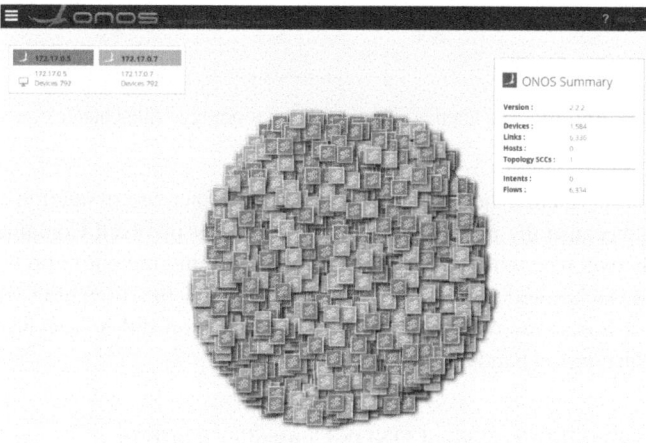

Fig. 14. The topology view after the takeover is completed.

5 Conclusion

This paper designs a satellite network simulation platform that supports distributed control, implements the simulation platform, and tests its functionality and performance. Furthermore, it conducts simulation tests on large-scale low Earth orbit satellite constellations using the simulation platform, validating the high availability of the ONOS distributed controller cluster.

Acknowledgment. This paper is supported by the research project fund of Songjiang Laboratory (No. SL20230104).

References

1. Zhan, Y., Wan, P., Jiang, C., Pan, X., Chen, X., Guo, S.: Challenges and solutions for the satellite tracking, telemetry, and command system. IEEE Wirel. Commun. **27**(6), 12–18 (2020)
2. Kreutz, D., Ramos, F.M.V., Veríssimo, P.E., Rothenberg, C.E., Azodolmolky, S., Uhlig, S.: Software-defined networking: a comprehensive survey. Proc. IEEE **103**(1), 14–76 (2015)
3. Kim, H., Feamster, N.: Improving network management with software defined networking. IEEE Commun. Mag. **51**(2), 114–119 (2013)
4. Xia, W., Wen, Y., Foh, C.H., et al.: A survey on software-defined networking. Commun. Surv. Tutorials IEEE **17**(1), 27–51 (2015)
5. Su, B., Zhao, L., Zhang, M., et al.: Research on the on-demand scheduling algorithm of intelligent routing load based on SDN. Int. J. Internet Protoc. Technol. **14**(1), 23 (2021)

Direct to Cell VLEO SatCom System Provide Low E2E Latency in STIN

Yuyan Ren[1], Meilin Xu[1], Yongkui Ma[1(✉)], Chengzhao Shan[1], Yunkai Guo[1], and Fan Zhang[2]

[1] Communication Research Center, Harbin Institute of Technology, Harbin, China
yk_ma@hit.edu.cn
[2] Shanghai Aerospace Electronics Co., Ltd., Shanghai, China

Abstract. Large scale low earth orbit (LEO) satellite constellations provide global Internet services for mobile terminals. In this paper, we first give an architectural model of the Direct to Cell satellite communications(SatCom) system. Then we analyze the terrestrial coverage and Doppler shift of the very low earth orbit (VLEO) satellites based on the abstracted geometric architecture. In particular, we simplify the Doppler shift closure expression compared to the conventional expression. We compare the end to end (E2E) latency of Satellite Terrestrial integrated network (STIN) and traditional terrestrial networks (TN). According to the different scenarios, we propose suitable location known and altitude known E2E transmission schemes. The proposed E2E transmission strategy based on maximum inter satellite links (ISLs) requires the least number of satellites and provides lower E2E transmission latency, with a 28% improvement over traditional terrestrial E2E transmission, which fully illustrate the E2E latency advantage of STIN. Finally, we obtain the areas of lower E2E latency for D2C VLEO SatCom transmissions.

Keywords: VLEO · STIN · Doppler shift · E2E latency · ISLs

1 Introduction

With the rapid development of the global economy, the realization of seamless communication on a global scale has become an essential requirement for future mobile communications [1]. One of the visions of 6th generation (6G) communication system is aiming to provide global coverage to support ubiquitous and seamless communications. STIN make seamless connection possible. The Direct to Cell(D2C) satellite communications(SatCom) system is a representative technology for global coverage and seamless communications in next generation communication systems [2]. Compared to terrestrial networks, satellites offer a broader coverage range [3]. Moreover, the 3rd Generation Partnership Project (3GPP) has explored several study items in Releases 15 and 16 [4,5] to examine the support about new radio non-terrestrial networks (NR-NTN), especially for SatCom issues. Subsequently, work items has been approved for the

© ICST Institute for Computer Sciences, Social Informatics and Telecommunications Engineering 2025
Published by Springer Nature Switzerland AG 2025. All Rights Reserved
H.-H. Chen and W. Meng (Eds.): WiSATS 2024, LNICST 605, pp. 42–52, 2025.
https://doi.org/10.1007/978-3-031-86196-3_4

standardization of 5G NR-NTN in Release 17 [6], giving priority to the satellite scenario, focusing on the transparent forwarding scenario of LEO, and further discussing the coverage enhancement and mobility enhancement of NTN. From early study items to recent work items, research on NTN has gained increasing attention. Previously, terrestrial fiber optic E2E transmission latency is high, which affects the delay sensitive services such as finance and intelligent medical care. The leading starlink GEN1 constellations have shortened the E2E latency [7], but they do not provide different strategies for different transmission distances in STIN. However, our proposed E2E transmission strategy based on maximum ISLs reduces the number of satellites and further shortens the end to end transmission delay on this basis.

The main contributions of this paper are summarized as follows. Firstly, in large scale VLEO SatCom systems, we analyze the terrestrial coverage and Doppler shift of VLEO communication satellite under the STIN architecture. In particular, we simplify the Doppler shift closure expression compared to the conventional expression in 3GPP [4]. Then, we compare the E2E latency between STN and TN. Appropriate low latency E2E transmission strategies for different situations have been determined for any given two points with least number of satellites, effectively highlighting the advantages of E2E latency through ISLs in D2C VLEO SatCom systems.

The rest of this paper is organized as follows. Section 2 analyzes the main parameters of the D2C VLEO SatCom systems. In Sect. 3, we introduce our proposed E2E transport latency and strategy. Section 4 provides the numerical results and compares the E2E latency between SatCom and TN. Finally, we conclude this paper in Sect. 5.

2   Main Parameters of SatCom System

2.1   Satellite Coverage

The geometric model of the SatCom system is given in Fig. 1. The coverage area of a single satellite R_{cover} is related to the orbit altitude h and the minimum elevation angle of the terrestrial terminal α as shown in Fig. 1. The coverage of the satellite R_{cover} can be further obtained by just figuring out the geocentric angle γ corresponding to the coverage. The simplification to obtain the geocentric angle γ can be defined as follows

$$\gamma = \arccos(\frac{r_E}{r_E + h} \cos \alpha) - \alpha \tag{1}$$

where r_E is the radius of Earth, h is the altitude of the satellite. Due to the limitations of the mechanical attitude, α represents the minimum elevation angle of the terrestrial terminal antenna. The terrestrial coverage of a single satellite can be expressed by the following equation

$$R_{cover} = 2r_E \cdot \gamma = 2r_E \cdot \left[\arccos \left(\frac{r_E}{r_E + h} \cos \alpha \right) - \alpha \right] \tag{2}$$

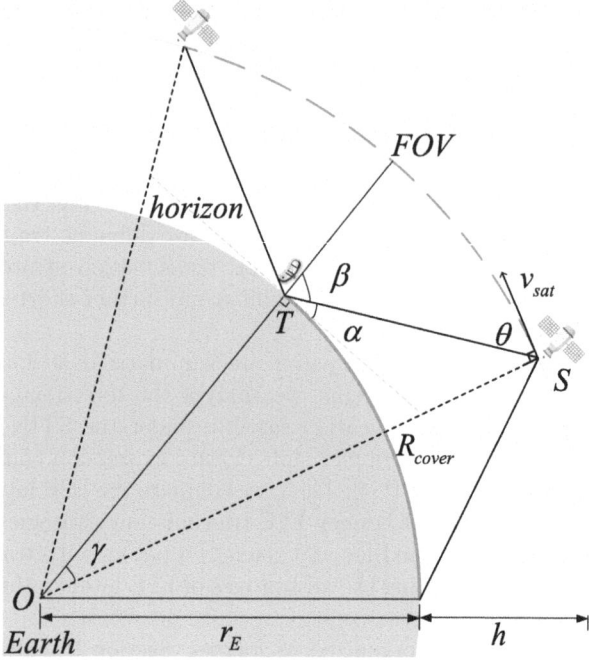

Fig. 1. The SatCom system geometric model.

Although the VLEO satellites are close to the Earth's surface and have low orbital altitudes, resulting in small communications coverage of a single satellite, it can be compensated by deploying large scale VLEO constellation and ISLs can be used to achieve wide coverage and make up for the small coverage area of a single D2C VLEO satellite.

2.2 Doppler Shift

Doppler shift is also one of the very real and difficult issues we need to consider [8]. Firstly, according to the cosine theorem we can calculate the distance between the satellite and the terrestrial terminal d_{ST} by Eq. (3)

$$d_{ST}^2 = (r_E + h)^2 + r_E^2 - 2r_E(r_E + h)\cos\gamma \tag{3}$$

Then according to the sine theorem we can get another representation of d_{ST} in the following equation

$$\frac{\sin\gamma}{d_{ST}} = \frac{\sin(\frac{\pi}{2} - \theta)}{r_E} \rightarrow d_{ST} = \frac{r_E \sin\gamma}{\cos\theta} \tag{4}$$

where θ is the angle between satellite velocity and terrestrial communications equipment. Bringing (4) back to (3) gives the relationship between θ and γ as shown in the following equation

$$\cos \theta = \frac{\sin \gamma}{\sqrt{1 + (\frac{r_E+h}{r_E})^2 - 2(\frac{r_E+h}{r_E}) \cos \gamma}} \tag{5}$$

And since the geocentric angle γ is unknown, it is further expressed using the terrestrial equipment elevation angle α to represent the geocentric angle γ by bringing (1), which then gives the relationship between θ and α, enables to calculate the Doppler shift.

The Doppler shift f_d due to satellite movement is formulated as follows

$$\begin{aligned}
f_d &= f_c v_{sat} \cos \theta / c \\
&= \frac{f_c v_{sat}}{c} \cdot \frac{\sin \gamma}{\sqrt{1 + (\frac{r_E+h}{r_E})^2 - 2(\frac{r_E+h}{r_E}) \cos \gamma}} \\
&= \frac{f_c}{c} \cdot \sqrt{\frac{GM_E}{r_E + h}} \cdot \frac{\sin \left[\arccos(\frac{r_E}{r_E+h} \cos \alpha) - \alpha\right]}{\sqrt{1 + (\frac{r_E+h}{r_E})^2 - 2(\frac{r_E+h}{r_E}) \cos \left[\arccos(\frac{r_E}{r_E+h} \cos \alpha) - \alpha\right]}}
\end{aligned} \tag{6}$$

where f_c is the frequency of carrier and c is the speed of light in vacuum. The higher the transmission frequency, the larger the Doppler shift will be. So we choose the lower frequency band of the S band, and the Doppler shift is also smaller. The relationship between θ and α is also derived in the 3GPP protocol [4]. However, we further found that the relationship between θ and α can be obtained directly through the sine theorem without the need for the intermediate variable geocentric angle γ to convert, as follows

$$\frac{\sin(\frac{\pi}{2} - \theta)}{r_E} = \frac{\sin(\frac{\pi}{2} + \alpha)}{r_E + h} \rightarrow \cos \theta = \frac{r_E}{r_E + h} \cos \alpha \tag{7}$$

Bringing (7) back to (6) gives a direct relationship as follows

$$f_d = f_c v_{sat} \cos \theta / c = \sqrt{\frac{GM_E}{(r_E + h)^3}} \cdot f_c r_E \cos \alpha / c \tag{8}$$

This greatly simplifies the computational complexity of solving the Doppler shift f_d, and numerical simulations show that the results of the two computational approaches (6) and (8) are consistent.

3   End to End Transport

3.1   Maximum ISL

We also consider the case where the ISL is blocked by the atmosphere, and the maximum ISL for a VLEO satellite can be easily calculated using the formula

$$ISL_{max} = 2 \left(\sqrt{(r_E + h)^2 - (r_E + a)^2} \right) \tag{9}$$

where a is the height of the atmospheric layer above the surface of Earth, generally taken as $a = 80\,\mathrm{km}$ [9]. The maximum ISL corresponding to the maximum geocentric angle γ_{max} can be expressed as

$$\gamma_{max} = 2\arccos(\frac{r_E + a}{r_E + h}) \tag{10}$$

3.2 End to End Transport Latency

Due to the different travel speeds of light in different media, when to choose SatCom and when to choose terrestrial communication in STIN is also a discussable point, and we will quantitatively analyze the effect of transmission distance on this.

First, we consider the case of a direct link with the least number of satellite. Let d_E represent the shortest transmission distance for E2E communication, not a physically true straight line, but the great circle surface distance of the shortest arc between two points around the Earth as a sphere. The distance between any two points on Earth is usually calculated using the Haversine Formula as follows

$$d_E = 2r_E \arcsin\left(\sqrt{\mathrm{hav}(\varphi_2 - \varphi_1) + \cos(\varphi_1)\cos(\varphi_2)\mathrm{hav}(\lambda_2 - \lambda_1)}\right) \tag{11}$$

where $\mathrm{hav}(x) = \sin^2\left(\frac{x}{2}\right)$ is the semipositive vector function, λ_1, λ_2 are the longitudes and φ_1, φ_2 are the latitudes of the two points.

In the single hop scenario when $d_E \leq R_{cover}$, user data can be transmitted directly from one satellite to another terrestrial gateway or terminal, without the need to relay flows on multiple satellites, this mode is also known as the bent pipe mode. However, if the operation is located on a GEO satellite, then the bent pipe mode can cause a large latency. And this is one of the advantages of the D2C VLEO SatCom system. Due to the movement of the satellite, the transmission between the satellite terrestrial link is constantly changing. The transmission latency is minimized when the distance between the satellite and the two users is equal. Assuming that the satellite needs to be switched to provide optimal network performance, the transmission latency is largest when the satellite is located directly above a user.

In the multi hop scenario, we assume that traffic relaying is completed by multiple satellites in the satellite network. The distance d_E needs to satisfy $R_{cover} < d_E \leq \pi r_E$ and corresponding to the geocentric angle is $\gamma_E = d_E/r_E$. Because d_E should be less than half of the Earth's perimeter. Divide γ_E into parts according to γ_{max} and calculate the minimum number of satellites needed to connect any two points

$$\begin{cases} n_{\gamma_{max}} = \lfloor \frac{\gamma_E}{\gamma_{max}} \rfloor \\ \gamma_f = \gamma_E - n_{\gamma_{max}} \times \gamma_{max} \end{cases} \tag{12}$$

where $\lfloor x \rfloor$ represents a downward rounding integer, $n_{\gamma_{max}}$ represents how many integer γ_{max} are contained in γ_E and γ_f is the remainder of γ_E divided by γ_{max}.

From this we obtain the minimum number of satellites required as $n_{\gamma_{max}} + \lceil \gamma_f \rceil +$ 1. The distance of the last segment of ISL corresponding to γ_f is

$$ISL_f = 2\left(r_E + h\right) sin(\gamma_f/2) \tag{13}$$

For computational comparison, based on the scenario where the satellites are directly above the gateway or the terminal, the E2E transmission latency with the minimum number of satellites is shown below

$$t_{n_{\gamma}} = d_{n_{\gamma}}/c = \left(n_{\gamma_{max}} ISL_{max} + ISL_f + 2 \times h\right)/c$$
$$= 2\left[n_{\gamma_{max}} \sqrt{(r_E + h)^2 - (r_E + a)^2} + (r_E + h)sin(\gamma_f/2) + h \right]/c \tag{14}$$

where $d_{n_{\gamma}}$ denotes the E2E transmission distance using the minimum number of satellites.In the next section, $t_{n_{\gamma}}$ also represents the E2E delay of our proposed strategy. Assuming the suitable density of satellites to be deployed in the ultra large scale constellations, satellite paths are composed of a series of point to point free space ISLs. The length of this series of connected links is approximately equal to the length of an arc in a sphere with a radius of the Earth's radius plus the altitude of the satellite. The corresponding E2E transmission latency for this scenario can be calculated by the following equation

$$t_{arc} = d_{arc}/c = \left(ISL_{arc} + 2h\right)/c = \left[d_E\left(r_E + h\right)/r_E + 2h\right]/c \tag{15}$$

where d_{arc} denotes the E2E transmission distance in this scenario and ISL_{arc} denotes the approximate arc length of ISLs. Compared to terrestrial fiber optic networks, latency is lower when the additional distance is shorter using a satellite network. However, the additional latency caused by this extra distance can be easily offset by communicating over long distances at the vacuum speed of light via satellite networks. The E2E transmission latency of the terrestrial network in the fiber optic can be expressed as

$$t_{TN} = d_E/v_{op} = d_E \cdot n_{op}/c \tag{16}$$

where v_{op} is the speed of light in optical fiber, n_{op} is the refractive index and $v_{op} = c/n_{op}$. This is the shortest transmission latency of the terrestrial fiber optic network in the most ideal case, since in practice it is not possible to lay fibers continuously over the most direct paths. We then consider the case $t_{arc} < t_{TN}$ where the E2E transmission latency in STIN is less than the minimum E2E transmission latency in the terrestrial fiber optic network. Given the terrestrial E2E communication distance d_E, the ISLs strategy for SatCom is chosen to have lower latency than the terrestrial fiber optic network when the orbital altitude h satisfies the following equation

$$h < \frac{(n_{op} - 1) \cdot r_E \cdot d_E}{d_E + 2r_E} \tag{17}$$

Bringing the previous maximum terrestrial E2E communication distance $d_{E_{max}} = \pi r_E$ into the above equation yields

$$h_{max} = \frac{(n_{op} - 1) \cdot r_E \cdot d_{E_{max}}}{d_{E_{max}} + 2r_E} = \frac{\pi \cdot (n_{op} - 1) \cdot r_E}{\pi + 2} \tag{18}$$

When the satellite orbit altitude is higher than $h_{max} = 1829\,\mathrm{km}$, SatCom loses its advantage in E2E transmission latency. When the satellite altitude h is given and the E2E communication distance d_E satisfies the following equation, the SatCom ISL latency is smaller than the terrestrial fiber optic network

$$d_E > \frac{2h \cdot r_E}{(n_{op} - 1)r_E - h} \tag{19}$$

where satellite orbit altitude $h < (n_{op} - 1)r_E$. The above analyses are all based on scenarios where the satellite is directly above the gateway or terminal. It should be noted that the actual total path length will likely be shorter. Ideally, the line from the gateway or terminal to the satellite is inclined at an angle to the terrestrial while $d_{ideal} = (r_E + h)d_E/r_E$ and t_{ideal} also can be calculated. However, it also depends on the relative location of the terrestrial gateway or terminals and the density of satellites. Due to the motion of the satellite with respect to the terrestrial gateway or terminal, the minimum latency occurs only briefly. The latency perceived by the user is subject to change, and the period of change is related to the altitude of the satellite. Still, we can estimate the minimum latency more accurately from this. Given any two points on Earth and the satellite altitude, the propagation latency of the satellite path can be calculated and compared to the terrestrial fiber path. Another variable is the satellite altitude, at a given distance between two points, we can determine whether satellite transmissions located at different altitudes are conducive to lowering the latency by comparing the terrestrial and satellite transmission latency.

3.3 End to End Transport Strategy

Based on the above analysis we give two different E2E transmission strategies, which are E2E transmission strategy based on given location and E2E transmission strategy based on given satellite altitude as shown in Algorithm 1 and Algorithm 2.

In Algorithm 1, after giving the latitude λ_1, λ_2 and longitude φ_1, φ_2 of the two points for E2E transmission, the E2E transmission distance d_E can be calculated. If the orbit altitude h of the satellite to be launched satisfies (17), we select the SatCom transmission strategy and give the corresponding E2E transmission latency t_{n_γ}, otherwise we select the TN transmission strategy and give the corresponding E2E transmission latency t_{TN}.

In Algorithm 2, given the orbit altitude h of the satellite to be launched, if the E2E transmission distance d_E satisfies (19), then we select the SatCom transmission strategy and give the corresponding E2E transmission latency t_{n_γ}, otherwise we select the TN transmission strategy and give the corresponding E2E transmission latency.

4   Simulation Results

The simulation parameters are shown in the Table 1. First, we analyze the Doppler shift of LEO satellite in dependence of the elevation angle α for

---

Algorithm 1 Location Known E2E strategy

Input: E2E transmission longitudes λ_1, λ_2, latitudes φ_1, φ_2, Earth radius r_E, light speed c, atmospheric height a, refractive index n_{op}.
Output: E2E strategy and E2E latency.
1: Calculate d_E by (11);
2: **if** altitude h meet (17) **then**
3:     Calculate $n_{\gamma_{max}}$ and γ_f by (12);
4:     Calculate t_{n_γ} by (14);
5:     **return** SatCom strategy and E2E latency t_{n_γ}.
6: **else**
7:     Calculate t_{TN} by (16);
8:     **return** TN strategy and E2E latency t_{TN}.
9: **end if**

Algorithm 2 Altitude Known E2E strategy

Input: Orbit altitude h, Earth radius r_E, light speed c, atmospheric height a, refractive index n_{op}.
Output: E2E strategy and E2E latency.
1: **if** E2E distance d_E meet (19) **then**
2:     Calculate $n_{\gamma_{max}}$ and γ_f by (12);
3:     Calculate t_{n_γ} by (14);
4:     **return** SatCom strategy and E2E latency t_{n_γ}.
5: **else**
6:     Calculate t_{TN} by (16);
7:     **return** TN strategy and E2E latency t_{TN}.
8: **end if**

Table 1. Simulation Parameters

System Parameters	Values
Earth radius r_E	6371 km
Orbit altitude h	550 km
Minimum elevation angle α	30°
Gravitational constant G	$6.6743 \times 10^{-11} N \cdot m^2/kg^2$
Earth mass M_E	$5.9722 \times 10^{24} kg$
Speed of light in vacuum c	$299,792,458 \, m/s$
Refractive index n_{op}	1.4675

different carrier frequency f_c and different orbit altitudes h according to (6) and (8) as shown in Fig. 2. We selected Gen1 and Gen2 Starlink user downlink frequencies and three different orbit altitude. From this figure, it is easy to see that the frequency selection has a much greater effect on the Doppler shift than the orbit height selection. Doppler shift f_d increases with increasing carrier frequency f_c. And Doppler shift f_d decreases with increasing orbit altitude h. The maximum Doppler shift happens when the satellite rises or sets since the relative velocity between the satellite and the terrestrial equipment is

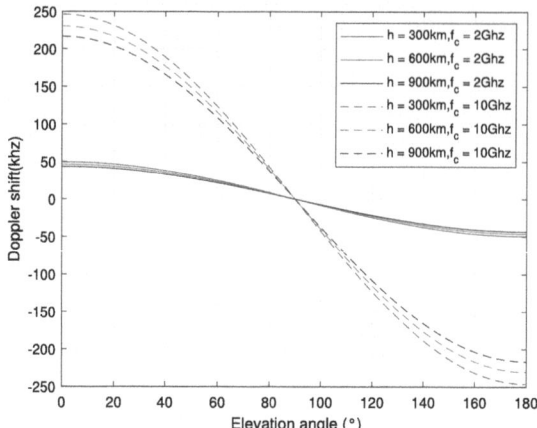

Fig. 2. Doppler shift of LEO satellite in dependence of the elevation angle α for different carrier frequency f_c and different orbit altitudes h.

maximized. The Doppler shift is minimized when the satellite passes over the top of the terrestrial equipment, where the angle between the terrestrial equipment and the direction of satellite motion is orthogonal. And since satellite motion is periodic, the change in Doppler shift is also periodic. Thus we can regularly estimate and pre-compensate for the Doppler shift due to satellite motion at the communication terminals. Obviously, the frequency shift caused by the satellite Doppler shift is much larger than that of the cellular network. After that we compare the E2E transmission latency of different schemes as shown in Fig. 3, where the ideal E2E transmission latency is the shortest. The satellite network in the comparison scenario uses the parameters of the SpaceX Gen1 Starlink constellation, i.e., an orbit altitude $h = 550$ km and a uniform spacing angle $\gamma_{Gen1} = 5°$ between the 72 satellites in the orbital plane [10]. Short distance communication while d_E is slightly smaller using terrestrial fiber optic networks with a slightly smaller transmission latency than STIN. When $d_E = 2900$ km, the communication latency of terrestrial fiber network and STIN is almost the same. However, as the communication distance increases, the advantages of STIN slowly show up. The longer the communication distance, the more latency is shortened, and the more obvious the advantages of STIN will be. The latency of our proposed scheme is slightly lower than the E2E latency of SpaceX Gen1 Starlink Constellation and uses fewer satellites. If we use the proposed scheme to transmit from New York to London by the shortest path, using the speed of light in a vacuum as the transmission speed, we can achieve a latency as low as 46 ms, which would take 59 ms even if we use fiber optic cables to take the shortest route, which is a 28% drop in speed. For the financial markets in both cities, millions of dollars can be transferred in a fraction of a second, and lower latency will provide a huge advantage in capitalizing on price volatility. These companies are already looking for technological solutions such as high-speed communication networks to reduce latency, and VLEO SatCom system may provide the perfect solution.

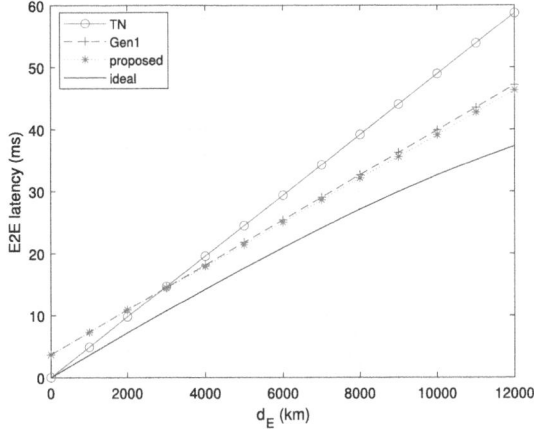

Fig. 3. Comparison of E2E transmission latency of different schemes.

Finally, the simulation analysis of Algorithm 1 and Algorithm 2 to obtain the areas of lower E2E latency for D2C VLEO SatCom transmissions is shown in Fig. 4. The parts above the blue curve are where our proposed solution is better in terms of E2E latency. For Algorithm 1, the transmission distance d_E is given, the E2E latency of SatCom strategy using ISLs is smaller while the orbit altitude h is lower than the blue curve meeting (17). For Algorithm 2, the orbit altitude h is given, the E2E latency of SatCom strategy using ISLs is smaller while the transmission distance d_E is longer than the blue curve that satisfies (19). Considering the limit cases, the lower the orbit altitude h, the longer the communication distance d_E, and the shorter the E2E latency, the more obvious the advantage of SatCom strategy with ISLs.

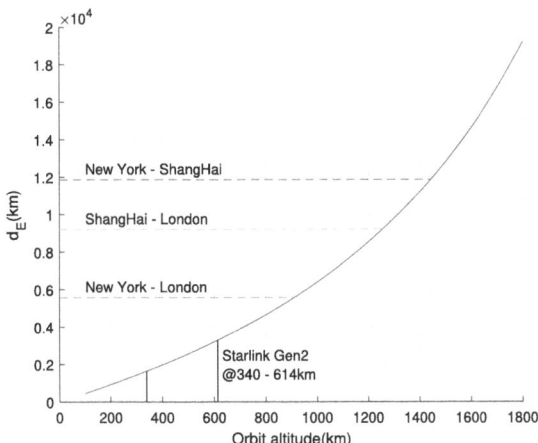

Fig. 4. Areas of lower E2E latency for VLEO SatCom transmissions.

5   Conclusion

In this paper, we analyze the terrestrial coverage and Doppler shift of D2C VLEO SatCom system to provide global coverage and low latency in STIN, especially simplify the closed expression for the Doppler shift compared to traditional methods. We also provide appropriate low latency E2E transmission strategies for different situations. The proposed E2E transmission strategy based on maximum ISLs requires fewer satellites and provides lower E2E transmission latency, which is 28% better than the conventional terrestrial E2E transmission, fully demonstrating the E2E latency advantage of the D2C VLEO SatCom system.

References

1. Kodheli, O., Lagunas, E., Maturo, N., et al.: Satellite communications in the new space era: a survey and future challenges. IEEE Commun. Surv. Tutor. **23**(1), 70–109 (2020)
2. Heo, J., Sung, S., Lee, H., Hwang, I., Hong, D.: MIMO satellite communication systems: a survey from the PHY layer perspective. IEEE Commun. Surv. Tutor. **25**, 1543–1570 (2023)
3. Li, S., Chen, Q., Meng, W., Li, C.: Civil aircraft assisted space-air-ground integrated networks: an innovative NTN of 5G and beyond. IEEE Wirel. Commun. **29**(4), 64–71 (2022)
4. 3GPP: Study on New Radio (NR) to support non-terrestrial networks. TR 38.811 V15.4.0 (2020)
5. 3GPP: Solutions for NR to Support Non-terrestrial Networks(NTN). TR 38.821 V16.0.0 (2020)
6. RP-213691: Solutions for NR to support non-terrestrial networks (NTN), Work Item description (2022). https://www.3gpp.org/ftp/tsg_ran/TSG_RAN/TSGR_94e/Docs/RP-213691.zip
7. Pachler, N., del Portillo, I., Crawley, E.F., Cameron, B.G.: An updated comparison of four low earth orbit satellite constellation systems to provide global broadband. In: 2021 IEEE International Conference on Communications Workshops (ICC Workshops), pp. 1–7. IEEE (2021)
8. Huang, M., Chen, J., Feng, S.: Synchronization for OFDM-based satellite communication system. IEEE Trans. Veh. Technol. **70**(6), 5693–5702 (2021)
9. Chaudhry, A.U., Yanikomeroglu, H.: Laser intersatellite links in a starlink constellation: a classification and analysis. IEEE Veh. Technol. Mag. **16**(2), 48–56 (2021)
10. Chaudhry, A.U., Yanikomeroglu, H.: Free space optics for next-generation satellite networks. IEEE Consum. Electron. Mag. **10**(6), 21–31 (2020)

Dynamic Beam Optimization and Interference Mitigation Methods for Multi-beam Satellite Systems

Yujie Ma, Xinting Song, Yixin Jiang, Huibin Liang, and Yunchao Song[(✉)] [ID]

Nanjing University of Posts and Telecommunications, 210023 Nanjing, China
{1022020635,1023020618,1023020617,2021020305,songyc}@njupt.edu.cn

Abstract. In multi-beam satellite system, dynamically adjusting the beams to meet the communication demands of ground users, adapt to changes in user distribution, and consider satellite hardware limitations is a technological challenge. To end this, this paper proposes an adaptive beamwidth design scheme. The scheme utilizes an enhanced K-means (called eK-means) clustering algorithm for user grouping and assigns suitable beams to each group, ensuring that all users within the same group are positioned within the primary radiation region of the beam. Also, a greedy frequency allocation strategy is introduced to mitigate inter-group interference. Given its capacity to dynamically tailor the number and coverage of beams based on user distribution and demands of communication, the proposed scheme greatly bolsters the flexibility of multi-beam satellite systems. Simulation results showcase its exceptional performance.

Keywords: Multi-beam satellite · User grouping · Beamwidth optimization

1 Introduction

With the advancement of future wireless networks, there is an increasing demand for broad coverage, high throughput, and ubiquitous large-scale connectivity. Under these circumstances, satellite communication has emerged as an ideal complement and extension to terrestrial communication networks, as it offers broader coverage and cost-effective internet access services to a large number of terminal devices [1]. Multi-beam satellite communication technology, as a crucial area of study, significantly enhances the flexibility and adaptability of satellite communication by employing spot beams to directly serve ground users [2].

To enhance communication capacity, multi-beam satellite communication systems implement frequency reuse techniques, including full frequency reuse

© ICST Institute for Computer Sciences, Social Informatics and Telecommunications Engineering 2025
Published by Springer Nature Switzerland AG 2025. All Rights Reserved
H.-H. Chen and W. Meng (Eds.): WiSATS 2024, LNICST 605, pp. 53–64, 2025.
https://doi.org/10.1007/978-3-031-86196-3_5

(FFR) and four color frequency reuse (FcFR) [3]. FFR technology allows for the reuse of frequencies within the same area, thereby maximizing the utilization of limited spectrum resources [4]. Nevertheless, this approach requires complex signal processing techniques to reduce the mutual interference between different beams. In contrast, FcFR technology effectively reduces the interference between beams by using different frequencies or polarizations in adjacent beams, thereby enhancing system capacity [5]. To implement these reuse technologies, satellites are typically equipped with multi-beam antennas such as phased array antennas and digital active antennas [6]. These antennas can generate multiple beams, each with its specific mainlobe and sidelobes. Users situated in the mainlobe encounter consistent service, whereas the sidelobes might introduce interference or diminish signal quality. Phased array antennas can adjust the direction and width of the beams. The wider the beam, the more users can be served, but the received power decreases. Therefore, a trade-off is needed between the number of users being served and the signal-to-interference-plus-noise ratio (SINR) of the beams, while also considering the gain characteristics of the mainlobe and sidelobes, to ensure communication performance.

To address the challenge of trade-off in multi-beam satellite communication systems, user grouping strategies and beam optimization techniques are utilized. Xu et al. proposed a method that utilizes deep reinforcement learning algorithms to optimize beam hopping scheduling and coverage control, in order to address the challenge of matching ground cell communication demands with dynamically beam transmission capabilities [7]. Liu et al. performed user grouping based on location information and optimized the direction and width of beams using time-division technology to maximize the average data rate of satellites [8]. In [9], the authors address the heterogeneous service requirements under satellite systems by employing two different sizes of beams, which are adjusted according to the users' demands dynamically. Honnaiah et al. proposed an adaptive multi-beam strategy for high-throughput satellite systems to address the uneven distribution of users and fluctuating service demands [10]. The aforementioned works did not comprehensively consider the balance between beamwidth, user requirements, and interference factors.

In this paper, we propose an adaptive beamwidth design scheme. The scheme groups users based on users' location information rather than their channel state information. Optimization of beam direction and beamwidth is conducted for each group to enhance system throughput and guarantee user Quality of Service (QoS). By employing FcFR, each group of users share the same time-frequency resources. We formulate an optimization problem that considers the trade-off among system throughput, user received SINR and satellite hardware constraints, which is known to be an NP-hard problem. To address this, we develop an algorithm that combines enhanced K-means (eK-means) clustering and greedy frequency allocation. The algorithm decomposes the problem into two stages: In the initial stage, due to the difficulties in directly acquiring inter-beam interference (IBI), we employ an iterative process with the objective of maximizing total received power. This process helps determine the optimal user grouping and beam radius for different group number. In the second stage, we utilize a graph-based greedy frequency allocation method to find the optimal frequency coloring solution for various group numbers. Finally, we compare and evaluate different designs to determine the optimal beamwidth that satisfies the given constraints. The effectiveness of the proposed scheme is validated and demonstrated through simulation results.

2 System Model and Problem Formulation

2.1 System Setup

This paper focuses on a downlink satellite communication system that comprises a satellite catering to K ground users indexed by $\mathcal{K} = \{1, 2, \ldots, K\}$ as shown in Fig. 1. Assuming the satellite is equipped with phased array antennas, it can provide flexible beam direction and beamwidth. The satellite payload generates a total of N beams on the ground. Here, N is not a fixed constant, but a variable, and $1 \leq N \leq K$. All ground users are situated within a common horizontal plane, and their positions are known. Denote $\mathbf{u}_k$ and $\mathbf{z}_k$ as the coordinates of the kth user and the coordinates of the beam center, respectively.

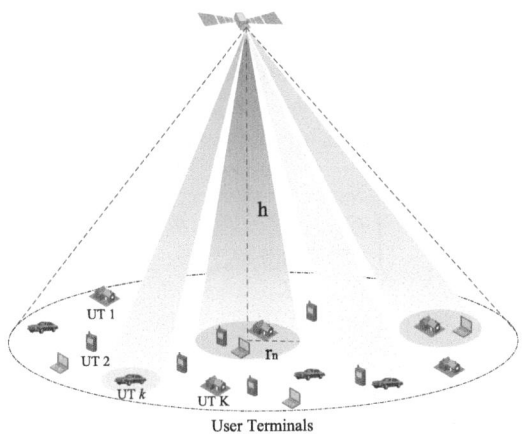

Fig. 1. System model.

Due to the inability of a single beam's mainlobe to cover all users simultaneously, it is necessary to group users and utilize multiple beams to provide services to the users. In this paper, the number of beams is equal to the number of user groups. We define a set of indicator variables, denoted as $b_{k,n}$, to describe the grouping of each user. Specifically, if the kth user belongs to the nth group, the value of $b_{k,n}$ is set to 1; otherwise, $b_{k,n}$ is set to 0. Each user can only be served by one beam, i.e.,

$$\sum_{n=1}^{N} b_{k,n} = 1, \quad \forall k. \tag{1}$$

Given the assumption that the beam coverage area has a circular shape, it is required that all users within the same group are positioned within the mainlobe of the beam. Then, we have

$$\sum_{n=1}^{N} b_{k,n} \|\mathbf{u}_k - \mathbf{z}_n\| \leq \sum_{n=1}^{N} b_{k,n} r_n, \quad \forall k, \tag{2}$$

where r_n is the coverage radius of nth beam.

In order to improve the communication throughput, this paper employs FcFR. Due to the reuse of frequencies in the downlink, the implementation of the multi-beam technique can result in IBI caused by the overlapping sidelobes in the radiation pattern.

Ground users employ omnidirectional antennas, and each user has the same gain of received antenna which is denoted as G^r. When the user is expected to locate at the center of the target beam, the received signal power of the expected user in the nth beam is

$$P_n^r = \frac{1}{2}\alpha G_{tx}^n(\phi_n) G^r P_n^t (\frac{\lambda}{4\pi l})^2, \tag{3}$$

where α is the power attenuation, G_{tx}^n is transmitter antenna gain, ϕ_n is the angle of the expected user from the antenna axis of the beam, P_n^t is the transmission power of the nth beam, λ is the wavelength, and l is the path length between the user and the satellite. The relationship between the offaxis angle θ and transmit antenna gain is denoted as [11].

$$G_{tx}(\theta) = \begin{cases} G_m, & \theta < \theta_b \\ G_m - 3(\theta/\theta_b)^2, & \theta_b \leq \theta \leq a\theta_b \\ G_m + L_s, & a\theta_b \leq \theta \leq b\theta_b \\ \max\{\delta, 0\}, & \text{else}, \end{cases} \tag{4}$$

where $a = 2.88$, $b = 6.32$, $L_s = -25\,\text{dB}$, θ_b denotes the angle corresponding to the 3dB beamwidth and $\delta = G_m + L_s + 20 - 25\log_{10}\left(\frac{\theta}{\theta_b}\right)$. G_m represents the maximum gain of the satellite's transmit antenna, and its form is given by [12]

$$G_m = 10\log_{10}\left[4.93\left(\frac{70}{\theta_b}\right)^2\right]. \tag{5}$$

The beam coverage radius is calculated by

$$r = h\tan\theta_b, \tag{6}$$

where h is the height of the satellite. The interference signal power affected by IBI of the nth beam is

$$P_n^I = \sum_{m=1}^{M} \frac{1}{2}\alpha G_{tx}^m(\phi_m) G^r P_n^t (\frac{\lambda}{4\pi l})^2, \tag{7}$$

where M denotes the total number of beams of the same color and ϕ_m represents the angle at which the expected user deviates from the axis of the nth beam of the same color. Then, the SINR of the nth beam is expressed as

$$\gamma_n = \frac{P_n^r}{N_0 W_n + P_n^I}, \tag{8}$$

where N_0 is the noise power spectral density and W_n represents the bandwidth allocated by the target beam n. So, the data rate of the nth beam can be expressed as

$$R_n = W_n \log_2(1 + \gamma_n). \tag{9}$$

2.2 Problem Formulation

Our goal is to comprehensively consider the limitations imposed by satellite hardware, dynamically adjust beams to meet the communication demands of ground users, adapt to changes in user distribution, and ultimately maximize system throughput. The problem is formulated as

$$
\begin{aligned}
\mathcal{P}_1 : &\max_{b,z,r} \sum_{n=1}^{N} R_n \\
\text{s.t. } C_1: &\sum_{n=1}^{N} b_{k,n} \left\| \mathbf{u}_k - \mathbf{z}_n \right\| \leq \sum_{n=1}^{N} b_{k,n} r_n, \quad \forall k \\
C_2: &\sum_{n=1}^{N} b_{k,n} = 1, \quad \forall k \\
C_3: &\, b_{k,n} \in \{0,1\}, \quad \forall k,n \\
C_4: &\, r_n \geq 0.443 \frac{\lambda}{D} h \\
C_5: &\, R_n \geq R_{th} \\
C_6: &\sum_{n=1}^{N} P_n^t \leq P_{total}
\end{aligned}
\tag{10}
$$

where D represents the diameter of the satellite phased array antenna, R_{th} denotes the minimum data rates and P_{total} is the total power of the satellite. The constraint C_4 means that the radius of the beam cannot be smaller than the beam resolution. Constraint C_5 indicates that the limitations for ensuring the minimum data rate for user QoS. C_6 represents that the total power allocated to all beams must not exceed the overall system power. The proposed problem $\mathcal{P}_1$ is a non-convex mixed integer programming problem, and its structure is similar to the problem discussed in [8], falling under the category of NP-hard.

3   Joint User Grouping and Dynamic Beam Resource Allocation Scheme

To solve problem $\mathcal{P}_1$, we adopt a staged strategy. Firstly, we perform a user grouping and determine the optimal beam coverage radius for each group to maximize the total received power. Then, we proposed a frequency allocation scheme based on graph theory, aiming to reduce IBIs. Through this approach, we aim to enhance the system throughput while ensuring the communication quality.

3.1   User Grouping Based on eK-Means Algorithm

Due to the inability to obtain the IBI, we adopted an alternative strategy that maximizes the total received power of all beams to improve system throughput. To achieve this, we fixed the total number of beams N in problem $\mathcal{P}_1$ and proceeded with the problem-solving process. Since $1 \leq N \leq K$, we perform a one dimensional exhaustive search over the range $[1, K]$ to find the optimal solution. Therefore, problem $\mathcal{P}_1$ can be transformed into K subproblems. Specifically, when N is fixed, we need to solve the following subproblem

$$\mathcal{P}_2 : \max \sum_{n=1}^{N} P_n^r \tag{11}$$

$$\text{s.t. } constrains \ \ C_1, C_2, C_3, C_4.$$

According to Eqs. (3)–(6), the strength of beam received power is closely related to the beam coverage radius. Therefore, a key aspect in solving problem $\mathcal{P}_2$ is to perform appropriate user grouping and select suitable beam coverage radius for each group.

The K-means algorithm has emerged as a highly favored data processing technique in recent years, known for its straightforward implementation and low computational complexity. However, the performance of this algorithm can be significantly influenced by the initial selection of cluster centers, which may lead to a local optimum instead of a global optimum [13]. The K-means++ algorithm enhances clustering quality by refining the selection of initial centroids based on the K-means algorithm. Nevertheless, this algorithm has higher complexity and its effectiveness is limited on certain datasets [14]. Based on these limitations, this paper proposes eK-means algorithm for user grouping.

Specifically, let $\mathcal{U} = \{\mathbf{u}_k\}, k = 1, ..., K$ be the set of user coordinates and the distance between $\mathbf{u}_k$ and $\mathcal{C}$ is defined as $d(\mathbf{u}_k, \mathcal{C}) = \min_{\mathbf{c}_y \in \mathcal{C}} ||\mathbf{u}_k - \mathbf{c}_y||$, where $\mathcal{C} = \{\mathbf{c}_1, ..., \mathbf{c}_Y\}$ is a set of points and $|| \cdot ||$ denotes the Euclidean distance. Then, we define the cost of $\mathcal{U}$ relative to $\mathcal{C}$ as

$$\Phi_{\mathcal{U}}(\mathcal{C}) = \sum_{\mathbf{u}_k \in \mathcal{U}} d^2(\mathbf{u}_k, \mathcal{C}) = \sum_{\mathbf{u}_k \in \mathcal{U}} \min_{y \in \{1, ..., Y\}} ||\mathbf{u}_k - \mathbf{c}_y||^2 \tag{12}$$

Then, for the proposed algorithm, we first randomly select a user from $\mathcal{U}$ as the initial center and add to the user center set $\mathcal{C}$. Subsequently, we calculate the initial clustering cost $\Phi_{\mathcal{U}}(\mathcal{C})$ according to (12), and perform $T = O(\log(\Phi_{\mathcal{U}}(\mathcal{C})))$ iterations. In each iteration, we sample each user point with the probability $p_{\mathbf{u}_k}$, which is given by

$$p_{\mathbf{u}_k} = \min \left\{ \frac{l \cdot d^2(\mathbf{u}_k, \mathcal{C})}{\Phi_{\mathcal{U}}(\mathcal{C})}, 1 \right\} \tag{13}$$

where l is an oversampling factor. Subsequently, we add the sampled points to $\mathcal{C}$, updating the value of $\Phi_{\mathcal{U}}(\mathcal{C})$. The final number of user centers is $|\mathcal{C}| = l \times T$, where $|\cdot|$ denotes the cardinality of the set. Then, we calculate the number of points in $\mathcal{U}$ closer to $\mathbf{c}_y$ than any other point in $\mathcal{C}$, denoted by ω_y. According to $\omega_y, y \in \{1, ..., Y\}$, we obtain the set of initial centroids from $\mathcal{C}$. Finally, we perform standard K-means algorithm for user grouping.

After user grouping, it is necessary to determine the radius of the beam serving per group. Considering that the beam received power decreases as the beam radius increases, we maximize the beam received power by selecting the minimum circle covering [15] that covers all users in the user group, satisfying the beam resolution. The section details are summarized in **Stage 1** of Algorithm 1.

3.2   Graph-Based Frequency Allocation Method

In order to effectively reduce IBI and enhance system throughput, we adopt a conventional FcFR scheme. In this scheme, the SINR of the nth beam is influenced not only by its own signal strength but also constrained by the sidelobe interference from beams of the same color. The level of sidelobe interference is closely related to the relative angle between beams. We define $\mathbf{G}$ as the adjacency matrix, where $[\mathbf{G}]_{n,m}$ represents the interference generated by the mth beam on the nth beam, i.e., $\frac{1}{2}\alpha G_{\text{tx}}^m(\phi_m) G^r P_n^t(\frac{\lambda}{4\pi l})^2$. It is worth noting that the gains of each beam vary depending on the angular difference of θ_b, resulting in the asymmetry of the adjacency matrix.

By grouping users and utilizing N beams to serve user groups, we consider a graph $\mathcal{G}$ with N vertices, defined the vertex set as $\mathcal{V} = \{v_1, \ldots, v_N\}$. In this graph, $[\mathbf{G}]_{n,m}$ represents the weight from vertex n to vertex m, constituting a directed weighted graph. We define $\bar{\mathbf{G}} = \mathbf{G} + \mathbf{G}^T$, converting the initial directed graph into an undirected graph for easier mathematical processing and analysis. This transformation facilitates subsequent mathematical processing and analysis while maintaining the basic structure.

In order to effectively utilize the FcFR technology, we first randomly select four vertices as initial points and assign them to four independent clusters. Next, for the remaining $N - 4$ vertices, we evaluate the sum of edge weights between each point and all points in the four clusters. Utilizing these sums, we assign every unassigned point to the cluster with the minimum sum of edge weights. After iteration, this allocation method reduces IBI of beams of the same color, thereby improving the overall communication performance. Define the ith cluster as $\mathcal{V}_i$, where $\sum_i |\mathcal{V}_i| = |\mathcal{V}|$. The section details are summarized in **Stage 2** of Algorithm 1.

Algorithm 1: Adaptive beamwidth design algorithm

Input: The user coordinates $\mathcal{U} = \{\mathbf{u}_k\}, k = 1, ..., K$

Output: The user group indicator $\{b_{k,n}\}$, the center coordinates $\{\mathbf{z}_n\}$, the beam coverage radius $\{r_n\}$ and the coloring solution Υ_N

1 **for** $N = 1 : K$ **do**
2   **Stage1** :
3   Choose a point at random from $\mathcal{U}$ and add to $\mathcal{C}$;
4   Calculate $\Phi_{\mathcal{U}}(\mathcal{C})$;
5   **for** $t = 1 : O(\log(\Phi_{\mathcal{U}}(\mathcal{C})))$ **do**
6   Calculate the chosen probability $p_{\mathbf{u}_k}$;
7   Sample each point from $\mathcal{U}$ independently with $p_{\mathbf{u}_k}$ and add to $\bar{\mathcal{C}}$;
8   Update $\mathcal{C} \leftarrow \mathcal{C} \cup \bar{\mathcal{C}}$;

9   Calculate ω_y and obtain the set of initial centroids from $\mathcal{C}$;
10   Perform standard K-means algorithm to divide users into N groups;
11   Calculate center coordinate $\mathbf{z}_n$, coverage radius r_n and received power P_n^r;
12   **Stage2** :
13   Calculate $\bar{\mathbf{G}}$ and let $\mathcal{V} = \{v_n\}, n = 1, ..., N$;
14   Choose four vertices randomly from $\mathcal{V}$ and assign them to four separate groups ;
15   Let $\tilde{\mathcal{V}} = \mathcal{V} - \bigcup_i \mathcal{V}_i$;
16   **for** $iter = 1 : N - 4$ **do**
17   Randomly choose $\tilde{v}_j \in \tilde{\mathcal{V}}$;
18         $\mathcal{V}_i = argmin\sum_{p \in \mathcal{V}_i} [\bar{\mathbf{G}}]_{\tilde{v}_j, p}$;
19         $\mathcal{V}_i = \mathcal{V}_i \cup \{\tilde{v}_j\}$;
20         $\tilde{\mathcal{V}} = \tilde{\mathcal{V}} - \{\tilde{v}_j\}$;

21   Obtain coloring solution Υ_N;
22   Calculate P_n^I;
23   **if** $R_n < R_{th}$ **then**
24         $\Sigma_{n=1}^N R_n = 0$;

25   **else**
26   Calculate $\Sigma_{n=1}^N R_n$;

27 Evaluate different designs and record the best $\{b_{k,n}\}$, $\{\mathbf{z}_n\}$, $\{r_n\}$, Υ_N;

---

4   Simulation Results

In this section, the simulation results are presented to evaluate the performance of the proposed scheme. We assume that user coordinates within the satellite coverage area follow a continuous uniform distribution. The satellite power and bandwidth are evenly allocated to each beam. The values of the major simulation setup parameters are summarized in Table 1. To validate the effectiveness of the proposed method, we compare it with the spiral algorithm [16], the K-means algorithm and the K-means++ algorithm [14].

Figure 2 illustrates the user grouping results of the three algorithms. A total of 180 users are randomly generated within a plane area (represented by black

Table 1. Simulation Parameters

Parameter	Value
The height of satellite h	35786 km
The covered radius of satellite	5000 km
Bandwidth W	200 MHz
Satellite power P_{total}	20 dBW
Phased array antenna diameter D	1 m
Frequency band f	20 GHz
User antenna gain G^r	40 dBi
Minimum data rates limitation R_{th}	70 kbps
Noise power spectral density N_0	−174 dBm

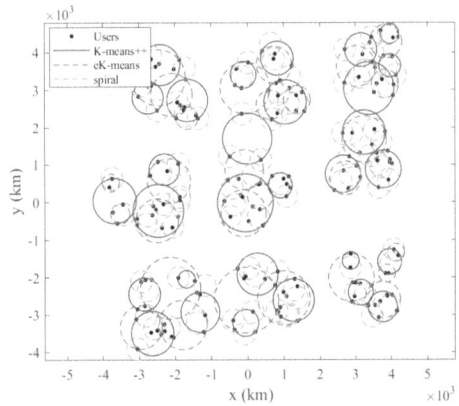

Fig. 2. User grouping of three algorithms with 180 users.

dots), with the number of groups set to 30. The beamwidth is dynamically adjusted based on the number of users in each group. In this case, the system throughput achieved with the eK-means, K-means++ and spiral algorithms is 53.8 Mbps, 52.1 Mbps and 47.5 Mbps, respectively. Therefore, the proposed scheme achieves a higher throughput at the same cost.

Figure 3 shows the correlation between the system throughput of all algorithms and the number of users, with each point representing the average results over 300 random instances. It can be observed that proposed algorithm consistently outperforms spiral, K-means and K-means++ algorithms and this advantage does not significantly diminish as the number of users increases. Moreover, eK-means, K-means and K-means++ algorithms exhibit superior performance compared to spiral algorithm, revealing that adjusting the beamwidth can effectively enhance system throughput. The superior performance of K-means++ over K-means is evident as discussed in detail in Sect. 3. Although K-means++ offers attractive simplicity and speed compared to the standard algorithm, it

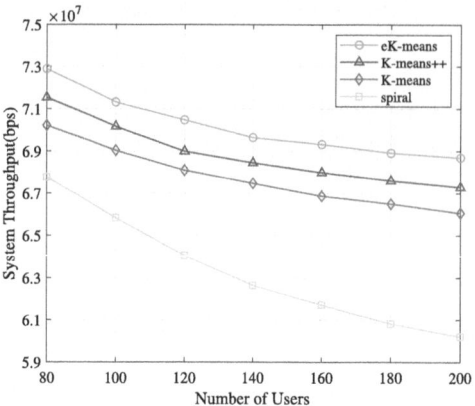

Fig. 3. Comparison of the system throughput under different number of users.

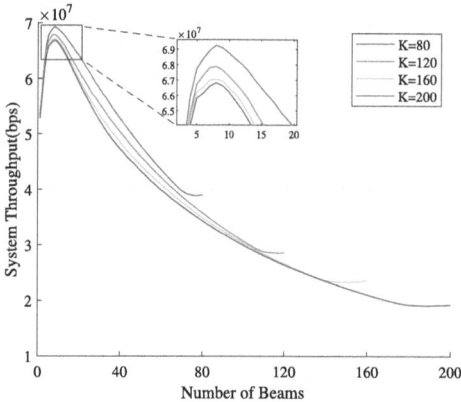

Fig. 4. System throughput verses number of beams with different number of users.

does not guarantee accuracy. The reasons why proposed algorithm outperforms K-means++ are as follows: (1) eK-means carefully selects centroids in both stages. In the first stage, it samples $l \times T$ centroids, which is more than N. In the second stage, K-means++ is applied to prune the centroids and select N centroids from the $l \times T$ centroids. (2) It may be due to the fact that eK-means updates the distribution function $\Phi_{\mathcal{U}}(\mathcal{C})$ only once per round, i.e., it recalculates $\Phi_{\mathcal{U}}(\mathcal{C})$ after selecting l centroids, whereas K-means++ recalculates $\Phi_{\mathcal{U}}(\mathcal{C})$ after selecting each centroid. It is observed that as the number of users increases, the system throughput tends to decrease. This is because the total transmit power of the system remains constant, and as the number of users increases, the distance between beam centers is more likely to be smaller than in the case of fewer users, resulting in increased IBI.

Furthermore, we conducted simulations to analyze the system throughput for different numbers of beams. Figures 4 and 5 present the results for different numbers of users and different minimum coverage radius of beams, respectively. The results indicate that typically about 10 beams are needed to achieve the highest system throughput. This suggests that it is possible to search for the optimal number of groups N within a smaller range without iterating over all possible values, significantly reducing the complexity.

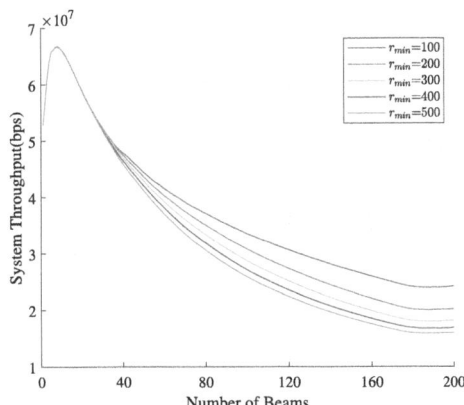

Fig. 5. System throughput verses number of beams with different minimum beam coverage radius.

5   Conclusion

This paper proposes an adaptive beamwidth design scheme that can adjust the number of beams and coverage range dynamically based on user distribution, communication requirements and satellite hardware constraints. This scheme enhances the flexibility of multi-beam satellite systems greatly. Compared to benchmark schemes, the proposed algorithm attains superior system throughput. In future research, we will explore integrating hybrid architectures and efficient user scheduling algorithms to further improve system throughput in large-scale user scenarios.

References

1. Dao, N.-N., et al.: Survey on aerial radio access networks: toward a comprehensive 6g access infrastructure. IEEE Commun. Surv. Tutor. **23**(2), 1193–1225 (2021)
2. Maral, G., Bousquet, M., Sun, Z.: Satellite Communications Systems: Systems, Techniques and Technology. John Wiley & Sons, Hoboken (2020)
3. Chang, S.-H., Park, H.-G., Kim, S.-H., Choi, J.P.: Study on coverage of full frequency reuse in FFR systems based on outage probability. IEEE Trans. Commun. **66**(11), 5828–5843 (2018)

4. Vázquez, M.Á., et al.: precoding in multibeam satellite communications: present and future challenges. IEEE Wirel. Commun. **23**(6), 88–95 (2016)
5. Maeng, S.J., Park, S.H., Moon, S.H., Cho, Y.S.: Inter-beam interference reduction technique for millimeter-wave cellular systems using hybrid beamforming. In: 2018 IEEE 88th Vehicular Technology Conference (VTC-Fall), pp. 1–5 (2018)
6. Hong, W., et al.: Multibeam antenna technologies for 5g wireless communications. IEEE Trans. Antennas Propag. **65**(12), 6231–6249 (2017)
7. Guoliang, X., Tan, F., Ran, Y., Zhao, Y., Luo, J.: Joint beam-hopping scheduling and coverage control in multibeam satellite systems. IEEE Wirel. Commun. Lett. **12**(2), 267–271 (2023)
8. Liu, B., Jiang, C., Kuang, L., Lu, J.: Joint user grouping and beamwidth optimization for satellite multicast with phased array antennas. In: GLOBECOM 2020 - 2020 IEEE Global Communications Conference, pp. 1–6 (2020)
9. Xu, C., Du, Q.: Resource allocation scheme in high throughput satellite systems based on dynamic beam-coverage algorithm. In: 2022 IEEE/CIC International Conference on Communications in China (ICCC), pp. 302–307 (2022)
10. Honnaiah, P.J., Maturo, N., Chatzinotas, S., Kisseleff, S., Krause, J.: Demand-based adaptive multi-beam pattern and footprint planning for high throughput geo satellite systems. IEEE Open J. Commun. Soc. **2**, 1526–1540 (2021)
11. Zhang, C., Jin, J., Zhang, H., Li, T.: Spectral coexistence between Leo and geo satellites by optimizing direction normal of phased array antennas. China Commun. **15**(6), 18–27 (2018)
12. Lin, Z., Ni, Z., Kuang, L., Jiang, C., Huang, Z.: Dynamic beam pattern and bandwidth allocation based on multi-agent deep reinforcement learning for beam hopping satellite systems. IEEE Trans. Veh. Technol. **71**(4), 3917–3930 (2022)
13. Ikotun, A.M., Ezugwu, A.E., Abualigah, L., Abuhaija, B., Heming, J.: K-means clustering algorithms: a comprehensive review, variants analysis, and advances in the era of big data. Inf. Sci. **622**, 178–210 (2023)
14. Li, Y., Zhu, S., Dai, J.: Joint user grouping and resource allocation for Leo satellite multicast. IEEE Syst. J. **17**(3), 4695–4702 (2023)
15. Welzl, E.: Smallest enclosing disks (balls and ellipsoids). In: 1991 Proceedings of New Results and New Trends in Computer Science: Graz, Austria, June 20–21, pp. 359–370 (2005)
16. Lu, W., et al.: Secure transmission for multi-UAV-assisted mobile edge computing based on reinforcement learning. IEEE Trans. Netw. Sci. Eng. **10**(3), 1270–1282 (2022)

Federated Learning-Based Cross-layer Security Design for Satellite Networks

Zhisheng Yin[1], Yonghong Liu[2], Nan Cheng[1(✉)], Linlin Liang[2], Wenbin Sun[3], and Tom H. Luan[4]

[1] School of Telecommunications Engineering, Xidian University, Xi'an 710071, China
zsyin@xidian.edu.cn, dr.nan.cheng@ieee.org
[2] School of Cyber Engineering, Xidian University, Xi'an 710071, China
23151214131@stu.xidian.edu.cn, llliang@xidian.edu.cn
[3] School of Electronics and Information, Northwestern Polytechnical University, 710072 Xi'an, China
sunwenbin@nwpu.edu.cn
[4] School of Cyber Science and Engineering, Xi'an Jiaotong University, Xi'an 710049, China
tom.luan@xjtu.edu.cn

Abstract. The extensive coverage of satellite networks robustly supports federated learning (FL) in multiple domains. This combination protects user privacy and enables extensive data training, with promising applications in remote healthcare, smart agriculture, and environmental monitoring. However, existing FL primarily focuses on data training and aggregation, with less attention given to the secure transmission of model data during upload and download processes. This paper explores cross-layer security in satellite networks, focusing on the physical and application layers. We propose a beamforming optimization scheme based on unsupervised neural network to guarantee secure transmissions without compromising FL training performance. Simulation results underscore the efficacy of our approach in securing physical layer transmissions and affirm its practicality in maintaining robust FL training outcomes.

Keywords: Satellite networks · Federated learning · Cross-layer security · Unsupervised learning

1 Introduction

In recent years, the proliferation of satellite networks (SN) has played a pivotal role in achieving ubiquitous global connectivity, particularly in remote and underserved regions. These networks, encompassing a vast array of connections, harbor substantial data volumes, significantly benefiting machine learning (ML)

© ICST Institute for Computer Sciences, Social Informatics and Telecommunications Engineering 2025
Published by Springer Nature Switzerland AG 2025. All Rights Reserved
H.-H. Chen and W. Meng (Eds.): WiSATS 2024, LNICST 605, pp. 65–76, 2025.
https://doi.org/10.1007/978-3-031-86196-3_6

applications driven by data [1]. However, due to privacy concerns inherent within SN, direct transmission of user data is impractical. Federated learning , as a distributed ML paradigm, emerges as a promising solution to enhance data privacy and reduce the latency associated with centralized data processing [2]. FL involves training across multiple dispersed edge devices or servers that hold local data samples without the need to exchange these samples [3]. This methodology is particularly suited to SN where data privacy and transmission costs are major concerns. Several studies have explored the initial integration of FL with SN, utilizing the distributed nature of these networks to enhance ML models by locally training on satellites and aggregating them through a central server. Notably, the authors of [4] introduced FedSat, which incorporates an asynchronous aggregation algorithm and a corresponding communication protocol, effectively accelerating FL training speeds. Addressing communication challenges in SN, [5] utilized optical relay links to reduce communication latency, alongside effective scheduling strategies for servers and Low Earth Orbit (LEO) satellites to minimize communication costs during FL training. Further, [6] tackled the issue of limited communication bandwidth by proposing SatelliteFL, which accelerates model convergence and enhances bandwidth utilization.

Despite these advancements, most research has primarily focused on optimizing resource allocation, improving data transmission efficiency, and enhancing the robustness of communication links under the unique constraints of SN. However, there remains a significant gap in discussions on the security of model parameter transmission between satellites and ground stations. Transmitting trained models via wireless communications to a central aggregator introduces potential vulnerabilities. Attackers could intercept or eavesdrop on the transmitted model parameters, leading to the leakage of sensitive user information. Some studies have addressed the security aspects of FL, where [7,8] introduced a method combining coding with differential privacy to secure the uplink transmission of model parameters, balancing model accuracy and security. In [9], the authors proposed uncoded wireless FL, implementing differential privacy and adaptive power control for secure transmission. Additionally, [10] focused on the physical layer security of FL in medical data analysis scenarios and proposed a framework based on clustering, along with a security analysis. The aforementioned articles focus on studying the security issues in the transmission process of federated learning models. However, the aforementioned works either focus primarily on physical layer security or on federated learning, without highlighting the importance and interrelationship of studying both aspects together.

Addressing these challenges, this paper proposes a novel secure transmission scheme for FL models in SN. Based on the channel state information (CSI) of both legitimate and wiretap channels, our approach optimizes the beamforming vectors of each client to maximize the minimum secrecy rate, thereby achieving physical layer secure transmission. This method offers superior physical layer security performance compared to traditional approaches. Furthermore, our results, which consider the actual transmission effects on the received model parameters, demonstrate that while there is a slight sacrifice in FL learning performance, the method significantly reduces the risk of eavesdropping. The main contributions of this paper are outlined as follows:

- **Novel Secure Transmission Scheme for FL in SN:** We introduce a new secure transmission scheme specifically designed for FL models in SN. This scheme leverages the CSI of both legitimate and wiretap channels. By optimizing the beamforming vectors of each client with the objective of maximizing the minimum secrecy rate, the scheme ensures enhanced physical layer security during the transmission of FL models.
- **Enhanced Physical Layer Security Performance:** The proposed method outperforms traditional physical layer security approaches by providing superior security performance. This is achieved through the strategic optimization of beamforming vectors based on the CSI, which not only secures the data transmission against eavesdropping but also maximizes the efficiency of the transmission by focusing the signal power in the direction of legitimate receivers while minimizing leakage to potential eavesdroppers.
- **Comprehensive Experimental Evaluation:** We conducted rigorous experiments to evaluate the impact of the secure transmission scheme on the learning performance and security of FL in satellite networks. The results indicate that our proposed unsupervised learning method outperforms traditional physical layer security methods in terms of secrecy rate performance, and the corresponding FL training performance is closer to the ideal scenario. This demonstrates the effectiveness and feasibility of our proposed method.

In Sect. 2, we introduce the system model, including the federated learning model, signal modeling, and problem formulation. In Sect. 3, we propose an unsupervised learning method for optimizing beamforming vectors and explain the integration of physical layer secure transmission schemes with federated learning training. Section 4 presents the simulation results and performance evaluations, followed by the conclusion and future research directions in Sect. 5.

2   System Model and Problem Formulation

2.1   FL Model

In this paper, we consider a scenario where each ground Access Point (AP) functions as a client in a FL framework. To achieve the aggregation of neural network parameters trained by each client, we utilize a LEO satellite as the FL server. The selection of LEO is due to its extensive coverage and ability to simultaneously receive neural networks transmitted by multiple ground APs and aggregate them effectively.

FL aims to enable collaborative model training across multiple decentralized devices without sharing raw data. Each client performs local training on its dataset, and only the model parameters are communicated to the server. The process begins with initializing the global model at the LEO server, which is then distributed to all ground APs. Each AP, acting as a client, trains the model locally using its dataset. Once local training is completed, the APs upload their

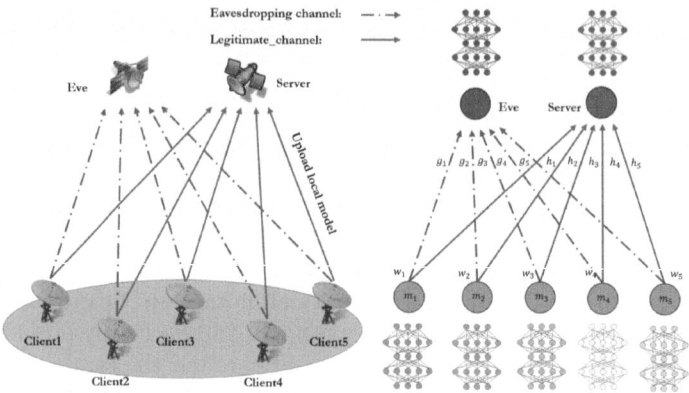

Fig. 1. Federated Learning with Satellite Networks

local models to the LEO satellite simultaneously. The LEO server aggregates these local models and sends the updated global model back to the ground APs. This process is iterated until the FL training converges, resulting in a robust and generalized global model. For the aggregation of the model parameters at the LEO satellite, we employ the Federated Averaging (FedAvg) algorithm. The principle of FedAvg is to compute a weighted average of the model parameters from all clients, effectively integrating the contributions from each client based on the size of their local datasets. The global loss function $F(\mathbf{m}^g)$ is defined as follows:

$$F(\mathbf{m}^g) = \frac{1}{S} \sum_{k=1}^{K} |S_k| F_k(\mathbf{m}^\ell) \tag{1}$$

where, $\mathbf{m}^g$ represents the global model parameter, and $S = \sum_k |S_k|$ refers to the total size of the distributed datasets. The local loss function for client k, $F_k(\mathbf{m})$, is defined as:

$$F_k(\mathbf{m}) = \frac{1}{|S_k|} \sum_{(\mathbf{u}_{k,j}, \mathbf{v}_{k,j}) \in S_k} f(\mathbf{m}; \mathbf{u}_{k,j}, \mathbf{v}_{k,j}) + \lambda R(\mathbf{m}) \tag{2}$$

In this context, $f(\mathbf{m}; \mathbf{u}_{k,j}, \mathbf{v}_{k,j})$ is the sample-wise loss function, $R(\mathbf{m})$ is a strongly convex regularization function, and $\lambda \geq 0$ is a regularization parameter used to prevent model overfitting during training. The goal of FL is to minimize the global loss function, which is given by:

$$\mathbf{m}^\star = \arg\min_{\mathbf{m}^g} F(\mathbf{m}^g) \tag{3}$$

The local model obtained by any client k in an iteration round μ is denoted as $\mathbf{m}^\ell_{k,\mu}$, and the aggregated global model $\mathbf{m}^g_\mu$ is computed as:

$$\mathbf{m}^g_\mu = \sum_{k=1}^{K} \mathbf{m}^\ell_{k,\mu} \frac{|S_k|}{S} \tag{4}$$

To minimize $F(\mathbf{m}^g)$, gradient descent is employed to update local model parameters, which are then utilized to update the global model parameters via Eq. (4). The local model parameters update process is described as follows:

$$\mathbf{m}_{k,\mu}^{\ell} = \mathbf{m}_{\mu-1}^{g} - \frac{\lambda_{lr}}{|S_k|} \sum_{j=1}^{|S_k|} \nabla f(\mathbf{m}_{\mu-1}^{g}; \mathbf{u}_{k,j}, \mathbf{v}_{k,j}) \tag{5}$$

where λ_{lr} denotes the learning rate, and $\nabla f(\mathbf{m}_{\mu-1}^{g}; \mathbf{u}_{k,j}, \mathbf{v}_{k,j})$ is the gradient of the loss function $f(\mathbf{m}_{\mu-1}^{g}; \mathbf{u}_{k,j}, \mathbf{v}_{k,j})$ with respect to $\mathbf{m}_{\mu-1}^{g}$. By repeating this process of local training, uploading, and aggregation, the FL training converges, resulting in an optimized global model that leverages the diverse datasets distributed across multiple ground APs. This approach ensures a scalable and efficient training process, facilitated by the comprehensive coverage of the LEO satellite.

2.2 Signal Model

In the context of Space-Air-Ground integrated networks, we investigate federated learning models in satellite-ground networks, as illustrated in Fig. 1. In low Earth orbit satellites, there are also eavesdropping satellites that exploit the broadcast nature of wireless transmissions to intercept information. Therefore, we focus on the security of the uplink transmission of local model parameters during the federated learning training process.

We assume that all clients are on the same frequency band, and the received signal at the satellite server can be represented as:

$$y = \sum_{k \in K} \mathbf{h}_k^{\dagger} \mathbf{w}_k x_k + n \tag{6}$$

where $\mathbf{h}_k$ denotes the CSI from the kth client to satellite, $(\cdot)^{\dagger}$ denotes the Hermitian transpose, $\mathbf{w}_k \in \mathbb{C}^{N \times 1}$ represents the beamforming vector at the kth client for shaping the uploading signal, x_k contains the confident information which represents the trained local model parameters, and n denotes the noise received by satellite.

Due to the openness of the wireless channel, the eavesdropping signal received by the non-cooperative satellite in the system can be represented as:

$$y_e = \sum_{k \in K} \mathbf{g}_k^{\dagger} \mathbf{w}_k x_k + n_e \tag{7}$$

where $\mathbf{g}_k$ denotes the CSI from the kth client to Eve and n_e represents the noise received by Eve.

2.3 Problem Formulation

Based on (6) and (7), we can calculate the uplink SINRs of the clients at satellite server and eavesdropping satellite, which are obtained as:

$$\gamma_k = \frac{\left\| \mathbf{h}_k^\dagger \mathbf{w}_k \right\|^2}{\sum\limits_{i \neq k, k \in K} \left\| \mathbf{h}_i^\dagger \mathbf{w}_i \right\|^2 + \delta_k^2} \tag{8}$$

$$\gamma_{k,e} = \frac{\left\| \mathbf{g}_k^\dagger \mathbf{w}_k \right\|^2}{\sum\limits_{i \neq k, k \in K} \left\| \mathbf{g}_i^\dagger \mathbf{w}_i \right\|^2 + \delta_e^2} \tag{9}$$

where $\delta_k^2 = \delta_e^2 = 1$ represent the noise power. This simplification assumes equal noise power for both variables.

The secrecy rate of transmission can be obtained as:

$$R_k = \left[\log_2 \left(1 + \gamma_k \right) - \log_2 \left(1 + \gamma_{k,e} \right) \right]^+ . \tag{10}$$

To enhance the secrecy rate of the uplink from clients to satellite server and ensure fairness in confidentiality, we design a problem formulation aimed at maximizing the minimum secrecy rate of the uplink transmission, which can be mathematically expressed as:

$$\mathcal{P}1 : \quad \mathrm{MaxMin}_{\{\mathbf{w}_k\}} \{R_k\}, \tag{11}$$

$$\mathrm{s.t.} : \quad \left\| \mathbf{w}_k \right\|^2 \leq P, \tag{11a}$$

$$\mathbf{w}_k \succ \mathbf{0}, \tag{11b}$$

in which (11a) constrains the total power of the system using P, and (11b) constrains the beamforming at the clients.

3   Federated Learning-Based Cross-Layer Security Design

In this section, we propose a beamforming vector optimization method to solve the non-convex problem presented in (11) and explain how to associate the physical layer secure transmission scheme with federated learning training performance.

3.1   Unsupervised Learning Methods for Beamforming

In this study, we utilize a deep complex network for training. We employ unsupervised deep learning to optimize the beamforming vectors in a wireless communication system. To address optimization problem $\mathcal{P}1$, the neural network needs to be trained based on legitimate and wiretap channel parameters. Since both legitimate and eavesdropping channel parameters are complex matrices, we utilize a deep complex network for training to avoid loss of important information due to operations such as extraction, concatenation, and unfolding.

The input to the network is a complex matrix $H = h_{real} + ih_{imag}$, where h_{real} and h_{imag} represent the real and imaginary parts of the legitimate and wiretap channel parameters, respectively. For convolution operations in the complex domain, the complex vector $z = x + iy$ is processed as:

$$H * z = (h_{real} * x - h_{imag} * y) + i(h_{imag} * x + h_{real} * y) \tag{12}$$

Complex convolution layers can thus perform equivalent operations by leveraging traditional real-valued convolution layers. We set up four complex convolution layers for training, with the output channel numbers of the first, second, and third layers being 32, 16, and 8, respectively. Each layer uses the LeakyReLU activation function, defined as:

$$\text{LeakyReLU}(x) = \begin{cases} x, & \text{if } x > 0 \\ \alpha x, & \text{if } x \leq 0 \end{cases} \tag{13}$$

Compared to the ReLU function, LeakyReLU effectively addresses the issue of gradient vanishing caused by negative input values. The Adam algorithm is employed throughout the training process to fine-tune the neural network's parameters and weights, ensuring stable convergence of the objective function and optimal secrecy rate performance. The network outputs beamforming vectors for five users. The neural network parameters, θ, are updated according to the gradient update rule:

$$\theta_t = \theta_{t-1} - \alpha \frac{\hat{m}_t}{\sqrt{\hat{v}_t} + \epsilon} \tag{14}$$

where, α represents the learning rate, ϵ is a small constant to prevent division by zero, and $\hat{m}_t$ and $\hat{v}_t$ are bias corrected estimates of the first moment (mean) and the second moment (uncentered variance), defined as:

$$\hat{m}_t = \frac{m_t}{1 - \beta_1^t}, \quad \hat{v}_t = \frac{v_t}{1 - \beta_2^t} \tag{15}$$

where β_1 and β_2 represent the decay rates for the first and second moment estimates, respectively. The estimates m_t and v_t are defined as:

$$m_t = \beta_1 m_{t-1} + (1 - \beta_1)\mathcal{L}(\boldsymbol{\theta}_t) \tag{16}$$

$$v_t = \beta_2 v_{t-1} + (1 - \beta_2)\mathcal{L}(\boldsymbol{\theta}_t)^2 \tag{17}$$

Since there is a constraint equation in the optimization problem $\mathcal{P}1$, a straightforward method is to use the Lagrangian dual method to transform the constrained optimization problem into an unconstrained one. The neural network training optimizes the Lagrangian dual function. However, the noninterpretability of the NN based on the statistical learning principle implies that the NN can only probabilistically optimize the Lagrangian dual function and cannot ensure that the output will always satisfy the constraint. Therefore, we design an efficient activation function $\mathcal{S}$ to ensure that the NN output adheres to the constraint.

The activation function $\mathcal{S}$ processes a complex vector as input and outputs a complex vector. If the square of the two-norm of the complex vector is less than P, it directly outputs the input complex vector. If the square of the two-norm exceeds P, it scales the complex vector by dividing it by the square of the two-norm and multiplying by P. This ensures that the square of the two-norm of the output complex vector is always less than or equal to P. Formally, $\mathcal{S}$ is defined as:

$$
\mathcal{S}(\mathbf{w}_k) = \begin{cases} \mathbf{w}_k, & \text{if } \|\mathbf{w}_k\|^2 \leq P \\ \mathbf{w}_k \frac{\sqrt{P}}{\|\mathbf{w}_k\|}, & \text{if } \|\mathbf{w}_k\|^2 > P \end{cases} \tag{18}
$$

The derivative of $\mathcal{S}$ with respect to the input complex vector $\mathbf{w}_k$ is given by:

$$
\frac{\partial \mathcal{S}(\mathbf{w}_k)}{\partial \mathbf{w}_k} = \begin{cases} 1, & \text{if } \|\mathbf{w}_k\|^2 \leq P \\ \frac{\sqrt{P}}{\|\mathbf{w}_k\|} - \frac{\mathbf{w}_k(\mathbf{w}_k^H \mathbf{w}_k)}{\|\mathbf{w}_k\|^3}, & \text{if } \|\mathbf{w}_k\|^2 > P \end{cases} \tag{19}
$$

This piecewise derivative confirms that $\mathcal{S}$ is differentiable. By incorporating the activation function $\mathcal{S}$ and defining the loss function as $\mathcal{L}(\boldsymbol{\theta}_t) = -\min R_k$, we ensure that the NN training process adheres to the constraints and achieves optimal performance. This allows for chain derivation to obtain the derivative of the NN parameter with respect to the loss function, facilitating unsupervised NN training.

To ensure the magnitude constraint on the beamforming vector of each client, we define a mask as follows:

$$
\text{mask}_k = \max\left(1, \frac{\|\mathbf{w}_k\|^2}{P}\right) \tag{20}
$$

The beamforming vector is then adjusted using the mask

$$
\mathbf{w_k}' = \frac{\mathbf{w_k}}{\text{mask}_k} \tag{21}
$$

By integrating the activation function $\mathcal{S}$ and the loss function $\mathcal{L}$, we ensure that the NN training process meets the constraints and achieves optimal performance in beamforming vector optimization, thus similar to [11,12] the gradient of objective function with respect to the parameters of NN can be obtained by chain rule, resulting in an unsupervised learning method.

3.2   Combination with Federated Learning

In an ideal federated learning model, the uplink transmission links where each client uploads local model parameters to the server are assumed to be perfectly transmitted. Thus, aggregation at the server can be directly computed using the formula. However, in actual transmission processes, signals are subject to attenuation, noise, and other influences. To simplify this process, it is understandable to directly add noise to the model parameters based on the SINR calculated from formulas (8) and (9), equivalent to the noise impact received during the uplink transmission process.

However, adding noise to model parameters $\mathbf{m}$ at the data level based on the signal level metric SINR is unreasonable. Therefore, we further model the relationship between SINR and the model parameters through bit error rate (BER) and parameter quantization with bit flipping, which can be calculated using the following formula:

$$BER = Q\left(\sqrt{2 \cdot SINR}\right) \tag{22}$$

The Q function is the Gaussian Q-function. Next, we use this BER model for parameter quantization and bit flipping. First, the model parameters are quantized. Assuming the model parameters are represented as a floating-point array $\mathbf{m}$, we quantize them into binary representation:

$$\mathbf{m}_{binary} = Binary(\mathbf{m}) \tag{23}$$

where $Binary(\cdot)$ denotes converting a floating-point number into its binary representation.

According to the BER calculated in (22) and the binary representation of the model parameters generated in (23), we generate a random flipping mask for each bit, defined as:

$$\mathbf{m}_{mask} = FlipMask(\mathbf{m}_{binary}, BER) \tag{24}$$

The rule for bit flipping the binary model parameters $\mathbf{m}_{binary}$ according to $\mathbf{m}_{mask}$ is defined as follows:

$$\mathbf{m}_{binary}[i] = \begin{cases} 1 - \mathbf{m}_{binary}[i], & \text{if } \mathbf{m}_{mask}[i] = 1 \\ \mathbf{m}_{binary}[i], & \text{otherwise} \end{cases} \tag{25}$$

After the binary model parameters have undergone bit flipping, they can be converted back to floating-point format for model aggregation at the server.

4 Numerical Results

In this section, we evaluate the secrecy performance of clients' uplink transmissions and compare the performance of federated learning models under different conditions. The simulation parameters are configured as follows: five clients are randomly distributed within a 1000 km radius area centered on the satellite server, with the satellite positioned at coordinates (0 km, 0 km, 600 km). All clients are equipped with 4 antennas. The channel power gains from clients to the satellite server and to the eavesdropping satellite at a reference distance of 1 meter are set to -40 dB. The Rician factors for the channels from clients to the satellite server and to the eavesdropping satellite are 10 dB and 5 dB, respectively, for the uplink transmissions.

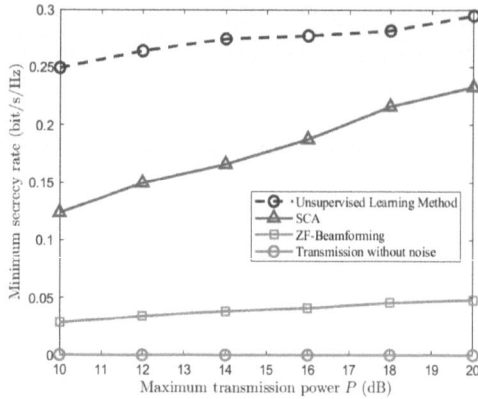

Fig. 2. Maximum transmission power P Vs. the minimum secrecy rate

Figure 2 shows the influence of the maximum transmission power on the minimum secrecy rate. As observed, the secrecy rate performance increases with the maximum transmission power. According to Theorem 1 in [13], as the maximum transmission power increases, more power will be allocated to clients, thereby improving the performance of secrecy rate. Compared to successive convex approximation(SCA) and Zero Forcing(ZF) beamforming, our proposed unsupervised learning method can optimize and achieve beamforming vector schemes with better secrecy rate performance. When PLS is not considered, the signal secrecy rate is essentially zero, making it vulnerable to eavesdropping attack.

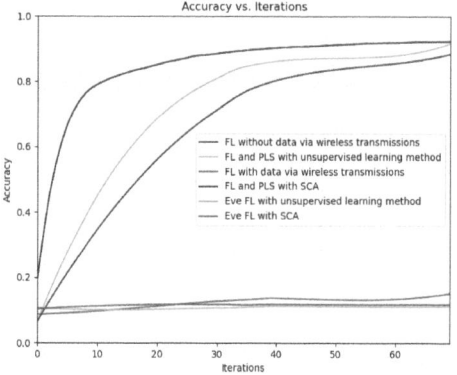

Fig. 3. Comparison of the accuracy

In Fig. 3, it can be observed that the unsupervised learning method we proposed achieves accuracy closer to the ideal scenario than SCA. This demonstrates that our proposed method can meet physical layer security standards while minimizing the impact on federated learning training accuracy performance. When noise during transmission is considered, federated learning training fails to converge. Similarly, eavesdroppers cannot train based on intercepted signals, demonstrating the effectiveness of the physical layer security transmission scheme in mitigating eavesdropping risks.

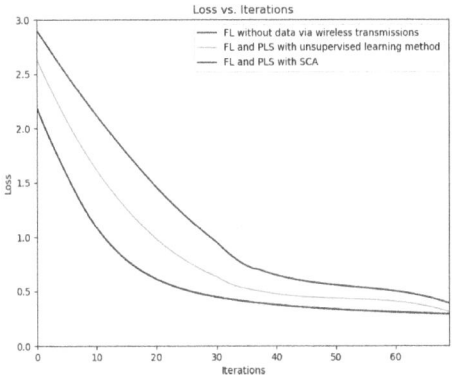

Fig. 4. Comparison of the loss

In Fig. 4, our proposed unsupervised learning method for optimizing beamforming vectors achieves physical layer security transmission while ensuring that the federated learning model achieves loss close to ideal conditions, which outperforms SCA in FL loss performance. Without any processing but considering noise during actual transmission, the FL losses corresponding to both beamforming vector optimization methods at the eavesdropping satellite are too large to be depicted in the figure, indicating their failure to achieve training effectiveness. This underscores the practical significance of beamforming vector optimization for secure model parameter transmission.

5   Conclusion

To achieve cross-layer security in satellite networks, this paper ensures the security of federated data uploads through secure transmission design while also considering FL learning performance. Particularly, an unsupervised learning approach for beamforming optimization in satellite uplinks is proposed, which achieves a superior secrecy rate. Simultaneously, its federated learning model performance decreases only slightly relative to ideal conditions. This demonstrates the feasibility and effectiveness of our proposed method, indicating that it is possible to enhance both secure transmission and federated learning performance in real wireless communication scenarios. In future work, the secure transmission of global model parameters in federated learning will be further investigated.

Acknowledgments. This work was supported in part by the National Natural Science Foundation of China (No. 62201432, 62071356, and 62101429).

References

1. Cheng, N., et al.: 6g service-oriented space-air-ground integrated network: a survey. Chin. J. Aeronaut. **35**, 1–18 (2022)
2. McMahan, B., Moore, E., Ramage, D., Hampson, S., Arcas, B.A.: Communication-efficient learning of deep networks from decentralized data. In: Singh, A., Zhu, J. (eds.) Proceedings of the 20th International Conference on Artificial Intelligence and Statistics. Proceedings of Machine Learning Research, vol. 54, pp. 1273–1282. PMLR, 20–22 April 2017
3. Shen, J., et al.: RingSFL: an adaptive split federated learning towards taming client heterogeneity. IEEE Trans. Mob. Comput. **23**(5), 5462–5478 (2024)
4. Razmi, N., Matthiesen, B., Dekorsy, A., Popovski, P.: Ground-assisted federated learning in LEO satellite constellations. IEEE Wirel. Commun. Lett. **11**(4), 717–721 (2022)
5. Chen, C.Y., Shen, L.H., Feng, K.T., Yang, L.L., Wu, J.M.: Edge selection and clustering for federated learning in optical inter-LEO satellite constellation. In: 2023 IEEE 34th Annual International Symposium on Personal, Indoor and Mobile Radio Communications (PIMRC), pp. 1–6 (2023)
6. Yang, C., et al.: Communication-efficient satellite-ground federated learning through progressive weight quantization. IEEE Trans. Mob. Comput. **23**, 1–14 (2024)
7. Zhang, H., Yang, C., Dai, B.: When wireless federated learning meets physical layer security: the fundamental limits. In: IEEE INFOCOM 2022 - IEEE Conference on Computer Communications Workshops (INFOCOM WKSHPS), pp. 1–6 (2022)
8. Zhang, H., Yang, C., Dai, B.: A finite blocklength approach for wireless hierarchical federated learning in the presence of physical layer security. In: IEEE INFOCOM 2023 - IEEE Conference on Computer Communications Workshops (INFOCOM WKSHPS), pp. 1–6 (2023)
9. Liu, D., Simeone, O.: Privacy for free: wireless federated learning via uncoded transmission with adaptive power control. IEEE J. Sel. Areas Commun. **39**(1), 170–185 (2021)
10. Ahmed, J., Nguyen, T.N., Ali, B., Javed, M.A., Mirza, J.: On the physical layer security of federated learning based IoMT networks. IEEE J. Biomed. Health Inform. **27**(2), 691–697 (2023)
11. Wang, X., et al.: Scalable resource management for dynamic MEC: an unsupervised link-output graph neural network approach. In: 2023 IEEE 34th Annual International Symposium on Personal, Indoor and Mobile Radio Communications (PIMRC), pp. 1–6. IEEE (2023)
12. Wang, X., et al.: Joint flying relay location and routing optimization for 6g UAV-IoT networks: a graph neural network-based approach. Rem. Sens. **14**(17), 4377 (2022)
13. Yin, Z., et al.: UAV-assisted secure uplink communications in satellite-supported IoT: secrecy fairness approach. IEEE Internet Things J. **11**(4), 6904–6915 (2024)

DRL Based Secure Optimization for RIS Aided SATINs with RSMA

Min Wu[1(✉)], Kefeng Guo[1], Zhi Lin[2], Huiyun Xia[3], Kang An[4,5], Liang Yang[5], and Jiangzhou Wang[6]

[1] School of Space Information, Space Engineering University, 101407 Beijing, China
1800022837@pku.edu.cn
[2] College of Electronic Engineering, National University of Defense Technology, 230037 Hefei, China
[3] College of Telecommunications and Information Engineering, Nanjing University of Posts and Telecommunications, 210003 Nanjing, China
[4] Sixty third Research Institute, National University of Defense Technology, 210007 Nanjing, China
ankang89@nudt.edu.cn
[5] College of Computer Science and Electronic Engineering, Hunan University, 410082 Changsha, China
liangy@hnu.edu.cn
[6] School of Engineering, University of Kent, CT2 7NT Canterbury, UK
j.z.wang@kent.ac.uk

Abstract. Amid the escalating demand for accessible users and security insurance in satellite aerial terrestrial integrated networks (SATINs), security and energy efficiency emerge as pivotal indicators. This paper proposes a secure beamforming scheme in reconfigurable intelligent surface (RIS) aided SATINs, in presence with multiple eavesdroppers, where rate splitting multiple access (RSMA) and RIS are adopted at the secondary UAV networks for achieving multiuser diversity and antijamming. To optimize the secrecy energy efficiency (SEE) for secondary networks while adhering to constraints on ground earth station (GES) secrecy rate, a deep reinforcement learning (DRL) framework is proposed to address the coupling between optimization variables through the improved proximal policy optimization (PPO) method, of which from existing DRL scheme is that the proposed one builds a unified learning framework. Simulation results indicate that the SEE derived by the proposed DRL scheme is superior to that of benchmark schemes, which validate the advantage of this work.

Keywords: Satellite aerial terrestrial integrated networks · reconfigurable intelligent surface · rate splitting multiple access · deep reinforcement learning · security

H.-H. Chen and W. Meng (Eds.): WiSATS 2024, LNICST 605, pp. 77–88, 2025.
https://doi.org/10.1007/978-3-031-86196-3_7

1 Introduction

Recently, satellite aerial terrestrial integrated networks (SATINs) has been recognized as a promising infrastructure for the next generation networks (NGs), where satellite and unmanned aerial vehicle (UAV) subnetworks employ cognitive radio (CR) technology to share the limited frequency spectrum under certain constraints [1,2]. But in this way, the challenge of preventing eavesdroppers (Eves) from intercepting private signals while ensuring the quality of service (QoS) of the primary network is a crucial one to be solved. As an effective supplement to cryptographic methods, physical layer security (PLS) has attracted extensive attention and investigation [3]. From this perspective, achieving an optimal balance between security and performance has become an important part of realizing the potential of the SATINs.

As well known that higher energy utilization efficiency is one of the inherent requirements of the NGs. Based on this consideration, reconfigurable intelligent surfaces (RISs) appear to tackle this issue. In contrast to traditional relays, RIS operates without the need for active radio frequency (RF) chains or complex signal processing components. This feature enables it to demonstrate significant capabilities in enhancing the PLS for SATINs. By strategically manipulating the phase shift of reflection elements, RIS facilitates constructive superimposition of direct and reflected signals at intended legitimate users, meanwhile inducing destructive interference for potential Eves [4–6]. Additionally, another method for energy efficiency improvement is multiple access, such as rate splitting multiple access (RSMA), which can split information into common and private parts for overlay transmission at the transmitter. This technique can leverage uses successive interference cancellation (SIC) at the receiver, which is considered a powerful approach for augmenting spectral efficiency (SE). Specifically, within the CR enabled NTNs, the design significance of this architecture lies in improving the performance of the unauthorized secondary network (SN). As a result, exploring the integration of RIS into SATINs to support RSMA in maximizing SEE of the SN while ensuring interference limitations becomes crucial.

Optimization problems in the RIS assisted SATINs under consideration are usually nonlinear and may contain a large number of variables. Traditional optimization methods often struggle to deal with this complexity. It is worth mentioning that in problems that require optimization of multiple variables, it is difficult to get optimized answers by traditional methods, and on this basis, model free artificial intelligence (AI) emerges. Based on the above, By establishing an appropriate Markov decision process (MDP), DRL has become a powerful technology for handling explosive communication data and finding optimal solutions through interaction with the environment continuously.

As discussed in the former paragraph, communication security is also the demand of the SATINs. This requirement highlights the significance of PLS in safeguarding transmissions against eavesdropping. Therefore, it can be seen that integrating multiple security enhancing technologies such as RIS and RSMA at different levels into SATINs will be a promising infrastructure. However, this amalgamation also presents several challenges that must be addressed to optimize security performance effectively. First of all, the foremost challenge lies in the inadequacy of traditional model based wireless technologies to meet the requirements of emerging RIS assisted SATINs, such as excessively complex communication scenarios with accurate mathematical description. Second, with the incorporation of RIS, the dynamic adjustments of its reflective elements add to the unpredictability of the wireless environment, complicating real time sensing. Finally, the dynamic multi channel access of CR technology in the process of spectrum sharing requires independent selection of access free spectrum resources under the condition of time varying spectrum occupancy. As an effective method to solve dynamic problems, DRL has been widely used in the wireless communication optimization.

There is currently researches on utilizing DRL in RIS aided secure SATINs with RSMA to maximize secure transmission performance of secondary networks. Our objective is to maximize the SEE by jointly designing the transmit beamforming of the UAV, RIS reflecting matrix and power splitting ratio, while guaranteeing the service quality of the primary network. Since there are several mutually coupled parameters in the formulated optimization problem, which are difficult to be solved using traditional algorithms, we develop a unified proximal policy optimization (PPO) learning framework based on the DRL method by designing dynamic reward functions that can seamlessly handle both continuous and discrete variables. Finally, simulation results demonstrate that our proposed PPO enabled framework exhibits greater adaptability than several benchmark approaches.

2   System Model and Problem Formulation

In this paper, we investigate the SEE optimization of secondary users in RIS aided SATINs in the presence of multiple eavesdroppers (Eves). In this setup, the whole integrated networks consists of two subnetworks, where the satellite sends multicast signals to multiple GESs and shares spectrum to UAV with overlay mode, which is denoted as the PN, while the UAV adopts the RSMA to serve N vehicle users with the aid of RIS, which is denoted as SN (Fig. 1).

2.1   Signal Model with RSMA

According to [7,8], it is assumed that $\mathbf{h}_{U,n} \in C^{N_U \times 1}$, $\mathbf{h}_{U,m} \in C^{N_U \times 1}$, $\mathbf{h}_{R,n} \in C^{K \times 1}$, $\mathbf{h}_{R,m} \in C^{K \times 1}$, $\mathbf{h}_{RG} \in C^{K \times 1}$, $\mathbf{H}_{UR} \in C^{N_U \times K}$ and $\mathbf{H}_{UG} \in C^{N_U \times K}$ are the channel gains from the UAV to the n th vehicle user (VU), from the UAV to the m th Eve, from the RIS to the n th VU, from the RIS to the m th Eve, from the RIS to the GES, from the UAV to the RIS, from the UAV to the GES, respectively. Meanwhile, $\mathbf{g}_{e,m}$, $\mathbf{g}_{c,n}$ denotes the channel gains from satellite to the m th Eve, the satellite to the n th VU. We assume that the satellite and the UAV are outfitted with array fed reflector antennas comprising N_S feeds and a uniform linear array (ULA) consisting of N_U antennas, respectively. In the transmission phase of the primary network from the satellite to a total of L

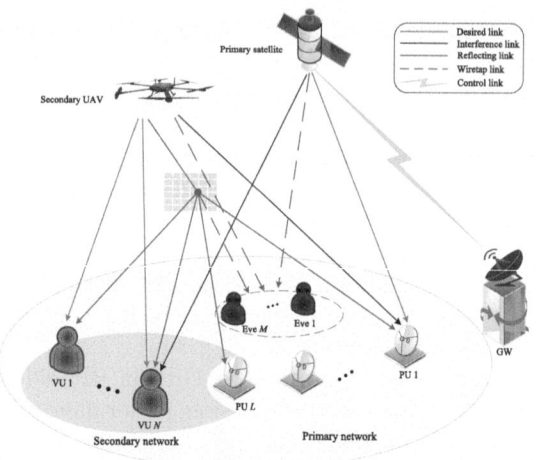

Fig. 1. Proposed system model.

ground earth stations (GESs) as PUs, the private multicast signal x is mapped to the satellite transmit beamforming precoding matrix $\mathbf{w} \in C^{N_S \times 1}$ in the presence of M Eves [9]. During the secondary network signalling process, the UAV can be described as utilizing its flexibility to serve N single antenna ground VUs, while the RIS equipped with $K = K_y \times K_z$ reflective elements is also deployed in the SN to enhance the expected signals at the VUs while suppressing the signals received by the Eves. Specifically, the reflecting phase shift matrix of RIS is given by $\mathbf{\Phi} = diag\left\{\beta_1 e^{j\theta_1}, \beta_2 e^{j\theta_2}, ..., \beta_K e^{j\theta_K}\right\}$, where β_k and θ_k are the amplitude factor and phase shift at the k th RIS element [10]. Meanwhile, applying the RSMA technology at the UAV, the unicast signal s_n designated for the n th VU gets divided into a common subsignal s_c with common transmit beamforming vector $\mathbf{v}_c \in \mathbb{C}^{N_U \times 1}$ and a private subsignal $s_{p,n}$ with the private beamforming vector $\mathbf{v}_n \in \mathbb{C}^{N_U \times 1}$. Utilizing a shared codebook among all VUs, the common subsignals are collectively encoded into a common signal stream s_c. The same frequency band is permitted to be shared by both satellites and the UAV within a specified interference tolerance in the GES of the primary network. Notably, a total of M Eves can also intercept signals transmitted by satellites and the UAV in a similar manner as legitimate VUs [11]. Consequently, the received signals at the GES, the m th Eve and the n th VU can be expressed as

$$y_G = \mathbf{g}^H \mathbf{w}x + \mathbf{z}_G^H \mathbf{v}_c s_c + \sum_{n=1}^{N} \mathbf{z}_G^H \mathbf{v}_n s_{p,n} + n_G, \tag{1}$$

$$y_{s,m} = \mathbf{g}_{e,m}^H \mathbf{w}x + \mathbf{z}_{e,m}^H \mathbf{v}_c s_c + \sum_{n=1}^{N} \mathbf{z}_{e,m}^H \mathbf{v}_n s_{p,n} + n_{e,m}, \tag{2}$$

$$y_{c,n} = \mathbf{g}_{c,n}^H \mathbf{w}x + \mathbf{z}_{c,n}^H \mathbf{v}_c s_c + \sum_{n=1}^{N} \mathbf{z}_{c,n}^H \mathbf{v}_n s_{p,n} + n_{c,n}, \tag{3}$$

where

$$\mathbf{z}_G = \left(\mathbf{H}_{UG} + \mathbf{h}_{RG}^H \mathbf{\Phi} \mathbf{H}_{UR}\right)^H, \tag{4}$$

$$\mathbf{z}_{e,m} = \left(\mathbf{h}_{U,m} + \mathbf{h}_{R,m}^H \mathbf{\Phi} \mathbf{H}_{UR}\right)^H, \tag{5}$$

$$\mathbf{z}_{c,n} = \left(\mathbf{h}_{U,n} + \mathbf{h}_{R,n}^H \mathbf{\Phi} \mathbf{H}_{UR}\right)^H. \tag{6}$$

Thus, the achievable rate of the GES, the m th Eves, the common signal s_c and the private subsignal stream of the n th VU can be expressed as

$$R_G = \log_2\left(1 + \frac{\left|\mathbf{g}^H \mathbf{w}\right|^2}{\left|\mathbf{z}_G^H \mathbf{v}_c\right|^2 + \sum_{n=1}^{N}\left|\mathbf{z}_G^H \mathbf{v}_n\right|^2 + \sigma_G^2}\right), \tag{7a}$$

$$R_{s,m} = \log_2\left(1 + \frac{\left|\mathbf{g}_{e,m}^H \mathbf{w}\right|^2}{\left|\mathbf{z}_{e,m}^H \mathbf{v}_c\right|^2 + \sum_{n=1}^{N}\left|\mathbf{z}_{e,m}^H \mathbf{v}_n\right|^2 + \sigma_{e,m}^2}\right), \tag{7b}$$

$$R_{c,n} = \log_2\left(1 + \frac{\left|\mathbf{z}_{c,n}^H \mathbf{v}_c\right|^2}{\left|\mathbf{g}_{c,n}^H \mathbf{w}\right|^2 + \sum_{n=1}^{N}\left|\mathbf{z}_{c,n}^H \mathbf{v}_n\right|^2 + \sigma_{c,n}^2}\right), \tag{7c}$$

$$R_{p,n} = \log_2\left(1 + \frac{\left|\mathbf{z}_{c,n}^H \mathbf{v}_n\right|^2}{\left|\mathbf{g}_{c,n}^H \mathbf{w}\right|^2 + \sum_{i \neq n}^{N}\left|\mathbf{z}_{c,n}^H \mathbf{v}_i\right|^2 + \sigma_{c,n}^2}\right). \tag{7d}$$

Meanwhile, we define $\chi_n \in (0, 1)$ as the common private power splitting ratio for the n th VU [12]. In this form, the above achievable rate of the common and private stream of the i th VU can be rewritten as

$$R_{c,i} = \log_2\left(1 + \frac{\chi_i \left|\mathbf{z}_{c,i}^H \mathbf{v}_c\right|^2}{\chi_i \sum_{n=1}^{N}\left|\mathbf{z}_{c,i}^H \mathbf{v}_n\right|^2 + \left|\mathbf{g}_{c,i}^H \mathbf{w}\right|^2 + \sigma_{c,i}^2}\right), \tag{8}$$

and

$$R_{p,i} = \log_2\left(1 + \frac{\chi_i \left|\mathbf{z}_{c,i}^H \mathbf{v}_i\right|^2}{\chi_i \sum_{n=1,n\neq i}^{N}\left|\mathbf{z}_{c,i}^H \mathbf{v}_n\right|^2 + \left|\mathbf{g}_{c,i}^H \mathbf{w}\right|^2 + \sigma_{c,i}^2}\right). \tag{9}$$

2.2   Problem Description

For secure and green communication, we need to codesign the UAV active secure beamforming vector $\mathbf{v} = [\mathbf{v}_c, \mathbf{v}_1, ..., \mathbf{v}_N]$ with $\mathbf{v}_c$ being the common stream beamforming vector, the RIS phase shift matrix $\mathbf{\Phi}$, and the transmit power splitting ratio χ_n to maximize the SN SEE, which can be defined as the ratio of the sum rate of the SN to the power consumption [13]. Besides, the achievable sum rate of the UAV enabled SN can be expressed as

$$R_U\left(\{\mathbf{v}_n, \mathbf{\Phi}\}, \chi_n\right) = \sum_{i=1}^{N} \left(c_i + R_{p,i}\right), \tag{10}$$

While satisfying the GES secrecy constraint, the mathematical expression for the SEE can be defined as

$$\text{SEE} = \frac{R_U - \sum_{m=1}^{M} \max R_{s,m}}{\left(\|\mathbf{v}_c\|^2 + \sum_{n=1}^{N} \|\mathbf{v}_n\|^2\right) + P_C}, \tag{11}$$

where P_C denotes the constant circuit power consumption at UAV. Here, we assume that the UAV provides communication services in a hovering state, and its energy consumption can refer to [14]. Mathematically, the whole optimization problem can be formulated as

$$\mathbf{P0} : \max_{\mathbf{v}_n, \mathbf{\Phi}, \chi_n} \max_{\mathbf{e}_{U,n}, \mathbf{e}_{R,n}} \text{SEE}, \tag{12a}$$

$$\text{s.t. } C1 : \min_{\mathbf{e}_{g,m}, \mathbf{e}_{z,m}} R_G - R_{s,m} \geq \Delta_U, \forall m, \tag{12b}$$

$$C2 : R_{c,n} \geq \Delta_c, \forall n, \tag{12c}$$

$$C3 : R_{p,n} \geq \Delta_p, \forall n, \tag{12d}$$

$$C4 : \|\mathbf{w}\|^2 \leq P_S, \|\mathbf{v}_c\|^2 + \sum_{n=1}^{N} \|\mathbf{v}_n\|^2 \leq P_U, \tag{12e}$$

$$C5 : \left|\exp\left(j\theta^k\right)\right| = 1, \forall k, \tag{12f}$$

$$C6 : \sum_{n=1}^{N} c_n \leq \min_n R_{c,n}\left(\{\mathbf{w}_l\}, \mathbf{\Phi}, \chi_n\right), \tag{12g}$$

where $\mathbf{e}_{U,n}$ and $\mathbf{e}_{R,n}$ denote the channel estimation error about $\mathbf{h}_{U,n}$ and $\mathbf{h}_{R,n}$. And, P_C denotes the constant circuit power consumption. Meanwhile, $C1$ denotes that the achievable rate of the secondary network users (SUs) must be less than the achievable rate of the PUs, and $C2$ and $C3$ denote the minimum rate requirement for the SN transmit signals. $C4$ is the transmit power limit for PN and SN, where P_S and P_U are the preset power caps for satellites and UAVs. $C6$ denotes that the VU of the SN is able to fully decode the common stream.

3   MDP for the Secrecy Energy Efficiency Maximization

As shown in Sect. 2, the problem **P0** is a high dimension complex problem that is difficult to solve directly, because it contains both discrete and continuous variables. In addition, in realistic RIS aided secure SATINs, the capabilities about obtaining information of VUs in the SN, the channel quality, and the service demand will change dynamically. Moreover, **P0** is an optimization problem confined to a single time slot. Its solution might converge to a suboptimal one, akin to a greedy search, given the overlooked historical environmental state and long term gains. Therefore, it is generally infeasible to employ conventional optimization techniques such as AO, SDP or SCA to achieve efficient and secure beamforming strategies in uncertain dynamic satellite wireless environments.

Model free reinforcement learning is a dynamic programming tool which can be continuously adopted to tackle decision making problems by learning optimal solutions in dynamic environments. Therefore, we model the secure beamforming optimization in RIS aided SATINs as an RL problem. In addition, in the model free RL family, the policy based learning approach, represented prominently by PPO, which solves the problem of difficult step size determination in policy gradient algorithms by using stochastic gradient ascent method to optimize instead of the objective function over, which can achieve small batch updates in multiple training steps. Here, the optimization problem **P0** is first transformed into MDP and then solved through by the proposed approach that supports a unified PPO framework [15]. By utilizing the PPO algorithm, the gradient is updated by employing a method that trims advantage functions. This is done to control the magnitude of each update, with the goal of maximizing the cumulative reward for agents across various states.

1) State space: For the designed state space, it contains, in principle, as much information as possible about the environment relevant to the problem **P0**. The effectiveness of the DRL algorithm is largely determined by the state space, which needs to include all participating states of the entire system, such as the current channel information of all users, all action vectors to be selected $\mathbf{A}$, and rewards $\mathbf{R} \in \mathcal{R}$ obtained after interaction. The current information about all users mainly includes the corresponding channel information, the achievable rate can be defined as

$$\mathbf{U} = \{\mathbf{g}, \mathbf{h}_n, \mathbf{h}_m, R_G, R_n, R_m\}, \tag{13}$$

where $\mathbf{g}$, $\mathbf{h}_n$ and $\mathbf{h}_m$ are the relevant channel coefficients of the GES, the n th VU and the mth Eve, respectively. As a consequence, the state space can be constructed as

$$\mathcal{S} = \{\mathbf{U}, \mathbf{A}, \mathbf{R}\}, \tag{14}$$

where we define $s^{(t)} \in \mathcal{S}$ to be the state of the representation at the t th time slot.

2) Action space: The action space can be designed as the UAV transmit beamforming vectors $\{\mathbf{v}_n\}$, the common private rate splitting ratio χ_n, the RIS phase shift $\mathbf{\Phi}$. Since deep neural networks can only accept real parts rather than complex valued parts as input or output, during the construction of the action $\mathcal{A}$, the real and imaginary parts are separated into separate input ports if complex numbers are involved. Given transmit symbols with unit variance, the transmit beamforming matrix $\{\mathbf{v}_n\}$ of the n th VU can be decomposed into two parts, i.e.,

$$\mathbf{v}_n = \|\mathbf{v}_n\| \bar{\mathbf{v}}_n, \tag{15}$$

where $\|\mathbf{v}_n\|$ and $\bar{\mathbf{v}}_n$ are the transmit power of the corresponding common stream at UAV and the normalized beam assignment characterizing the beamforming direction.

Following [12], we simplified the beamforming direction to facilitate the learning of approximate optimal mapping from state to action by agents, as it is easier to implement and can be represented as

$$\bar{\mathbf{v}}_n = \begin{cases} \frac{\sum_{i=1}^{N} \mathbf{z}_{c,n}^H}{\|\sum_{i=1}^{N} \mathbf{z}_{c,n}^H\|}, n = 0, \\ \frac{\mathbf{V}_n}{\|\mathbf{V}_n\|}, n \neq 0, \end{cases} \tag{16}$$

where $\mathbf{V}_n$ denotes the V th column of $\mathbf{V} = [\mathbf{V}_1, ..., \mathbf{V}_N]$ where $\mathbf{V} = \mathbf{Z}^H (\mathbf{Z}\mathbf{Z}^H)^{-1}$ and $\mathbf{Z} = [\mathbf{z}_{c,1}, ..., \mathbf{z}_{c,N}]$.

In this regard, the action space can be expressed as

$$\mathcal{A} = \{\{\mathbf{v}_n\}, \{\chi_n\}, \{c_n\}, \{\theta_k\}\}, \tag{17}$$

where χ_n is the generation of hyperbolic tangent functions, θ_k indicates the amount of phase shift change. Besides, we define $a^{(t)} \in \mathcal{A}$ to be the chosen action at the tth time slot of the subsequent representation.

3) Reward function: The constraints of the objective problem P0 need to be considered simultaneously in the reward function we have designed. It can be composed of two items, i.e., the instant reward term that represents the expression of unconstrained emotion and the penalty term that ensures various constraints can be satisfied. The main purpose of the reward function is to guide the agent to learn towards the desired goal. Instant rewards can help the agent to get positive feedback quickly and accelerate the learning process. The penalty terms, on the other hand, can avoid the agent from adopting bad behaviors or actions with large errors, thus helping the agent to better explore and optimize the strategy. Thus, to further strike a balance between the instant reward and penalty terms, the reward function can be defined as

$$\mathcal{R} = \text{SEE} (\{\mathbf{v}_n, \{\chi_n\}, \{c_n\}\}, \mathbf{\Phi}) \\ \times (\varsigma_e \times \varsigma_c \times \varsigma_r), \tag{18}$$

where

$$\varsigma_e = \begin{cases} 1, \min R_G - R_{s,m} \geq \Delta U, \\ 0, \min R_G - R_{s,m} < \Delta U, \end{cases} \tag{19a}$$

$$\varsigma_c = \begin{cases} 1, \|\mathbf{v}_c\|^2 + \sum_{n=1}^{N} \|\mathbf{v}_n\|^2 \leq P_U, \\ 0, \|\mathbf{v}_c\|^2 + \sum_{n=1}^{N} \|\mathbf{v}_n\|^2 > P_U, \end{cases} \tag{19b}$$

$$\varsigma_r = \begin{cases} 1, \sum_{n=1}^{N} c_n - \min_n R_{c,n} \leq 0, \\ 0, \sum_{n=1}^{N} c_n - \min_n R_{c,n} > 0, \end{cases} \tag{19c}$$

where ς_e, ς_c and ς_r are the penalties for the selected actions that do not satisfy the QoS requirements of the PN, the transmit power budget requirements of the SN, and the common message decoding requirements of the SN, respectively.

Within the PPO enabled framework, the collected state information from the UAV transmit beamforming matrix, RIS phase shift matrix, and power splitting ratio serves as input. During each learning iteration, the agent undergoes alternating phases of sampling and optimization over T time slots. For the training phase, let us denote the size of the training layer as L. The input layer size, which is dependent on the number of states, is denoted as Z_I. Additionally, Z_l represents the number of neurons in the l th layer of the DNN. It should be noted that at this point, the computational complexity of the agent at each time step can be calculated as $\mathcal{O}\left(Z_I Z_l + \sum_{l=1}^{L} Z_l Z_{l+1}\right)$. Assuming N^{epi} episodes with each episodes in each mini batch being $T_{\max}$ time steps, each training model iteration is completed when the algorithm reaches convergence. As a result, the total computational complexity in this proposed scheme can be computed as $\mathcal{O}\left(N^{\mathrm{epi}} T_{\max}\left(Z_I Z_l + \sum_{l=1}^{L} Z_l Z_{l+1}\right)\right)$. Clarifying this streamlined time complexity is crucial for ensuring efficient processing, especially in real time applications where fast decision making is crucial.

4 Numerical Results

In this Sect. 4, we present the simulation results to further demonstrate the performance and validate the superiority of our proposed algorithm. Taking the satellite beam center as the origin, the PUs are evenly distributed at a distance of 50 m from the beam center. The position coordinate of the UAV beam center is (5,100), and that of VUs are (5,125), (5,145) and (5,165) [16]. RIS is located near VUs, with the coordinate being (20,125).

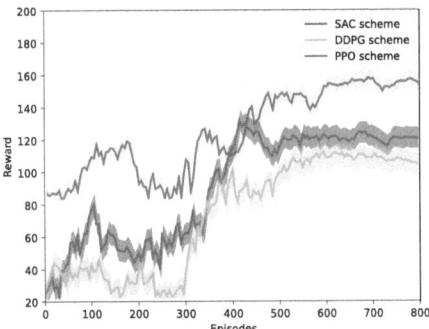

Fig. 2. Convergence comparison between different algorithms.

Figure 2 demonstrates how the proposed PPO based approach converges over the course of the training phase compared to DDPG and SAC algorithms, with a total time slot T set to 100. It can be seen that the proposed PPO enabled algorithm achieves higher rewards, followed by SAC, with DDPG yielding the lowest

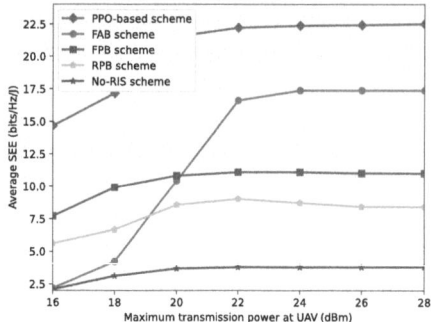

Fig. 3. Comparison of SEE with UAV maximum transmit power.

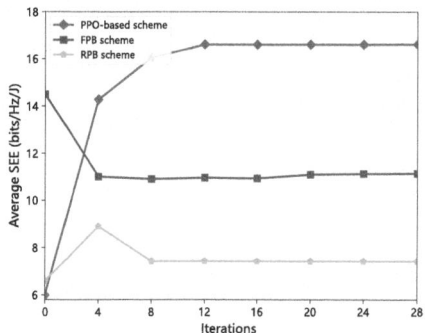

Fig. 4. Comparison of average SEE under different algorithms.

rewards. This visualization highlights the algorithm's steady progress toward optimal performance, clearly showing the effectiveness of our method in enhancing learning and decision making accuracy.

Furthermore, the comparisons between the four benchmark algorithms and our proposed algorithm are provided. In particular, our proposed algorithm is labeled as PPO based scheme. The first benchmark algorithm is marked as FAB (fixed active beamforming) scheme, where the UAV transmit active beamforming is fixed. The second and third benchmark algorithms are labeled as FPB (fixed passive beamforming) and RPB (random passive beamforming), which refer to the optimization problem solved by designing active beamforming and power splitting ratio with fixed and random phase shift matrix. Finally, the fourth benchmark algorithm is marked as No RIS scheme, i.e., without the aid of RIS. Figure 3 shows the variation of the SEE with the maximum transmit power of the UAV. It can be seen that the SEE increases with the increase of the maximum transmit power and tends to converge when the maximum transmit power reaches 22 dBm [17].

Figure 4 shows the variation of different SEE with the number of algorithm iterations under different algorithms. It can be seen that after the 8th iteration, all the proposed algorithms can converge to a fixed value. Here, the main purpose of this article is to verify the improvement in system performance after introducing RIS. Therefore, we focus on studying three phase shift schemes. We only list three RIS phase shift change schemes, which are optimizing RIS phase shift using PPO algorithm, FPB scheme, and RPB scheme. It can be seen that the SEE of the PPO algorithm mentioned is higher than the other two algorithms, which verifies the superiority of this algorithm [18].

Figure 5 clearly illustrates the trend of the average worst secrecy rate as the number of secondary vehicle users varies. The graph reveals that, as the user count increases, the average worst secrecy rate corresponding to all optimization strategies exhibits a decreasing trend. The average worst secrecy rate is defined as the expected secrecy rate between legitimate users and eavesdropping users, computed across all possible channel conditions. This phenomenon underscores the challenges posed by secure communication in multi user environments, specifically the overall deterioration in security performance stemming from user interference and competition for channel resources.

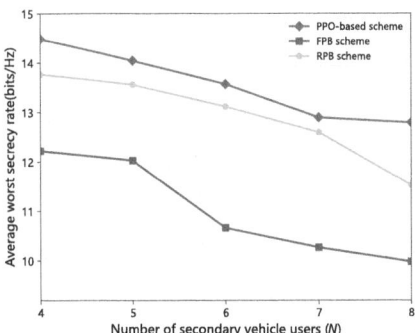

Fig. 5. Comparison of the average worst secrecy rate under different numbers of secondary vehicle users.

5 Conclusion

In the paper, we proposed a new infrastructure by combining SATINs with RSMA for supporting massive connectivity, and with RIS for enhancing the security. Different from existing works focusing on SE or EE separately, we formulated a SEE maximization problem, and then proposed a unified PPO learning framework based on DRL to further handle both continuous and discrete optimization variables. Specifically, this framework designed state action pairs to determine UAV transmit beamforming, RIS reflected beamforming, and power splitting ratio. The simulation results showed that the proposed scheme outperforms the benchmark scheme in terms of achievable SEE performance and computational complexity.

References

1. Liu, R., et al.: RIS-empowered satellite-aerial-terrestrial networks with PD-NOMA. IEEE Commun. Surv. Tutor. **26**, 2258–2289 (2024). https://doi.org/10.1109/COMST.2024.3393612
2. An, K., et al.: Secure transmission in cognitive satellite terrestrial networks. IEEE J. Sel. Areas Commun. **34**(11), 3025–3037 (2016)
3. Ma, R., et al.: Covert mmWave communications with finite blocklength against spatially random wardens. IEEE Internet Things J. **11**(2), 3402–3416 (2024)
4. Xu, J., et al.: Sum secrecy rate maximization for IRS-aided multi-cluster MIMO-NOMA Terahertz systems. IEEE Trans. Inf. Forensics Secur. **18**, 4463–4474 (2023)
5. Wu, Q., Zhang, R.: Towards smart and reconfigurable environment: intelligent reflecting surface aided wireless network. IEEE Commun. Mag. **58**(1), 106–112 (2020)
6. Li, X., et al.: Exploiting benefits of IRS in wireless powered NOMA networks. IEEE Trans. Green Commun. Netw. **6**(1), 175–186 (2022)
7. Guo, K., et al.: Outage performance of RIS-assisted cognitive non-terrestrial network with NOMA. IEEE Trans. Veh. Tech. **73**(4), 5953–5958 (2024)
8. Sun, Y., et al.: Energy-efficient hybrid beamforming for multilayer RIS-assisted secure integrated terrestrial-aerial networks. IEEE Trans. Commun. **70**(6), 4189–4210 (2022)
9. Li, X., et al.: Secure communication of active RIS assisted NOMA networks. IEEE Trans. Wirel. Commun. **23**(5), 4489–4503 (2024)
10. Huang, C., et al.: Reconfigurable intelligent surfaces for energy efficiency in wireless communication. IEEE Trans. Wirel. Commun. **18**(8), 4157–4170 (2019)
11. Dong, R., et al.: Secure transmission design of RIS enabled UAV communication networks exploiting deep reinforcement learning. IEEE Trans. Veh. Tech. **73**, 8404–8419 (2024). https://doi.org/10.1109/TVT.2024.3357821
12. Zhang, R., et al.: Energy efficiency maximization in RIS-assisted SWIPT networks with RSMA: a PPO-based approach. IEEE J. Sel. Areas Commun. **41**(5), 1413–1430 (2023)
13. Lin, Z., et al.: Refracting RIS-aided hybrid satellite-terrestrial relay networks: joint beamforming design and optimization. IEEE Trans. Aerosp. Electron. Syst. **58**(4), 3717–3724 (2022)
14. Mozaffari, M., Saad, W., Bennis, M., Debbah, M.: Wireless communication using unmanned aerial vehicles (UAVs): optimal transport theory for hover time optimization. IEEE Trans. Wirel. Commun. **16**(12), 8052–8066 (2017)
15. An, H., Wang, L.: Robust topology generation of internet of things based on PPO algorithm using discrete action space. IEEE Trans. Ind. Inform. **20**(4), 5406–5414 (2024)
16. Hao, W., et al.: Securing reconfigurable intelligent surface-aided cell-free networks. IEEE Trans. Inf. Forensics Secur. **17**, 3720–3733 (2022)
17. Zhou, C., et al.: Energy-efficient maximization for RIS-aided MISO symbiotic radio systems. IEEE Trans. Veh. Technol. **72**(10), 13689–13694 (2023)
18. Wu, M., et al.: Deep reinforcement learning-based energy efficiency optimization for RIS-aided integrated satellite-aerial-terrestrial relay networks. IEEE Trans. Commun. **72**(7), 4163–4178 (2024)

Research on the Signal Detection in an Uplink Ground-to-Satellite UDC-FSO System with Optical Path Difference

Ya-Tian Li[1], Zhi-Qiang Xu[1(✉)], Kai-Nan Yao[1,2], Rui-Peng Li[1,2], Lu Chen[1], and Hong-Zhuang Li[1]

[1] Changchun Institute of Optics, Fine Mechanics and Physics, Chinese Academy of Sciences, Changchun 130033, China
xuzhiqiang@ciomp.ac.cn
[2] University of Chinese Academy of Sciences, Beijing 100049, China

Abstract. This paper focuses on the optical path difference (OPD) in a 2×1 uplink ground-to-satellite free space optics (FSO) system with uniquely decodable codes (UDC), where the different data from transmitters (TXs) are superimposed asynchronously due to the OPD. We first analyze the influence of OPD on the uplink UDC-FSO system. Then the suboptimal minimal detection for moved patterns (MDMP) and optimal minimal metric-based pattern detection (MMPD) algorithms are proposed for mitigating the OPD-introduced interference, which are based on the minimum distance criterion and maximum likelihood sequence detection, respectively. Simulation results of symbol error rate (SER) and mutual information show that both of them outperform the case of directly detection notably. A desktop equivalent experiment is also built to verify the effectiveness of the proposed algorithms. It also promotes the potential for practical application of the UDC-FSO system.

Keywords: Free Space Optics · Uniquely Decodable Code · Optical Path Difference

1 Introduction

1.1 Background and Related Works

With the increasing demands for bandwidth and capacity, free space optics (FSO) has become a hot topic in the field of wireless communications, which

---

This work is supported by the National Natural Science Foundation of China (NO. 62101527).

H.-H. Chen and W. Meng (Eds.): WiSATS 2024, LNICST 605, pp. 89–101, 2025.
https://doi.org/10.1007/978-3-031-86196-3_8

has the advantages of easy placement, free of spectrum license, and small divergence angle to prevent interception [1,2]. Benefiting from these superiorities, FSO is widely used in ground-to-satellite links. Recently, the National Aeronautics and Space Administration (NASA) has conducted the Terabyte Infrared Delivery (TBIRD) program, achieving the burst rates up to 200 Gbps for optical communication links from low-Earth orbit to ground stations. This marks a new milestone in rate/throughput for point-to-point optical communications [3].

In further pursuit of higher data rates, different types of multiplexing techniques have been applied in FSO systems to improve throughput, such as using wavelength multiplexing [4], frequency multiplexing [5], angular momentum multiplexing [6], polarization multiplexing [7], and mode multiplexing [8]. The mentioned multiplexing techniques increase channel capacity by introducing additional parallel degrees of freedom. However, a single degree of freedom still has the potential to be exploited.

As a result, researchers invented the non-orthogonal multiple access (NOMA) techinique. Different from conventional orthogonal multiple access technique, NOMA technique enhances channel capacity by fully utilizing each degree of freedom [9]. NOMA technique can be categorized into power-domain (PD-NOMA) and code domain (CD-NOMA) according to the way of implementation. In the field of optical communications, PD-NOMA is primarily used for visible light communications (VLC), where the modulation method is always orthogonal frequency division multiplexing (OFDM) [10]. In FSO systems, which usually employ on-off keying (OOK) modulation, the transceiver structure and channel model are different from those in VLC. As a result, PD-NOMA is not commonly used in FSO.

On the basis that power signal superposition is mathematically consistent with code word superposition, CD-NOMA is an option for FSOs. Focusing on the area of CD-NOMA, our previous work [11–13] integrate the FSO and uniquely decodable codes (UDC) with the aim of leveraging the non-orthogonality of UDC to enhance channel capacity. We demonstrate that UDC codewords remain uniquely decodable (UD) even after passing through the fading channel in [11]. To quantitatively analyze the system performance, we deduce the theoretical value of the symbol error rate (SER) and calculate the channel capacity in [12]. Further, considering the multi-receiver scenario, two combination methods are proposed in [13], i.e., distance-based optimal candidate selection method and suboptimal maximization minimum distance combination method, both of which perform better than the traditional maximal ratio combining (MRC) method.

1.2   Motivation and Contribution

In our previous studies on UDC and FSO [11–13], it is assumed that the distances between all transmitters (TXs) and receiver (RX) are equal, which ensures synchronized superposition of the UDC codewords. However, in practice, especially in the ground-satellite uplinks, the optical path difference (OPD) is inevitable due to the fact that the satellite moves continuously while the ground stations are stationary, thus causing the signals from different TXs cannot be synchronized superimposed on the RX [14, 15]. Therefore, this paper focuses on a 2×1 uplink UDC-FSO scenario with OPD, aiming at designing signal detection algorithms to promote the practical application of UDC-FSO. The main contributions of this paper are illustrated as follows.

■ Different from the synchronous superposition cases, this paper investigates an asynchronous superposition scenario caused by the OPD between different TXs and RX.

■ We analyze the influence of OPD on the superimposed patterns in a uplink 2×1 UDC-FSO system.

■ To mitigate the interference, two signal detection algorithms are proposed, namely, the suboptimal minimal distance for moved patterns (MDMP) and optimal minimal metric-based pattern detection (MMPD).

■ By the simulations and experiments, the validity and feasibility of the proposed methods are verified by measuring the metrics such as the SER and the mutual information.

It is also worth noting that although both traditional optical code-division multiple-access (OCDMA) technique and UDC [16] are multiple access codes for FSOs, they are different. Since UDC is non-orthogonal and traditional OCDMA is always orthogonal. Another point that needs to be mentioned is that UDC is not a multi-decimal system, rather it can be constructed even under ternary or higher multi-decimal domains [17]. Moreover, common multiplexing techniques can be incorporated into the UDC-FSO system to further enhance channel capacity.

The structure of this paper is organized as follows. Section 2 briefly depicts the system model of a 2×1 uplink UDC-FSO links with OPD, as well as the channel model. Section 3.1 presents the influence of OPD on UDC-FSO. Section 3.2 and Sect. 3.3 cover the suboptimal MDMP and optimal MMPD algorithms, respectively. Section 4 shows the simulation results, while Sect. 5 illustrates the experimental ones. In the end, Sect. 6 concludes this paper.

2   System Model of a 2×1 Uplink UDC-FSO with OPD

2.1   System Structure and Influence of the OPD

This paper considers a 2×1 ground-to-satellite uplink UDC-FSO with OPD, where the UDC is utilized to allow the 2 TXs to transmit different data in a non-orthogonal way. For the sake of exposition, this paper considers a simple UDC codeword sets, i.e., $\mathbb{C}_1 = \{00, 01, 10\}$ and $\mathbb{C}_2 = \{00, 11\}$, respectively. According to [11], upper bounds on the amount of mutual information is equal to $\frac{1}{2}\log_2 6 = 1.2925$ bit/symbol (larger than 1 bit/symbol in the orthogonal case). The front coefficient $1/2$ means that it takes 2 slots to transmit a UDC codeword. As shown in Fig. 1, baseband data $\mathbf{x_1}$ (or $\mathbf{x_2}$) in TX-1 (or TX-2) are first encoded into $\mathbf{c_1}$ or $(\mathbf{c_2})$ by UDC codeword sets, and then modulated and amplified. These signals out of the transmitting lens are further passing through the optical fading channels. Different from our previous works [11–13], where it's assumed that the UDC signals are superimposed synchronously at the RX, this paper considers the case that there is a OPD between 2 uplinks. It's mentioned that we only need to consider the fractional part, due to the UDC codewords still maintain the UD feature after moving several integer codewords. Thus, this paper studies the case of fractional OPD and defines τ as the OPD of TX-1 to RX with respect to the TX-2 to RX link, satisfying $0 < \tau < 1$. Note that τ is a quantity in the time dimension, which has been normalized by the period time corresponding to the symbol clock rate. For the sake of analysis, it's also assumed that there is no frequency difference between the clocks at the TXs and RX, which can be reached by timing operation or timing recovery.

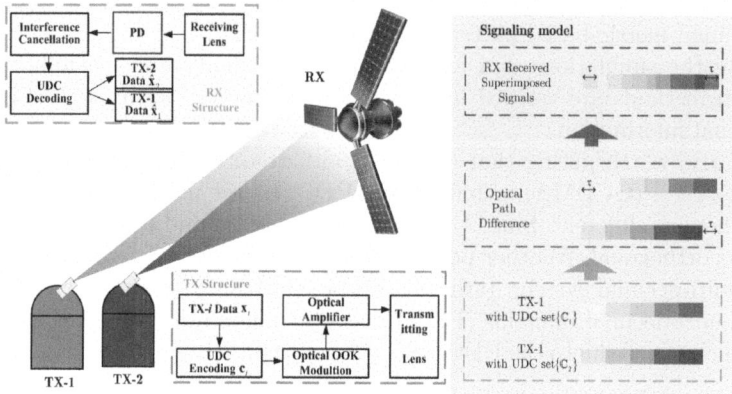

Fig. 1. System model of a 2×1 uplink UDC-FSO with OPD.

From Fig. 1, the OPD τ cause interference to neighbor signals, and the received signals at RX (called as superimposed signals) can be expressed as

$$\mathbf{y}^k = \eta h_1^k \left[(1-\tau)\,\mathbf{c}_1^k(1) + \tau \mathbf{c}_1^k(2), (1-\tau)\,\mathbf{c}_1^k(2) + \tau \mathbf{c}_1^{k+1}(1) \right] + \eta h_2^k \mathbf{c}_2^k + \mathbf{n}_{\text{eq}}^k, \quad (1)$$

where the superscript k corresponds to k-th codeword. η stands for the photon-electric conversion ratio. $\mathbf{c}(1)$ (or $\mathbf{c}(2)$)is the first (or second) symbol in UDC codeword $\mathbf{c}$. $\mathbf{n}_{\text{eq}}^k$ represents equivalent Gaussian noise with the variance σ_n^2. It is worth mentioning that noted that the length of each vector in Eq. (1) is the exactly the same as the UDC codeword length. Due to the interference introduced by OPD, the RX tries to cancel the interference, and then decoding the UDC codewords from the superimposed symbols.

2.2   Channel Model

Considering link attenuation, Malaga turbulence and pointing errors [18], the probability distribution function (PDF) $f_h(h)$ of the channel gain h is shown below,

$$f_h(h) = \frac{\xi^2 A}{2h} \sum_{m=1}^{\beta} b_m \cdot \mathbf{G}_{1,3}^{3,0} \left[\frac{\alpha\beta}{(g\beta+\Omega')} \frac{h}{h_l A_0} \,\middle|\, \xi^2+1; \xi^2, \alpha, m \right], \quad (2)$$

where $\mathbf{G}_{p,q}^{m,n}(\cdot)$ is the Meijier'G function. α, β, g and Ω' are fading parameters of Malaga turbulence. A and b_m can be obtained from these parameters, by $\frac{2\alpha^{\alpha/2}}{g^{1+\alpha/2}\Gamma(\alpha)}\left(g\beta/g\beta+\Omega'\right)^{\beta+\alpha/2}$ and $a_m[\alpha\beta/\left(g\beta+\Omega'\right)]^{-(\alpha+m)/2}$, respectively. a_m denotes $\left(\frac{\beta-1}{m-1}\right)\left(g\beta+\Omega'\right)^{1-m/2}/(m-1)!\left(\Omega'/g\right)^{m-1}(\alpha/\beta)^{m/2}$. Both A_0 and ξ means the pointing error parameters. Specifically, A_0 defines the pointing loss, while ξ is the ratio between the receiver's equivalent beam radius and pointing error displacement standard deviation.

3 Signal Detection Algorithms for UDC-FSO with OPD

In this section, the influence of OPD τ is first discussed. Then the suboptimal and optimal algorithms for signal detection are illustrated, respectively.

3.1 Influence of OPD on UDC-FSO

Before discussing the OPD on UDC-FSO, we need to review the definition of superimposed patterns. The superimposed patterns are the superimposed UDC codewords after fading channels, i.e., $\eta h_1^k \mathbf{c}_1^k + \eta h_2^k \mathbf{c}_2^k$ in the ideal UDC-FSO case, where there are $2 \times 3 = 6$ superimposed patterns (labeled as $\varphi_1, ..., \varphi_6$) as shown in the first line of Fig. 2. It can be also defined that φ^k is the corresponding k-th superimposed pattern in the ideal UDC-FSO without OPD. The UD characteristic of UDC ensures that the superimposed pattern corresponds one-to-one with the UDC codewords from TXs. This means that the receiver can still recover the original data from the superimposed signals.

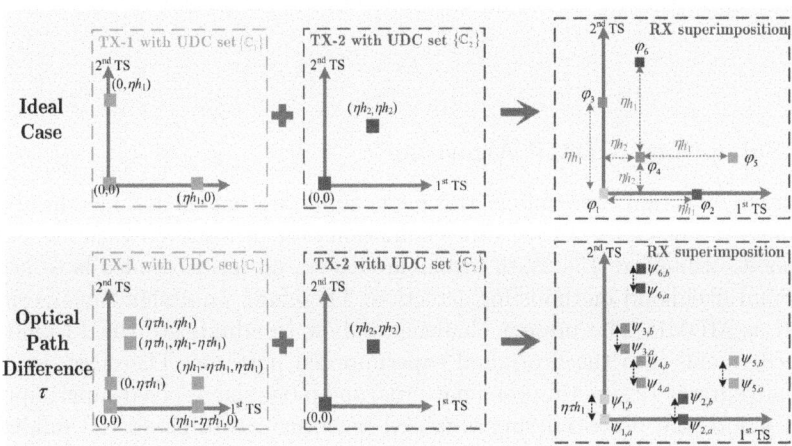

Fig. 2. The influence of OPD on superimposed patterns of UDC-FSO systems.

Under the circumstances of OPD $0 < \tau < 1$, the part τ of the first symbol in each superimposed pattern contributes to the previous superimposed pattern. So does the next superimposed patterns. The moved superimposed patterns can be defined as $\eta h_1^k \left[(1 - \tau) \, \mathbf{c}_1^k(1) + \tau \mathbf{c}_1^k(2), (1 - \tau) \, \mathbf{c}_1^k(2) + \tau \mathbf{c}_1^{k+1}(1) \right] + \eta h_2^k \mathbf{c}_2^k$. Due to the fact of $\mathbf{c}_1^{k+1}(1) = 0$ or 1, the number of superimposed patterns has doubled. For ease of presentation, $\psi_{i,a}$ (or $\psi_{i,b}$) represents the changed superimposed patterns with the subsequent codeword starting with symbol "0" (or "1"), as given in Fig. 2's second line. It shows how the superimposed patterns will be changed when there is OPD. It's apparent that the locations of superimposed symbol have moved, where distance between these superimposed patterns is also shortened. It will certainly result in poorer SER and mutual information.

However, the changed superimposed patterns can still be categorized into 6 parts (defined as $\psi_i = \{\psi_{i,a}, \psi_{i,b}\}, i = 1, \ldots, 6$), which are also corresponding to the original ideal superimposed patterns. We also define the operation $\mathcal{D}[\bullet]$ to be the mapping from moved superimposed pattern $\psi_{i,j}$ to original superimposed pattern and next codeword $\mathbf{c}_1^{k+1}$, i.e., $\psi_{i,j} = \mathcal{D}\left(\varphi^k, \mathbf{c}_1^{k+1}\right)$. The mapping relationship is summarized in Table 1.

Table 1. Superimposed patterns after OPD

$\psi_{i,j} = \mathcal{D}\left(\varphi^k, \mathbf{c}_1^{k+1}\right)$	$\mathbf{c}_{k+1} = [0,0]$ or $[0,1]$ $(\varphi^{k+1} = \varphi_1, \varphi_3, \varphi_4, \varphi_6)$	$\mathbf{c}_{k+1} = [1,0]$ $(\varphi^{k+1} = \varphi_2, \varphi_5)$
$\varphi^k = [0,0]$	$\psi_{1,a} = [0,0]$	$\psi_{1,b} = [0, \eta\tau h_1]$
$\varphi^k = [\eta h_1, 0]$	$\psi_{2,a} = [\eta h_1(1 - \tau), 0]$	$\psi_{2,b} = [\eta h_1(1 - \tau), \eta\tau h_1]$
$\varphi^k = [0, \eta h_1]$	$\psi_{3,a} = [\eta\tau h_1, \eta h_1(1 - \tau)]$	$\psi_{3,b} = [\eta\tau h_1, \eta h_1]$
$\varphi^k = [\eta h_2, \eta h_2]$	$\psi_{4,a} = [\eta h_2, \eta h_2]$	$\psi_{4,b} = [\eta h_2, \eta h_2 + \eta\tau h_1]$
$\varphi^k = [\eta h_1 + \eta h_2, \eta h_2]$	$\psi_{5,a} = [\eta h_1(1 - \tau) + \eta h_2, \eta h_2]$	$\psi_{5,b} = [\eta h_1(1 - \tau) + \eta h_2, \eta h_2 + \eta\tau h_1]$
$\varphi^k = [\eta h_2, \eta h_1 + \eta h_2]$	$\psi_{6,a} = [\eta h_2 + \eta\tau h_1, \eta h_1 + \eta h_2 - \eta\tau h_1]$	$\psi_{6,b} = [\eta h_2 + \eta\tau h_1, \eta h_1 + \eta h_2]$

3.2   Suboptimal MDMP Algorithm

In order to detection the symbols, this paper supposes that the RX has the ability of estimating the OPD τ, where the estimation may be achieved with maximum likelihood estimation [15]. With available OPD τ, an intuitive idea is to utilize maximum likelihood methods for detection. Therefore, we design the algorithm named as MDMP. The present challenge is how to adjudicate the 12 kinds of received signals into the 6 original superimposed patterns. Therefore, we first calculate current 12 superimposed patterns, and judge the received superimposed signal $\mathbf{y}$ into the potential superimposed patterns according to the minimum distance criterion.

$$\hat{\psi}_{i,j} = \arg\min_{i,j} |\mathbf{y} - \psi_{i,j}|, i = 1, \ldots, 6; j = a \text{ or } b. \tag{3}$$

Then we correspond the obtained $\hat{\psi}_{i,j}$ to the ideal superimposed pattern ψ_i by Table 1. The data can be further decoded by regular UDC decoders [11–13].

3.3   Optimal MMPD Algorithm

As mentioned above, the suboptimal MDMP algorithm considers the moved superimposed pattern. However, the effect of each judged codeword on neighboring codewords is not fully utilized. Thus we propose the MMPD algorithm based on maximum likelihood sequence detection. Given the one-to-one correspondence between the UDC and the original data $\mathbf{x}_k$, the $\hat{\mathbf{x}}_k$ can be obtained by adjudicating the correct superimposed pattern.

$$\hat{\varphi}^k = \arg \max_{\varphi^k} \sum_{k=1} \ln \left[P \left(\mathbf{y}^k \mid \varphi^k, \mathbf{c}_1^{k+1}, \tau \right) \right], \tag{4}$$

where $P \left(\mathbf{y}^k \mid \varphi^k, \mathbf{c}_1^{k+1}, \tau \right)$ is the conditional PDF, given as

$$P \left(\mathbf{y}^k \mid \varphi^k, \mathbf{c}_1^{k+1}, \tau \right) = \frac{1}{\sqrt{2\pi}\sigma_n} \exp \left[-\frac{1}{2\sigma_n^2} \cdot \left| \mathbf{y}^k - \psi_{i,j}^k \right|^2 \right], \psi_{i,j} = \mathcal{D} \left(\varphi^k, \mathbf{c}_1^{k+1} \right). \tag{5}$$

By substituting Eq. (5) to Eq. (4),

$$\hat{\varphi}_i^k = \arg \min_{\varphi_i^k} \sum_{k=1} \left| \mathbf{y}^k - \psi_{i,j} \right|^2, \psi_{i,j} = \mathcal{D} \left(\varphi^k, \mathbf{c}_1^{k+1} \right). \tag{6}$$

Table 2. Pseudo-code diagram of the MMPD algorithm

Input:$\{\mathbf{y}_k\}$, h_1^k, h_1^k τ (k=1,2,,N_c).
Output: Detected signals $\hat{\mathbf{x}}_1^k$ and $\hat{\mathbf{x}}_2^k$.

1: Initialize $\mathcal{A}_p = \infty$ for p =2,6, $\mathcal{A}_p = 1$, $\mathcal{R} = \text{zeros} \left(6, N_c \right)$, $\mathcal{B}_p = \infty$ for $p = 1, 2, , 6$.
2: **FOR** $k = 1 : N_c$
3:     **FOR** $p = 1 : 6, q = 1 : 6$
4:         Calculate current distance $\mu_{p,q} = \left| \mathbf{y}^k - \psi_{p,j}^k \right|, j = a \ (q = 2,5), j = b \ (q = 1, 3, 4, 6)$.
5:         **IF** $\mathcal{B}_p > \mathcal{A}_p + \mu_{p,q}$
6:             Update the current distance value by $\mathcal{B}_p = \mathcal{A}_p + \mu_{p,q}$.
7:             Record the current path node $\mathcal{R}_q^k = p$.
8:         **END IF**
9:     **END FOR**
10:    Update cumulative distance $\mathcal{A}_p = \mathcal{B}_p$ for $p = 1, , 6$.
11: **END FOR**
12: Find $p = \arg \min_{p} \{\mathcal{A}_p\}$.
13: **FOR** $k = N_c$: -1: 1
14:    Obtain the judged superimposed patterns $\hat{\varphi}_i^k = \mathcal{R}_p^k$.
15:    Update the index $p = \mathcal{R}_p^k$.
16: **End FOR**
17: Decode from ideal UDC superimposed patterns $\hat{\varphi}_i^k$ to $\hat{\mathbf{x}}_1^k$ and $\hat{\mathbf{x}}_2^k$ for $k = 1, , N_c$.

By observing the form of Eq. (6), it is equivalent to minimizing the sum of distances between the superimposed signal $\mathbf{y}^k$ and the superimposed patterns $\psi_{i,j}^k$. In other words, the key merit is the summation of the distances. Therefore, we can model the MMPD algorithm after the Viterbi method by recording lattice graph paths. Each step in the lattice graph has six nodes, and each node corresponds to a kind of superposition pattern. Due to the uniformity and traversal of the code word, each node has 6 possible paths.

We Define $\mathcal{A}_p$ to represent the previous cumulative distance on the p-th node. Similarly we define $\mathcal{B}_p$ to be the current cumulative distance value on the p-th node. Also the register $\mathcal{R}_p^k$ ($p = 1, \ldots, 6; k = 1, \ldots, N_c$) represents the stacked node number corresponding to ψ_p in the k-th transmission codeword. The pseudo-code diagram is shown in Table 2, where N_c denotes the number of transmitted codewords in each TX. For ease of representation, we may suppose that the first codeword sent to be [0,0] for both TXs, i.e., $\psi^{k=1} = \psi_1$.

4   Simulation Results

Simulations of a 2×1 uplink UDC-FSO with OPD are carried out in this section. The simulation parameters are summarized in Table 3. It is also important to mention here that unlike conventional RF communication systems, the signal-to-noise ratio (SNR) is proportional to the transmit power. In intensity-modulated/direct-detection (IM/DD) FSO systems, the SNR will be proportional to the square of the transmit power [19]. Therefore, SNR from 0 to 50 dB is a suitable range.

Table 3. Simulation Parameters

Parameters	Values
Link distance	4000 km
Beam Divergence Angle	30 μrad
Malaga Turbulence	$(\alpha, \beta, g, \Omega') = (8, 4, 0.02, 1)$
Pointing Errors	$A_0 = 1$, $\xi = 6.7$
OPD	$\tau = 0.2$

Figure 3 depicts the SER of a 2×1 uplink UDC-FSO system with OPD $\tau = 0.2$, as well as the mutual information. It's found that both the MDMP and MMPD algorithms outperform the direct detection (unknown τ, as a control group). The optimal MMPD can approach the ideal UDC-FSO without OPD in case of high SNR, while the suboptimal MDMP still has a gap with the ideal UDC-FSO even though the SNR is high enough. It's obtained that the slopes of the SERs of MDMP, MMPD, ideal UDC-FSO and the ideal point-to-point (P2P) FSO case are almost the same when τ is equal to 0.2, which indicates that they have almost the same diversity order of 1. This is easy to understand since the employment of UDC in 2×1 links is to apply its CD-NOMA property, where the TXs send different messages with no diversity gain. In addition, the direct detection with unknown τ has an error floor in the SER curve, which owes to the OPD's interference to neighbor superimposed patterns. As can be also found from Fig. 3(b), the mutual information of UDC-FSO with OPD τ can still approach the upper bound of ideal UDC-FSO systems, i.e. $\frac{1}{2}\log_2 6 = 1.2925$ bit/symbol, when the MDMP or MMPD are employed. It's implied that the effectiveness of the proposed algorithms.

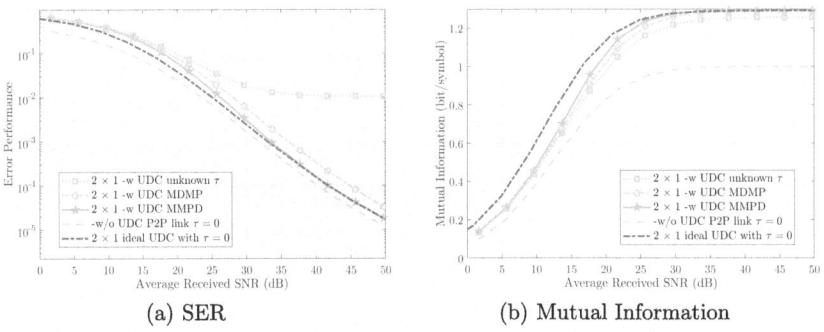

(a) SER   (b) Mutual Information

Fig. 3. Simulation Performance of different algorithms with $\tau = 0.2$.

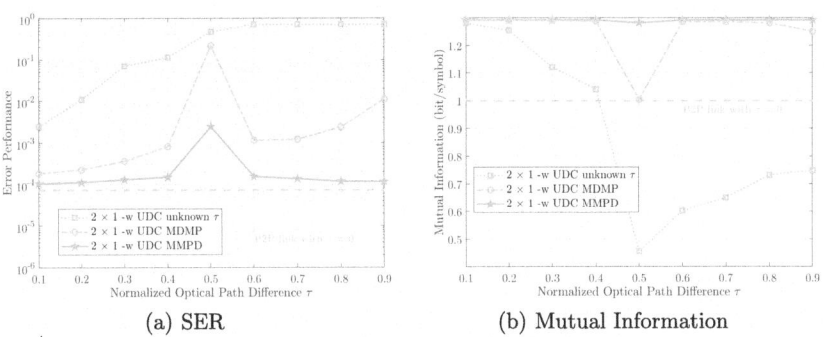

(a) SER   (b) Mutual Information

Fig. 4. Simulation performance versus different τ.

Considering that Fig. 3 only considers the case when $\tau = 0.2$, we explore the performance of the UDC-FSO system for different OPD τ in Fig. 4. Similar to Fig. 3, the curves of SER and mutual information are represented in Figs. 4(a) and 4(b), respectively. It's seen that the gap between optimal MMPD and suboptimal MDMP becomes larger with increasing OPD τ. Specifically, for the SER metric, the suboptimal MDMP performs barely acceptably when the OPD τ is less than 0.4, while the optimal MMPD consistently exhibits excellent performance and is close to the traditional P2P case. From both Figs. 4(a) and 4(b), it can be found that OPD $\tau = 0.5$ is the worst case, because under this condition, superimposed patterns $\psi_{2,b}$ and $\psi_{3,a}$ will overlap, so will $\psi_{5,b}$ and $\psi_{6,a}$. Misclassification will often occur leading to performance degradation. This also implies why the MMPD performance is positively correlated with $|\tau - 0.5|$ for the same SNR.

5   Experimental Results

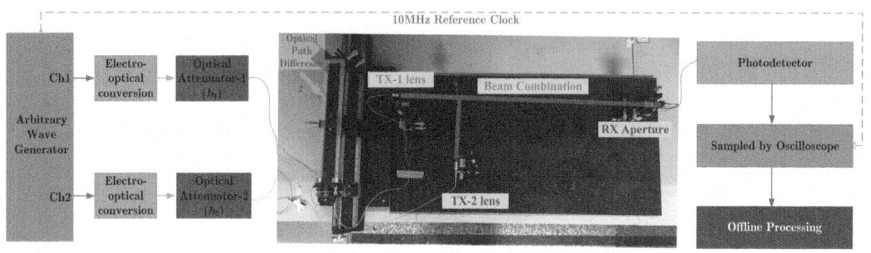

Fig. 5. Experiment scene of a desktop equivalent 2×1UDC-FSO system with OPD.

After simulations analysis, a 2×1 UDC-FSO equivalent desktop experiment is built, as shown in Fig. 5. Two homologous channels of the Arbitrary Wave Generator (AWG, Tektronix AWG70002A) produce the UDC-encoded electrical signals which are further modulated by the electro-optical modulator. There is an optical attenuator in each TX where the attenuation values consist of the path loss and channel fading introduced by turbulence and pointing errors. By adjusting the optical attenuator and the transmitting power, it makes the desktop experiment similar as the slant ground-to-satellite link. It's also noted that the OPD is achieved by a linear guideway, where the optical beam in TX-1 enters a collimator after passing through one transmitting lens and two 45-degree mirrors. The OPD is set to be 67.5 cm, i.e., $\tau = 0.45$ for symbol rate of 200 MHz. The signals from 2 TXs are combined and then coupled into a multimode fiber at the RX, which are converted to electrical signals. These electrical signals are further sampled and stored by an oscilloscope (Tektronix, DPO7354). The AWG also provides a 10 MHz reference clock for the oscilloscope to ensure that there is no frequency difference between the TXs and RX. The collected data are first transmitted to a computer and further processed in an offline way.

The experimental results are shown in Fig. 6. As can be seen from Fig. 6(a), the number of superimposed signals has doubled, compared to the case of no OPD, which is consistent with the analysis in Fig. 2. Figure 6(b) provides both the SER and mutual information of optimal MMPD and suboptimal MDMP algorithms, where the direct detection with unknown τ is also depicted. We

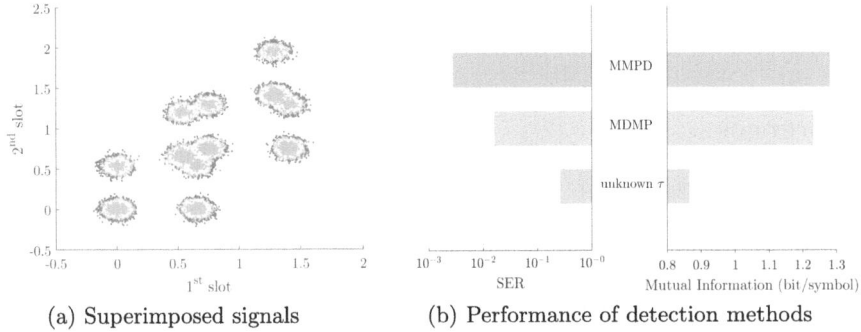

(a) Superimposed signals   (b) Performance of detection methods

Fig. 6. Experimental Results of UDC-FSO with OPD.

can obtain similar conclusions to the simulations that the proposed MMPD and MDMP methods can both mitigate the interference introduced by the OPD τ. The mutual information after optimal MMPD is close the upper bound of ideal UDC-FSO systems. Additionally, the experiments also imply that the proposed algorithms can enhance the tolerability of the UDC-FSO system for real asynchronous situations, thus increasing its potential for application in real systems.

6   Conclusion

Our previous works have verified the feasibility of UDC-FSO systems, whose main advantage is to allow TXs to transmit different data in a CD-NOMA way. This paper considers an actual scene of a 2×1 ground-to-satellite UDC-FSO link, where there is an OPD between the 2 uplinks. It's discovered that the OPD not only doubles the number of superimposed patterns, but also shifts the locations of the superimposed patterns. Consequently, the minimum distance between the superimposed patterns becomes smaller, thus degrading the system SER and the amount of mutual information. In order to more accurately detect the signals with interference, this paper proposes the suboptimal MDMP and optimal MMPD algorithms, which are based on the minimum distance criterion and maximum likelihood sequence detection, respectively. Both simulation and experimental results show that the SER and mutual information by the proposed algorithms outperform the traditional direct detection method. Specifically speaking, the optimal MDMP can approach the ideal UDC-FSO case in case of high SNR, while the suboptimal MDMP still has a gap compared with the optimal MDMP even in the high SNR case. The suboptimal MDMP is bearable with $\tau < 0.4$. The gap between the suboptimal MDMP and optimal MMPD becomes larger with increasing OPD τ. Besides, it's also found the worst situation is the OPD $\tau = 0.5$ for all the mentioned algorithms, owing to the overlap of superimposed patterns $\psi_{2,b}$ and $\psi_{3,a}$ (also $\psi_{5,b}$ and $\psi_{6,a}$). Overall, this paper serves as a starting point and enhances the possibility of applying the UDC-FSO system in practical scenarios. Subsequent works may focus on further investigation in scenarios where there are clock frequency differences between the transceivers or non-perfect estimation of the OPD.

References

1. Jahid, A., Alsharif, M.H., Hall, T.J.: A contemporary survey on free space optical communication: potentials, technical challenges, recent advances and research direction. J. Netw. Comput. Appl. **200**, 103311 (2022)
2. Karmous, S., Adem, N., Atiquzzaman, M., Samarakoon, S.: How can optical communications shape the future of deep space communications? A Survey. IEEE Commun. Surv. Tutor. 1 (2024). https://doi.org/10.1109/COMST.2024.3403873.
3. Schieler, C M., et al.: 200 Gbps TBIRD CubeSat downlink: pre-flight test results. In: Hemmati, H., Robinson, B.S. (eds.) Free-Space Laser Communications XXXIV, 119930P, SPIE (2022)
4. Fadil, E.A., Abass, A.K., Tahhan, S.R.: Secure WDM-free space optical communication system based optical chaotic. Opt. Quantum Electron. **54**(8), 477 (2022)
5. Ahmed, M.S., Gucluoglu, T.: Maximum ratio transmission based generalized frequency division multiplexing over gamma-gamma channel. Opt. Commun. **492**, 126965 (2021)
6. Zhao, L., et al.: High-accuracy mode recognition method in orbital angular momentum optical communication system. Chin. Opt. Lett. **20**(2), 020601 (2022)
7. Singh, M., Aly, M.H., El-Mottaleb, S.A.A.: Performance analysis of a 448 GBPS PDM/WDM/16-QAM hybrid SMF/FSO system for last mile connectivity. Opt. Quantum Electron. **55**(3), 231 (2023)
8. Kakati, D., Minz, M., Sonkar, R.K.: Performance analysis of grating-assisted passive mode-division multiplexing device using silicon photonics for high-speed RoF/RoFSO communication. Opt. Eng. **60**(1), 016102 (2021)
9. Liu, Y., et al.: Evolution of NOMA toward next generation multiple access (NGMA) for 6G. IEEE J. Sel. Areas Commun. **40**(4), 1037–1071 (2022)
10. Vappangi, S., Deepa, T., Mani, V.V., Bharathiraja, N.: On the performance of delta sigma modulators for DCO-OFDM based NOMA visible light communication systems. Opt. Laser Technol. **167**, 109653 (2023)
11. Li, Y., Geng, T., Gao, S.: Improve the throughput of M-to-1 free-space optical systems by employing uniquely decodable codes. Chin. Opt. Lett. **21**(3), 030603 (2023)
12. Li, Y., Geng, T., Gao, S.: On the error performance and channel capacity of a uniquely decodable coded FSO system over Malaga turbulence with pointing errors. Opt. Express **31**(21), 34264–34279 (2023)
13. Li, Y., Geng, T., Gao, S.: On the signal combinations for a uniquely decodable coded MIMO-FSO communication system. Opt. Laser Technol. **172**, 110533 (2024)
14. Liu, Y., He, Y., Chen, K., Guo, L.: Asynchronous transmission for cooperative free-space optical communication system. IEEE Wirel. Commun. Lett. **11**(4), 766–770 (2022)
15. Li, Y., Geng, T., Gao, S.: Likelihood based synchronization algorithms in optical pulse position modulation systems with photon-counting receivers. Opt. Express **30**(17), 31472–31485 (2022)
16. Hacini, L., Aissaoui, A.: Performance evaluation of SAC-OCDMA-FSO system based on LSC code under fog conditions. Opt. Quantum Electron **55**(2), 189 (2023)

17. Lu, S., Hou, W., Cheng, J., Kamabe, H.: Recursive construction of k-ary uniquely decodable codes for multiple-access adder channel. In: 2018 International Symposium on Information Theory and Its Applications, pp. 565–569, Singapore. IEEE (2018)
18. Ansari, I.S., Yilmaz, F., Alouini, M.-S.: Performance analysis of free-space optical links over Malaga (M) turbulence channels with pointing errors. IEEE Trans. Wireless Commun. **15**(1), 91–102 (2016)
19. Uysal, M., Capsoni, C., Ghassemlooy, Z., Boucouvalas, A., Udvary, E.: Optical Wireless Communications: An Emerging Technology. Springer, Cham (2016)

A High Precision Satellite Beam Agility Control Method

Jian Wang[1,2], Siyue Sun[1,2,3(✉)], Linchen Ku[1,2], Chunxin Mu[3], and Yimeng Luo[1,2]

[1] Innovation Academy for Microsatellites of Chinese Academy of Sciences, Shanghai 201204, China
sunmissmoon@163.com
[2] University of Chinese Academy of Sciences, Beijing 100049, China
[3] Shanghai Engineering Center for Microsatellites, Shanghai, China

Abstract. This paper proposes a high precision satellite beam agility control system that accounts for the satellite-ground time delay error caused by the rotation of the Earth. It is aimed to achieve high precision beam hopping of the phased array with sub-millisecond time granularity between multiple ground terminals in satellite communication. This system integrates a highly stable clock with a global navigation system to optimally calculate the satellite-ground transmission delay, correcting the orbital position through a two-iteration process. Simulation results show that the method can further improve the estimation accuracy of the satellite ground signal transmission delay under the satellite computationally constrained conditions. It achieves high time synchronization of the satellite-ground communication beam time and improves the efficiency of satellite-ground communication.

Keywords: Satellite Beam Agility control · Time Delay Compensation · High Time Synchronization

1 Introduction

Research on satellite Internet and its key technologies has created a worldwide research boom in academia and industry. Onboard multibeam phased array antenna technology is widely recognized as a core key technology for improving the performance of low orbit satellite communication systems. However, traditional low orbit satellites mostly use fixed beam coverage, and the total available frequency band of the system is multiplexed in all beams according to a certain multiplexing factor, which results in low spectral efficiency [1–4]. This fixed communication resource sharing mechanism will restrict the service capability of space Internet based on low orbit satellite constellations, making it difficult to meet the communication needs of the proliferation of the number of service users, data volume, and types of services of low orbit satellite constellations. It is a bottleneck technical problem restricting the development of space multimedia Internet. The hopping beam coverage technology of satellite-carried multibeam phased

© ICST Institute for Computer Sciences, Social Informatics and Telecommunications Engineering 2025
Published by Springer Nature Switzerland AG 2025. All Rights Reserved
H.-H. Chen and W. Meng (Eds.): WiSATS 2024, LNICST 605, pp. 102–110, 2025.
https://doi.org/10.1007/978-3-031-86196-3_9

array antenna is a real-time adjustment of the beam service object for the current communication demand of the active users under the satellite taking into account the system throughput under the constraints of system resources and service fairness. This technology can not only reduce inter-beam interference and improve spectrum utilization and system trigger capacity, but also use fewer beam to achieve the same coverage effect as more fixed beams, thus improving satellite resource efficiency [5].

For a beam hopping system, the onboard beam switches between multiple ground terminals at a sub-millisecond time granularity, while the signal transmission delay between the satellite and the ground varies between 0 to 10 ms. Therefore, it is necessary to accurately adjust the beam hopping time on the satellite, fully considering the satellite-ground transmission delay and clock errors, to ensure that the beams transmitted by the satellite can be accurately received by the ground terminals even after sub-millisecond level hopping and millisecond level spatial transmission. Similarly, the signals transmitted by the ground terminals can still be accurately received by the receiving beam on the satellite even after sub-millisecond level hopping and millisecond level transmission [6].

There are not many domestic and foreign reports of hopping-beam based real-time communication system related technologies being applied on low orbit satellites. There is no reference system protocol for the management and control of satellite-ground communication resources under this system. The research on core key technologies and engineering practicality needs to be deepened urgently [7]. The general method of calculating the satellite-ground delay is to use the satellite's ephemeris to obtain the coordinate information of the satellite position and the coordinate information of the ground station to calculate the Euclidean distance divided by the speed of light. However, this method ignores the factor of the rotation of the Earth, and the obtained satellite-ground transmission delay causes errors. This paper proposes a method for satellite communication beam hopping control using a highly stable onboard clock and a global navigation system to achieve time synchronization. It improves the control accuracy of the phased-array beam agility time and achieves the alignment of the onboard beam hopping time to the ground terminal time.

2 Design of Beam Agility Control System

The satellite communication beam agility control system for time synchronization is shown in Fig. 1. It's supposed that the beam hopping requires alignment to the hop time T_0 of the ground communication system's time system. For downlink communication, it is required to generate an onboard transmitting beam hopping control pulse, the time of which must ensure that the signal is transmitted to the ground terminal through the transmitting beam of the phased array at the moment of T_0. For uplink communication, it is required to generate an onboard receiving beam hopping control pulse, the time of which must ensure that the signal transmitted from the ground station at time T_0 can be accurately received by the phased array receive beam after space transmission. This system consists of a phased array antenna, a beam agility control pulse generation module, a beam agility time calculation module, a time maintenance module, and a GNSS (Global Navigation Satellite System) receiver.

The GNSS receiver obtains the satellite's orbital position in the WGS-84 coordinate system by receiving navigation satellite signals and decoding the navigation message.

It sends the current onboard time t and the corresponding satellite orbital position $B(t)$ $= (X_B, Y_B, Z_B)$ to the beam agility control pulse generation module every second, and outputs a 1 Hz pulse to the time maintenance module every second. The rising edge of the 1 Hz pulse is aligned to the navigation system time.

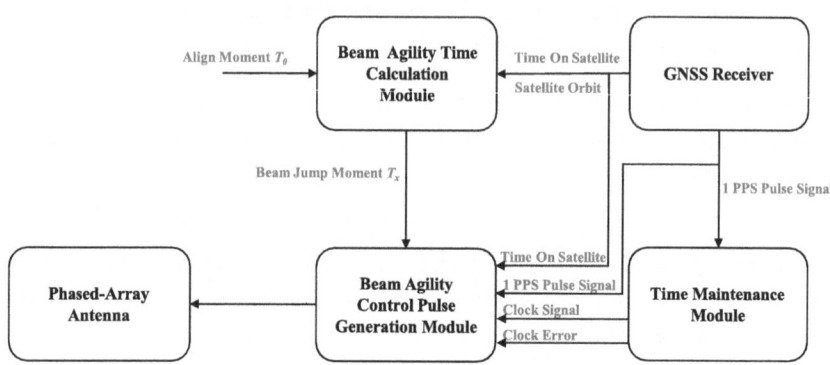

Fig. 1. Design of beam agility control system for satellite communication

The time maintenance module has a highly stable local indicator clock with a frequency of 100 MHz, but the clock accuracy does not meet the time control requirements. The clock error needs to be obtained based on the exact 1 s duration output from the GNSS. When the rising edge of each second pulse arrives, it starts counting based on the local clock until the rising edge of the next second pulse arrives. The count of the t th second is N_t, and the local clock error is E after accumulating W seconds. The time maintenance module sends the local clock error E to the beam agility control pulse generation module. E can be determined by

$$E = \frac{1}{W} \sum_{t=1}^{W} (10^8 - N_t) \tag{1}$$

The beam agility time calculation module calculates the signal space transmission delay according to the beam agility time T_0 aligned to the ground communication system annotated on the ground operation and control system, the position of the ground station $A(t) = (X_A, Y_A, Z_A)$, and the orbit $B(t) = (X_B, Y_B, Z_B)$ of the satellite at the time t. The beam agility time calculation module calculates the onboard beam hopping time to meet the signal hopping time alignment to the ground time. Finally, the beam agility time calculation module sends the onboard beam hopping time T_x to the beam agility control pulse generation module.

3 Time Delay Theory Analysis and Compensation Methods

3.1 Time Delay Theory Analysis

The satellite dynamically calculates the time delay according to the satellite-ground distance change and aligns the ground-based base station time slots to each time slot. The actual start time of each time slot is delayed in uplink communication and advanced in downlink communication. This paper analyses the uplink communication scenario.

The beam hopping time T_x is determined by the following four variables: (1) The time in the beam hopping table, which is the ground base station signal transmission time T_0. (2) The signal transmission delay from the ground base station to the ground feeder antenna interface T_1. (3) The signal transmission delay through the air interface T_2. (4) The signal transmission delay from the satellite feeder antenna to the phased array antenna T_3. The relationship between them is as follows:

$$T_x = T_0 + T_1 + T_2 + T_3 \qquad (2)$$

This paper completes the error compensation of the transmission delay T_2 due to the rotation of the Earth. Suppose the delay is calculated directly using the orbit at the moment of signal initiation. In that case, the signal space transmission delay is calculated using the position of the ground station $A(t) = (X_A, Y_A, Z_A)$, and the satellite's orbit $B(t) = (X_B, Y_B, Z_B)$ at the moment t. Signal space transmission T_2' delay can be determined by

$$T_{2'} = \frac{\sqrt{(X_B - X_A)^2 + (Y_B - Y_A)^2 + (Z_B - Z_A)^2}}{c} \qquad (3)$$

where c denotes the speed of light, is $3*10^8$ m/s. If the maximum speed of the satellite is v m/s, then the maximum position error Δ_p during transmission time can be determined by

$$\Delta_p = v * T_2' \qquad (4)$$

Then the corresponding time delay error Δ_t can be determined by

$$\Delta_t = \frac{\Delta_p}{c} \qquad (5)$$

3.2 Time Delay Compensation Methods

For uplink communication, the base station sends a signal at the moment T_0, which can be accurately received by the beam of the receiving phased array after spatial transmission, and the time at which the signal is received is T_x.

The WGS-84 coordinate of the satellite at T_0 is $B(T_0) = (X_B(T_0), Y_B(T_0), Z_B(T_0))$. Due to the limitation of computational resources, it is necessary to linearly interpolate the orbit to compensate the orbit error for the signal transmission delay T_1 from the ground base station to the ground feed antenna. The corrected orbit is $B(T_0 + T_1) =$

$(X_B(T_0 + T_1), Y_B(T_0 + T_1), Z_B(T_0 + T_1))$. The coarse delay T_2')between the satellite and the ground station at the time can be determined by

$$T_2' = \frac{\sqrt{(X_B(T_0 + T_1) - X_A)^2 + (Y_B(T_0 + T_1) - Y_A)^2 + (Z_B(T_0 + T_1) - Z_A)^2}}{c} \quad (6)$$

Linear extrapolation of the orbit $B(T_0 + T_1 + T_2')$ is to get the position of the orbit after experiencing a coarse time delay. Due to the rotation of the Earth, it is necessary to correct the coordinates of the satellite in the inertial coordinate system to the coordinates in the Earth-Fixed coordinate system. The corrected orbit can be $B'(T_0 + T_1 + T_2') = (X_B'(T_0 + T_1 + T_2'), Y_B'(T_0 + T_1 + T_2'), Z_B'(T_0 + T_1 + T_2'))$.

The signal transmission precision delay T_2 can be calculated by the corrected orbit. T_2 can be expressed as:

$$T_2 = \frac{\sqrt{[X_B'(T_0 + T_1 + T_2') - X_A]^2 + [Y_B'(T_0 + T_1 + T_2') - Y_A]^2 + [Z_B'(T_0 + T_1 + T_2') - Z_A]^2}}{c} \quad (7)$$

Assuming that T_0, T_1, and T_3 are known, Eq. (1) gives T_x.

The Beam Agility Control Pulse Generation Module generates the received signal pulse at T_x. Since the clock stability of the time maintenance module does not meet the time control requirements, the clock error needs to be considered when controlling the pulse generation. Assuming T_a is the whole second part of T_x and $T_b = T_x - T_a$ is the non-whole second part of T_x, the whole second starting point of T_x is determined by the on-board time and PPS. After the whole second starting point, the time when the hopping beam pulse is generated is the time when the local clock count is N. N can be expressed as

$$N = \left\lfloor T_b * (10^8 - E) \right\rfloor \quad (8)$$

where $\lfloor . \rfloor$ denotes the operation of rounding down.

In this paper, the position of the ground station is unchanged, and only the change of the satellite position is considered. The method of delay compensation for downlink and uplink is largely the same. For downlink communication, when calculating the delay compensation, to ensure that the onboard transmitting beam is received by the ground station at the time T_0, the extrapolated orbit needs to be modified to $B(T_0 - T_1 - T_2')$. And when correcting the orbit change due to rotation in the transmission process, α needs to be modified to $-\alpha$. The beam hopping time T_x can be written as $T_x = T_0 - T_1 - T_2 - T_3$.

4 System Performance Analysis

4.1 Visibility Analysis

The premise of communication between the satellite and the ground is that the ground station is within the coverage of the satellite. It can be assumed that the satellite's trajectory is a circular arc within the visible time range of the satellite to the ground station. It can be assumed that the radius of the Earth is r and the ground antenna pitch angle is θ. Setting the center of the Earth coordinate is $O = (X_o, Y_o, Z_o)$. There are the following relations.

$$|OB|^2 = |AB|^2 + r^2 + 2 * |AB| * r * \sin\theta \quad (9)$$

Equation (9) has two solutions that satisfy the conditions for the position of the satellite at the time of entry and the position of the satellite at the time of exit, which in turn allows the calculation of the visible period.

4.2 Analysis of Time Delay Error Estimation

In this paper, a section of the satellite orbital position visible to the station for 9.910 min is selected for simulation. We mainly analyze the satellite-ground transmission delay due to the rotation of the Earth and use the theoretical value to compare with the result value of orbit information simulation. As shown in Fig. 2, the maximum satellite-ground transmission delay is 8.38 ms during the period when the satellite is visible to the Earth. The maximum speed of the satellite is 7.3 km/s. Substituting the two into Eq. (4), we can get that the maximum position theoretical error is 61.17 m. The corresponding time delay theoretical error is 203.913 ns which is a non-negligible error. Therefore, it is necessary to correct the orbit once according to the coarse estimated time delay. Correcting the coordinates of the satellite in the inertial coordinate system to the coordinates in the Earth-Fixed coordinate system., and then we calculate the satellite-ground transmission delay for the first iteration based on the corrected orbital position. The maximum transmission is 8.38ms, which generates a maximum error of 203.913 ns in transmission delay. If we iterate the orbit one more time, the transmission delay of the first iteration of the orbit is used to recalculate the coordinates in the Earth-Fixed coordinate system, which is equivalent to an accurate transmission delay of 203.913 ns. The error in transmission delay is 203.913 ns, and the maximum theoretical error of the position is 0.001489 m, which corresponds to the time delay theoretical error is 0.04962 ns. So the error is negligible. Therefore, another iteration of track position is needed to satisfy the calculation accuracy.

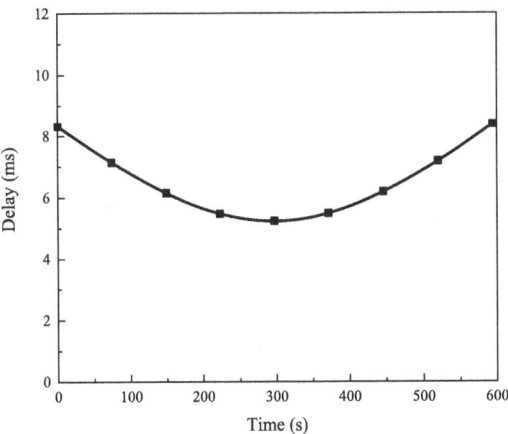

Fig. 2. Satellite to ground transmission delay.

The following analysis compares the transmission delay calculated by iterating the orbit position once with the coarse estimated delay with the coarse delay. As shown in Fig. 3, the red line shows the difference in simulation delay between the delay of the first iteration of the track position and the coarse delay, while the black line shows the difference in theoretical delay. It can be found that the maximum simulation error between the delay calculated by iterating the orbit position once and the coarse delay is 148.06 ns. Which has a gap compared with the theoretical value of 203.913 ns.

As shown in Fig. 4, the red line shows the difference in simulation delay between the first and second iterations of the track position, while the black line shows the difference in theoretical delay. It can be seen that the maximum delay error of the simulation result is 0.0026 ns which has a gap compared with the theoretical value of 0.4926 ns.

It can be seen that there are some deviations between the theoretical values and simulated results. This is due to the fact that the orbit position used in the calculation of the coarse delay is the orbit position at the moment of T0. In addition, due to the limitation of computational resources, the orbit value is calculated by linear interpolation rather than introduced by orbit dynamics.

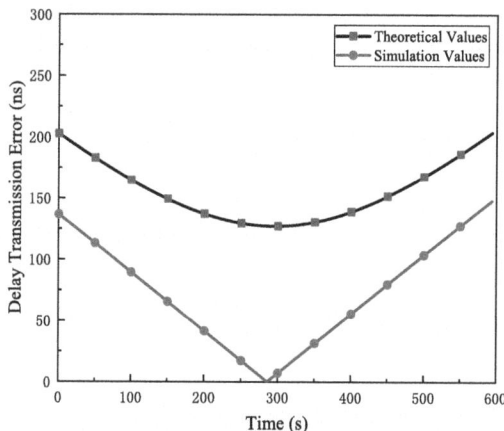

Fig. 3. Difference in time delay between iterating the orbit once and not iterating the orbit.

In summary, the delay compensation method proposed in this paper effectively improves the accuracy of the satellite-ground delay by correcting the orbital position through a two-iteration process compared with the direct calculation. It realizes that the signals transmitted from the ground station can still be accurately received by the sub-millisecond hopping receiving beam on the satellite even if they undergo millisecond transmission. This method helps save the expenses of communication resources.

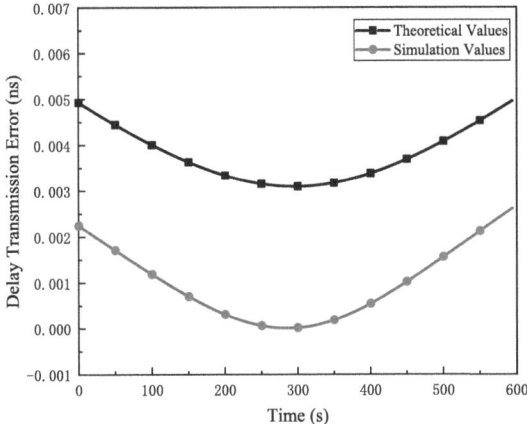

Fig. 4. Difference in time delay between iterating the orbit once and iterating the orbit twice.

5 Conclusion

This paper proposes a satellite communication beam agility control method for time synchronization using a highly stable clock and a global navigation system. The method first utilizes orbital information to calculate the coarse time delay between the satellite and the ground. Then, the orbital interpolation module is used to determine the orbital position of the received signal and corrections are made for the changes in the position of orbit in WGS-84 due to the rotation of the Earth during the transmission time. This allows for the calculation of the precise transmission delay of the signal. To ensure the signal is accurately received by the satellite's beam hopping within sub-millisecond precision, the orbital position needs to be iterated twice to enhance compensation accuracy. Simulation results show that this method improves the time delay accuracy by 148.06 ns compared to the traditional method. After two iterations of orbital position, the transmission delay error can be reduced to 0.0026 ns, meeting the required calculation precision.

Acknowledgments. This study was funded by The Chinese Academy of Sciences focuses on the deployment of scientific research projects (No. KGFZD-145-23-14) and Youth Innovation Promotion Association CAS (NO. 2020294).

References

1. Li, K.L., Li, Y.T., Qiu, Z.K., et al.: Handover procedure design and performance optimization strategy in LEO-HAP system. In: 2019 11th International Conference on Wireless Communications and Signal Processing (WCSP), pp. 1–7. IEEE, Xi'an (2019)
2. Miao, J.S., Wang, P.J., Yin, H.Q. et al.: A multi-attribute decision handover scheme for LEO mobile satellite networks. In: 2019 IEEE 5th International Conference on Computer and Communications (ICCC), pp. 938–942. IEEE, Chengdu (2019)
3. Wang, L., Zhang, N.T.: Dynamic location management in LEO networks. In: The 13th IEEE International Symposium on Personal. Indoor and Mobile Radio Communications, pp. 1397–1401. IEEE, Lisbon (2002)

4. Musumpuka, R., Walingo, T.M., Smith, J.M.: Performance analysis of correlated handover service in LEO mobile satellite systems. IEEE Commun. Lett. **20**(11), 2213–2216 (2016)
5. Sun, S.H., Hou, L.M., Miao, D.S.: Beam switching solutions for beam-hopping based LEO system. In: 2021 IEEE 94th Vehicular Technology Conference (VTC2021-Fall), pp. 1–5. IEEE, Norman (2021)
6. Wang, Y.X., Bian, D.M., Hu, J., et al.: A flexible resource allocation algorithm in full bandwidth beam hopping satellite systems. In: 2019 IEEE 3rd Advanced Information Management, Communicates, Electronic and Automation Control Conference (IMCEC), pp. 920–927. IEEE Chongqing (2019)
7. Liu, W.Y., Xia, S.Y., Jiang, Q.J., et al.: Hop-beam based resource scheduling algorithm for low orbit satellite networks. J. Chin. Acad. Sci. Univ. **37**(6), 9 (2020)

Design of an Electro-Optical Hybrid Switching Architecture for Satellite Internet

Zhenhua Zhang[1,2]([✉]) [ORCID], Siyue Sun[1,2], Xiangyu Gan[1,2], Yimeng Luo[1,2], Jian Wang[1,2], and Linchen Ku[1,2]

[1] Innovation Academy for Microsatellites of Chinese Academy of Sciences, Shanghai, China
nmwjasdf@163.com
[2] University of Chinese Academy of Sciences, Beijing, China

Abstract. The establishment of satellite Internet is a crucial step in the future development of the satellite communications industry. Therefore, in the current inter-satellite link environment where laser links and microwave links coexist, a new switching system architecture is needed. This paper summarizes the business capabilities that satellite Internet must meet based on the current development status of satellite communications, as well as the characteristics and transmission requirements of satellite Internet services. It also investigates and analyzes the current state of switching technology, summarizing the applicability of existing switching technologies in the construction of satellite Internet. Based on the analysis results, an end to end network on the satellite is constructed, leading to the design of a satellite optical-electrical hybrid architecture.

Keywords: Satellite Internet · Electro-Optical Hybrid Switching · Intersatellite link

1 Introduction

Satellite Internet is a satellite-based communication system that provides services such as processing, storing, and forwarding operational data through artificial satellites, enabling the interconnection and interoperability of air, sky, earth, and sea. Satellite Internet is not a new concept; from the inception of the Iridium system to today's Starlink, more than 30 years have passed. Early satellite communications primarily involved geostationary orbit (GEO) satellites, which used single satellites to relay data.

As satellite communication technology has evolved, the limitations of ground networks have become more apparent. For instance, high-speed mobile aircraft communication services struggle to maintain high communication quality, and extreme areas such as polar regions, deserts, and oceans remain uncovered. Lower satellite orbits, with their low cost, low latency, large scale, and high bandwidth, have garnered increasing attention from researchers [1].

© ICST Institute for Computer Sciences, Social Informatics and Telecommunications Engineering 2025
Published by Springer Nature Switzerland AG 2025. All Rights Reserved
H.-H. Chen and W. Meng (Eds.): WiSATS 2024, LNICST 605, pp. 111–124, 2025.
https://doi.org/10.1007/978-3-031-86196-3_10

Today's satellite communication systems are utilizing progressively lower orbits. Systems like O3b use medium Earth orbit (MEO), while the second-generation Iridium system, OneWeb, Starlink, and similar constellations use low Earth orbit (LEO). The advent of LEO satellite Internet has triggered a global surge in research and development.

Leveraging the research and development surge in satellite constellations, this paper aims to design a switching architecture that meets the current information transmission needs of satellite constellations and is scalable for future satellite Internet development. The paper first summarizes the business requirements and characteristics of existing satellite constellations based on the current state of satellite development. It then investigates various existing switching technologies, comparing their advantages and disadvantages to identify a switching form suitable for the future development of satellite Internet. Ultimately, this study proposes an Electro-Optical Hybrid switching architecture.

2 Status of Satellite Internet Development

Low orbit satellite communications initiated a significant boom as early as the 1990s, with Motorola's Iridium system being the most notable example. However, due to the high development costs and the rapid advancement of terrestrial cellular networks, the Iridium project ultimately went bankrupt. In recent years, the development of small satellites and the reduction in launch costs have highlighted the advantages of deploying low orbit satellites. As a result, nearly 30 companies worldwide are now engaged in deploying satellite Internet, with plans to launch more than 100,000 satellites globally . Among these, over 10 companies have proposed non-geostationary orbit (NGSO) satellite systems, involving approximately 80,000 satellites [1]. The main constellations are presented in Table 1.

Table 1. Satellite Internet Constellation.

Satellite Constellation	ballpark	frequency band	service
Iridium	66	L/Ka	voice communication
Starlink	42000	Ku/Ka/V	high speed Internet
OneWeb	882	Ku/Ka/V	high speed Internet
Kuiper	3236	Ka	Internet
HongYun	156	Ka	Internet
HongYan	324	L/Ka	Internet

Early satellite communications primarily utilized the transparent forwarding method for data transmission, with information processing mainly conducted at ground stations. This approach significantly limited the satellite information processing capacity. Additionally, using ground stations as forwarding nodes increased communication delays and adversely affected transmission quality. In recent years, the number of access users has risen, and the frequency of information interaction and sharing has increased. Consequently, the transparent forwarding method no longer meets the needs of the evolving communication industry. Therefore, there is a need to develop satellites with information processing capabilities, such as multimedia satellites.

At present, satellite communication systems primarily use microwave links for star to Earth connections, while laser links have been added for intersatellite connections alongside microwave links. However, microwave links are limited by frequency constraints, leading to bottlenecks in transmission rates and communication capacity, making it difficult to meet the demand for distributing and transmitting various types of services. In recent years, the continuous development of optical communication technology has provided a solution to the limitations of microwave links. On-planet laser links offer advantages such as large capacity, small equipment size, and strong anti-interference capabilities, which can effectively supplement microwave links for information transmission [3]. Therefore, the development of space laser communication is crucial for realizing satellite Internet. Table 2 shows the current status of satellite links.

Table 2. Satellite link status

Satellite orbit type	Link Type	transmission medium	single-port rate
intersatellite orbit	Same orbit, different orbits, cross-layer link building	Laser/Microwave	multirate 100 Mbps, 2.5 Gbps, 5 Gbps, 10 Gbps, 100 Gbps
access link orbit	Establishing links to users	Microwave	Multi-user, multi-band Wide range of rates (1 Mbps-20 Gbps)
Feeder link orbit	Implementing links	Microwave	Ka band 10 Gbps-20 Gbps

Satellite switching technology can effectively reduce the satellite system's dependence on ground stations and, at the same time, reduce communication delays. Currently, satellites mainly use microwave links to transmit information, and the primary switching method on satellite is electric domain switching. However, electric switching faces an electronic bottleneck, making it difficult to improve communication rates and capacity. Additionally, the electric switching devices on-satellite have a relatively large volume, which increases the design requirements of the satellite's interior. In contrast, optical switching devices are relatively smaller in volume and offer advantages such as large transmission capacity and good information confidentiality. Therefore, studying satellite optical switching will lay the foundation for improving satellite Internet performance in the future. The service model shown in Table 3 will further constrain the switching system of satellite Internet [4].

At present, the development of all optical switching is constrained by optical devices and other factors, making it difficult for available optical switching methods to flexibly handle multiple types and granularities of services on satellites. Therefore, to meet the service forwarding requirements of satellite Internet, it

Table 3. Satellite business model.

data type	Resource type	packet delay	packet loss	Guaranteed bandwidth
signaling	Non-GBR	100 ms	10^{-6}	shared bandwidth
conversational speech	GBR	100 ms	10^{-2}	shared bandwidth
Conversation videos	GBR	150 ms	10^{-6}	shared bandwidth
Non-conversational videos	GBR	300 ms	10^{-6}	shared bandwidth
multimedia video	Non-GBR	300 ms	10^{-6}	shared bandwidth
TCP, P2P file sharing	Non-GBR	300 ms	10^{-6}	shared bandwidth
Dedicated line business	GBR	100 ms		Exclusive bandwidth

is necessary to use optical-electrical hybrid switching on satellites. The application of optical-electrical hybrid switching combines the advantages of both optical and electrical switching. Electrical switching, with its flexible forwarding capabilities and mature technology, is used for handling a large number of transmissions with small information streams [5]. Meanwhile, high capacity optical switching is employed for dealing with a small number of transmissions with large information streams. This approach effectively meets the high efficiency transmission requirements of various types and granularities of services in space.

3   Current Status of Research on Switching Technology and Analysis of Its Applicability

3.1   Electrical Switching Technology

The Optical Transport Network (OTN) is based on wavelength division multiplexing technology within the optical layer of the network. Its standardization began in 1998. Prior to 2000, the design philosophy of OTN was similar to that of the Synchronous Digital Hierarchy (SDH) system. According to the principles of optical network layering, OTN was defined in terms of network node interfaces, physical layer interfaces, network jitter performance, and other aspects. The main standards for OTN were largely finalized by 2003.

The OTN is divided into two layers: the optical layer and the electrical layer, which together facilitate the transmission of services, as shown in Fig. 1. The optical layer primarily functions as a transmission pipeline for information, performing optical layer scheduling and enabling the cross scheduling of optical signals. The core unit for optical signal scheduling is the Reconfigurable Optical Add Drop Multiplexer (ROADM). The ROADM receives OTU optical signals and then routes these signals to specified egress points by creating internal optical cross paths, with each egress corresponding to a different line.

However, with the accelerating pace of informatization, various video services have been growing rapidly in recent years. These services are characterized by small bandwidth and large numbers, necessitating simple and fast flexible bandwidth adjustments. Traditional OTN technology has become insufficient

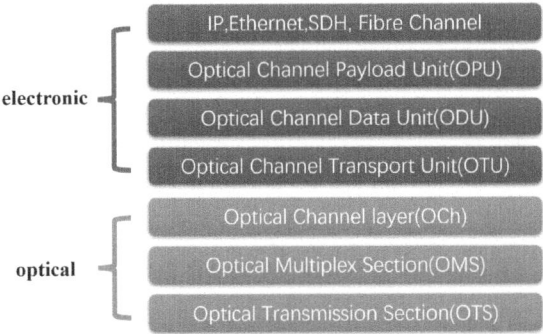

Fig. 1. OTN structure

for efficiently transmitting these types of services. Consequently, Optical Service Unit (OSU) technology was developed. In January 2020, the ITU-T adopted the Optical Service Unit path layer network (OSU) standard during a plenary meeting in Geneva to initiate standard research on OTN's capability to carry small granular services.

OSU, as a technological expansion of the optical transport network (OTN), can efficiently transmit small grained services on the ground with high technological maturity and well developed corresponding devices. However, in traditional terrestrial networks, completing end to end communication is more complex. First, the user terminal sends information to the access network. Then, through the wireless access network and IP IPRAN, information is transmitted to the core network, where the fiber optic channel completes the transmission of high capacity information. Finally, the information is processed and forwarded back through IP bearer in the core network. OTN, as a technology for bearing high traffic, long distance services, is only part of the ground network, whereas constructing a star network requires encompassing the entire ground architecture's content and function.

In a satellite network, there is no division into access network, bearer network, and core network. Services uploaded to the satellite require new routing and switching for transmission. Therefore, the use of OSU technology in satellite networks requires consideration of the functional design of core and access networks, which puts high demands on network protocol optimization and network planning, especially under the constraint of fast switching in satellite networks.

OSU technology is essentially a switching technology for optical layer transmission and electrical layer switching. The application prospects and efficiency of optical switching technology are higher than those of electrical domain switching. In the optical layer, OSU needs to establish channels in advance to meet end to end communication. The variety of business needs on the star require flexible network bandwidth for efficient transmission. While OSU pipeline switching has advantages in leased line business, it struggles to effectively respond to scenarios with a large number of user terminals requiring flexible access. Additionally, the delay and bandwidth utilization in pipeline establishment and dismantling are disadvantages compared to optical layer switching.

To summarize, OSU technology in the context of OTN is more reliable for star applications due to its mature application on the ground and the availability of well developed devices. However, future optical domain switching holds better development prospects.

3.2   Optical Switching Technology

At present, optical switching technology is mainly divided into: optical circuit switching, optical burst switching and optical packet switching. Among them, optical circuit switching has been studied the most and is relatively mature, optical packet switching inherits the characteristics of traditional electric domain packet switching, and optical burst switching is closer to the former two performance of the compromise program.

Optical Circuit Switching(OCS). Optical Circuit Switching, a mature optical switching technology, inherits the characteristics of traditional circuit switching. The transmission and exchange of services require a link building process, where each link is assigned a dedicated wavelength from the source to the destination. During the switching process, establishing a link necessitates a bidirectional bandwidth application to complete the request and response process. Once established, only the two parties involved can transmit information, and resources are released only after the link is dismantled.

Although OCS can transmit information at high speed and high capacity, it is not suitable for most current business types, such as video services, which require high frequency and low transmission capacity. OCS technology is more suitable for high capacity service transmission pipelines and has a significant advantage in transmitting on-satellite services that are not sensitive to large-granularity delay. Additionally, OCS can be used for some on-satellite private line services, where channel resources are individually allocated to ensure high reliability transmission. However, when handling small grained, delay sensitive services, OCS technology struggles to provide flexible and efficient transmission.

Optical Burst Switching(OBS). Optical Burst Switching is a technology in which the control packet enters the optical switching node first, followed by the data packet for forwarding. The switching unit of OBS, called an Optical Burst (OB), includes two parts: the Burst Data Packet (BDP) and the Burst Control Packet (BCP). The BDP is a re-encapsulation of the data in the network, based on attributes such as the destination address and QoS requirements. The BCP contains the routing information of the BDP, its length, offset time, priority, and quality of service. The BCP and the corresponding BDP are transmitted in separate optical channels, with the BCP leading the BDP by an offset delay [6].

This offset delay allows the reservation of the resources required by the BDP in the absence of optical caching and optical synchronization. By the time the

BDP arrives at the node, the corresponding optical path has been established, ensuring the efficient switching and transmission of the BDP [7].

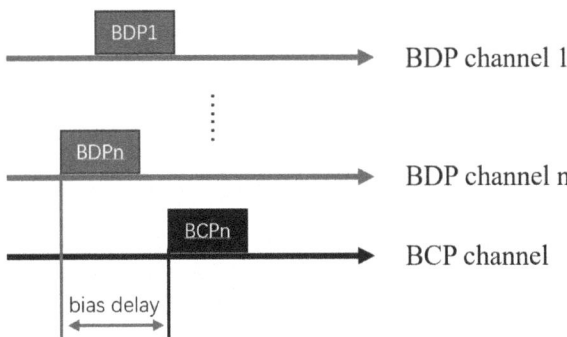

Fig. 2. OTN structure

As shown in Fig. 2, the OBS switching process requires setting an offset delay between the BCP and the BDP. The offset delay is configured to ensure that the BCP has reserved the necessary resources before any BDP arrives. This design allows for a unidirectional reservation process without needing a buffer for the switching technology [8]. However, once blocking occurs in the network, the packet loss rate increases. Different network structures can lead to blocking, making it difficult to guarantee transmission quality even with optical delay lines. Therefore, developing strategies to manage blocking is critical.

The switching granularity of Optical Burst Switching (OBS) can vary from a few IP packets to hundreds of IP packets, reducing control overhead. The separate transmission of burst data packets (BDPs) and burst control packets (BCPs) on the physical channel allows the switching node to reserve resources for the BDP after the BCP's arrival. This ensures that the BDP can be transmitted directly without undergoing optoelectronic conversion, facilitating the efficient transmission of high bandwidth services. However, when the frequency of service transmission is high, congestion and conflicts can prevent OBS from achieving high-reliability service transmission, which is unacceptable when such reliability is required.

Currently, the application of Optical Burst Switching (OBS) technology on satellites primarily needs to focus on the optical delay line and the optical switching matrix. OBS requires an anti-blocking design, and the design of the optical delay line significantly impacts the performance of the entire on-board network. The optical switching matrix is the core device of the OBS system, directly influencing the performance of the switching network. Presently, the typical structures of the optical burst switching matrix include spatial optical switching matrices and arrayed waveguide grating (AWG)-based optical burst switching structures.

The burst packet granularity of OBS technology is moderate, which can adequately support the transmission of small granularity services, such as video services on satellites. Additionally, OBS offers higher channel resource utilization since it does not require the traditional circuit switched form's chain building process and resource monopolization. Regarding delay, the primary delay in OBS arises from the processing and switching delay of the BCP at each node. Each node only needs to perform optoelectronic and optical (O/E/O) conversion for the BCP without analyzing the BDP.

In summary, OBS technology has a foundational level of engineering implementation for satellite use. While it is not as mature as Optical Transport Network (OTN) technology, which is better suited for satellite service transmission, OBS offers high bandwidth utilization. However, a reasonable anti-blocking strategy is necessary to optimize its performance.

Optical Packet Switching(OPS). Traditional packet switching employs the store and forward method, wherein messages sent from the source node are segmented into fixed format packets. Each packet is appended with the destination node's address in the packet header and transmitted using a virtual circuit. Upon receiving a packet, the network switch temporarily stores it, then searches for an available switching path within the network to forward the packet to its destination, as illustrated in Fig. 3. This approach significantly enhances line utilization [9].

Optical packet switching, a technology based on optical signal transmission, inherits the characteristics of electronic packet switching. Compared to traditional networks, optical packet switching networks exhibit higher resource utilization and better adaptability to sudden data and information surges [10]. OPS

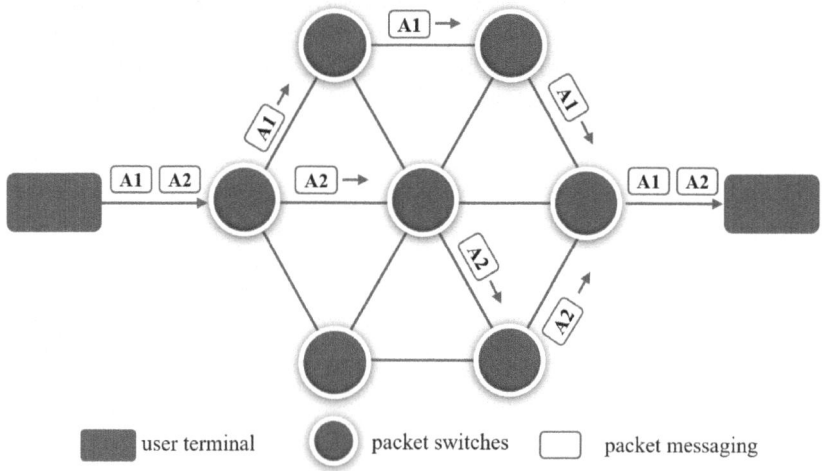

Fig. 3. OTN structure

technology, inherited from the domain of electric packet switching, can adeptly handle the corresponding services of satellite Internet due to its efficient and flexible information transmission capabilities. However, a primary challenge facing OPS technology lies in the absence of an efficient optical caching mechanism [11].

While terrestrial network's electrical switching technology can achieve electrical caching, replicated circuit block switching, and read-as-you-go functions, the current research on optical caching in optical networks primarily relies on optical delay lines for brief caching. Under ideal conditions, altering crystal lattice structures and increasing micro-ring resonance cavities can extend caching times to up to an hour, with caching rates reaching 1 Gbit/s. However, relying on optical delay lines for caching fails to effectively address cache contention issues, as this technology cannot ensure meeting the delay disparities inherent in the switching process.

In summary, due to the development of optical caching devices is not mature, want to complete the optical caching process can only use the optical delay line, so OPS technology, although in the theoretical level than the OBS and OCS technology is more efficient, more flexible, more suitable for the optical network as a switching technology, but subject to the immaturity of the physical level of the device is very difficult to be effectively applied to the network on the satellite [12].

Table 4. Switching Technology Comparison

Switching Technology	switching Form	Device Capabilities	capability	Satellite-based applicability
OSU	electrical	maturity	Better performance, but limited by electronic bottlenecks	applicable
OCS	optical	maturity	High transmission capacity, but inflexible	inapplicable
OBS	optical	comparatively maturity	Moderate business granularity and high transmission efficiency	applicable
OPS	optical	immaturity	Subject to the immaturity of the optical device can not meet the business requirements	inapplicable

As depicted in Table 4, at this juncture, while OSU technology exhibits viability within the electric domain for satellite Internet networking, it confronts electronic bottlenecks as communication capacity escalates. Conversely, the optical domain presently demonstrates proficiency in engineering OBS technology, rendering it more apt for satellite applications. Should mature development products for optical cache devices materialize in the future, OPS technology would emerge as a more fitting solution for the networking demands of satellite Internet.

4   Electro-Optical Hybrid Switching Architecture

At this stage, the construction of satellite Internet is primarily focused on low-orbit satellites. Consequently, numerous data transmission services have opted to utilize low orbit satellites, which facilitate easier acquisition of high resolution images and other data. These satellites are also suitable for measurement and control purposes. High-speed convergence business scenarios from space to the core network include applications such as general aviation aircraft networking and entertainment, rescue medical police aviation networking, broadband communications for ocean-going vessels, polar scientific research communications, and land emergency command communications. The data types transmitted in these scenarios encompass signaling, session-based voice, session-based video, and non-session-based video. Measurement and control services comprise remote control and telemetry services, where telemetry is predominantly employed for the centralized detection of dispersed or inaccessible objects, including those that are distant, in harsh environments, or moving at high speeds. Beyond fulfilling basic data transmission and measurement and control requirements, satellite Internet also necessitates network management and safeguard functions.

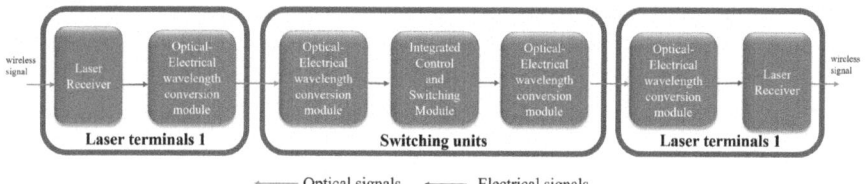

Fig. 4. Current satellite Switching processes

As shown in Fig. 4, laser links have been incorporated into current satellites to facilitate inter-satellite connections. However, due to the lack of optical wavelength conversion devices, six photoelectric conversions are necessary to complete the information processing at satellite switching nodes. While the use of laser links enhances the satellite's signal transmission capacity, the excessive photoelectric conversions significantly increase overhead and transmission delay. Consequently, this architecture is not an efficient switching solution.

Figure 5 depicts the ground optical switching model, where ground optical switching nodes utilize wavelength routing. This allows multi service flow switching across fibers carrying hundreds of channels, primarily serving backbone networks. The optical switching speed requirements for these networks range from seconds to milliseconds. However, in satellite networks, services are carried on a single wavelength, necessitating shorter response times for optical switching. Additionally, the diversity of data granularity in satellite networks requires precise and synchronized optical switching, which ground switching nodes struggle to achieve. Therefore, this paper proposes the following switching architecture

Figure 6 depicts the design of an optical and electrical hybrid architecture based on service type. This design features both an external electrical interface and an optical terminal capable of simultaneously establishing laser links and microwave links. The electrical interface supports microwave links across various frequency bands, while the optical terminal receives laser signals via an

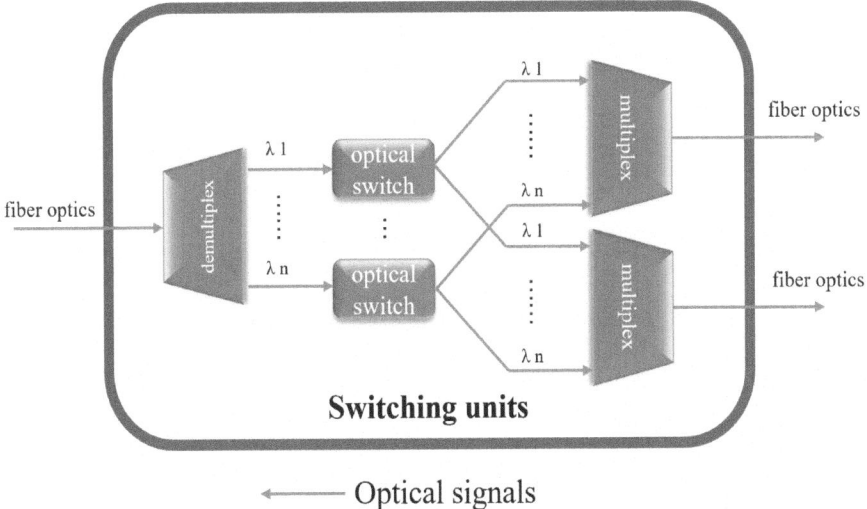

Fig. 5. Current satellite Switching processes

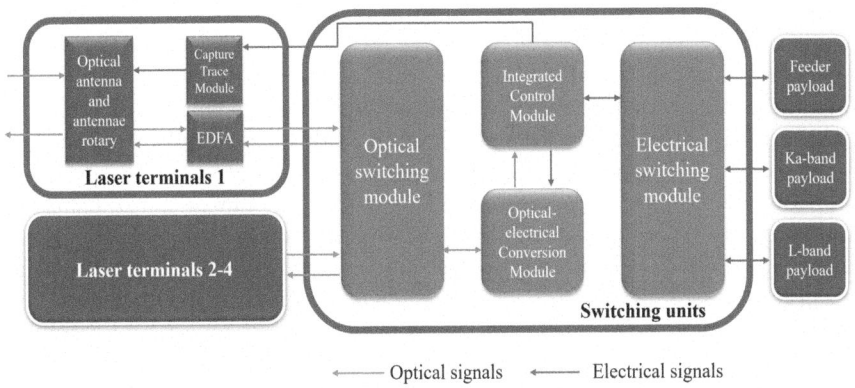

Fig. 6. Electro-Optical Hybrid Switching Architecture

optical antenna and manages the antenna using a capture and tracking module. The electrical switching module handles the monitoring and control of user-side access, the combination and splitting of packet-switched packets, and transmission control. The integrated control module's functions include packet classification, forwarding table generation and configuration, call processing, traffic control, routing, switching control, system configuration, and management. The Electro-Optical Switching module is primarily responsible for the convergence and divergence of optical and electrical signals, including optical-to-electrical and electrical-to-optical conversions. The optical switching module encompasses optical switching and protocol processing, ensuring the adaptation of light emitting signals, data generation and disassembly, and queue control.

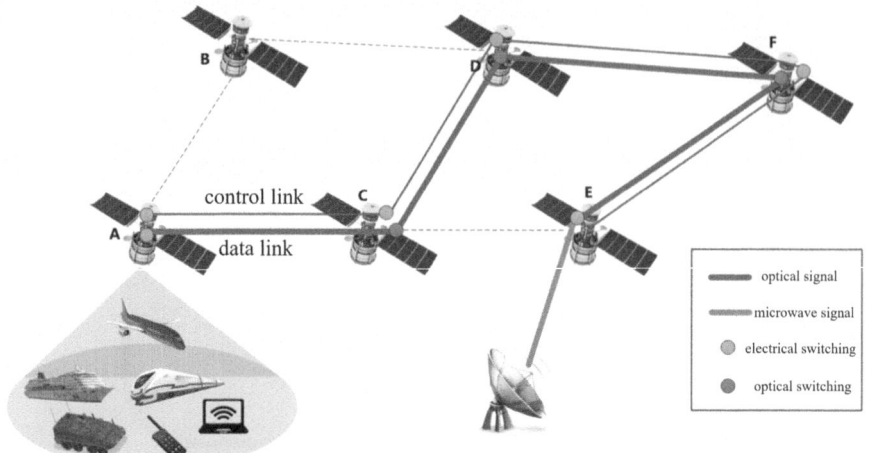

Fig. 7. switching unit works in a satellite internet

Figure 7 illustrates the working principle of a switching unit employing the optical burst switching regime in a satellite Internet system, utilizing both data and control channel transmissions. The control channel employs an electrical switching module to manage its forwarding, while the data channel directly uses an optical switching module for transmission. Additionally, both upstream and downstream feeder links utilize microwave links to facilitate transmission.

The introduction of the optical switching module enables signal transmission without requiring photoelectric conversion, thereby reducing overhead and transmission delay associated with multiple photoelectric conversions. Moreover, since the satellite laser link operates using a single wavelength transmission system, this architecture is compatible with the wavelength transmission of satellites, making it particularly suitable for constructing satellite Internet systems utilizing laser links. This approach allows the satellite Internet to move beyond the original satellite function of merely transparent forwarding, enabling some of the ground station's functions to be performed directly by the satellite's switching node. As a result, this reduces the reliance on ground stations.

5   Conclusion

Switching technology is crucial for building satellite Internet. In this paper, we first examine and analyze the switching requirements for satellite Internet. We investigate the current mainstream switching technologies and summarize the advantages and disadvantages of each when applied on satellite.

Electric domain switching, a mature technology, is well developed in terms of transmission systems and switching equipment, making it easier to implement at the application level. In contrast, optical domain switching, which can overcome electronic bottlenecks, offers superior performance and represents a future oriented technology. However, its implementation on satellites is currently hampered by underdeveloped devices and systems.

The adoption of hybrid switching in this paper is primarily based on previous research, current switching technology, satellite links, and existing data formats. Among switching technologies, optical switching is significantly constrained by the lack of engineered optical cache devices and optical wavelength conversion devices, making it challenging to construct fully optical switching nodes at the physical layer. Satellite communication links currently use both microwave and laser links; thus, introducing a hybrid architecture can accommodate these two forms of links to a certain extent, enhancing their efficiency. Moreover, given the variable types and granularity of services, the hybrid switching architecture can flexibly manage diverse service types. Therefore, this paper anticipates that optoelectronic hybrid switching will have a broader application prospect. Finally there are many more key elements worth studying for satellite internet

1 Design of transmission protocols in satellite constellations.
2 Engineering of optical caching devices and all-optical wavelength conversion devices.
3 Design of multi-wavelength laser terminals
4 Fast capture and tracking of inter-satellite laser links.

References

1. Chen, Q., Giambene, G., Yang, L., et al.: Analysis of inter-satellite link paths for LEO mega-constellation network. IEEE Trans. Veh. Technol. **70**(3), 2743–55 (2021)
2. Chaudhry, A.U., Yanikomeroglu, H.: Free space optics for next-generation satellite networks (2020)
3. Susilo, H.E., Suryana, J.: Research on LPWAN direct to satellite IoT: a survey technology and performance on LEO satellite. In: 2023 29th International Conference on Telecommunications (ICT), Toba, Indonesia, pp. 1–7 (2023). https://doi.org/10.1109/ICT60153.2023.10374072. keywords: Surveys;Satellites;Power demand;Low earth orbit satellites;Telecommunications;Internet of Things;Doppler effect;LEO Satellite;Internet of Things;Low Power Wide Area Network (LPWAN);Satellite-Based IoT,
4. Ding, R., et al.: 5G integrated satellite communication systems: architectures, air interface, and standardization. In: 2020 International Conference on Wireless Communications and Signal Processing (WCSP), Nanjing, China, pp. 702–707 (2020). https://doi.org/10.1109/WCSP49889.2020.9299757. keywords: Satellite broadcasting;5G mobile communication;Satellites;Protocols;Communication channels;Optical switches;Logic gates;Satellite-terrestrial networks;5G;air interface;satellite communications,
5. Zhou, W., Hong, T., Ding, X., Zhang, G.: LoRa performance analysis for LEO satellite IoT networks. In: 2021 13th International Conference on Wireless Communications and Signal Processing (WCSP), Changsha, China, pp. 1–5 (2021). https://doi.org/10.1109/WCSP52459.2021.9613680. keywords: Wireless communication;Satellites;Interference cancellation;Silicon carbide;Simulation;Low earth

orbit satellites;Mathematical models;Internet of Things;satellite IoT;LoRa;Uplink Performance;successive interference cancellation,

6. Papazoglou, C., Sarigiannidis, P.G., Papadimitriou, G.I., Pomportsis, A.S.: Techniques for improved scheduling in optical burst switched networks. In: International Symposium on Autonomous Decentralized Systems, vol. 2009, pp. 1–4 (2009). https://doi.org/10.1109/ISADS.2009.5207359

7. de Pedro, L., Aracil, J., Hernandez, J.A., Garcia-Dorado, J.L.: Analysis of the processing and sojourn times of Burst Control Packets in Optical Burst Switches. In: International Conference on Optical Network Design and Modeling, vol. 2008, pp. 1–3 (2008). https://doi.org/10.1109/ONDM.2008.4578393

8. Li, C.Y., Li, G., Wai, P.K.A., Li, V.O.K.: Optical burst switching with large switching overhead. J. Lightwave Technol. **25**(2), 451–462 (2007). https://doi.org/10.1109/JLT.2006.889427

9. Chen, K.S., Yang, C.C.: An application of spectral-amplitude-coding labels in optical signal buffering over optical packet-switching networks. IEEE Commun. Lett. **24**, 2020–2023 (2020)

10. Liu, W., Romeira, B., Li, M., et al.: A wavelength tunable optical buffer based on self-pulsation in an active microring resonator. J. Lightwave Technol. **34**(14), 1 (2016)

11. Ma, Y., Ma, Y.Z., Zhou, Z., et al.: One-hour coherent optical storage in an atomic frequency comb memory. Nat. Commun. **12**, 2381 (2021)

12. Zhang, Z., et al.: A survey of optical/electric hybrid switching technology for satellite Internet. Telecommun. Sci. **38**(11), 1–10 (2022)

Genetic Algorithm-Based Inter-Satellite Link Establishment and Routing Scheme for Satellite Networks

Kaiyuan Zhang[1]📷, Shuai Li[2], Ruisong Wang[1(✉)]📷, Gongliang Liu[1(✉)]📷, Di Ren[2], and Xingxing Wang[3]

[1] School of Information Science and Engineering, Harbin Institute of Technology, Weihai 264209, China
mathwrs@163.com, liugl@hit.edu.cn
[2] Qian Xuesen Laboratory, CAST, Beijing 100094, China
flutedi@sina.com
[3] China National Space Administration Earth Observation and Data Center, Beijing 100101, China
wangxx@radi.ac.cn

Abstract. In recent years, because of their advantages in coverage and throughput compared to traditional fiber and mobile networks, satellite networks have garnered increasing attention. However, satellite networks have limited resources such as storage, power, and frequency bands. Therefore, how to maximize network transmission capacity under limited communication resources is a key to the practical application of satellite networks. To enhance the throughput of the satellite network, we have devised a multicast satellite network that incorporates network coding. Additionally, we have further bolstered the network capacity by optimizing its topology and refining the routing of information flow. In order to find a better topology structure, we design a Genetic Algorithm based topology construction method which decode the topology as the chromosome and finding topologies with higher performance by mimicking biological genetic meritocracy. Ultimately, the simulation outcomes demonstrate that the introduced method substantially outperforms traditional approaches in augmenting the network's capacity.

Keywords: Network Coding · Inter-Satellite Link(ISL) Establishment · Genetic Algorithm · Satellite Network · Routing Scheme

1 Introduction

During the past few years, satellite networks have received more focus and attention due to their ability to provide greater coverage and throughput compared

This work was supported in part by the National Natural Science Foundation of China under Grants 61971156 and 61801144, in part by Shandong Provincial Natural Science Foundation under Grants ZR2020MF141 and ZR2019MF035.

H.-H. Chen and W. Meng (Eds.): WiSATS 2024, LNICST 605, pp. 125–137, 2025.
https://doi.org/10.1007/978-3-031-86196-3_11

to traditional fiber and mobile networks, especially in remote locations, including mountainous regions and vast oceans, without incurring additional deployment costs. As a result, satellite networks have become an integral part of next-generation communication networks. However, satellite networks have limited resources such as storage, power, and frequency bands, while high-bandwidth transmission tasks like streaming video, VR/AR, and large language models are essential services provided by current and future networks. Therefore, how to maximize network transmission capacity under limited communication resources is a current research hotspot within the realm of satellite communication and a key to the practical application of satellite networks.

Traditional methods often improve network capacity by optimizing the allocation of communication resources, such as the author in [1] craft a gain function for multi-service characterization and devise a multi-beam resource allocation scheme to boost satellite network capacity. Although these studies have achieved some capacity optimization by investigating resource allocation issues, they lack consideration of the dynamic characteristics of satellite networks. In actual transmission scenarios, due to the continuous changes in environment and tasks, resource optimization strategies also need to be updated in real-time. However, most of the optimization algorithms used in these studies take too long to compute and occupy significant memory in larger constellations, making it difficult to maintain high real-time performance. Therefore, improving the characteristics of the network itself is a more practical research direction.

Network coding is an effective tool for enhancing network performance in multicast scenarios, with numerous studies demonstrating its ability to improve network capacity. In [2], author proposes a co-oprative multicast scheme for content delivery in the integrated terrestrial-satellite networks which is further enhanced by network coding, and the experimental data show that network throughput was enhanced. The random linear network coding (RLNC) was used to improve the sceurity and performance of data transmission in [3]. According to current research, the network topology has a significant impact on the effectiveness of network coding in improving network capacity, such as the authors in [4] analyz the eddect of network topology on RLNC system and found that it may be having advantage in reducing the failure probability. Because of this, in the study [5], the authors utilized a topology construction technique rooted in the Lagrangian relaxation approach to optimize secure multicasting. This approach to topology construction serves as an effective means of enhancing the performance of network coding systems. However, the inherently dynamic nature of satellite systems necessitates a continuously evolving network topology over time. Adding the time dimension to the network model makes it difficult to represent and optimize. By using a time-expanded graph to describe the storage, communication, and other behaviors between satellites As demonstrated in [6,7], the time-varying network model is simplified into a directed graph.

Drawing from the preceding analysis, this paper represents the dynamic changes and network connections between satellites using a time-expanded graph and employs an improved genetic algorithm for topology optimization and flow allocation in satellite networks. This approach aims to enhance the multicast performance of satellite networks under the network coding mechanism by transmitting content from several source satellites to various multiple destination satellites, thereby improving network capacity from the fundamental network topology perspective. Simulation results show that when using the topology-optimized network coding scheme, network capacity is significantly increased.

2 System Model and Problem Formulation

2.1 System Model

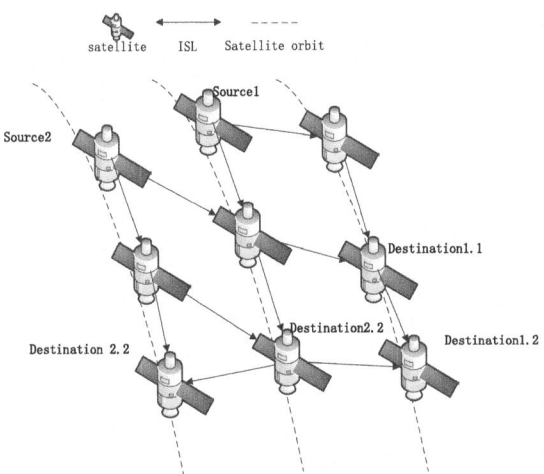

Fig. 1. Multicast satellite network model, Source1 transmits data to Destination1.1 and Destination1.2, Source2 transmits data to Destination2.1 and Destination2.2.

This paper considers a wireless multicast satellites network model depicted in Fig 1. It is composed of multiple communications satellites, every satellites can build several wireless inter satellite links (ISL) with other satellites and thus become a network node. Every node is fully equipped with communication and computation functions and can be a source, relay or destination node as required. During a multicast transmission with network coding, several source satellites are first encode and transmit the information to the relay satellite which is connected by the builded link, the relay satellites are tasked with eoncoding once more and relaying these packets, the destination satellites that want to acquire data from one of the source satellite collect the packets from the relay satellites and decode them to get the orginal information.

Consider the dynamic characterization of the satellites, the period motion of the satellites will cause the periodic and predictable performance changes of

ISLs, even wheteher it exists or not over time. For ease of analysis, we consider the network over a short period as a static. Therefore, we divided the total transmission timeframe T into N time slots, each time slot lasts for $\tau = T/N$. When τ is small enough that the change of the character of ISLs can be ignored. Thus, The satellite network's topology can be structured as a time expanded graph $G = (V, E)$ representation. Where $V = \{v_i^{(t)} | v_i^{(t)} \in ST, t \in N\}$ is a set representing vertices, $v_i^{(t)}$ represents i-th satellite nodes in the time slot t and $ST = S \cup R \cup D$ where S is a collection comprising source satellite nodes, R is composed of relay satellite nodes, and D is composed of destination satellite nodes. E is composed of edges that contain the communication edges between two satellites in one slot and the storage edges between two slots in one satellite. The capacity of communication edges is defined as the data transfer rate achievable through the ISL connecting two satellites. The representation of edge $e(v_i^{(t)}, v_j^{(t)})$'s capacity is as follows:

$$C_{i,j}^{(t)} = \tau B \log(1 + \frac{p_{i,j}^{(t)} G_{i,j}^{(t)}}{n}) \tag{1}$$

B signifies the bandwidth of the ISL, $p_{i,j}^{(t)}$ indicates the transmission power utilized by i-th satellite, $n_{i,j}^{(t)}$ represents the average noise power and $G_{i,j}^{(t)}$ is the gain of ISL between i-th satellite and j-th satellite, that can be calculated as

$$G_{i,j}^{(t)} = \frac{\lambda^2 G^{tr} G^{re}}{\left(4\pi d_{i,j}^{(t)}\right)^2} \tag{2}$$

$$n = \kappa B \Gamma \tag{3}$$

Where κ and Γ represent the Boltzmann constant and noise temperature, respectively. λ represents the wavelength used for ISLs, the transmit gain and receive gain during communication can be represented by G^{tr} and G^{re}, respectively. $d_{i,j}^{(t)}$ represents the straight-line distance between i-th satellite and j-th satellite.

For the storage edge which is presented as $e(v_i^{(t)}, v_i^{(t+1)})$, it's capacity is the storage capacity STO_i of the i-th satellite.

2.2   Problem Formulation

After establishing the graph G that represents the time-varying topology of the satellite network, we can convert the programming issue of multicasting data from several source satellite nodes to their respective multiple destination satellite node into a problem of allocationg flows in the time expanded graph G between the vertex set S and D that represent source satellite nodes and destination satellite nodes respectively. In order to introduce the network topology into G, we define a binary set $\mathbf{A} = \{a(v_i^{(t)}, v_j^{(t)}) = \begin{cases} 1, if \; establish \; e(v_i^{(t)}, v_j^{(t)}) \\ 0, otherwise \end{cases} \}$ to describe whether the ISL $e(v_i^{(t)}, v_j^{(t)})$ will be established. Taking into account the finite number of antennas available on each satellite node, we have the constraint as

$$\sum_{v_j^{(t)} \in ST} a(v_i^{(t)}, v_j^{(t)}) \leq A_{out} \tag{4}$$

$$\sum_{v_j^{(t)} \in ST} a(v_j^{(t)}, v_i^{(t)}) \leq A_{in} \tag{5}$$

Unlike traditional transimission modes, due to the information packets has been encoded by source satellite and relay satellites, the information packets has been compressed and harmonized. Thus the common flow balance constraint, which stipulates that in each relay satellites, inflow and outflow must be equal, does not hold true in the context of our problem. But we can still figure that the inflow and outflow of data destined for the same destination satellite node remain equal at each relay satellites. To represent the information flow that has been transmitted from source satellite $\tilde{s}$, through relay satellites $v_i^{(t)}$ nad $v_j^{(t)}$ and finally collected by destination satellite $\tilde{d} \in D_s$, the $D_s \in D$ is the set of destination satellites receiving data from $\tilde{s}$, we define $x(v_i^{(t)}, v_j^{(t)}, \tilde{s}, \tilde{d})$. Now we can express the flow balance constraint of each relay satellite as

$$\sum_{v_j^{(t)} \in ST} x(v_i^{(t)}, v_j^{(t)}, \tilde{s}, \tilde{d}) + x(v_i^{(t)}, v_i^{(t+1)}, \tilde{s}, \tilde{d})$$
$$= \sum_{v_j^{(t)} \in ST} x(v_j^{(t)}, v_i^{(t)}, \tilde{s}, \tilde{d}) + x(v_i^{(t-1)}, v_i^{(t)}, \tilde{s}, \tilde{d}), v_i^{(t)} \notin S, t \in \mathcal{N} \tag{6}$$

In addition, all information is sent by the source satellite and collected by destination in a given time, thus we have another flow constraint as follow:

$$\sum_{v_j^{(t)} \in ST} x(v_i^{(t)}, v_j^{(t)}, \tilde{s}, \tilde{d}) = R_{\tilde{s},\tilde{d}}, v_i^{(t)} = \tilde{s}, t = 1 \tag{7}$$

$$\sum_{v_j^{(t)} \in \mathcal{D}} x(v_j^{(t)}, v_i, \tilde{s}, \tilde{d}) = R_{\tilde{s},\tilde{d}}, v_i = \tilde{d} \tag{8}$$

Based on the characteristics of linear network coding [8], during the transmission over ISL $e(v_i^{(t)}, v_j^{(t)})$, The total quantity of data transmitted precisely matches the maximum allowable flow volume over this ISL to all disparate destination satellites, remaining within the ISL's capacity limits. Thus, we have

$$\sum_{\tilde{s} \in S} \max_{\tilde{d} \in \mathcal{D}_s} x(v_i^{(t)}, v_j^{(t)}, \tilde{s}, \tilde{d}) \leq a(v_i^{(t)}, v_j^{(t)}) C_{i,j}^{(t)} \tag{9}$$

Likewise, for an edge $e(v_i^{(t)}, v_i^{(t+1)})$ which representing the data has been stored by satellite i instead of being transmitted, the total quantity is less than the maximum cache capacity carried by this satellite. Thus, we have

$$\sum_{\tilde{s} \in S} \max_{\tilde{d} \in \mathcal{D}_s} x(v_i^{(t)}, v_j^{(t)}, \tilde{s}, \tilde{d}) \leq STO_i \tag{10}$$

After find the constraints, we can build the optimization problem for our model. The optimization problem is optimizing the plan of establishment ISLs $\mathbf{A} = \{a(v_i^{(t)}, v_j^{(t)})\}$, the flow ditribution $\mathbf{X} = \{x(v_i^{(t)}, v_j^{(t)})\}$ and the data requirements $\mathbf{R} = \{R_{\tilde{d}}\}$ to maximize the coding capacity $\sum_{\tilde{s} \in \mathcal{S}} \min_{\tilde{d} \in \tilde{D}} R_{\tilde{s}, \tilde{d}}$which is in accordance with the linear network coding theory. Overall, we have the optimization problem as

$$\max_{\mathbf{A}, \mathbf{X}, \mathbf{R}} \sum_{\tilde{s} \in \mathcal{S}} \min_{\tilde{d} \in \mathcal{D}_s} R_{\tilde{d}}$$

$$s.t.(4) - (10) \tag{11}$$

$$a(v_i^{(t)}, v_j^{(t)}) \in \{0, 1\}$$

This problem is a integer linear programming, which is obviously a NP-hard problem, therefore, this optimization problem is difficult to effectively solve through traditional methods. So, we design an efficient algorithm to obtain sub optimal solutions. We will divide this problem into two sub-problems, namely a topology construction problem and a maximum flow problem. The second sub problem is easy to be solved, therefore we need to find a method to construct a efficient topology $\mathbf{A}$.

3   GA-Based ISLs Construction Method

In this section, we design a Genetic Algorithm (GA) based ISLs construction method that is a search algorithm inspired by the theory of natural evolution, which searches for high-quality solutions by simulating the processes of biological evolution in nature.

Individuals with different chromosomes are randomly generated to form the initial population. By evaluating the transmission performance of the network topology represented by each individual as its fitness function, we determine which individuals can reproduce. The chromosomes of these individuals are crossed to simulate sexual reproduction in nature, thus searching for other better solutions under the premise of retaining the partial advantages of the current network topology. At the same time, the population is randomly updated periodically to simulate genetic mutations, encouraging the search in unknown regions of the solution space and preventing the algorithm from falling into local optimal solutions. The above process is repeated iteratively, and after the population characteristics tend to be stable or the algorithm has completed M iterations, reaching its predefined maximum, the individual with the highest fitness is selected, and the set $\mathbf{A}$ of ISL establishment it represents is the solution obtained by this algorithm. Specifically, A GA encompasses the subsequent stages:

1) Generating the initial cohort of candidates. The initial population is a randomly selected set of individuals that represent acceptable proposals for selection. Every individuals have different chromosomes which are randomly generated. We need to build a complete topology to get the optimization variable $\mathbf{A}$.

If and only if both satellites are visible to one another, we build the ISL and add the ISL as a element into set $\mathbf{A}$, and encode $\mathbf{A}$ into chromosomes g_i as shown in Fig. 2. If we have P individuals, we have the population $\mathbf{G} = \{g_i | i \in P\}$.

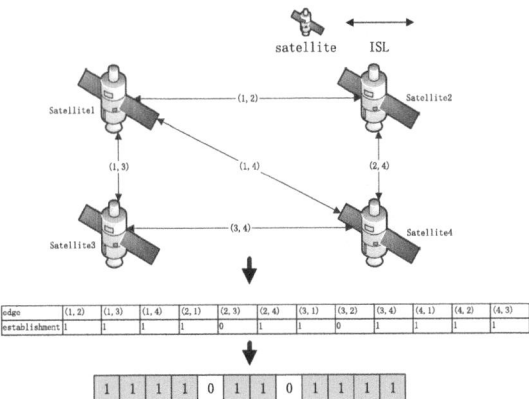

Fig. 2. Traverse a network topology into a set $\mathbf{A}$ and then into a chromosomeg_i^j.

2) Calculating fitness. Each individual's suitability is assessed using the fitness function, initially for the entire starting population, and afterwards for every newly generated population following the application of genetic operators like selection, genetic recombination, and mutation. Given the independence of individual fitness assessments, the calculations can be efficiently executed in parallel, enhancing the overall performance of the process. With the aim of finding a solution to our problem, we use the optimization problem as the fitness function to obtain the maximum multicast capacity with network coding that can be achieved by the network topology represented by each individual chromosome, and to jude the value of an individual. Due to the variable $\mathbf{A}$ has benn given by chromosomes, the fitness function can be calculated as follow.

$$f(g_i) = \max_{\mathbf{X},\mathbf{R}} \sum_{\tilde{s}\in\mathcal{S}} \min_{\tilde{d}\in\mathcal{D}_{\tilde{s}}} R_{\tilde{d}}$$

$$s.t.(6) - (10) \tag{12}$$

$$a(v_i^{(t)}, v_j^{(t)}) \in \{0,1\}$$

This problem is difficult to solve directly, so we design a multi-source and multi-objective flow allocation method. The main idea of the method is first determine how to allocate information flows in order to maximize throughput, by solving the maximum flow problem, for each source node separately, and accumulate the solved flows to find the edges that overflow. A subgraph is created based on the maximum flows of different source nodes, and the capacity of the

---

Algorithm 1. Multi-source Flow Allocation Methods

Input: The set of source nodes $\mathcal{S}$, the set of destination nodes $\mathcal{D}$, the GVE G
Output: flow allocation result **x** and the sum of network coding capacity values
1: **for** $\tilde{s}$ in S **do**
2:     **for** $\tilde{d}$ in D **do**
3:         Solving the Maximum Flow Problem between $\tilde{s}$ and $\tilde{d}$
4:         Add the flow of $\tilde{s}$ and $\tilde{d}$ to the subgraph $G_{\tilde{s}}$ according to the formula (9)
5:     **end for**
6:     Accumulate the flow of subgraph$G_{\tilde{s}}$ on graph G
7: **end for**
8: **for** Iterate over the set of edges E of the graph G **do**
9:     **if** Constraint (9) Constraint (10) is not satisfied **then**
10:         Subtract the capacity of the corresponding edge in the subgraphs, Sub-
     tracted capacity value $C_{\tilde{s}} = \frac{C_{\tilde{s}}}{\sum\limits_{\tilde{s} \in S} C_{\tilde{s}}} C_{overflow}$
11:     **end if**
12: **end for**
13: **for** $\tilde{s}$ in S **do**
14:     **for** $\tilde{d}$ in D **do**
15:         Solving the Maximum Flow Problem between $\tilde{s}$ and $\tilde{d}$
16:         Add the solution to the result **x** and $R_{\tilde{d}}$
17:     **end for**
18: **end for**
19: **return x**, $\sum\limits_{\tilde{s} \in \mathcal{S}} \min\limits_{\tilde{d} \in \mathcal{D}_s} R_{\tilde{d}}$

---

corresponding edges in the subgraph is reduced according to the exceeded capacity. Finally, solve the maximum flow problem separately on the new subgraphs. The entire procedure can be encapsulated in Algorithm 1.

3) Selection, genetic recombination and mutation. Employing the evolutionary principles of selection, recombination, and mutation on a population leads to the emergence of a subsequent generation, optimized through the inheritance of favorable traits from the preceding generation's most fit individuals. Selection is aimming to choose the individuals that have advantages in current population. The probability that i-th individual's chromosome is selected for reproduction is proportional to its fitness $f(g_i)$. The set p_i is the probability that the i-th individual's chromosome is selected, we have:

$$p_i = \frac{f(g_i)}{\sum_{j=1}^{P} f(g_j)} \tag{13}$$

Genetic recombination progeny by blending the genetic information of chosen individuals, a process that is accomplished by two chosen individuals interchanging segments of their chromatids results in the formation of two distinct chromosomes, each serving as the genetic blueprint for a new individual. If the intersection is k and the chromosomes from parents are g_i and g_j, offspring g_new can be experessed as:

$$g_{new} = (g_{i1}, g_{i2}, ..., g_{ik}, g_{j(k+1)}, ..., g_{jn}) \tag{14}$$

To make it easier to understand, this process has been shown in Fig. 3.

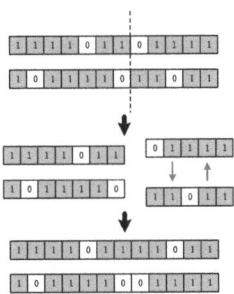

Fig. 3. Procedure for genetic recombination operations.

During the generation of new individuals, a mutation process is applied with a minute chance of randomly altering one or several genetic within their chromosomes. This mutation mechanism operates infrequently. We used the uniform mutation that replace the original chromosome at each locus in an individual with random numbers conforming to a uniform distribution within a certain range, respectively, with some smaller probability. The above process can be expressed as:

$$g'_{nk} = g_{nk} + \delta, \quad \text{with probability} \mu \tag{15}$$

Now we summarized the whole algorithm as Algorithm 2.

Algorithm 2. Genetic ISLs Construction Algorithm

Input: The satellites' visually represented and the ISL capacity
Output: The ISLs construction **A**
1: intialize the initial population
2: $k=0$
3: **while** max $f(g_i)$ tends to be stable or $k < M$ **do**
4:     **for** $i = 1$ to P **do**
5:         evalute fitness of $f(g_i)$ by Equation 12
6:     **end for**
7:     **for** $i = 1$ to P **do**
8:         Select operation of g_i by Equation 13
9:     **end for**
10:    **for** $i = 1$ to P **do**
11:        Crossover operation of g_i by Equation 14
12:    **end for**
13:    **for** $i = 1$ to P **do**
14:        Mutation operation of g_i by Equation 15
15:    **end for**
16:    $k = k + 1$
17: **end while**
18: Converting arg max $f(g_i)$ into **A**
19: **return A**

---

4   Analysis and Interpretation of Simulation Outcomes

With the objective of assessing the efficacy of our ISLs construction algorithm, we have implemented a Walker-Delta satellite constellation with 3 robits of 20 LEO satellite each. We choose source satellites and destination satellites randomly from all satellites, and repeated the process for 50 rounds to obtain the average results. We will then evaluate the performance in terms of multi-source coding capacity, i.e., the sum of coding capacity from different sources. The parameters of the simulate environment are show in the Table 1.

Table 1. The parameters of the simulate environment.

Parameters	Value
Maximum number of iterations M	200
population size P	100
Channel bandwith B	20 MHZ
Wavelength λ	0.125 m
Length of a time slot ΔT	30 s
The temperature of noise Γ	354.81 K
Transimission antenna gain G^{tr}	10 dB
Receiving antenna gain G^{re}	10 dB
The upper limit of transmission antenna count A_{out}	2
The lower limit of receiving antenna count A_{out}	2
Orbital height of the satellite	1300 km
The orbital tilt of the satellite	60 deg

First, we choose two source satellites and two destination satellites for each source satellites randomly, set the transmission power to 80 W, and the storage capacity of satellite to 2000 Mbits and perform 200 iterations. The data in training is obtained as in Fig. 4.

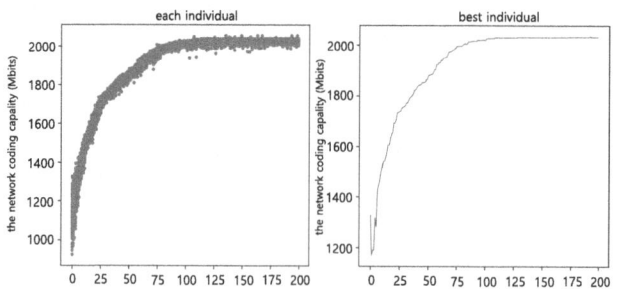

Fig. 4. Multi-source Network coding capacity versus iterations.

It is observable that the capacity rises gradually with the number of iterations and levels off after 125 generations and finally settles at 2032.437 Mbits at 150 generations. We can consider the population after 125 generations as a solution to the problem and apply it to the subsequent simulations. We can consider the population after 125 generations as a solution to the problem and apply it to the subsequent simulations.

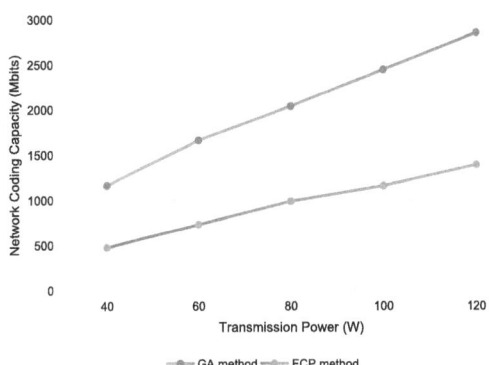

Fig. 5. Multi-source Network coding capacity versus transmission power

Figure 5 demonstrate a direct link between network coding capacity and the transmission power. Obviously, as the increasing transmission power increase the capacity of all ISLs, the network coding capacity also be increased. Compared with the baseline method, our method has obvious advantage.

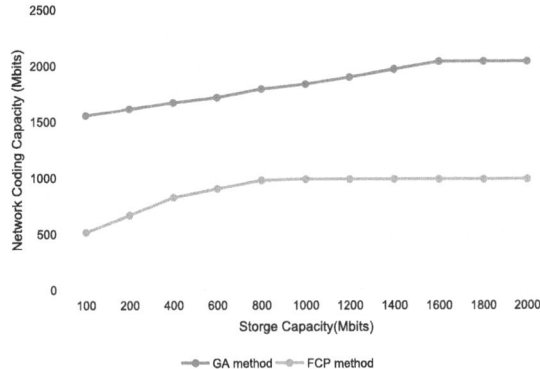

Fig. 6. Multi-source Network coding capacity versus storage capacity

As shown in Fig. 6, Obviously the storage capacity has a notable influence on network throughput when it is low. The reason of this is that not sufficient storage capacity forces some data packets that can't wait for more suitable time slots for transmission by be cached in relay satellites. In addition, as the storage capacity reaches a certain level, the network coding capacity becomes almost independent of the storage capacity, which can be interpreted that the ISLs' throughput became the weak link in improving the performance.

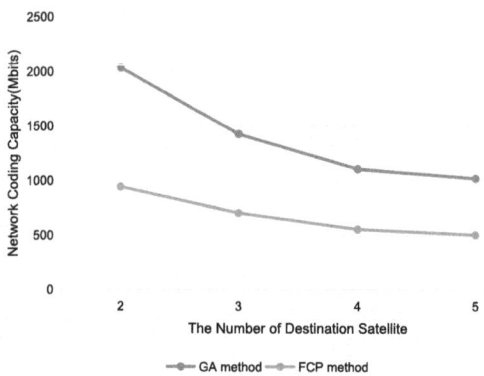

Fig. 7. Multi-source Network coding capacity versus destination number

As depicted in Fig. 7, When the quantity of destination nodes increases, the capacity decreases. We argue that this is because, according to coding theory, algorithms will tend to construct topologies that equalize the traffic of different destination satellites, resulting in a non-optimal traffic for each destination satellite.

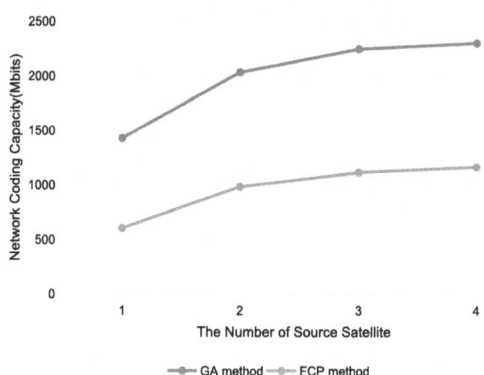

Fig. 8. Multi-source Network coding capacity versus source number

As depicted in Fig. 8, the number of source satellites increases, the total coding capacity of the multisource network rises, but at a significantly lower rate.

it is because that as the quantity of source satellites increases, the quantity of ISLs being used by multiple source satellites also increases. While the capacity of these ISLs remains constant, it can only reduce the traffic of each source satellite, so the rate of rise of the total coding capacity decreases.

Based on the above multiple comparisons, it can be seen that in almost any scenario, our method is significantly better compared to the baseline method.

5 Conclusions

This article explores how to enhance the throughput performance of satellite networks through network topology construction and network coding techniques. By leveraging the encoding process, we effectively compress multiple data streams transmitted via satellites, effectively enhances the utilization efficiency of on-satellite resources during the communication process. Additionally, we present a GA-based approach for network topology design and flow allocation, aimed at enhancing the efficacy of network coding. Our simulation results underscore the substantial augmentation in network capacity achieved through the optimization of topology construction..

References

1. Li, Y., Wang, S., Zhou, W.: A novel dynamic resource optimization method in LEO-MSS downlink with multi-service based on handover forecasting. In: 5th International Conference on Computer and Communications, pp. 809–814. IEEE, Chengdu (2019)
2. Wang, X., Li, H., Tong, M., Pan, K., Wu, Q.: Network coded cooperative multicast in integrated terrestrial-satellite networks. In: Symposium on Computers and Communications, pp. 1–6. IEEE, Barcelona(2019)
3. Wu, R., Ma, J., Tang, Z., Li, X., Choo, K.K.R.: A generic secure transmission scheme based on random linear network coding. IEEE-ACM Trans. Netw. **30**(2), 855–866 (2021)
4. Li, D., Guang, X., Zhou, Z., Li, C., Tan, C.: Hierarchical performance analysis on random linear network coding. IEEE Trans. Commun. **66**(5), 2009–2021 (2018)
5. Zhao, R., Wang, J., Lu, K., Chang, X., Jia, J., Zhang, S.: Optimal transimission topology construction and secure linear network coding design for virtualsource multicast with integral link rates. IEEE Trans. Multimedia **20**(11), 3069–3083 (2018)
6. Zhou, D., Sheng, M., Wang, X., Xu, C., Liu, R., Li, J.: Mission aware contact plan design in resource-limited small satellite networks. IEEE Trans. Commun. **65**(6), 2451–2466 (2017). 3083 (2018)
7. Zhou, D., Sheng, M., Liu, R., Wang, Y., Li, J.: Channel-aware mission scheduling in broadband data relay satellite networks. IEEE J. Sel. Areas Commun. **36**(5), 1052–1064 (2018)
8. Ahlswede, R., Ning, C., Li, S.Y.R.: Network information flow. IEEE Trans. Inf. Theory. **46**(4), 1204–1216 (2000)

Kolmogorov-Arnold Networks Based Signal Detection for OTFS Systems in LEO Satellite Communications

Yakai Zhang[1], Jiayi He[1], and Zhiyong Liu[1,2,3]($\boxtimes$)

[1] School of Information Science and Engineering of HIT, Weihai 264209, China
lzyhit@hit.edu.cn
[2] Shandong Provincial Key Laboratory of Marine Electronic Information
and Intelligent Unmanned Systems, Weihai 264209, China
[3] Key Laboratory of Cross-Domain Synergy and Comprehensive Support
for Unmanned Marine Systems of Ministry of Industry and Information Technology,
Weihai 264209, China

Abstract. In numerous studies, orthogonal time-frequency space (OTFS) has been utilized in satellite-terrestrial communication systems with high mobility due to its strong adaptability to Doppler shifts and delays. Signal detection, a crucial technology influencing OTFS performance, is often hindered by high complexity or suboptimal detection capabilities. To address this, we propose a Kolmogorov-Arnold Networks (KANs)-based OTFS signal detection method for low Earth orbit satellite (LEO-Sat) communication systems. KANs employ learnable activation functions instead of traditional learnable linear weights between network nodes, enabling dynamic activation functions to enhance model accuracy. We integrate KANs, trained offline, into the LEO-Sat system to recover distorted signals at the receiver, facilitating effective signal detection. Compared to conventional detection algorithms, the proposed method demonstrates superior Bit Error Rate (BER) performance. Additionally, KANs are more parameter-efficient than DNNs, using significantly fewer parameters.

Keywords: OTFS · Kolmogorov-Arnold networks(KANs) · satellite · signal detection

1 Introduction

Unlike traditional terrestrial communication systems, low Earth orbit satellite (LEO-Sat) communications provide extensive coverage unimpeded by terrain,

This research was partially funded by the National Natural Science Foundation of China under Grant 61871148; the Major Scientific and Technological Innovation Project of Shandong Province under Grants 2020CXGC010705, 2021ZLGX05, and 2022ZLGX04; and the Strategic Rocketry Innovation Fund Project under Grant ZH2022007.

© ICST Institute for Computer Sciences, Social Informatics and Telecommunications Engineering 2025
Published by Springer Nature Switzerland AG 2025. All Rights Reserved
H.-H. Chen and W. Meng (Eds.): WiSATS 2024, LNICST 605, pp. 138–149, 2025.
https://doi.org/10.1007/978-3-031-86196-3_12

ensuring reliable services in remote and underdeveloped regions. This capability makes it an essential element of the next-generation global communication network [1]. However, the LEO satellite-terrestrial communication environment differs significantly from terrestrial systems due to high Doppler shift characteristics that disrupt subcarrier orthogonality in conventional OFDM systems, resulting in considerable performance degradation [2]. Recently, the orthogonal time-frequency space (OTFS) 2D modulation technique has been introduced, converting time-varying channels into nearly time-invariant ones in the delay-Doppler (DD) domain. This conversion enables data symbols to be multiplexed in this stable DD domain [3,4], effectively combating Doppler frequency shift interference and greatly enhancing system performance. Studies in references [5–8] have shown that OTFS performs better than OFDM in satellite-terrestrial high dynamics scenarios.

Signal detection is a crucial technology influencing the performance of LEO-Sat communication systems utilizing OTFS. Traditional detection methods are typically divided into linear and nonlinear algorithms. Linear methods include the Minimum Mean Square Error (MMSE) algorithm [9] and the Zero Forcing (ZF) algorithm [10], both requiring matrix inversion and having high computational complexity. Nonlinear approaches involve the Markov Monte Carlo detection algorithm [11] and the message passing detection algorithm [12]. However, the former does not exploit the sparse nature of the channel in the delay-Doppler (DD) domain and also has high complexity. In contrast, the latter approximates the interference term as Gaussian noise, which does not accurately reflect the actual interference distribution in satellite-ground communication systems, leading to performance degradation.

In wireless communication systems, algorithms based on deep learning exhibit strong nonlinear representation capabilities, enabling effective detection in non-ideal assumption models [13]. Research [14–16] has utilized different neural networks, including DNN, CNN, and LSTM, for OTFS signal detection, resulting in better bit error rate (BER) performance than conventional approaches. Specifically, reference [14] proposed two DNN-based detection strategies: one utilizes a fully connected DNN to frame the detection task as a multi-class classification problem, while the other employs multiple DNNs, each responsible for detecting an individual symbol within the transmission vector. Reference [15] implemented the MP algorithm to preprocess the two-dimensional OTFS frame signal at the receiver, subsequently feeding it into a two-dimensional CNN for detection, resulting in a BER performance nearly identical to that of the MAP detector but with reduced complexity. Furthermore, reference [16] proposed a Bi-LSTM-based detection method for underwater OTFS signals, resulting in a lower symbol error rate (SER) compared to traditional algorithms. Despite these advancements, all the aforementioned neural networks rely on Multi-Layer Perceptron (MLP) architecture with fixed activation functions at the nodes and linear functions along the edges [17], which leads to low convergence speeds and increased model complexity.

A recent study [17] introduced Kolmogorov-Arnold Networks (KANs), an innovative neural network architecture aimed at replacing conventional MLPs. Unlike MLPs, which rely on the universal approximation theorem, KANs are grounded in the Kolmogorov-Arnold representation theorem [18,19] and utilize learnable activation functions instead of conventional linear weights between nodes. In KANs, fixed activation functions are replaced by additive operations, resulting in a faster neural scaling law, enhanced accuracy, and improved interpretability. Notably, KANs can achieve similar or better prediction results than MLPs while using a smaller network size. Reference [20] shows that KANs are effective for time series prediction, offering more precise results than traditional MLPs with fewer parameters. Nevertheless, to the best of the authors' knowledge, applying KANs for signal detection in OTFS systems within LEO satellite communications remains unexplored.

Given the benefits of OTFS and the exceptional capabilities of KANs, this paper proposes an OTFS signal detection algorithm for the LEO-Sat system, utilizing KANs to enhance the overall performance of satellite-terrestrial communication systems.

2   System Model

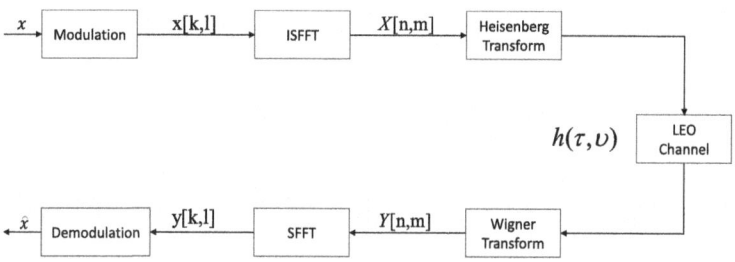

Fig. 1. OTFS based LEO-Sat communication system block diagram.

2.1   Basic Principle of OTFS

Figure 1 presents the block diagram of the LEO-Sat communication system utilizing OTFS. At the transmitter, binary bit information x is modulated into DD domain symbol $x[k, l]$, where $k = 0, 1, 2, ..., N - 2, N - 1; l = 0, 1, 2, ..., M - 2, M - 1$, These DD domain signals are organized into squares to create a frame of OTFS symbols. Each OTFS symbol undergoes an inverse symplectic finite Fourier transform (ISFFT) to yield the time-frequency(TF) domain symbol $X[n, m]$:

$$X[n, m] = \frac{1}{\sqrt{MN}} \sum_{k=0}^{N-1} \sum_{l=0}^{M-1} x[k, l] e^{j2\pi(\frac{nk}{N} - \frac{ml}{M})} \tag{1}$$

The time-frequency (TF) domain signals are mapped to the time domain transmitted signal $s(t)$ using the Heisenberg transform along with windowing techniques:

$$s(t) = \sum_{n=0}^{N-1} \sum_{m=0}^{M-1} X[n,m] g_{tx}(t-nT) e^{j2\pi m \Delta f(t-\Delta f)} \tag{2}$$

where g_{tx} represents the transmit pulse, T indicates the duration of the subframe, and $\Delta f = 1/T$ signifies the subcarrier interval.

The channel impulse response in the DD domain can be articulated as follows:

$$h(\tau, \upsilon) = \sum_{i=1}^{p} h_i \delta(\tau - \tau_i) \delta(\upsilon - \upsilon_i) \tag{3}$$

where h_i represents the channel gain of the ith path, while τ_i and υ_i denote the time delay and frequency offset of the ith path, respectively. The values of τ_i and υ_i can be determined by

$$\tau_i = \frac{l_i}{M\Delta f}, \nu_i = \frac{k_i + \kappa_i}{NT} \tag{4}$$

where k_i and κ_i represent the integer and fractional Doppler indices of the ith path, respectively.

The transmitted symbols arrive at the receiver after traversing the channel characterized by the above impulse response, and the received symbols can be expressed as follows:

$$r(t) = \int_{\nu} \int_{\tau} h(\tau, \nu) s(t-\tau) e^{j2\pi\nu(t-\tau)} d\tau d\nu + n(t) \tag{5}$$

where $n(t)$ represents the additive white Gaussian noise. Plugging Eq. (3) into Eq. (4):

$$r(t) = \sum_{i=1}^{p} h_i e^{j2\pi\nu_i(t-\tau_i)} s(t-\tau_i) + n(t) \tag{6}$$

By sampling at $t = nT$ and $f = m\Delta f$, the received symbols are transformed into the TF domain symbols using the Wenger transform:

$$Y[n,m] = \int g_{rx}^*(t-nT) r(t) e^{-j2\pi m \Delta f(t-nT)} dt \tag{7}$$

where g_{rx} denotes the receive pulse. The TF domain symbols $Y[n,m]$ are converted to the DD domain signal using the symplectic finite Fourier transform (SFFT):

$$y[k,l] = \frac{1}{\sqrt{MN}} \sum_{n=0}^{N-1} \sum_{m=0}^{M-1} Y[n,m] e^{-j2\pi(\frac{nk}{N} - \frac{ml}{M})} \tag{8}$$

Ultimately, the binary data information $\hat{x}$ is derived through equalization and demodulation of the DD domain symbols at the receiver.

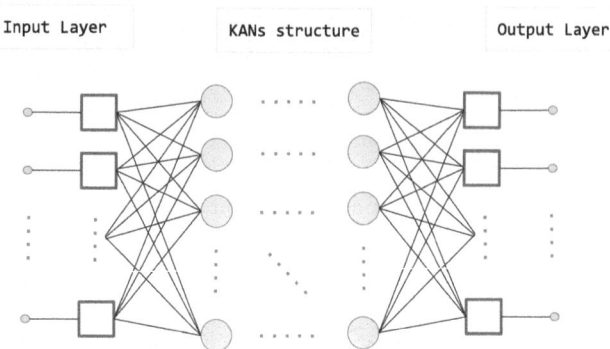

Fig. 2. Multiple-input multiple-output KAN network structure diagram.

2.2 Kolmogorov-Arnold Networks (KANs)

The Kolmogorov-Arnold representation theorem, independently developed by Andrey Kolmogorov and Vladimir Arnold, states that any multivariate continuous function u defined on a bounded domain can be represented as a finite composition of single-variable continuous functions combined with the operation of addition [18]. Specifically, for a smooth function $u : [0,1]^n \to \mathbb{R}$,

$$u(\mathbf{x}) = u(x_1, \cdots, x_n) = \sum_{p=1}^{2n+1} \Phi_p \left(\sum_{q=1}^{n} \phi_{p,q}(x_q) \right) \qquad (9)$$

where $\Phi_p : \mathbb{R} \to \mathbb{R}$ and $\phi_{p,q} : [0,1] \to \mathbb{R}$. Inspired by Kolmogorov-Arnold representation theorem, literature [17] proposed Kolmogorov-Arnold network architecture. The network structure is shown in Fig. 2, the width and depth of the network are arbitrary, and the nodes represent additive operations, while the connections between them utilize learnable activation functions. In reference [17], the learnable activation function is defined as a B-spline function, where the spline curve is a smooth, continuous curve defined by a series of control nodes. This is defined by the order k and the number of intervals G. The parameter k indicates the order of the polynomial function used to approximate the curve between control nodes, while G specifies the number of subintervals between adjacent control points. The lth KAN layer can be represented as the function matrix Φ_p composed by univariate functions $\phi_{p,q}(\cdot)$ with $p = 1, 2, 3, ..., N_{in}$ and $q = 1, 2, 3, ..., N_{out}$, where N_{in} and N_{out} denote the dimension of inputs and outputs, respectively, and $\phi_{p,q}(\cdot)$ are the trainable spline functions. The structure of a KAN is represented by an integer array $[n_0, n_1, n_2, n_3, ..., n_{L-1}, n_L]$. A general KAN network consists of L layers:

$$\mathbf{y} = u_{KAN}(\mathbf{x}) = (\mathbf{\Phi}_{L-1} \circ \cdots \circ \mathbf{\Phi}_0)\mathbf{x} \qquad (10)$$

It is essential to highlight that above operations are differentiable, enabling KANs to be trained through backpropagation.

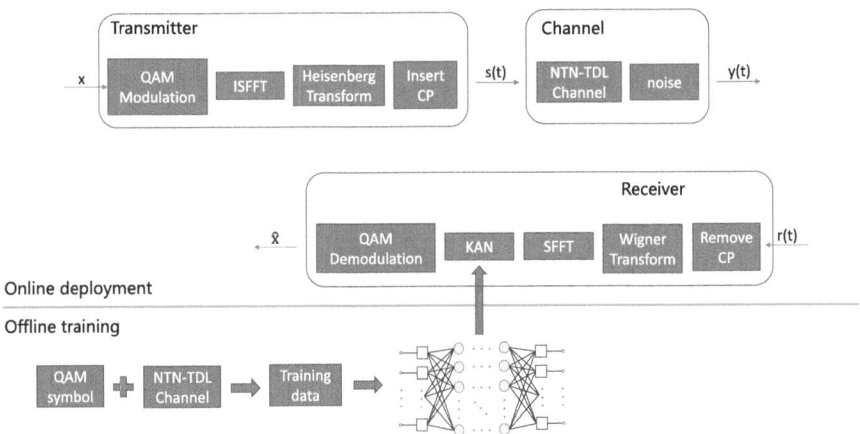

Fig. 3. KANs based OTFS signal detection in LEO-Sat system structure diagram.

3 KANs Based OTFS Signal Detection in LEO-Sat System

Figure 3 presents the system block diagram for the OTFS signal detection algorithm designed for the LEO-Sat system, which utilizes a KAN network. The transmitter operates similarly to a conventional OTFS system; however, a signal detection module based on the KAN network is integrated at the receiver to identify the distorted signal. The system model is organized into two stages. In the first stage, the OTFS samples generated by the model are used to train the KAN network. The second stage involves online deployment, where the trained KAN network is employed to recover the original transmitted data in the OTFS system, enabling effective signal detection.

During the model training phase, the transmitter generates pseudo-random input data and subsequently travels through the channel to reach the receiver, resulting in the received signal. The original transmitted data and the received signal y together constitute the training data set. The model is trained to minimize the discrepancies between the neural network's output and the transmitted data, represented by a loss function $L(loss)$:

$$L(loss) = \frac{1}{M} \sum_{j=0}^{M-1} (\hat{x}(j) - x(j))^2 \tag{11}$$

The system model is composed of MN data symbols within a frame, where both the real and imaginary parts of each symbol serve as input to the network. The output of the network consists of $2MN$ data, corresponding to the real and imaginary components of the MN symbols. Training and testing of the network are carried out using the PyTorch framework.

4   Numberical Results

4.1   System Setup

To assess the performance of the proposed OTFS signal detection algorithm for the LEO-Sat communication system utilizing KANs, this section computes the bit error rate (BER) through MATLAB simulations and contrasts it with traditional methods such as ZF, MMSE, and DNN. The channel model employs the NTN-TDL-D model as outlined in the 3GPP TR 38.811 protocol [21], with channel parameters presented in Table 1. This model features three taps: the first tap follows a Rician distribution with a K factor of 11.707 dB, while the remaining two taps adhere to a NLOS Rayleigh fading distribution.

Table 1. The power delay profile of the LEO-Sat communication channel.

Tap	delay	Power(dB)	Fading distribution
1	0	−0.284	Rician
	0	−11.991	Rayleigh
2	0.5596	−9.887	Rayleigh
3	7.3340	−16.771	Rayleigh

The parameters of the LEO-Sat system are presented in Table 2. In the LEO-Sat channel model, the Doppler shift for each tap is determined using the formula [22]:

$$f_d = (f_{\text{sat}} + f_c)\frac{V_t}{c}\cos\alpha\cos\phi, \quad f_{\text{sat}} = \frac{f_c \nu_{\text{sat}}}{c} \cdot \frac{R}{R+h}\cos\alpha \quad (12)$$

where c represents the speed of light, h is the altitude of the LEO satellite, α indicates the elevation angle of the LEO satellite, f_c is the carrier frequency, R denotes the Earth's radius, and ϕ is the angle between the direction of the user's equipment (UE) movement and the satellite's projected plane. Utilizing the parameters mentioned above, the model system generates 50,000 frames of training data, with the size ratio of the training set, validation set, and test set being 4:1:1. The structure of the KANs presented in this paper is [256, 256], which can be expressed as follows:

$$\mathbf{y} = \text{KAN}(\mathbf{x}) = \Phi\mathbf{x} \quad (13)$$

The DNN architecture consists of 4 layers, with the number of neurons in each layer being 256, 512, 512, and 256, respectively, and the activation function employed is LeakyReLU. The loss function utilized is MSELoss. All networks were trained for 500 epochs with the Adam optimizer, and the learning rate is 0.001.

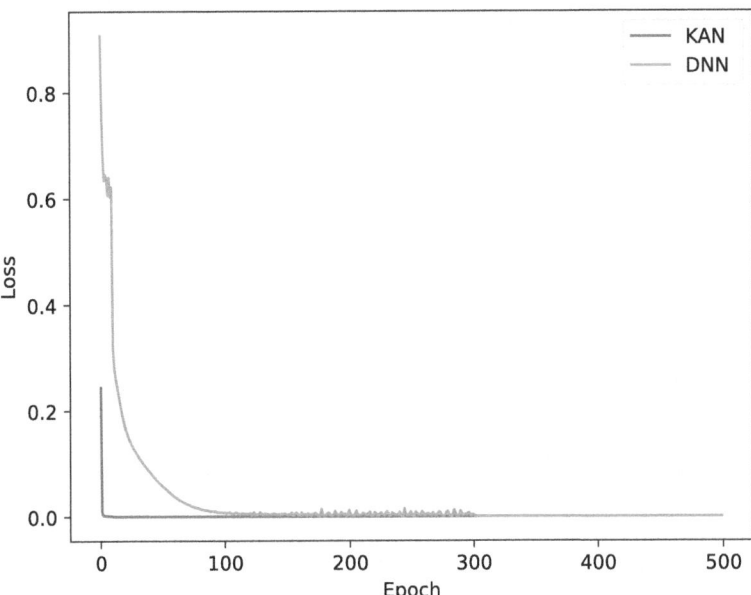

Fig. 4. Comparison of convergence speed of KAN and DNN loss functions on the validation dataset.

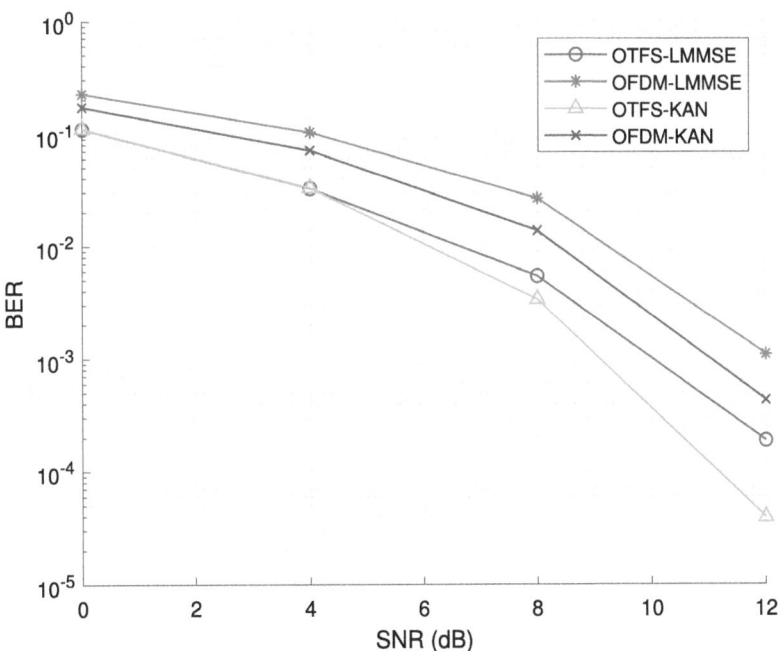

Fig. 5. 4-QAM BER performance comparison of the OTFS and OFDM in LEO-Sat system, $M = 16, N = 8, CP = 5$.

Table 2. Parameters for OTFS in LEO-Sat system.

Parameter	Value
Earth radius, R	6371 km
Satellite height, h	1500 km
Elevation angle, α	50°
User Moving Direction, ϕ	40°
Satellite speed, v_{sat}	7.11 km/s
UE speed, V_t	500 km/hr
Carrier frequency, f_c	20 GHz
Subcarrier frequency, Δf	60 kHz

4.2   Simulation Results

Figure 4 illustrates the trend of the loss function for both KAN and DNN as training epochs grows on the validation dataset. The blue curve indicates the loss function of the KAN, while the orange curve represents that of the DNN. The KAN network achieves convergence around 5 training epochs, whereas the DNN converges approximately at 100 epochs, demonstrating that the KAN converges more quickly than the DNN. This increased speed is attributed to the learnable activation function of the KAN, which allows for more efficient learning of the intrinsic data relationships compared to the DNN.

To validate the BER performance of the proposed algorithm, KAN, DNN, LMMSE, and ZF algorithms are employed for OTFS signal detection in LEO-Sat system.

Figure 5 illustrates the BER performance comparison of OTFS and OFDM with KAN and LMMSE. It shows that whether KAN or LMMSE, OTFS performance is better than OFDM, and KAN performance is better than LMMSE. Specifically, at BER $= 1 \times 10^{-3}$, the OTFS performance gain both are about 2 dB compared to OFDM with KAN and LMMSE. This is because that high speed satellite motion generates high Doppler shift, while OTFS transmits data in the DD domain and its resistance to Doppler interference is higher than OFDM.

Figure 6 presents the BER performance comparison of OTFS signal detection using different algorithms within the LEO-Sat communication system. The simulation results demonstrate that the proposed detection algorithm outperforms the others across all SNR levels. Specifically, both the KAN and DNN algorithms, which are based on deep learning, show improved performance compared to the traditional ZF and LMMSE algorithms as SNR increases, with the KAN algorithm achieving better BER performance than DNN. Notably, targeting the BER of 1.1×10^{-4}, the KAN achieves a gain of approximately 1 dB over DNN. This advantage arises because KAN employs nonlinear kernel functions to replace linear functions on the edges of the DNN, incorporating learnable activation functions between nodes and substituting fixed activation functions with simple addition operations. This adjustment enhances KAN's prediction

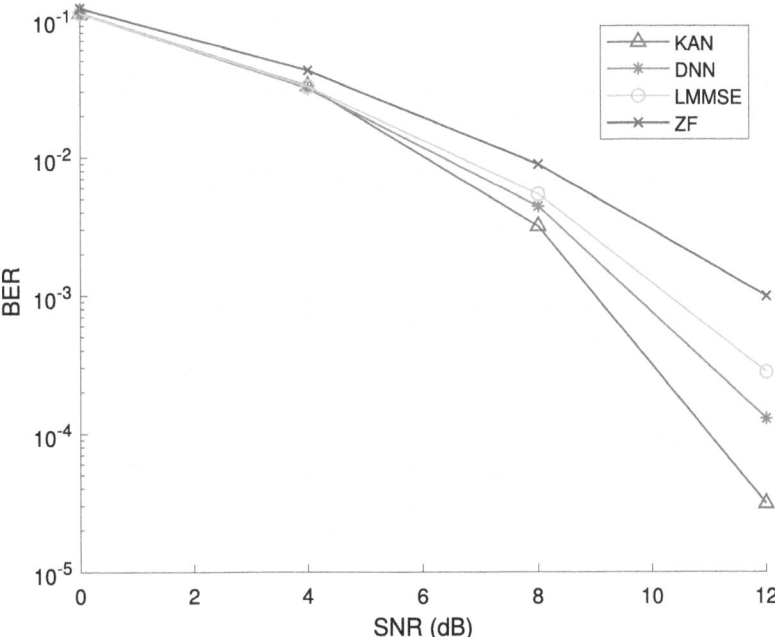

Fig. 6. 4-QAM BER comparison of the proposed KAN-based OTFS detector with LMMSE, ZF, DNN in LEO-Sat system, $M = 16, N = 8, CP = 5$.

accuracy. In contrast, due to their weaker nonlinear representation capabilities, the traditional LMMSE and ZF algorithms experience losses of 1 dB and 3 dB, respectively, compared to the KAN detector at the BER of 1×10^{-3}.

Additionally, the parameter count indicates a notable difference in the complexity of the algorithms, KAN has significantly fewer parameters than DNN, with about 328 k parameters compared with about 524 k parameters for DNN, KAN achieves more accurate results with fewer parameters, the KAN is significantly more parameter-efficient. Flexible and learnable activation functions allow KAN to achieve similar or higher prediction accuracy than DNN with fewer parameters. This makes KAN more suitable for deployment in satellite scenarios with limited computing and storage resources.

5 Conclusion

In this paper, an OTFS signal detection method for LEO-Sat system based on KAN network is proposed. Deploying the KAN completed with offline training online to the LEO-Sat communication system, the distorted signal at the receiver side can be effectively recovered and the system performance can be improved. Numerical results show that KAN has better BER performance than DNN, LMMSE and ZF. KAN achieve higher prediction accuracy with fewer parameters than DNN. The proposed method effectively solves the problems existing in other traditional OTFS system signal detection methods, such as low detection accuracy and slow convergence speed. In this paper, the feasibility of KANs in LEO satellite communication signal detection research is proved, which offers a novel approach for future research in OTFS-based signal detection for LEO-Sat systems.

References

1. You, L., Li, K.X., Wang, J., Gao, X., Xia, X.G., Ottersten, B.: Massive MIMO transmission for LEO satellite communications. IEEE J. Sel. Areas Commun. **38**(8), 1851–1865 (2020)
2. Su, Y., Liu, Y., Zhou, Y., Yuan, J., Cao, H., Shi, J.: Broadband LEO satellite communications: architectures and key technologies. IEEE Wirel. Commun. **26**(2), 55–61 (2019)
3. Hadani, R., Monk, A.: OTFS: a new generation of modulation addressing the challenges of 5G. arXiv preprint arXiv:1802.02623 (2018)
4. Hadani, R., et al.: Orthogonal time frequency space modulation. In: 2017 IEEE Wireless Communications and Networking Conference (WCNC), pp. 1–6. IEEE (2017)
5. Devarajalu, S.K., Jose, D.: Performance evaluation of OTFS under different channel conditions for LEO satellite downlink. In: 2023 10th International Conference on Wireless Networks and Mobile Communications (WINCOM), pp. 1–6. IEEE (2023)
6. Gunturu, A., Godala, A.R., Sahoo, A.K., Chavva, A.K.R.: Performance analysis of OTFS waveform for 5G NR MMWAVE communication system. In: 2021 IEEE Wireless Communications and Networking Conference (WCNC), pp. 1–6. IEEE (2021)
7. Liu, Y., Chen, M., Pan, C., Gong, T., Yuan, J., Wang, J.: OTFS vs OFDM: which is superior in multiuser leo satellite communications. arXiv preprint arXiv:2403.02012 (2024)
8. Shi, J., et al.: OTFS enabled LEO satellite communications: a promising solution to severe doppler effects. IEEE Netw. (2023)
9. Raviteja, P., Phan, K.T., Jin, Q., Hong, Y., Viterbo, E.: Low-complexity iterative detection for orthogonal time frequency space modulation. In: 2018 IEEE Wireless Communications and Networking Conference (WCNC), pp. 1–6 (2018). https://doi.org/10.1109/WCNC.2018.8377159
10. Raviteja, P., Viterbo, E., Hong, Y.: OTFS performance on static multipath channels. IEEE Wirel. Commun. Lett. **8**(3), 745–748 (2019)
11. Murali, K.R., Chockalingam, A.: On OTFS modulation for high-doppler fading channels. In: 2018 Information Theory and Applications Workshop (ITA), pp. 1–10. IEEE (2018)
12. Raviteja, P., Phan, K.T., Hong, Y., Viterbo, E.: Interference cancellation and iterative detection for orthogonal time frequency space modulation. IEEE Trans. Wireless Commun. **17**(10), 6501–6515 (2018)
13. Zhang, X., Zhang, S., Xiao, L., Li, S., Jiang, T.: Graph neural network assisted efficient signal detection for OTFS systems. IEEE Commun. Lett. (2023)
14. Naikoti, A., Chockalingam, A.: Low-complexity delay-doppler symbol DNN for OTFS signal detection. In: 2021 IEEE 93rd Vehicular Technology Conference (VTC2021-Spring), pp. 1–6. IEEE (2021)

15. Enku, Y.K., et al.: Two-dimensional convolutional neural network-based signal detection for OTFS systems. IEEE Wirel. Commun. Lett. **10**(11), 2514–2518 (2021)
16. Tang, Y., Li, Y., Wang, X., Li, D.: Bi-lstm-based signal detection method for underwater acoustic OTFS communication system. In: 2023 International Conference on Microwave and Millimeter Wave Technology (ICMMT), pp. 1–3. IEEE (2023)
17. Liu, Z., et al.: KAN: Kolmogorov-Arnold networks. arXiv preprint arXiv:2404.19756 (2024)
18. Kolmogorov, A.N.: On the representation of continuous functions of several variables by superpositions of continuous functions of a smaller number of variables. American Mathematical Society (1961)
19. Braun, J., Griebel, M.: On a constructive proof of kolmogorov's superposition theorem. Constr. Approx. **30**, 653–675 (2009)
20. Vaca-Rubio, C.J., Blanco, L., Pereira, R., Caus, M.: Kolmogorov-Arnold networks (KANS) for time series analysis. arXiv preprint arXiv:2405.08790 (2024)
21. 3GPP TR 38.811 V15.4.0. Study on new radio (NR) to support non-terrestrial networks
22. Bora, A.S., Phan, K.T., Hong, Y.: Spatially correlated MIMO-OTFS for LEO satellite communication systems. In: 2022 IEEE International Conference on Communications Workshops (ICC Workshops), pp. 723–728. IEEE (2022)

Joint Computation Offloading and Resource Allocation for Low-Earth Orbit Satellites MEC Networks

Meng Wang[1,2], Yaqiong Wang[1(✉)], Cheng Zhang[1,2], Hui Zhou[1],
and Longteng Yi[1,2]

[1] Institute of Telecommunication and Navigation Satellites, China Academy of Space
Technology, Beijing 100094, China
wangmeng_1996@hit.edu.cn, wangyaqiong83@163.com
[2] Innovation center for Satellite Communication Systems, Beijing 100094, China

Abstract. This study addresses the challenges of joint computation
offloading and resource allocation in low-earth orbit (LEO) satellite networks. To effectively manage the computational demands of LEO satellites, we propose a collaborative framework that allows each LEO satellite to offload tasks either to high-earth orbit (GEO) satellites or to
multi-access edge computing (MEC) servers on the ground. Our goal is
to jointly optimize the offloading ratio, computational frequency, transmission power, and bandwidth utilization of the LEO satellites, aiming
to minimize the overall energy consumption while adhering to latency
requirements. We formulate this challenge as a non-convex optimization
problem and introduce an energy-efficient layered optimization approach
to address it with reduced complexity. This involves breaking down the
original problem into several manageable subproblems, which are solved
sequentially to achieve a suboptimal solution. The simulation results confirm the effectiveness of our method, demonstrating its advantages over
existing benchmark algorithms.

Keywords: Computation offloading · Resource allocation · Low-orbit
Satellite network · Multi-access edge computing

1 Introduction

Multi-access Edge Computing (MEC) has emerged as an effective framework in
the architecture of next-generation networks, facilitating efficient, low-latency
data processing at the network's edge. By shifting computation-heavy tasks to
remote MEC servers equipped with adequate processing capabilities, MEC can
significantly lower the energy consumption of mobile users (MUs) [1]. Within
the MEC framework, two primary challenges arise: computation offloading and

This work is supported by the pre-research project on Civil Aerospace Technologies,
grant number D010203.

H.-H. Chen and W. Meng (Eds.): WiSATS 2024, LNICST 605, pp. 150–160, 2025.
https://doi.org/10.1007/978-3-031-86196-3_13

resource allocation. Computation offloading involves deciding where mobile users should execute their tasks, while resource allocation focuses on how these tasks are managed to ensure compliance with Quality of Service (QoS) standards [2].

In traditional Mobile Edge Computing (MEC) setups, users are mainly ground-based intelligent terminals, with MEC servers located in nearby base stations. However, the rapid advancement of satellite communication, particularly with low-Earth orbit (LEO) satellite constellations, has broadened MEC application scenarios. LEO satellites, especially remote sensing ones, handle computational tasks like image processing and large-scale routing. With the end-to-end transmission delay between LEO satellites and ground stations reduced to 4–30 ms, LEO satellites can act as users, while geostationary Earth orbit (GEO) satellites with ample computational resources serve as MEC servers. Integrating MEC with LEO satellite networks can enhance their performance, particularly for computationally intensive tasks. Nonetheless, joint computation offloading and resource allocation in LEO satellite MEC networks remain unresolved challenges.

Several previous studies have explored this topic [4–10]. Jing et al. [4] examined a single LEO-assisted MEC system, aiming to minimize the combined energy consumption of users and the LEO-MEC server by optimizing computation offloading decisions, utilizing a federated learning approach. Cao et al. [5] built on this work, focusing on maximizing the weighted sum computation rate through the optimization of radio and computational resources in both binary and partial offloading scenarios. However, neither study addressed task execution constraints. Dong et al. [6] took communication quality into account, investigating the joint optimization of offloading strategies and resource allocation in LEO-enabled MEC systems, with the goal of minimizing user delay in each time slot. In contrast, Zhang et al. [7] aimed to enhance the energy efficiency (EE) of LEOs, formulating a non-convex EE maximization problem under users' QoE requirements, and optimizing LEO positions, user transmit power, and computational load iteratively. Unlike the aforementioned studies that considered only a single LEO-MEC server, Minglei et al. [8] analyzed a multi-LEO framework, minimizing the overall power consumption of LEOs and users by jointly optimizing user associations, power control, computation capacity, and GEO positions. While the previous studies focused solely on LEOs as MEC servers, [9] and [10] introduced scenarios in which a BS-MEC server collaborates with LEO-MEC servers for data offloading. Specifically, Rodrigues et al. [9] explored a tethered LEO-assisted MEC system where tasks could be offloaded to both LEO-MEC and BS-MEC servers simultaneously, aiming to minimize the weighted-sum system delay of mobile users by optimizing LEO positions, time slot allocations, and task splitting ratios. Hao et al. [10] investigated a collaborative multi-LEO MEC system, minimizing the total execution latency for all users by jointly optimizing offloading decisions alongside communication and computing resources.

Unlike the previous studies, this paper introduces a novel MEC scenario where LEO satellites function as users, while GEO satellites and ground gateway stations serve as MEC servers. In this setup, LEOs operate with partial offloading, allowing them to either execute tasks locally or offload them to MEC servers. We jointly optimize the offloading ratio, transmit power, transmission bandwidth, and computational frequency to minimize energy consumption while meeting latency constraints. This leads to a non-convex optimization problem, which we address by decomposing it into several subproblems, solving each sequentially. Simulation results demonstrate that our approach significantly reduces energy consumption compared to benchmark algorithms.

2   System Model and Problem Formulation

We investigate a satellite-terrestrial cooperative MEC system comprising one BS-MEC server, M GEO-MEC server and N LEOs as depicted in Fig. 1. The set of LEOs is defined as $\mathcal{N} \triangleq \{1, \cdots, N\}$, while the MEC servers are defined as $\mathcal{M} \triangleq \{0, \cdots, M\}$, where the index '0' represents the BS-MEC server. To model dynamic characteristics, we consider a time-slotted system of T time slots, each of equal length ΔT, denoted as $\mathcal{T} \triangleq \{1, \cdots, T\}$. In this paper, we assume that LEOs hover at a fixed height H above the ground. To represent the positions of LEOs and GEO-MEC servers, we utilize a three-dimensional coordinate system. The BS-MEC server is positioned at $(X_0, Y_0, 0)$, while the coordinates of the j-th GEO-MEC server and the i-th LEO in the t-th time slot are denoted as $\mathbf{q}_j(t) = (X_j(t), Y_j(t), Z_j(t)), \forall j \in \mathcal{M}$ and $\mathbf{q}_i(t) = (x_i(t), y_i(t), z_i(t)), \forall i \in \mathcal{N}$, respectively. Following the approach in [10], we assume that the locations of LEOs and GEOs remain fixed within a time slot, but may vary between different time slots. In our model, the k-th task of the i-th LEO in the t-th time slot is characterized as $(S_{i,k}(t), C_{i,k}(t), T_{i,k}(t))$, where $S_{\min} \leq S_{i,k}(t) \leq S_{\max}, C_{\min} \leq C_{i,k}(t) \leq C_{\max}, T_{\min} \leq T_{i,k}(t) \leq T_{\max}$ denote the data size (bits), the number of CPU cycles required for executing a single bit and the maximum tolerable delay (ms) with respect to the k-th task of the i-th LEO, respectively. LEOs can partially offload tasks to the BS-MEC server and GEO-MEC servers via a wireless uplink channel in a partial offloading manner [4,6]. The offloading ratio of all LEOs in the t-th time slot are denoted as $\beta_{k,j,i}(t), k \in [1, A_i(t)], j \in \mathcal{M}, i \in \mathcal{N}$, where $0 \leq \beta_{k,j,i}(t) \leq 1$ indicates the k-th task's offloading ratio to the j-th MEC server in the t-th time slot.

To streamline the analysis, we focus on a single-input single-output (SISO) channel between the LEOs and the MEC servers. Additionally, we assume that different LEOs access the MEC servers using an orthogonal multiple access (OMA) scheme. The uplink channel capacity between the i-th LEO and the BS-MEC server in t-th time slot is given by

$$R_{i,g}(t) = \alpha_{0,i}(t) B_g \log \left(1 + \frac{|h_{i,g}(t)|^2 p_{i,0}(t)}{N_0 B_g \alpha_{0,i}(t)} \right), \tag{1}$$

where B_g is the total bandwidth allocated between LEOs and BS, N_0 is the white noise power spectrum density, $0 \leq \alpha_{j,i}(t) \leq 1, \forall j \in \mathcal{M}, \forall i \in \mathcal{N}$ is the ratio of the j-th MEC server's bandwidth allocated to the i-th LEO in the t-th time

GEO-MEC Servers

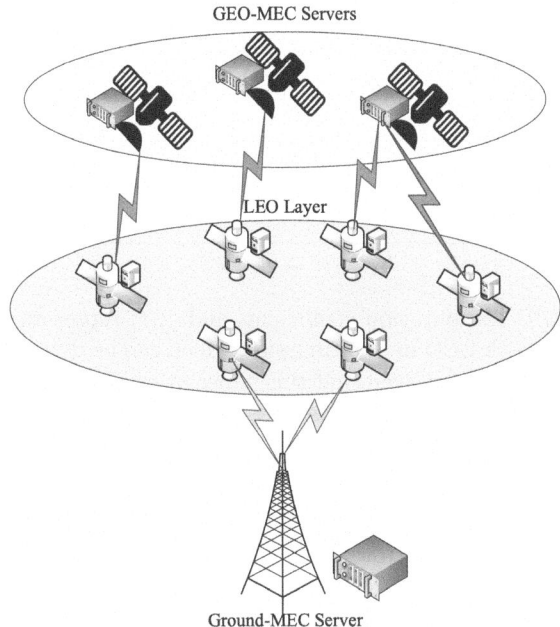

LEO Layer

Ground-MEC Server

Fig. 1. An illustration of the considered satellite-terrestrial collaborative Networks.

slot, $0 \leq p_{i,j}(t) \leq p_{\max}, \forall i \in \mathcal{N}, \forall j \in \mathcal{M}$ is the transmit power of the i-th LEO to the j-th MEC server. The channel gain between the i-th LEO and the BS-MEC server in the t-th time slot is denoted as $h_{i,g}(t)$. Thus, the uplink offloading time for the k-th task of the i-th LEO in the t-th time slot is expressed as

$$T_{k,0,i}(t) = \frac{\beta_{k,0,i}(t)S_{i,k}(t)}{R_{i,g}(t)}, \forall k \in [1, A_i(t)]. \tag{2}$$

The maximum total transmit energy consumption of the i-th LEO during the t-th time slot can be expressed as

$$E_i^r(t) = \Delta T \sum_{j=0}^{M} p_{i,j}(t). \tag{3}$$

The channel between i-th LEO and j-th GEO can be modeled as a free space loss channel. The uplink channel capacity between i-th LEO and j-th GEO can be expressed as

$$R_{i,j}(t) = \alpha_{j,i}(t)B_u \log\left(1 + \frac{|h_{i,j}(t)|^2 p_{i,j}(t)}{N_0 B_u \alpha_{j,i}(t)}\right), \forall j \in [1, M], \tag{4}$$

where B_u is the total bandwidth between each LEO and GEOs, $h_{i,j}(t)$ is the channel gain. Therefore, the uplink offloading time for k-th task of i-th LEO in

t-th time slot is given by

$$T_{k,j,i}(t) = \frac{\beta_{k,j,i}(t)S_{i,k}(t)}{R_{i,j}(t)}, \forall k \in [1, A_i(t)], \tag{5}$$

According to [11], during the t-th time slot, the computational energy consumed by the i-th LEO is expressed as

$$E_i^l(t) = \Delta T \epsilon f_i(t)^3, \tag{6}$$

where ϵ is the CPU computation coefficient, and $f_i(t)$ represents the computational frequency of i-th LEO in t-th time slot, which can be dynamically adjusted based on the task load [12]. Given that this paper primarily focuses on the energy consumption of LEOs, we do not consider the computational energy in MEC servers. The local computing time consumed by i-th LEO when executing k-th task is expressed as

$$T_{i,k}^l(t) = \frac{\left(1 - \sum\limits_{j=0}^{M} \beta_{k,j,i}(t)\right) S_{i,k}(t)C_{i,k}(t)}{f_i(t)} \tag{7}$$

We aim to minimize the total energy consumption of all LEOs while satisfying the latency constraints. Therefore, the optimization problem can be formulated as

$$(\textbf{P1}): \min_{\{\mathbf{X}(t)\}} \sum_{t=1}^{T} \sum_{i=1}^{N} \left\{E_i^l(t) + E_i^r(t)\right\}, \tag{8a}$$

$$\text{s.t. } 0 \le f_i(t) \le f_{\max}, \forall i \in \mathcal{N}, \forall t \in \mathcal{T} \tag{8b}$$

$$0 \le \beta_{k,j,i}(t) \le 1, \forall t \in \mathcal{T}, \forall i \in \mathcal{N}, \forall j \in \mathcal{M}, k \in [1, A_i(t)], \tag{8c}$$

$$\sum_{j=0}^{M} \beta_{k,j,i}(t) \le 1, t \in \mathcal{T}, \forall i \in \mathcal{N}, k \in [1, A_i(t)], \tag{8d}$$

$$0 \le p_{i,j}(t) \le p_{\max}, \forall t \in \mathcal{T}, \forall i \in \mathcal{N}, \forall j \in \mathcal{M}, \tag{8e}$$

$$0 \le \alpha_{j,i}(t) \le 1, \forall t \in \mathcal{T}, \forall i \in \mathcal{N}, \forall j \in \mathcal{M}, \tag{8f}$$

$$\sum_{i=1}^{N} \alpha_{j,i}(t) \le 1, \forall t \in \mathcal{T}, \forall i \in \mathcal{N}, \tag{8g}$$

$$\frac{\left(1 - \sum\limits_{j=0}^{M} \beta_{k,j,i}(t)\right) C_{i,k}(t)S_{i,k}(t)}{f_i(t)} \le T_{i,k}(t), \forall t \in \mathcal{T}, \forall i \in \mathcal{N}, k \in [1, A_i(t)], \tag{8h}$$

$$\frac{\beta_{k,0,i}(t)S_{i,k}(t)}{R_{i,g}(t)} + \sum_{j=1}^{M} \frac{\beta_{k,j,i}(t)S_{i,k}(t)}{R_{i,j}(t)} \le T_{i,k}(t), \forall t \in \mathcal{T}, \forall i \in \mathcal{N}, k \in [1, A_i(t)], \tag{8i}$$

We denote the system operation at the t-th time slot as $\mathbf{X}(t) \triangleq [\boldsymbol{f}(t), \boldsymbol{\beta}(t), \boldsymbol{P}(t), \boldsymbol{\alpha}(t)]$, where $\boldsymbol{f}(t) = \{f_i(t)|, \forall i \in \mathcal{N}\}$ denotes the computational frequency allocation factor, $\boldsymbol{\beta}(t) = \{\beta_{k,j,i}(t)|, \forall k \in [1, A_i(t)], \forall j \in \mathcal{M}, \forall i \in \mathcal{N}\}$ denotes the task offloading decision, $\boldsymbol{P}(t) = \{p_{i,j}(t)|, \forall i \in \mathcal{N}, \forall j \in \mathcal{M}\}$ denotes the transmit power allocation factor and $\boldsymbol{\alpha}(t) = \{\alpha_{j,i}(t)|, \forall j \in M, \forall i \in N\}$ denotes the bandwidth resource allocation factor. (8b) gives the range constraint on computational frequency for all LEOs. (8c) and (8d) give the constraints on offloading ratio. (8e) indicates that the transmit power of all LEOs cannot exceed the maximum transmit power. (8f) and (8g) give constraints on the radio resource allocation factor. (8h) and (8i) show that the total local computing and remote offloading time of each task should be less than the maximum tolerant delay.

Note that (**P1**) is a non-convex optimization problem which is highly challenging to solve directly. Thus, it is necessary to design an algorithm to solve (**P1**) efficiently.

3   Proposed Energy-Efficient Layered Optimization Method

In this section, we present the solution to problem (**P1**) using the block coordinate descent method. We decompose (**P1**) into two subproblems: the optimization of computation resources and task offloading, and the optimization of radio resources. For each subproblem, we derive the optimal solution.

3.1   Computation Resource and Task Offloading Optimization

By substracting terms related to $\boldsymbol{f}(t)$ and $\boldsymbol{\beta}(t)$ in (**P1**), the computation resource and task offloading optimization sub-problem is formulated as follows.

$$(\textbf{P2}): \min_{\boldsymbol{f}(t), \boldsymbol{\beta}(t)} \sum_{t=1}^{T} \sum_{i=1}^{N} \epsilon \left(f_i(t)^3 \right) \tag{9a}$$

$$\text{s.t. } 0 \leq f_i(t) \leq f_{\max}, \forall i \in \mathcal{N}, \forall t \in \mathcal{T} \tag{9b}$$

$$0 \leq \beta_{k,j,i}(t) \leq 1, \forall t \in \mathcal{T}, \forall i \in \mathcal{N}, \forall j \in \mathcal{M}, k \in [1, A_i(t)], \tag{9c}$$

$$\sum_{j=0}^{M} \beta_{k,j,i}(t) \leq 1, t \in \mathcal{T}, \forall i \in \mathcal{N}, k \in [1, A_i(t)], \tag{9d}$$

$$\frac{(1 - \sum_{j=0}^{M} \beta_{i,j,k}(t)) C_{i,k}(t) S_{i,k}(t)}{f_i(t)} \leq T_{i,k}(t), \forall i \in \mathcal{N}, \forall t \in \mathcal{T}, k \in [1, A_i(t)]. \tag{9e}$$

$$\frac{\beta_{k,0,i}(t) S_{i,k}(t)}{R_{i,g}(t)} + \sum_{j=1}^{M} \frac{\beta_{k,j,i}(t) S_{i,k}(t)}{R_{i,j}(t)} \leq T_{i,k}(t), \forall t \in \mathcal{T}, \forall i \in \mathcal{N}, k \in [1, A_i(t)], \tag{9f}$$

It is observed that (9a) is a convex function with respect to $\boldsymbol{f}(t)$ and (9b), (9c), (9d), (9f) are all convex constraints. In (9e), $\boldsymbol{f}(t), \boldsymbol{\beta}(t)$ are coupled, however, since $f_i(t) \geq 0$, (9e) can be transformed as $(1 - \sum_{j=0}^{M} \beta_{i,j,k}(t))C_{i,k}(t)S_{i,k}(t) - f_i(t)T_{i,k}(t) \leq 0, \forall i \in \mathcal{N}, \forall t \in \mathcal{T}, k \in [1, A_i(t)]$, which is a linear constraint with respect to $\boldsymbol{f}(t), \boldsymbol{\beta}(t)$. Therefore, by reformulating constraint (9e), (**P2**) can be regarded as a convex optimization problem, thus can be solved by CVX using interior points method.

3.2   Radio Resource Optimization

In this paper, radio resource optimization includes bandwidth and transmit power allocation. For fixed $\boldsymbol{f}(t)$ and $\boldsymbol{\beta}(t)$, the joint optimization of $\boldsymbol{\alpha}(t)$ and $\boldsymbol{P}(t)$ can be formulated as

$$(\textbf{P3}): \min_{P(t), \alpha(t)} \Delta T \sum_{i=1}^{N} \left(\sum_{j=0}^{M} p_{i,j}(t) \right) \tag{10a}$$

$$\text{s.t.} \, 0 \leq p_{i,j}(t) \leq p_{\max}, \forall t \in \mathcal{T}, \forall i \in \mathcal{N}, \forall j \in \mathcal{M}, \tag{10b}$$

$$0 \leq \alpha_{j,i}(t) \leq 1, \forall t \in \mathcal{T}, \forall i \in \mathcal{N}, \forall j \in \mathcal{M}, \tag{10c}$$

$$\sum_{i=1}^{N} \alpha_{j,i}(t) \leq 1, \forall t \in \mathcal{T}, \forall i \in \mathcal{N}, \tag{10d}$$

$$\frac{\beta_{k,0,i}(t)S_{i,k}(t)}{R_{i,g}(t)} + \sum_{j=1}^{M} \frac{\beta_{k,j,i}(t)S_{i,k}(t)}{R_{i,j}(t)} \leq T_{i,k}(t), \forall t \in \mathcal{T}, \forall i \in \mathcal{N}, k \in [1, A_i(t)], \tag{10e}$$

It is observed that (10a) is convex function with respect to $\boldsymbol{P}(t)$, and (10b), (10c), (10d) are convex constraints. Therefore, the main difficulty is to deal with (10e). To address this issue, we present the following lemma:

Lemma 1. $R_{i,g}(t)$ *and* $R_{i,j}(t)$ *are all jointly concave functions with respect to* $\boldsymbol{P}(t), \boldsymbol{\alpha}(t)$.

Proof. According to [13], we can use the property of perspective function to prove Lemma 1. Since $g(x,t) = tf(x/t)$, if f is a concave function, then $g(x,t)$ is a jointly concave function with respect to x, t. It is observed that $R_{i,g}(t)$ and $R_{i,j}(t)$ have the same mathematical property. Therefore, we only prove $R_{i,g}(t)$ for brevity. Specifically, by letting $x = p_{i,0}(t), t = \alpha_{0,i}(t), z = \dfrac{p_{i,0}(t)}{\alpha_{0,i}(t)}$, we have $f(z) = B_g \log \left(1 + \frac{z|h_{i,g}(t)|^2}{N_0 B_g} \right)$,. It is trivial to observe that $f(z)$ is a standard log function, and thus $f(z)$ is a concave function, according to the property of perspective function, $g(x,t)$ is a concave function, which indicates $R_{i,g}(t)$ is a concave function. Lemma 1 has been proved.

Algorithm 1. Block Coordinate Descent Method for (**P1**)

1: Observe ,$A_i(t)$, $h_{i,g}(t)$ and $h_{i,j}(t)$ in the current time slot.
2: Set $w = 0$ and the tolerance threshold ξ. Initialize task offloading matrix $\boldsymbol{f}^0(t), \boldsymbol{\beta}^0(t), \boldsymbol{\alpha}^0(t), \boldsymbol{P}^0(t)$.
3: **repeat**
4:   Find $\boldsymbol{f}^{w+1}(t), \boldsymbol{\beta}^{w+1}(t)$ by solving (**P2**) with given $\boldsymbol{\alpha}^w(t), \boldsymbol{P}^w(t)$.
5:   Obtain $\boldsymbol{\alpha}^{w+1}(t), \boldsymbol{P}^{w+1}(t)$ by solving (**P3**) with given $\boldsymbol{f}^{w+1}(t), \boldsymbol{\beta}^{w+1}(t)$.
6:   Denote the objective funtion of **P1** as $O_{P_1}(t)$. Compute $O_{P_1}^{w+1}(t)$ using $\boldsymbol{f}^{w+1}(t)$, $\boldsymbol{\beta}^{w+1}(t)$, $\boldsymbol{\alpha}^{w+1}(t)$, $\boldsymbol{P}^{w+1}(t)$.
7:   $w \leftarrow w + 1$.
8: **until** $\left| O_{P_2}^{w+1}(t) - O_{P_2}^{w+1}(t) \right| \leq \xi$
9: **Output:** $\boldsymbol{f}^\star(t), \boldsymbol{\beta}^\star(t), \boldsymbol{P}^\star(t), \boldsymbol{\alpha}^\star(t)$.

Since $R_{i,g}(t)$ and $R_{i,j}(t)$ are all concave functions, $\frac{\beta_{k,0,i}(t)S_{i,k}(t)}{R_{i,g}(t)}$ and $\frac{\beta_{k,j,i}(t)S_{i,k}(t)}{R_{i,j}(t)}$ are all convex functions, and thus (10e) is a convex constraint, (**P3**) is a convex optimization problem with respect to $\boldsymbol{P}(t), \boldsymbol{\alpha}(t)$. Therefore, (**P3**) can be optimally solved using interial points method. By solving the above two subproblems in a iterally manner, we can obtain a near-optimal solution, the detailed procedure is given in Algorithm 1.

4   Simulation Results

The main parameters are given in Table 1.

To show the effectiveness of the proposed method, we compare our method with the following four benchmark algorithms.

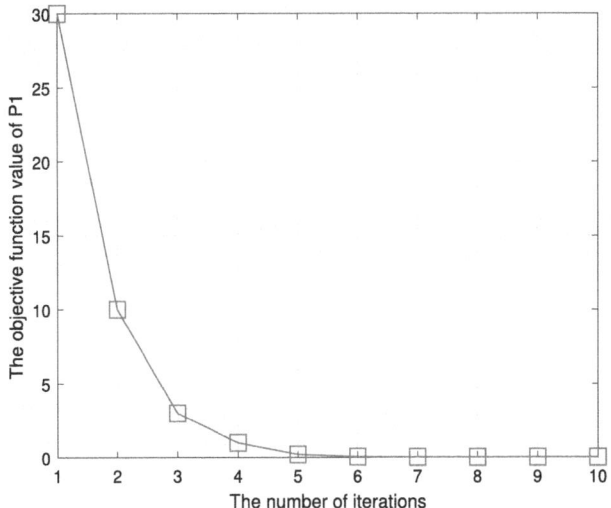

Fig. 2. The convergence performance of the proposed method.

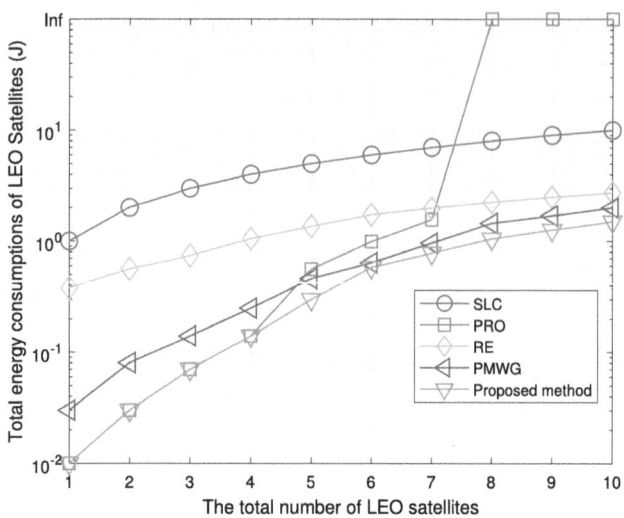

Fig. 3. The total energy consumptions of the proposed method compared with benchmark algorithms.

1. *Satellite local computing (SLC)*: This corresponds to the case where all computational tasks are executed locally. Specifically, we set $\beta(t) = \mathbf{0}, \mathbf{P}(t) = \mathbf{0}, \alpha(t) = \mathbf{0}$ and solve (**P1**) in each time slot.
2. *Pure Remote offloading (PRO)*: In this case, the tasks are all offloaded to MEC servers. Specifically, we set $\sum_{j=0}^{M} \beta_{k,j,i}(t) = 1, \forall k \in [1, A_i(t)], \forall i \in \mathcal{N}, \forall t \in \mathcal{T}$ and solve (**P2**) and (**P3**) in each time slot.
3. *Random execution (RE)*: In this case, $\mathbf{f}(t), \beta(t), \mathbf{P}(t), \alpha(t)$ are set randomly in the feasible region. (**P2**), (**P3**) are solved according to Algorithm 1.
4. *The proposed method without GEO-MEC servers (PMWG)*: This method corresponds to the case where the LEOs are not assisted by GEO-MEC servers. Specifically, we set $M = 0$ and solve (**P2**), (**P3**) in each time slot.

Figure 2 illustrates the convergence performance of the proposed method. It is evident that the method converges after approximately 5 to 6 iterations. The simulation is conducted with $N = 5$, and upon convergence, the objective value of (**P1**) is 0.036. This indicates that the proposed method effectively reaches a near-optimal solution.

Figure 3 shows the performance of the proposed method compared with the 4 benchmark algorithms. It is observed that the proposed method outperforms the benchmark algorithms in terms of total energy consumptions. In Fig. 3, "Inf" means the constraints of P1 are not satisfied, resulting in a infeasible solution. With the increase of LEO satellites, the bandwidth resource is limited which limits the uplink channel capacity. Therefore, the PRO method may not satisfy the latency constraint, by contrast, the proposed method can adjust the offloading ratio according to the current state. It is also observed that the performance

Table 1. Main Simulation Parameters

Parameters	Value
Ground bandwidth B_g	20 MHz
Inter-satellite bandwidth B_u	20 MHz
Number of GEO-MEC Servers M	3
The height of LEO satellites H	600 km
Maximum transmission power p_{max}	23 dBm
Noise power spectral density N_0	–174 dBm/Hz
Computational coefficient ϵ	10^{-26}
Maximum computational frequency f_{max}	2 GHz
The size of the input tasks $S_{i,k}(t)$	$[5 \times 10^5, 5 \times 10^6]$ bits
The maximum tolerant latency $L_{i,k}(t)$	$[0.01, 0.1]$ s
CPU cycles for a unit bit $C_{i,k}(t)$	500 cycles/bit
The threshold of Algorithm 1 ξ	0.001

of the proposed method is better than PMWG, which indicates the importance of GEO-MEC servers.

5   Conclusion

In this paper, we address the joint computation offloading and resource allocation problem in LEO-MEC networks. We formulate the problem as a non-convex optimization problem and propose an energy-efficient layered optimization method to solve it effectively. Specifically, the original problem is decomposed into three subproblems: offloading ratio optimization, computation frequency optimization, and radio resource optimization. For each subproblem, we derive the optimal solution, and the final solution is obtained by iteratively solving these subproblems. Simulation results demonstrate the method's convergence and effectiveness.

For future work, we plan to extend the study to more realistic scenarios where LEO satellites can offload tasks to multiple GEO satellites and ground MEC servers. Additionally, we will explore using geometric methods to account for the visible time between LEO satellites, ground servers, and GEO satellites.

References

1. Abbas, N., Zhang, Y., Taherkordi, A., Skeie, T.: Mobile edge computing: a survey. IEEE Internet Things J. **5**(1), 450–465 (2018)
2. Taleb, T., et al.: On multi-access edge computing: a survey of the emerging 5G network edge cloud architecture and orchestration. IEEE Commun. Surv. Tutor. **19**(3), 1657–1681 (2017)

3. Song, Z., Hao, Y., Liu, Y., Sun, X.: Energy-efficient multiaccess edge computing for terrestrial-satellite Internet of Things. IEEE Internet Things J. **8**(18), 14202–14218 (2021)
4. Jing, Y., Wang, J., Jiang, C., Zhan, Y.: Satellite MEC with federated learning: architectures, technologies and challenges. IEEE Netw. **36**(5), 106–112 (2022)
5. Cao, X., et al.: Edge-assisted multi-layer offloading optimization of LEO satellite-terrestrial integrated networks. IEEE J. Sel. Areas Commun. **41**(2), 381–398 (2023)
6. Dong, Q., Xu, X., Han, S., Liu, R., Zhang, X.: 'DDPG-based task offloading in satellite-terrestrial collaborative edge computing networks. In: 2023 IEEE International Conference on Communications Workshops (ICC Workshops), Rome, Italy (2023)
7. Zhang, X., et al.: Energy-efficient computation peer offloading in satellite edge computing networks. IEEE Trans. Mob. **23**(4), 3077–3091 (2024)
8. Minglei, T., Song, L., Wanjiang, H., Xiaoxiang, W.: Online learning-based offloading decision and resource allocation in mobile edge computing-enabled satellite-terrestrial networks. China Commun. **21**(3), 230–246 (2024)
9. Rodrigues, T.K., Kato, N.: Hybrid centralized and distributed learning for MEC-equipped satellite 6G networks. IEEE J. Sel. Areas Commun. **41**(4), 1201–1211 (2023)
10. Hao, Y., Song, Z., Zheng, Z., Zhang, Q., Miao, Z.: Joint communication, computing, and caching resource allocation in LEO satellite MEC networks. IEEE Access **11**, 6708–6716 (2023)
11. Yang, Z., Bi, S., Zhang, Y.-J.A.: Dynamic offloading and trajectory control for LEO-enabled mobile edge computing system with energy harvesting devices. IEEE Trans. Wirel. Commun. **21**(12), 10515–10528 (2022)
12. Wang, Y., Sheng, M., Wang, X., Wang, L., Li, J.: Mobile-edge computing: partial computation offloading using dynamic voltage scaling. IEEE Trans. Commun. **64**(10), 4268–4282 (2016)
13. Boyd, S., Vandenberghe, L.: Convex Optimization. Cambridge University Press, Cambridge (2004)

Key Technologies and Future Developments in the Design of Spaceborne Digital Transparent Processors

Zhongyue Liu[1(✉)], Jiatao Cui[1], Jiayu Wang[2], and Yuqian Liu[1]

[1] Institute of Telecommunication and Navigation Satellites of CAST, Beijing 100094, China
liuzhongyue_hit@163.com
[2] Xi'an Institute of Space Radio Technology, Xi'an 710100, Shaanxi, China

Abstract. With the continuous development of satellite communication technology, the people of the traditional commercial communications satellite can only provide service pattern fixed repeater, now already far cannot satisfy the current needs of satellite communications, now the high flux of satellites at the same time of increasing system capacity, has a higher requirement to the flexibility, which uses digital transparent processor (DTP, Digital Transparent Processor and other digital flexible load become the inevitable trend of today's development. This paper introduces the component interface and basic functions of a typical spaceborne digital transparent processor. The key technologies in DTP design are analyzed and the future development of DTP is described. The results and benefits of spaceborne DTP in practical application are explained.

Keywords: DTP · communication satellites · key technologies · future development

1 Introduction

With the rapid development of ground satellite communication application technology, traditional civilian commercial communication satellites can only provide fixed service mode transponders, which are far from meeting the needs of practical applications. It is required to digitize analog transponders and use digital payloads to provide sufficient flexibility for satellite communication systems.

The transponder is realized by three technical routes: analog transparent transponder, regenerative processing transponder and digital transparent forwarding. The traditional analog transparent transponder is limited by the performance of analog filter and microwave exchange matrix, the exchange particle size is coarse, and the adjustment ability is limited, which restricts the system performance. The regenerative process transponder has the guarantee of single channel, high speed and good real-time performance. However, due to the need for signal modulation and demodulation and encoding and decoding, it has high dependence on the system, but the system flexibility is low,

© ICST Institute for Computer Sciences, Social Informatics and Telecommunications Engineering 2025
Published by Springer Nature Switzerland AG 2025. All Rights Reserved
H.-H. Chen and W. Meng (Eds.): WiSATS 2024, LNICST 605, pp. 161–171, 2025.
https://doi.org/10.1007/978-3-031-86196-3_14

the equipment complexity is relatively high, and the weight and power consumption are large.

It is hoped that the civil commercial communication satellite can ensure the flexibility of the system with high capacity, and has the advantages of analog transparent transponder and regenerative processing transponder. The Digital Transparent Processor (DTP) appears in the alternative scheme.

Compared with the analog transparent transponder, DTP has the advantages of supporting any subchannel crosslink, upstream spectrum detection, adjustable subchannel gain, flexible use, etc. It is especially suitable for the application scenarios with multi-communication system, multiservice bandwidth and one hop transmission requirements. At the same time, through the management of the subchannel, the resource utilization of the system is improved, and the shortcoming of the analog transparent transponder is overcome.

Compared with the regenerative transponder, DTP does not need to perform signal modulation and demodulation, encode and decode, and only completes the processing of physical subchannels, which is independent of the system and has higher flexibility. It saves a lot of regenerative processing resources for digital channel processing, and the total capacity of the system is large.

The digital transparent processor uses the flexible onboard channelized filtering technology to support information interaction between any frequency band and any bandwidth on board and flexible cross beam interaction, and can flexibly realize the integrated processing of high speed information acquisition services, broadband communication services and measurement and control services, so that the system has the ability to flexibly select the appropriate communication system, divide the best channel and temporary networking. Improve the flexibility and reliability of communication, and realize the flexible exchange of satellite signals and resources. DTP products will gradually replace satellite analog transparent transponders to a certain extent, representing the technical trend of the digital development of satellite payloads in the future, and is extremely important for the subsequent development of military and civilian satellites [1–3].

This paper first introduces the architecture design of DTP, introduces the basic functions, interfaces and components of digital transparent processor, then analyzes the key technologies in DTP design, and finally expounds the future development of DTP, explaining the achievements and benefits of spaceborne DTP in practical applications in the future.

2 Digital Transparent Processor Architecture Design

In the high throughput communication satellite, the DTP link can realize the flexible forward and backward cross-link of user beam, and the traditional "two hop" communication mode of "forward link + backward link" can be changed to the "one hop" communication mode of client to end. Figure 1 shows the information flow of DTP link in USERS to USERS mode.

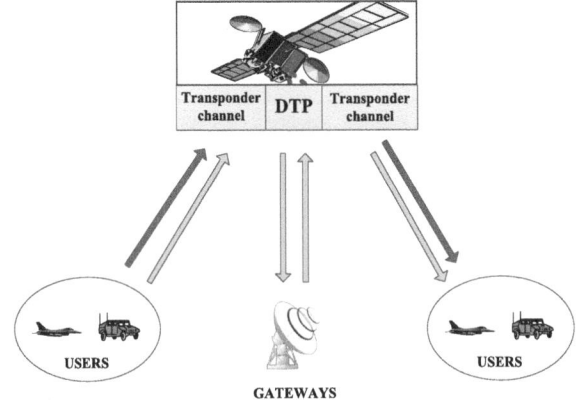

Fig. 1. "One hop" and "two hop" mode information flow diagram

2.1 DTP Components and Interfaces

DTP is mainly composed of channel processing, switch processing, control, frequency synthesizing and power supply, as shown in Fig. 2. Each branch transmits signals through an internal connector, and the channel processing branch is equipped with a special Application Specific Integrated Circuit (ASIC) chip, which has the ability to complete the digital channelization of the input channel and the digital channel synthesis processing of the output channel. At the same time, ADC/DAC(Analog to Digital Converter/Digital to Analog Converter) chip is configured to complete the channel analog to digital and digital to analog conversion function. An extension switch is configured with an ASIC for switching processing and has the ability to perform switching processing on a certain scale of subbands. The control branch completes the receiving and parsing of service remote control instructions, and distributes the corresponding service remote control instructions to the corresponding channel processing ASics and switch processing ASics. At the same time, the working states of channel processing ASics and switch processing ASics are collected and then output after frame processing [4].

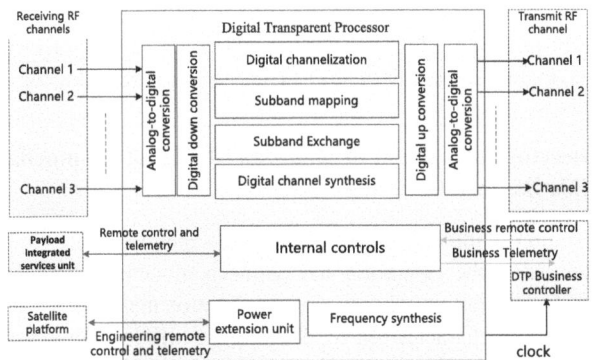

Fig. 2. DTP components and interfaces

The digital transparent processor is connected to the transmitting and receiving radio frequency channel, and there are data and control interfaces between the platform digital tube system, load integrated service unit, DTP service controller and other devices.

2.2 Basic DTP Functions

The basic function of DTP is to process the input upstream IF analog signal through analog to digital conversion, digital channolization, subband mapping, subband switching, subband gain control, digital channel synthesis and digital to analog conversion, and finally output the downstream IF analog signal, as shown in Fig. 3. At the same time, DTP receives external service remote control commands, completes subband mapping, subband switching, and subband gain control of a single machine, monitors the internal working status of a single machine, completes subband and channel power estimation, and frames the status information of a single machine into telemetry information for output.

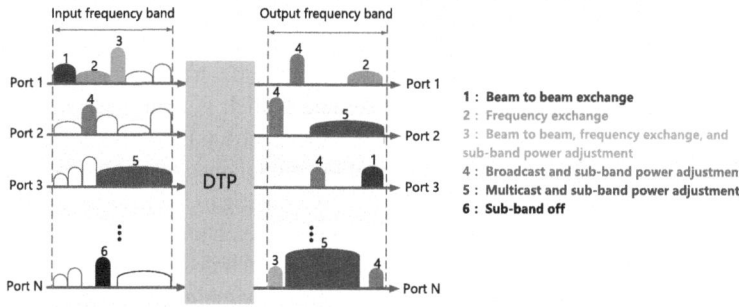

Fig. 3. DTP basic functional mode diagram

3 Digital Transparent Processor Key Technologies

Digital transparent processing transponder technology, involving electrical design and core components, mainly including the following seven aspects of technical difficulties.

3.1 The Engineering Realization of High Speed Digital Channelization with Flexible Bandwidth Configuration

Digital channelization is the realization of channel separation and synthesis in digital domain, and then realize the separation and synthesis of subband signals with dynamic variable bandwidth. The traditional digital channelization method is based on polyphase filter structure, which is characterized by dividing the whole sampling bandwidth into the required number of subchannels in one step. At the same time, because FFT can be used for calculation, the system resource utilization can be greatly reduced [5].

How to ensure the perfect reconstruction of the process of "wideband signal - multiple subbands - wideband signal" without distortion has become an urgent problem to be solved. In the traditional digital channelization technology, the filter obtained according to the perfect filter design method has been developed into a perfect filter bank. The perfect filter bank divides a complete broadband signal into multiple subbands through the filter bank, and then the subband signal passes through the filter bank, which can be nearly perfectly restored to the original information. Figure 4 below shows the subband splicing diagram and the amplitude-frequency response of the spliced subband after channelization and synthesis [6].

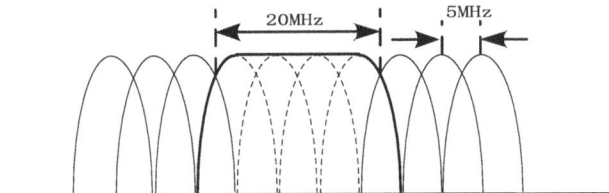

Fig. 4. Subband splicing diagram

Through the design method of the perfect reconstructed prototype filter, the whole frequency resource can be divided into multiple resource blocks according to the subband granularity. The nearly perfect reconstructed complex exponential modulation filter bank means that each filter is obtained by complex exponential modulation of a prototype filter. This filter bank can make use of the polyphase structure in engineering implementation, reduce the filter's demand for system resources, and facilitate engineering implementation as shown in Fig. 5.

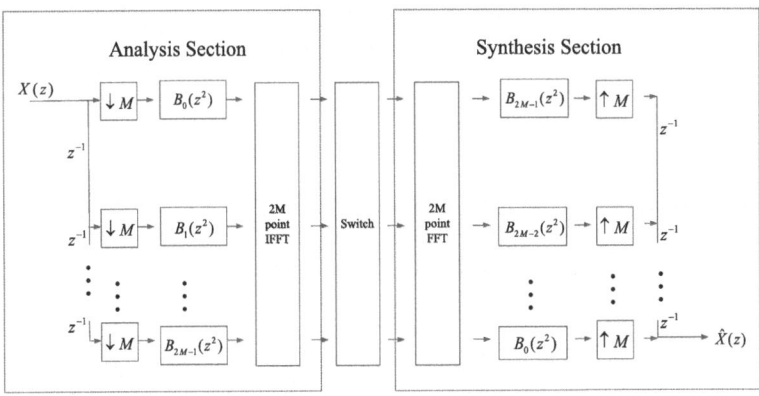

Fig. 5. The engineering implementation of nonuniform bandwidth digital channelizers

3.2   Engineering Implementation of Routing and Switching Technology of Super Large Capacity Subchannel

DTP forwarding of subband information of different frequencies is a subband switching process. Because the complexity of subband switching unit is proportional to the square of the number of switching ports, the number of switching unit ports should be reduced as much as possible in implementation.

Through the introduction of time division multiplexing mechanism, the subband switching unit needs to deal with both time division switching and space division switching. The time division in the subband switching unit is converted into T level and the space division is converted into S level, so the subband switching unit needs to contain at least 1 T level and 1 S level. According to the different connection modes of T-level and S-level, there are two ways to implement the subband switching unit, namely T-S-T and S-T.

The implementation of T-S-T switching structure is simple, and non-blocking switching can be realized by scheduling algorithm. The constraints on the implementation of T-S-T switching structure mainly include synchronization between switching units, the cache rate of time-division switching units and the switching capacity of air-division switching units. Figure 6 below shows the T-S-T implementation of the subband switching unit [7].

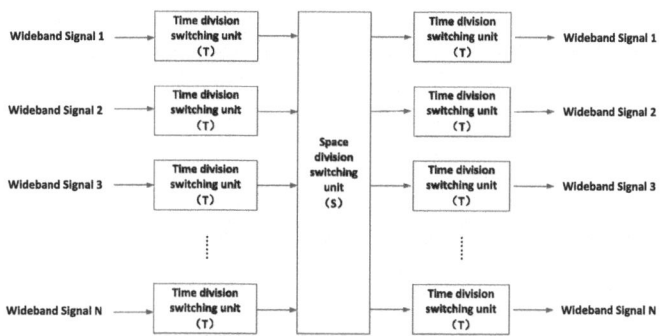

Fig. 6. T-S-T structure of subband switching unit

The S-T switching structure is similar to the T-S-T switching structure. The difference is that the first level time division switching unit is replaced with the input processing unit, as shown in Fig. 7, to complete the packet encapsulation and forwarding path search of subband data, the second level air division switching unit and the third level time division switching unit are changed to asynchronous working mode, and the whole switching structure no longer needs synchronous allocation modules.

Compared with the T-S-T switching structure, the S-T switching structure adopts the packet switching mode and lacks the first-level intermediate slot scheduling, resulting in the output port conflict and loss of switching packets. In order to cope with the output port conflict, the switching capacity of the air division switching unit needs to be further improved. As a result, the data rate between the input processing unit, the air division switching unit and the time division switching unit also needs to be further improved.

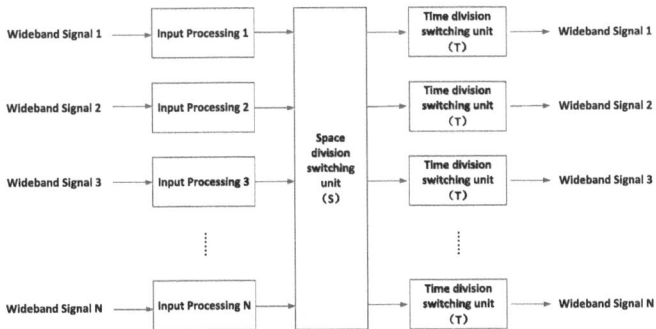

Fig. 7. S-T structure of subband switching unit

For different switching structures, how to optimize the network topology in engineering implementation, improve the reliability and availability of the whole network, and ensure non-blocking high speed channel switching under the condition of network element failure will become the focus of future development.

3.3 The Engineering Realization of Large Scale Complex Digital Integrated Single Machine

For complex integrated single machine, it is required that the power supply network conversion efficiency is high, the energy loss is reduced, and the network is stable and reliable. At the same time, it is necessary to ensure the reliability of the clock and data transmission network, and has self-check and recovery functions. In addition, for very large scale complex integrated digital integrated single-machine, for high integrated circuit boards, large power consumption devices, new and more efficient heat dissipation methods need to be adopted.

At present, the heat dissipation of large power devices in spaceborne single machine mainly depends on the heat dissipation copper or aluminum sheet, one end of the heat sink is crimped on the large-power device, and the other end is connected to the reinforcement bar of the single machine structure. This method mainly relies on copper or aluminum with high thermal resistance for heat conduction, and the heat dissipation path is mainly the reinforcement bar of the single machine structure, which is limited by the design of the reinforcement bar. Generally, there is a narrow heat dissipation path and a long path, and the overall heat dissipation efficiency is low. The current heat dissipation mode cannot meet the heat dissipation requirements of boards with large power consumption.

The heat pipe heat dissipation efficiency is several orders of magnitude higher than that of conventional materials such as copper and aluminum. The heat pipe technology is applied to the heat dissipation of large power components in a single machine. For example, the heat pipe is directly laid on the large-power components (ASICs), which can solve the heat dissipation problem of large power components and improve the overall heat dissipation efficiency of a single machine.

3.4   High Speed and Reliable Data Transmission Technology

At present, there are two technical ways to realize data transmission: optical transmission and electrical transmission. The electrical interface technology is mature and heavy, and the backplane has the advantage of power consumption [8]. The optical interface is less reliable and lighter, and has the advantage over the cable transmission.

At present, according to the calculation of data throughput, the data rate of a single data transmission link between the channelized processor and the switching processor will reach more than 20Gbps in the future, so the data transmission between the processors will be achieved by optical fiber transmission [9].

3.5   Multilevel Clock Allocation Network Management Technology

Under the board architecture based on backplane and high speed connector, the high speed cooperation between the board and the board module puts forward higher requirements for the allocation and management of clock network. The use of the one-level clock allocation management network brings the following two problems to provide clock for all processing modules:

1) The clock path is too long, resulting in a serious decline in the quality of the clock signal waveform;
2) With the limited adjustment ability of the clock allocation management module, the clock signal transmission path between each module is difficult to synchronize.

This problem is solved by using a two level clock allocation management network. As shown in Fig. 8 below, a first level clock allocation management module completes the system clock management of large functional modules between subboards, and multiple second level clock allocation management modules complete the board level clock management between subboards.

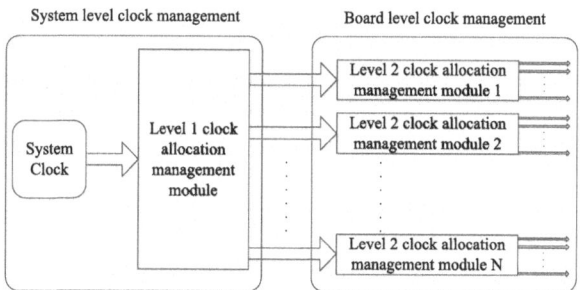

Fig. 8.   Schematic diagram of a two level clock allocation management network

3.6   High Speed Signal Transmission Delay Control Technology

In a digital system that works synchronously, the actions of all system components that use clock signals must be coordinated, and the working system will have normal timing.

When the phase difference between clock signals and high speed parallel data signals reaching different IC input clock pins exceeds the maximum tolerance range, various abnormal phenomena will appear in the system.

The main purpose of using high-speed signal transmission delay control technology is to minimize the phase difference between multiple clock signals or parallel data signals. The phase difference can not be eliminated, can only be minimized in the design, the main technical means are as follows:

1) In the two level clock allocation management module, a clock management chip with small difference and adjustable is used.
2) Considering the layout of the subboard and high speed PCB design, SI simulation is carried out on all clock signals and high speed parallel data signal networks by means of high speed signal integrity analysis to ensure that the transmission delay of the physical path is as consistent as possible.

3.7 High Speed ADC/DAC Conversion

With the improvement of digital signal processing technology and digital circuit working speed, as well as the continuous improvement of system sensitivity and other requirements, high requirements are put forward for high-speed and high-precision ADC/DAC indicators.

According to the Nyquist sampling law, the sampling rate must be at least twice the bandwidth of the signal. At the same time, in order to support the flexible standard, the transceiver modules of modern communication are more and more common to use digital IF direct sampling, which further improves the performance requirements for high speed analog to digital conversion chips [10].

In the development process of DTP, analog to digital conversion chips need to sample or output signals of higher and higher frequencies and higher and higher bandwidth. The noise and signal distortion caused by analog to digital or digital to analog conversion are often difficult to compensate for and can have a significant impact on system performance. Therefore, the performance of high speed ADC chip in sampling or analog to digital conversion is very important to the system index. At the same time, in order to complete the complex system function, the power consumption of each submodule in the large system should be as low as possible, so low power ADC/DAC conversion is essential. In short, an ADC/DAC chip with large broadband, low power consumption, high dynamic range and sample rate is one of the key core technologies in the development of DTP.

4 Future Development of Digital Transparent Processors

DTP is the most complex and most powerful spaceborne processing products at present, which uses a large number of advanced processing technologies, and is the concentrated embodiment of the comprehensive development level of aerospace products.

4.1 Future Trends of DTP

At present, the three major satellite manufacturers: Boeing, ADS, and TAS have developed DTP products. DTP technology has gradually expanded from early mobile communications satellites to Ku and Ka band broadband missions, as well as the latest HTS/VHTS missions. Each company has different standards for DTP generation. At present, DTP products can be divided into five generations according to single-port processing bandwidth, as shown in Table 1.

Table 1. DTP generation typical indicators

Argument	The first generation	The second generation	The third generation	The fourth generation	The fifth generation
Number of ports	120	20	14	48 & 128	reachable 160
Port processing bandwidth	30 MHz	125 MHz	250MHz	500 MHz	2.9 GHz
Subchannel spacing	200 kHz	2.6 MHz	250kHz	312.5kHz	3.515 MHz
Weight	160 kg	/	21kg	58 kg & 154 kg	371.2 kg
Power dissipation	1800 W	/	270W	792 W & 2112 W	/
Structure	Discrete vertical + backplane	/	Integrated planking	Discrete vertical	Discrete vertical
Manufacturer	Astrium	Boeing	Astrium	Thales	Thales

In the future, DTP will develop towards greater bandwidth, more functions, lower weight and power consumption. No matter which generation of products, in the era of emergence are very large scale complex integrated digital processing machine, representing the highest level of digital load in aerospace manufacturing at that time.

4.2 Application Result Benefit

DTP is used to enhance the capability of satellite ground integrated satellite communication applications, realize the system integration of various services, build high orbit space based infrastructure, promote the integration of military communications and civil and commercial communications, and realize the autonomous and controllable HTS satellite system.

The breakthrough of DTP technology can form and enhance the development and research capacity of domestic spaceborne super large scale complex processing products, drive the upgrading of high performance and high quality products of related product supporting units of the whole domestic industry chain, and lead the core technology level improvement and products of domestic technical advantage units. Optimize the product development process, improve the product output efficiency, reduce the weight and power consumption ratio of the product per unit bandwidth, improve the international competitiveness and influence of the product, and lay the technical foundation for the subsequent development of the fifth generation product.

5 Conclusions

This paper introduces the component interface and basic functions of a typical space-borne digital transparent processor. The key technologies of DTP implementation are analyzed and the future development of DTP is described, and the achievements and benefits of spaceborne DTP in practical application in the future are explained.

References

1. Morelli, G., Mainguet, A., Eustace, M.: Automated operations of large geo telecom satellites with digital transparent processors (DTP). In: Challenges and Lessons Learned. In: SpaceOps Conferences, Marseille, pp. 2666–2680 (2018)
2. Butash, T., Marshall, J.: Leveraging digital on-board processing to increase communications satellite flexibility and effective capacity. In: Aiaa International Communications Satellite Systems Conference (2013)
3. Pera A.L., Forni F., Grossi M., et al.: Digital transparent processor for satellite telecommunication services. In: IEEE Aerospace Conference, Big Sky, pp. 1–9 (2007)
4. Sulli, V., Giancristofaro, D., Santucci, F., et al.: Design of digital satellite processors: from communications link performance to hardware complexity. IEEE J. Sel. Areas Commun. **36**(2), 338–350 (2018)
5. Mishra, N., Mishra, P., Shah, H., et al.: A design method using a set of objective functions for near-perfect reconstruction filter bank based transmultiplexer for onboard transparent processor. In: International Conference on Signal Processing and Communications (ICSC), Noida, pp. 271–275 (2013)
6. Shin, H., Harjani, R.: Low-power wideband analog channelization filter bank using passive polyphase-FFT techniques. J. Solid-State Circ. **52**(7), 1753–1767 (2017)
7. Dawei, Z., Jing, Y., Rui, C., et al.: The implementation of routing information protocol porting to the switching system. In: Seventh International Conference on Measuring Technology and Mechatronics Automation, Nanchang, pp. 1220–1223 (2015)
8. Veneta, N., Enjolrasa, V., Nicolasa, C., Voisina, P.: Spaceflex onboard digital transparent processor: a new generation of DTP with optical digital interconnects. In: International Conference on Space Optics (2018)
9. Shao, Y., Li, X.C., Wang, N., et al.: Theoretical and experimental investigation of HMSIW-based high-speed data transmission system using QPSK scheme. Trans. Compon. Packag. Manuf. Technol. **8**(11), 1938–1947 (2018)
10. Drenski, T., Rasmussen, J.C.: ADC/DAC and ASIC technology trends. In: 24th OptoElectronics and Communications Conference (OECC) and 2019 International Conference on Photonics in Switching and Computing (PSC), Fukuoka, pp. 1–3 (2019)

A Solution to the Problem of Retail Credit Risk Pricing Problem Based on the Machine Learning XGBoost Algorithm

Jingxuan Ma[1] , Xin Li[1] , Jiajie Guo[2] , and Qiuyue Li[1(✉)]

[1] College of Science, China Agricultural University, Beijing, China
lqyue@cau.edu.cn
[2] School of Electronics and Information Engineering, Harbin Institute of Technology, Harbin, China
23S005086@stu.hit.edu.cn

Abstract. Machine learning algorithms, represented by logistic regression and decision tree algorithms, have a wide range of applications in retail credit risk management, such as anti fraud models, application scoring models, behavioural scoring models and overdue collection scoring models, which are used to assess the credit risk level of customers at different stages of the retail credit process. The integrated decision tree model, represented by the XGBoost algorithm, constructs the model using more variables and although it lacks the necessary interpretability, its predictions are more accurate. Traditional retail risk pricing typically uses a preapplication scoring model to enforce different product prices for customers with different risk ratings. Based on the XGBoost algorithm and personal credit information from the People's Bank of China and other tripartite credit bureaus, we attempt to develop a retail risk pricing model based on the actual loan disbursement of the customers, which is used to apply different product prices to customers with different risk ratings, while at the same time remarketing to customers who have not disbursed historically. The data for the construction of the retail risk pricing model are taken from a retail personal loan business of a financial institution, and customers who are approved but not actually withdraw money are marked as 1, while those who are approved and actually withdraw money are marked as 0.

Keywords: Retail credit risk pricing · Machine learning XGBoost algorithm · Personal credit data

1 Introduction

As a multidisciplinary field that encompasses probability theory, statistics, approximation theory and complex algorithms, machine learning uses computers

---

J. Ma and X. Li—Co-First Author.

© ICST Institute for Computer Sciences, Social Informatics and Telecommunications Engineering 2025
Published by Springer Nature Switzerland AG 2025. All Rights Reserved
H.-H. Chen and W. Meng (Eds.): WiSATS 2024, LNICST 605, pp. 172–186, 2025.
https://doi.org/10.1007/978-3-031-86196-3_15

as tools to realistically simulate the way humans learn and to structure existing content in a way that effectively improves learning efficiency. Machine learning has a very wide range of applications in daily life, such as in intelligent finance [1,2], intelligent healthcare [3,4], intelligent transport [5,6], image recognition [7,8] and many other fields [9,10], and it has brought very many changes to our lives. In the field of machine learning, machine learning methods usually include supervised learning, unsupervised learning, semisupervised learning, and reinforcement learning, where supervised learning includes algorithms such as Linear Regression, Logistic Regression, Decision Trees, Random Forests, Support Vector Machines, Naive Bayes, and other algorithms, while unsupervised learning includes K-Means Clustering, Hierarchical Clustering, Gaussian Mixture Models, Principal Component Analysis, Association Rule Learning, etc. Decision tree algorithms include ID3 algorithm, C4.5 algorithm, CART (Classification and Regression Trees) algorithm, C5.0 algorithm and also integrated algorithms such as GBDT (Gradient Boosting Decision Tree) [11,12], XGBoost (Extreme Gradient Boosting) [13,14], LightGBM (Light Gradient Boosting Machine) [15,16] through are also considered as decision tree algorithms.

In the field of retail credit, the most widely used algorithms are logistic regression algorithm and XGBoost algorithm [13], for example, personal credit application scorecard constructed by using logistic regression algorithm can use fewer variables to evaluate the credit risk level of retail customers, For example, the personal credit application scorecard constructed by using logistic regression algorithm can use fewer variables to evaluate the credit risk level of retail customers, and it can be very intuitive to understand the factors that affect the evaluation results, while the personal credit application scorecard constructed by using XGboost algorithm [13] can autonomously find the factors that affect the evaluation results of customers from thousands of variables, which avoids a lot of human intervention, thus it can achieve the rapid iteration of the model. Retail credit risk pricing refers to the application of different pricing strategies to different risk segments in the consumer credit market in order to improve profitability. Typical risk pricing strategies are based on a retail credit application scorecard, whereby customers with high scores, i.e. those with a low risk of default, are offered lower prices and customers with low scores, i.e. those with a high risk of default, are offered higher prices.

In this paper, based on a financial institution's customer credit application data, including credit data from the People's Bank of China (PBOC) and third party credit bureaus A, B and C, we use the XGBoost algorithm [13] to build a retail credit risk pricing model, which not only allows us to implement different risk pricing strategies for different customers, but also allows us to remarket to customers who have passed credit approval but have not withdrawn their money. The modelling sample includes all approved customers, and the risk pricing model predictions are targeted at customers who have no actual credit transactions among the approved customers, and it should be noted that customers who have been rejected during the credit approval process are excluded from the sample for this modelling. This paper is organised as follows:

- In Sect. 2, we provide a brief overview of common machine learning algorithms.
- In Sect. 3, we provide a brief description of the methodology of the retail credit risk pricing model.
- In Sect. 4, we give the validation metrics of the retail credit risk pricing model and the effect of the applications.
- In Sect. 5, we present the conclusions of the retail credit risk pricing model and its shortcoming.

2   Related Work

In recent years, machine learning algorithms have been used more and more widely, both in traditional financial institutions such as banks [23–25], and in the retail credit segment of some Internet. Commonly used machine learning algorithms include logistic regression algorithms and integrated decision tree algorithms, of which integrated decision tree algorithms include GBDT, XGBoost and LightGBM.

2.1   Logistic Regression Algorithms

Logistic regression is a commonly used binary classification model [17,18], which is usually used to predict binary classification problems, such as whether a customer will click on a product link, whether a credit customer will default on a loan, whether a certain evaluation is positive or negative, and so on. In the financial field, logistic regression is widely used in credit assessment, default prediction, and customer value analysis. Logistic regression is used to predict the value of an output variable by learning the relationship between input features and output labels, and its loss function is usually the cross entropy loss function. The difference between logistic regression and linear regression is that linear regression is used to predict continuous variables where the output variable is a continuous value, such as the price of a commodity, wage income, while logistic regression is used to solve binary problems where the output variable is a binary value, such as whether or not to buy a product, whether or not to default on a contract, and so on. The core principle of the logistic regression algorithm can be expressed as

$$P(y = 1|x; w) = \frac{1}{1 + e^{-(w_0 + w_1 * x_1 + w_2 * x_2 + ... + w_n * x_n)}} \tag{1}$$

where $P(y = 1|x; w)$ denotes the probability that the output variable is 1 when the input feature is x, and $x_1, x_2, ..., x_n$ denote the input features, while $w_0, w_1, w_2, ..., w_n$ denote the weight vectors. We use stochastic gradient descent to optimise the loss function $L = -(ylog(p) + (1 - y)log(1 - p))$ until the optimal weight parameters are found. The advantages of using logistic regression to construct a retail credit risk scorecard are that the modelling process is simple and efficient, it is easy to understand and implement, and it directly predicts classification probabilities without making prior assumptions about the data distribution, thus avoiding problems associated with inaccurate assumptions about the distribution, and the parameters it fits represent the impact of each feature on the results. Similarly, its disadvantages are more obvious, such as the model is easily underfitting, in most cases manual feature engineering is required to construct the combination of features, the classification accuracy may not be high, it is essentially a linear classifier which does not deal well with the correlation between the features, and it is very sensitive to covariance, but there may be multiple covariance which needs to be tested by the VIF (Variance Inflation Factor) test.

2.2 Gradient Boosting Decision Tree

Gradient Boosting Decision Tree (GBDT) is an iterative decision tree algorithm that effectively combines decision trees with integration ideas by constructing a set of weak learners and accumulating the results of multiple decision learners as the final prediction output. The decision tree used by GBDT is a CART regression tree [28,29], whether the problem is regression, binary classification or multiple classification. The core idea is that each tree learns the residuals of all previous decision trees, and the residuals are essentially the difference between the true value and the predicted value. In the learning process, it first learns a regression tree and then subtracts the true value from the predicted value to get the residuals, and then takes the residuals as a learning target to learn the next regression tree, and so on, until the residuals are less than a certain threshold close to 0, or the number of regression trees reaches a certain threshold. The core idea is to reduce the loss function by fitting the residuals in each round. It uses a gradient descent algorithm to optimise the loss function. It approximates the loss function with a firstorder Taylor expansion of the loss function during model optimisation, which can reduce the amount of computation in the model optimisation process. The GBDT model has high accuracy, it performs well on both training and test sets, while it can handle complex problems such as high dimensionality [35,36], sparse features [37,38] and nonlinear relationships, and it also has strong generalisation ability as it reduces the risk of overfitting by combining several weak classifiers into a single strong classifier. However, as GBDT is a serial algorithm, it needs to construct each decision tree sequentially, so the training time is long, while it is sensitive to outliers, and it is easily affected by outliers during the training process, which may lead to the degradation of the model's performance. In addition, although the generalisation ability of GBDT model is better, when the model has less sample data or the number of model features is small, it is easy to have overfitting problem.

2.3 Extreme Gradient Boosting

Extreme Gradient Boosting (XGBoost) is an efficient gradient boosting decision tree algorithm [26,27] that uses the second order Taylor expansion of the loss function to approximate the loss function, which greatly improves the model performance compared to GBDT. As a forward additive model [33,34], it adopts the same integration idea as GBDT, which works by integrating multiple weak learners into one strong learner by certain methods, and uses multiple trees for joint decision making. In the XGBoost model, the prediction result of each decision tree is the difference between the target value and the prediction results of all previous decision trees, so the final prediction result of the model is obtained by adding the prediction results of all decision trees. Unlike other models, which typically require a separate preprocessing step, XGBoost can handle the missing value problem internally, with the algorithm finding the best imputation values for the missing values and then storing them for future prediction. Although the augmentation algorithm is prone to overfitting problems, XGBoost improves the generalisation of the model by incorporating the L1 (lasso) [19,20] and L2 (ridge) [21,22] regularisations directly into the objective function during training. For sparse data problems, XGBoost uses compressed, memory efficient data structures and its algorithm is designed to efficiently traverse sparse matrices. Most integrated methods provide feature importance metrics, but XGBoost provides a more comprehensive set of feature importance metrics, including gain, frequency and coverage, which allows for a more detailed interpretation of the model. For categorical variable problems, XGBoost's treatment of categorical variables is more nuanced than simple binary partitioning, allowing complex relationships to be captured without additional preprocessing.XGBoost's unique capabilities make it not only a state of art machine learning algorithm in terms of predictive accuracy, but also efficient and customisable. Its ability to handle real world data complexities such as missing values, sparsity and multicollinearity, while being computationally efficient and providing detailed interpretability, makes it an invaluable tool for a wide range of data science tasks.

2.4   Light Gradient Boosting Machine

Light Gradient Boosting Machine (LightGBM) [30,32] is an efficient and scalable machine learning algorithm based on Gradient Boosted Decision Trees, which combines the advantages of the GBDT algorithm and the XGBoost algorithm with a series of optimisations to the model. In order to solve the problem of the GBDT algorithm framework's computational inefficiency [39] when dealing with large amounts of data, LightGBM greatly improves the computational efficiency of GBDT at the expense of a very small computational accuracy. Despite the sacrifice in computational accuracy, the actual modelling effect of LightGBM is almost at the same level as XGBoost. From another perspective, although LightGBM sacrifices computational accuracy to a certain extent, it suppresses the overfitting problem [40,41] of the model. Therefore, in many scenarios, the algorithmic effect of LightGBM will even be better than XGBoost. In terms of algorithmic principles, LightGBM also adopts a gradient based boosting algorithm, but it uses the optimisation technique of Gradient based One Side Sampling (GOSS) to speed up the training process by retaining samples with larger gradients. In terms of data processing, when the amount of data is very large,

XGBoost may face the problem of insufficient memory, but LightGBM significantly improves the data processing capability by adopting the GOSS technique, and is able to process larger data sets efficiently, while outperforming XGBoost in terms of computational speed and memory consumption. In addition, LightGBM uses the histogram algorithm for node splitting, which can take full advantage of the parallel computing capabilities of multi core CPUs and significantly accelerate the training speed. LightGBM uses a leaf wise growth strategy to find a leaf node with the largest splitting gain from all the current leaves, then splits it, and then loops to execute this strategy. However, this strategy grows deeper decision trees, which in turn creates an overfitting problem, so LightGBM adds a maximum depth limit on top of leaf wise to prevent overfitting while maintaining high efficiency.

3   Methodology

Retail credit risk pricing is an assessment of the price of a risky asset. In order to maximise operating profit, financial institutions usually implement different pricing strategies for customers with different levels of credit risk, whereby customers with lower credit risk usually receive financing services at lower prices, while those with higher credit risk usually need to receive financing services at higher prices, i.e., users with poorer levels of risk need to be supplemented with a risk premium. In this paper, based on the actual business data of financial institutions, including customers' application information data, approval result data, credit data from the People's Bank of China and credit data from other three party financial institutions, we use the XGBoost machine learning algorithm to construct a retail credit risk pricing model that evaluates the customer's withdrawal propensity by predicting whether the customer who passed the credit approval will have an actual withdrawal behaviour in the next three months. Based on the results of the model's prediction, a higher pricing strategy is implemented for customers with a high propensity to withdraw, while a relatively lower pricing strategy is implemented for customers with a relatively low propensity to withdraw.

3.1   Model Sample Segmentation Strategies

We randomly selected 10,000 customers from all retail credit approvals for use in building the retail credit risk pricing model. 77% of the 10,000 customers modelled made a withdrawal within three months of being approved, but the remaining 23% did not actually make a withdrawal within three months of being approved for credit. In order to test the actual predictive power of the model and whether there is an overfitting or underfitting problem in the model, we divided all the model samples into training and test sets according to a 2:1 ratio, where the number of training sets totals 6667, while the numbers of samples in the test set totals 3333. As a total of 23% of the 10,000 customers modelled did not make an actual withdrawal, the percentages of target customers in both the training and test sets are about 23%.

The model feature variables used in this modelling are mainly from four parts, which are the credit data of the People's Bank of China (PBOC), the data of the three party credit agency A, the data of the three party credit agency B and the data of the three party credit agency C. The data of the PBOC contains about 15,000 feature variables, the data of the three party credit agency A contains about 1,250 model variables, the data of the three party credit agency B contains about 410 model variables, while the data of the three party credit agency C contains about 60 model variables. We categorise the PBOC's credit data according to their actual business meanings, with a total of 15 different categories, where the business meanings of the feature variables within each category were similar or the same, and the businmess meanings of the feature variables differe significantly of different categories. With 15 categories of PBOC credit data and 3 categories of credit data from tripartite credit agencies, we have a total of 18 categories of credit feature variables to construct the retail credit risk pricing model.

3.2   Model Indicator Screening Strategies

When faced with a large number of features, relying on all of them for modelling can lead to dimensional disaster and overly complex models, while also introducing redundant or irrelevant features, reducing the accuracy and interpretability of the model [42,43]. The goal of multi feature screening [46,47] is to select the subset of features from all available features that are most important for credit risk model building and prediction. By properly selecting and carefully screening features, we can improve the predictive power of the model, simplify the model complexity, reduce the risk of overfitting, and better explain the model predictions. These optimisations will help to improve the stability, reliability and practicality of the credit risk model and provide effective support for risk management and decision. In total, there are about 17,000 different feature variables in the 18 different categories of credit data mentioned above, and there is a high degree of multicollinearity among feature variables in the same category. Although the XGBoost algorithm can theoretically handle an infinite number of different feature variables and does not need to preprocess the multicollinearity problem, from a practical application point of view, we need to filter the feature variables to some extent to ultimately achieve lightweight deployment.

For each set of feature variables of different categories, we use the XGBoost algorithm to model the target customers on the training set and perform parameter tuning by adjusting the different model hyperparameters, in particular, we can adjust the weight coefficients of the different variables by adjusting the L1 regularity coefficients and the L2 regularity coefficients. The L1 regularity is the sum of the absolute values of the elements in the pointers, also known as Lasso regularisation, in the high dimensional case, if a feature is unimportant, even if the weights of that feature are large, it has a small impact on the loss function but a large impact on the regularity term, which is then filtered out in the presence of the regularity term. L2 regularisation, also known as ridge regression, is the process of summing the squares of the elements of a quantity and then finding the square root, the effect of the L2 regular term is to keep all the parameters close to 0 so that the model isn't particularly sensitive to any particular feature, i.e. when running on a test set, even if there is unusually strong noise on one of the features, that noise won't have a big effect on the result for the output of the overall model. The process of feature screening using the XGBoost algorithm is as follows:

- Train the initial XGBoost model based on the feature variables to be screened.u
- Rank the feature variables according to the importance of the feature variable [44,45], eliminate the variables with lower importance rankings.
- Continue to perform feature variables and screening, and so on, until the number of retained variables reaches a certain threshold or a significant degradation in model performance occurs after modelling the excluded feature variables.

3.3   Model Training Strategies

Machine learning models are trained using specific algorithms and data to create a model that can solve a specific problem. Throughout the model training process, the model learns the associative relationships hidden behind the data from the training data set, with the goal of being able to accurately predict or classify new data. The model training process typically involves selecting model training data, dividing the model samples into training and test sets, tuning the model parameters, and testing the model. Through model training, the model is able to learn the laws of the feature variables and use these laws to make predictions or decisions on new data. Ultimately, the model obtained through training determines a set of parameter values at which the model is better able to handle new data.

In the process of model training, the model training data we use includes 10,000 training samples, in which the proportion of the prediction target in the whole sample is about 23%, and these 10,000 data are divided into two parts, the training set and the test set, according to the ratio of 2:1, in which the training set is used to adjust the parameters of the model, and the test set is used to evaluate the generalisation ability of the model. In the process of model training, we always consider factors such as the model's KS value (Kolmogorov Smirnov value), AUC (Area Under Curve) value the accuracy rate and the actual percentage of customer withdrawals in different probability intervals, and at the same time we evaluate the model's generalisation ability by comparing the model's performance in the training set and the test set. Overall, model training is a process of constantly adjusting model parameters, and this process requires making full use of the data set to evaluate model performance in order to obtain a well performing model with good generalisation ability.

3.4   Model Testing Strategies

The testing of machine learning models consists of two aspects: on the one hand, it refers to whether the model's performance on the training set is stable and the prediction results are up to the expected standard; on the other hand, it refers to whether the model trained on the training set has a good generalisation on the test data set. The performance of the model on the training set can indicate whether the model has sufficiently learned the rules hidden behind the training data, while the performance of the model on the test set can indicate whether the performance of the model can achieve stable performance on new data. Through several rounds of tuning the model parameters, we finally retained 34 feature variables as the final model features, and the KS values of the model on the training and test sets are 0.28 and 0.26, while the AUC values are 0.69 and 0.67, respectively.

The KS curves of the model on the training and test sets are shown in Fig. 1:

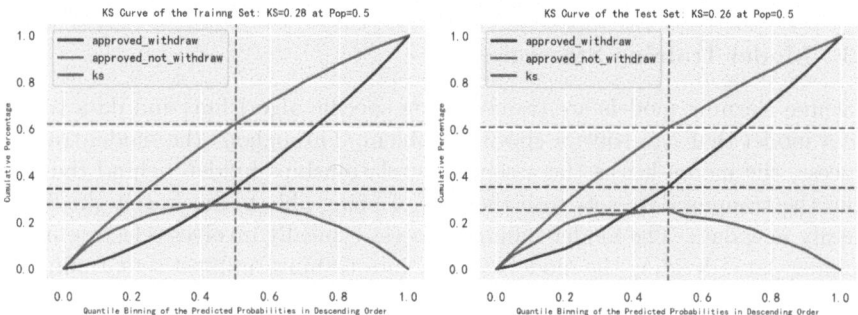

Fig. 1. KS curves of the training set and test set

The AUC curves of the model on the training and test sets are shown in Fig. 2:

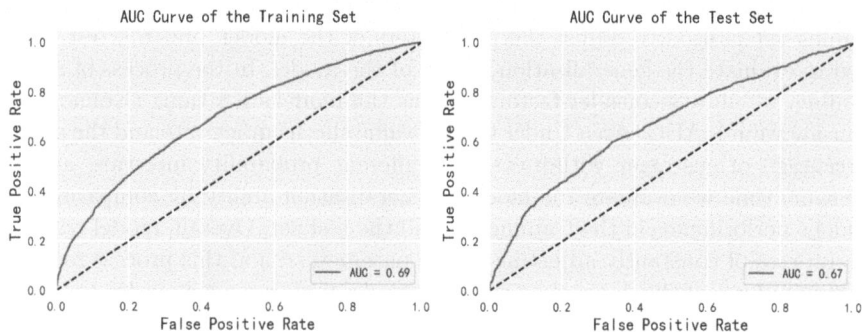

Fig. 2. AUC curves of the training set and test set

The probability of withdrawals in different probability intervals for training set customers and test set customers as shown in Fig. 3:

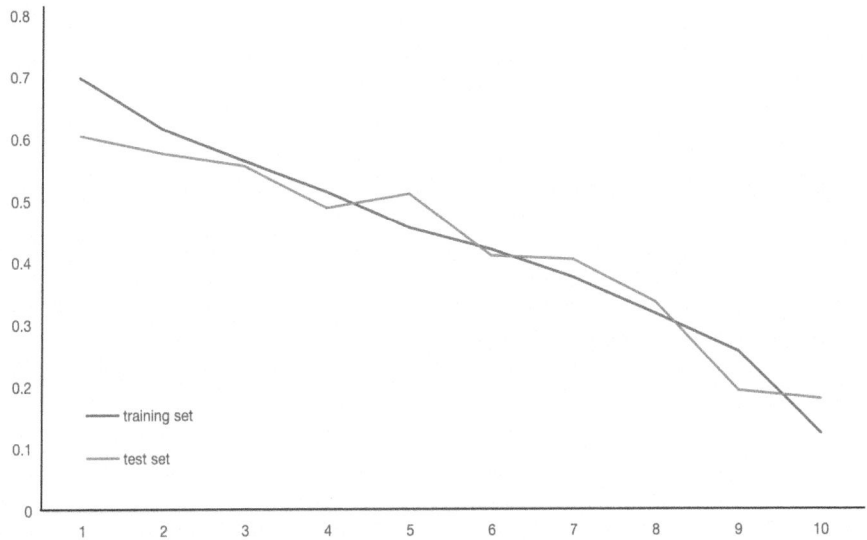

Fig. 3. Withdrawal probabilities for different probability intervals

From the perspective of model generalisation, the metrics of the training set and the test set are relatively close to each other, i.e. there is no obvious over-fitting phenomenon. The results are in line with expectations, and the model results can be practically applied. From the perspective of model metrics, the KS of the training set is about 0.28, with an accuracy of about 69%, and the KS of the test set is about 0.26, with an accuracy of about 67%, which is a little lower than expected, but can be worth trying to apply. From the perspective of the future extension space, we only use the credit data of the People's Bank of China (PBOC) and the credit data of three third party credit agencies, although the number of feature variables of the PBOC credit data is large, but the meanings of most of the feature variables are overlapping. There are more feature variables related to customers' credit risk, but fewer characteristic variables related to customers' willingness to withdraw money, so there is some room for improvement.

4 Applications

In this paper, the application of the retail credit risk pricing model has two aspects: firstly, we develop a differentiated pricing strategy for new customers based on their propensity to withdraw, and secondly, we remarket historically approved but underserved customers by lowering the credit price.

4.1 Differentiated Pricing Strategies

For credit customers with low withdrawal propensity, the price of credit products can be lowered to increase the turnover rate under the premise of protecting the credit risk of the customers, while for customers with high withdrawal propensity, the price of credit products can be raised under the premise of protecting the turnover rate and credit risk of the customers to increase the return of the customers, so as to achieve the effective distribution of funds and the optimal allocation of resources. In addition, for customers with poor credit qualifications, differentiated pricing can be used to allow more people to receive financial services, thus achieving the purpose of true financial inclusion.

From the Fig. 4, we can see that, overall, for retail credit customers in different willingness bands, customers' willingness to withdraw decreases and then slowly increases as the interest rate on the loan increases. However, customers' willingness to withdraw decreases rapidly when the interest rate increases from 16% to 17% and does not decrease with the increase in the interest rate when the interest rate is above 17%. That is to say, the lower the interest rate, the higher the willingness of customers to withdraw money, but once the interest rate level reaches a certain level, the willingness of customers to withdraw money no longer decreases as the interest rate rises, and even increases to a certain extent.

Generally speaking, the willingness of customers to withdraw has a correlation with their credit qualification, i.e. the better the credit qualification, the lower the willingness to withdraw, while the worse the credit qualification, the higher the willingness to withdraw. For customers with higher credit qualification, they have more channels to obtain credit products, so they are more sensitive to the interest rate of credit products, while for customers with lower credit qualification, they have fewer channels to obtain credit products, so they are not sensitive to the interest rate of credit products. In the past, during the stage of rough development, financial institutions usually offered low interest rate products to customers with better credit qualifications and high interest rate products to customers with poorer credit qualifications. Therefore, in the low interest rate band, the overall customer qualification is relatively good, and they are more sensitive to interest rates, so when the interest rate is raised, the probability of withdrawal is significantly reduced. However, when the interest rate is higher than a certain level, the customers' credit qualifications are relatively poor and they are not sensitive to interest rates, so when the interest rate is raised, the withdrawal rate of the customers does not decrease, but rather, it is raised to a certain extent. Thus, for customers in different willingness zones, the actual probability of withdrawal first decreases significantly when the interest rate level of the credit product goes from low to high, but then increases slightly when the interest rate rises to a certain level.

We know from detailed calculations that implementing a differentiated pricing strategy can increase the profitability of a single transactional customer by 15%.

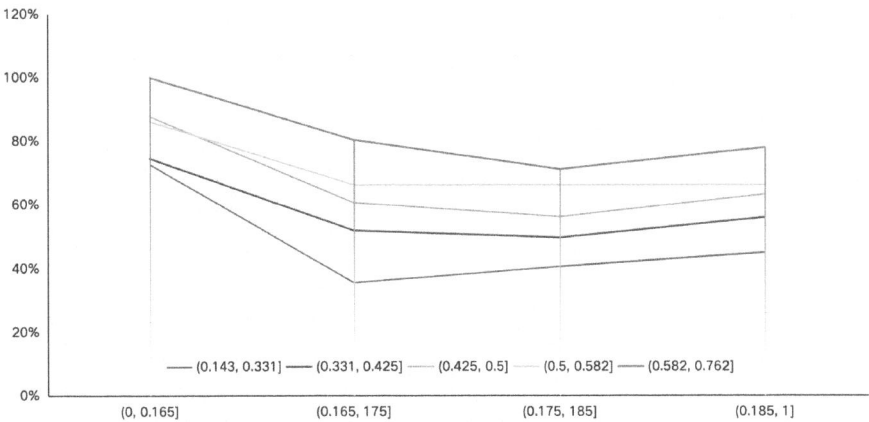

Fig. 4. Willingness to withdraw under different interest rate bands

4.2 Remarketing to Unwithdrawn Customers

For customers whose credit approvals have been passed, whether or not the customer actually takes out the loan is closely related to the price of the credit product. In the pass through case, the lower the price of the credit product, the higher the probability that the customer will complete the transaction and, conversely, the higher the price of the credit product, the lower the probability that the customer will draw down the loan.

For all 10,000 samples used to construct the retail credit risk pricing model, we divide them into five parts according to their withdrawal propensity, from low to high, and label them A1, A2, A3, A4 and A5. If we conduct secondary marketing for customers in groups A1, A2, and A3 who do not make withdrawals, and implement differentiated interest rates of 14%, 15%, and 16% for customers in groups A1, A2, and A3 who do not make withdrawals, and assume that they have response probabilities of 5%, 6%, and 7%, respectively, we can add ¥410,000, ¥350,000, and ¥320,000, respectively, to our additional profits. The overall withdrawal probability of customers in A4 and A5 is relatively high, and based on the results in Fig. 4, it can be seen that if we increase the effective interest rate for the interest rate insensitive customers in this segment, the withdrawal probability of customers does not decrease . For this group of customers, if we increase the effective interest rate by 1 per cent, it is calculated that this group of customers can increase their income by about ¥ 4,500,000.

5   Conclusions

In this paper, we describe the construction of a retail credit pricing model using the XGBoost machine learning algorithm. The entire model construction process includes identifying the model data, defining the prediction target of the model, dividing the model samples into training and test sets, performing feature variable screening, performing model training, performing model testing, and applying the model. However, this method of pricing retail credit risk only models the customer's propensity to withdraw and does not take into account corporate social responsibility and national policies. In fact, the pricing of credit products by financial institutions should not only consider the business cost, risk and necessary profit from their own actual situation, but also make the price acceptable to customers from the customers' point of view, and also consider the competitors' pricing strategy and the price level of the market.

References

1. Liu, X., Salem, S., Bian, L., Seong, J.T., Alshanbari, H.M.: Application of machine learning algorithms in the domain of financial engineering. Alexandria Eng. J. **95**, 94–100 (2024)
2. Nazareth, N., Reddy, Y.V.R.: Financial applications of machine learning: a literature review. Expert Syst. Appl. **219**, 119640 (2023)
3. Ponsiglione, A.M., et al.: Combining simulation models and machine learning in healthcare management: strategies and applications. Prog. Biomed. Eng. **6**(2), 022001 (2024)
4. Yaghoobpoor, S., et al.: Machine learning approaches in the prediction of positive axillary lymph nodes post neoadjuvant chemotherapy using MRI, CT, or ultrasound: a systematic review. Eur. J. Radiol. Open **12**, 100561 (2024)
5. Agarwal, S., Gupta, S., Kachroo, P., Dhingra, N.: A machine learning based approach for smart and automated data collection: applications in transportation. Transport. Dev. Econ. **10**(1), 15 (2024)
6. Durlik, I., Miller, T., Dorobczyński, L., Kozlovska, P., Kostecki, T.: Revolutionizing marine traffic management: a comprehensive review of machine learning applications in complex maritime systems. Appl. Sci. **13**, 8099 (2023)
7. Wu, C.W., et al.: Recognition of glaucomatous fundus images using machine learning methods based on optic nerve head topographic features. J. Glaucoma, 10-1097 (2024)
8. Li, H., Li, R.W., Shu, P., Li, Y.Q.: Machine learning-based identification of contaminated images in light curve data preprocessing. Res. Astron. Astrophys. **24**(4), 045025 (2024)
9. Singh, K.N., Mantri, J.K.: An intelligent recommender system using machine learning association rules and rough set for disease prediction from incomplete symptom set. Decis. Anal. J. **11**, 100468 (2024)
10. Qian, R., et al.: Predictive value of machine learning for the severity of acute pancreatitis: a systematic review and meta-analysis. Heliyon **10**, e29603 (2024)
11. Xie, F., Wang, H., Ni, S., An, C.: Efficiency optimization control of permanent magnet synchronous motors for pure electric vehicles based on GBDT. J. Power Electron. **24**(2), 215–226 (2024)
12. Zhang, G.: Application of project-based learning model based on GBDT model in higher vocational civics classes at the time of innovation. Appl. Math. Nonlinear Sci. **9** (2024)
13. Chen, T., Guestrin, C.: XGBoost: a scalable tree boosting system. CoRR arxiv:1603.02754 (2016)

14. Wu, Z., Zhao, J., Li, Y., Wang, Z., He, B., Chen, L.: A GAN-BO-XGBoost model for high-quality patents identification. Sci. Rep. **14**(1), 9560 (2024)
15. Ke, G., et al.: LightGBM: a highly efficient gradient boosting decision tree. Neural Inf. Process. Syst. (2017)
16. Lu, Y., Wang, J., Wang, D., Yoo, C., Liu, H.: Incorporating temporal multi-head self-attention convolutional networks and LightGBM for indoor air quality prediction. Appl. Soft Comput. **157**, 111569 (2024)
17. Zhou, B., Yuan, Y., Song, Q.: A proximal forward-backward splitting based algorithmic framework for Wasserstein logistic regression using heavy ball strategy. Int. J. Syst. Sci. **55**(4), 644–657 (2024)
18. Huang, Y.: Analysis of the impact of ADDIE education model based on logistic regression model on teaching contemporary cultural and creative product design. Appl. Math. Nonlinear Sci. **9** (2024)
19. Binns, M., Usai, A., Theodoropoulos, C.: Identifiability methods for biological systems: determining subsets of parameters through sensitivity analysis, penalty-based optimisation, profile likelihood and LASSO model reduction. Comput. Chem. Eng. **186**, 108683 (2024)
20. Han, D., Modisette, V., Forthofer, M., Paul, R.: Hierarchical Bayesian adaptive lasso methods on exponential random graph models. Appl. Netw. Sci. **9**(1), 9 (2024)
21. Han, F., Cheng, C.: The innovation path of virtual practice teaching in college Civics class based on the Ridge regression model. Appl. Math. Nonlinear Sci. **9** (2024)
22. Selman, M., Özge, A., Atila, G., Necla, G.: A new robust ridge parameter estimator having no outlier and ensuring normality for linear regression modele. J. Radiat. Res. Appl. Sci. **17**, 100788 (2024)
23. Coskun, T., Murat, D.: Constructing early warning indicators for banks using machine learning models. North Am. J. Econ. Finan. **69**, 102018 (2024)
24. Gaurav, K., Ramizur, R.M., Abhinav, R., Kumar, M.A.: Predicting systemic risk of banks: a machine learning approach. J. Model. Manag. **19**, 441–469 (2024)
25. Nguyen, L.Q.T., Matousek, R., Muradoglu, G.: Bank capital, liquidity creation and the moderating role of bank culture: an investigation using a machine learning approach. J. Finan. Stabil. **72**, 101265 (2024)
26. Li, X., et al.: An improved method for broiler weight estimation integrating multi-feature with gradient boosting decision tree. Animals **13**(23), 3721 (2023)
27. Ait Naceur, H., Abdo, H.G., Igmoullan, B., Namous, M., Alshehri, F., Albanai, J.A.: Implementation of random forest, adaptive boosting, and gradient boosting decision trees algorithms for gully erosion susceptibility mapping using remote sensing and GIS. Environ. Earth Sci. **83**(3), 121 (2024)
28. Dacko, M., Oleksy, A., Synowiec, A., Klimek-Kopyra, A., Kulig, B., Zajac, T.: Plant-architectural and environmental predictors of seed mass of winter oilseed rape in southern Poland based on the CART trees regression model. Ind. Crops Prod. **192**, 116109 (2023)
29. Sharma, D.N., Iqbal, S.I.M.: Applying decision tree algorithm classification and regression tree (CART) algorithm to gini techniques binary splits. Int. J. Eng. Adv. Technol. **12**(5), 77–81 (2023)
30. Zhang, S., Hu, Y., Tan, Z.: Research on borrower's credit classification of P2P network loan based on LightGBM algorithm. IJES **11**, 602–612 (2019)
31. Guo, Q., et al.: Mobile user credit prediction based on LightGBM. In: Proceedings of 2019 International Conference on Big Data, Electronics and Communication Engineering (BDECE 2019) (2019)

32. Mao, X., et al.: A variable weight combination prediction model for climate in a greenhouse based on BiGRU-Attention and LightGBM. Comput. Electron. Agric. **219**, 108818 (2024)
33. Lahiri, A., Paria, B., Biswas, P.K.: Forward stagewise additive model for collaborative multiview boosting. IEEE Trans. Neural Netw. Learn. Syst. **29**(2), 470–485 (2016)
34. Zhong, W., Duan, S., Zhu, L.: Forward additive regression for ultrahigh-dimensional nonparametric additive models. Stat. Sin. **30**(1), 175–192 (2020)
35. Telea, A., Machado, A., Wang, Y.: Seeing is learning in high dimensions: the synergy between dimensionality reduction and machine learning. SN Comput. Sci. **5**(3), 279 (2024)
36. Tan, W.G.Y., Xiao, M., Wu, Z.: Robust reduced-order machine learning modeling of high-dimensional nonlinear processes using noisy data. Dig. Chem. Eng. **11**, 100145 (2024)
37. Hiyama, K., Takeuchi, K., Omodaka, Y., Srisamranrungruang, T.: Operation strategy for engineered natural ventilation using machine learning under sparse data conditions. Jpn. Arch. Rev. **5**(1), 119–126 (2022)
38. Chen, X., Chen, H., Nan, S., Kong, X., Duan, H., Zhu, H.: Dealing with missing, imbalanced, and sparse features during the development of a prediction model for sudden death using emergency medicine data: machine learning approach. JMIR Med. Inf. **11**, e38590 (2023)
39. Zhang, L., Csányi, G., van der Giessen, E., Maresca, F.: Efficiency, accuracy, and transferability of machine learning potentials: application to dislocations and cracks in iron. Acta Mater. **270**, 119788 (2024)
40. Chao, B, Zhang, Z.: Research on overfitting problem and correction in machine learning. In: Journal of Physics: Conference Series, vol. 1693, p. 012100 (2020)
41. Salam, M.A., Azar, A.T., Elgendy, M.S., Fouad, K.M.: The effect of different dimensionality reduction techniques on machine learning overfitting problem. Int. J. Adv. Comput. Sci. Appl. **12**(4), 641–655 (2021)
42. Presciuttini, A., Cantini, A., Costa, F., Portioli-Staudacher, A.: Machine learning applications on IoT data in manufacturing operations and their interpretability implications: a systematic literature review. J. Manuf. Syst. **74**, 477–486 (2024)
43. Baur, L., et al.: Explainability and interpretability in electric load forecasting using machine learning techniques–a review. Energy AI **16**, 100358 (2024)
44. Wen, H.T., Wu, H.Y., Liao, K.C.: Using XGBoost regression to analyze the importance of input features applied to an artificial intelligence model for the biomass gasification system. Inventions **7**(4), 126 (2022)
45. Song, T., Yan, Q., Fan, C., Meng, J., Wu, Y., Zhang, J.: Significant wave height retrieval using XGBoost from polarimetric Gaofen-3 SAR and feature importance analysis. Remote Sens. **15**(1), 149 (2022)
46. Jovanovic, L., et al.: Improving phishing website detection using a hybrid two-level framework for feature selection and xgboost tuning. J. Web Eng. **22**(3), 543–574 (2023)
47. Abbas, Z., ur Rehman, M., Tayara, H., Zou, Q., Chong, K.T.: XGBoost framework with feature selection for the prediction of RNA N5-methylcytosine sites. Molec. Therapy J. Am. Soc. Gene Therapy **31**(8), 2543–2551 (2023)

Physical Layer

A Cooperative Spectrum Sensing Method Based on Feature Extraction and Fusion Clustering

Jian Li, Yue Li$^{(\boxtimes)}$, and Xiaoxu Chen

Heilongjiang University, Harbin 150080, China
2017021@hlju.edu.cn

Abstract. To improve the performance of spectrum sensing at low SNR, a collaborative spectrum sensing method based on feature extraction and fusion clustering is proposed (FEFC). First, the sampling matrix of the received signal is vectorially decomposed to obtain the I and Q component signals. Second, Cholesky decomposition is applied to the covariance matrices of the I and Q signals to fully extract their features and construct the two dimensional feature vectors. The K-Means clustering algorithm is used to optimize the initial parameters of the Gaussian Mixture Model (GMM), effectively preventing it from falling into local minima under low SNR. Finally, the feature vectors of the signals are classified using GMM clustering optimized by the K-Means algorithm to obtain the final spectrum sensing results. Simulation results show that this method reduces the convergence time of GMM and improves the accuracy of model classification. It effectively enhances the performance of spectrum sensing compared to other mainstream methods.

Keywords: cooperative spectrum sensing · Cholesky · K-Means · Gaussian mixture model

1 Introduction

In recent years, the rapid development of wireless communications and the surge in spectrum demand have outpaced the available spectrum resources, which can no longer meet user needs. Cognitive Radio (CR) technology is a key solution to alleviate spectrum resource scarcity. This technology intelligently detects unused frequency bands, efficiently allocates and fully utilizes spectrum resources, and enhances band utilization. Traditional spectrum sensing techniques include Energy Detection (ED), Matched Filter (MF) detection, and

This work was supported in part by Heilongjiang provincial Internet of things perception layer and sensor network technology innovation service platform, and in part by the Basic scientific research project of Heilongjiang province [grant number 2020-KYYWF-1003].

Cyclostationary Feature (CF) detection [1]. However, traditional spectrum sensing techniques have shortcomings. For example, ED cannot distinguish between signal and noise at low SNR [2]. MF requires prior knowledge of the primary user signal and the channel response [3]. CF is characterized by high complexity and latency [4]. Stochastic theory based and machine learning based methods are employed for spectrum sensing.

1.1   Random Matrix Theory Based Approaches

Spectrum sensing schemes based on random matrix theory have been applied [5], such as Ratio of Maximum and Minimum Eigenvalue (MME), Difference between the Maximum Eigenvalue and the Average Eigenvalues (DMEAE), Difference of Maximum and Minimum Eigenvalues (DMM), and Ratio between Maximum Eigenvalue and the Trace (RMET). These blind spectrum sensing methods extract eigenvalues from the received signal covariance matrix to obtain statistical properties, without requiring any prior information about the PU signal and noise variance. However, these schemes require the calculation of precise judgment thresholds in practice.

1.2   Machine Learning Based Approaches

Machine Learning (ML) based spectrum sensing techniques avoid the issue of judgment threshold calculation [6]. Recent studies have combined covariance based spectrum sensing techniques with ML by extracting eigenvalues from the covariance matrix to generate a training set, thus obtaining a spectrum sensing model. An unsupervised spectrum sensing technique based on K-Means, using the MME of the covariance matrix as the training input for the classifier [7]. In [8], eigenvalues are extracted through the covariance matrix after I Q decomposition and a perception scheme based on K-Means clustering is analyzed with different statistical properties. In [9], eigenvalue computation are realized using the Decomposition and Reorganization (DAR) method for random matrices, increasing the amount of SUs from the theoretical derivation by constructing two covariance submatrices. In [10], the received signal is first preprocessed to generate a feature vector, which is then classified using a Support Vector Machine (SVM), and this approach ultimately yields an effective spectrum sensing result.

1.3   Our Contributions

In order to solve the problem of poor sensing ability and inaccurate threshold estimation at low SNR in traditional spectrum sensing system. This paper proposes a cooperative spectrum sensing method based on feature extraction and fusion clustering (FEFC). The main components are as follows:

1. Vector decomposition is performed on the acquired signals to obtain I and Q components.

2. Construct the I and Q signals feature matrices, and use Cholesky to decompose the feature matrices to fully extract the features of the signals and construct two dimensional feature vectors.
3. Optimization of the GMM using the K-Means algorithm can effectively prevent the GMM from falling into local minima at low SNR, thus improving the performance of spectrum sensing under low SNR conditions.

In the experimental part, we compare the method of this paper with other spectrum sensing methods. Experimental results show that the algorithm avoids the setting of classification thresholds and exhibits good perceptual performance at low SNR compared to traditional algorithms, and the improvement in perceptual performance is more significant in the case of fewer secondary users.

2   System Model

In cognitive radio, the secondary user (SU) senses the primary user (PU) signal, which is easily affected by multipath effects, shadowing, and channel fading, increasing the detection difficulty. To address this, a multiuser collaborative spectrum sensing model is proposed. Signal sensing through multiple users and paths reduces environmental influences and improves system performance. The model is illustrated in Fig. 1.

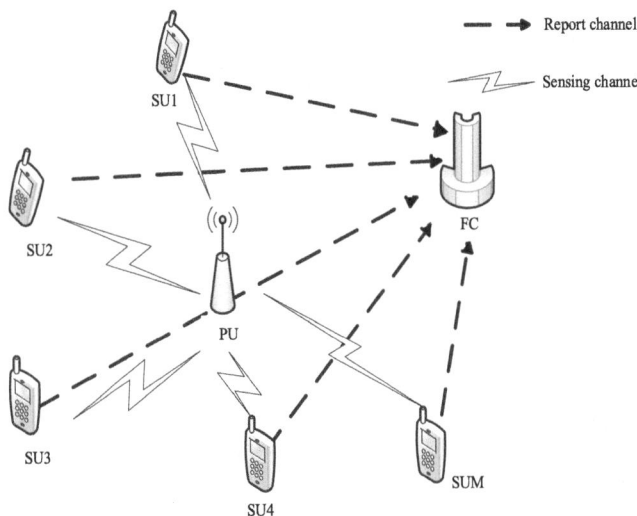

Fig. 1. Cooperative spectrum sensing model

The cognitive radio network consists of 1 PU and M SUs. The detection of the PU signal by the SU can be expressed as a binary hypothesis model.

$$x(t) = \begin{cases} w(t), & H_0 \\ s(t) + w(t), & H_1 \end{cases} \tag{1}$$

In Eq. (1), $x(t)$ represents the received signal of the SU at time t, $s(t)$ represents the PU signal at time t, and $w(t)$ represents additive Gaussian white noise with a mean of 0 and a variance of δ_x^2. The PU signal and the noise are independently distributed. H_0 indicates that the PU signal is absent, while H_1 indicates that the PU signal is present. Assuming $S=0$ and $S=1$ correspond to the channel's available states, respectively, they can be represented as:

$$S = \begin{cases} 0, H_0 \\ 1, H_1 \end{cases} \tag{2}$$

Thus, the false alarm probability (P_f) and the detection probability (P_d) are defined as:

$$\begin{aligned} P_f &= p[S = 1 \, S = 0] \\ P_d &= p[S = 1 \, S = 1] \end{aligned} \tag{3}$$

In a spectrum sensing system, the signals sensed by M SUs form a vector matrix $X = [\boldsymbol{x}_1, \boldsymbol{x}_2, ..., \boldsymbol{x}_M]^T$, where the signal sensed by the mth SU is $\boldsymbol{x}_m = [\boldsymbol{x}_m(1), \boldsymbol{x}_m(2), ..., \boldsymbol{x}_m(N)]$, and N is the number of samples. This results in an $M \times N$ dimensional signal matrix.

$$\mathbf{X} = [\boldsymbol{x}_1, \boldsymbol{x}_2, ..., \boldsymbol{x}_M]^T = \begin{bmatrix} x_1(1) & x_1(2) & \cdots & x_1(N) \\ x_2(1) & x_2(2) & \cdots & x_2(N) \\ \vdots & \vdots & \ddots & \vdots \\ x_M(1) & x_M(2) & \cdots & x_M(N) \end{bmatrix} \tag{4}$$

3   Feature Extraction

3.1   Signal Decomposition

In signal analysis, the signal is typically decomposed into two components with the same peak amplitude and frequency but with a 90° phase difference, known as I Q decomposition. This method provides a comprehensive description of the signal's amplitude, frequency, and phase. To fully utilize the received signal information, the signal matrix X is vectorially decomposed:

$$\begin{aligned} X^I &= \sin(\tfrac{2\pi f_c n}{f_s})X \\ X^Q &= \cos(\tfrac{2\pi f_c n}{f_s})X \end{aligned} \tag{5}$$

In Eq. (5), f_c and f_s denote the carrier frequency and sampling frequency, respectively. Thus, the signal matrix X is vectorially decomposed into two $M \times N$ signal matrices:

$$X^I = \begin{bmatrix} x_1^I(1) & x_1^I(2) & \cdots & x_1^I(N) \\ x_2^I(1) & x_2^I(2) & \cdots & x_2^I(N) \\ \vdots & \vdots & \ddots & \vdots \\ x_M^I(1) & x_M^I(2) & \cdots & x_M^I(N) \end{bmatrix} \tag{6}$$

$$X^Q = \begin{bmatrix} x_1^Q(1) & x_1^Q(2) & \cdots & x_1^Q(N) \\ x_2^Q(1) & x_2^Q(2) & \cdots & x_2^Q(N) \\ \vdots & \vdots & \ddots & \vdots \\ x_M^Q(1) & x_M^Q(2) & \cdots & x_M^Q(N) \end{bmatrix} \tag{7}$$

3.2   Feature Extraction

Using the X^I and X^Q matrices from Eq. (6) and (7), we can calculate the corresponding covariance matrices R^I and R^Q as follows:

$$R^I = \tfrac{1}{N} X^I (X^I)^H$$
$$R^Q = \tfrac{1}{N} X^Q (X^Q)^H \tag{8}$$

In Eq. (8), $(\cdot)^H$ represents the conjugate transpose operation, and the covariance matrices R^I and R^Q are both $M \times M$ dimensional. Next, the two matrices undergo Cholesky decomposition, as shown in Eq. (9).

$$R^I = Y^I (Y^I)^T$$
$$R^Q = Y^Q (Y^Q)^T \tag{9}$$

Both Y^I and Y^Q are lower triangular matrices, expressed as:

$$Y^I = \begin{bmatrix} y_{11}^I & 0 & \cdots & 0 \\ y_{21}^I & y_{22}^I & \cdots & 0 \\ \vdots & \vdots & \ddots & \vdots \\ y_{M1}^I & y_{M2}^I & \cdots & y_{MM}^I \end{bmatrix} \tag{10}$$

$$Y^Q = \begin{bmatrix} y_{11}^Q & 0 & \cdots & 0 \\ y_{21}^Q & y_{22}^Q & \cdots & 0 \\ \vdots & \vdots & \ddots & \vdots \\ y_{M1}^Q & y_{M2}^Q & \cdots & y_{MM}^Q \end{bmatrix} \tag{11}$$

The signal features G^I are extracted using the lower triangular matrix Y^I after Cholesky decomposition, represented by Eq. (12) as follows:

$$G^I = \frac{\sum_{1 \leq i \leq j \leq M} | y_{ij}^I |}{\sum_{1 \leq i \leq M} | y_{ii}^I |} \tag{12}$$

$y_{ij}^I \geq 0$ is calculated by Eq. (13).

$$\begin{cases} y_{ij}^I = \sqrt{\left(r_{ij}^I - \sum_{k=1}^{i-1}\left(y_{ki}^I\right)^2\right)} & i = j \\ y_{ij}^I = \left[r_{ij}^I - \sum_{k=1}^{j-1}\left(y_{ki}^I y_{kj}^I\right)\right] /y_{jj}^I & i > j \end{cases} \tag{13}$$

where r_{ij}^I represents the element in the ith row and jth column of matrix R^I. Similarly, Cholesky decomposition of the covariance matrix Y^Q is performed, and the signal feature G^Q is extracted, represented as:

$$G^Q = \frac{\sum_{1 \leq i \leq j \leq M} | y_{ij}^Q |}{\sum_{1 \leq i \leq M} | y_{ii}^Q |} \tag{14}$$

Thus, based on G^Q and G^Q, the two dimensional feature vector G of the signal can be constructed.

$$G = [G^I, G^Q] \tag{15}$$

Since many training feature vectors are needed to train the clustering algorithm, all training feature vectors **G** must first be constructed as a training feature vector set $\tilde{G}$:

$$\tilde{G} = \{G_1, G_2, ..., G_B\} \tag{16}$$

where G_b ($b = 1, 2, \ldots, B$) is the two dimensional feature vector computed in Eq. (16), and B denotes the number of feature vectors in the training set.

4   A Fusion Clustering-Based Approach to Spectrum Sensing

In this paper, the K-Means clustering algorithm is used to optimize the initial parameters of the Gaussian Mixture Model (GMM), effectively preventing it from falling into local minima under low SNR. The optimized GMM model is then used to classify the constructed signal feature vectors, yielding the spectrum sensing results. Figure 2 shows the system modeling based on the fusion clustering algorithm.

4.1   Training Process of K-Means Clustering Algorithm

For the input set of training feature vectors $\tilde{G} = \{G_1, G_2, ..., G_B\}$, the K-Means clustering algorithm divides the set into multiple clusters. The objective function of the K-Means clustering algorithm is as follows:

$$J = \sum_{i=1}^{k} \sum_{G_b \in C_i} \|G_b - \beta_i\|^2 \tag{17}$$

Here, k is the number of clustering centers, which is set to 2. C_i represents the ith cluster, G_b denotes the sample points in the C_i cluster, and β_i is the center

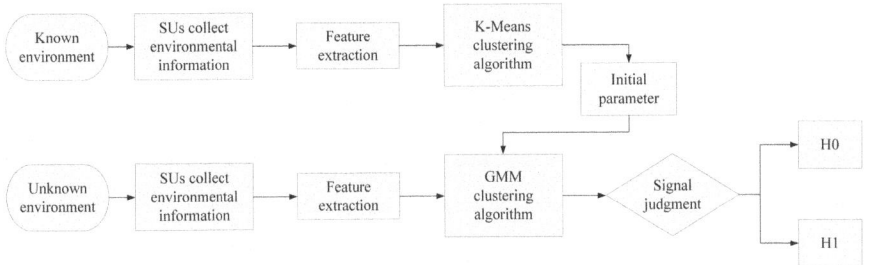

Fig. 2. System modeling based on fusion clustering algorithm

of mass of C_i. The final division of clusters is achieved when the iterative results of the algorithm no longer produce significant changes. At this point, the optimal center of mass β_k^{ψ} is calculated using Eq. (18).

$$\beta_k^{\psi} = \frac{1}{|C_k|} \sum_{G_b \in C_k} G_b \tag{18}$$

In the final clustering result, cluster k contains B_k data points out of a total of B data points. The weight of the cluster corresponding to the best quality center is calculated using Eq. (19):

$$\alpha_k^{\psi} = \frac{B_k}{B} \tag{19}$$

The corresponding covariance matrix of the corresponding K-Means is as follows:

$$\Sigma_k^{\psi} = \frac{1}{N_k - 1} \sum_{i=1}^{B_k} (G_i - \beta_k^{\psi})(G_i - \beta_k^{\psi})^T \tag{20}$$

4.2   Training Process of Fusion Clustering Algorithm

The GMM clustering algorithm is initialized using the optimal centroids, weights, and covariance matrices obtained from the convergence of the K-Means clustering algorithm. The GMM measures the affiliation category of each data point in terms of probability, with its probability density distribution given by the following form:

$$q(G) = \sum_{k=1}^{K} \pi_k \mathcal{N}(G|\mu_k, \Sigma_k), \sum_{k=1}^{K} \pi_k = 1 \tag{21}$$

where K is the number of models, π_k denotes the mixture weights, $\mathcal{N}(G|\mu_k, \Sigma_k)$ denotes the kth Gaussian distribution, μ_k is the mean vector, Σ_k is the covariance matrix of the GMM, and the D-dimensional Gaussian distribution takes the following form:

$$\mathcal{N}(G \mid \mu_k, \Sigma_k) = \frac{1}{(2\pi)^{D/2}} \frac{1}{|\Sigma_k|^{1/2}} \exp\left\{ -\frac{1}{2}(G - \mu_k)^T \Sigma_k^{-1}(G - \mu_k) \right\} \tag{22}$$

The GMM determines the parameters of each distribution using the maximum likelihood function, which is formulated as follows:

$$\ln q(G|\pi, \mu, \Sigma) = \sum_{b=1}^{B} \ln(\sum_{k=1}^{K} \pi_k \mathcal{N}(G_b|\mu_k, \Sigma_k)) \qquad (23)$$

The maximum likelihood function is solved using the Expectation -Maximization algorithm (EM), and the specific implementation process is shown in Table 1:

Table 1. GMM Expectation-Maximization algorithm

Expectation-Maximization algorithm steps
Step 1   Use the K-Means clustering algorithm to initialize the GMM algorithm
$\mu_k = \beta_k^\psi, \Sigma_k = \Sigma_k^\psi, \pi_k = \alpha_k^\psi$
Step 2   Desired Steps :
$\gamma(z_k \mid G_b) = \frac{\pi_k \mathcal{N}(G_b|\mu_k, \Sigma_k)}{\sum_{j=1}^{k} \pi_j \mathcal{N}(G_b|\mu_j, \Sigma_j)}$
Step 3   Maximization step:
$\mu_k = \frac{1}{B} \sum_{b=1}^{B} \gamma(z_k \mid G_b) G_b$
$\Sigma_k = \frac{1}{B} \sum_{b=1}^{B} \gamma(z_k \mid G_b)(G_b - \mu_k)(G_b - \mu_k)^{\mathrm{T}}$
$\pi_k = \frac{B_k}{B}$
$B_k = \sum_{b=1}^{B} \gamma(z_k|G_b)$
Step 4   until the parameters converge, otherwise return to step 2.

4.3   Perceptual Decision

The optimal solutions $(\mu_k^*, \Sigma_k^*, \pi_k^*)$ for the relevant parameters of the $\tilde{G}$ training vectors are obtained using Expectation-Maximization algorithm. The test vectors are then partitioned using the final clustering model, represented by the following mathematical model of perceptual judgment:

$$\omega = \ln \frac{\pi_1^* N(Q|\mu_1^*, \Sigma_1^*)}{\pi_2^* N(Q|\mu_2^*, \Sigma_2^*)} \qquad (24)$$

In the above equation, Q is the test vector, ω denotes the detection probability, and β is the threshold which controls the false alarm probability P_f. The detection and judgment process does not require retraining the model. If $\omega > \beta$, the judgment is H_1. Here, H_0 and H_1 denote channel unavailability and availability.

4.4   Complexity Analysis

The model training time overhead of this paper's approach consists of the computation of the covariance matrix, the feature extraction and the computation of fusion clustering,the complexities are $O(M^2N)$, $O(M^3)+O(M^2)$ and

Table 2. Comparison of complexity of different methods

Methods	Complexity
DMM+IQ	$O(N^2L) + O(M^3) + O(CdL)$
DMEAE+DAR	$O(M^2L) + O(M^3) + O(CdL)$
GMM	$O(M^2N) + O(M^3) + O(M^2) + O(CdL + CL) + O(2CdL)$
FEFC	$O(M^2N) + O(M^3) + O(M^2) + O(CdL) + O(2CdL)$

$O(CdL) + O(2CdL)$, where d denotes the dimension, C is the number of clustering centers and L is the length of the training data.

We also compare the complexity of the method in this paper with other methods with better performance, as shown in Table 2. The clustering method in this paper has lower complexity compared to traditional GMM clustering, comparing with the other two algorithms, the complexity of this paper's method is higher, but the proposed method has better detection performance due to the use of GMM clustering.

5   Simulation Experiments

To demonstrate the spectrum sensing performance of the proposed method, its performance is analyzed through MATLAB simulations and compared with other spectrum sensing techniques. To ensure the accuracy and reliability of the experimental results, the simulated primary user signal used in the experiments is a BPSK signal, with a signal activity probability of 0.5. Additionally, a flat Rayleigh fading channel is assumed between the primary user (PU) and the secondary user (SU). The noise is an additive white Gaussian noise (AWGN) signal with a mean of 0 and a variance of 1, and it is independently distributed with ideal Gaussian white noise. Experimentally, 2000 signal feature vectors were extracted for clustering to obtain a classification model, and another 1000 signal feature vectors were extracted to analyze the perceptual performance of the model.

5.1   Classification Effect Based on Feature Extraction and Fusion Clustering

Figure 3 shows 2000 feature vectors that have not been classified by the clustering algorithm, with 1000 being noise feature vectors and the remaining 1000 being signal plus noise feature vectors. Figure 4 shows the results of clustering 2000 feature vectors using the proposed method. In the figure, red indicates the channel available class, while blue represents the channel unavailable class.

5.2   Spectrum Sensing Performance Comparison

Figure 5 compares the channel classification accuracy of the proposed fusion clustering method with traditional GMM clustering at different SNR. The SNR

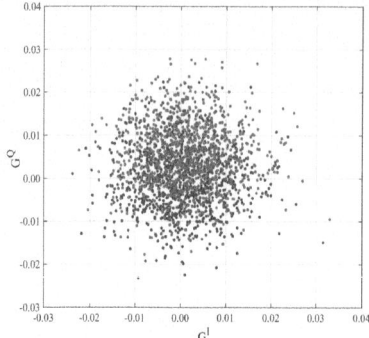 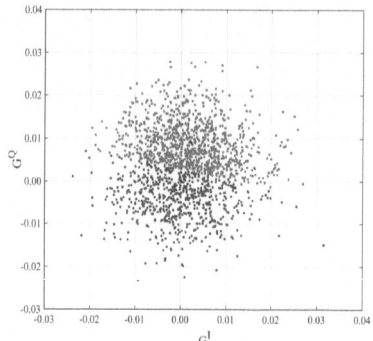

Fig. 3. Raw signal feature vector (Color figure online)

Fig. 4. Clustered signal feature vector (Color figure online)

was varied from -20 dB to -6 dB, with the number of SUs $M = 5$ and the number of samples $N=2000$. From the figure, it can be seen that the classification accuracy of this paper's algorithm is close to 100% when $SNR = -8$ dB, 97.6% when $SNR = -10$ dB, and 62.75% in the worse environment with SNR of -20 dB. When the SNR is higher than -10 dB, the accuracy of the two algorithms in the figure is comparable. However, when the SNR is lower than -12 dB, the classification accuracy of the proposed method is significantly better than that of traditional GMM clustering.

To evaluate the performance of our proposed method, we compare it with other mainstream spectrum sensing techniques, including the Maximum to Minimum Eigenvalue ratio (MME), the Difference between Maximum and Minimum Eigenvalues (DMM), and the Ratio of Maximum Eigenvalue to Trace (RMET).

Figure 6 shows the spectrum sensing performance of various algorithms with the number of SUs $M = 5$, the SNR is set to be -12 dB and the number of samples N equals 2000. When the false alarm probability P_f is 0.1, the detection probability P_d reaches 89%, representing a 9% improvement over the DMM based K-Means clustering method. Figure 7 shows the spectrum sensing performance of various algorithms at an SNR of -14 dB. When the false alarm probability P_f is 0.1, the detection probability P_d reaches 78.5%, representing an 8% improvement over the DMM based K-Means clustering method.

Figure 8 shows the performance analysis of different number of SU with $SNR = -16$ dB and $N = 2000$. From Fig. 8, it can be seen that the number of secondary SUs M is highly related to the detection probability of the algorithm, and the perceived performance of the FEFC algorithm improves with the increase of M.

Figure 9 shows the performance analysis of different sampling points with $SNR = -16$ dB and $M = 5$. From Fig. 9, it can be seen that the perceptual performance of the FEFC algorithm improves with the increase in the number of sampling points.

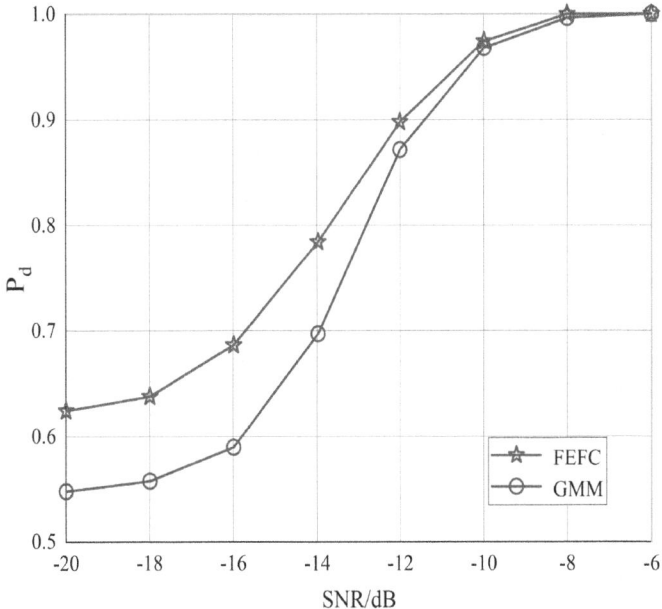

Fig. 5. Comparison of classification accuracy

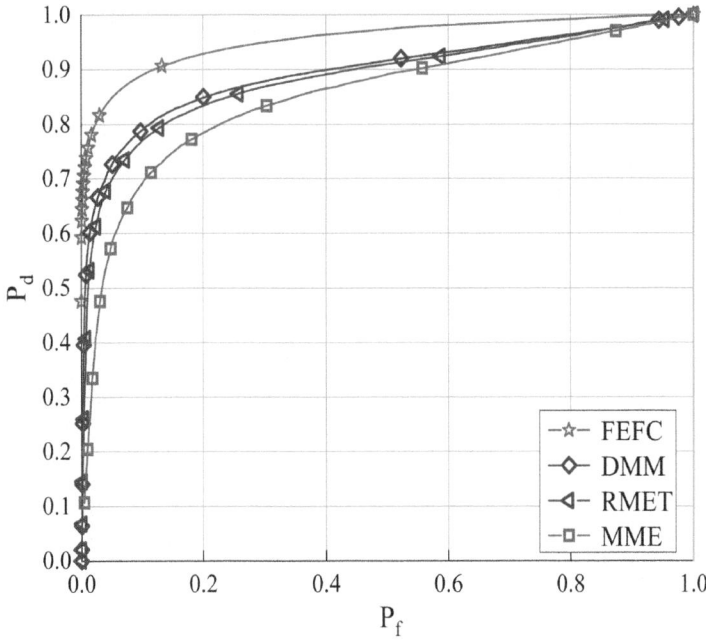

Fig. 6. ROC curves for each algorithm with $SNR = -12$ dB and $M = 5$

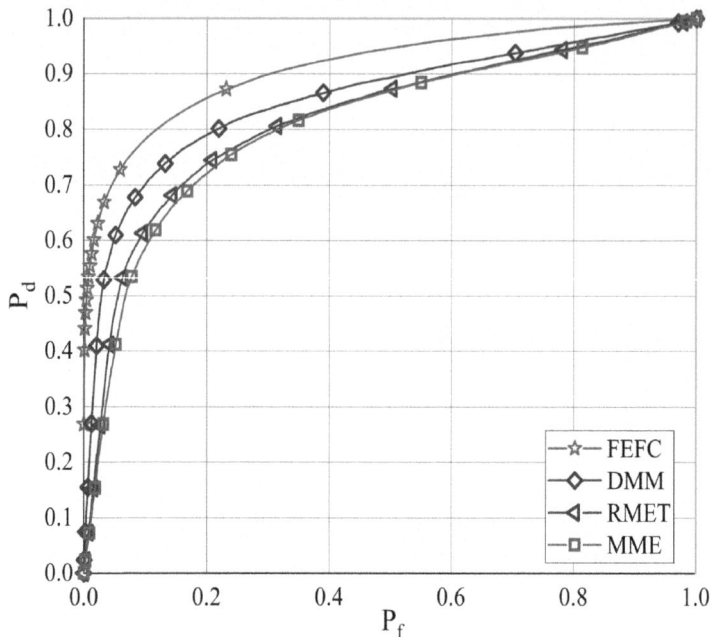

Fig. 7. ROC curves for each algorithm with $SNR = -14$ dB and $M = 5$

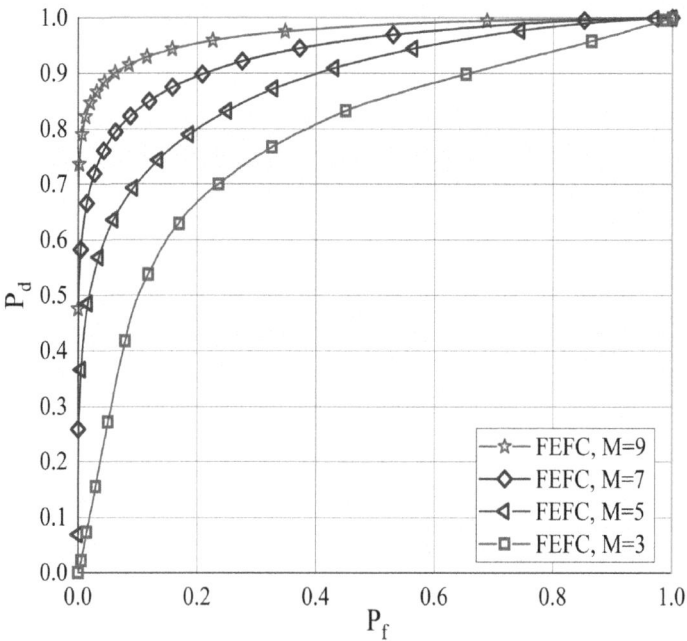

Fig. 8. Performance analysis of different number of SU with $SNR = -16$ dB

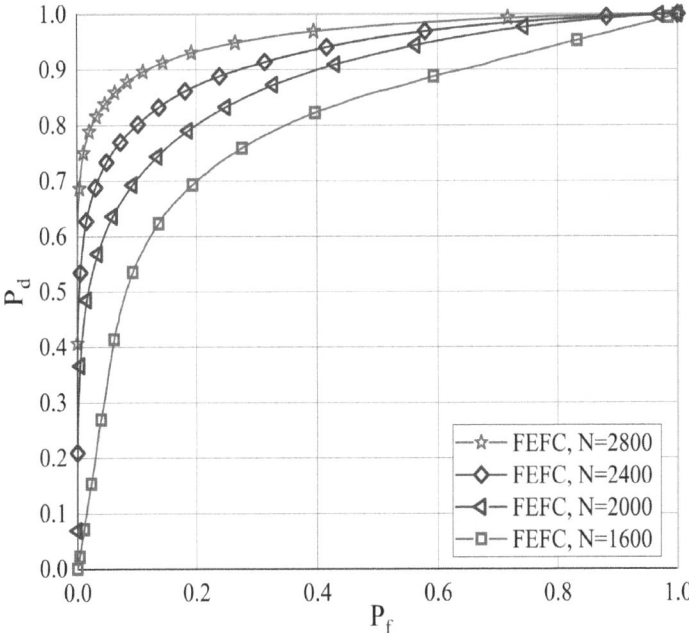

Fig. 9. Performance analysis of different sampling points with $SNR = -16$ dB

The experimental results indicate that the detection performance of the method proposed in this paper is significantly improved compared to other spectrum sensing methods across a range of SNR.

5.3   Conclusions

This paper proposes a spectrum sensing method based on feature extraction and fusion clustering to address spectrum sensing problem under low SNR conditions. First, the sampling matrix of the received signal is vectorially decomposed to obtain the I and Q component signals. Then, the information of the signal matrix is fully extracted using the cholesky decomposition of the covariance matrix of the I and Q signals. Finally, the GMM model, optimized by the K-Means algorithm, is used to classify the signal samples and determine the channel state. Simulation results indicate that the algorithm exhibits good perceptual performance. In this paper, we have not considered the problem of forging data by malicious users in the system, which can generate outliers and thus affect the performance of clustering, and further research will be conducted on this issue in the subsequent work.

References

1. Digham, F.F., Alouini, M.S., Simon, M.K.: On the energy detection of unknown signals over fading channels. IEEE Trans. Commun. **55**(1), 21–24 (2007)
2. Pan, J., Zhai, X.: Spectrum sensing in cognitive radio based on energy detection. J. Shanghai Univ. **15**(1), 54–59 (2016)
3. Sardana, M., Vohra, A.: Analysis of different spectrum sensing techniques. In: 2017 International Conference on Computer, Communications and Electronics (Comptelix), Jaipur, India, pp. 422–425. IEEE (2017). https://doi.org/10.1109/COMPTELIX.2017.8004006
4. Gardner, W.A.: Exploitation of spectral redundancy in cyclostationary signals. IEEE Signal Process. Mag. **8**(2), 14–36 (1991)
5. Zhao, W., Li, H., Jin, M.: Fusion spectrum sensing algorithm based on eigenvalues. J. Commun. **40**(11), 57–64 (2019)
6. Zhang, G.: Researches on wireless network sensing technology based on AI: an overview. Telecommun. Eng. **62**(5), 686–694 (2022)
7. Sobabe, G.C., Song, Y., Bai, X., et al.: A cooperative spectrum sensing algorithm based on unsupervised learning. In: 2017 10th International Congress on Image and Signal Processing, BioMedical Engineering and Informatics (CISP-BMEI), pp. 1–6. IEEE (2018). https://doi.org/10.1109/CISP-BMEI.2017.8302156
8. Zhang, Y., Wan, P., Zhang, S., Wang, Y., Li, N.: A spectrum sensing method based on signal feature and clustering algorithm in cognitive wireless multimedia sensor networks. Adv. Multimedia **2017**, 2895680, 10 (2017)
9. Wang, Y., Zhang, Y., Zhang, S., et al.: A cooperative spectrum sensing method based on a feature and clustering algorithm. In: 2018 Chinese Automation Congress (CAC), pp. 1029–1033. IEEE (2018). https://doi.org/10.1109/CAC.2018.1234567
10. Bao, J., Nie, J., Liu, C., Jiang, B., Zhu, F., He, J.: Improved blind spectrum sensing by covariance matrix Cholesky decomposition and RBF-SVM decision classification at low SNRs. IEEE Access **7**, 97117–97129 (2019)

An Optimized Design of Golden Angle Modulation SCMA Codebook Based on Genetic Algorithms

Jingqiu Ren, Sen Li, Guanghua Zhang$^{(\boxtimes)}$, and Shang Liu

Northeast Petroleum University, DaQing, China

dazgh@nepu.com.cn

Abstract. Sparse Code Multiple Access (SCMA) is a novel non-orthogonal muti-ple access scheme, which maps information on different resources into mutidi-mensional codewords to improve system mapping diversity. However, the per-formance of the same codebook may vary greatly between different channels, so we propose a new SCMA codebook optimization design for the difference of the codebook, It can be used in the codebook generation process of multiple channels, and optimize the minimum Euclidean distance between code words by genetic algorithm to achieve the effect of improving the codebook performance. In this paper, based on the codebook design of Golden Angle Modulation (GAM), we optimize GAM with the help of genetic algorithm. The simulation results show that in the process of SCMA system simulation using the codebook generated by the optimized parameters in Gaussian channel and Rayleigh fading channel, the BER performance of the codebook is significantly improved.

Keywords: Sparse Code Multiple Access · Genetic algorithm · Minimum Euclidean distance · Codebook optimization · Rayleigh fading channel

1 Introduction

Non-orthogonal multiple access (NOMA) is a communication technology that allows multiple users to occupy the same resource for transmission in 5G and other net-works. Recently, NOMA has attracted more and more researchers' attention because it meets various stringent requirements proposed in Massive machine type commu-nication (mMTC). Its excellent characteristics such as very high spectrum efficiency, unscheduled delivery of small data packets at irregular times, large user capacity and ultra-low access delay make it considered as a very promising communication tech-nology. NOMA requires specific technologies to realize, among which power domain non-orthogonal multiple access (PD-NOMA) distinguishes users by power, and code domain non-orthogonal multiple access (CD-NOMA) by code are two specific technical solutions for the implementation of NOMA. As a kind of CD-NOMA, SCMA is devel-oped on the basis of Low density signature (LDS) [1, 2]. Different from LDS, SCMA directly maps user's bit information into a multidimensional complex sequence using a

© ICST Institute for Computer Sciences, Social Informatics and Telecommunications Engineering 2025
Published by Springer Nature Switzerland AG 2025. All Rights Reserved
H.-H. Chen and W. Meng (Eds.): WiSATS 2024, LNICST 605, pp. 203–213, 2025.
https://doi.org/10.1007/978-3-031-86196-3_17

codebook, making it easier to distinguish at the receiver, and allocates the transmission of the user on multiple resource blocks to achieve higher spectral efficiency and improved BER performance. In SCMA, research mainly focuses on the codebook design, decoding algorithm and practical application of SCMA technology. The codebook design of SCMA mainly determines the BER performance of the system [3]. In recent years, many codebooks have been designed. Most of the codebooks generate the initial mother constellation by maximizing the minimum Euclidean distance (MED) index, and then perform a series of transformations on the mother constellation to generate the user's codebook. Since these codebooks are used in a specific channel, the same codebook in different channels may not show excellent performance, and may even increase the BER.

So the codebook design approach of GAM is adopted in this paper [4], Because in the two categories of codebooks design methods in GAM, codebooks with one and two optimization parameters, respectively, can construct codebooks for Rayleigh fading channels in the uplink and downlink. After testing, the performance of the optimized codebook in Gaussian channel is also improved compared with other methods. We first generate GAM codebooks for different channels, and then use Genetic Algorithm (GA) to optimize the parameters during the generation process, because GA is easy to optimize the number of parameters, it shows good optimization performance in this methods. Simulation results show that our codebooks optimized by GA significantly improves the performance over existing codebooks used in both Gaussian and Rayleigh fading channels.

The SCMA codebooks design is an important and challenging problem, Taherzadeh and Nikopour et al. first proposed SCMA method and basic codebook construction method [5]. Following this direction, many codebook design methods were proposed based on various theories came into being. In Downlink, Yu et al. proposed a design to generate the mother constellation based on the star-QAM signal constellation [6], and then generate the user codebook through some operators. However, although three operators were proposed in the paper, no specific design indicators were given. In Uplink, Tian, Zhong et al. formulated the design of the multidimensional mother constellation as a nonconvex optimization problem [7] to obtain a suboptimal solution, so as to obtain better coding gains. Gao et al. proposed an algorithm to construct a multidimensional mother constellation by using a two dimensional lattice constellation [8] and design of the uplink SCMA codebook in a multilevel optimization manner. However, most of the design work for uplink SCMA codebook needs to solve complex optimization problems, and there are few related works proposed for uplink. In the codebook design method under Gaussian channel, Zhou et al. proposed a codebook design method based on constellation rotation [9]. And Cai et al. further proposed a codebook generation method by adding interweaving after rotation. [10] However, in the above papers, the codebook was only generated for a certain channel, and it may not have excellent effects in other channel.

In this paper we propose the design method can use a simple algorithm to generate suitable codebooks between channels with different performance, so as to reduce the bit error rate during transmission. The rest of this paper is organized as follows: Sect. 2 introduces the traditional system model of SCMA, Sect. 3 describes the method of using GA to optimize the GAM codebook, Sect. 4 describes the comparison of different codebooks and BER simulation and analysis in different channels, and Sect. 5 concludes the paper.

2 SCMA System Model

The SCMA encoder is defined as a mapping from $\log_2(M)$ bits to a K-dimensional complex codebook of size M. In the downlink SCMA system, each SCMA encoder consists of J Internet of Things (IOT) devices (users) occupying K orthogonal resource nodes. Among them, orthogonal resources can be subcarriers, time slots, etc. Each user has a multidimensional SCMA codebook with M codewords x_j of length K. The SCMA encoder for user j is defined as the mapping:

$$f_j : \mathbb{B}^{\log_2(M)} \to \chi_j \tag{1}$$

where χ_j is the set of codebooks, M is the modulation order, $\mathbb{B}^{\log_2(M)}$ is the binary bit at the encoder side, and x_j is extracted from $\chi_j \in \mathbb{C}^{K \times M}$. Set of codebooks:

$$\chi_j = \left\{ x_{j,1}, x_{j,2}, \ldots, x_{j,M} \right\} \in \mathbb{C}^{K \times M}, i.e. x_j = f_j b_j \tag{2}$$

$$b_j = \left[b_{j,1}, b_{j,2}, \ldots, b_{j,\log_2(M)} \right]^\top \in \mathbb{B}^{\log_2(M)} \tag{3}$$

where b_j is the incoming binary message vector from the jth user.

A K-dimensional complex codeword of a codebook is a sparse vector with $N < K$ nonzero entries. All codewords in the codebook contain zeros in the same $K - N$ dimension. The nonzero dimensions of the mapping matrix V are mapped to the K-dimensional complex domain. Let C_j be the N-dimensional compound constellation obtained by removing all zero elements in χ_j. Define the mapping from $\mathbb{B}^{\log_2(M)}$ to C_j:

$$g_j : \mathbb{B}^{\log_2(M)} \to C_j, i.e. c_j = g_j b_j. \tag{4}$$

$$C_j \subset \mathbb{C}^{N \times M} \tag{5}$$

Then the SCMA encoder in (1) can be redefined as

$$f_j : V_j g_j, i.e. x_j = V_j g_j b_j \tag{6}$$

where $V_j \in \mathbb{B}^{K \times N}$ is a binary mapping matrix that maps N-dimensional constellation points to K-dimensional SCMA codewords. The mapping matrix V_j contains $K - N$ all zero rows. The inclusion of a row $r \in \{1, \ldots, K\}$ with value 1 in V_j means that user j is using the rth resource. Thus, the set of resources occupied by user j depends on V_j. Define the factor matrix F as follows:

$$F_{K \times J} = \left[f_1, \ldots, f_2 \right] \subset \mathbb{B}^{K \times J}, f_j = diag\left(V_j V_j^\top \right) \tag{7}$$

User node j is connected to resource node k if and only if $f_{k,j} = 1$. An example of a factor graph representation of F is shown in Fig. 1. There are 6 symbol nodes and 4 resource nodes (Fig. 2).

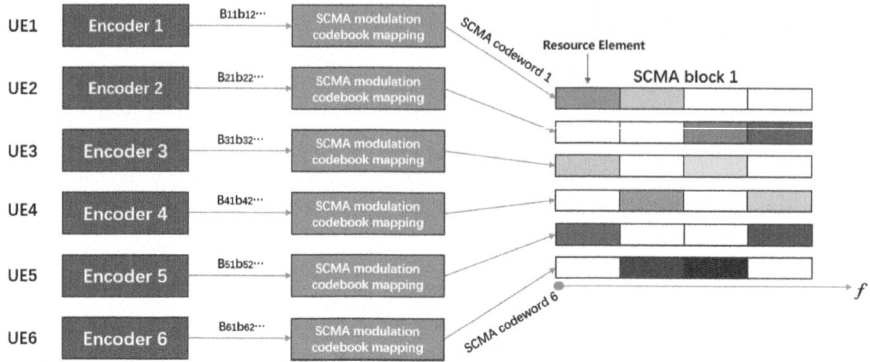

Fig. 1. SCMA system model

$$F_{4\times 6} = \begin{bmatrix} 0 & 1 & 1 & 0 & 1 & 0 \\ 1 & 0 & 1 & 0 & 0 & 1 \\ 0 & 1 & 0 & 1 & 0 & 1 \\ 1 & 0 & 0 & 1 & 1 & 0 \end{bmatrix}$$

Fig. 2. Factor graph F

For a known channel h and a received signal y, a near optimal detection of layers J can be performed iteratively by applying a message passing algorithm (MPA). The complexity of MPA is proportional to Md_f where d_f is the number of branches reaching the resource node. The sparse codebook can effectively control the number of branches at each resource node, thus limiting the complexity of the MPA receiver. The data of J users are first superimposed at the base station and then transmitted over K resource blocks, with a total of M^J superimposed codewords. The signal received by the user can be written as

$$y = diag(h_j) \sum_{j=1}^{J} x_j + n \tag{8}$$

where $x_j = V_j g_j b_j$ is the vector of SCMA codewords of user J, h_j is the channel vector of layer J, and n is the ambient noise. In the case where all layers transmit from the same transmitting point, all channels to the destination receiver are the same, $i.e.$ $h_j = h, \forall j$. The overload factor of the code is defined as $\lambda = J/K$ by multiplexing J layers on K resources.

3   The Optimized GAM Codebook

3.1   Mathematical Model

The GAM structure proposed in [1] is adopted, which can design the downlink and uplink SCMA codebooks based on golden Angle modulation [11]. One optimization parameter (θ) and two optimization parameters (θ, ρ) are used respectively to optimize the codebook design for the downlink and uplink. The optimization parameter is independent of the codebook and system parameters, so a simple optimization method can be used to optimize the parameters to design a better codebook. By adjusting the value of θ and ρ, the BER of the proposed codebook can be reduced and the minimum normalized Euclidean distance can be improved.

The specific codebook design method of GAM is provided in [1], no further details here. GAM point x_n is generated as follows.

$$x_n = r_{n+\rho} e^{i2(\pi+\theta)n}, n = 1, \ldots, N_p \tag{9-a}$$

$$r_{n+\rho} = c_{norm}\sqrt{n+\rho} \tag{9-b}$$

$$c_{norm} = \sqrt{\frac{2P}{N_P+1}} \tag{9-c}$$

where $N_p = N \cdot \frac{M}{2}$, θ and ρ are the free parameters proposed in θ-GAM, which can be optimized to improve the codebook performance, x_n are used to generate the mother constellation to design SCMA codebook (Fig. 3).

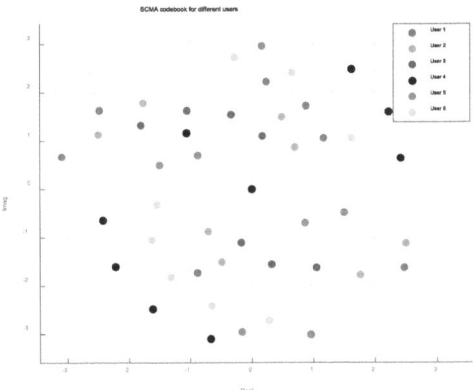

Fig. 3. The user codebook constellation points generated using GAM in the Rayleigh channel downlink, $\theta = -2.8329$, $\rho = 0$.

3.2 Optimization Algorithm

GA optimizes the θ and ρ parameters of GAM in a simple optimization manner [12]. For convenience, in this paper, the normalized minimum Euclidean distance $\tilde{d}_{\min}$ is used as the fitness to calculate the θ and ρ that are optimal for the GAM points.

$$\tilde{d}_{\min} = \min\left\{ \frac{|x_i - x_j|}{\sqrt{E}}, \forall x_i x_j \in x_n, x_i \neq x_j \right\} \tag{10}$$

where x_n denotes the nth codeword in the GAM constellation point, E is the average power of the codeword. Before obtaining the codebook, we propose Algorithm 1 to optimize the parameters, which is used to build the codebook of each user later. In GA, we try to increase the initial population size, and appropriately adjust the crossover probability, mutation probability and generation gap value to prevent the generation of local optimal solution in the iterative process. The algorithm steps are as follows:

1) Population initialization. It is Set that *NIND* individuals (chromosomes) need to be initialized as the population number, so n numbers are randomly generated at first, and each number is tested whether it satisfies the range constraint of θ. According to this method, all *NIND* individuals are initialized, and the initialization of *Chrom* of the parent population is completed after the completion.
2) Fitness function. A proper evaluation of each chromosome is needed to find the optimal value in the GA optimization process. The design criterion of the optimal θ value is to maximize the minimum Euclidean distance between codewords [13]. Therefore, $\tilde{d}_{\min}$ is used as the evaluation index, and the Fitness function is calculated as follows:

$$Fitness = \max\left(\tilde{d}_{\min}|\theta_i\right) \ i = 1, ..., NIND \tag{11}$$

3) Selection. From the biological point of view, although there are *NIND* individuals in the population, not all of them can give birth to offspring, so instead of selecting out *NIND* individuals, but $Nsel = NIND \times GGAP$ individuals. *GGAP* is the generation gap, and the selection method uses the roulette wheel selection strategy. Specifically, the probability of being selected is assigned to each different individual, and which one is selected is decided by rotating the roulette wheel. in conclusion, the selected individuals need to be rotated Nsel times to form the *SelCh*(select Chrom).
4) Crossover and mutation. The genes of the offspring population individuals generated by the selection operation have not changed, and the individual genes need to be changed to make the population evolve. The first operation is crossover, which usually requires two objects, but there is only one parameter for the optimization of θ, so the crossover adopts a simple parameter perturbation. The second operation is mutation, which takes a small value in code because mutation is less common in nature.
5) Reorganization and update. Nsel individuals are obtained through the above series of operations, and the individuals with the top $NIND - Nsel$ fitness rank are found out from the parent population *Chrom* and added to the child population *SelCh*. Then the new parent population *Chrom* is updated and used as the population in the next selection operation. The reproduction algebra *MAXGEN* was set, which was the number of iterations. Finally, the optimal individual generated in each iteration was recorded and updated to generate the optimal individual value.

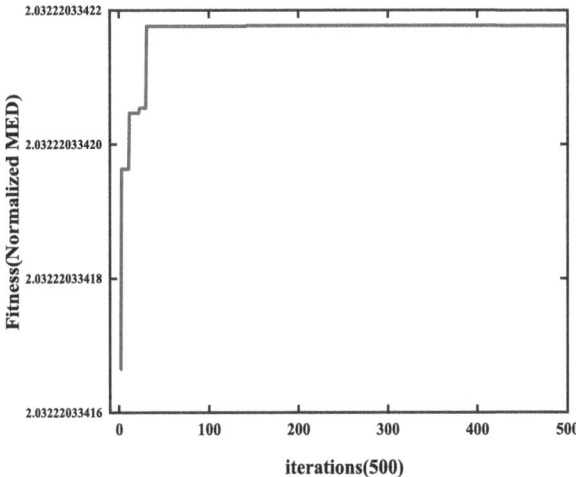

Fig. 4. Diagram of iterative process of GA minimum Euclidean distance iterations $= 500$

4 Simulation and Numerical Analysis

In this section, the performance of codebooks generated using GA optimized parameters θ, ρ is evaluated under different channels. We take the classic case of 6 users, 4 resource blocks, and the number of resources used by each user $N = 2$ to evaluate the average BER of the codebook. Figure 1 represents the factor matrix. According to GA in Gauss and downlink, the minimum Euclidean distance is optimized to generate parameters as $\theta_1 = -2.8329$, $\rho = 0$.The optimized parameter in the uplink is $\theta_2 = 3.9549$, where is the value of θ selected for the best performance, because the optimization of θ does not depend on the system. Then we fix the θ_2 and optimize ρ separately to produce $\rho = 1.054$. Using the above optimized parameters in the GAM method, three different codebooks are generated in the Gaussian channel and Rayleigh fading channel up/downlink, and their performance is compared with other codebooks. Figure 4, Fig. 5, and Fig. 6 show the BER performance of the GAM codebook optimized using GA, tentatively referred to as GA-GAM, compared with the original GAM and the proposed codebook in [6, 14, 15] in different channels. We observe that The $\tilde{d}_{min}$ between the GA-GAM codewords is larger under Gaussian and Rayleigh channels, and this codebook has a lower BER than other codebooks (Fig. 7).

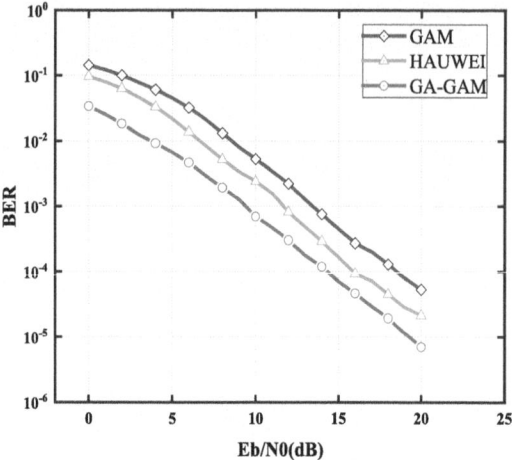

Fig. 5. Performance comparison of GAM codebook in [4], Huawei codebook in [15] and GA-GAM in Rayleigh downlink channel with diversity, θ = -2.8329 and ρ = 0 after optimization.

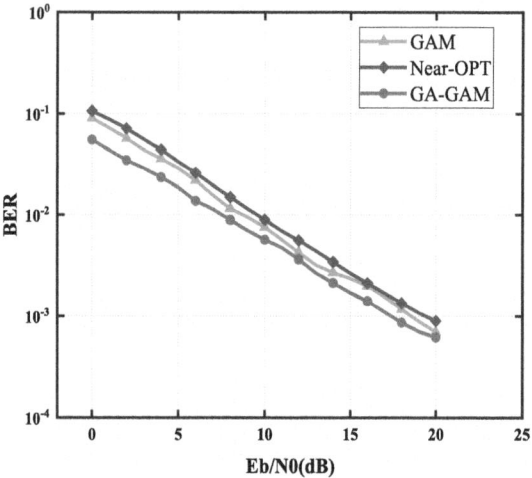

Fig. 6. Performance comparison of GAM codebook in [4], Near-OPT codebook in [14] and GA GAM in Rayleigh fading uplink channel with diversity, θ = 3.9549 and ρ = 1.054 after optimization

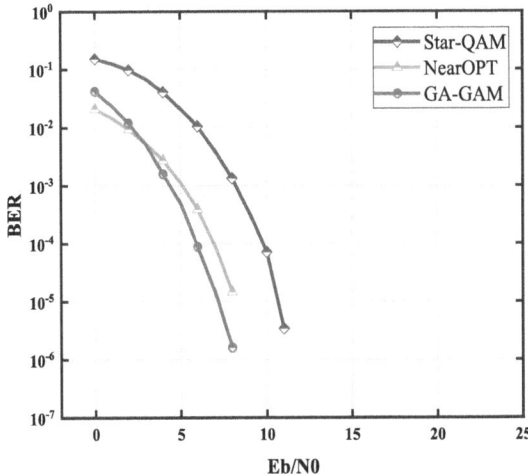

Fig. 7. Performance comparison of the Star-QAM codebook in [6], Near-OPT codebook in [14] and GA-GAM in Gaussian channel codebook, θ = −2.8329 and ρ = 0 after optimization

Table 1. Comparison of BER and $\tilde{d}_{\min}$ for different SNR in uplink/downlink of Rayleigh channel

DOWNLINK				UPLINK			
BER \ Eb/No	5dB	15 dB	$\tilde{d}_{\min}$	BER \ Eb/No	5dB	15dB	$\tilde{d}_{\min}$
[4]	0.06051	0.00045	1.2886	[4]	0.03335	0.00266	1.4120
[15]	0.03298	0.00017	1.4142	[14]	0.02873	0.00235	1.8354
This work	0.0092	0.00007	1.8068	This work	0.01858	0.0017	2.0322

Table 2. Comparison of BER and $\tilde{d}_{\min}$ for different SNR in Gaussian channel

AWGN			
BER \ Eb/No	5dB	10dB	$\tilde{d}_{\min}$
[6]	0.02078	0.0000712	1.4426
[14]	0.00113	0.00000046	1.6135
This work	0.0005	0	1.6348

5 Conclusion

Based on the method of GAM codebook design, we use GA to optimize its proposed θ, ρ, and thus propose an optimal SCMA codebook design method for different channels. Our proposed method optimizes one parameter (θ) or two parameters (θ, ρ) respectively by maximizing the minimum Euclidean distance. The results of numerical experiments on codebooks show that the GA method can easily find better optimization parameters. Table 1 and Table 2 show that the optimized codebook is used to compare the Huawei generated codebook, the approximate optimal algorithm [14], star-QAM and the original GAM method under the Gaussian channel and Rayleigh channel down/uplink. It is proved that the proposed codebook optimization method has larger $\tilde{d}_{min}$ value and better BER performance. However, the codebook proposed in this scheme is still limited to the three commonly used channels, and whether it can maintain good flexibility and robustness when the channel changes remains to be tested and studied (Table 3).

Table 3. A θ is optimized by the GA algorithm.

1: Set Chrom $=$ InitPop (NIND, θ − range)
2: Set gen $=$ 1
3: bestIndividual $=$ Chrom（1, : ）
4: while gen $<=$ MAXGEN do
5:    for i $=$ 1: NIND do
6:       CB $=$ GenerateCB(Chrom(i))
7:       Obj $=$ CalculateMED（Chrom(i)）
8:       FitnV $=$ Obj
9:    end for
10:    SelCh = Select (Chrom, FitnV, GGAP)
11:    SelCh $=$ Mutate (SelCh, θ − range)
12:    Chrom $=$ Reins (Chrom, SelCh, Obj)
13:    BestObj(gen, 1) $=$ bestObj
14:    gen $=$ gen + 1
15: end while
16: Output the best individual

References

1. Hoshyar, R., Razavi, R., et al.: LDS-OFDM an efficient multiple access technique. In: 2010 IEEE 71st Vehicular Technology Conference, pp. 1–5. IEEE (2010)
2. Bayesteh, A., Nikopour, H., et al.: Low complexity techniques for SCMA detection. In: 2015 IEEE Globecom Workshops (GC Wkshps), pp. 1–6. IEEE (2015)
3. Alam, M., Zhang, Q.: Performance study of SCMA codebook design. In: 2017 IEEE Wireless Communications and Networking Conference (WCNC), pp. 1–5. IEEE (2017)
4. Mheich, Z., Wen, L., et al.: Design of SCMA codebooks based on golden angle modulation. IEEE Trans. Veh. Technol. **68**(2), 1501–1509 (2018)
5. Taherzadeh, M., Nikopour, H., et al.: SCMA codebook design. In: 2014 IEEE 80th Vehicular Technology Conference (VTC2014-Fall), pp. 1–5. IEEE (2014)

6. Yu, L., Lei, X., et al.: An optimized design of SCMA codebook based on star-QAM signaling constellations. In: 2015 International Conference on Wireless Communications & Signal Processing (WCSP), pp. 1–5. IEEE (2015)

7. Tian, L., Zhong, J., et al.: A suboptimal algorithm for SCMA codebook design over uplink Rayleigh fading channels. In: 2018 IEEE 87th Vehicular Technology Conference (VTC Spring), pp. 1–5. IEEE (2018)

8. Gao, M., Ge, W., et al.: An efficient codebook design for uplink SCMA. IEEE Access 8, 211665–211675 (2020)

9. Zhou, Y., Yu, Q., et al.: SCMA codebook design based on constellation rotation. In: 2017 IEEE International Conference on Communications (ICC), pp. 1–6. IEEE (2017)

10. Cai, D., Fan, P., et al.: Multi-dimensional SCMA codebook design based on constellation rotation and interleaving. In: 2016 IEEE 83rd Vehicular Technology Conference (VTC Spring), pp. 1–5. IEEE (2016)

11. Larsson, P.: Golden angle modulation. IEEE Wirel. Commun. Lett. 7(1), 98–101 (2017)

12. Chu, P.C., Beasley, J.E.: A genetic algorithm for the multidimensional knapsack problem. J. Heurist. 4, 63–86 (1998)

13. Liu, S.L., et al.: Optimized SCMA codebook design by QAM constellation segmentation with maximized MED. IEEE Access 6, 63232–63242 (2018)

14. Chen, Y.M., et al.: On the design of near-optimal sparse code multiple access codebooks. IEEE Trans. Commun. 68(5), 2950–2962 (2020)

15. Luo, Q., Liu, Z., et al.: A design of low-projection SCMA codebooks for ultra-low decoding complexity in downlink IoT networks. IEEE Trans. Wirel. Commun. (2023)

Bidirectional Backscatter NOMA Schemefor Efficient CDRT Systems

Rongfei Hu[1,2], Yao Xu[1(✉)], Jianyue Zhu[1], Jichong Guo[3], Shaobo Jia[4], Yi Lou[5], and Chengzhao Shan[5]

[1] Nanjing University of Information Science and Technology, Nanjing 210044, China
yaoxu@nuist.edu.cn
[2] NUIST-TianChang Research Institute, Tianchang 239300, China
[3] Suzhou University of Science and Technology, Suzhou 215009, China
[4] Zhengzhou University, Zhengzhou 450001, China
[5] Harbin Institute of Technology, Harbin 150001, China

Abstract. Non-orthogonal multiple access (NOMA) based coordinated direct and relay transmission (CDRT) is recognized as one of the enabling technologies for effectively enhancing spectral efficiency and coverage range in mobile communication systems. However, most conventional NOMA based CDRT schemes only support cellular data transmission. To simultaneously support both cellular and Internet of Things (IoT) data transmission and further improve the spectral efficiency of the system, this paper proposes a novel bidirectional backscatter NOMA scheme for CDRT systems. Specifically, the proposed scheme utilizes both uplink NOMA and downlink NOMA to facilitate the sharing of spectrum and time resources between cellular information and IoT data reflected by users. To accurately characterize the effectiveness of the proposed scheme, the closed-form expressions for the ergodic sum capacity (ESC) are derived. Simulation experiments validate the correctness of theoretical analysis and demonstrate that the proposed scheme can achieve better ESC performance than the conventional NOMA based CDRT and orthogonal multiple access.

Keywords: Non-orthogonal multiple access · Coordinated direct and relay transmission · Backscatter communication · Ergodic sum capacity

This work was supported in part by the Natural Science Foundation of Jiangsu Province under Grants BK20220438 and BK20220439; in part by National Natural Science Foundation of China under Grant 62301268; in part by the Natural Science Foundation of the Higher Education Institutions of Jiangsu Province under Grants 22KJB510033 and 22KJB10005; and in part by the Startup Foundation for Introducing Talent of NUIST under Grant 2023r015.

© ICST Institute for Computer Sciences, Social Informatics and Telecommunications Engineering 2025
Published by Springer Nature Switzerland AG 2025. All Rights Reserved
H.-H. Chen and W. Meng (Eds.): WiSATS 2024, LNICST 605, pp. 214–225, 2025.
https://doi.org/10.1007/978-3-031-86196-3_18

1   Introduction

The sixth generation (6G) mobile communication urgently requires enhancements in system spectral efficiency and communication coverage to support diverse vertical applications [1–3]. Integrating non-orthogonal multiple access (NOMA) and coordinated direct and relay transmission (CDRT) enables the exploitation of power domain NOMA to serve multiple users within the same time/frequency/code resources, while also supporting direct transmission and relay communication simultaneously [4,5]. Thus, NOMA based CDRT, renowned for its high spectral efficiency and broad coverage, has become a focal point of academic interest in recent years. For instance, significant research efforts have been dedicated to studying various aspects of NOMA based CDRT systems, such as efficient aggregate transmission [6], physical layer security [7], and high speed mobile applications [8]. However, existing NOMA based CDRT schemes encounter challenges due to limited spectrum resources and inter-user interference. These challenges hinder the simultaneous support for the fusion transmission of cellular information and low rate Internet of Things (IoT) sensing information, thus impeding the heterogeneous fusion development of future mobile communications.

Fortunately, backscatter NOMA offers a novel approach to address the aforementioned issues. Backscatter communication utilizes ambient radio frequency (RF) signals and adjusts the matching state between load impedance and antenna impedance to reflect low rate IoT information to the receiver without consuming additional energy [9]. When the receiver is equipped with both the conventional transceiver circuits and backscatter circuits, it can decode its own information using a portion of the received signal, while the remaining part is used to modulate its own information for transmission [10].

Motivated by these observations, this paper proposes a novel bidirectional backscatter NOMA scheme for CDRT systems to simultaneously support the fusion transmission of cellular and IoT information, thereby further enhancing spectral efficiency. The contributions of this paper are summarized as follows. (1) This paper proposes a bidirectional backscatter NOMA scheme for CDRT systems. In the proposed scheme, the base station (BS) collects IoT information from both the cell center user (CCU) and relay user (RU) using uplink backscatter NOMA, and then the CCU collects IoT information from the RU and cell edge user (CEU). Meanwhile, the BS employs downlink NOMA to serve the three users in the two time slots. (2) To characterize the performance of the proposed scheme, we derived the closed-form expressions for the ergodic sum capacity (ESC) using Gamma-Gamma distribution and Gaussian-Chebyshev quadrature. (3) Simulations demonstrate that the proposed scheme achieves superior ESC performance compared with the conventional NOMA based CDRT and orthogonal multiple access (OMA) under various parameter settings.

2   System Model

As depicted in Fig. 1, we investigate a CDRT system using backscatter NOMA, consisting of one BS, one RU, one CCU, and one CEU. In this system, it is feasible for the BS to communicate directly with RU and CCU. However, the BS can only communicate with the CEU with the assistance of RU. This is because the link between the BS and CEU has a long distance, severe deep fading, or obstruction. All nodes operate with a single antenna, and the RU employs a decode and forward (DF) protocol. Additionally, the BS is capable of full duplex communication, while the other nodes operate in half duplex mode. To improve the system spectral efficiency under the same energy supply conditions, each user node is equipped with a hybrid wireless circuit, which includes a transceiver circuit and a backscatter circuit. Specifically, the users can adaptively switch between transceiver mode and backscatter mode. In the transceiver mode, the users can complete general communication sending and receiving functions. When the users switch to backscatter mode, it can complete decoding of the received signals while reflecting its own information.

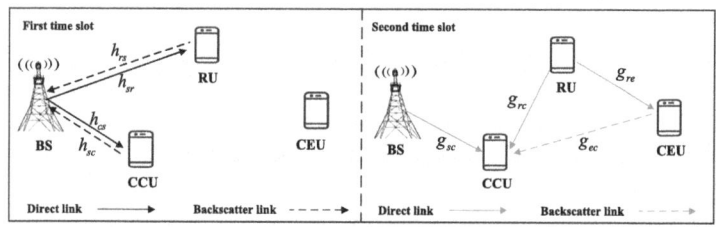

Fig. 1. Illustration of the considered system model.

Assume that all channel links experience quasi-static Rayleigh block fading. Subsequently, subscripts s, r, c, and e are used to denote the BS, RU, CCU, and CEU, while superscripts 1 and 2 are utilized to distinguish the first and second time slots, respectively. Define nodes w and v in the first time slot satisfy $w \in \{s, r, c\}$ and $v \in \{s, r, c\}$, nodes i and j in the second time slot meet $i \in \{s, r, e\}$ and $j \in \{c, e\}$. Let h_{wv} and H_{wv}, $w \neq v$, represent the channel coefficient and channel power between w and v in the first time slot, and let g_{ij} and G_{ij}, $i \neq j$, denote the channel coefficient and channel power between i and j in the second time slot. The channel coefficients h_{wv} and g_{ij} follow complex Gaussian distribution, i.e., $h_{wv} \sim CN(0, \Omega_{wv})$ and $g_{ij} \sim CN(0, \Omega_{ij})$. Without loss of generality, it is assumed that the channel configuration satisfies the conditions $\Omega_{sc} > \Omega_{sr}$, $\Omega_{cs} > \Omega_{rs}$, and $\Omega_{sc} > \Omega_{rc}$.

3   Transmission Protocol

3.1   First Time Slot

In the first time slot, the BS operates in full duplex mode and performs superposition coding on the power-normalized signals xc, xr, and x_e according to downlink NOMA. The CCU and RU operate in the backscatter mode. The signals x_c, x_r, and x_e are needed by the CCU, RU, and CEU, respectively. The signal to be transmitted at the BS can be represented as $S_s^1 = \sqrt{\alpha_c}x_c + \sqrt{\alpha_r}x_r + \sqrt{\alpha_e}x_e$, where α_c, α_r, and α_e represent the power allocation coefficients (PACs) corresponding to the signals x_c, x_r, and x_e, respectively.

Due to $\Omega_{sc} > \Omega_{sr}$ and the absence of a direct link between the BS and the CEU, the PACs should meet $0 < \alpha_c < \alpha_r < \alpha_e < 1$ and $\alpha_e + \alpha_r + \alpha_c = 1$. The CCU and RU can leverage a fraction of the RF signals from the BS for backscatter modulation to convey their individual uplink signals u_c and u_r. Subsequently, the residual portion of the incoming signals can be used for self-information decoding. The received signals at the CCU, RU, and BS are given by $y_c^1 = h_{sc}\sqrt{(1-a_c)P_s}S_s^1 + n_c^1$, $y_r^1 = h_{sr}\sqrt{(1-a_r)P_s}S_s^1 + n_r^1$, and $y_s^1 = h_{sc}h_{cs}\sqrt{a_c P_s}S_s^1 u_c + h_{sr}h_{rs}\sqrt{a_r P_s}S_s^1 u_r + S_{SI} + n_s^1$, respectively, where $0 < a_c < 1$ and $0 < a_r < 1$ are the reflection coefficients at the CCU and RU, and P_s is the transmit power at the BS. The term $n_w^1 \sim CN(0, \sigma^2)$ denotes the additive white Gaussian noise (AWGN) at the node $w \in \{s, c, r\}$. Moreover, $S_{SI} \sim CN(0, \varepsilon P_s \Omega_{ss})$ is the self-interference term due to the full duplex, where $0 \le \varepsilon \le 1$ represents the residual interference level, and Ω_{ss} is the channel power of the self-interference channel of the BS.

According to downlink NOMA, the CCU needs to decode x_e, x_r, and x_c using successive interference cancellation (SIC). Thus, the signal-to-interference plus noise ratios (SINRs) for decoding x_e, x_r, and x_c at the CCU are given by

$$\gamma_{c,x_e}^1 = \frac{H_{sc}(1-a_c)\alpha_e\rho_s}{H_{sc}(1-a_c)(\alpha_c + \alpha_r)\rho_s + 1}, \tag{1}$$

$$\gamma_{c,x_r}^1 = \frac{H_{sc}(1-a_c)\alpha_r\rho_s}{H_{sc}(1-a_c)\alpha_c\rho_s + 1}, \tag{2}$$

$$\gamma_{c,x_c}^1 = H_{sc}(1-a_c)\alpha_c\rho_s, \tag{3}$$

where $\rho_s \triangleq \frac{P_s}{\sigma^2}$ represents the transmit SNR at the BS. Based on (3), the achievable rate associated with x_c is $R_{x_c} = \frac{1}{2}\log_2(1+\gamma_{c,x_c}^1)$. Meanwhile, the RU decodes the signals x_e and x_r via SIC, and the corresponding SINRs can be written as

$$\gamma_{r,x_e}^1 = \frac{H_{sr}(1-a_c)\alpha_e\rho_s}{H_{sr}(1-a_c)(\alpha_c + \alpha_r)\rho_s + 1}, \tag{4}$$

$$\gamma_{r,x_r}^1 = \frac{H_{sr}(1-a_c)\alpha_r\rho_s}{H_{sr}(1-a_c)\alpha_c\rho_s + 1}. \tag{5}$$

Since the CCU needs to successfully decode x_r in the first time slot before decoding x_c, the achievable rate for x_r is limited to γ_{c,x_r}^1. Based on (2) and (5), the achievable rate for x_r is given by $R_{x_r} = \frac{1}{2}\log_2(1 + \min\{\gamma_{c,x_r}^1, \gamma_{r,x_r}^1\})$.

By recalling y_s^1, the signal S_s^1 can be considered as a virtual fast fading channel gain for decoding u_c and u_r, where $S_s^1 \sim CN(0, 1)$. The process of the BS receiving the reflected uplink signals from the CCU and RU can be regarded as an uplink NOMA transmission. Due to $\Omega_{sc} > \Omega_{sr}$ and $\Omega_{cs} > \Omega_{rs}$, the reflection coefficient is set to $a_c > a_r$. Thus, the BS can use SIC to decode u_c and u_r sequentially. The SINRs for the BS to decode u_c and u_r are given by

$$\gamma^1_{s,u_c} = \frac{H_{sc}H_{cs}a_c\rho_s|S^1_s|^2}{H_{sr}H_{rs}a_r\rho_s|S^1_s|^2 + \varepsilon\rho_s H_{ss} + 1}, \tag{6}$$

$$\gamma^1_{s,u_r} = \frac{H_{sr}H_{rs}a_r\rho_s|S^1_s|^2}{\varepsilon\rho_s H_{ss} + 1}, \tag{7}$$

where $H_{ss} \sim \exp(\Omega_{ss})$. The achievable rates for u_c and u_r are given by $R_{u_c} = \frac{1}{2}\log_2(1 + \gamma^1_{s,u_c})$ and $R_{u_r} = \frac{1}{2}\log_2(1 + \gamma^1_{s,u_r})$, respectively.

3.2   Second Time Slot

In the second time slot, the CCU and RU switch to the transceiver mode, while the CEU operates in the backscatter mode. To fully utilize the time resources of the BS, a new downlink signal x'_c is transmitted to the CCU from the BS with the power P_s. The RU broadcasts the decoded signal x_e and the new signal x_{rc} by using superposition encoding with the transmit power P_r, where x_{rc} contains the environmental information that be collected for the CCU from the RU. Therefore, the superimposed encoded signal at the RU can be given by $S^2_r = \sqrt{\beta_{rc}}x_{rc} + \sqrt{\beta_e}x_e$, where β_{rc} and β_e denote the PACs corresponding to x_{rc} and x_e, respectively. Since the signal x_e is transmitted through a dual-hop link, the decoding requirement of x_e is higher than that of x_{rc}, the PACs should satisfy $0 < \beta_{rc} < \beta_e < 1$ and $\beta_{rc} + \beta_e = 1$. Assume that the normalized reflection coefficient at the CEU is b_e. The signal x_{ec} containing environmental information is loaded onto a part of received signal via backscatter modulation and reflected to the CCU. The remaining part of the received signal is used for information decoding. Based on this, the received signal at the CEU is given by $y^2_e = g_{re}\sqrt{(1 - b_e)P_r}S^2_r + n^2_e$, where $P_r = \vartheta P_s$, $0 < \vartheta \leq 1$ denotes the power scaling factor, and $n^2_e \sim CN(0, N_0)$ is the AWGN at the CEU. The CEU decodes x_e by treating x_{rc} as interference, and the corresponding SINR is given by

$$\gamma^2_{e,x_e} = \frac{G_{re}(1 - b_e)\beta_e\rho_r}{G_{re}(1 - b_e)\beta_{rc}\rho_r + 1}, \tag{8}$$

where $\rho_r \triangleq \frac{P_r}{N_0}$ denotes the transmit SNR at the RU. In the first time slot, the CCU needs to decode x_e before performing SIC. Because the RU adopts the DF protocol, the achievable rate for x_e is constrained by the weaker link in the BS to RU and RU to CEU connections. Thus, by using (1), (4) and (8), the achievable rate for x_e is given by $R_{x_e} = \frac{1}{2}\log_2(1 + \min\{\gamma^1_{c,x_e}, \gamma^1_{r,x_e}, \gamma^2_{e,x_e}\})$.

The received signal at the CCU is written as $y^2_c = g_{sc}\sqrt{P_s}x'_c + g_{rc}\sqrt{P_r}S^2_r + g_{re}g_{ec}\sqrt{b_e P_r}S^2_r x_{ec} + n^2_c$, where $n^2_c \sim CN(0, \sigma^2)$ denotes the AWGN at the CCU. Since x_e has been decoded at the CCU in the first time slot, the CCU can utilize the side information of x_e to eliminate the term $g_{rc}\sqrt{\beta_e P_r}x_e$ in y^2_c. Furthermore, y^2_c is rewritten as $y^2_c = g_{sc}\sqrt{P_s}x'_c + g_{rc}\sqrt{\beta_{rc}P_r}x_{rc} + g_{re}g_{ec}\sqrt{b_e P_r}S^2_r x_{ec} + n^2_c$. The condition $\Omega_{sc} > \Omega_{rc}$ holds and P_s is usually higher than P_r. Besides, the reflected signal x_{ec} experience a dual-fading channel, resulting in a corresponding lower received signal power level. Therefore, the decoding sequence of the SIC applied by the CCU is x'_c, x_{rc}, and x_{ec}. Specifically, the CCU first decodes x'_c by considering x_{rc} and x_{ec} as interference, with the corresponding SINR of

$$\gamma^2_{c,x'_c} = \frac{G_{sc}\rho_s}{G_{rc}\beta_{rc}\vartheta\rho_s + G_{re}G_{ec}b_e\vartheta\rho_s + 1}. \tag{9}$$

Similarly, the SINR for the CCU to decode x_{rc} can be given by

$$\gamma^2_{c,x_{rc}} = \frac{G_{rc}\beta_{rc}\vartheta\rho_s}{G_{re}G_{ec}b_e\vartheta\rho_s + 1}. \tag{10}$$

When decoding x_{ec}, the CCU treats S^2_r as a known virtual fast fading channel coefficient. The corresponding SINR is given by

$$\gamma^2_{c,x_{ec}} = G_{re}G_{ec}b_e\vartheta\rho_s|S^2_r|^2. \tag{11}$$

Based on (9), (10) and (11), the achievable rates corresponding to the signal x'_c, x_{rc}, and x_{ec} are given by $R_{x'_c} = \frac{1}{2}\log_2(1 + \gamma^2_{c,x'_c})$, $R_{x_{rc}} = \frac{1}{2}\log_2(1 + \gamma^2_{c,x_{rc}})$, and $R_{x_{ec}} = \frac{1}{2}\log_2(1 + \gamma^2_{c,x_{ec}})$, respectively.

4 Performance Analysis

This section analyzes the ESC for the proposed scheme. Because this paper considers Rayleigh block fading channels and assumes that $S^1_s \sim CN(0,1)$ and $S^2_r \sim CN(0,1)$ hold, both the channel power and signal power follow exponential distributions. Using (3) and R_{x_c}, the ergodic capacity for x_c is calculated as

$$\begin{aligned}
C_{x_c} &= \frac{1}{2\ln 2}\int_0^\infty \frac{1}{1+x}\big(1 - F_{\gamma^1_{c,x_c}}(x)\big)dx \\
&= \frac{1}{2\ln 2}\int_0^\infty \frac{1}{1+x}e^{-\frac{v}{(1-a_c)\alpha_c\rho_s\Omega_{sc}}}dx \\
&= -\frac{1}{2\ln 2}e^{\frac{1}{(1-a_c)\alpha_c\rho_s\Omega_{sc}}}\text{Ei}(-1/((1-a_c)\alpha_c\rho_s\Omega_{sc})),
\end{aligned} \tag{12}$$

where $\text{Ei}(\cdot)$ is the exponential integral function [[11], eq.3.352.4].

Let $Z_1 \triangleq \min\{\gamma^1_{c,x_r}, \gamma^1_{r,x_r}\}$. Based on the order statistics, the cumulative distribution function (CDF) of Z_1 is obtained as $F_{Z_1}(z) = 1 - (1 - F_{\gamma^1_{c,x_r}}(z))(1 - F_{\gamma^1_{r,x_r}}(z))$, where $F_{\gamma^1_{c,x_r}}(x) = 1 - \exp\big(-\frac{x}{(1-a_c)\rho_s\Omega_{sc}(\alpha_r - \alpha_c x)}\big)$ and $F_{\gamma^1_{r,x_r}}(x) = 1 - \exp\big(-\frac{x}{(1-a_c)\rho_s\Omega_{sr}(\alpha_r - \alpha_c x)}\big)$ for $x < \frac{\alpha_r}{\alpha_c}$, while $F_{\gamma^1_{c,x_r}}(x) = 1$ and $F_{\gamma^1_{r,x_r}}(x) = 1$ for $x \geq \frac{\alpha_r}{\alpha_c}$. Therefore, using Gaussian-Chebyshev quadrature, the ergodic capacity for x_r is given by

$$\begin{aligned}
C_{x_r} &= \frac{1}{2\ln 2}\int_0^{\frac{\alpha_r}{\alpha_c}} \frac{1}{1+z}(1 - F_{Z_1}(z))dz \\
&= \frac{\alpha_r\pi}{4\ln 2\alpha_c M_{x_r}}\sum_{m_{x_r}=1}^{M_{x_r}}\sqrt{1 - Q_{x_r}^2}(1 - F_{Z_1}(q_{x_r}))\frac{1}{1+q_{x_r}},
\end{aligned} \tag{13}$$

where $Q_{x_r} = \cos(\frac{2m_{x_r}-1}{2M_{x_r}}\pi)$, $q_{x_r} = \frac{\alpha_r(1+Q_{x_r})}{2\alpha_c}$, M_{x_r} is a complexity-accuracy tradeoff parameter.

Let $Z_2 \triangleq \min\{\gamma^1_{c,x_e}, \gamma^1_{r,x_e}, \gamma^2_{e,x_e}\}$. Similar to Z_1, applying the order statistics, then we can calculate the CDF of Z_2 as $F_{Z_2}(z) = 1 - (1 - F_{\gamma^1_{c,x_e}}(z))(1 - F_{\gamma^1_{r,x_e}}(z))(1 - F_{\gamma^2_{e,x_e}}(z))$, where $F_{\gamma^1_{c,x_e}}(x) = 1 - \exp\left(-\frac{x}{(\alpha_e-(\alpha_c+\alpha_r)x)(1-a_c)\rho_s\Omega_{sc}}\right)$ and $F_{\gamma^1_{r,x_e}}(x) = 1 - \exp\left(-\frac{x}{(\alpha_e-(\alpha_c+\alpha_r)x)(1-a_c)\rho_s\Omega_{sr}}\right)$ for $x < \frac{\alpha_e}{\alpha_c+\alpha_r}$, while $F_{\gamma^1_{c,x_e}}$ and $F_{\gamma^1_{r,x_e}}(x)$ equal one for $x \geq \frac{\alpha_e}{\alpha_c+\alpha_r}$. The CDF of γ^2_{e,x_e} is $F_{\gamma^2_{e,x_e}}(x) = 1 - \exp\left(-\frac{x}{(1-b_e)\rho_r(\beta_e-\beta_{rc}x)\Omega_{re}}\right)$ and $F_{\gamma^2_{e,x_e}}(x) = 1$ for $x < \frac{\beta_e}{\beta_{rc}}$ and $x \geq \frac{\beta_e}{\beta_{rc}}$, respectively. Therefore, using Gaussian-Chebyshev quadrature, the ergodic capacity for x_e can be obtained as

$$C_{x_e} = \frac{1}{2\ln 2}\int_0^{\varphi_{x_e}} \frac{1}{1+z}(1 - F_{Z_2}(z))dz$$
$$= \frac{\varphi_{x_e}\pi}{4\ln 2 M_{x_e}}\sum_{m_{x_e}=1}^{M_{x_e}}\sqrt{1-Q_{x_e}{}^2}(1-F_{Z_2}(q_{x_e}))\frac{1}{1+q_{x_e}}, \qquad (14)$$

where $\varphi_{x_e} = \min\{\frac{\alpha_e}{\alpha_c+\alpha_r}, \frac{\beta_e}{\beta_{rc}}\}$, $Q_{x_e} = \cos(\frac{2m_{x_e}-1}{2M_{x_e}}\pi)$, $q_{x_e} = \frac{\varphi_{x_e}(1+Q_{x_e})}{2}$, and M_{x_e} denotes the complexity-accuracy tradeoff parameter.

Theorem 1. *The ergodic capacity for u_c can be written as*

$$C_{u_c} = \Xi_{11} - \Xi_{12} - \Xi_2, \qquad (15)$$

where

$$\Xi_{11} = -\frac{1}{2\ln 2}\frac{\pi^2}{4M_{\Xi_{11}}}\sum_{m_{\Xi_{11}}=1}^{M_{\Xi_{11}}}\sqrt{1-Q_{\Xi_{11}}{}^2}e^{\frac{1}{2\tan q_{\Xi_{11}}}}$$
$$\times \mathrm{Ei}(-1/(2\tan q_{\Xi_{11}}))f_{V_1}(\tan q_{\Xi_{11}})(\sec q_{\Xi_{11}})^2, \qquad (16)$$

$$\Xi_{12} = \frac{\pi^4}{64\ln 2 M_{\theta'}M_\theta}\sum_{m_{\theta'}=1}^{M_{\theta'}}\sum_{m_\theta=1}^{M_\theta}\sqrt{1-(Q_{\theta'})^2}\sqrt{1-(Q_\theta)^2}$$
$$\times e^{\frac{1+\tan q_{\theta'}}{\varepsilon\rho_s\Omega_{ss}}-\frac{\tan q_\theta}{2\tan q_\theta}}\mathrm{Ei}\left(-\frac{1+\tan q_{\theta'}}{\varepsilon\rho_s\Omega_{ss}}\right)\frac{1}{\tan q_\theta}(\sec q_{\theta'})^2(\sec q_\theta)^2 f_{V_1}(\tan q_\theta), \qquad (17)$$

$$\Xi_2 = \Xi_1(f_{V_1}(\cdot) \to f_{V_2}(\cdot)), \qquad (18)$$

where $f_{V_1}(v) = 2\sum_{j_1=1}^2\left\{\prod_{j_2=1 \neq j_1}^2 \frac{\tilde{\Omega}'_{j_1}}{\tilde{\Omega}'_{j_1}-\tilde{\Omega}'_{j_2}}(\frac{2}{\tilde{\Omega}'_{j_1}})^{\frac{3}{2}}v^{\frac{1}{2}}K_1(2\sqrt{\frac{2}{\tilde{\Omega}'_{j_1}}v})\right\}$, $f_{V_2}(v) = \frac{2}{\Omega_{sr}}K_0(2\sqrt{\frac{v}{\Omega_{sr}}})$, *and* $(f_{V_1}(\cdot) \to f_{V_2}(\cdot))$ *represent that* Ξ_2 *can be obtained by replacing* $f_{V_1}(\cdot)$ *to* $f_{V_2}(\cdot)$ *in* Ξ_1. *The functions* $K_1(\cdot)$ *and* $K_0(\cdot)$ *represent the first-order and zero-order modified Bessel functions of the second kind, respectively. Besides,* $Q_\theta = \cos(\frac{2m_\theta-1}{2M_\theta}\pi)$, $Q_{\theta'} = \cos(\frac{2m_{\theta'}-1}{2M_{\theta'}}\pi)$, $Q_{\Xi_{11}} = \cos(\frac{2m_{\Xi_{11}}-1}{2M_{\Xi_{11}}}\pi)$, $q_{\Xi_{11}} = \frac{\pi(1+Q_{\Xi_{11}})}{4}$, $q_\theta = \frac{\pi}{4}(1+Q_\theta)$, *and* $q_{\theta'} = \frac{\pi}{4}(1+Q_{\theta'})$, *where* $M_{\theta'}$, M_θ, *and* $M_{\Xi_{11}}$ *are complexity-tradeoff parameters.*

Proof. See Appendix A.   □

Using a derivation method similar to Theorem 1, we can calculate C_{u_r} as $C_{u_r} = \Xi_2 - \Xi_3$, where $\Xi_3 = -\frac{1}{2\ln 2}e^{\frac{1}{\varepsilon\rho_s\Omega_{ss}}}\mathrm{Ei}(-\frac{1}{\varepsilon\rho_s\Omega_{ss}})$. Applying the Gaussian-Chebyshev quadrature with variable substitution $x = \tan\theta$,we can approximate the ergodic capacity for x'_c as

$$C_{x'_c} = \frac{1}{2\ln 2}\int_0^{\frac{\pi}{2}}\frac{1 - F_L(\tan\theta)}{1 + \tan\theta}(\sec\theta)^2 d\theta$$

$$= \frac{1}{2\ln 2}\frac{\pi^2}{4M_{x'_c}}\sum_{m_{x'_c}=1}^{M_{x'_c}}\sqrt{1 - Q_{x'_c}^2}\frac{1 - F_L(\tan q_{x'_c})}{1 + \tan q_{x'_c}}(\sec q_{x'_c})^2, \quad (19)$$

where $F_L(l) = 1 + \frac{\Omega_{sc}^2}{(\Omega_{rc}\beta_{rc}\vartheta l + \Omega_{sc})\Omega_{re}\Omega_{ec}b_e\vartheta l}e^{\frac{\Omega_{sc}}{\Omega_{re}\Omega_{ec}b_e\vartheta l} - \frac{l}{\Omega_{sc}\rho_s}}\mathrm{Ei}\left(-\frac{\Omega_{sc}}{\Omega_{re}\Omega_{ec}b_e\vartheta l}\right)$, $Q_{x'_c} = \cos(\frac{2m_{x'_c}-1}{2M_{x'_c}}\pi)$, $q_{x'_c} = \frac{\pi}{4}(1 + Q_{x'_c})$, and $M_{x_c'}$ is a accuracy-complexity tradeoff parameter.

Similarly, using [[11], 3.352.4], the variable substitution $x = \tan\theta$, and Gaussian-Chebyshev quadrature, we can calculate $C_{x_{ec}}$ as

$$C_{x_{ec}} = \frac{1}{2\ln 2}\int_0^\infty\int_0^\infty e^{-\frac{u}{b_e\vartheta\rho_s x}}/(1 + u)f_{G_{re}G_{ec}}(x)du$$

$$= \frac{1}{2\ln 2}\int_0^\infty -e^{\frac{1}{b_e\vartheta\rho_s x}}\mathrm{Ei}(-\frac{1}{b_e\vartheta\rho_s x})f_{G_{re}G_{ec}}(x)dx$$

$$= -\frac{1}{2\ln 2}\frac{\pi^2}{4M_{x_{ec}}}\sum_{m_{x_{ec}}=1}^{M_{x_{ec}}}\sqrt{1 - Q_{x_{ec}}^2}e^{\frac{1}{b_e\vartheta\rho_s\tan q_{x_{ec}}}}$$

$$\times \mathrm{Ei}(-\frac{1}{b_e\vartheta\rho_s\tan q_{x_{ec}}})f_{G_{re}G_{ec}}(\tan q_{x_{ec}})(\sec(q_{x_{ec}}))^2, \quad (20)$$

where $Q_{x_{ec}} = \cos(\frac{2m_{x_{ec}}-1}{2M_{x_{ec}}}\pi)$, $q_{x_{ec}} = \frac{\pi}{4}(1 + Q_{x_{ec}})$, $f_{|S_r^2|^2}(x) = e^{-x}$, $f_{G_{re}G_{ec}}(x) = \frac{2}{\Omega_{re}\Omega_{ec}}K_0\left(2\sqrt{\frac{x}{\Omega_{re}\Omega_{ec}}}\right)$, and $M_{x_{ec}}$ is a accuracy-complexity tradeoff parameter.

Similarly, the ergodic rate for x_{rc} can be calculated as

$$C_{x_{rc}} = \frac{1}{2\ln 2}\int_0^\infty\frac{1 - F_T(t)}{1 + t}dt$$

$$= \frac{\pi^2}{8\ln 2M_{x_{rc}}}\sum_{m_{x_{rc}}=1}^{M_{x_{rc}}}\sqrt{1 - Q_{x_{rc}}^2}\frac{1 - F_T(\tan q_{x_{rc}})}{1 + \tan q_{x_{rc}}}(\sec q_{x_{rc}})^2, \quad (21)$$

where $F_T(t) = 1 + \frac{\beta_{rc}\Omega_{rc}}{b_e\Omega_{re}\Omega_{ec}t}e^{\frac{\beta_{rc}\Omega_{rc}}{b_e\Omega_{re}\Omega_{ec}t} - \frac{t}{\beta_{rc}\vartheta\rho_s\Omega_{rc}}}\mathrm{Ei}(-\frac{\beta_{rc}\Omega_{rc}}{b_e\Omega_{re}\Omega_{ec}t})$, $q_{x_{rc}} = \frac{\pi}{4}(1 + Q_{x_{rc}})$, $Q_{x_{rc}} = \cos(\frac{2m_{x_{rc}}-1}{2M_{x_{rc}}}\pi)$, and $M_{x_{rc}}$ is a accuracy-complexity tradeoff parameter. Based on the above analysis, the ESC for the proposed scheme is given by $C_{\mathrm{sum}} = C_{x_c} + C_{x_r} + C_{x_e} + C_{u_c} + C_{u_r} + C_{x'_c} + C_{x_{ec}} + C_{x_{rc}}$.

5   Simulation Results

This section evaluates the ESC of the proposed scheme (i.e., Prop.), the conventional NOMA based CDRT (i.e., CNC), and OMA under the same parameter

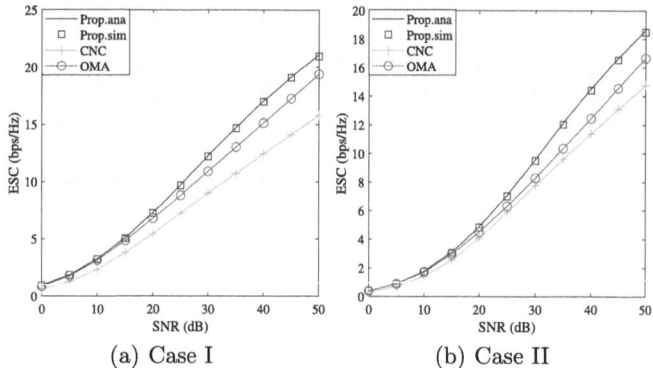

(a) Case I   (b) Case II

Fig. 2. ESC versus transmit SNR in two cases

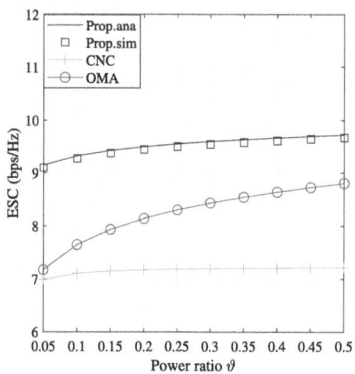

Fig. 3. ESC versus power ratio ϑ in Case I.

settings. We consider two cases, where Case I is set to $\Omega_{sc} = \Omega_{cs} = \Omega_{ss} = 1$, $\Omega_{sr} = \Omega_{rs} = \Omega_{rc} = \Omega_{re} = \Omega_{ec} = 0.8$, and $\vartheta = 0.5$, and Case II is set to $\Omega_{sc} = \Omega_{cs} = \Omega_{re} = \Omega_{ec} = 0.5$, $\Omega_{sr} = \Omega_{rs} = \Omega_{rc} = 0.25$, $\Omega_{ss} = 1$, and $\vartheta = 0.1$. The PACs are set to $\alpha_c = 0.01$, $\alpha_r = 0.09$, $\alpha_e = 0.9$, $\beta_e = 0.9$, and $\beta_{rc} = 0.1$. The reflection coefficients are set to $a_c = a_r = a_e = 0.6$. For fair comparison, the PACs for the NOMA-based CDRT are consistent with the proposed scheme.

Figure 2 illustrates the relationship between the ESC and ρ_s. The figure shows a significant overlap between the simulated values and the theoretical curves, which indicates the correctness of the theoretical analysis. Moreover, the proposed scheme outperforms other benchmarks in terms of ESC in different cases. This is because the proposed scheme simultaneously applies NOMA and backscatter communication to the system, which improves the system ESC. Since OMA transmits as many signals as the proposed scheme without inter-user interference, it can achieve higher ESC than the CNC. Figure 3 depicts the ESC under different power ratio ϑ. From the figure, it can be seen that the proposed scheme still achieves the best ESC with ϑ. As the ρ_r increases, the ESCs for all the three schemes are improved to different degrees. This is due to the fact that the increase of transmit power at the RU can improve the information rate of the CEU in all the schemes, thus increasing the overall ESC.

6   Conclusions

This paper investigated a NOMA based CDRT system comprising one full duplex BS, one RU, one CCU, and one CEU. To enhance the system SE, we proposed a bidirectional backscatter NOMA scheme, wherein the BS employs downlink NOMA and uplink NOMA to serve three users and collect information from the RU and CCU. Simultaneously, the CCU collects information from the RU and CEU. The closed-form expressions for the ESC of the proposed scheme were derived to evaluate system performance. Simulation results demonstrate that the proposed analytical framework accurately characterizes system performance. Moreover, the ESC performance of the proposed scheme outperforms both the NOMA-based CDRT and OMA schemes.

A   Proof of Theorem 1

Denote $A \triangleq H_{sr}H_{rs}a_r\rho_s|S_s^1|^2 + H_{sc}H_{cs}a_c\rho_s|S_s^1|^2 = |\sum_{n=1}^2 \tilde{h}_n\hat{h}_n\sqrt{a_n\rho_s}S_s^1|^2$, $B \triangleq H_{sr}H_{rs}a_r\rho_s|S_s^1|^2$, and $C \triangleq \varepsilon\rho_s H_{ss}$, where $\tilde{h}_1 = h_{sr}$, $\hat{h}_1 = h_{rs}$, $\tilde{h}_2 = h_{sc}$, $\hat{h}_2 = h_{cs}$, $a_1 = a_r$, and $a_2 = a_c$. Based on this, the probability density functions (PDFs) of A, B, and C can be written as $f_A(a) = \frac{1}{2V_1}e^{-\frac{a}{2V_1}}$, $f_B(b) = \frac{1}{2V_2}e^{-\frac{b}{2V_2}}$, and $f_C(c) = \frac{1}{\varepsilon\rho_s\Omega_{ss}}e^{-\frac{c}{\varepsilon\rho_s\Omega_{ss}}}$, where $V_1 = \frac{\sum_{n=1}^2 a_n\rho_s|\tilde{h}_n\hat{h}_n|^2}{2}$ and $V_2 = \frac{a_r\rho_s|h_{sr}h_{rs}|^2}{2}$. Based on γ_{s,u_c}^1, the ESC for u_c can be rewritten as

$$
\begin{aligned}
C_{u_c} =& \frac{1}{2\ln 2}E\left\{\ln(A+C+1) - \ln(B+C+1)\right\} \\
=& \frac{1}{2\ln 2}\underbrace{\int_0^\infty\int_0^\infty\int_0^\infty \ln(a+c+1)f_A(a)f_C(c)f_{V_1}(v)dadcdv}_{\Xi_1} \\
& - \frac{1}{2\ln 2}\underbrace{\int_0^\infty\int_0^\infty\int_0^\infty \ln(b+c+1)f_B(b)f_C(c)f_{V_2}(v)dbdcdv}_{\Xi_2}. \quad (22)
\end{aligned}
$$

Considering A as a function of variable S_s^1, we have $\mathrm{Re}\{\sum_{n=1}^2 \tilde{h}_n\hat{h}_n\sqrt{a_n\rho_s}S_s^1\} \sim N(0,V_1)$ and $\mathrm{Im}\{\sum_{n=1}^2 \tilde{h}_n\hat{h}_n\sqrt{a_n\rho_s}S_s^1\} \sim N(0,V_1)$. Specifically, V_1 and V_2 can be equivalently written as $V_1 = \sum_{n=1}^2 |\tilde{h}_n'\hat{h}_n'|^2$ and $V_2 = |\tilde{h}_{sr}\hat{h}_{rs}|^2$, where $\tilde{h}_n' \sim CN(0,\tilde{\Omega}_n')$, $\hat{h}_n' \sim CN(0,1)$, $\tilde{h}_{sr} \sim CN(0,\tilde{\Omega}_{sr})$, $\hat{h}_{rs} \sim CN(0,1)$, $\tilde{\Omega}_n' = \frac{a_n\rho_s\tilde{\Omega}_n\hat{\Omega}_n}{2}$, and $\tilde{\Omega}_{sr} = \frac{a_r\rho_s\Omega_{sr}\Omega_{rs}}{2}$. According to [12], the PDFs of V_1 and V_2 are given in

Theorem 1. Substituting $f_C(c)$ and [[11], 4.337.1] to (22), we have

$$
\Xi_1 = \underbrace{\frac{1}{2\ln 2} \int_0^\infty \int_0^\infty \ln(1+a) f_A(a) f_{V_1}(v) da dv}_{\Xi_{11}}
$$

$$
- \underbrace{\frac{1}{2\ln 2} \int_0^\infty \int_0^\infty e^{\frac{1+a}{\varepsilon \rho_s \Omega_{ss}}} \operatorname{Ei}\left(-\frac{1+a}{\varepsilon \rho_s \Omega_{ss}}\right) f_A(a) f_{V_1}(v) da dv}_{\Xi_{12}}. \qquad (23)
$$

Furthermore, applying [[11], 4.337.1], the variable substitution $\theta = \arctan v$, and the Gaussian-Chebyshev quadrature to Ξ_{11}, we can obtain Ξ_{11} as (16). Similarly, we can use the variable substitutions $\theta = \arctan v$ and $\theta' = \arctan a$, and the Gaussian-Chebyshev quadrature to obtain Ξ_{12} as (17). Since Ξ_1 and Ξ_2 have similar integral forms, we can easily obtain $\Xi_2 = \Xi_1(f_{V_1}(\cdot) \to f_{V_2}(\cdot))$. Substituting Ξ_{11}, Ξ_{12}, and Ξ_2 into (19), we obtain C_{u_c}.

References

1. Han, S., Li, Z., Xue, Q., Meng, W., Li, C.: Joint broadcast and unicast transmission based on RSMA and spectrum sharing for integrated satellite-terrestrial network. IEEE Trans. Cognitive Commun. Netw. (2024). https://doi.org/10.1109/TCCN. 2024.3350596
2. Zhang, R., et al.: Integrated sensing and communication with massive MIMO: a unified tensor approach for channel and target parameter estimation. IEEE Trans. Wireless Commun. (2024). https://doi.org/10.1109/TWC.2024.3351856 Early Access
3. Wu, C., You, C., Liu, Y., Han, S., Renzo, M.D.: Two-timescale design for STAR-RIS-aided NOMA systems. IEEE Trans. Commun. **72**(1), 585–600 (2024)
4. Kim, J.-B., Lee, I.-H.: Non-orthogonal multiple access in coordinated direct and relay transmission. IEEE Wireless Commun. Lett. **19**(11), 2037–2040 (2015)
5. Xu, Y., et al.: Coordinated direct and relay transmission with NOMA and network coding in Nakagami-m fading channels. IEEE Trans. Commun. **69**(1), 207–222 (2021)
6. Xu, Y., Cheng, J., Wang, G., Leung, V.C.M.: Adaptive coordinated direct and relay transmission for NOMA networks: a joint downlink-uplink scheme. IEEE Trans. Wireless Commun. **20**(7), 4328–4346 (2021)
7. Lei, H., et al.: On secure CDRT with NOMA and physical-layer network coding. IEEE Trans. Commun. **71**(1), 381–396 (2023)
8. Xu, Y., Du, Z., Yuan, W., Jia, S., Leung, V.C.M.: Performance of OTFS-NOMA scheme for coordinated direct and relay transmission networks in high-mobility scenarios. IEEE Wireless Commun. Lett. **12**(12), 2268–2272 (2023)
9. Liang, Y.-C., Long, R., Zhang, Q., Niyato, D.: Symbiotic communications: where Marconi meets Darwin. IEEE Wireless Commun. **29**(1), 144–150 (2022)
10. Chen, W., et al.: Backscatter cooperation in NOMA communications systems. IEEE Trans. Wireless Commun. **20**(6), 3458–3474 (2021)

11. Gradshteyn, I.S., Ryzhik, I.M.: Tables of Integrals, Series, and Products, 7th edn. Academic Press, New York (2007)
12. Chatzidiamantis, N.D., Karagiannidis, G.K.: On the distribution of the sum of gamma-gamma variates and applications in RF and optical wireless communications. IEEE Trans. Commun. **59**(5), 1298–1308 (2011)

Joint Equalization and Multi-phase Tracking Based on MCC Criterion for Underwater Acoustic Communication

Miao Ke[1] and Zhiyong Liu[1,2,3](✉)

[1] Harbin Institute of Technology (Weihai), Weihai, China
lzyhit@hit.edu.cn
[2] Shandong Provincial Key Laboratory of Marine Electronic Information and Intelligent Unmanned Systems, Weihai 264209, China
[3] Key Laboratory of Cross-Domain Synergy and Comprehensive Support for Unmanned Marine Systems of Ministry of Industry and Information Technology, Weihai 264209, China

Abstract. In this paper, a multi-phase tracking (MT) structure based on decision feedback equalization is studied, which can solve the problem of strong multipath and phase offset in time varying underwater acoustic communication. Further, the joint equalization and multi-phase Tracking algorithm (JEMT) is proposed. The MT structure not only accelerates the convergence speed of phase tracking but also achieves better steady-state mean square error in equalization. In addition, considering that the noise in the actual underwater acoustic environment has obvious impulse noise characteristics rather than the Gaussian noise, this paper further proposes the JEMT algorithm based on the maximum correntropy criterion (JEMTMCC) to make it more suitable for the underwater acoustic environment. Finally, simulation results show that the JEMTMCC algorithm can achieve better bit error performance.

Keywords: Underwater Acoustic Time Varying Channel · Non-Gaussian Noise · Multi-Phase Tracking · Maximum Correntropy Criterion

1 Introduction

Underwater acoustic communication technology is the main way of long distance information transmission in the marine environment. However, compared with the environment of terrestrial wireless communication, the marine environment has the characteristics of strong multipath, time varying, and non-Gaussian noise, which leads to the degradation of communication quality.

Depending on the difference in transmission rate in underwater acoustic communication, the inter-symbol interference (ISI) caused by the multipath effect can span up to several tens of symbol intervals. To solve this problem, equalization is one of the commonly used research ways. However, perfect carrier recovery and symbol timing

© ICST Institute for Computer Sciences, Social Informatics and Telecommunications Engineering 2025
Published by Springer Nature Switzerland AG 2025. All Rights Reserved
H.-H. Chen and W. Meng (Eds.): WiSATS 2024, LNICST 605, pp. 226–236, 2025.
https://doi.org/10.1007/978-3-031-86196-3_19

are assumed in most research. The time varying ISI is the main reason for the bad capabilities of synchronization systems which are dominated by phase-locked loop (PLL) structure. In [1], phase parameter estimation and decision feedback equalization are jointly implemented to solve the problem of performance degradation caused by the interaction between equalization and phase estimation, and an adaptive algorithm combining phase estimation and equalization is designed. The second order PLL is used to estimate the phase parameters, the fractionally spaced decision feedback equalization (DFE) eliminates the need for symbol timing estimation, and the recursive least squares (RLS) algorithm with faster convergence speed improves the ability of fast-tracking. Subsequently, the authors extended this algorithm to spatial diversity and proposed an adaptive multichannel equalization and phase estimation algorithm [2]. Since the second order PLL and RLS algorithm increase a certain algorithm complexity compared with the conventional algorithm, some researchers consider the complexity of the system and algorithm and use different equalization algorithms (such as fast self-optimizing least mean square, FOLMS) and the structure of the first order PLL to study the joint phase estimation and equalization.

Another characteristic of the underwater acoustic environment is that underwater noise has obvious impulse noise characteristics, which do not conform to the nature of Gaussian distribution. Most equalization algorithms are based on the MSE standard and are carried out under the Gaussian assumption, which will lead to errors in the system performance when used in the actual system. To overcome this effect, some algorithms that can combat impulse noise, such as the affine projection algorithm and least mean M-estimation algorithm, have been introduced to deal with non-Gaussian noise [3, 4]. In recent years, an adaptive algorithm based on the maximum correntropy criterion (MCC) has been proposed to maximize the entropy between the desired signal and the output of the equalizer, which can effectively suppress impulse noise. After proving the mean square deviation (MSD) of the MCC in the adaptive filter, there have been several research directions on adaptive filtering algorithms for MCC. Kernel adaptive filtering [5, 6], convex merging optimization [7], and sparse adaptive filtering [8, 9].

As far as we know, the joint equalization and phase tracking algorithm based on MCC has not been studied yet, and the non-Gaussian noises in underwater acoustic communication cannot be ignored. Therefore, this paper will first study the joint equalization and single phase tracking algorithm based on MCC (JESTMCC). In addition, considering that the phase effect caused by the strong multipath effect in the underwater acoustic environment is the cumulative sum of the phase offset of multiple paths, and the single phase tracking structure cannot achieve the best phase compensation result, this paper plans to propose a multi-phase tracking (MT) structure to deal with the phase offset effect of multipath separately and combine this structure with MCC. To further improve the processing method for non-Gaussian and time varying multipath problems in underwater acoustic communication, the proposed joint equalization and multi-phase tracking algorithm based on MCC (JEMTMCC) will be verified by simulation.

The structure of this paper is as follows. Section 2 describes the time varying underwater acoustic multipath channel model and the adopted signal frame structure. In Sect. 3, We analyzed the channel model used in our research, the decision feedback equalization with the MT structure is introduced, and the JEMTMCC algorithm is described. The steady state error performance analysis is presented. In Sect. 4, the algorithm is simulated and compared with other algorithms. Finally, Sect. 5 summarizes the main conclusions of this paper as well as future research directions.

2 System Model

In this paper, the equalization algorithm of underwater acoustic communication receivers is mainly considered. In the whole system model, transmitted data bits are in turn passed through the modulation and waveform. The time varying channel and non-Gaussian noises will be considered. The simplified system model is shown in Fig. 1.

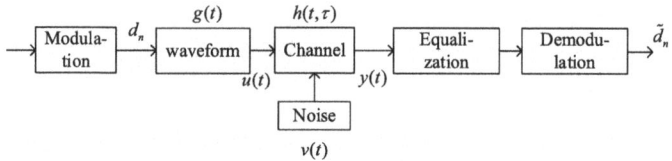

Fig. 1. System model

The purpose of the system design in Fig. 1 is that the original data bits can be recovered by the equalization algorithm at the receiver so that the probability $P(d_n \neq \tilde{d}_n)$ is minimized. Where d_n denotes the modulation symbol, $g(t)$ denotes the transmitted signal waveform, $u(t)$ denotes the baseband signal, $h(t, \tau)$ denotes the underwater acoustic channel model, $v(t)$ denotes the non-Gaussian noise, and $y(t)$ denotes the received signal.

In the modulation part, the carrier modulation part is ignored, and the modulated signal is expressed $\{+1, -1\}$ in the form of a constellation diagram. In this paper, QPSK modulation is used, and the baseband signal is specifically expressed as follows:

$$u(t) = \sum_n d_n g(t - nT) \tag{1}$$

where T denotes the symbol duration.

The underwater acoustic channel model is specifically expressed as formula (2).

$$h(t, \tau) = \sum_{p=1}^{L} A_P(t)\delta(\tau - \tau_p(t))e^{-j\varphi_p(t)} \tag{2}$$

where L denotes the number of multipath, $A_P(t)$ denotes the amplitude of the pth path, $\tau_p(t)$ denotes the delay of the pth path, $\varphi_p(t)$ denotes the phase offset of the pth path, and $\delta(\tau)$ is the unit impulse function.

The received signal can be expressed as follows.

$$y(t) = \sum_n \sum_{p=1}^{L} d_n A_P(t)g(\tau - nT - \tau_p(t))e^{-j\varphi_p(t)} + v(t) \tag{3}$$

The received signal is affected by channel fading, and the amplitude is generally small. Between equalization, we amplify the received signal by a certain proportion of power to avoid the situation that equalization is difficult to handle small values. In addition, the input method of equalization can be sampled with a symbol interval, but the best can be achieved only when the equalization length is infinite. In this paper, the fractional interval sampling method which is smaller than the symbol interval is used as the input signal of equalization, which can achieve better equalization performance.

The whole data frame can be divided into two parts. The first is the initial training phase, which may have multiple channel changes. The purpose is to make the equalization performance approach to the steady state, to facilitate the subsequent equalization and the tracking of the PLL. The second phase is the data phase, in which a small number of training sequences are used for supplementary training between each data packet, and the channel can be changed between any data packets.

3 Proposed Algorithm

3.1 Preprocessing

Firstly, this section will analyze the phase offset of the multipath channel. Under the condition of the underwater acoustic channel model described in Eq. (2), taking only two paths and the signal waveform represented by a rectangle as an example. When the phase offset of the first path is not affected by the phase offset of the following path, the phase compensation at the beginning of the second path has not eliminated the phase offset of the first path, so the PLL cannot achieve the desired effect.

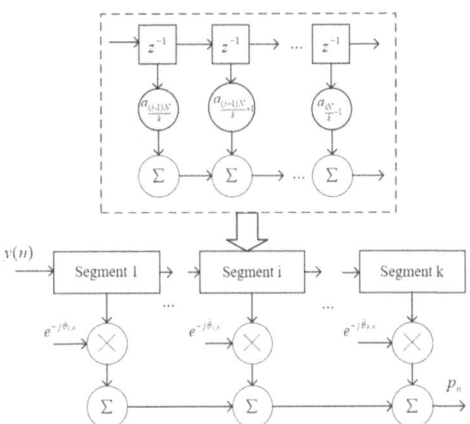

Fig. 2. MT Structure in Feedforward.

However, the inter-symbol interference is generally 20 ms above in the underwater acoustic channel, and the number of main paths of multipath is more than 5, which leads to the phase offset of more than one path when dealing with phase offset. Therefore, we further analyze and adjust the phase compensation in the specific equalization structure, and propose the MT structure, as shown in Fig. 2.

The input signal of equalization is generally obtained by sampling the received signal. In this paper, the received signal is sampled in the fractional interval mode, which is less than the symbol interval, and the sampling result of the received signal is represented. Then the output of feedforward equalization can be expressed as (4).

$$
p_n = \sum_{i=0}^{N/k-1} y(n-i)e^{-j\widehat{\theta}_{1,n}}a_i + \cdots + \sum_{i=N/k}^{2N/k-1} y(n-i)e^{-j\widehat{\theta}_{2,n}}a_i + \cdots +
$$

$$
\sum_{i=(k-1)N/k}^{N-1} y(n-i)e^{-j\widehat{\theta}_{2,n}}a_i = \sum_{l=1}^{k} (\sum_{i=(l-1)N/k}^{lN/k-1} y(n-i)a_i) \cdot e^{-j\widehat{\theta}_{l,n}}
\tag{4}
$$

Due to the existence of the segmented structure, the signal vector of the ith received signal at time n can be denoted as $\mathbf{y}_n[i] = [y(n-(i-1)N/k), \cdots, y(n-iN/k+1)]$, $\mathbf{a}_n[i] = [a_{(i-1)N/k}, \cdots, a_{iN/k-1}]$ denote the tap vector of the ith received signal at time n, N denotes the total length of the balanced taps, and k denotes the number of segments, which will be used in the following algorithm part. The above equation is further expressed in the form of vectors.

$$
p_n = \mathbf{y}_n^T \Phi \mathbf{a}_n
\tag{5}
$$

where $\Phi = diag[\underbrace{e^{-j\widehat{\theta}_{1,n}}}_{N/k}, \underbrace{e^{-j\widehat{\theta}_{2,n}}}_{N/k}, \cdots, \underbrace{e^{-j\widehat{\theta}_{k,n}}}_{N/k}]$ denotes the matrix consisting of phase offsets which is a diagonal matrix.

3.2 JEMTMCC Algorithm

This section introduces the JEMTMCC algorithm. MT structure is an improvement of the equalization structure. As decision feedback equalization is used in this paper, MT is mainly used in the feedforward part of the equalization, and the feedback part is consistent with the original equalization structure. The whole equalization structure will be shown in Fig. 3.

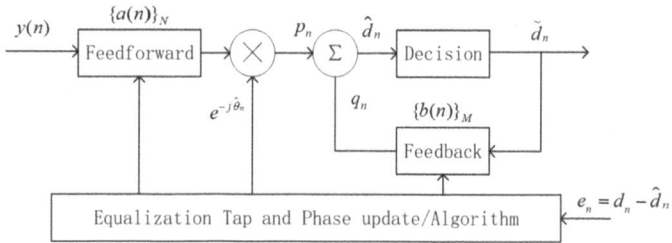

Fig. 3. Decision Feedback Equalization.

The input and tap of feedforward equalization and feedback equalization are represented by a vector.

$$\mathbf{w}_n = [\mathbf{a}_n, \mathbf{b}_n] \tag{6}$$

$$\mathbf{x}_n = [\mathbf{y}_n, -\widetilde{\mathbf{d}}_n] \tag{7}$$

The corresponding phase matrix is denoted as

$$\mathbf{\Phi} = diag[\underbrace{e^{-j\hat{\theta}_{1,n}}}_{N/k}, \underbrace{e^{-j\hat{\theta}_{2,n}}}_{N/k}, \cdots, \underbrace{e^{-j\hat{\theta}_{k,n}}}_{N/k}, \underbrace{1}_{M}] \tag{8}$$

where M denotes the length of the feedback equalization. The error of equalization output can be expressed as follows.

$$e_n = d_n - \mathbf{w}_n^T \mathbf{\Phi} \mathbf{x}_n \tag{9}$$

The optimization criterion of the JEMTMCC algorithm is maximization $\exp(-e_n^2/2\sigma^2)/\sqrt{2\pi}\sigma$, the corresponding partial derivatives are as follows

$$\partial/\partial\mathbf{w}_n = \exp(-e_n^2/2\sigma^2)\mathbf{\Phi}\mathbf{x}_n e_n^*/\sqrt{2\pi}\sigma^3 \tag{10}$$

$$\partial/\partial\hat{\theta}_{i,n} = -2\mathrm{Im}\{\exp(-e_n^2/2\sigma^2)/\sqrt{2\pi}\sigma^3 \cdot \mathbf{y}_n^T[i]\mathbf{a}_n[i]\cdot e^{-j\hat{\theta}_{i,n}})e_n^*\} \tag{11}$$

Table 1. The proposed JEMTMCC algorithm

Initialization	$\mathbf{a}_0[i] = \mathbf{0}, \ \mathbf{b}_0[i] = \mathbf{0}$
Parameter	μ, η
	for n =1,2,3,... $\mathbf{y}_n[i] = [y(n - (i-1)N/k), \cdots, y(n - iN/k + 1)]$ $\widetilde{\mathbf{d}}_n[i] = [\tilde{d}_{(i-1)N/k}, \cdots, \tilde{d}_{iN/k-1}]$ $\mathbf{x}_n = [\mathbf{y}_n, -\widetilde{\mathbf{d}}_n]$ $\mathbf{\Phi} = diag[\underbrace{e^{-j\hat{\theta}_{1,n}}}_{N/k}, \underbrace{e^{-j\hat{\theta}_{2,n}}}_{N/k}, \cdots, \underbrace{e^{-j\hat{\theta}_{k,n}}}_{N/k}, \underbrace{1}_{M}]$ $e_n = d_n - \mathbf{w}_n^T \mathbf{\Phi} \mathbf{x}_n$ $\mathbf{w}_{n+1} = \mathbf{w}_n + \mu \exp(-e_n^2/2\sigma^2)\mathbf{\Phi}\mathbf{x}_n e_n^*/\sqrt{2\pi}\sigma^3$ $\hat{\theta}_{i,n+1} = \hat{\theta}_{i,n} - \eta\mathrm{Im}\{\exp(-e_n^2/2\sigma^2)/\sqrt{2\pi}\sigma^3 \cdot \mathbf{y}_n^T[i]\mathbf{a}_n[i]\cdot e^{-j\hat{\theta}_{i,n}})e_n^*\}$ *end*

3.3 Steady-State Mean Square Error Performance Analysis

The inputs of the feedforward filter and the feedback filter of the equalizer are combined, and the input of the feedforward part is multiplied by the phase compensation x_n, which can be expressed as

$$x_n = [a_n e^{-j\hat{\theta}_n}, b_n] \tag{12}$$

The error term in the tap coefficient update formula is represented by $f(e_n) = \exp(-e_n^2/2\sigma^2)e_n$, and the step size is denoted by $\eta = \mu/\sqrt{2\pi}\sigma^3$, , then (10–11) can obtain the following tap coefficient update formula

$$w_{n+1} = w_n + \eta f(e_n)x_n \tag{13}$$

Assuming that the optimal tap coefficient is w_0, after n times iterations the tap coefficient is w_n, n times iterations the systematic error can be expressed as

$$e_n = (w_0^T - w_n^T)x_n + v_n = \tilde{w}_n^T x_n + v_n = e_n^a + v_n \tag{14}$$

where e_n^a is the error of the equalization at the n iterations and v_n is the channel error.

Taking the expectation of Eq. (13), assuming that the input signal and channel noise are zero-mean and satisfy independent and identically distributed.

$$E[||\tilde{w}_{n+1}||^2] = E[||\tilde{w}_n||^2] + \eta^2 E[f^2(e_n)||x_n||^2] - 2\eta E[f(e_n)\tilde{w}_n^T x_n]$$
$$= E[||\tilde{w}_n||^2] + \eta^2 Tr(x)E[f^2(e_n)] - 2\eta E[f(e_n)e_n^a] \tag{15}$$

When the number of iterations is sufficient, the equalizer can be regarded as having reached the steady state, and then the tap coefficient satisfies the following

$$\lim_{n\to\infty} E[||\tilde{w}_{n+1}||^2] = \lim_{n\to\infty} E[||\tilde{w}_n||^2] \tag{16}$$

$$2 \lim_{n\to\infty} E[f(e_n)e_n^a] = \eta Tr(x) \lim_{n\to\infty} E[f^2(e_n)] \tag{17}$$

We simplified the left equation of Eq. (17), and let $E[||e_n^a||^2] = S$, (18) can be obtained.

$$\lim_{n\to\infty} E[f(e_n)e_n^a] = S \lim_{n\to\infty} E[f'(e_n)] \tag{18}$$

Using the expectation calculation formula, (18) can be simplified further.

$$f'(e_n) = (\exp(\frac{-e_n^2}{2\sigma^2})e_n)' = (1 - \frac{e_n^2}{\sigma^2})\exp(\frac{-e_n^2}{2\sigma^2}) \tag{19}$$

$$\lim_{n\to\infty} E[f'(e_n)] = \int_{-\infty}^{\infty} f(x)f_X(x)dx = \frac{1}{\sqrt{2\pi}\sigma_e} \int_{-\infty}^{\infty} (1 - \frac{e_n^2}{\sigma^2})\exp(-(\frac{\sigma^2 + \sigma_e^2}{2\sigma^2\sigma_e^2})e_n^2)de_n \tag{20}$$

Through a series of complicated integrals and simplifications.

$$\lim_{n \to \infty} E[f(e_n)e_n^a] = S\sigma^3/(\sigma^2 + S + \sigma_v^2)^{3/2} \tag{21}$$

$$\lim_{n \to \infty} E[f^2(e_n)] = \sigma^3(S + \sigma_v^2)/(2S + 2\sigma_v^2 + \sigma^2)^{3/2} \tag{22}$$

Substitute (21) and (22) into Eq. (17), lastly steady-state mean square error can be simplified as (23)

$$S = \frac{\eta\lambda Tr(\mathbf{x})\sigma_v^2}{2 - \eta\lambda Tr(\mathbf{x})}, \ \lambda = (\frac{\sigma^2 + S + \sigma_v^2}{2S + 2\sigma_v^2 + \sigma^2})^{3/2} \tag{23}$$

When $\lambda = 1$ the steady-state error of the equalizer satisfying the JEMTMCC algorithm is equal to that of the LMS algorithm. Then $\lambda < 1$, we have

$$S_{JEST-MCC} < S_{LMS} = \frac{\eta Tr(\mathbf{x})\sigma_v^2}{2 - \eta Tr(\mathbf{x})} \tag{24}$$

4   Simulation Results and Analysis

4.1   Underwater Acoustic System Model Simulation

The statistical time varying underwater acoustic channel model proposed in [10] is used for the algorithm considered in this paper, while the symmetric α-stable ($S\alpha S$) model is used for the non-Gaussian noise model. The non-Gaussian noise waveform with symmetry parameter 0, offset parameter 1, and different characteristic parameters, represents the composition of large amplitude noise in non-Gaussian noise. The specific situation will be analyzed by simulation. In general, the range of values α in the $S\alpha S$ model is between 1 and 2.

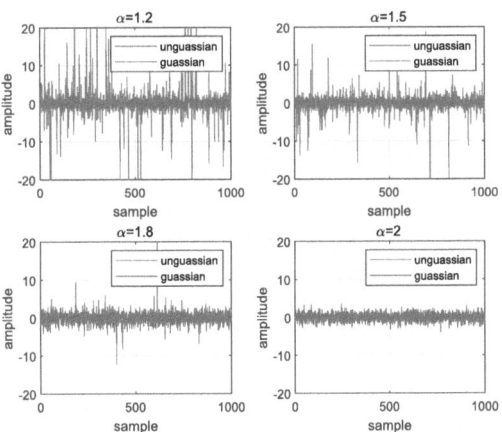

Fig. 4. Different α in $S\alpha S$ model

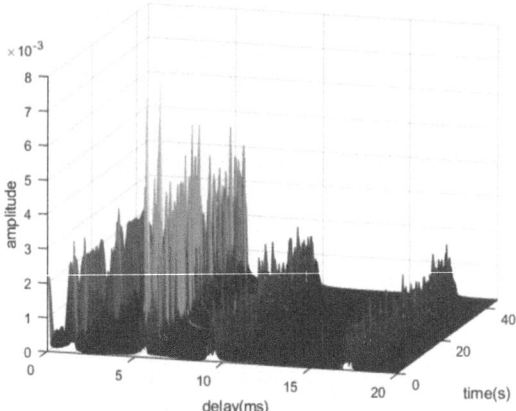

Fig. 5. Time varying underwater acoustic channel

Figure 4 in right above shows that when $\alpha = 2$, there is no large value amplitude noise, compared with Gaussian noise, which can be considered as Gaussian noise. With the decrease of α, when $\alpha = 1.8$, individual large amplitude noise appears; when $\alpha = 1.5$, the number of large amplitude noise increases; when $\alpha = 1.2$, larger amplitude noise appears, and the Gaussian component accounts for a small proportion. In the simulation, we adopt this model with $\alpha = 1.2$, 1.5, and 1.8 to simulate the non-Gaussian noise in the underwater acoustic communication algorithm test. Similarly, the underwater acoustic time varying model adopted in the simulation, as shown in Fig. 5. Multipath effect, which is mainly composed of five main paths, the arrival time of each main path will have a certain offset, and then the amplitude of different main paths will also change with time, which is in line with the characteristics of the underwater acoustic time varying channel.

4.2 Simulation of the Performance of the JEMTMCC Algorithm

The initial training consists of 1000 symbols, followed by symbols containing 1000 valid data to complete the information transmission process, and the simulation is repeated 300 times. The mixed signal-to-noise ratio (MSNR) is the ratio to the power of non-Gaussian noise Under this condition, the performance comparison between the JESTMCC algorithm and the JESTNLMS algorithm with different values is tested, and the results are shown in Fig. 6. In the models with different α, the BER performance of the two algorithms also becomes worse as the value decreases, which verifies that the large non-Gaussian value in the $S\alpha S$ model increases as the α decreases. In addition, the performance of the JESTMCC algorithm is slightly better than the JESTNLMS algorithm in the same model.

This result shows that the MCC algorithm achieves better BER performance than the MSE algorithm when the system noises are considered as non-Gaussian noise. We will consider the case of α 1.8 later in the validation of the algorithm.

In the same simulation environment, we continue to simulate and analyze the JEMTMCC algorithm proposed in this paper and the results are shown in Fig. 7.

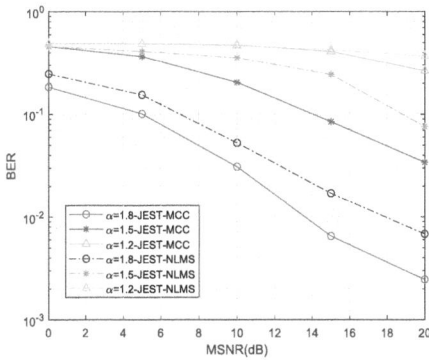

Fig. 6. Differences α in the JEST algorithm

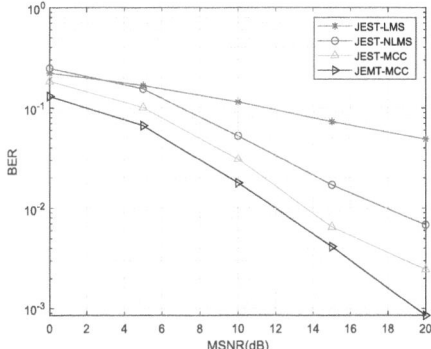

Fig. 7. BER performance of JEMT algorithms

From Fig. 7, we conclude that both JEMT and JEST algorithms fail to meet the desired system performance requirements at low SNR, and there is no significant difference in performance. However, compared with the MSE algorithm, the MCC algorithm still has a performance advantage. With the increase of SNR, JEMTMCC achieves an improvement compared to JESTMCC, which verifies the advantages of the MT structure proposed in this paper when facing time varying multipath channels.

5 Conclusion

In this paper, the non-Gaussian noise interference in time varying underwater acoustic communication systems is considered, and the multipath and phase offset problems in the actual channel are analyzed. An MT structure is proposed, and the JEMTMCC algorithm is proposed on this basis. The performance of the algorithm is tested under different non-Gaussian noise, different packet sizes, and different time varying factors. The results show that the JEMTMCC algorithm has the best robustness.

References

1. Stojanovic, M., Catipovic, J.A., Proakis, J.G.: Phase-coherent digital communications for underwater acoustic channels. IEEE J. Oceanic Eng. **19**(1), 100–111 (1994)
2. Stojanovic, M., Catipovic, J., Proakis, J.G.: Adaptive multichannel combining and equalization for underwater acoustic communications. J. Acoust. Soc. Am. **94**(3), 1621–1631 (1993)
3. Shao, T., Zheng, Y.R., Benesty, J.: An affine projection sign algorithm robust against impulsive interferences. IEEE Signal Process. Lett. **17**(4), 327–330 (2010)
4. Song, P., Zhao, H.: Affine-projection-like M-estimate adaptive filter for robust filtering in impulse noise. IEEE Trans. Circuits Syst. II Express Briefs **66**(12), 2087–2091 (2019)
5. Ma, W., Qu, H., Gui, G., Xu, L., Zhao, J., Chen, B.: Maximum correntropy criterion based sparse adaptive filtering algorithms for robust channel estimation under non-Gaussian environments. J. Franklin Inst. **352**(7), 2708–2727 (2015)
6. Chen, B., Xing, L., Liang, J., et al.: Steady-state mean-square error analysis for adaptive filtering under the maximum correntropy criterion. IEEE Signal Process. Lett. **21**(7), 880–884 (2014)
7. Chen, B., Xing, L., Zhao, H., et al.: Generalized correntropy for robust adaptive filtering. IEEE Trans. Signal Process. **64**(13), 3376–3387 (2016)
8. Shi, L., Lin, Y.: Convex combination of adaptive filters under the maximum correntropy criterion in impulsive interference. IEEE Signal Process. Lett. **21**(11), 1385–1388 (2014)
9. Li, Y., Jiang, Z., Shi, W., Han, X., Chen, B.: Blocked maximum correntropy criterion algorithm for cluster-sparse system identifications. IEEE Trans. Circuits Syst. II Express Briefs **66**(11), 1915–1919 (2019)
10. Wang, J., et al.: A novel underwater acoustic signal denoising algorithm for Gaussian/non-Gaussian impulsive noise. IEEE Trans. Veh. Technol. **70**(1), 429–445 (2020)

ISAC Beamforming in Connected Autonomous Vehicles

Jian Zhang, Chenguang He$^{(\boxtimes)}$, Weixiao Meng, and Yuchuan Ma

School of Electronics and Information Engineering, Harbin Institute of Technology, 150001 Harbin, China
{hechenguang,wxmeng}@hit.edu.cn

Abstract. Connected Automated Vehicles (CAV) is a promising application for connected vehicles. However, in the automatic driving scenario, the sensor blind area will lead to serious security risks, and the existing vehicle-to-vehicle technology is difficult to break through the sensor blind area and ensure the reliability of the perceptual information. To overcome these problems, based on Integrated sensing and communication (ISAC) technology, it is feasible to treat infrastructure as a means to extend the sensing range. The base station transmits a number of beams, including a sensing beam and a communication beam. The sensing beam is responsible for sensing the target in the sensing blind area, and the communication beam is responsible for transmitting the sensed information to the CAV. However, there may be interference in the transmission process. In this paper, the beamforming algorithm of communication beam and sensing beam is designed to reduce the interference, and the communication signal-to-noise ratio (SINR) at the autonomous vehicle and the sensing signal-to-noise ratio (SNR) returned at the base station are guaranteed.

Keywords: Integrated Sensing And Communication · Connected Automated Vehicles · Beamforming

1 Introduction

With the development of the fifth generation of mobile communication, the sixth generation of mobile communication and artificial intelligence technology, the autonomous vehicle industry is developing rapidly. Autonomous vehicles need continuous real-time sensing of the surrounding environment, but it is difficult to achieve it only by on-board functions, because the sensing function of autonomous vehicles is mainly realized by multiple on-board sensors. Under the influence of obstacles and bad weather, vehicles often have a sensing blind area, which will lead to the self-driving car can not obtain a full range of perceptual information, and it is impossible to predict the possible danger. In addition, the

This work is supported by the Key R&D Program of Heilongjiang Province under Grant JD22A001.

© ICST Institute for Computer Sciences, Social Informatics and Telecommunications Engineering 2025
Published by Springer Nature Switzerland AG 2025. All Rights Reserved
H.-H. Chen and W. Meng (Eds.): WiSATS 2024, LNICST 605, pp. 237–245, 2025.
https://doi.org/10.1007/978-3-031-86196-3_20

data format of each sensor on the car is not uniform, and it is difficult to process a large number of sensor data for the vehicle computing system [6].

Beamforming technology is a multi-channel signal processing method that generates synthetic beams through the combination of multiple antennas to improve the performance of the system. Its basic principle is to make the radiation direction of the synthetic beam point to the target. By using this technology, the detection range and anti-interference ability of the system can be improved, and the mutual interference between receivers can be significantly reduced, so a higher signal-to-noise ratio can be obtained. In recent years, the application of beamforming technology in the integration of communication perception [1] has also received a lot of attention. While solving the shortage of wireless communication spectrum resources, beamforming design can be used to reduce the impact of interference. In the scenario of vehicle networking in this subject, the application of this technology can also effectively improve the accuracy of sensing information and expand the range of sensing. The introduction of trade-off factors can also effectively balance communication performance and sensing performance.

In recent years, efficient sensor data sharing between vehicles through integrated communication and sensing systems has become the key to improving the performance and safety of autonomous driving [5], and this scheme has attracted wide attention. With the progress of technology, many technologies have emerged to realize the integrated function of communication sensing, such as using radar detection information to assist millimeter wave communication [4], embedding communication data in radar signals to design integrated communication sensing waveform [2], and designing integrated communication perception function based on IEEE 802.11ad standard [3].

Based on the above beamforming technology and integrated sensing and communication technology, the main research content of this paper is the research of joint communication and perceptual beamforming algorithm based on ISAC in the scenario of networked autonomous driving, with the purpose of achieving maximum communication SINR at the user and maximum sensing SNR at the base station.

The rest of this paper is organized as follows. In Sect. 2, the system model used in this paper is introduced, in Sect. 3, the beamforming algorithm for joint sensing and communication is designed, and in Sect. 4, the simulation results and analysis are given.

2   System Model

The system model considered in this paper is five autonomous vehicles on a road, two base stations are placed 50 m away from the autonomous vehicle, and there is a sensing blind area 60 m away from the base station, as shown in the Fig. 1 below. In the downlink, assuming that M_t access points are sending communication and sensing beams to jointly serve U users, and M_r access points are used to receive beams sent or reflected by various targets and users in the environment, M_t and M_r can have no overlap, partial overlap or complete overlap.

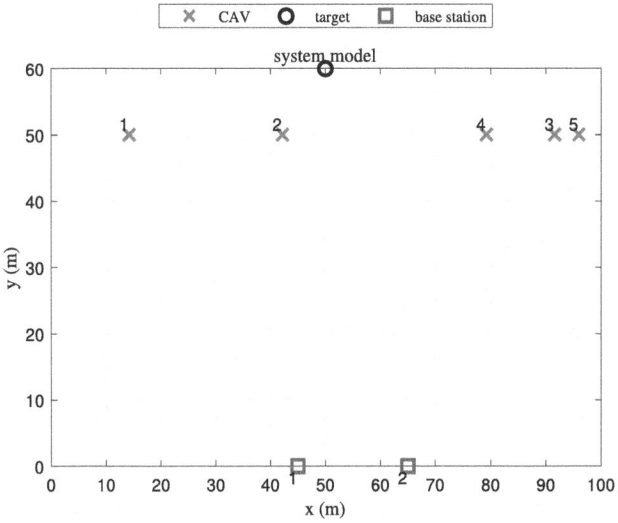

Fig. 1. System model

There are N_t antennas for transmitting and N_r antennas for receiving, assuming that each antenna has a dedicated RF link, that is, each access point has digital beamforming capability.

2.1 Signal Model

The base station transmits the communication beam and the sensing beam, Communication beam $\{x_u[l]\}_{u \in U}$, sensing of beam is $\{x_q[l]\}_{q \in Q}$, then send signals with beam forming vector can be expressed as

$$x_m[l] = \sum_{u \in U} f_{mu} x_u[l] + \sum_{q \in Q} f_{mq} x_q[l] = \sum_{s \in S} f_{ms} x_s[l] \tag{1}$$

The power of the beamforming vector is limited by the total power constraint P_m, There is the following formula

$$E\left[\|x_m[l]\|^2\right] \le P_m \tag{2}$$

In the following calculation process, the beamforming vectors are stacked into matrix form.

2.2 Communication Model

Assume that the channel between the base station and the self-driving car remains constant during signal transmission. Next, considering a block fading channel model. Then the received signal at CAV can be expressed as

$$y_u[l] = \sum_{m \in M_t} h_{mu}^H x_m[l] + n_u \tag{3}$$

By further dividing the signal part into the communication beam for this vehicle, the communication beam for other vehicles and the sensing beam, the formula can be further transformed into

$$y_u[l] = \sum_{m \in M_t} h_{mu}^H f_{mu} x_u[l] + \sum_{u^* \in U u^* \neq u} \sum_{m \in M_t} h_{mu}^H f_{mu^*} x_{u^*}[l] + \sum_{q \in Q} \sum_{m \in M_t} h_{mu}^H f_{mq} x_q[l] + n_u[l] \tag{4}$$

$n_u[l] \sim CN\left(0, \sigma_u^2\right)$ is receiver noise at CAV, so we can calculate the SINR at CAV

$$SINR = \frac{\left|h_u^H f_u\right|^2}{\sum_{u^* \in U, u^* \neq u} \left|h_u^H f_{u^*}\right|^2 + \sum_{q \in Q} \left|h_u^H f_q\right|^2 + \sigma_u^2} \tag{5}$$

2.3   Sensing Model

The following formula is adopted in this paper for the sensing channel between transmitting sensor beam and receiving echo of the base station

$$G_{m_t m_r} = \alpha_{m_t m_r} a\left(\theta_{m_r}\right) a^H\left(\theta_{m_t}\right) \tag{6}$$

$\alpha_{m_t m_r} \sim CN\left(0, \zeta_{m_t m_r}^2\right)$ is combined sensing channel gain, The effects of path loss and RCS are included, $a\left(\theta\right)$ represents the array response vector. θ_{m_t} and θ_{m_r} represents the Angle of transmitting beam and receiving beam of the base station respectively. Therefore, the echo signal received at the base station can be expressed as

$$y_{m_r}[l] = \sum_{m_t \in M_t} G_{m_t m_r} x_{m_t}[l] + n_{m_r}[l] \tag{7}$$

$n_{m_r}[l]$ is noise at the receiving end of the base station, obey the $CN\left(0, \zeta mr^2\right)$ distribution. First, the vector is compressed into the matrix form $F_m = [f_{m_1}, \ldots, f_{m_s}]$, $X = [x_1, \ldots, x_s]$, $N_{m_r} = [n_{m_r}[1], \ldots, n_{m_r}[L]]$, and then the sensor SNR is represented as

$$SNR = \frac{\sum_{m_r \in M_r} \sum_{m_t \in M_t} \zeta_{m_t m_r}^2 \left\|a^H\left(\theta_{m_t}\right) F_{m_t}\right\|^2}{\sum_{m_r \in M_r} \zeta_{m_r}^2} \tag{8}$$

The above formula is derived from the original definition by F norm expansion, expectation and multiple trace operations [1].

3   Beamforming Algorithm Design

3.1   Optimization Problem Modeling

The main method to be designed in this paper is to jointly optimize communication and sensing beams, The goal is to maximize sensing SNR and communication SINR. Therefore, the optimization problem can be modeled as the following formula

$$\max_{f_{ms}} SNR \tag{9}$$

$$s.t. SINR_u \geq \gamma, \forall u \in U \tag{10}$$

$$\sum_{s \in S} \|f_{ms}\|^2 \leq P_m, \forall m \in M_t \tag{11}$$

The objective function of the desired solution is non-convex, so consider transforming this problem into a semidefinite programming problem, and then apply semidefinite relaxation to the non-convex objective function to transform the non-convex problem into a convex problem, and further use a convex solver to solve this problem(Table 1).

In order to transform the above problems into semi-definite programming problems, the beamforming vector is first redefined as $F_s = f_s f_s^H$, This form of construction can eliminate the influence of quadratic terms in SNR and SINR. However, the construction of this formula introduces two new constraints: (1) Semi-definite constraint of Hermitian matrix $F_s \in S^+$; (2) Rank-1 constraint $rank(F_s) = 1$.

For ease of calculation, artificial definition

$$D_{m_t} = diag(d_{m_t}) \otimes I^{N_t \times N_t} \tag{12}$$

$$A = aa^H \tag{13}$$

$d_m = [d_{m1}, \ldots, d_{mM_t}]$, $d_{mm} = 1, d_{mm'} = 0$, $\forall m, m' \in M_t, m \neq m'$, moreover $a = \left[a(\theta_1)^T, \ldots, a(\theta_{M_t})^T \right]^T$, Based on these variables, the objective function sensing SNR can be rerepresented as

$$SNR = \frac{\sum_{m_r \in M_r} \sum_{m_t \in M_t} \zeta_{m_t m_r}^2 Tr\left(D_{m_t} A D_{m_t} \sum_{s \in S} F_s\right)}{\sum_{m_r \in M_r} \zeta_{m_r}^2} \tag{14}$$

For constraints in optimization problems, define $Q_u = h_u h_u^H$. Therefore, the communication SINR can be reformulated as

$$SINR = \frac{Tr(Q_u F_u)}{\sum_{u^* \in U, u^* \neq u} Tr(Q_u F_{u^*}) + \sum_{q \in Q} Tr(Q_u F_q) + \sigma_u^2} \tag{15}$$

Therefore, the optimization problem can be further transformed into

$$SINR_u = \frac{Tr(Q_u F_u)}{\sum_{u^* \in U, u^* \neq u} Tr(Q_u F_{u^*}) + \sum_{q \in Q} Tr(Q_u F_q) + \sigma_u^2} \tag{16}$$

Therefore, this paper further deforms the constraint conditions, and the optimization problem after transformation can be obtained as

$$\max_{\{F_s\}} SNR \tag{17}$$

$$s.t. \left(1 + \gamma^{-1}\right) Tr\left(Q_u F_u\right) - Tr\left(Q_u \sum_{s \in S} F_s\right) \geq \sigma_u^2 \tag{18}$$

$$\sum_{s \in S} Tr\left(D_m F_s\right) \leq P_m, \forall m \in M_t \tag{19}$$

$$rank\left(F_s\right) = 1, \forall s \in S \tag{20}$$

$$F_s \in S^+, \forall s \in S \tag{21}$$

Therefore, algorithm can be used to solve this problem.

3.2   Joint Sensing and Communication Beamforming Algorithm

Table 1. Joint Sensing and Communication Beamforming Algorithm

Algorithm: Semi-definite Relaxation Algorithm for Joint Sensing and Communication(JSC) Beamforming
Input: N_t, N_r, M_t, M_r
Initialization: F_u and F_q
1. for rep=1:n
2. Generate user, target, and base station locations
3. Calculate communication SINR and sensing SNR using (5) and (8)
4. Formulate the joint optimization problem (9) to (11)
5. Transform into the semi-definite programming problem shown in (17) to (21)
6. Relax the rank-1 constraint in (20)
7. Solve the semi-definite programming problem using convex optimization toolbox CVX
8. Apply eigenvalue decomposition to generate an approximate optimal solution for the original optimization problem
9. end
Output: F_u and F_q

4   Simulation Result

In this section, we consider the effects of different number of antennas and different number of users on the designed algorithm when the proportion of communication power to total power ranges from 0 to 1 respectively.

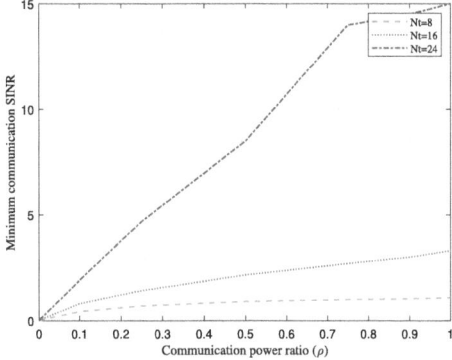

Fig. 2. Effect of different antenna number on JSC algorithm (SINR ρ)

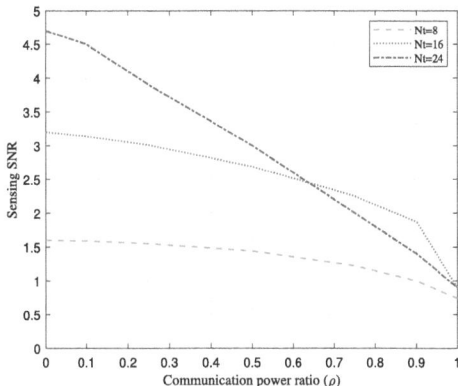

Fig. 3. Effect of different antenna number on JSC algorithm(SNR ρ)

4.1   The Effect of Different Number of Antennas

It can be seen from Fig. 2 and Fig. 3 that when the influence of communication power ratio on minimum communication SINR and sensing SNR is studied, with the constant number of users, the more antennas there are, the larger the minimum communication SINR will be as the communication power ratio increases. In addition, with a higher number of antennas, sensing performance degrades faster as more power is allocated to the communication beam. It can be seen that the more antennas there are, the faster the communication or sensing performance changes when the power distribution between communication and sensing changes. With the increase of the communication power ratio, the communication SINR and sensing SNR curves with different antenna numbers have excellent convergence performance.

In addition, with the increase of the communication power ratio, the power allocated to the communication beam gradually increases, and the power allocated to the sensing beam gradually decreases. Therefore, when the communication power ratio increases, the minimum communication SINR shows an upward trend, while the sensing SNR shows a downward trend. At this time, the communication performance becomes better and better, and the sensing performance gradually deteriorates.

4.2   The Effect of Different Number of Users

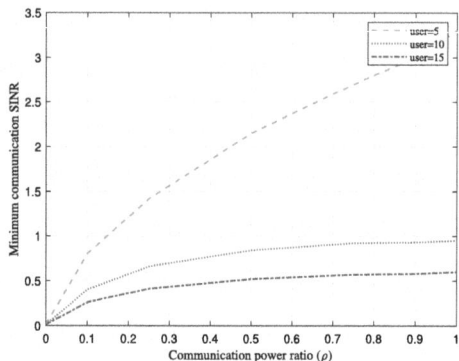

Fig. 4. The influence of different number of users on JSC algorithm (SIN ρ)

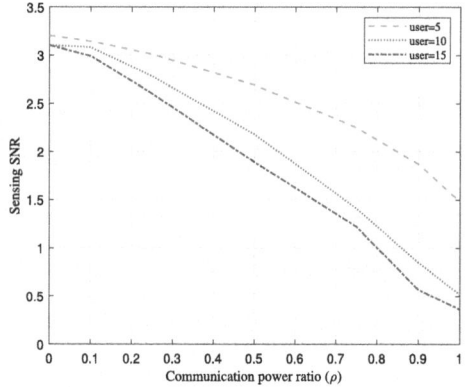

Fig. 5. The influence of different number of users on JSC algorithm (SNR ρ)

As can be seen from the simulation results in Fig. 4 and Fig. 5, when the number of antennas remains unchanged, the smaller the number of users, the larger the minimum communication SINR and sensing SNR will be when the communication power ratio increases. This is because when the number of antennas is fixed, the fewer the number of users means that each user can get more antenna resources, thereby increasing the quality of its received signal. Therefore, the minimum communication SINR will be relatively large, and when the number of users increases, each user will need to share more antenna resources, resulting in a decline in signal quality, the minimum communication SINR will be relatively reduced, and the impact on the sensing SNR is relatively small. With the increase of the communication power ratio, the communication SINR and sensing SNR curves of different users tend to be stable and still have excellent convergence performance.

It can be seen from the above results that the algorithm has good convergence under different number of antennas and different number of users.

5   Conclusion

In this paper, an ISAC beamforming algorithm for joint sensing and communication is designed to solve the problem of sensor blind spot in the network of vehicles. The algorithm has better communication and sensing performance, and has better convergence when the number of antennas and the number of users are different.

References

1. Demirhan, U., Alkhateeb, A.: Cell-free ISAC MIMO systems: joint sensing and communication beamforming. arXiv preprint arXiv:2301.11328 (2023)
2. Hassanien, A., Amin, M.G., Zhang, Y.D., Ahmad, F.: Signaling strategies for dual-function radar communications: an overview. IEEE Aerosp. Electron. Syst. Mag. **31**(10), 36–45 (2016)
3. Kumari, P., Choi, J., González-Prelcic, N., Heath, R.W.: IEEE 802.11 ad-based radar: an approach to joint vehicular communication-radar system. IEEE Trans. Veh. Technol. **67**(4), 3012–3027 (2017)
4. Liu, F., Masouros, C.: A tutorial on joint radar and communication transmission for vehicular networks-part II: state of the art and challenges ahead. IEEE Commun. Lett. **25**(2), 327–331 (2020)
5. Liu, F., Masouros, C., Petropulu, A.P., Griffiths, H., Hanzo, L.: Joint radar and communication design: applications, state-of-the-art, and the road ahead. IEEE Trans. Commun. **68**(6), 3834–3862 (2020)
6. Liu, S., Hao, Q., Zhang, Q., Liu, J., Jiang, Z.: Integrated sensing and communication enabled multiple beamwidth and power allocation for connected automated vehicles. China Commun. **20**(9), 46–58 (2023)

Model-Driven Deep Learning for MIMO Signal Detection

GuangHua Zhang$^{(\boxtimes)}$, Fan Yang, and Sen Li

Northeast Petroleum University, DaQing, China
dqzgh@nepu.edu.cn

Abstract. Multiple Input Multiple Output (MIMO) technology is widely applied in various wireless communication systems, significantly improving communication efficiency and reliability. Signal detection is critical for MIMO systems. However, with the increasing integration of deep learning into MIMO signal detection algorithms, challenges such as high complexity and limited interpretability have emerged. To address this, this paper proposes a model driven trainable approximate message passing (AMP) algorithm that combines the iterative process of AMP with deep learning techniques. By introducing trainable parameters and optimizing them through training, and incorporating an attention mechanism to enhance channel feature extraction, the detection accuracy is improved, and the algorithm's generalization capability is enhanced. Simulation results demonstrate that AMP Attention Net achieves lower bit error rates compared to traditional detection algorithms. Furthermore, the proposed algorithm exhibits robust performance under different configurations of transmitting and receiving antennas.

Keywords: MIMO · Deep Learning · Signal Detection

1 Introduction

MIMO technology holds an important position in modern wireless communications [1,2]. It utilizes multiple transmitting and receiving antennas to achieve higher data transmission rates without increasing the spectral bandwidth, thereby meeting the growing demand for data. Signal detection is crucial for the stable operation and efficient transmission of MIMO communication systems.

Maximum Likelihood (ML) detection is a commonly used algorithm [3]. Its basic principle is to select the most likely transmitted symbol combination from the received signal, which has the highest likelihood, as the final detection result. However, Maximum Likelihood algorithms require enumerating all possible symbol combinations, resulting in exponentially increasing computational complexity as the number of antennas and modulation symbols in the MIMO system increases, making it impractical for real world applications. Zero Forcing (ZF) detection is a common linear detection algorithm that eliminates interference through linear transformations to accurately detect the transmitted symbols [4],

© ICST Institute for Computer Sciences, Social Informatics and Telecommunications Engineering 2025
Published by Springer Nature Switzerland AG 2025. All Rights Reserved
H.-H. Chen and W. Meng (Eds.): WiSATS 2024, LNICST 605, pp. 246–254, 2025.
https://doi.org/10.1007/978-3-031-86196-3_21

While simple and easy to implement, it is highly susceptible to noise. The Minimum Mean Square Error (MMSE) detection algorithm improves the quality and performance of received signals by minimizing the mean square error between the received and estimated signals [5,6]. However, it involves complex matrix inversion, leading to high complexity.

Data driven neural networks are often referred to as black boxes due to their complex structures and highly nonlinear mapping relationships. This characteristic implies that while the model can make predictions based on input data, its internal structure is often inexplicable or difficult to understand [7,8]. Model driven deep learning can reduce training volume and provide stronger interpretability, becoming a research hotspot. In [9], the authors use the Orthogonal Approximate Message Passing (OAMP) algorithm as a detector prototype, replacing matrix inversion with the Conjugate Gradient method to reduce OAMP complexity, further extending the Conjugate Gradient based OAMP algorithm into a network and enhancing detection performance through deep learning. In [10], the authors combine the OAMP algorithm with sparse connected neural networks (ScNet) to form a trainable network structure, proposing the ScNet OAMP network to enhance the detection capability of the MMSE estimator in the OAMP process, improving detection accuracy.

Inspired by the aforementioned work, a new network model, AMP Attention Net, is proposed for signal detection. Specifically, the AMP iterative process is improved by adding several trainable parameters to enhance the accuracy of signal detection, reducing the network complexity and making it easier to implement. Additionally, an attention mechanism is incorporated to extract channel features, thereby enhancing the network's generalization capability.

2   System Model

This paper considers a single cell massive MIMO communication system with N_t transmitting antennas and N_r receiving antennas. The received signal vector $\overline{y} \in C^{N_r}$ can be expressed as:

$$\overline{y} = \overline{H}\,\overline{x} + \overline{n} \tag{1}$$

where $\overline{H} \in C^{N_r \times N_t}$ is the channel gain matrix, $\overline{n} \sim CN\left(0, \sigma^2 I_{N_r}\right)$ is Gaussian white noise, σ^2 is noise variance, $\overline{x} \in C^{N_t}$ represents the transmitted signal.

Since the vectors and matrices in (1) are complex numbers, they can be converted to real numbers for easier processing in deep learning:

$$y = Hs + n \tag{2}$$

Specifically expressed as:

$$y = \begin{bmatrix} \Re(\overline{y}) \\ \Im(\overline{y}) \end{bmatrix}, H = \begin{bmatrix} \Re\left(\overline{H}\right) & -\Im\left(\overline{H}\right) \\ \Im\left(\overline{H}\right) & \Re\left(\overline{H}\right) \end{bmatrix}, s = \begin{bmatrix} \Re(\overline{s}) \\ \Im(\overline{s}) \end{bmatrix}, n = \begin{bmatrix} \Re(\overline{n}) \\ \Im(\overline{n}) \end{bmatrix} \tag{3}$$

Here the real and imaginary parts of a complex matrix or vector are tabulated by $\Re(\cdot)$ and $\Im(\cdot)$, respectively.

3   Model Driven for Signal Detection

3.1   Approximate Message Passing

The core idea of the AMP is to approximate the posterior probability distribution through iterative message updates, with low computational complexity and good convergence. It is widely used in signal detection.

Assume the signal $x = [x_1, x_2, \cdots, x_N]^T \in R^N$, the Gaussian random observation matrix $A \in R^{M \times N}$, then the measurement vector can be expressed as:

$$y = Ax + w \tag{4}$$

where $w \in R^M$ represents noise. The algorithm initializes with the reconstructed vector $x^0 = A^t y$ and residual vector $z^{-1} = y$. The t $(t \geq 0)$-th iteration can be expressed as:

$$z^t = y - Ax^t + b_t z^{t-1} \tag{5}$$

$$x^{t+1} = \eta_t(x^t + A^T z^t; \lambda_t) \tag{6}$$

where x^t is the reconstructed vector after the t-th iteration, and $b_t z^{t-1}$ is the Onsager correction term. $b_t = \frac{1}{N_r}\|x^t\|_0, \lambda_t = \frac{\alpha}{\sqrt{N_r}}\|z^t\|_2, \alpha$ is an adjustable value related to the sparsity and the observation vector. The existence of the Onsager correction term allows the AMP to converge quickly (Table 1).

Table 1. Approximate message passing algorithm

Input: y, A, Output: x^{t+1}
Initialize: $x^0 = A^T y, z^{-1} = y, t = 1$
$z^t = y - Ax^t + b_t z^{t-1}$
$x^{t+1} = \eta_t(x^t + A^T z^t; \lambda_t)$
Condition met, exit iteration

3.2   Channel Attention Mechanism

In the signal detection task, the channel information is often complex and changeable. By introducing an attention mechanism, the network can dynamically adjust its attention to different channels, enabling it to pay more attention to the channel information that is critical to the detection task. A channel attention mechanism (CAM) is commonly used in deep learning, and its structure is shown in Fig. 1.

First, apply global max pooling and global average pooling along the spatial dimensions to the input features of size $H \times W \times C$, resulting in two $1 \times 1 \times C$ feature maps. This step compresses the spatial dimensions, making it easier to learn the channel features in subsequent steps. Next, feed the results of global

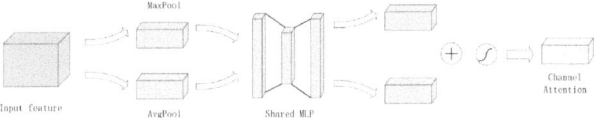

Fig. 1. The structure of channel attention mechanism.

max pooling and global average pooling into a shared multi layer perceptron (MLP) to learn, resulting in two $1 \times 1 \times C$ feature maps. Finally, perform an element wise addition on the outputs of the multi-layer perceptron, followed by a Sigmoid activation function to map the results, ultimately obtaining the channel attention weight matrix.The specific calculation process is expressed as:

$$M_c = \sigma \left(MLP \left(AvgPool \left(F \right) \right) + MLP \left(MaxPool \left(F \right) \right) \right)$$
$$= \sigma \left(W_1 \left(W_0 \left(F_{avg}^c \right) \right) + W_1 \left(W_0 \left(F_{\max}^c \right) \right) \right) \tag{7}$$

3.3 Amp Attention Net

Due to the significant influence of parameters on the convergence speed and accuracy of the AMP algorithm, and the complex and variable channel information in communication environments, these issues are addressed by unfolding the AMP detector and adding several trainable parameters. Additionally, an attention mechanism is incorporated to extract channel information features, thereby improving the generalization of the detection algorithm. The specific network structure is shown in Fig. 2. For the overall network, the input is the received signal y and the signal matrix H, and the output is the estimated input signal x. For the $t + 1$-th layer of the network, the input is the estimated signal x_t from the t-th layer, and the network at this layer performs an iteration to obtain the output x_{t+1}. Compared to the Approximate Message Passing algorithm, AMP NET adds trainable parameters ω_t, ψ_t. Each layer of the network has the same structure but different learnable parameters. The iterative process can be expressed as:

$$z^t = y - Ax^t + \omega_t b_t z^{t-1} \tag{8}$$
$$x^{t+1} = \eta_t(x^t + A^T z^t; \psi_t \lambda_t) \tag{9}$$

Adding a learnable parameter ω_t is to provide a more suitable step size for the update of the residual z^t, while adding parameter ψ_t dynamically selects the threshold. Thus, the MIMO detection problem is transformed into finding the most suitable learnable parameters through deep learning to reduce the error rate.

During the training of the parameters, the gradient descent algorithm is used, and its convergence behavior and performance depend on the appropriate step size for moving to the search point. The optimal step size ω_t can be learned from the data for updating the residual, and ψ_t follows the same training process.

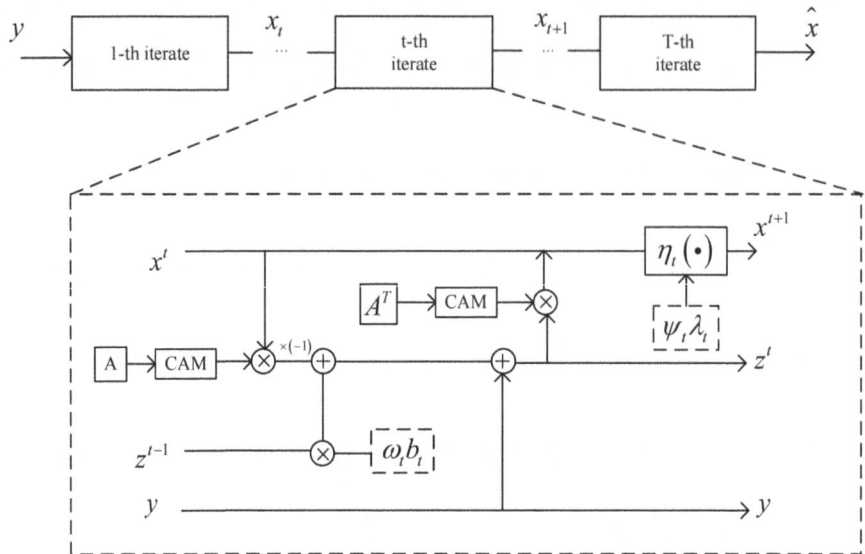

Fig. 2. The network structure of the algorithm that combines the AMP algorithm with deep learning.

4   Simulation Analysis

4.1   Parameter Settings

In practical applications, the dataset used to train the model and the data distribution faced by the model during actual deployment or testing may not match. This mismatch can be caused by various factors, such as the time varying nature of communication channels, changes in noise levels, and differences in hardware devices. To maintain the generalization ability of the model, various experiments are conducted for research.

The wireless communication simulation parameters and network model parameters are shown in Table 2. The number of antennas at the system's transmitter is set to 48, and at the receiver, it is set to 64. The channel model is set to a Rayleigh fading channel, and QPSK modulation is used. A total of 125,000 simulation experiments are conducted. For the network model parameters, 3/5 of the data obtained from the wireless communication simulation is set as the training set, 1/5 as the validation set (used to select the best network during the training phase), and the remaining 1/5 as the test set (used to test the network model). The Adam optimizer and gradient descent method are used for training the network, with the learning rate set to 0.001. The initial values of the variables ω_t and ψ_t are set to 1, and the batch size is set to 100. The optimizer chosen is the gradient descent method, and the loss function is set to the square of the difference between the predicted values and the true values.

Table 2. Simulation Parameters and Network Model Parameters

Parameter Name	Parameter Value
Number of Transmit Antennas	48
Number of Receive Antennas	64
Learning Rate	0.001
Loss Function	MSE
Batch Size	100
Optimizer	Gradient Descent
Number of Training Iterations	500
Training Set Size	7500
Validation Set Size	2500

4.2 Complexity Analysis

For algorithms, the standard measure of complexity generally uses real multiplications. However, the complexity of signal detection algorithms also depends on parameters such as the number of transmit antennas MT, receive antennas MR, modulation order M, and the number of iterations $iter$. ZF and MMSE detection algorithms require matrix inversion operations on the signal matrix. The main complexity of ML algorithm arises from enumerating all possible transmitted symbols and comparing them with the received vector. In cases where the number of transmit and receive antennas is large, the complexity of these three algorithms becomes extremely high, making practical implementation difficult.

The main complexity of the AMP algorithm comes from iterative processing of the channel matrix. In contrast, the complexity of Amp Attention Net mainly depends on the dimensions of matrices and iterations, especially the input matrix and the dimensions of hidden layer variables. Generally, in practical application scenarios, the complexity of Amp Attention Net remains within acceptable limits. Specific complexities are detailed in Table 3.

Table 3. Algorithm Complexity

MIMO Detection Algorithm	Complexity
ZF	$O\left(MR^3\right)$
MMSE	$O\left(MR^3 + MT^3\right)$
ML	$O\left(M^{MT} \times MT \times MR\right)$
AMP	$O\left(iter \times MT \times MR\right)$
AMP Attention Net	$O\left(M^2 \times N + iter \times M^2\right)$

4.3   Performance Analysis

To determine the detection effectiveness of different unfolded layers, the Amp Attention Net with different layers was validated on the validation set, and their bit error rate (BER) were compared. The specific results are shown in Fig. 3. From Fig. 3, it is evident that when the network has 1 layer, the BER on the validation set is significantly higher than that of networks with more layers. When the network has 2 or 3 layers, the BER decreases significantly compared to the 1-layer network but still lags behind networks with more layers. As the number of unfolded layers continues to increase, the overall difference in BER is not substantial. Therefore, considering overfitting and training complexity, the optimal number of unfolded layers is set to 4.

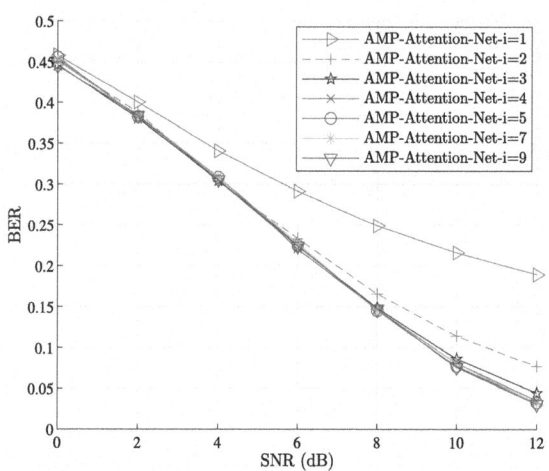

Fig. 3. Comparison of BER for Different Layers of AMP Attention Net.

Figure 4 compares the BER performance of the 3-layer Amp Attention Net with the AMP, MMSE, and ZF algorithms. Overall, the ZF algorithm performs the worst. At low SNRs, the performance of MMSE, AMP, OAMP and Amp Attention Net is similar, but as the SNR increases, the BER of Amp Attention Net becomes significantly lower than that of the other algorithms. When the BER is 0.17, Amp Attention Net achieves approximately 1.8dB performance gain compared to AMP, about 0.3dB performance gain compared to OAMP, and about 0.5dB performance gain compared to MMSE. This demonstrates that Amp Attention Net can significantly improve the performance of AMP detection and has strong detection capabilities in MIMO signal detection.

Figure 5 shows the BER of Amp Attention Net for different antenna configurations 64×64 and 128×128. The results show that although the antenna configuration is different in the simulation, the overall bit error rate is about the same, which shows that the algorithm has strong detection performance and good generalization ability.

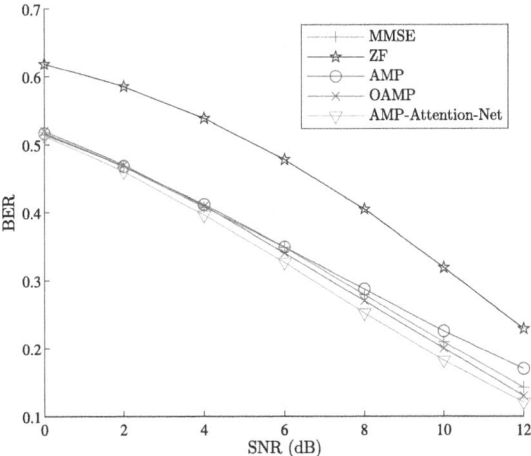

Fig. 4. Comparison of BER for MMSE, ZF, AMP, OAMP and AMP Attention Net Detection Algorithms

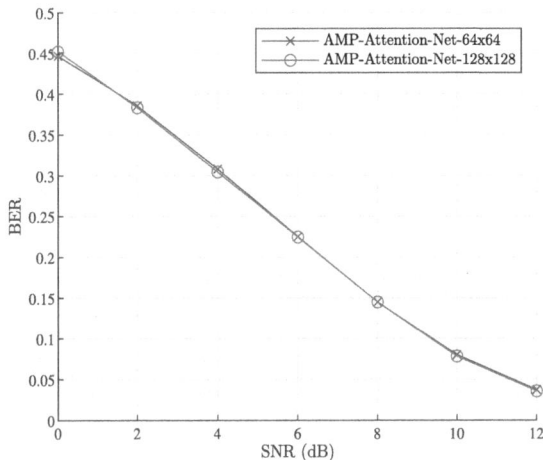

Fig. 5. Comparison of BER Under Different Numbers of Antennas

5   Analysis

This paper conducts research on signal detection algorithms and proposes a model driven Amp Attention Net signal detection algorithm based on the AMP detection algorithm. This algorithm unfolds the iterative process of the AMP algorithm, adds trainable parameters, and introduces an attention mechanism to enhance the extraction of channel features. By training to obtain the optimal parameters, the accuracy of signal detection is improved. Simulation results indicate that the proposed algorithm has a lower error rate compared to traditional detection algorithms, and it performs well with different numbers of transmit and receive antennas. Additionally, the algorithm model proposed in this paper is relatively easy to implement and has low cost.

References

1. Lu, L., Li, G.Y., Swindlehurst, A.L., Ashikhmin, A., Zhang, R.: An overview of massive MIMO: benefits and challenges. IEEE J. Sel. Top. Sig. Process. **8**(5), 742–758 (2014)
2. Larsson, E.G., Edfors, O., Tufvesson, F., Marzetta, T.L.: Massive MIMO for next generation wireless systems. IEEE Commun. Mag. **52**(2), 186–195 (2014)
3. He, K., He, L., Fan, L., Deng, Y., Karagiannidis, G.K., Nallanathan, A.: Learning-based signal detection for MIMO systems with unknown noise statistics. IEEE Trans. Commun. **69**(5), 3025–3038 (2021)
4. Liu, Y.: A massive MIMO signal detection method based on ZF method. In: 2021 5th International Conference on Imaging, Signal Processing and Communications (ICISPC), pp. 71–76. IEEE (2021)
5. Khoso, I.A., Kang, C.G.: Extrapolation principle-based low-complexity signal detection in massive MIMO systems. IEEE Wirel. Commun. Lett. **13**(1), 123–130 (2024)
6. Zhao, S., Shen, B., Hua, Q.: A comparative study of low-complexity MMSE signal detection for massive MIMO systems. KSII Trans. Internet Inf. Syst. (TIIS) **12**(4), 1504–1526 (2018)
7. Baek, M.-S., Kwak, S., Jung, J.-Y., Kim, H.M., Choi, D.-J.: Implementation methodologies of deep learning-based signal detection for conventional MIMO transmitters. IEEE Trans. Broadcast. **65**(3), 636–642 (2019)
8. Nguyen, L.V., Nguyen, N.T., Tran, N.H., Juntti, M., Swindlehurst, A.L., Nguyen, D.H.N.: Leveraging deep neural networks for massive MIMO data detection. IEEE Wirel. Commun. **30**(1), 174–180 (2022)
9. Karahan, S.N., Kalaycıoğlu, A., Taşcıoğlu, S.: MIMO detection algorithms–Deep learning based and traditional methods. In: 2022 International Conference on Electrical, Computer and Energy Technologies (ICECET), pp. 1–4. IEEE (2022)
10. Zhou, X., Zhang, J., Syu, C.W., Wen, C.K., Zhang, J., Jin, S.: Model-driven deep learning-based MIMO-OFDM detector: design, simulation, and experimental results. IEEE Trans. Commun. **70**(8), 5193–5207 (2022)

Integrated Sensing and Communication Empowered Secure Computation Offloading in Integrated Satellite-Terrestrial Networks

Chenglong Dou[1] , Xumin Huang[1] , Jiawen Kang[2] , Yuan Wu[1,3(✉)] ,
and Liping Qian[4]

[1] State Key Laboratory of Internet of Things for Smart City, University of Macau,
Macau, China
[2] School of Automation, Guangdong University of Technology, Guangzhou 510006,
China
kavinkang@gdut.edu.cn
[3] Zhuhai UM Science and Technology Research Institute, Zhuhai 519301, China
yuanwu@um.edu.mo
[4] College of Information Engineering, Zhejiang University of Technology,
Hangzhou 310023, China
lpqian@zjut.edu.cn

Abstract. Integrated satellite-terrestrial edge computing networks have emerged as a promising solution to enhance data processing capabilities and connectivity in remote and underserved areas. However, the physical layer security of computation offloading in such networks is increasingly challenged by potential eavesdroppers. In this paper, we propose an integrated sensing and communication (ISAC) empowered secure computation offloading in integrated satellite-terrestrial networks, in which the satellite can utilize the ISAC signal to sense the malicious eavesdropper with an uncertain location while offloading data with improved secrecy rates. To investigate this problem, we formulate a joint optimization of the transmit beamforming, the receive beamforming, the computation offloading strategies and the associated allocations of the communication and computing resources, with the objective of maximizing the minimum sensing performance for all possible eavesdropper locations, while guaranteeing the secrecy offloading transmission rate. Despite the nonconvexity of the formulated problem, we propose an efficient algorithm to obtain its solutions. Numerical results validate the performance advantages of our ISAC empowered secure computation offloading in secrecy and robustness.

Keywords: Integrate satellite-terrestrial networks · Edge computing ·
Integrated sensing and communication · Physical layer security

© ICST Institute for Computer Sciences, Social Informatics and Telecommunications Engineering 2025
Published by Springer Nature Switzerland AG 2025. All Rights Reserved
H.-H. Chen and W. Meng (Eds.): WiSATS 2024, LNICST 605, pp. 255–268, 2025.
https://doi.org/10.1007/978-3-031-86196-3_22

1 Introduction

With the rapid development of satellite communication and edge computing technologies, integrated satellite-terrestrial networks have emerged as a promising solution to enhance data processing capabilities and provide seamless connectivity, especially in remote and underserved areas [1]. These networks leverage the unique advantages of low Earth orbit (LEO) satellites and terrestrial infrastructures to support a wide range of applications such as real time data analytics. However, the proliferation of such networks also poses significant security challenges, especially in the case of computation offloading of privacy sensitive data [2].

With the increased computation capacity of eavesdroppers, traditional secure communications based on cryptographic techniques in the upper layers of the protocol stack become increasingly unreliable. To this end, physical layer security approaches have been proposed as the promising solution, particularly in integrated satellite-terrestrial networks [3]. Numerous studies have demonstrated the effectiveness of physical layer security in improving communication confidentiality and eavesdropping resistance. In [4], Liu et al. proposed an access authentication protocol in integrated satellite-terrestrial networks with user anonymity and traceability. In [5], An et al. proposed to employ the source of green interference to enhance secure transmission in integrated satellite-terrestrial networks. In [6], Lin et al. investigated secrecy energy efficient hybrid beamforming schemes for integrated satellite-terrestrial networks. Nevertheless, due to the unpredictable locations of eavesdroppers, the above approaches are insufficient to address the security challenges comprehensively. Thus, a more adaptable security solution is necessitated.

Integrated sensing and communication (ISAC), which allows simultaneous transmission and sensing on the same resource block, provides a promising avenue for dynamically adapting to the presence of eavesdroppers and obtaining their accurate information [7]. Due to its great potential, ISAC attracts wide research interests for various wireless services [8–10]. In this paper, we propose an ISAC empowered secure computation offloading in integrated satellite-terrestrial networks. By deploying ISAC on the LEO satellite, it can simultaneously perform data offloading and eavesdropper detection. The integration of sensing capabilities allows the satellite to accurately locate potential eavesdroppers and adapt its computation offloading strategies accordingly. Moreover, the use of dedicated sensing signal not only aids in eavesdropper detection but also generates intentional interference, which further protects the offloaded data from interception. Our contributions can be summarized as follows.

- We propose an ISAC empowered secure computation offloading in the integrated satellite-terrestrial network, in which the satellite can utilize the ISAC signal to sense the malicious eavesdropper with an uncertain location while offloading data with improved secrecy rates.
- We formulate a joint optimization problem with the objective of maximizing the minimum sensing performance for all possible eavesdropper locations,

while guaranteeing the secrecy offloading transmission rate. We design the surrogate functions and present a convex surrogate problem for this nonconvex problem, based on which we propose an efficient algorithm for solving it.

– We present the numerical results to verify the performance superiority of leveraging ISAC for secure computation offloading in integrated satellite-terrestrial networks. The results demonstrate that our scheme outperforms the benchmark schemes in both secrecy and robustness.

The remainder of this paper is organized as follows. Section 2 depicts the system model and problem formulation. Section 3 proposes an efficient algorithm for solving the formulated problem. Section 4 presents the numerical results. Section 5 concludes this work and discusses the future directions.

2 System Model and Problem Formulation

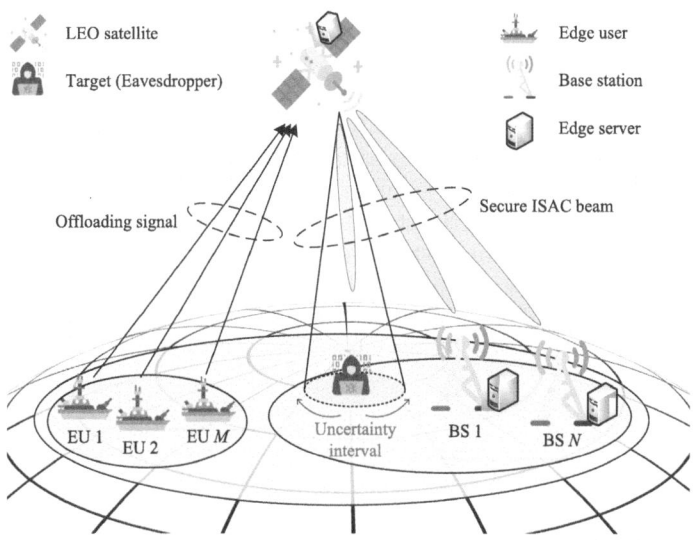

Fig. 1. Illustrative system model

As shown in Fig. 1, we consider an ISAC empowered integrated satellite-terrestrial edge computing network, which includes an LEO satellite with N_t transmit antennas and N_r receive antennas, a group of edge users (EUs) represented by $\mathcal{M} = \{1, 2, ..., M\}$, and a group of base stations (BSs) with N_r receive antennas represented by $\mathcal{N} = \{1, 2, ..., N\}$. In this network, the LEO satellite provides the computational task offloading services for the EUs (e.g., the unmanned surface vehicles), and it can further offload the workloads to the

BSs for efficient processing. Furthermore, we consider the presence of a potential malicious eavesdropper with an uncertain location that may intercept the data offloaded by the LEO satellite. To achieve secure computation offloading, ISAC is deployed on the LEO satellite to sense the location of the eavesdropper and prevent information leakage while offloading to the BSs.

2.1   Signal Model

In this work, we consider that the EUs offload their entire task workloads $\{D_m^{\text{tot}}\}_{m \in \mathcal{M}}$ to the LEO satellite due to their limited computation capacities. The transmitted signal of EU m is given by

$$x_m = \sqrt{p_m} s_m, \tag{1}$$

where p_m denotes the transmit power for delivering the information symbol s_m with $\mathbb{E}\{|s_m|^2\} = 1$. The task workloads at the LEO satellite can be further offloaded to a group of BSs via the ISAC signal. The transmitted ISAC signal of the LEO satellite is given by

$$\mathbf{x} = \sum_{n \in \mathcal{N}} \mathbf{u}_n z_n + \mathbf{v}_0, \tag{2}$$

where $\mathbf{u}_n \in \mathbb{C}^{N_t \times 1}$ denotes the transmit beamforming for BS n, and z_n with $\mathbb{E}\{|z_n|^2\} = 1$ denotes the symbol for BS n. In Eq. (2), $\mathbf{v}_0$ denotes the dedicated sensing signal, which is exploited to enhance the sensing performance towards the eavesdropper and serve as a jamming to the eavesdropper.

We consider that the uncertainty interval of the eavesdropper is $\theta_0 \in \Phi = [\theta_e - \Delta\theta, \theta_e + \Delta\theta]$, and there exists I clutters under the angles of $\{\theta_i\}_{i=1}^I$. The received signal at the LEO satellite consists of three parts, including the offloading signal from M EUs, the sensing echo from the eavesdropper, and the clutter interference from I clutters and noise. It can be expressed as

$$\mathbf{y}_0 = \underbrace{\sum_{m \in \mathcal{M}} \mathbf{h}_m \sqrt{p_m} s_m}_{\text{signal from all EUs}} + \underbrace{\kappa_0 \mathbf{a}_r(\theta_0) \mathbf{a}_t^H(\theta_0) \mathbf{x}}_{\text{sensing echo from the eavesdropper}}$$

$$+ \underbrace{\sum_{i=1}^{I} \kappa_i \mathbf{a}_r(\theta_i) \mathbf{a}_t^H(\theta_i) \mathbf{x} + \mathbf{n}_0}_{\text{clutter interference and noise}}, \tag{3}$$

where $\mathbf{h}_m \in \mathbb{C}^{N_r \times 1}$ denotes the channel from EU m to the LEO satellite. The complex amplitudes $\{\kappa_i\}_{i=0,1,\dots,I}$ are primarily determined by the factors such as the path loss and radar cross section. $\mathbf{n}_0$ denotes the noise with variance σ_0^2. In Eq. (3), $\mathbf{a}_t(\theta)$ and $\mathbf{a}_r(\theta)$ are the steering vectors of uniform linear array antenna with half wavelength antenna spacing, and can be respectively defined as

$$\mathbf{a}_t(\theta) = \frac{1}{\sqrt{N_t}} \left[1, e^{j\pi \sin\theta}, \dots, e^{j\pi(N_t-1)\sin\theta} \right]^T, \tag{4}$$

$$\mathbf{a}_r(\theta) = \frac{1}{\sqrt{N_r}} \left[1, e^{j\pi \sin\theta}, ..., e^{j\pi(N_r-1)\sin\theta} \right]^T. \tag{5}$$

For the sake of clear notations, we further define $\mathbf{A}_s = \kappa_0 \mathbf{a}_r(\theta_0)\mathbf{a}_t^H(\theta_0)$ and $\mathbf{A}_c = \sum_{i=1}^{I} \kappa_i \mathbf{a}_r(\theta_i)\mathbf{a}_t^H(\theta_i)$.

We use $\mathbf{G}_n \in \mathbb{C}^{N_r \times N_t}$ to denote the channel from the LEO satellite to BS n. Then, the received signal at BS n can be expressed as

$$\mathbf{y}_n = \mathbf{G}_n \mathbf{u}_n z_n + \sum_{j \in \mathcal{N}, j \neq n} \mathbf{G}_n \mathbf{u}_j z_j + \mathbf{n}_n, \tag{6}$$

where n_n denotes the noise with variance σ_n^2.

2.2   Computation Offloading Model

Based on Eq. (3), the offloading transmission rate from EU m to the LEO satellite is given by

$$R_m^u = B^u \log_2 \left(1 + \frac{p_m \mathbf{c}_m^H \mathbf{h}_m \mathbf{h}_m^H \mathbf{c}_m}{\mathbf{c}_m^H \mathbf{\Gamma}_m \mathbf{c}_m} \right), \tag{7}$$

where B^u denotes the channel bandwidth between the EUs and LEO satellite, and $\mathbf{c}_m \in \mathbb{C}^{N_r \times 1}$ denotes the LEO satellite's receive beamforming for EU m's data. In Eq. (7), $\mathbf{\Gamma}_m$ denotes the total interference for receiving EU m's data, and it can be expressed as

$$\mathbf{\Gamma}_m = \sum_{j \in \mathcal{M}, j \neq m} p_j \mathbf{h}_j \mathbf{h}_j^H + (\mathbf{A}_s + \mathbf{A}_c)\mathbf{x}\mathbf{x}^H \left(\mathbf{A}_s^H + \mathbf{A}_c^H \right) + \sigma_0^2 \mathbf{I}_N. \tag{8}$$

According to the minimum variance distortionless response (MVDR) beamforming problem, the optimal receiver $\mathbf{c}_m^*$ is given by

$$\mathbf{c}_m^* = \arg\max \frac{p_m \mathbf{c}_m^H \mathbf{h}_m \mathbf{h}_m^H \mathbf{c}_m}{\mathbf{c}_m^H \mathbf{\Gamma}_m \mathbf{c}_m} = \mathbf{\Gamma}_m^{-1} \mathbf{h}_m, \forall m \in \mathcal{M}. \tag{9}$$

By substituting $\mathbf{c}_m^*$ into Eq. (7), the offloading transmission rate R_m^u can be rewritten as

$$R_m^u = B^u \log_2 \left(1 + p_m \mathbf{h}_m^H \mathbf{\Gamma}_m^{-1} \mathbf{h}_m \right), \forall m \in \mathcal{M}. \tag{10}$$

We use B^d to denote the channel bandwidth between the LEO satellite and the BSs. Based on Eq. (6), the offloading transmission rate from the LEO satellite to BS n is given by

$$R_n^d = B^d \log_2 \left(1 + \frac{\mathbf{q}_n^H \mathbf{G}_n \mathbf{u}_n \mathbf{u}_n^H \mathbf{G}_n^H \mathbf{q}_n}{\mathbf{q}_n^H \mathbf{\Lambda}_n \mathbf{q}_n} \right), \tag{11}$$

where $\mathbf{q}_n \in \mathbb{C}^{N_r \times 1}$ denotes the receive beamforming of BS n. $\mathbf{\Lambda}_n$ is the inference of BS n for receiving the offloaded workloads from the LEO satellite, and it can be expressed as

$$\mathbf{\Lambda}_n = \mathbf{G}_n \left(\sum_{j \in \mathcal{N}, j \neq n} \mathbf{u}_j \mathbf{u}_j^H \right) \mathbf{G}_n^H + \mathbf{G}_n \mathbf{v}_0 \mathbf{v}_0^H \mathbf{G}_n^H + \sigma_n^2. \tag{12}$$

The optimal receiver $\mathbf{q}_n^*$ is given by

$$\mathbf{q}_n^* = \arg\max \frac{\mathbf{q}_n^H \mathbf{G}_n \mathbf{u}_n \mathbf{u}_n^H \mathbf{G}_n^H \mathbf{q}_n}{\mathbf{q}_n^H \mathbf{\Lambda}_n \mathbf{q}_n} = \frac{\mathbf{\Lambda}_n^{-1} \mathbf{G}_n \mathbf{u}_n}{\mathbf{u}_n^H \mathbf{G}_n^H \mathbf{\Lambda}_n^{-1} \mathbf{G}_n \mathbf{u}_n}. \tag{13}$$

By substituting $\mathbf{q}_n^*$ into Eq. (11), the offloading transmission rate R_n^d can be rewritten as

$$R_n^d = B^d \log_2 \left(1 + \mathbf{u}_n^H \mathbf{G}_n^H \mathbf{\Lambda}_n^{-1} \mathbf{G}_n \mathbf{u}_n \right), \forall n \in \mathcal{N}. \tag{14}$$

The latency for completing EU m's workloads is determined by two parts, including the latency l_m^{LS} for processing at the LEO satellite, and the latency l_m^{BS} for processing at the BSs. We use d_{mn} to denote the EU m's workloads offloaded from the LEO satellite to BS n. The latency for processing EU m's workloads at the LEO satellite is given by

$$l_m^{\mathrm{LS}} = \frac{D_m^{\mathrm{tot}}}{R_m^u} + \frac{\nu_m(D_m^{\mathrm{tot}} - \sum_{n \in \mathcal{N}} d_{mn})}{\varrho_m}, \tag{15}$$

where ν_m denotes the number of CPU cycles for processing one bit of D_m^{tot}, and ϱ_m denotes the processing rate of the LEO satellite for processing EU m's offloaded workloads. We use t_n to denote the transmission duration from the LEO satellite to BS n. The latency for processing EU m's workloads at the BSs is given by

$$l_m^{\mathrm{BS}} = \frac{D_m^{\mathrm{tot}}}{R_m^u} + \max_{n \in \mathcal{N}}\{t_n + \frac{\nu_m d_{mn}}{\zeta_{mn}}\}, \tag{16}$$

where ζ_{mn} denotes the processing rate of BS n allocated for processing the offloaded workloads from EU m.

The power consumption of the LEO satellite can be expressed as

$$P_0 = \sum_{n \in \mathcal{N}} \mathbf{u}_n^H \mathbf{u}_n + \mathbf{v}_0^H \mathbf{v}_0 + \sum_{m \in \mathcal{M}} \epsilon_0 \varrho_m^3, \tag{17}$$

where ϵ_0 denotes the power consumption coefficient of the LEO satellite.

2.3   Sensing and Interception Model

With the sensing receive beamforming $\mathbf{w}$, the output sensing SINR is given by

$$\mathrm{SINR}(\theta_0) = \frac{\mathbf{w}^H \mathbf{A}_s \mathbf{x} \mathbf{x}^H \mathbf{A}_s^H \mathbf{w}}{\mathbf{w}^H (\mathbf{A}_c \mathbf{x} \mathbf{x}^H \mathbf{A}_c^H + \sigma_0^2 \mathbf{I}_N) \mathbf{w}}. \tag{18}$$

Due to the presence of the potential malicious eavesdropper, the data offloaded by the LEO satellite is at risk of leakage. We use $\mathbf{\Theta}$ to denote the estimated channel from the LEO satellite to the eavesdropper. Considering the uncertainty of target location, the bounded channel state information (CSI) error for $\mathbf{\Theta}$ is given by

$$\mathbf{\Theta} = \overline{\mathbf{\Theta}} + \Delta\mathbf{\Theta}, \Delta\mathbf{\Theta} \in \mathcal{J}_\mathbf{\Theta} = \{\|\Delta\mathbf{\Theta}\|_F \leq \varepsilon\}. \tag{19}$$

The received SINR at the eavesdropper for intercepting the data offloaded from the LEO satellite to BS n is expressed as

$$\gamma_n^e = \frac{|\mathbf{\Theta}^H \mathbf{u}_n|^2}{\sum_{j \in \mathcal{N}, j \neq n} |\mathbf{\Theta}^H \mathbf{u}_j|^2 + |\mathbf{\Theta}^H \mathbf{v}_0|^2 + \sigma_e^2}. \tag{20}$$

2.4   Coverage Model

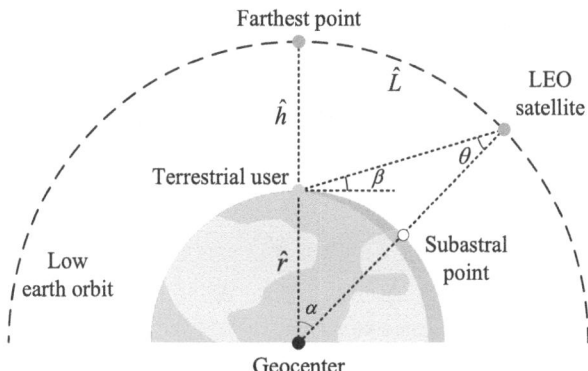

Fig. 2. Space geometric relationship

Different from the terrestrial edge computing networks, the communication link between the EUs and the LEO satellite is available only if the EUs are within the coverage area of the LEO satellite. Figure 2 shows the space geometric relationship between the EUs and the LEO satellite. In Fig. 2, $\hat{h}$ denotes the distance between the terrestrial user and the LEO, $\hat{r}$ denotes the radius of the earth, β denotes the elevation angle between the terrestrial user and the LEO satellite, α denotes the geocentric angle of the LEO satellite coverage area. After some math manipulations, α can be given by

$$\alpha = \arccos\left(\frac{\hat{r}}{\hat{r} + \hat{h}} \cos \beta\right) - \beta. \tag{21}$$

Then, the distance $\hat{L}$ from the LEO satellite to the farthest orbital point where it can maintain the available communication link with terrestrial users can be expressed as

$$\hat{L} = 2 \cdot (\hat{r} + \hat{h}) \cdot \alpha. \tag{22}$$

Based on the above model, the available communication duration for computation offloading of EU m is given by

$$T_m = \frac{\hat{L}_m}{v_s}, \tag{23}$$

where v_s denotes the speed of the LEO satellite.

2.5   Problem Formulation

To guarantee the secure computation offloading (SCO) in integrated satellite-terrestrial networks with the location uncertain malicious eavesdropper, the objective of this paper is to maximize the minimum sensing SINR for all possible eavesdropper locations within Φ, while maintaining the secrecy offloading transmission rate of the LEO satellite. To accomplish this objective, we jointly optimize the transmit beamforming $\{\mathbf{u}_n\}_{\forall n}$ and $\mathbf{v}_0$, the sensing receive beamforming $\mathbf{w}$, the offloading strategies $\{d_{mn}\}_{\forall m,n}$ of the LEO satellite for EUs' workloads, the offloading durations $\{t_n\}_{\forall n}$ from the LEO satellite to the BSs, and the computation rate $\{\varrho_m\}_{\forall m}$ allocated by the LEO satellite as follows.

$$\text{(SCO):} \quad \max \quad \min_{\theta_0 \in \Phi} \quad \text{SINR}(\theta_0)$$

$$\text{subject to:} \quad \max\{l_m^{\text{LS}}, l_m^{\text{BS}}\} \leq T_m, \forall m \in \mathcal{M}, \tag{24}$$

$$\gamma_n^e \leq \gamma_n^{e,\max}, \forall n \in \mathcal{N}, \Delta\Theta \in \mathcal{J}_\Theta, \tag{25}$$

$$R_n^d \geq R_n^{d,\min}, \forall n \in \mathcal{N}, \tag{26}$$

$$R_n^d t_n \geq \sum_{m \in \mathcal{M}} d_{mn}, \forall n \in \mathcal{N}, \tag{27}$$

$$0 \leq \sum_{n \in \mathcal{N}} d_{mn} \leq D_m^{\text{tot}}, \forall m \in \mathcal{M}, \tag{28}$$

$$P_0 \leq P_0^{\max}, \tag{29}$$

$$\text{variables:} \quad \{\mathbf{u}_n\}_{\forall n}, \mathbf{v}_0, \mathbf{w}, \{d_{mn}\}_{\forall m,n}, \{t_n\}_{\forall n}, \text{ and } \{\varrho_m\}_{\forall m}.$$

Constraint (24) guarantees that the overall latency in completing EU m's workloads cannot exceed the maximum available communication duration T_m. Constraint (25) represents the maximum tolerable leakage for the computation offloading. Constraint (26) represents the minimum offloading transmission rate required by the BSs. Constraint (29) provides an upper bound for the LEO satellite's power consumption. Notice that the secrecy offloading transmission rate for BS n can be guaranteed by constraints (25) and (26), and it is bounded by $R_n^{d,\min} - \log_2(1 + \gamma_n^{e,\max})$.

3   Proposed Algorithms

It can be identified that Problem (SCO) is a strictly nonconvex optimization problem due to the fractional objective function and the strong coupling of the variables. Thus, it is very difficult to be solved directly. We next transform Problem (SCO) into a tractable form.

After some math manipulations, constraint (24) can be transformed into the following two inequalities.

$$\frac{D_m^{\text{tot}}}{T_m - \frac{\nu_m(D_m^{\text{tot}} - \sum_{n \in \mathcal{N}} d_{mn})}{\varrho_m}} - R_m^u \leq 0, \forall m \in \mathcal{M}, \tag{30}$$

$$\frac{D_m^{\text{tot}}}{T_m - t_n - \frac{\nu_m d_{mn}}{\zeta_{mn}}} - R_m^u \leq 0, \forall m \in \mathcal{M}, \forall n \in \mathcal{N}. \tag{31}$$

By observing Problem (SCO) with constraints (30) and (31), we conclude that given the other variables, the optimal solutions of the sensing receive beamforming $\mathbf{w}^*$ and the computation rate $\{\varrho_m^*\}_{\forall m}$ are respectively given by

$$\mathbf{w}^* = (\mathbf{A}_c \mathbf{x} \mathbf{x}^H \mathbf{A}_c^H + \sigma_0^2 \mathbf{I}_N)^{-1} \mathbf{a}_r(\theta_0), \tag{32}$$

$$\varrho_m^* = \frac{\nu_m (D_m^{\text{tot}} - \sum_{n \in \mathcal{N}} d_{mn})}{T_m - \frac{D_m^{\text{tot}}}{R_m^u}}, \forall m \in \mathcal{M}. \tag{33}$$

It can be identified that constraints (30) and (31) are difference of convex forms. To transform them into convex functions, we perform the first order Taylor expansion of $\mathbf{h}_m^H \mathbf{\Gamma}_m^{-1} \mathbf{h}_m$, for the τ-th iteration of the SCA, we obtain the lower bound as

$$\mathbf{h}_m^H \mathbf{\Gamma}_m^{-1} \mathbf{h}_m \geq \Omega_m^{\text{lb}} \triangleq \mathbf{h}_m^H (\mathbf{\Gamma}_m^{\tau-1})^{-1} \mathbf{h}_m - \mathbf{h}_m^H (\mathbf{\Gamma}_m^{\tau-1})^{-1} (\mathbf{\Gamma}_m - \mathbf{\Gamma}_m^{\tau-1}) (\mathbf{\Gamma}_m^{\tau-1})^{-1} \mathbf{h}_m, \tag{34}$$

where $\mathbf{\Gamma}_m^{\tau-1}$ denotes the solution obtained in the $(\tau - 1)$th iteration and it can be expressed as

$$\mathbf{\Gamma}_m^{\tau-1} = (\mathbf{A}_s + \mathbf{A}_c) \mathbf{x}^{\tau-1} (\mathbf{x}^{\tau-1})^H (\mathbf{A}_s^H + \mathbf{A}_c^H) + \sum_{j \in \mathcal{M}, j \neq m} p_j \mathbf{h}_j \mathbf{h}_j^H + \sigma_0^2 \mathbf{I}_N. \tag{35}$$

Then, constraints (30) and (31) are replaced by the following two convex constraints

$$\frac{D_m^{\text{tot}}}{T_m - \frac{\nu_m (D_m^{\text{tot}} - \sum_{n \in \mathcal{N}} d_{mn})}{\varrho_m}} - \tilde{R}_m^u \leq 0, \forall m \in \mathcal{M}, \tag{36}$$

$$\frac{D_m^{\text{tot}}}{T_m - t_n - \frac{\nu_m d_{mn}}{\zeta_{mn}}} - \tilde{R}_m^u \leq 0, \forall m \in \mathcal{M}, \forall n \in \mathcal{N}, \tag{37}$$

where

$$\tilde{R}_m^u = B^d \log_2 \left(1 + p_m \Omega_m^{\text{lb}} \right). \tag{38}$$

With Eq. (20), constraint (25) is transformed into

$$\frac{1}{\gamma_n^{e,\max}} |\mathbf{\Theta}^H \mathbf{u}_n|^2 - \sigma_e^2 \leq \sum_{j \in \mathcal{N}, j \neq n} |\mathbf{\Theta}^H \mathbf{u}_j|^2 + |\mathbf{\Theta}^H \mathbf{v}_0|^2. \tag{39}$$

By performing the first order Taylor expansion of the right hand side in Eq. (39), for the τth iteration of the SCA, we obtain the lower bound as

$$\sum_{j \in \mathcal{N}, j \neq n} |\mathbf{\Theta}^H \mathbf{u}_j|^2 + |\mathbf{\Theta}^H \mathbf{v}_0|^2 \geq \Psi_n^{\text{lb}} \triangleq 2\text{Re}\{(\mathbf{\Theta}^H \mathbf{v}_0^\tau)^\dagger (\mathbf{\Theta}^H \mathbf{v}_0)\} - |\mathbf{\Theta}^H \mathbf{v}_0^\tau|^2$$
$$+ \sum_{j \in \mathcal{N}, j \neq n} \left(2\text{Re}\{(\mathbf{\Theta}^H \mathbf{u}_j^\tau)^\dagger (\mathbf{\Theta}^H \mathbf{u}_j)\} - |\mathbf{\Theta}^H \mathbf{u}_j^\tau|^2 \right), \tag{40}$$

where $\mathbf{u}_n^\tau$ and $\mathbf{v}_0^\tau$ denote the solutions obtained in the $(\tau - 1)$th iteration. Then, constraint (25) can be replaced by the convex function as

$$\frac{1}{\gamma_n^{e,\max}}|\mathbf{\Theta}^H\mathbf{u}_n|^2 - \mathit{\Psi}_n^{\text{lb}} - \sigma_e^2 \le 0, \forall n \in \mathcal{N}. \tag{41}$$

Then, we address nonconvex constraint (26). By using Lagrangian dual transform method, we introduce the auxiliary variables $\{\lambda_n\}_{\forall n}$ and rewrite R_n^d in Eq. (14) as

$$\bar{R}_n^d = B^d(1 + \lambda_n)\mathbf{u}_n^H\mathbf{G}_n^H\mathbf{E}_n^{-1}\mathbf{G}_n\mathbf{u}_n + B^d\log_2(1 + \lambda_n) - B^d\lambda_n, \tag{42}$$

where $\mathbf{E}_n$ is given by

$$\mathbf{E}_n = \mathbf{G}_n\mathbf{u}_n\mathbf{u}_n^H\mathbf{G}_n^H + \mathbf{\Lambda}_n. \tag{43}$$

It can be identified that $\bar{R}_n^d$ is a concave function of $\{\lambda_n\}_{\forall n}$ under the given $\{\mathbf{u}_n\}_{\forall n}$. The first derivative of $\bar{R}_n^d$ regarding $\{\lambda_n\}_{\forall n}$ is given by

$$\frac{\partial \bar{R}_n^d}{\partial \lambda_n} = B^d\mathbf{u}_n^H\mathbf{G}_n^H\mathbf{E}_n^{-1}\mathbf{G}_n\mathbf{u}_n - \frac{B^d\lambda_n}{(1 + \lambda_n)}. \tag{44}$$

By using Sherman Morrison formula, Eq. (44) can be rewritten as

$$\begin{aligned}
\frac{\partial \bar{R}_n^d}{\partial \lambda_n} &= -\frac{B^d\mathbf{u}_n^H\mathbf{G}_n^H\mathbf{\Lambda}_n^{-1}\mathbf{G}_n\mathbf{u}_n\mathbf{u}_n^H\mathbf{G}_n^H\mathbf{\Lambda}_n^{-1}\mathbf{G}_n\mathbf{u}_n}{(1 + \mathbf{u}_n^H\mathbf{G}_n^H\mathbf{\Lambda}_n^{-1}\mathbf{G}_n\mathbf{u}_n)} \\
&\quad + B^d\mathbf{u}_n^H\mathbf{G}_n^H\mathbf{\Lambda}_n^{-1}\mathbf{G}_n\mathbf{u}_n - \frac{B^d\lambda_n}{(1 + \lambda_n)} \\
&= \frac{B^d\mathbf{u}_n^H\mathbf{G}_n^H\mathbf{\Lambda}_n^{-1}\mathbf{G}_n\mathbf{u}_n}{(1 + \mathbf{u}_n^H\mathbf{G}_n^H\mathbf{\Lambda}_n^{-1}\mathbf{G}_n\mathbf{u}_n)} - \frac{B^d\lambda_n}{(1 + \lambda_n)}.
\end{aligned} \tag{45}$$

Let $\frac{\partial \bar{R}_n^d}{\partial \lambda_n} = 0$, we can derive that the optimal solution of $\{\lambda_n\}_{\forall n}$ can be expressed as

$$\lambda_n^* = \mathbf{u}_n^H\mathbf{G}_n^H\mathbf{\Lambda}_n^{-1}\mathbf{G}_n\mathbf{u}_n. \tag{46}$$

Since Eq. (42) is still nonconvex, we further use multiple dimensional quadratic transformation method to rewrite $\bar{R}_n^d$ as

$$\tilde{R}_n^d = 2\sqrt{B^d(1 + \lambda_n)}\text{Re}\{\mathbf{u}_n^H\mathbf{G}_n^H\mathbf{f}_n\} - \mathbf{f}_n^H\mathbf{E}_n\mathbf{f}_n + B^d\log_2(1 + \lambda_n) - B^d\lambda_n, \tag{47}$$

where $\{\mathbf{f}_n\}_{\forall n} \in \mathbb{C}^{N_r \times 1}$ are the auxiliary vectors. By substituting Eq. (43) into Eq. (47), we obtain

$$\begin{aligned}
\tilde{R}_n^d = {}&2\sqrt{B^d(1 + \lambda_n)}\text{Re}\{\mathbf{u}_n^H\mathbf{G}_n^H\mathbf{f}_n\} - |\mathbf{f}_n^H\mathbf{G}_n\mathbf{u}_n|^2 - \sum_{j \in \mathcal{N}, j \ne n}|\mathbf{f}_n^H\mathbf{G}_n\mathbf{u}_j|^2 \\
&- |\mathbf{f}_n^H\mathbf{G}_n\mathbf{v}_0|^2 - \sigma_n^2\|\mathbf{f}_n\|_F^2 + B^d\log_2(1 + \lambda_n) - B^d\lambda_n.
\end{aligned} \tag{48}$$

According to the criterion of multiple dimensional quadratic transformation, the optimal solution of $\{\mathbf{f}_n\}_{\forall n}$ is given by

$$\mathbf{f}_n^* = \sqrt{B^d(1+\lambda_n)}\mathbf{E}_n^{-1}\mathbf{G}_n\mathbf{u}_n. \tag{49}$$

After the above operations, the nonconvex constraint (26) is equivalently transformed into

$$\tilde{R}_n^d \geq R_n^{d,\min}, \forall n \in \mathcal{N}. \tag{50}$$

We next address the fractional form of the objective function. By introducing the auxiliary variables $\{\varpi_{\theta_0}\}_{\theta_0 \in \Phi}$ and using the quadratic transformation, the objective function of Problem (SCO) can be equivalently rewritten as

$$\max \min_{\theta_0 \in \Phi} 2\varpi_{\theta_0}\sqrt{|\mathbf{w}^H\mathbf{A}_s\mathbf{x}|^2} - \varpi_{\theta_0}^2\mathbf{w}^H(\mathbf{A}_c\mathbf{x}\mathbf{x}^H\mathbf{A}_c^H + \sigma_0^2\mathbf{I}_N)\mathbf{w} \tag{51}$$

The optimal solution of ϖ_{θ_0} can be updated by

$$\varpi_{\theta_0}^* = \frac{\sqrt{|\mathbf{w}^H\mathbf{A}_s\mathbf{x}|^2}}{\mathbf{w}^H(\mathbf{A}_c\mathbf{x}\mathbf{x}^H\mathbf{A}_c^H + \sigma_0^2\mathbf{I}_N)\mathbf{w}}. \tag{52}$$

To tackle the *max-min* form of the objective function (51), we further introduce an auxiliary variable μ which satisfies

$$\mu \leq \min_{\theta_0 \in \Phi} 2\varpi_{\theta_0}\sqrt{|\mathbf{w}^H\mathbf{A}_s\mathbf{x}|^2} - \varpi_{\theta_0}^2\mathbf{w}^H(\mathbf{A}_c\mathbf{x}\mathbf{x}^H\mathbf{A}_c^H + \sigma_0^2\mathbf{I}_N)\mathbf{w}. \tag{53}$$

Then, the objective function (51) can be equivalently transformed into

$$\max \mu \tag{54}$$

with the following constraint

$$2\varpi_{\theta_0}\sqrt{|\mathbf{w}^H\mathbf{A}_s\mathbf{x}|^2} - \varpi_{\theta_0}^2\mathbf{w}^H(\mathbf{A}_c\mathbf{x}\mathbf{x}^H\mathbf{A}_c^H + \sigma_0^2\mathbf{I}_N)\mathbf{w} \geq \mu, \forall \theta_0 \in \Phi. \tag{55}$$

Constraint (55) is still nonconvex. Thus, we perform the first order Taylor expansion of the first term of $|\mathbf{w}^H\mathbf{A}_s\mathbf{x}|^2$, we obtain its lower bound as

$$|\mathbf{w}^H\mathbf{A}_s\mathbf{x}|^2 \geq \psi^{\text{lb}} \triangleq 2\text{Re}\{(\mathbf{w}^H\mathbf{A}_s\mathbf{x}^\tau)^\dagger(\mathbf{w}^H\mathbf{A}_s\mathbf{x})\} - |\mathbf{w}^H\mathbf{A}_s\mathbf{x}^\tau|^2. \tag{56}$$

Based on the following operations, the surrogate problem for Problem (SCO) can be established as

(SCO-Sur): $\max \mu$

subject to: constraints $(28), (29), (36), (37), (41)$, and (50),

$$-\varpi_{\theta_0}^2\mathbf{w}^H(\mathbf{A}_c\mathbf{x}\mathbf{x}^H\mathbf{A}_c^H + \sigma_0^2\mathbf{I}_N)\mathbf{w} + 2\varpi_{\theta_0}\sqrt{\psi^{\text{lb}}} \geq \mu, \forall \theta_0 \in \Phi, \tag{57}$$

$$R_n^{d,\min}t_n \geq \sum_{m \in \mathcal{M}} d_{mn}, \forall n \in \mathcal{N}, \tag{58}$$

variables: $\{\mathbf{u}_n\}_{\forall n}, \mathbf{v}_0, \mathbf{w}, \{d_{mn}\}_{\forall m,n}, \{t_n\}_{\forall n}, \{\lambda_n\}_{\forall n}, \{\mathbf{f}_n\}_{\forall n}, \{\varpi_{\theta_0}\}_{\forall \theta_0}, \{\varrho_m\}_{\forall m},$ and μ.

It can be identified that Problem (SCO-Sur) is a strict convex optimization problem, since the objective function is affine, and all constraints compose a convex feasible region. Therefore, we cam obtain the solution of Problem (SCO) by solving Problem (SCO-Sur) with CVX in an iterative manner. The details for solving Problem (SCO) are shown as follows.

Algorithm 1 : To solve Problem (SCO).

1: **Initialization:** Initialize $\{d_{mn}[0]\}_{\forall m,n}$, $\{\mathbf{u}_n[0]\}_{\forall n}$ and $\mathbf{v}_0[0]$. Set $k = 0$.
2: **repeat**
3:    Set $k = k + 1$.
4:    Update $\mathbf{w}[k]$ according to Eq. (32).
5:    Update $\{\varrho_m[k]\}_{\forall m}$ according to Eq. (33).
6:    Update $\{\lambda_n[k]\}_{\forall n}$ according to Eq. (46).
7:    Update $\{\mathbf{f}_n[k]\}_{\forall n}$ according to Eq. (49).
8:    Update $\{\varpi_{\theta_0}[k]\}_{\forall \theta_0}$ according to Eq. (52).
9:    Solve Problem (SCO-Sur) with $\{\mathbf{w}[k]\}$, $\{\varrho_m[k]\}_{\forall m}$, $\{d_{mn}[k-1]\}_{\forall m,n}$, $\{\mathbf{u}_n[k-1]\}_{\forall n}$, $\mathbf{v}_0[k-1]$, $\{\lambda_n[k]\}_{\forall n}$, $\{\mathbf{f}_n[k]\}_{\forall n}$, and $\{\varpi_{\theta_0}[k]\}_{\forall \theta_0}$ by using CVX and obtain $\{d_{mn}[k]\}_{\forall m,n}$, $\{\mathbf{u}_n[k]\}_{\forall n}$, $\mathbf{v}_0[k]$, and $\{t_n\}_{\forall n}$.
10: **until** *Convergence*
11: Set $\{d^*_{mn} = d_{mn}[k]\}_{\forall m,n}$, $\{\mathbf{u}^*_n = \mathbf{u}_n[k]\}_{\forall n}$, $\mathbf{v}^*_0 = \mathbf{v}_0[k]$, $\{\varrho^*_m = \varrho_m[k]\}_{\forall m}$, $\{t^*_n = t_n[k]\}_{\forall n}$ and $\mathbf{w}^* = \mathbf{w}[k]$.
12: **Output:** $\{d^*_{mn}\}_{\forall m,n}$, $\{\mathbf{u}^*_n\}_{\forall n}$, $\mathbf{v}^*_0$, $\{\varrho^*_m\}_{\forall m}$, $\{t^*_n\}_{\forall n}$, $\mathbf{w}^*$.

---

4   Numerical Results

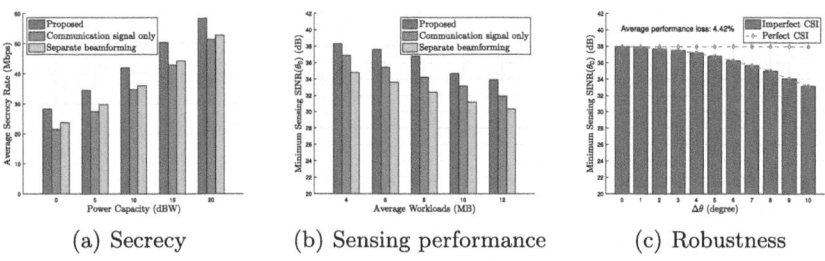

(a) Secrecy   (b) Sensing performance   (c) Robustness

Fig. 3. Performance advantages of our ISAC empowered secure computation offloading

We present numerical results to demonstrate the performance advantages of our ISAC empowered secure computation offloading in the integrated satellite-terrestrial network. We consider the tested scenario of $M = 4$ EUs and $N = 2$ BSs. We set $N_t = 10$ transmit antennas and $N_r = 15$ receive antennas. We assume that the communication link between the LEO satellite and the terrestrial transceiver is dominated by the line of sight component. The channels between the satellite and terrestrial in this work are set according to [11]. Moreover, We set bandwidth $B^u = B^d = 10$ MHz, $\Delta\theta = 5°$, $\epsilon_0 = 1 \times 10^{-28}$, and set $\sigma_0^2 = \sigma_n^2 = -80$ dBm.

To verify the performance advantages of the ISAC empowered secure computation offloading, we consider the following benchmarks for comparison.

- Communication signal only: In this benchmark scheme, we only use the communication signal as the integrated signal (i.e., without the dedicated sensing signal) for both sensing and offloading.
- Separate beamforming: In this benchmark scheme, we use the conventional separate design of the communication signal and the sensing signal.

Figure 3 demonstrates the performance superiority of our proposed approach. Figure 3(a) shows the average secrecy offloading rate of the LEO satellite with different power capacities. It can be seen that the average secrecy rate is increasing with respect to the value of the LEO satellite's power capacity $P_0^{\max}$. Figure 3(b) shows the minimum sensing performance within the eavesdropper's uncertain region under different average task workloads. It can be observed that the minimum sensing performance is decreasing with respect to the workloads due to the fact that the increased workloads result in more resources being allocated for computation offloading. The results in Figs. 3(a) and 3(b) verify that our proposed scheme outperforms the benchmark schemes in security. Figure 3(c) shows the minimum sensing performance with different uncertain regions. The red dashed line represents the case in which the satellite has perfect CSI about the eavesdropper. In particular, the average performance loss of our proposed scheme in the case of eavesdropper location uncertainty compared to the perfect eavesdropper CSI is marked at the top of Fig. 3(c). The results show that the average loss does not exceed 5%, which verifies the robustness of our scheme.

5 Conclusions

In this paper, we have proposed an ISAC empowered secure computation offloading in integrated satellite-terrestrial networks, in which the ISAC signal transmitted by the LEO satellite can be used for sensing the potential eavesdropper with an uncertain location while improving secrecy offloading transmission rates. We have proposed a joint optimization of the transmit beamforming, the receive beamforming, the computation offloading strategies and the associated allocations of communication and computing resources, with the aim of achieving the robust security of the network. Despite the nonconvexity of the formulated problem, we have proposed an efficient algorithm to obtain its solutions. In our future work, we will investigate the integration of quantum cryptographic techniques and covert communication methods within integrated satellite-terrestrial networks to further enhance security against sophisticated eavesdroppers.

Acknowledgement. This work was supported in part by National Natural Science Foundation of China under Grants 62122069, 62072490, and 62071431, in part by the Guangdong Basic and Applied Basic Research Foundation (2022A1515011287), in part by Science and Technology Development Fund of Macau SAR under Grant FDCT 0158/2022/A, and in part by MYRG-GRG2023-00083-IOTSC-UMDF.

References

1. Chen, Q., Meng, W., Quek, T.Q.S., Chen, S.: Multi-tier hybrid offloading for computation-aware IoT applications in civil aircraft-augmented SAGIN. IEEE J. Sel. Areas Commun. **41**(2), 399–417 (2023). https://doi.org/10.1109/JSAC.2022. 3227031

2. Liu, Y., Chen, H.H., Wang, L.: Physical layer security for next generation wireless networks: theories, technologies, and challenges. IEEE Commun. Surv. Tutorials **19**(1), 347–376 (2017). https://doi.org/10.1109/COMST.2016.2598968

3. Liu, Y., et al.: Physical layer security assisted computation offloading in intelligently connected vehicle networks. IEEE Trans. Wireless Commun. **20**(6), 3555–3570 (2021). https://doi.org/10.1109/TWC.2021.3051772

4. Liu, Y., Ni, L., Peng, M.: A secure and efficient authentication protocol for satellite-terrestrial networks. IEEE Internet Things J. **10**(7), 5810–5822 (2023). https://doi.org/10.1109/JIOT.2022.3152900

5. An, K., Lin, M., Ouyang, J., Zhu, W.P.: Secure transmission in cognitive satellite terrestrial networks. IEEE J. Sel. Areas Commun. **34**(11), 3025–3037 (2016). https://doi.org/10.1109/JSAC.2016.2615261

6. Lin, Z., Lin, M., Champagne, B., Zhu, W.P., Al-Dhahir, N.: Secrecy-energy efficient hybrid beamforming for satellite-terrestrial integrated networks. IEEE Trans. Commun. **69**(9), 6345–6360 (2021). https://doi.org/10.1109/TCOMM.2021.3088898

7. Dou, C., Huang, N., Wu, Y., Qian, L., Quek, T.Q.S.: Sensing-efficient NOMA-aided integrated sensing and communication: a joint sensing scheduling and beamforming optimization. IEEE Trans. Veh. Technol. **72**(10), 13591–13603 (2023). https://doi.org/10.1109/TVT.2023.3277734

8. Yuan, W., Wei, Z., Li, S., Yuan, J., Ng, D.W.K.: Integrated sensing and communication-assisted orthogonal time frequency space transmission for vehicular networks. IEEE J. Sel. Top. Sig. Process. **15**(6), 1515–1528 (2021). https://doi.org/10.1109/JSTSP.2021.3117404

9. Lyu, Z., Zhu, G., Xu, J.: Joint maneuver and beamforming design for UAV-enabled integrated sensing and communication. IEEE Trans. Wireless Commun. **22**(4), 2424–2440 (2023). https://doi.org/10.1109/TWC.2022.3211533

10. Dou, C., Huang, N., Wu, Y., Qian, L., Quek, T.Q.S.: Channel sharing aided integrated sensing and communication: an energy-efficient sensing scheduling approach. IEEE Trans. Wireless Commun. **23**(5), 4802–4814 (2024). https://doi.org/10.1109/TWC.2023.3322680

11. Yin, Z., et al.: UAV-assisted physical layer security in multi-beam satellite-enabled vehicle communications. IEEE Trans. Intell. Transp. Syst. **23**(3), 2739–2751 (2022). https://doi.org/10.1109/TITS.2021.3090017

Rotator-Aided RIS Beam Stabilization Method in UAV Communications

Jingwei Hu[1,2(✉)] [iD], Mingcheng Shen[1], Chunxia Su[1] [iD], Yao Xu[3] [iD], and Jichong Guo[1] [iD]

[1] Suzhou University of Science and Technology, Suzhou 215009, China
javery_hu@163.com, guojichong@usts.edu.cn
[2] University of Glasgow, Glasgow G12 8QQ, UK
[3] Nanjing University of Information Science and Technology, Nanjing 210044, China
yaoxu@nuist.edu.cn

Abstract. Unmanned Aerial Vehicle (UAV) air-to-ground communication plays a significant role in the integrated information network. Reconfigurable Intelligent Surface (RIS), a passive antenna array, is particularly well-suited for UAV applications. However, airflow induced UAV wobbling can significantly damage the performance of the RIS enabled beamforming. In this paper, we investigate a robust beamforming method that employs a Rotator-Aided RIS (R-RIS), introducing a novel approach to mitigating disturbances. The design problem is non-convex, prompting the proposal of a heuristic strategy that effectively decouples the original problem. The simulation results validate the effectiveness of the proposed scheme, highlighting its ability to enhance the beam stabilization.

Keywords: UAV communications · RIS · Beamforming

1 Introduction

RIS is a planar metasurface capable of controlling the properties of electromagnetic waves, typically composed of a large array of specially designed passive reflecting elements. Each element can independently modulate the characteristics of the incident signal by applying the required phase shift or tunable amplitude to it [1]. Due to its high energy efficiency and hardware utilization in reshaping the electromagnetic environment, RIS is considered to be one of the most crucial supporting technologies for future 6G networks [2].

UAV, with its high flexibility and low deployment costs, is widely employed in wireless communications [3], such as assisting two-way relaying networks [4].

The work was supported in part by the National Natural Science Foundation of China (Grant No. 62271085), and in part by the Natural Science Foundation of the Higher Education Institutions of Jiangsu Province, China (Grant No. 22KJB510033, 23KJB510031, and 23KJB520035).

H.-H. Chen and W. Meng (Eds.): WiSATS 2024, LNICST 605, pp. 269–278, 2025.
https://doi.org/10.1007/978-3-031-86196-3_23

Different from terrestrial communications and high altitude platform based communications, systems equipped with low altitude UAVs may benefit from short range Line-of-Sight (LoS) links, potentially resulting in better communication channels. Moreover, such systems generally boast quicker deployment speeds and more flexible reconfigurations [5].

The diversification and complexity of application scenarios in next generation wireless communications presents new challenges for the development of wireless communications. For instance, to meet the demands of mobile communications, both mobility and reliability of the system are forced to adapt to higher standards [6]. Building on the discussions above, the integration of RIS and UAV in wireless communications is a natural progression. Given the numerous uncertainties in the aerial environment, it is worth considering how to address the impacts of UAV jitters. Indeed, a substantial body of research is already based on the combination of RIS and UAV and aimed at tackling the challenges from UAV jittering. Authors in [6] present the UAV's energy consumption model and an algorithm to optimize its trajectory. The work in [4] investigates the effects of jittering UAV on the capacity of UAV assisted communication systems and derives an expression for the system's capacity, taking into account the unique properties of UAV jitters. In [7], an anti-jamming approach is proposed by adjusting the UAV's trajectory. Authors in [8] introduce a strategy designed to reduce energy used in UAV equipped multi-user RIS wireless networks, especially for the challenges posed by UAV jitters and considering the effects of imperfect hardware.

As discussed above, most existing studies focus on adjusting the UAV's position and the RIS's phase shift, potentially increasing system latency. Therefore, inspired by [9], a heuristic approach that installs a mechanical rotator between the UAV and RIS is proposed in this paper, which aims to enhance system performance when the UAV jitters.

Here is the structure of this paper: The first section outlines the background and research significance of RIS and UAV. It reviews existing studies on dealing with UAV jitter based on the integration of the two, identifies their shortcomings and leads into the research content of this paper. In the second section, the system model and signal transmission model are introduced, and the necessary expressions are listed to lay the foundation for the subsequent research. In order to mitigate the effects of UAV jitter on the system and enhance the beam stability, the third section investigates a heuristic method that decouples the problem into two manageable subproblems, determining the optimal azimuth and elevation angles for the R-RIS firstly and configuring the phase shift matrix secondly. The fourth section illustrates the setting parameters and simulation results, which demonstrate the effectiveness of the proposed scheme through comparative performance analyses. The final section provides a conclusion of the entire paper.

Note 1. Lowercase bold letters are used to describe vectors, whereas uppercase bold letters denote matrices. The operation $(x \mod y)$ is defined as the remainder of x divided by y, $\mathbb{E}[\cdot]$ denotes the expectation operation. The superscript

$[\cdot]^{\mathrm{T}}$ signifies the transpose operation and the superscript $[\cdot]^{\mathrm{H}}$ indicates the conjugate transpose operation. The complex normal distribution is represented by $\mathcal{CN}(\mu, \sigma^2)$, where μ and σ^2 stand for the mean and variance, respectively. The floor function is denoted by $\lfloor \cdot \rfloor$ and the absolute value is expressed as $|\cdot|$. Finally, $\| \cdot \|$ symbolizes the l_2 norm and the imaginary unit is defined as $j \triangleq \sqrt{-1}$.

2   System Model

The model of the UAV air-to-ground communication system is introduced in Fig. 1, which includes the process of transmitting and receiving signals. Here considers a down link transmission model in an air disturbance environment where the UAV employs an R-RIS with $M \times N$ reflective elements. The R-RIS, configured as a uniform planar array, is organized on a rectangular grid with gaps of a and b. The center of the R-RIS serves as the origin for the three-dimensional Cartesian coordinate system, and the initial pose of RIS coincides with the $x - y$ plane. Both the Base Station (BS) and the User Equipment (UE) are equipped with a single isotropic antenna. Their positions can be described as $\boldsymbol{p}_{\mathrm{BS}} = [x_{\mathrm{BS}}, y_{\mathrm{BS}}, z_{\mathrm{BS}}]^{\mathrm{T}}$ and $\boldsymbol{p}_{\mathrm{UE}} = [x_{\mathrm{UE}}, y_{\mathrm{UE}}, z_{\mathrm{UE}}]^{\mathrm{T}}$, respectively. Additionally, it is assumed that partial Channel State Information (CSI) is available in advance.

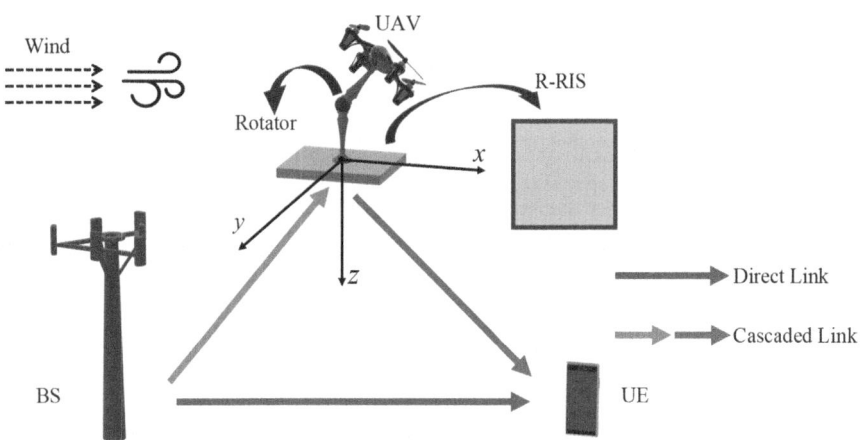

Fig. 1. Transmission model.

The element R-RIS(m, n) denotes the (m, n)-th unit of the R-RIS, the position of which on the $x - y$ plane is

$$\hat{\boldsymbol{p}}_{m,n} = [\omega(m, \alpha, M), \omega(n, b, N), 0]^{\mathrm{T}}, \tag{1}$$

where $\omega(m, \alpha, M) = a(m - 0.5((M + 1) \bmod 2))$, $m \in \omega(M)$ with $\omega(M) = \{((M + 1) \bmod 2)) - \lfloor \frac{M}{2} \rfloor, \dots, \lfloor \frac{M}{2} \rfloor\}$ [10]. Similarly, we can obtain $\omega(n, b, N)$.

In this paper, the rotator is assumed as a mechanical structure for connecting the UAV and the RIS, allowing the R-RIS to freely rotate beneath the UAV. It is similar to the axis structure of a camera gimbal, which would enable the R-RIS to adjust its orientation in the air. In the environment where the UAV is subject to disturbances from air flow, since the attitude changes of which follow a stochastic process, it is more practical to model and analyze the changes with discrete data block i rather than continuous time. Consequently, the actual position vector of R-RIS(m, n) can be described as

$$\boldsymbol{p}_{m,n}(i) = \boldsymbol{\Gamma}^{\mathrm{T}}(i)\hat{\boldsymbol{p}}_{m,n}, \tag{2}$$

where $\boldsymbol{\Gamma}(i)$ is

$$
\boldsymbol{\Gamma}(i) =
\begin{bmatrix}
\cos(\theta_i^{\mathrm{RIS}} + \theta_i) & -\sin(\theta_i^{\mathrm{RIS}} + \theta_i)\cos(\varphi_i^{\mathrm{RIS}} + \varphi_i) & \sin(\theta_i^{\mathrm{RIS}} + \theta_i)\sin(\varphi_i^{\mathrm{RIS}} + \varphi_i) \\
\sin(\theta_i^{\mathrm{RIS}} + \theta_i) & \cos(\theta_i^{\mathrm{RIS}} + \theta_i)\cos(\varphi_i^{\mathrm{RIS}} + \varphi_i) & -\cos(\theta_i^{\mathrm{RIS}} + \theta_i)\sin(\varphi_i^{\mathrm{RIS}} + \varphi_i) \\
0 & \sin(\varphi_i^{\mathrm{RIS}} + \varphi_i) & \cos(\varphi_i^{\mathrm{RIS}} + \varphi_i)
\end{bmatrix}.
$$
$$\tag{3}$$

As the jitter of the R-RIS is modeled as $\mathcal{CN}(0, \sigma_1{}^2)$ ($\theta_i \sim \mathcal{CN}(0, \sigma_1{}^2)$ and $\varphi_i \sim \mathcal{CN}(0, \sigma_1{}^2)$), $\boldsymbol{p}_{m,n}(i)$ may change at each different data block i. In other words, the azimuth angle θ_i^{RIS} and elevation angle φ_i^{RIS} for the R-RIS vary at different block i. In addition, small-scale fading is negligible [9] and the channels are supposed to be exclusively LoS. Therefore, for data block i, the instantaneous gain of the direct link between the BS and the UE can be expressed as

$$A_d = \frac{\lambda_c}{4\pi d_{\mathrm{BS}}^{\mathrm{UE}}}, \tag{4}$$

where λ_c represents the wavelength of the carrier signal, and ($d_{\mathrm{BS}}^{\mathrm{UE}} = \|\boldsymbol{p}_{\mathrm{UE}} - \boldsymbol{p}_{\mathrm{BS}}\|$) denotes the Euclidean distance between the BS and the UE. Since the relative position between the BS and the UE does not change, Eq. (4) can be considered a constant for the sake of simplifying calculations.

Similarly, the instantaneous gain of the cascaded link for block i is regarded as

$$A_{m,n}(i) = \frac{\lambda_c^2 \sqrt{G_{m,n}^{\mathrm{BS}}(i) G_{m,n}^{\mathrm{UE}}(i)}}{16\pi^2 d_{\mathrm{BS}}^{m,n}(i) d_{m,n}^{\mathrm{UE}}(i)}, \tag{5}$$

where $d_{\mathrm{BS}}^{m,n}(i) = \|\boldsymbol{p}_{m,n}(i) - \boldsymbol{p}_{\mathrm{BS}}\|$ represents the distance from R-RIS(m, n) to the BS, and $d_{m,n}^{\mathrm{UE}}(i) = \|\boldsymbol{p}_{\mathrm{UE}} - \boldsymbol{p}_{m,n}(i)\|$ denotes the distance from the UE to R-RIS(m, n). In addition, $G_{m,n}^{\mathrm{BS}}(i)$ is the gain of R-RIS(m, n) with the BS as the observation point, and $G_{m,n}^{\mathrm{UE}}(i)$ indicates the gain of R-RIS(m, n) with the UE as the observation point. Since the initial conditions are undisturbed, it is assumed that the initial localization points of the BS, the center of the R-RIS, and the UE are aligned on the same plane, namely $x - z$ plane. Thus, $G_{m,n}^{\mathrm{BS}}(i) \approx \frac{4\pi}{\lambda_c^2} ab \cos(\theta_i^{\mathrm{BS}}) \cos(\varphi_i^{\mathrm{BS}})$ and $G_{m,n}^{\mathrm{UE}}(i) \approx \frac{4\pi}{\lambda_c^2} ab \cos(\theta_i^{\mathrm{UE}}) \cos(\varphi_i^{\mathrm{UE}})$, where

θ_i^{BS} and φ_i^{BS} are the azimuth and elevation angles of the BS, respectively, and they can be written as

$$\theta_i^{\mathrm{BS}} = \arccos(\frac{x_{\mathrm{BS}}}{\|\boldsymbol{p}_{\mathrm{BS}}\|}) \in [0, \theta_{max}^{\mathrm{BS}}], \varphi_i^{\mathrm{BS}} = \arccos(\frac{z_{\mathrm{BS}}}{\|\boldsymbol{p}_{\mathrm{BS}}\|}) \in [0, \varphi_{max}^{\mathrm{BS}}]. \quad (6)$$

Similarly, for the UE, the azimuth angle θ_i^{UE} and elevation angle φ_i^{UE} are described as

$$\theta_i^{\mathrm{UE}} = \arccos(\frac{x_{\mathrm{UE}}}{\|\boldsymbol{p}_{\mathrm{UE}}\|}) \in [0, \theta_{max}^{\mathrm{UE}}], \varphi_i^{\mathrm{UE}} = \arccos(\frac{z_{\mathrm{UE}}}{\|\boldsymbol{p}_{\mathrm{UE}}\|}) \in [0, \varphi_{max}^{\mathrm{UE}}], \quad (7)$$

where $\theta_{max}^{\mathrm{BS}}$, $\varphi_{max}^{\mathrm{BS}}$, $\theta_{max}^{\mathrm{UE}}$ and $\varphi_{max}^{\mathrm{UE}}$ are the maximum angle limits. It is important to note that this setup incorporates a specific transformation relationship between the azimuth and elevation angles of the BS, the R-RIS and the UE, which can be expressed as

$$k^{\mathrm{BS}}\theta_i^{\mathrm{BS}} + k^{\mathrm{UE}}\theta_i^{\mathrm{UE}} = \theta_i^{\mathrm{RIS}} \quad (8)$$

and

$$l^{\mathrm{BS}}\varphi_i^{\mathrm{BS}} + l^{\mathrm{UE}}\varphi_i^{\mathrm{UE}} = \varphi_i^{\mathrm{RIS}}, \quad (9)$$

where k and l are adjustment coefficients. Due to the presence of disturbances, $d_{\mathrm{BS}}^{m,n}(i)$ and $d_{m,n}^{\mathrm{UE}}(i)$ may change. Therefore, Eq. (5) can be reformulated as

$$A_{m,n}(i) \approx \frac{ab}{4\pi d_{\mathrm{BS}}^{m,n}(i)d_{m,n}^{\mathrm{UE}}(i)} \sqrt{\cos(\theta_i^{\mathrm{BS}})\cos(\varphi_i^{\mathrm{BS}})\cos(\theta_i^{\mathrm{UE}})\cos(\varphi_i^{\mathrm{UE}})}. \quad (10)$$

Assume that the change of $d_{\mathrm{BS}}^{m,n}(i)d_{m,n}^{\mathrm{UE}}(i)$ induced by the rotator adjustments is very limited, that is to say, $d_{\mathrm{BS}}^{m,n}(i)d_{m,n}^{\mathrm{UE}}(i) \approx d_1 d_2$, where d_1 and d_2 are the distances from the BS to the R-RIS center and from the R-RIS center to the UE, respectively.

Different from the normal fixed RIS, the proposed R-RIS can be controlled by operating the mechanical structure between it and the UAV, which means it is possible to find the certain azimuth and elevation angles to maximize $A_{m,n}(t)$. However, it should be mentioned that the optimal azimuth and elevation angles are impossible to be obtained, since the R-RIS can only be rotated once at each data block i, while the R-RIS is equipped with $M \times N$ elements and each of them has its own optimal azimuth and elevation angles. Therefore, the design considers the R-RIS center as the reference point for calculating the azimuth and elevation angles, with small expected losses.

The latency for the direct link is

$$\tau_d = \frac{d_{\mathrm{BS}}^{\mathrm{UE}}}{c}, \quad (11)$$

where c represents the speed of light. Similarly, the time delay for the cascaded link at data block i is

$$\tau_{m,n}(i) = \frac{d_{\mathrm{BS}}^{m,n}(i) + d_{m,n}^{\mathrm{UE}}(i)}{c}, \quad (12)$$

If $\Phi_{i,mn} \in (0, 2\pi]$ represents the continuous phase adjustment of R-RIS(m, n), $\Phi_d \triangleq e^{-j2\pi f_c \tau_d}$ is the direct link phase part and $\Phi_{m,n}(i) \triangleq e^{-j2\pi f_c \tau_{m,n}(i) - j\Phi_{i,mn}}$ denotes the cascaded link phase part. Therefore, the received complex base band signal is given by

$$y(i) = S_d(i)\Phi_d + \sum_{m=1,n=1}^{M,N} S_{m,n}(i)\Phi_{m,n}(i) + w(i), \tag{13}$$

where

$$S_d(i) = A_d \left\{ \sqrt{P_t} x(i - \tau_d) \right\}, \tag{14}$$

and

$$S_{m,n}(i) = A_{m,n}(i) \left\{ \sqrt{P_t} x(i - \tau_{m,n}(i) - \frac{\Phi_{i,mn}}{2\pi f_c}) \right\}. \tag{15}$$

$x(i)$ denotes the modulated signal with $\mathbb{E}\{|x(i)|^2\} = 1$, and P_t is the transmission power budget. $w(i)$ and f_c are white Gaussian noise at data block i and the carrier frequency, respectively. It is assumed that all devices in this paper are free from hardware impairments.

To evaluate the performance of the UAV air-to-ground communication system, a complex normal distribution $\mathcal{CN}(0, \sigma_2{}^2)$ is introduced to describe the noise affecting the system. Accordingly, the Signal-to-Noise Ratio (SNR) of the UE at data block i is derived as

$$\gamma_i = \frac{P_t \left| A_d + \sum_{m=1,n=1}^{M,N} A_{m,n}(i) \right|^2}{\sigma_2{}^2}, \tag{16}$$

3   Design of Anti-Jitter Scheme

In order to mitigate the effects of UAV jitter caused by air shakes and enhance the stability of communication, it is necessary to design a robust beamforming scheme based on the UAV equipped with the R-RIS. The rotatable feature of the R-RIS can be utilized to improve the performance. Ideally, the R-RIS would dynamically adjust in response to UAV vibrations immediately, in which case the normal beamforming works well. However, considering that the R-RIS is operated by the mechanical rotator that requires reaction time , the ideal situation may not always be satisfied. Therefore, it becomes critically important to explore a joint suppression method of beamforming and rotation, which is detailed in the following.

Considering that the Minimum Mean Square Error (MMSE) criterion effectively balances Bit Error Ratio (BER) and Spectral Efficiency (SE), it is employed as the design criteria in this section. To begin with, the sum of Mean Square Error (MSE) over the entire service period is required to be calculated, which, based on the signal received by the UE in the UAV air-to-ground communication system, can be described as

$$\epsilon = \mathbb{E}\left[\sum_{i=1}^{I} ||y(i) - x(i)||^2\right] = \sum_{i=1}^{I} \mathbf{H}_2(i)\varPhi(i)\mathbf{H}_1(i) + IA_d^2 P_t + I\sigma_2{}^2, \qquad (17)$$

$\mathbf{H}_1(i)$ and $\mathbf{H}_2(i)$ denote the channel matrices for the two hops in the communication link, from the BS to the R-RIS and from the R-RIS to the UE, respectively. $\varPhi(i)$ represents the phase shift matrix applied by the R-RIS for the i-th data block.

With the MSE defined, it is able to formulate the design problem, which is

$$(\theta_i^{\mathrm{RIS}})^*, (\varphi_i^{\mathrm{RIS}})^*, \varPhi(i)^* = \min_{\theta_i^{\mathrm{RIS}}, \varphi_i^{\mathrm{RIS}}, \varPhi(i)} \epsilon$$

$$\begin{aligned} \mathrm{s.}t.C1 &: \mathbb{E}\{|x(i)|^2\} = 1 \\ C2 &: \gamma_i \geq \gamma_0 \\ C3 &: \varPhi(i) = diag\{\varPhi_{1,1}(i), \varPhi_{1,2}(i), \cdots, \varPhi_{M,N}(i)\} \\ C4 &: 0 \leq \theta_i^{\mathrm{RIS}} \leq \theta_{max}, 0 \leq \varphi_i^{\mathrm{RIS}} \leq \varphi_{max} \end{aligned} \qquad (18)$$

In this formulation, constraint $C1$ imposes a power limit on transmitted data. $C2$ states that the received SNR should surpass a predefined threshold to assure communication quality. $C3$ confines adjustments to phase shifts alone within the R-RIS. And constraint $C4$ means that the range of the angles is limited.

Obviously, the problem outlined in (18) is non-convex, making it intractable to achieve an optimal solution. Consequently, a heuristic scheme is researched, which decouples the design of rotary angles and hybrid beamforming.

*Step*1: Suppose that the R-RIS's diagonal phase shift matrix is given, the task then revolves around the azimuth and elevation angles, described as:

$$(\theta_i^{\mathrm{RIS}})^*, (\varphi_i^{\mathrm{RIS}})^* = \min_{\theta_i^{\mathrm{RIS}}, \varphi_i^{\mathrm{RIS}}} \epsilon$$

$$C4 : 0 \leq \theta_i^{\mathrm{RIS}} \leq \theta_{max}, 0 \leq \varphi_i^{\mathrm{RIS}} \leq \varphi_{max} \qquad (19)$$

While the vibration condition of UAV can be detected by tools such as Inertial Measurement Unit (IMU) [11], formulating a precise design for rotation angles remains a challenge. As mentioned above, the mechanized nature of R-RIS rotation introduces a notable delay relative to communication time.

Therefore, we turn to explore the block rotation angle, which remains constant for a set period. According to the ergodic MSE, the rotation angles are designed as

$$(\theta_i^{\mathrm{RIS}})^*, (\varphi_i^{\mathrm{RIS}})^* = \min_{\theta_i^{\mathrm{RIS}}, \varphi_i^{\mathrm{RIS}}} (1/I)\mathbb{E}\left[\left(\sum_{i=1}^{I} \mathbf{H}_2(i)\right)\varPhi\left(\sum_{i=1}^{I} \mathbf{H}_1(i)\right)\right]. \qquad (20)$$

Considering that probability distribution of vibration is of significance and the Gaussian random distribution works well, the vibration condition of UAV is assumed to follow $\mathcal{CN}(0, \sigma_3{}^2)$, where $\sigma_3{}^2$ is the variance achieved by experience. Unfortunately, acquiring a closed-form solution is found to be challenging, a numerical solution is taken instead.

*Step*2: Once the rotation angles are given, we proceed to design the R-RIS's diagonal phase shift matrix according to the detected instantaneous vibration condition of the UAV. The design problem can be written as

$$\Phi(i)^* = \min_{\Phi_i(i)} \epsilon_i$$
$$s.t. C1 : \mathbb{E}\{|x(i)|^2\} = 1 \tag{21}$$
$$C2 : \gamma_i \geq \gamma_0$$
$$C3 : \Phi(i) = diag\{\Phi_{1,1}(i), \Phi_{1,2}(i), \cdots, \Phi_{M,N}(i)\}$$

Based on MMSE rule, the design matrix can be formulated as

$$\mathbf{W}(i) = \mathbf{H}_1(i)^{\mathrm{H}} \big(\mathbf{H}_1(i)\mathbf{H}_1(i)^{\mathrm{H}} + \sigma_2{}^2\mathbf{I}\big)^{-1} \big(\mathbf{H}_2(i)^{\mathrm{H}}\mathbf{H}_2(i)\big)^{-1}\mathbf{H}_2(i)^{\mathrm{H}} \tag{22}$$

Subsequently, the R-RIS's diagonal phase shift matrix is derived by extracting the angle of $\mathbf{W}(i)$, that is to say, $\Phi(i) = e^{-j \arg(\mathbf{W}(i))}$.

4   Simulation Results

In this section, the impact of UAV jitter on the SE is examined. To begin with, some parameters of the simulation environment are presented in Table 1. For the number of elements on the R-RIS, $M = N = 64$ is set. Assume that the BS and the UE are both positioned at the ground level, and the length of the mechanical structure connecting the UAV to the R-RIS is considered negligible, the altitude of the UAV can be regarded as the absolute values $|z_{\mathrm{BS}}|$ or $|z_{\mathrm{UE}}|$. Furthermore, the values of the carrier frequency f_c and the transmit power P_t are also specified.

Table 1. Simulation Parameters.

Parameters	Values
Number of elements on R-RIS	$M \times N = 64 \times 64$
Altitude of UAV	$|z_{\mathrm{UE}}| = 20$ meters
Carrier frequency	$f_c = 2.4$ GHz
Transmit power	$P_t = 20$ dBm

The simulation results are shown in Fig. 2. To verify the effectiveness of the proposed scheme, a comparative scheme, termed 'without anti-jitter scheme', is considered. Additionally, the proposed scheme is assessed under two typical conditions.

As the variance of disturbance increases, the SE of all three schemes deteriorates due to the mismatch of the R-RIS phase matrix when the UAV jitters. The comparative scheme suffers the most significant degradation in performance. In contrast, as a result of considering anti-jitter, the proposed schemes with both tested conditions consistently perform better than the comparative one. Among the conditions, the scenario where $\sigma_1 = \sigma_3$ achieves superior performance. This is attributed to the fact that $\sigma_1 \neq \sigma_3$ represents a non-ideal situation, implying errors existing in the empirical variance values used to design the block rotation angle. This situation is inevitable given the reliance on numerical solutions, which highlights the necessity for a reliable mathematical derivation of the variance to optimize the performance.

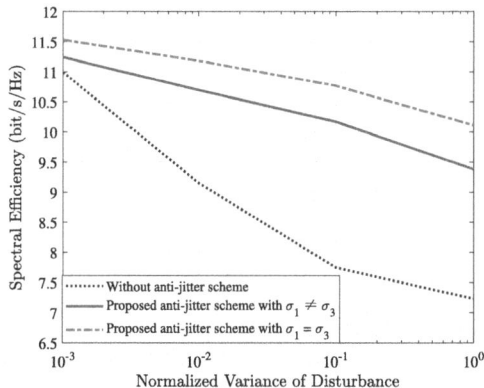

Fig. 2. Effect of UAV jitter on SE with different disturbance variances.

5   Conclusion

In this paper, a novel R-RIS approach for stabilizing the beamforming in UAV air-to-ground communications is presented, which aims to address the challenge of airflow induced UAV wobbling. The proposed method integrates the operation of the mechanical rotator with the phase shift of the R-RIS, enabling dynamic orientation adjustments to optimize beam direction when the UAV jitters.

Firstly, we formulate the system model incorporating the rotator's mechanical properties and derive the signal model considering the UAV's jittering effects as a stochastic process. Secondly, we propose a heuristic strategy that decouples the complex problem into subproblems including the rotation angle adjustments and the R-RIS's phase shift configurations.

Simulation results show that the proposed method effectively improves the system performance under UAV jitter conditions, demonstrating the effectiveness of the proposed scheme in enhancing beam stability.

Future work could explore more advanced dynamic control algorithms that further minimize the response time of the rotator and refine the phase adjustment process of the RIS. Moreover, the system model in this paper is simple, a mobile UE and the UAV with a wide range of movement could be introduced in the future.

References

1. Pan, C., et al.: Reconfigurable intelligent surfaces for 6g systems: principles, applications, and research directions. IEEE Commun. Mag. **59**(6), 14–20 (2021). https://doi.org/10.1109/MCOM.001.2001076
2. Liu, R., Li, M., Luo, H., Liu, Q., Swindlehurst, A.L.: Integrated sensing and communication with reconfigurable intelligent surfaces: opportunities, applications, and future directions. IEEE Wirel. Commun. **30**(1), 50–57 (2023). https://doi.org/10.1109/MWC.002.2200206
3. Sun, W.-B., Zhou, R., Yang, X., Zhang, J., Wang, L.: UAV-assisted opportunistic beamforming in internet of things networks. IEEE Internet Things J. **10**(17), 15393–15407 (2023). https://doi.org/10.1109/JIOT.2023.3263879
4. Sheng, Z., Tuan, H.D., Duong, T.Q., Hanzo, L.: UAV-aided two-way multi-user relaying. IEEE Trans. Commun. **69**(1), 246–260 (2021). https://doi.org/10.1109/TCOMM.2020.3030679
5. Zeng, Y., Zhang, R., Lim, T.J.: Wireless communications with unmanned aerial vehicles: opportunities and challenges. IEEE Commun. Mag. **54**(5), 36–42 (2016). https://doi.org/10.1109/MCOM.2016.7470933
6. Liu, Y., Wang, S., Ma, L., Huang, Y., Xing, W.: Energy-Efficient RIS-UAV relay with trajectory optimization and fair communication. In: Proceedings of the 2022 IEEE 8th International Conference on Computer and Communications (ICCC), pp. 339–343 (2022). https://doi.org/10.1109/ICCC56324.2022.10065829
7. Wang, H., Chen, J., Ding, G., Sun, J.: Trajectory planning in UAV communication with jamming. In: Proceedings of the 10th International Conference on Wireless Communications and Signal Processing (WCSP), pp. 1–6 (2018). https://doi.org/10.1109/WCSP.2018.8555700
8. Adam, A.B.M., et al.: Intelligent and robust UAV-aided multiuser RIS communication technique with jittering UAV and imperfect hardware constraints. IEEE Trans. Veh. Technol. **72**(8), 10737–10753 (2023). https://doi.org/10.1109/TVT.2023.3255309
9. Wang, K., Lam, C.-T., Ng, B.K.: Reconfigurable intelligent surface assisted communications using dynamic rotations. In: Proceedings of the 22nd IEEE International Conference on Communication Technology (ICCT), pp. 652–656 (2022). https://doi.org/10.1109/ICCT56141.2022.10072753
10. Wang, K., Lam, C.-T., Ng, B.K.: IRS-aided predictable high-mobility vehicular communication with doppler effect mitigation. In: Proceedings of the IEEE 93rd Vehicular Technology Conference (VTC2021-Spring), pp. 1–6 (2021). https://doi.org/10.1109/VTC2021-Spring51267.2021.9448955
11. Abiko, S., Tashiro, K.: Fundamental numerical and experimental evaluation of attitude recovery control for a quad tilt rotor UAV against disturbance. In: Proceedings of the 16th International Conference on Control, Automation and Systems (ICCAS), pp. 709–712 (2016). https://doi.org/10.1109/ICCAS.2016.7832396

A Massive MIMO Antenna Array Loaded with Quadruple Sequentially Rotated Square SRR for 5G Base Station

Asad Ali Khan[1] (ID), Zhenyong Wang[1,2(✉)] (ID), Dezhi Li[1], and Ali Ahmad[3]

[1] School of Electronics and Information Engineering, Harbin Institute of Technology,
Harbin 150001, China
asadali@stu.hit.edu.cn, ZYWang@hit.edu.cn
[2] Songjiang Laboratory, Harbin Institute of Technology, Harbin 150001, China
[3] Advanced Communications and Electronics Systems (ACES), Riyadh 12326, Saudi Arabia
ali.ahmed@aces-co.com

Abstract. A 4 × 4 multiple input multiple output (MIMO) rectangular patch antenna array loaded with massive sequentially rotated split ring resonators (SRR) operating at 3.5 GHz is presented for 5G new radio (NR) frequency range 1 (FR1) n77 mid band base station application. SRR are placed in such a novel arrangement to avoid radiation pattern overlapping and improve overall gain of antenna array. Each sub array consists of three layers, top layer is made up of 2 × 2 patch elements each surrounded with four rings of sequentially rotated split ring resonators to support high port pattern isolation, middle layer act as ground plane, bottom layer consists of calculated corporate feeding network which feed antenna elements using via through ground plane at an optimized location to achieve impedance matching. More than 100 MHz impedance bandwidth, at least 14.47 dBi gain for any sub array, more than 90% of efficiency, 0.0027 of envelop correlation coefficient (ECC) and port isolation less than −25 dB is achieved using proposed MIMO array system. Overall, 20.6 dBi gain is achieved for whole array system. Leveraging a novel interlaced subarray topology, this work achieves superior port to port isolation and improved gain compared to prior state of the art MIMO designs. These optimistic results make proposed array an excellent candidate for 5G base station application.

Keywords: Massive MIMO · SRR (Split Ring Resonator) · NR (New Radio) · FR1 (Frequency Range 1) · High Efficiency · Port Isolation · High Gain

1 Introduction

Massive MIMO antenna arrays have emerged as a key technology for meeting the high data rate and reliability demands of next generation wireless communications [1, 2]. Integrating metamaterial split ring resonators into massive MIMO antenna arrays unlocks new potential for enhanced efficiency and reconfigurability. Researchers at LUND university in 2010 analyzed performance and practical feasibility of very large MIMO arrays

© ICST Institute for Computer Sciences, Social Informatics and Telecommunications Engineering 2025
Published by Springer Nature Switzerland AG 2025. All Rights Reserved
H.-H. Chen and W. Meng (Eds.): WiSATS 2024, LNICST 605, pp. 279–288, 2025.
https://doi.org/10.1007/978-3-031-86196-3_24

at base station [3]. Up until mid of last decade massive MIMO was incorporated by 3GPP to standardize for 5G communication system. In 3GPP release 15 5G massive MIMO standards are specified [4]. Complementary split ring resonators (CSRR) are etched in ground plane [5] and also used co planar as radiating elements [6, 7] with defective ground plane [8, 9]. A variety of distinct designs are documented in the references [10–14]. Reported arrays show some notable deficiencies which need further research to optimize realized gain, unacceptable side lobe levels, manufacturability constraints for massive MIMO 5G base stations.

To address the limitations of prior works and meet the demanding requirements of massive MIMO systems, this paper presents a novel 4 × 4 antenna array with split ring resonators to enhance port isolation while maintaining broadside radiation with high efficiency, very low envelop correlation coefficient less than 0.0027 and high gain up to 20.5 dBi. Proposed antenna array system is designed using CST Studio Suit. Remaining sections of article is organized as follows. Section II gives details on design and optimization of antenna unit cell. Section III covers design and results comparison of 4 × 4 array. Finally, last section concludes the paper.

2   Design and Optimization of Antenna

2.1   Design of Unit Cell

A unit cell consists of three layers top layer is 2 × 2 rectangular linearly polarized elements surrounded by four sequentially rotated SRR, bottom layer is corporate feeding network and middle layer act as ground layer for both patch and feeding network. Four via from feeding network to patches through two layers of Rogers RT-5880 (dielectric constant 2.2, height 1.73) as shown in Fig. 1. The length and width of a single element is calculated using following Eq. 1 and 2 defined in [15].

$$\text{Width} = \frac{c}{2f_o\sqrt{\frac{\varepsilon_r+1}{2}}} \tag{1}$$

$$\varepsilon_{\text{eff}} = \frac{\varepsilon_r+1}{2} + \frac{\varepsilon_r-1}{2}\left[\frac{1}{\sqrt{1+12\left(\frac{h}{W}\right)}}\right]$$

$$\text{Length} = \frac{c}{2f_o\sqrt{\varepsilon_{\text{eff}}}} - 0.824h\left(\frac{\left(\varepsilon_{\text{eff}}+0.3\right)\left(\frac{W}{h}+0.264\right)}{\left(\varepsilon_{\text{eff}}-0.258\right)\left(\frac{W}{h}+0.8\right)}\right) \tag{2}$$

Detailed parameters and corresponding values to design unit cell and full array is mentioned in Table 1, while size of unit cell with two layers of substrate is 137 × 137 × 3.46.

Table 1. Unit cell and 4 × 4 array values and dimensions.

Parameter	Value (mm)	Parameter	Value (mm)	Element	Dimension (mm^2)
Wp	33.86	Rs	5	N-Line	36.73 × 1.55
Lp	26.04	Rg	1	F-Line	70.08 × 1.55
Wg	137.05	Rw	1.5	M-Line1	14.88 × 5.34
Lg	137.05	L	274.1	M-Line2	15.12 × 3.06
Sx	14.67	W	274.1		
Sy	22.48	h	1.73		

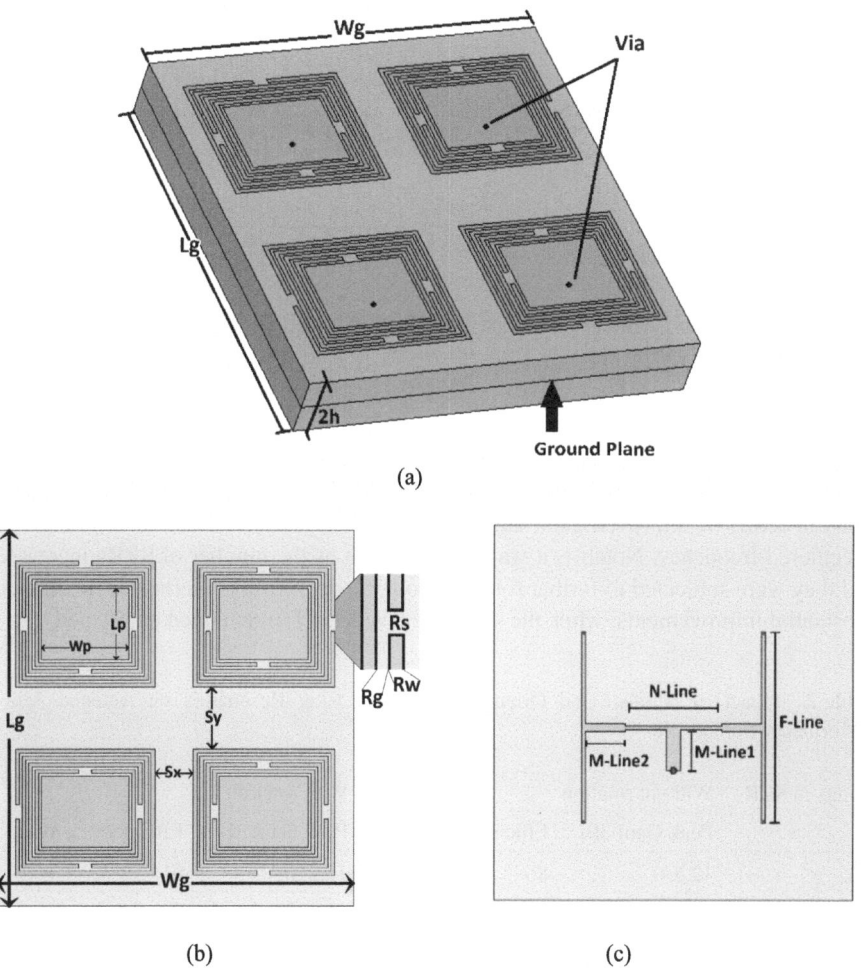

(a)

(b)   (c)

Fig. 1. Unit Cell structure. (a) Side view (b) Top View (c) Bottom View

Figure 2 presents a comprehensive comparison of the results in terms of achieving the required bandwidth, efficiency, and gain. The analysis reveals that when employing the Split Ring Resonator (SRR) antenna, a total efficiency exceeding 90% is attained across the entire band of concern. Furthermore, within the specified band, the SRR antenna exhibits an enhanced gain of 1 to 1.5 dBi compared to its counterpart without the SRR. Figure 3 illustrates the radiation patterns, where (a) and (b) depict the 3D radiation patterns of the unit cell with and without the incorporation of SRR, respectively. Additionally, Fig. 3(c) provides a detailed comparison of the 2D radiation patterns for the unit cell with and without the SRR implementation.

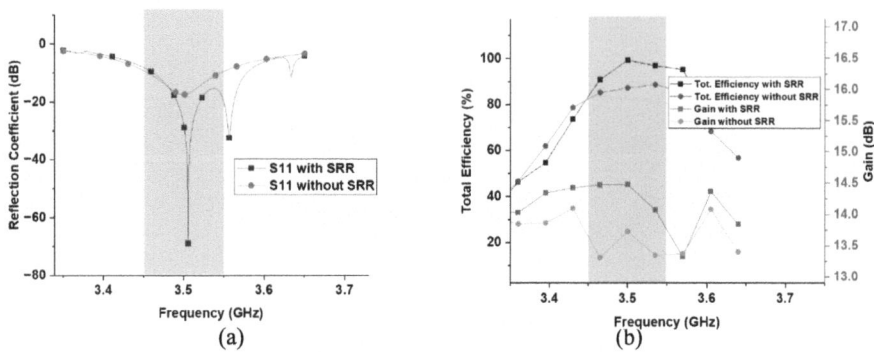

Fig. 2. (a) Reflection Coefficient with and without SRR (b) Efficiency and Gain plot with and without SRR

To further enhance the gain and efficiency each surrounding SRR was rotated by 90 degrees relative to the preceding one. Table 2 provides a comprehensive rationale for the utilization of SRR rotation within the base structure, elucidating the associated gains in terms of improved gain, augmented efficiency, and reduced side lobe levels at centered frequency. Notably, it was observed that as the number of SRRs increased and they were subjected to further rotation, both the peak gain and efficiency exhibited substantial improvements, while the side lobe levels (SLLs) remained unaffected.

Table 2. Impact of Number and Orientation of Split Ring Resonators on Antenna Array Performance Parameters.

Rings in SRR	Without rotation			With rotation		
	Peak Gain dBi	Efficiency	SLL	Peak Gain dBi	Efficiency	SLL
1	12.567	86	−9.5	13.256	91	−9.6
2	13.4014	86	−9.5	14.4499	92	−9.6
3	12.7798	87	−9.6	14.3805	94	−9.7
4	13.5364	87	−9.6	14.4774	98	−9.7

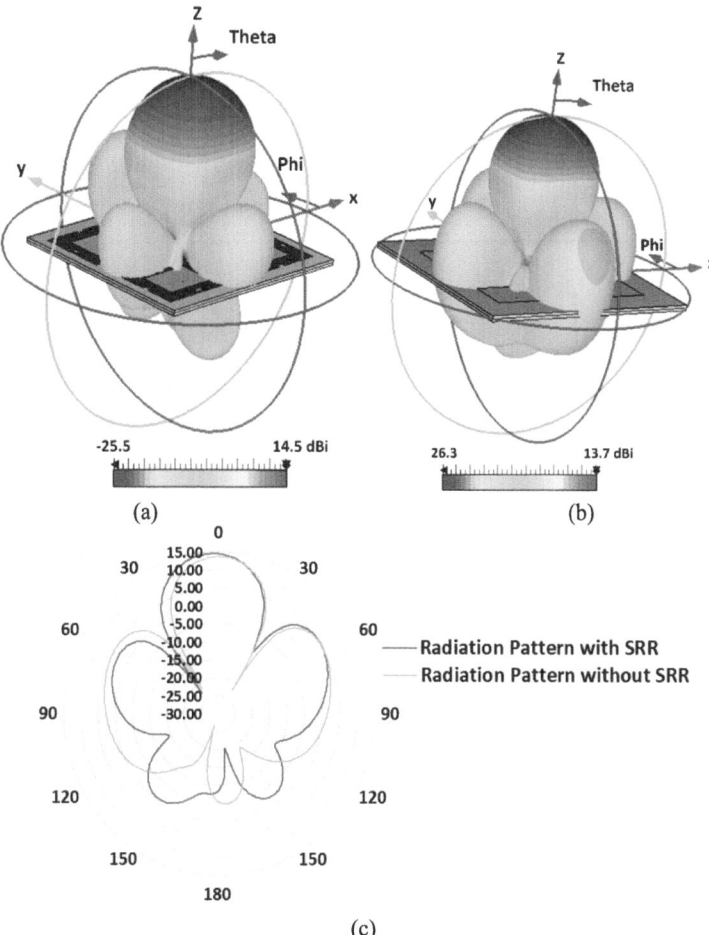

Fig. 3. 3D radiation pattern at 3.5 GHz a) with SRR b) without SRR c) 2D Radiation pattern comparison

2.2 Design of Array

The proposed antenna array is configured as a 4×4 element rectangular lattice, comprising 4 ports arranged in a 2×2 layout. Each port and its associated feeding network are responsible for exciting four antenna elements, with each element being encircled by four rectangular, sequentially rotated split ring resonators (SRRs). Figure 4 illustrates the top and bottom views of the complete array model. Furthermore, Fig. 5 depicts the 3D and 2D radiation patterns of the full array with and without the incorporation of SRRs at the centered frequency of 3.5 GHz. It is evident from the analysis that the implementation of SRRs around the rectangular patch antenna array results in a substantial enhancement of the gain.

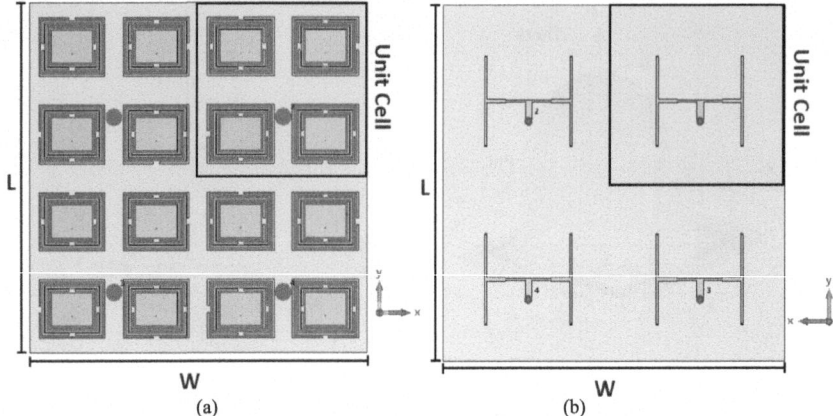

Fig. 4. 4x4 Array(a) Top view (b) Bottom view

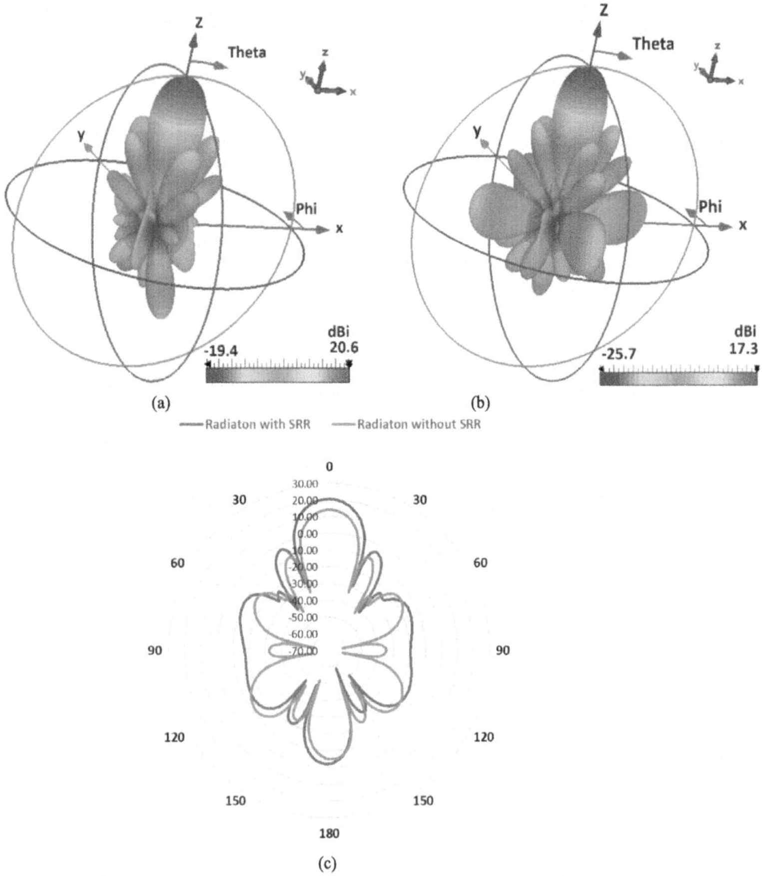

Fig. 5. Array factor (a) 3D radiation pattern with SRR (b) 3D radiation pattern without SRR (c) 2D radiation pattern comparison

Figure 6 presents a comparative analysis of the reflection coefficient, efficiency, and overall gain of the full MIMO array, both with and without the incorporation of SRRs. Port isolation and the envelope correlation coefficient (ECC) are regarded as the most crucial MIMO parameters for evaluating the array's performance.

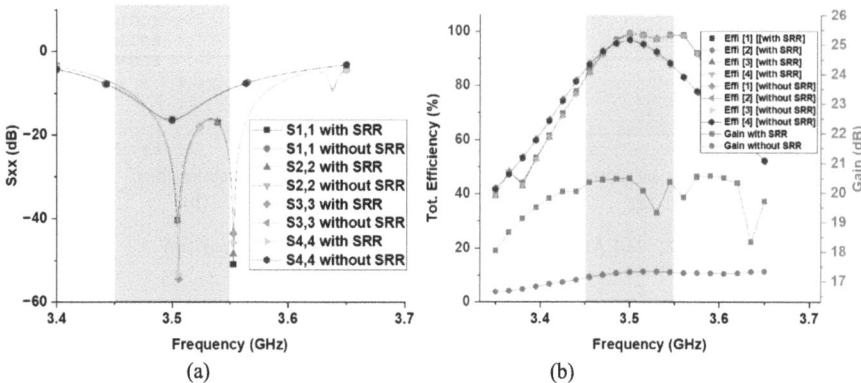

(a)   (b)

Fig. 6. 4x4 Array (a) Reflection Coefficient (b) Efficiency and Gain

ECC quantifies the statistical correlation between the signal envelopes received by the individual antennas. Mutual coupling in antenna arrays represents the electromagnetic interaction between the individual antenna elements. Figure 7 illustrates a comparison of port isolation and ECC for the full array, with and without the utilization of SRRs. Notably, it is observed that the mutual coupling remains below −25 dBi across the band of concern, spanning from 3.45 to 3.55 GHz. Furthermore, the MIMO antenna array employing SRRs exhibits a lower ECC in comparison to its counterpart without SRRs, indicating an improved performance. Table 3 presents a comparative analysis of the proposed antenna and MIMO system with previously reported base station antennas, evaluating critical performance parameters. The results demonstrate that the proposed antenna exhibits superior performance across the majority of the considered parameters, evidencing its enhanced capabilities.

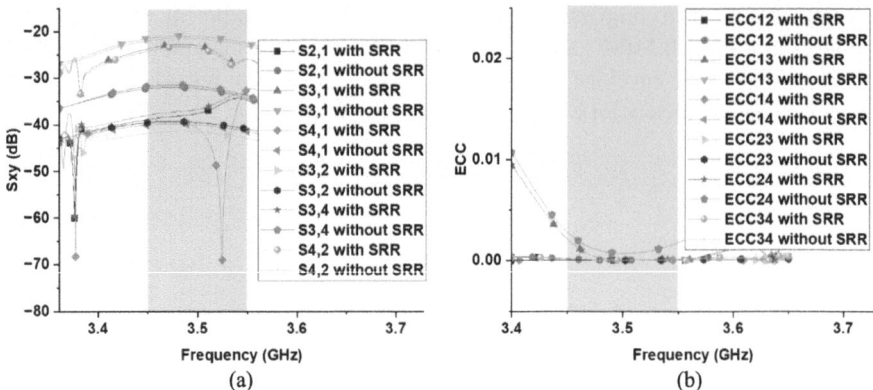

Fig. 7. 4x4 Array (a) Mutual Coupling (b) ECC comparison

Table 3. Comparison of proposed structure with previously reported MIMO antenna arrays.

Ref.	Operating Band (GHz)	MIMO Model	Array Size (mm3)	Elements per port	Max. Gain per port (dBi)	Total Gain Array (dBi)	Total Efficiency	Port Isolation (dB)	ECC
[10]	2.8–4	4 × 4	200 × 200 × 32	-	–	9.1	-	−27	-
[12]	3.3–3.87	4 × 4	147.41 × 147.41 × 3.2	2 × 2	8.1	8.72	> 92	< −32	0.001
[13]	3.1–11	1 × 2	26 × 31 × 0.8	1	–	5.67	85.5	< −25	0.001
[16]	3.3–5	4 × 4	76.2 × 76.2 × 13.9	1	–	7.9	>90	< −30	<0.1
[17]	3.35–3.65	2 × 8	8(36 × 23 × 1.5)	1 × 2	–	6.5	65	28	<0.1
This work	3.45–3.55	4 × 4	274.1 × 274.1 × 3.46	2 × 2	14.473	20.5	>91	< −25	<0.0027

3 Conclusion

In this research endeavor, a 4 ports 16 elements antenna array has been designed on a Rogers 5880 substrate, incorporating a corporate feeding network in which each port excites four radiating elements surrounded with rotating SRR to operate within the frequency range of 3.45 to 3.55 GHz. Each unit cell exhibits a peak gain of 14.47 dBi and achieves a total efficiency surpassing 90% across the band of concern, spanning from 3.45 to 3.55 GHz. For the full 16 elements array, a directional beam is formed, attaining a high gain of 20.5 dBi, low mutual coupling up to -25 dB and an exceptionally low ECC below 0.0025 have been realized within the band of concern. Overall, antenna array possesses attractive features for next generation 5G base stations.

Acknowledgement. This paper is supported by the research project fund of Songjiang Laboratory (No. SL20230104).

Data Availability. The data used to support the findings of this study are included within the paper.

Conflict of Interest. The authors declare that they have no conflicts of interest.

References

1. Huang, H., Li, X., Liu, Y.: 5G MIMO antenna based on vector synthetic mechanism. IEEE Antennas Wirel. Propag. Lett. **17**(6), 1052–1055 (2018)
2. Zada, M., Shah, I.A., Yoo, H.: Integration of sub-6-GHz and mm-wave bands with a large frequency ratio for future 5G MIMO applications. IEEE Access **9**, 11241–11251 (2021)
3. Marzetta, T.L.: Noncooperative cellular wireless with unlimited numbers of base station antennas. IEEE Trans. Wireless Commun. **9**(11), 3590–3600 (2010)
4. 3GPP, D.: Study on new radio access technology physical layer aspects. Tech. Report (TR) 38.802, V14. 2.0 (2017)
5. Bait-Suwailam, M.M., Siddiqui, O.F., Ramahi, O.M.: Mutual coupling reduction between microstrip patch antennas using slotted-complementary split-ring resonators. IEEE Antennas Wirel. Propag. Lett. **9**, 876–878 (2010)
6. Karthigaiveni, S., Pandeeswari, R., Deivalakshmi, S.: Miniaturized MIMO antenna with complementary split ring resonators loaded superstrate for x-band applications. Wireless Pers. Commun., 1–19 (2022)
7. Dave, K., et al.: Graphene-based double-loaded complementary split ring resonator (CSRR) slotted MIMO patch antenna for spectroscopy and imaging THZ applications. Appl. Phys. A **128**(8), 656 (2022)
8. Patchala, K., Rao, Y.R., Prasad, A.: Triple band notch compact MIMO antenna with defected ground structure and split ring resonator for wideband applications. Heliyon **6**(1) (2020)
9. Atallah, H.A., Abdel-Rahman, A.B., Yoshitomi, K., Pokharel, R.K.: Mutual coupling reduction in MIMO patch antenna array using complementary split ring resonators defected ground structure. Appl. Comput. Electromagnetics Soc. J. **31**(7) (2016)
10. Vadlamudi, R., Kumar, D.S.: Very novel design and mutual coupling analysis of a wideband, tightly arranged DP massive MIMO (32t and 32r) antenna array for 5G base station application. In: 2020 IEEE International Students' Conference on Electrical, Electronics and Computer Science (SCEECS), pp. 1–5. IEEE (2020)
11. Sufian, M.A., Hussain, N., Askari, H., Park, S.G., Shin, K.S., Kim, N.: Isolation enhancement of a metasurface-based MIMO antenna using slots and shorting pins. IEEE Access **9**, 73533–73543 (2021)
12. Khan, A., Bashir, S., Ghafoor, S., Qureshi, K.K.: Mutual coupling reduction using ground stub and EBG in a compact wideband MIMO-antenna. IEEE access **9**, 40972–40979 (2021)
13. Zhu, Y., Chen, Y., Yang, S.: Integration of 5G rectangular MIMO antenna array and gsm antenna for dual-band base station applications. IEEE Access **8**, 63175–63187 (2020)

14. Shabbir, T., et al.: 16-port non-planar MIMO antenna system with near-zero-index (NZI) metamaterial decoupling structure for 5G applications. IEEE Access **8**, 157946–157958 (2020)
15. Garg, R.: Microstrip antenna design handbook. Artech house (2001)

Sum Rate Maximization
for NOMA-Aided Cell-Free System

Qiling Gao$^{(\boxtimes)}$, Zhongming Feng, and Yun Lin

School of Information and Communication Engineering, Harbin Engineering
University, Harbin 150001, China
`qilinggao@outlook.com`, {`fzm98,linyun`}`@hrbeu.edu.cn`

Abstract. In this paper, a downlink non-orthogonal multiple access
(NOMA)-aided cell-free system is proposed. Multiple access points (APs)
are distributed in a wide area and cooperatively serve users using NOMA.
A sum rate maximization problem is formulated, where the beamforming coefficients at APs are jointly optimized subject to the minimum rate
requirements and decoding order of NOMA users. An iterative algorithm
is proposed, where semi-definite programming (SDP) and penalty based
methods are employed to address the resultant non-convex problem.
Numerical results show that our proposed algorithm converges within 10
iterations, and the sum rate enhancement can be achieved with the aid
of our proposed algorithm compared to the orthogonal multiple access
(OMA) system. Furthermore, NOMA achieves better user fairness compared with spatial domain multiple access (SDMA), while may suffer a
sum rate loss.

Keywords: Beamforming design · Cell-free · Non-orthogonal multiple
access

1 Introduction

The envisaged future wireless communications systems are expected to satisfy
tens of Gbps peak data rate and massive connectivity demands [1–3]. However,
the inefficient usage of radio resources in orthogonal multiple access (OMA)
techniques is the main bottleneck of communication performance enhancement
[4]. Therefore, non-orthogonal multiple access (NOMA) techniques have been
proposed for attaining high spectral efficiency (SE), high connectivity and har-
monious integrity [5,6]. Particularly, by serving users via the same radio resource,
NOMA has been widely advocated for the improved SE as well as the number of
users supported [7]. Furthermore, the cell-free network infrastructure has been
proposed as a beneficial technique recently [8]. In this kind of infrastructure, a
number of access points (APs) equipped with a small number of antennas are
geographically distributed and connected to a central processing unit (CPU) for
signal processing [9]. These APs serve users in the same time and within the
same frequency bands without cell classification, hence leading to benefits such
as low propagation and low inter-cell interference [10].

© ICST Institute for Computer Sciences, Social Informatics and Telecommunications Engineering 2025
Published by Springer Nature Switzerland AG 2025. All Rights Reserved
H.-H. Chen and W. Meng (Eds.): WiSATS 2024, LNICST 605, pp. 289–300, 2025.
https://doi.org/10.1007/978-3-031-86196-3_25

Given the distinctive benefits of cell-free and NOMA, several works have employed NOMA in cell-free systems for the their advantages [11,12]. The authors of [13] analyzed the sum rate achieved by the cell-free MIMO-NOMA system with three linear precoders. The authors of [14] proposed a machine learning based user clustering algorithm in the cell-free NOMA system for maximizing the sum-rate. Most of studies focus on the performance analysis of the NOMA assisted cell-free system with each AP equipped with a single antenna. To our best knowledge, there is no existing work on the beamforming coefficients optimization for NOMA-aided cell-free system, which motivates this work.

In this paper, we propose a downlink NOMA aided cell-free system in order to amalgamate their advantages. A sum rate maximization problem for the optimization of the beamforming coefficients at APs is formulated, and an iterative based algorithm is developed by employing the successive convex approximation (SCA) and penalty based methods. We focus on verifying the performance enhancement of our proposed system in terms of the sum rate. Simulation results unveil that aided by our proposed algorithm, the sum rate is significantly enhanced by amalgamating cell-free and NOMA compared with conventional OMA and cell-based counterparts.

Notations: Lower case letters and bold face letters denote scalars and matrices, respectively. $\mathbb{C}^{M \times N}$ denotes the space of $M \times N$ complex valued matrices, $(\cdot)^T$ and $(\cdot)^\dagger$ denote the transpose and conjugate transpose operations, respectively, Rank$(\cdot)$ and Tr$(\cdot)$ denote the rank and the trace of the matrix, respectively, $\mathbf{A} \succeq 0$ indicates that $\mathbf{A}$ is a positive semi-definite matrix.

2   System Model and Problem Formulation

We consider a a downlink NOMA-aided cell-free system as illustrated in Fig. 1. In this setup, M distributed N_t-antenna APs cooperatively serve N single-antenna users over the same radio resources. A central processing unit (CPU) is deployed for control and planning, to which APs are connected by optical cables [15]. The NOMA is employed at APs in the cell-free system, where each user is served with a beamformer at each AP. Let $\mathcal{N} = \{1, ..., N\}$ and $\mathcal{M} = \{1, .., M\}$ denote the index set of users and APs, respectively.

The received signal of the n-th user is the superposition of the signals transmitted by M APs, which can be expressed as:

$$y_n = \sum_{m=1}^{M} \mathbf{h}_{m,n}^\dagger \mathbf{w}_{m,n} s_n + \sum_{m=1}^{M} \sum_{n' \neq n} \mathbf{h}_{m,n}^\dagger \mathbf{w}_{m,n'} s_{n'} + n_n, \tag{1}$$

where $\mathbf{w}_{m,n} \in \mathbb{C}^{M \times 1}$ denotes the beamforming coefficients at the m-th AP, to the n-th user, s_n denotes the signal of the n-th user, $\mathbf{h}_{m,n} \in \mathbb{C}^{M \times 1}$ is the channel between the m-th AP and the n-th user, n_n is the additive white Gaussian noise (AWGN) at the n-th user with variance δ_n^2.

Based on the NOMA principle, the successive interference cancellation (SIC) is employed at users for signal detection, the users with high decoding order

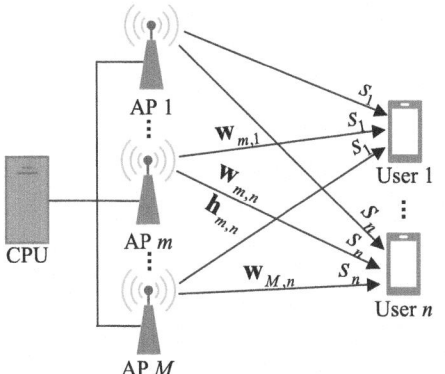

Fig. 1. Illustration of NOMA-aided cell-free system.

decode the signals of the users with low order before detecting their own signals. To be specific, define $\pi(n)$ as the decoding order of the user n, for any two users n' and n with $\pi(n') > \pi(n)$, the user n' will detect its own signal after detecting the signals of the user n. An important observation is the decoding order is a essential problem to be considered, and an efficient NOMA user ordering design is proposed in Sect. 3.3.

For ease of exposition, we assume that the decoding order is $\pi(n) = n$, $\forall n \in \mathcal{N}$ in the following, the achievable rate at the user n after SIC operation is given by

$$R_{n \to n} = \log_2 \left(1 + \frac{\left| \sum_{m=1}^{M} \mathbf{h}_{m,n}^\dagger \mathbf{w}_{m,n} \right|^2}{\sum_{\tilde{n}=n+1}^{N} \left| \sum_{m=1}^{M} \mathbf{h}_{m,n}^\dagger \mathbf{w}_{m,\tilde{n}} \right|^2 + \delta_n^2} \right). \tag{2}$$

In addition, for any user n' with $\pi(n') > \pi(n)$, they need to decode user n's signal and perform SIC before detecting their own signals, the rate for the user n' to decode the message of user n is

$$R_{n' \to n} = \log_2 \left(1 + \frac{\left| \sum_{m=1}^{M} \mathbf{h}_{m,n'}^\dagger \mathbf{w}_{m,n} \right|^2}{\sum_{\tilde{n}=n+1}^{N} \left| \sum_{m=1}^{M} \mathbf{h}_{m,n'}^\dagger \mathbf{w}_{m,\tilde{n}} \right|^2 + \delta_{n'}^2} \right), \tag{3}$$

Once the condition $R_{n' \to n} \geq R_{n \to n}, \forall n \in \mathcal{N}, \pi(n') > \pi(n)$ is satisfied, user n' is able to perform SIC, then detect their own signals. Therefore, both the rates of *desired messages* $(R_{n \to n})$ and *other users' messages* $(R_{n' \to n})$ decide the rate of user n, which can be expressed as

$$R_n = \min \left(R_{n \to n}, R_{(n+1) \to n} .., R_{N \to n} \right), \ n = 1, ..., N - 1. \tag{4}$$

Note that for the user N with the highest decoding order, its achievable rate can be expressed as

$$R_{N \to N} = \log_2(1 + \frac{\left| \sum_{m=1}^{M} \mathbf{h}_{m,N}^{\dagger} \mathbf{w}_{m,N} \right|^2}{\delta_N^2}), \tag{5}$$

and since no user n' need to detect the signal of user N, we have $R_N = R_{N \to N}$.

Then, we formulate the sum rate maximization problem by optimizing the beamformer at each AP as:

$$\max_{\mathbf{w}_{m,n}} \sum_{n=1}^{N} R_n \tag{6a}$$

$$\text{s.t.} \quad R_n \geq R_n^{\min}, \ \forall n \in \mathcal{N}, \tag{6b}$$

$$\sum_{n=1}^{N} \|\mathbf{w}_{m,n}\|^2 \leq P_s, \ \forall m \in \mathcal{M}, \tag{6c}$$

where P_s denotes the maximal transmit power of each AP, (6b) is the quality of service (QoS) requirements of each user, and (6c) is the transmit power constraint of each AP.

3   Proposed Beamforming and User Ordering Design

3.1   Beamforming Coefficients Design

To address the non-convex problem 6, we first introduce a slack vector $\mathbf{r} \in \mathbb{R}_+^N$, and problem (6) can be equivalently written as

$$\max_{\mathbf{w}_{m,n},\mathbf{r}} \sum_{n=1}^{N} r_n \tag{7a}$$

$$\text{s.t.} \quad \sum_{n=1}^{N} \|\mathbf{w}_{m,n}\|^2 \leq P_s, \ \forall m \in \mathcal{M}, \tag{7b}$$

$$R_n \geq r_n, \ n \in \mathcal{N}, \tag{7c}$$

$$r_n \geq R_n^{\min}, \ n \in \mathcal{N}, \tag{7d}$$

$$(6c). \tag{7e}$$

Here, the overall problem still remains intractable, and we further develop an iterative algorithm as follows. Define $\mathbf{h}_n = [\mathbf{h}_{1,n}^T, ..., \mathbf{h}_{M,n}^T]^T$ as the channel between all APs to the n-th user, and $\mathbf{w}_n = [\mathbf{w}_{1,n}^T, ..., \mathbf{w}_{M,n}^T]^T \in \mathbb{C}^{MN_t \times 1}$ as the beamformer of all APs to the n-th user, which can be generated by the CPU. Then, by denoting $\mathbf{W}_n = \mathbf{w}_n \mathbf{w}_n^{\dagger}$, which satisfies $\mathbf{W}_n \succeq 0$ and $\text{Rank}(\mathbf{W}_n) = 1$, $R_{n \to n}$ in (2) can be reformulated as

$$R_{n \to n} = \log_2 \left(1 + \frac{\text{Tr}(\mathbf{H}_n \mathbf{W}_n)}{\sum_{\tilde{n}=n+1}^{N} \text{Tr}(\mathbf{H}_n \mathbf{W}_{\tilde{n}}) + \delta_n^2} \right), \tag{8}$$

similarly, $R_{n' \to n}$ can be reformulated by

$$R_{n' \to n} = \log_2 \left(1 + \frac{\text{Tr}(\mathbf{H}_{n'} \mathbf{W}_n)}{\sum_{\tilde{n}=n+1}^{N} \text{Tr}(\mathbf{H}_{n'} \mathbf{W}_{\tilde{n}}) + \delta_n'^2} \right), \tag{9}$$

where $\mathbf{H}_n = \mathbf{h}_n \mathbf{h}_n^\dagger$. The optimization problem in ((7)) can be equivalently expressed as

$$\max_{\mathbf{W}_n, \mathbf{r}} \sum_{n=1}^{N} r_n \tag{10a}$$

$$\text{s.t.} \quad r_n \geq R_n^{\min}, \tag{10b}$$

$$R_{n \to n} \geq r_n, \; n \in \mathcal{N}, \tag{10c}$$

$$R_{n' \to n} \geq r_n, \; \pi(n') > \pi(n), \; n = 1, ..., N-1, \tag{10d}$$

$$\sum_{n=1}^{N} \text{Tr}\left([\mathbf{W}_n]_{(m-1)N_t+1:mN_t, (m-1)N_t+1:mN_t} \right) \leq P_s, \tag{10e}$$

$$\forall m \in \mathcal{M},$$

$$\mathbf{W}_n \succeq 0, \; \forall n \in \mathcal{N}, \tag{10f}$$

$$\text{Rank}(\mathbf{W}_n) = 1, \; \forall n \in \mathcal{N}, \tag{10g}$$

where $[\mathbf{W}_n]_{(m-1)N_t+1:mN_t, (m-1)N_t+1:mN_t}$ denotes the elements between the index $((m-1)N_t + 1, (m-1)N_t + 1)$ and (mN_t, mN_t) of matrix $\mathbf{W}_n$, which implies the transmit power of the m-th AP to the n-th user. However, the problem (10) is still non-convex due to the non-convex constraints.

We first tackle the non-convex rank one constraint by replacing (10g) as

$$\text{Tr}(\mathbf{W}_n) - \max[\text{eig}(\mathbf{W}_n)] \leq 0, \; \forall n \in \mathcal{N}, \tag{11}$$

where $\max[\text{eig}(\mathbf{W}_n)]$ denotes the maximum eigenvalue of $\mathbf{W}_n$. An important note is that $\text{Tr}(\mathbf{W}_n) - \max[\text{eig}(\mathbf{W}_n)] \geq 0$ holds for any $\mathbf{W}_n$, thus the equality of (11) holds if and only if $\mathbf{W}_n$ is a rank one matrix with one non-zero eigenvalue. Therefore, the rank one constraint can be guaranteed by making $\text{Tr}(\mathbf{W}_n) - \max[\text{eig}(\mathbf{W}_n)]$ as small as possible. We introduce a penalty based method, by substituting the penalty function into the (10a), we obtain the new objective function as

$$f \triangleq \sum_{n=1}^{N} r_n - \eta_n \left(\text{Tr}(\mathbf{W}_n) - \max[\text{eig}(\mathbf{W}_n)] \right), \tag{12}$$

where η_n is the paucity factor. Due to the non-differentiable expression $\max[\mathrm{eig}(\mathbf{W}_n)]$, we further employ its approximation as

$$\max[\mathrm{eig}(\mathbf{W}_n)] = \tilde{\mathbf{w}}_n^\dagger \mathbf{W}_n \tilde{\mathbf{w}}_n, \tag{13}$$

where $\tilde{\mathbf{w}}_n$ is the eigenvector corresponding to the maximum eigenvalue of $\mathbf{W}^{(\tau)}$ in the τ-th iteration. Finally, the rank one constraint can be released by reformulating the objective function as

$$f \triangleq \sum_{n=1}^N r_n - \eta_n \left(\mathrm{Tr}\,(\mathbf{W}_n) - \mathrm{Tr}\left(\left(\tilde{\mathbf{w}}_n \tilde{\mathbf{w}}_n^\dagger\right)^\dagger \mathbf{W}_n \right) \right). \tag{14}$$

Then, to tackle the non-convex constraint (10c), we introduce slack variables $\{x_n\}$ and $\{y_n\}$ as

$$x_n = \frac{1}{\mathrm{Tr}\,(\mathbf{H}_n \mathbf{W}_n)}, \tag{15}$$

$$y_n = \sum_{\tilde{n}=n+1}^N \mathrm{Tr}\,(\mathbf{H}_n \mathbf{W}_{\tilde{n}}) + \delta_n^2, \tag{16}$$

therefore, $R_{n\to n}$ in (2) can be rewritten as $R_{n\to n} = \log_2\left(1 + \frac{1}{x_n y_n}\right)$. The optimization problem can be reformulated as

$$\max_{\mathbf{W}_n, \mathbf{r}, \{x_n\}, \{y_n\}} f \tag{17a}$$

$$\mathrm{s.t.} \quad r_n \geq R_n^{\min}, \tag{17b}$$

$$r_n \leq \log_2\left(1 + \frac{1}{x_n y_n}\right), \ \forall n \in \mathcal{N}, \tag{17c}$$

$$\frac{1}{x_n} \leq \mathrm{Tr}\,(\mathbf{H}_n \mathbf{W}_n), \ \forall n \in \mathcal{N}, \tag{17d}$$

$$y_n \geq \sum_{\pi(\tilde{n}) > \pi(n)} \mathrm{Tr}\,(\mathbf{H}_n \mathbf{W}_{\tilde{n}}) + \delta_n^2, \ \forall n \in \mathcal{N}, \tag{17e}$$

$$(10d) - (10f). \tag{17f}$$

Since the function $f(x,y) \triangleq \log(\frac{1}{xy})$ is a joint convex function with respect to x and y, the lower bound of the right-hand-side of (17c) can be given by

$$\log_2\left(1 + \frac{1}{x_n y_n}\right) \geq \log_2\left(1 + \frac{1}{\tilde{x}_n \tilde{y}_n}\right) - \frac{\log_2 e\,(\tilde{x}_n - x_n)}{\tilde{x}_n\,(1 + \tilde{x}_n \tilde{y}_n)}$$
$$- \frac{\log_2 e\,(\tilde{y}_n - y_n)}{\tilde{y}_n\,(1 + \tilde{x}_n \tilde{y}_n)} \triangleq \tilde{R}_{n\to n}, \ \forall n \in \mathcal{N}, \tag{18}$$

where $(\tilde{x}_n, \tilde{y}_n)$ is the feasible point of the first order Taylor expansion. Then the problem (17) can be rewritten as

$$\max_{\substack{\mathbf{W}_n, r_n, \\ \{x_n\}, \{y_n\}}} \quad f \tag{19a}$$

$$r_n \leq \tilde{R}_{n \to n}, \ \forall n \in \mathcal{N}, \tag{19b}$$

$$(10d) - (10f), (17d) - (17e). \tag{19c}$$

Similarly, to address the non-convex constraint (10d), we introduce slack variables $x_{n,n'}$ and $y_{n,n'}$ such that

$$\frac{1}{x_{n,n'}} \leq \operatorname{Tr}(\mathbf{H}_{n'} \mathbf{W}_n), \ \pi(n') > \pi(n), \tag{20}$$

$$y_{n,n'} \geq \sum_{\tilde{n}=n+1}^{N} \operatorname{Tr}(\mathbf{H}_{n'} \mathbf{W}_{\tilde{n}}) + \delta_{n'}^2, \ \pi(n') > \pi(n), \tag{21}$$

we can readily obtain that

$$
\begin{aligned}
r_n \leq &\log_2\left(1 + \frac{1}{\tilde{x}_{n,n'}\tilde{y}_{n,n'}}\right) - \frac{\log_2 e\,(\tilde{x}_{n,n'} - x_{n,n'})}{\tilde{x}_{n'}\,(1 + \tilde{x}_{n,n'}\tilde{y}_{n,n'})} \\
&- \frac{\log_2 e\,(\tilde{y}_{n,n'} - y_{n,n'})}{\tilde{y}_{n,n'}\,(1 + \tilde{x}_{n,n'}\tilde{y}_{n,n'})}, \ \pi(n') > \pi(n),
\end{aligned}
\tag{22}
$$

where $(x_{n,n'}, y_{n,n'})$ denotes the feasible point of the first-order Taylor expansion. Finally, the considered problem becomes a convex SDP problem, which is given as

$$\max_{\substack{\mathbf{W}_n, \mathbf{r}, \{x_n\}, \{y_n\} \\ \{x_{n,n'}\}, \{y_{n,n'}\}}} \quad f \tag{23a}$$

$$\text{s.t.} \quad r_n \geq R_n^{\min}, \ \forall n \in \mathcal{N}, \tag{23b}$$

$$(10b) - (10f), (17d), (17e), (19b), (20) - (22). \tag{23c}$$

The problem (23) is now convex and can be efficiently solved by CVX. Furthermore, due to the replacement of lower bound in (18) and (22), problem (23) is a lower bound approximation of the origin problem, and its solution ia guaranteed to converge to a locally optimal solution.

3.2 Complexity Analysis

The complexity of solving the SDP problem (23) is $\mathcal{O}[\tau \max(MN_t, 2N + 1)^4 \sqrt{MN_t} \log_2 \frac{1}{\epsilon}]$, where τ is the number of iterations for obtaining convergent solutions of (23), and ϵ is the solution accuracy, The complexity of the proposed ordering design is $\mathcal{O}(1)$.

3.3   Proposed NOMA User Ordering Design

In Sect. 3.1, the optimization problem is solved for a given decoding order. Normally, in the two user case, the optimal decoding order can be found by exhaustively searching all possible candidates. However, the complexity of exhaustive search is unacceptable with the increasing of users. Therefore, we propose an efficient user ordering scheme based on the geometry mean of the distances between users and APs. To be specific, a user can be simultaneously served by all distributed APs in our proposed system, and the decoding order can be determined by

$$
\pi\left(\tilde{n}\right) > \pi\left(n\right), \text{ if } \left(\prod_{m=1}^{M} d_{m,n}\right)^{\frac{1}{M}} > \left(\prod_{m=1}^{M} d_{m,\tilde{n}}\right)^{\frac{1}{M}}, \ \forall n \in \mathcal{N}, \tag{24}
$$

where $d_{m,n}$ denotes the distance between the n-th user and the m-th AP, Eq. (24) means that the user with small geometry-mean distance to all APs has higher decoding order.

4   Numerical Results

In this part, numerical results are provided to evaluate the effectiveness of our proposed design. We consider a scenario that all APs and users are randomly deployed within the circle whose radius is $R = 100$ m, the noise power is set to $\delta_n^2 = -80$ dBm. Furthermore, the channel between APs and users can be modeled as the Rayleigh fading, and the large scale path loss can be expressed as

$$
L_{m,n} = 10^{\frac{PL_{m,n}+\sigma_{sh}}{10}}, \tag{25}
$$

where σ_{sh} is the shadow fading parameter follows the logarithmic normal distribution, $PL_{m,n}$ denotes the path-loss between the m-th AP and the n-th user, which can be expressed as

$$
PL_{m,n} = -140.7 - 35 \lg d_{m,n} + 20c_0 \lg \frac{d_{m,n}}{d_0} + 15c_1 \lg \frac{d_{m,n}}{d_1}, \tag{26}
$$

where $d_{m,n}$ is the distance between the m-th AP and the n-th user, $c_i = \max\{0, \frac{d_i - d_{m,n}}{|d_i - d_{m,n}|}\}$, d_i is the reference distance, $i \in \{0,1\}$. In simulation, the reference distance d_0 and d_1 are set to $d_0 = 10$ m and $d_1 = 50$ m, the mean and the standard deviation of σ_{sh} are set to 1 and $10^{1.6}$, respectively.

Figure 2 illustrates the convergence of the proposed algorithm. Both the performance of the fixed decoding order and of the proposed ordering design is studied. The transmit power of each AP is set to 40 dBm. Observe that the proposed algorithm converges in less than 10 iterations, and our proposed ordering scheme outperforms the fixed order design.

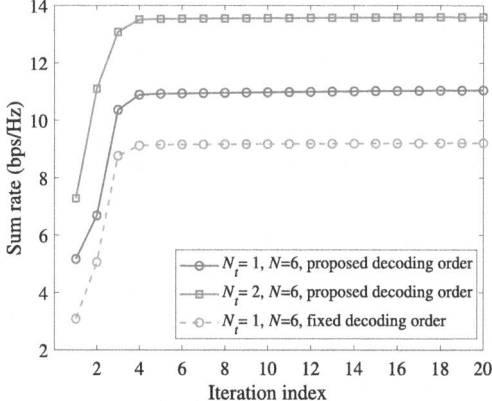

Fig. 2. Convergence of the proposed algorithm.

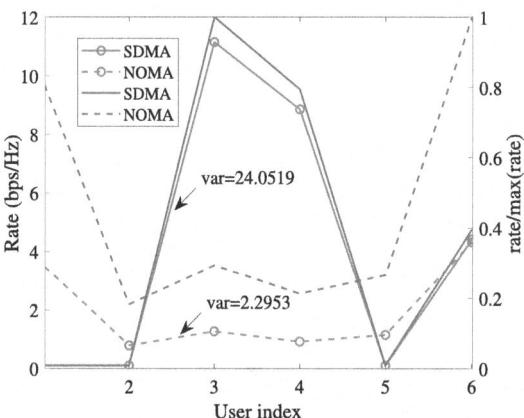

Fig. 3. Rate performance at each user.

Figure 3 shows the rate and the normalized rate of each user in NOMA and spatial domain multiple access (SDMA) scheme, where $P_s = 40$ dBm, the QoS requirements of users is set to $R^{\min} = 0.1$ bps/Hz. It can be found that SDMA can achieve the higher sum rate performance compared with NOMA system with poor fairness among users, i.e., the 1st, 2nd and 5th users only served with the minimal data rates 0.1 bps/Hz. We use the variance of users' rates to describe the fairness, the higher variance implies the poorer fairness. It can be observe that the variance of SDMA is about $var = 24$, much higher than that in NOMA-aided system, which demonstrates the effectiveness of NOMA.

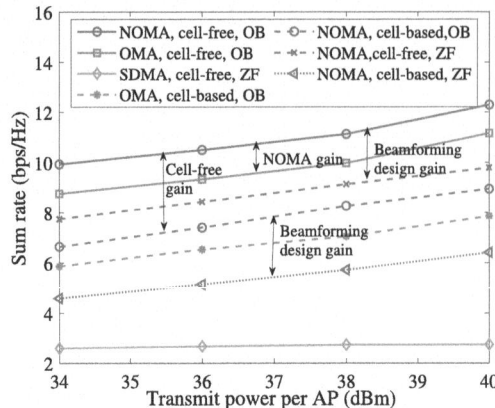

Fig. 4. Sum rate performance versus the transmit power per AP.

Figure 4 plots the sum rate performance versus the total transmit power of all APs, where $N_t = 1$. The results indicate that the sum rate performance increases linearly with the total transmit power. Note that for the cell-central system, users are served by a single AP equipped with 4 antennas and MP_s transmit power. The following insights can be observed: 1) both NOMA and OMA aided cell-free systems outperforms the cell-based system, that is because the cell-free system is capable of deploying antennas closer to users, hence decrease the propagation fading; 2) NOMA-aided cell-free system achieves better performance compared to OMA-aided system with the aid of our proposed optimized beamforming (OB) algorithm; 3) our proposed algorithm out performs the zero forcing (ZF) beamforming benchmark in both OMA and NOMA-aided system, which illustrates the effectiveness of our proposed beamforming coefficient design.

In Fig. 5, the transmit power at each AP for NOMA and OMA schemes is plotted in a 2 user case. The maximal transmit power at each AP is set to 40 dBm, and the number of APs is set to $M = 8$, the minimal required rate of users is set to $R_n^{\min} = R^{\min} = 1$ bps/Hz. The results indicate that the APs allocate average transmit power to NOMA users while allocate almost all power to a user in frequency division multiple access (FDMA). To be specific, AP prefers to provide service to its nearest user in OMA scheme. This can be explained: assume any two NOMA users n' and n with $\pi(n') > \pi(n)$, the user n' has to recover user n's signal after detecting its own signal according to the SIC principle, and the rate for the user n' to detect user n has a great impact on the achievable sum rate. Therefore, the optimized beamforming not only guarantees the achievable rate at user n and n', but also the decoding rate of user n at user n'. However, there is no need for OMA users to decode each other's signals, hence the APs only serve their closest user can achieve higher sum rate performance.

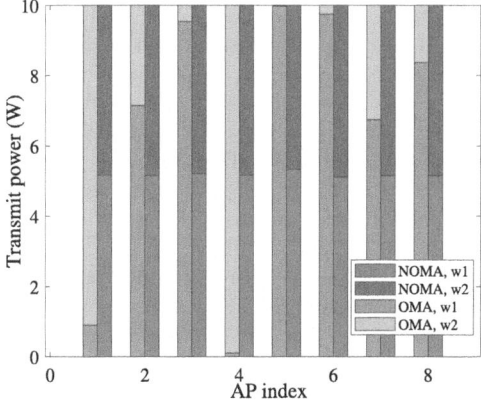

Fig. 5. Transmit power at each AP in NOMA and OMA scheme.

5 Conclusion

In this letter, we proposed a downlink NOMA assisted cell-free system, where each AP served multiple users via NOMA downlink, and users received the superposition of all APs' transmitted signals. To enhance the communication performance, a sum rate optimization problem was formulated for optimizing the beamforming coefficients at each AP. Due to the non-convex objective function as well as constraints, IPF and SDP methods were employed to make the problem tractable. Simulation results confirmed the sum rate improvement of the interplay between cell-free and NOMA compared with the OMA assisted networks. Furthermore, results revealed that NOMA and OMA prefer different resource allocation strategies at APs. Additionally, the better fairness among users' rates can be achieved by employing NOMA.

References

1. Wu, Q., et al.: Intelligent surfaces empowered wireless network: recent advances and the road to 6G. In: Proceedings of the IEEE (2024)
2. Lin, Y., Tu, Y., Dou, Z.: An improved neural network pruning technology for automatic modulation classification in edge devices. IEEE Trans. Veh. Technol. **69**(5), 5703–5706 (2020). https://doi.org/10.1109/TVT.2020.2983143
3. Lin, Y., Wang, M., Zhou, X., Ding, G., Mao, S.: Dynamic spectrum interaction of UAV flight formation communication with priority: a deep reinforcement learning approach. IEEE Trans. Cognit. Commun. Netw. **6**(3), 892–903 (2020). https://doi.org/10.1109/TCCN.2020.2973376
4. Cui, H., Niu, K., Ren, M., Huo, J.: Polar coded power domain non-orthogonal multiple access system: construction and optimization. IEEE Commun. Lett. **28**(3), 607–611 (2024). https://doi.org/10.1109/LCOMM.2024.3353728
5. Sun, X., et al.: Joint beamforming and power allocation in downlink NOMA multiuser MIMO networks. IEEE Trans. Wireless Commun. **17**(8), 5367–5381 (2018)

6. Li, W., Liang, H., Dong, C., Xu, X., Zhang, P., Liu, K.: Non-orthogonal multiple access enhanced multi-user semantic communication. IEEE Trans. Cognit. Commun. Netw. 9(6), 1438–1453 (2023). https://doi.org/10.1109/TCCN.2023.3306852

7. Mu, X., Wang, Z., Liu, Y.: Noma for integrating sensing and communications toward 6G: a multiple access perspective. IEEE Wirel. Commun. 31(3), 316–323 (2024). https://doi.org/10.1109/MWC.015.2200559

8. Liu, Z., et al.: Cell-free xl-mimo meets multi-agent reinforcement learning: architectures, challenges, and future directions. IEEE Wirel. Commun., 1–8 (2024). https://doi.org/10.1109/MWC.007.2300176

9. Shi, E., et al.: Ris-aided cell-free massive mimo systems for 6G: fundamentals, system design, and applications. Proc. IEEE 112(4), 331–364 (2024)

10. Nguyen, T.K., Nguyen, H.H., Tuan, H.D.: Max-min QoS power control in generalized cell-free massive MIMO-NOMA with optimal backhaul combining. IEEE Trans. Veh. Technol. 69(10), 10949–10964 (2020). https://doi.org/10.1109/TVT.2020.3006054

11. Zhang, R., Xiong, K., Lu, Y., Ng, D.W.K., Fan, P., Letaief, K.B.: Swipt-enabled cell-free massive mimo-noma networks: a machine learning-based approach. IEEE Trans. Wirel. Commun., 1 (2023). https://doi.org/10.1109/TWC.2023.3327596

12. Gao, Q., Jia, M., Guo, Q., Gu, X., Hanzo, L.: Jointly optimized beamforming and power allocation for full-duplex cell-free noma in space-ground integrated networks. IEEE Trans. Commun. 71(5), 2816–2830 (2023). https://doi.org/10.1109/TCOMM.2023.3251342

13. Rezaei, F., Tellambura, C., Tadaion, A.A., Heidarpour, A.R.: Rate analysis of cell-free massive MIMO-NOMA with three linear precoders. IEEE Trans. Commun. 68(6), 3480–3494 (2020). https://doi.org/10.1109/TCOMM.2020.2978189

14. Le, Q.N., Nguyen, V.D., Dobre, O.A., Nguyen, N.P., Zhao, R., Chatzinotas, S.: Learning-assisted user clustering in cell-free massive MIMO-NOMA networks. IEEE Trans. Veh. Technol. 70(12), 12872–12887 (2021). https://doi.org/10.1109/TVT.2021.31212

15. Jin, S.N., Yue, D.W., Nguyen, H.H.: RIS-aided cell-free massive MIMO systems: joint design of transmit beamforming and phase shifts. arXiv preprint arXiv:2112.06593 (2021)

Research on RIS Assisted Vehicle Communication Method Based on Deep Learning

Hua Tan, Chenguang He[✉], and Dezhi Li

School of Electronics and Information Engineering, Harbin Institute of Technology, Harbin 150001, China
1201051820@stu.hit.edu.cn, {hechenguang,lidezhi}@hit.edu.cn

Abstract. This thesis proposes an innovative system framework for vehicular communication utilizing Reconfigurable Intelligent Surfaces (RIS) to support millimeter-wave (mmWave) scenarios, addressing the high transmission rate demands of 6G communication. Due to significant path loss in mmWave propagation, RIS is introduced to enhance coverage and communication rates. Additionally, the thesis employs a deep learning-based Graph Neural Network (GNN) algorithm to optimize beamforming at the base station and phase shift matrices at the RIS, bypassing complex channel estimation processes. Simulation results demonstrate that the proposed algorithm exhibits excellent performance and generalization capabilities, enabling rapid response in vehicular communication scenarios.

Keywords: reconfigurable intelligent surface · deep learning graph neural network architecture · vehicle communication

1 Introduction

Advancements in mobile communication have equipped modern vehicles with capabilities for positioning, V2V communication, vehicle perception, autonomous driving, and intelligent transportation systems, enhancing traffic safety. Millimeter-wave (mmWave) communication, operating in the 30 GHz to 300 GHz range, meets the demand for higher transmission rates and throughput using advanced beamforming techniques to counter high propagation losses, achieving wireless data rates exceeding 6 GHz [1]. These technologies enable precise vehicle positioning, essential for autonomous driving [1,2].

However, urban environments with obstructions, reflections, and high vehicle mobility causing rapid channel changes can degrade communication links. Reliable communication requires strategic planning and infrastructure. Fast channel

---

This work is supported by the Key R&D Program of Heilongjiang Province under Grant JD22A001.

H.-H. Chen and W. Meng (Eds.): WiSATS 2024, LNICST 605, pp. 301–311, 2025.
https://doi.org/10.1007/978-3-031-86196-3_26

switching during vehicle movement affects communication quality and rate. Limited spectrum and hardware resources demand innovative methods to enhance performance by increasing data rates, reducing power consumption, and minimizing latency.

Reconfigurable Intelligent Surfaces (RIS) offer a solution for energy-efficient communication, mitigating high attenuation in mmWave and terahertz systems [3]. Comprising many independently controlled reflective elements, RIS enhances signal-to-noise ratio (SNR) at the receiver by adjusting the phase of reflected signals [5]. Placed between the base station and the target user, RIS redirects multipath signals to supplement the communication path when direct links are obstructed, creating passive beams aimed at the user. RIS can establish a smart radio environment (SRE) to address 6G network limitations [4].

A challenge in SRE-assisted vehicular communication is dynamically adjusting RIS elements in complex and variable channels. Each RIS element has an independent channel, requiring knowledge of the communication channel parameters for each antenna and reflecting element. Optimizing the reflected signal and enhancing SNR involves extensive, high-complexity computations [6].

To address this, this thesis introduces deep learning methods to accelerate optimization. Deep learning models, capable of extracting features from raw data, handle complex data and improve through parameter tuning [7]. They reduce computational complexity compared to traditional methods [8]. This thesis proposes a deep learning-based approach for RIS-assisted vehicular communication systems, training models on real-world datasets to enhance communication stability and reliability in high-mobility scenarios, thereby maximizing data rates.

2   System Model

This chapter designs a distributed RIS-assisted communication system, consisting of a base station (BS), which communicates with user equipment (UE) through direct links and RIS-cascaded links with the assistance of N distributed RISs $(R_n, n = 1, \ldots, N)$. As shown in Fig. 2.

2.1   Communication Model for Reconfigurable Intelligent Surfaces

In this system, the nth Reconfigurable Intelligent Surface (RIS) consists of L passive reflective units capable of altering both the amplitude and phase of electromagnetic waves. Each RIS, regardless of its location, has the same number of reflective units. Both the transmitter and receiver employ single-antenna systems. The phase shift matrix at the nth RIS is denoted as $\Theta_n = \mathrm{diag}([k_{n1}e^{j\theta_{n1}}, \ldots, k_{nl}e^{j\theta_{nl}}, \ldots, k_{nL}e^{j\theta_{nL}}])$, where $k_{nl} \in (0, 1]$ and $\theta_{nl} \in [0, 2\pi)$ represent the amplitude reflection coefficient and phase shift of the lth reflective unit on the nth RIS, respectively (Fig. 1).

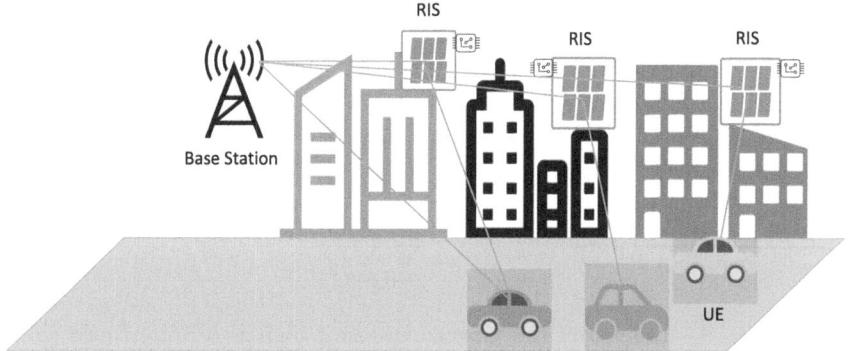

Fig. 1. System Model for Multi-RIS Assisted Communication

Each RIS is equipped with low-power communication and control modules to enable straightforward interaction with the base station, which handles the computation and distribution of phase shift matrices. RIS deployment ensures line-of-sight communication for both uplink and downlink channels, enhancing transmission rate and reliability by creating additional propagation paths and adjusting the phase of reflected waves. The base station, with perfect global Channel State Information (CSI), can directly compute and deploy the necessary phase shift matrices to the RISs. The single-antenna configuration at both transmitter and receiver simplifies optimization, facilitating easier validation of the performance of multiple RISs.

Define h_{nl} and g_{nl} as the complex channel coefficients from the base station to the nth reflective unit's lth reflection and from that reflective unit to the user equipment (UE), respectively. h_0 represents the channel coefficient of the direct link from the base station to the UE. x_S denotes the transmission symbol at the base station (with $E[|x_S|^2] = 1$), P_S is the transmission power at the base station (in dBm), and ω_D is the additive white Gaussian noise (AWGN) at the UE, with zero mean and variance σ_D^2, i.e., $\omega_D \sim \mathcal{CN}(0, \sigma_D^2)$.

As the user equipment (UE) employs a single antenna for signal reception, the signal takes the form of a direct superposition of all multipath signals. Consequently, the received signal at the UE is composed of both the direct signal and the reflected signals from all N Reconfigurable Intelligent Surfaces (RISs), and can be expressed in the form of Eq. (1).

$$y_r = \sqrt{P_S} \left(h_0 + \sum_{n=1}^{N} \sum_{l=1}^{L_n} g_{nl} k_{nl} e^{j\theta_{nl}} h_{nl} \right) x_S + \omega_D \tag{1}$$

Expressing the complex channel coefficients in polar coordinates, the Signal-to-Noise Ratio (SNR) received at the User Equipment (UE) location can be represented as Eq. (2).

$$SNR_r = \bar{\rho}\left|\left(h_0 e^{j\phi_0} + \sum_{n=1}^{N}\sum_{l=1}^{L_n} g_{nl}k_n h_{nl} e^{j(\theta_{nl}+\alpha_{nl}+\beta_{nl})}\right)\right|^2 \tag{2}$$

$$SNR_r = \bar{\rho}\left|\left(e^{j\phi_0}\right)\right|^2\left|\left(h_0 + \sum_{n=1}^{N}\sum_{l=1}^{L_n} g_{nl}k_{nl} h_{nl} e^{j\delta_{nl}}\right)\right|^2 \tag{3}$$

$$SNR_r = \bar{\rho}\left|e^{j\phi_0}\right|^2\left|h_0 + \sum_{n=1}^{N}\sum_{l=1}^{L_n} g_{nl}k_{nl} h_{nl} e^{j\delta_{nl}}\right|^2 \tag{4}$$

Here, $\bar{\rho} = \frac{P_S}{\sigma_D^2}$ represents the average transmit Signal-to-Noise Ratio (SNR) in dB, $\delta_{nl} = \theta_{nl} + \alpha_{nl} + \beta_{nl} - \phi_0$ denotes the phase error of the lth reflection element of the nth RIS relative to the direct link channel parameters. Since both the transmitter and receiver are single-antenna systems, the direct link channel conditions contain only one amplitude and phase information. Thus, the direct link channel can serve as a reference for designing the phase adjustment parameters for the reflection elements on the RIS.

Based on this analysis, the ideal phase shift configuration for the lth reflection element of the nth RIS can be represented as Eq. (5).

$$\theta_{nl}^* = \arg\max_{\theta_{nl}\in\mathcal{Q}} SNR_r(\theta_{nl}), \quad \forall l \forall n \tag{5}$$

2.2 RIS-Assisted Communication Optimization Problem Modeling

Based on the aforementioned system model architecture, the Reconfigurable Intelligent Surface (RIS) is integrated into the vehicular communication system. This integration enables communication targets with high mobility to maintain good line-of-sight communication with the base station through the RIS. According to Shannon's formula, combined with the previously derived signal propagation paths and channel model, the achievable maximum rate R (bits/sec/Hz) of the communication target in this system architecture can be expressed as:

$$R = \log_2\left(1 + \bar{\rho}\left|e^{j\phi_0}\right|^2\left|h_0 + \sum_{n=1}^{N}\sum_{l=1}^{L_n} g_{nl}k_{nl} h_{nl} e^{j\delta_{nl}}\right|^2\right) \tag{6}$$

Among them, $\bar{\rho}\left|e^{j\phi_0}\right|^2\left|h_0 + \sum_{n=1}^{N}\sum_{l=1}^{L_n} g_{nl}k_{nl} h_{nl} e^{j\delta_{nl}}\right|^2$ represents the Signal-to-Noise Ratio (SNR) of the receiving user, and $\bar{\rho} = \frac{P_S}{\sigma_D^2}$ is the average transmission SNR. For ease of calculation, we consider the amplitude reflection coefficient of the RIS to be 1, and the phase error of the l-th reflecting element of the RIS is defined as $\delta_l \triangleq \theta_l + \alpha_l + \beta_l - \phi_0$. By optimizing the reflection coefficients, the above rate can be maximized, and the problem can be formulated as follows:

$$\delta_{nl}^\star = \arg\max\left(\log_2\left(1 + \bar{\rho}\left|h_0 + \sum_{n=1}^{N}\sum_{l=1}^{L_n} g_{nl}h_{nl} e^{j\delta_{nl}}\right|^2\right)\right) \tag{7}$$

3 RIS Implicit Channel Estimation Algorithm

The paper proposes using a neural network-trained model to represent the mapping function in an optimization problem. Extensive channel data, including transmitter pilot sequences, receiver signals, and known channel parameters, train the neural network. The objective is for the neural network to learn the mapping from received pilot signals to the RIS phase shift matrix and the base station's beamforming vector, maximizing network utility while bypassing the channel estimation stage.

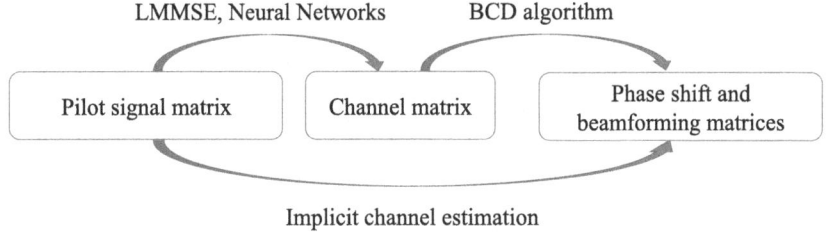

Fig. 2. Different algorithms

In multi-user cellular networks, addressing inter-user interference is critical, especially in dense environments, as it significantly impacts system performance, including user throughput and connection quality. To address this, we employ Graph Neural Networks (GNNs) to model and optimize user beamformers and reflection matrices. GNNs are adept at handling graph-structured data, facilitating effective learning of intricate relationships between network nodes.

We construct a graph with $K + 1$ nodes representing users and an RIS, with edges depicting interactions symbolizing physical-layer assistance or interference. Each node is characterized by a vector z_k, where k denotes the node index. GNNs iteratively update node representation vectors through multiple layers to capture useful information. Using current node representations, GNNs apply graph neural network operations at each layer for iterative refinement.

By integrating beamformer and phase shift matrix collaboration at the RIS and leveraging GNNs for graphical representation and optimization, we manage inter-user interference, thereby enhancing network performance and capacity. This approach promises improved communication quality and user experience.

The GNN structure comprises three main layers: the initialization layer, the data separation and aggregation layer, and the normalization final layer. The initialization layer uses pilot signals as input, denoted as z_k^0. The data separation and aggregation layer aggregates and transmits information between nodes, yielding updated representation vectors z_k^d, where $d = 1, \ldots, D$. Finally, the linear layer generates $z_k^{(D+1)}$, mapped to beamformer matrices w_k and the phase shift matrix v through normalization. This architecture enables GNNs to flexibly adapt to problems of varying scales and complexities, effectively representing and learning graph structures through parameter sharing and feature extraction. The overall architecture is depicted in Fig. 3.

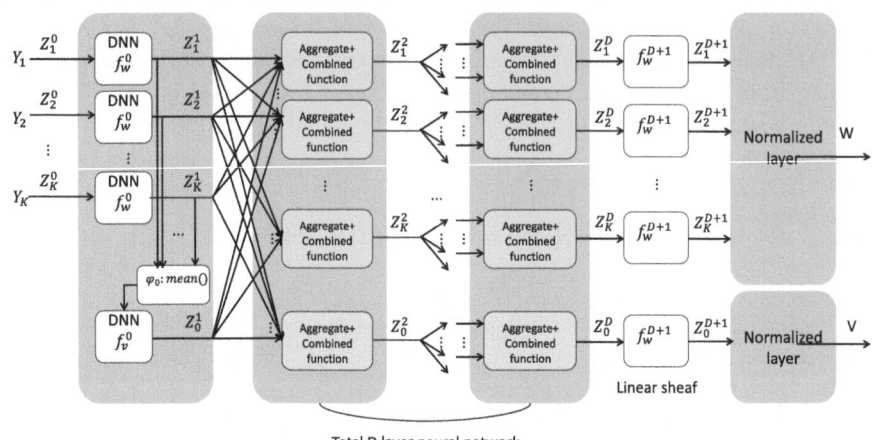

Fig. 3. Overall graph neural network architecture

3.1   Neural Network Training Parameter Setting

For the proposed 2-layer GNN with $D = 2$, where $k = 0, \ldots, 4$ and $d = 1, 2$. TensorFlow, a deep learning library, will be utilized to implement the proposed network. During the training process, the Adam optimizer will be employed to iteratively update the parameters, with an initial learning rate set to 10^{-3}. The learning rate will decrease by a factor of 0.98 after 300 iterations. In each training epoch, the parameters of the neural network will be updated through 100 iterations, and 1024 training samples will be used to compute the gradient at each iteration. The training process will terminate if the loss function does not significantly improve on the validation dataset over 10 consecutive training points.

3.2   Deep Learning Performance Analysis

Generate Training and Test Datasets. This paper focuses on a deep learning-based Reconfigurable Intelligent Surface (RIS) assisted vehicular communication system. In urban environments, vehicular communication faces significant challenges due to complex electromagnetic conditions and a high density of users, leading to substantial interference and channel blockages. Therefore, this research primarily targets urban communication scenarios. Given the mobility of vehicles, it is crucial to rapidly respond to changing channel conditions by synchronously updating the RIS reflection matrices and beamforming vectors following vehicle position updates.

The DeepMIMO dataset, published by the Information Theory and Applications Workshop, provides various scenarios, including indoor, outdoor, urban, and suburban settings. Each scene has distinct characteristics and channel properties, including channel matrices and Channel State Information (CSI), aligning well with the requirements of this study.

Using the DeepMIMO dataset involves two main steps: first, selecting and downloading the appropriate scenario and corresponding Python package from the official website; second, inputting scenario parameters to generate channel information. The general framework is depicted in Fig. 4. For this study, the "O1" outdoor ray-tracing scenario is chosen to generate channel information. This dataset operates at a frequency of 60GHz, which is within the millimeter-wave communication range.

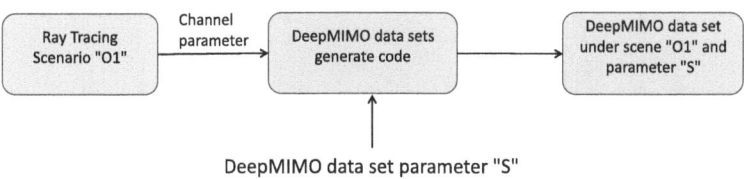

Fig. 4. Generate DeepMIMO dataset framework

The following Table 1 introduces the specific settings of the scenario used in this article.

Table 1. DeepMIMO dataset parameter setting

DeepMIMO dataset parameters	Numeric
Number of base station antennas	1,8,1
Number of RIS antennas	1,10,10
System bandwidth	100 MHz
Consider the number of strongest signal components	1
Antenna spacing	0.5λ

3.3 Performance Comparison of Different Algorithms

Next, the training data will be fed into the neural network, and the system performance will be evaluated against the following benchmarks during the testing phase:

Benchmark 1: Perfect CSI with BCD: Solving the rate maximization problem using block coordinate descent (BCD) algorithm with perfect CSI.

Benchmark 2: LMMSE Channel Estimation with BCD: Estimating channels using the LMMSE estimator, then employing the BCD algorithm for rate maximization.

Benchmark 3: Deep Learning-based Channel Estimation with BCD: Implementing a neural network for explicit channel estimation, followed by BCD-based design of phase shifts and beamformers. Comparing its performance against the proposed implicit channel estimation strategy in this paper to understand the advantages of implicit channel estimation over explicit channel estimation.

Firstly, in Fig. 5, the impact of the length of uplink pilots on downlink throughput and rate is demonstrated.

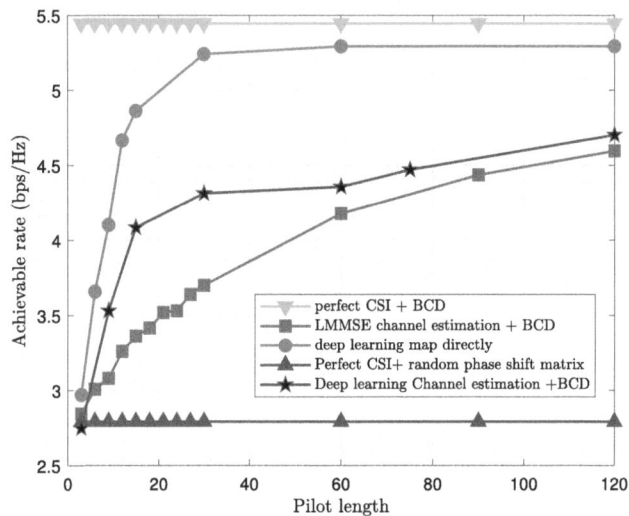

Fig. 5. Performance comparison of different algorithms

Figure 5 demonstrates that the BCD algorithm with perfect CSI (Benchmark 1) achieves the theoretical upper bound of the achievable rate. The deep learning approach proposed in this paper achieves approximately 90% of Benchmark 1's total rate with only 40 pilot signals, with further increases in pilot signals resulting in marginal rate improvements. In contrast, traditional explicit channel estimation methods (Benchmarks 2 and 3) require at least 120 pilot signals to achieve similar rates. While the deep learning algorithm initially requires longer training, its direct mapping for channel estimation is faster than the LMMSE algorithm once trained. Overall, the GNN architecture effectively learns the mapping from pilot signals to optimization, significantly reducing pilot training costs.

Next, we will compare the computational time of different algorithms. In vehicular communication, rapid channel changes necessitate real-time adjustments by the RIS, requiring high computational efficiency from optimization algorithms. We will calculate the total time spent by each algorithm for 1000 sample data points under various pilot signal scenarios.

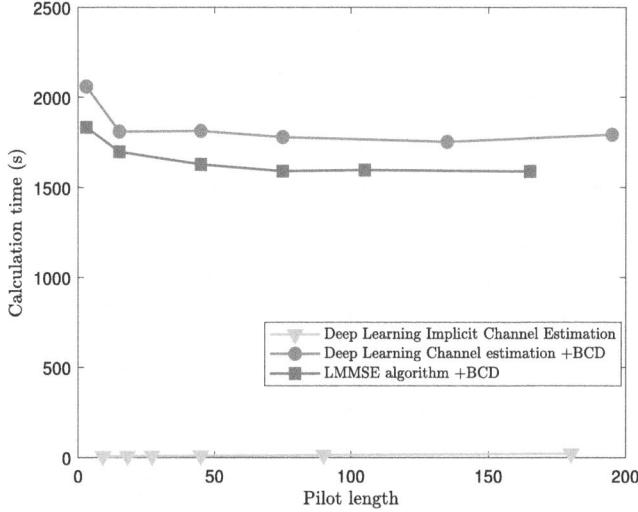

Fig. 6. Comparison of time consumption of different algorithms

Figure 6 demonstrates that, with a trained deep learning model, the time required for beamforming vector and phase shift matrix calculations significantly decreases compared to using the BCD algorithm. Deploying deep learning models at the BS enables rapid adjustment of the RIS phase shift matrix for vehicles entering a specific area, enhancing communication quality. However, as the length of pilot signals increases, the computational time for deep learning-based implicit channel estimation also increases due to the larger input vectors, while the BCD algorithm converges faster with longer pilot signals.

To evaluate the generalization capability of the GNN model and to compare user performance at different distances from the RIS and BS, we consider a scenario where a vehicle gradually approaches a high-demand communication intersection. In the DeepMIMO dataset, only the data from the intersection center is used for training, while the test dataset includes users at various positions. The pilot signal is input into the trained neural network to obtain the achievable rate. The simulation results are shown in Fig. 7, where the 50 m in the simulation parameters represent the center of the intersection. This area is unobstructed with strong signals, while the range from 0 to 150 m depicts the process of moving from a heavily obstructed area into the intersection center and then driving away.

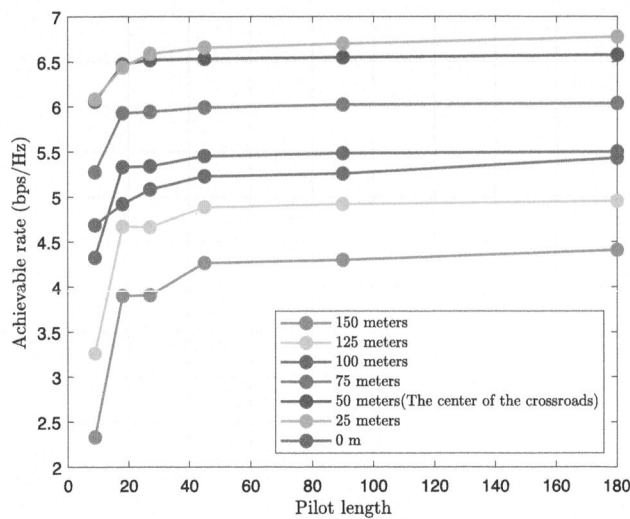

Fig. 7. Relationship between user distance and achievable rate

The simulation results indicate that as the vehicle approaches the intersection from a farther distance, the communication rate gradually increases when using the model trained with the intersection position data. This suggests that deploying the model at the current intersection can effectively enhance communication rate and stability as vehicles enter high-demand communication intersections. Performance is notably good at both 25 m and 75 m. Additionally, when the vehicle is in a heavily signal-blocked area, appropriately increasing the length of the pilot signal can significantly improve the achievable rate, addressing the millimeter-wave blockage issue.

4   Conclusion

This study focuses on a deep learning-based approach for RIS-assisted vehicular communication systems. Throughout this process, a system model for RIS-assisted communication is established, and the performance of deep learning algorithms is compared under different conditions.The research findings are summarized as follows:

Based on the RIS-assisted communication system architecture, a model for deep learning optimization problems is developed. The model is trained using appropriate datasets and tested against traditional algorithms. Results show that the deep learning method closely approximates the theoretical achievable rate upper bound with minimal training costs, exhibiting superior performance. Additionally, in vehicular communication scenarios, the method responds rapidly to vehicle channel switching and effectively enhances achievable rates and stability in high-demand communication areas.

References

1. Lavdas, S., Gkonis, P.K., Tsaknaki, E., Sarakis, L., Trakadas, P., Papadopoulos, K.: A deep learning framework for adaptive beamforming in massive mimo millimeter wave 5g multicellular networks. Electronics **12**(17), 3555 (2023)
2. Hashida, H., Kawamoto, Y., Kato, N.: Intelligent reflecting surface placement optimization in air-ground communication networks toward 6g. IEEE Wirel. Commun. **PP**(99), 1–6 (2020)
3. Bjornson, E., Ozdogan, O., Larsson, E.G.: Reconfigurable intelligent surfaces: three myths and two critical questions. IEEE Commun. Mag. **58**(12), 90–96 (2020). https://doi.org/10.1109/MCOM.001.2000407
4. Di Renzo, M., et al.: Smart radio environments empowered by reconfigurable intelligent surfaces: How it works, state of research, and the road ahead. IEEE J. Selected Areas Commun. 38(11), 2450–2525 (2020)
5. Albinsaid, H., Singh, K., Biswas, A.B.S., et al.: Multiple antenna selection and successive signal detection for smbased irs-aided communication. IEEE Signal Process. Lett. **28**, 813–817 (2021)
6. Wang, Z., Liu, L., Cui, S.: Channel estimation for intelligent reflecting surface assisted multiuser communications: Framework, algorithms, and analysis[J]. IEEE Trans **19**(10), 6607–6620 (2020)
7. Jia, C., Gao, H., Chen, N., et al.: Machine learning empowered beam management for intelligent reflecting surface assisted mmwave networks. China Commun. **17**(10), 100–114 (2020)
8. Kadhim, J.Q., Sallomi, A.H.: Enabling deep learning and swarm optimization algorithm for channel estimation for low power RIS assisted wireless communications. Int. J. Interact. Mobile Technol. (iJIM) (2023)

Deep Joint Source Channel Coding via Attention for Wireless Image Transmission

Haoze Chang[ID], Lin Ma[(✉)][ID], and Xuedong Wang

School of Electronics and Information Engineering,
Harbin Institute of Technology, Harbin, China
malin@hit.edu.cn

Abstract. In digital communication, efficiently transmitting image and video data through constrained channels remains challenging nowadays. Traditional methods using separate source and channel coding often fail in dynamic environments. In this paper, we introduce a novel deep learning based (DL) attention joint source channel coding (AttenJSCC) approach, which enhances robustness and efficiency in wireless image transmissions. By integrating source and channel coding into a unified framework and incorporating our Enhanced Attention Feature (EAF) modules and the ECA attention mechanism, our method outperforms some of the existing JSCC techniques, especially in low SNR conditions. Our framework not only overcomes the limitations of current technologies but also reduces the storage and computational needs on edge devices, facilitating more efficient real time communication.

Keywords: JSCC · Deep Learning · Wireless Image Transmission · Attention Mechanisms

1 Introduction

With the rapid advancement of modern computer science and the growing demands of users, the rise of Internet of Things applications is pushing the limits for transmitting image/video data under the strict conditions of latency, bandwidth, and energy consumption [1]. Contemporary communication frameworks employ a dual phase encoding method for distributing image/video content, known as source coding and channel coding [2], as illustrated in Fig. 1. Although this encoding process is highly optimized and widely adopted in image transmission systems, its performance can be significantly compromised when the channel conditions deviate from those for which the system was optimized. Such performance degradation is known as the *cliff effect*, which has been seen as a common problem in the digital communication scheme.

To address the limitations posed by traditional separate source channel coding schemes, several deep learning based joint source channel coding (JSCC) methods have been introduced [3–5]. Due to the strong encoding and decoding

© ICST Institute for Computer Sciences, Social Informatics and Telecommunications Engineering 2025
Published by Springer Nature Switzerland AG 2025. All Rights Reserved
H.-H. Chen and W. Meng (Eds.): WiSATS 2024, LNICST 605, pp. 312–323, 2025.
https://doi.org/10.1007/978-3-031-86196-3_27

ability of deep learning architecture, the joint source channel coding architecture can help capture the most important features in the original image. The feature vector is mapped to the complex value channel sample. The DeepJSCC [6] scheme, specifically tailored for wireless image transmission, has demonstrated significant potential by directly mapping image pixels to complex value channel input symbols. Building on the pioneering work of DeepJSCC, numerous related JSCC projects have been developed. For instance, DeepJSCC-f [7] leverages feedback from the receiver, utilizing the feedback information through deploying a decoder at the transmitter end to modify the outgoing data based on the received information. To align with modern hardware capabilities, DeepJSCC-Q [8] has been proposed to map complex value signals into constellation signals with fixed positions, thereby circumventing the quantization process. However, some of the approaches mentioned above require training across multiple channel SNRs to adapt to diverse channel conditions. Such designs necessitate increased storage capacity on edge devices and precise channel estimation prior to image transmission. Although some models are trained within a predefined SNR range to accommodate channel variability, their performance is often compromised under low SNR conditions, leading to diminished effectiveness.

In this study, we leverage recent advancements in deep learning methodologies within the realms of image compression and communication systems to introduce a cutting-edge joint source channel coding algorithm designed for image transmission across wireless communication channels. We proposed a new module based on the attention mechanism to recalibrate the weight of feature map and thus amplify the core features under different channel SNRs.

The remainder of the paper is organized as follows: Sect. 2 discusses the theoretical foundation and the model overview of our proposed JSCC algorithm. Section 3 presents the proposed Enhanced Attention Feature module and gives a detailed description on the model architecture. Section 4 gives a detailed explanation on experimental setup, including the datasets used, training procedures, and the evaluation metrics. Finally, the conclusions and future research directions are summarized in Sect. 5.

2   System Overview

In this section, we will give a detailed introduction of the proposed end-to-end image wireless transmission. In the traditional transmission method, the message is firstly encoded to remove the redundancies in the message and thus reduce the bits needed to be sent. The channel coding is done next to add protective bits to detect and correct possible mistakes. The process can be represented as:

$$\mathbf{b} = \mathbf{c}_\beta(\mathbf{s}_\alpha(M)) \tag{1}$$

where $\mathbf{c}_\beta(\cdot)$ denotes the channel coding algorithm β, and $\mathbf{s}_\alpha(\cdot)$ denotes the source coding algorithm α. M denotes the message to be sent. The encoded information is further processed through modulation and frequency up conversion before being transmitted in the high frequency band. At the receiver end, the received bits are first frequency shifted to the base band and the rest process is done reversely, that is, the protective channel coding bits are first removed to restore the original message after source coding. The sent message is restored through the source decoding. The process can be presented as:

$$\hat{M} = \mathbf{s}_\alpha^{-1}(\mathbf{c}_\beta^{-1}(\hat{\mathbf{b}}))$$ (2)

where $\mathbf{c}_\beta^{-1}(\cdot)$ denotes the decoding algorithm based on the channel coding algorithm β and $\mathbf{s}_\alpha^{-1}(\cdot)$ denotes the source decoding algorithm based on the source coding algorithm α. The $\hat{M}$ denotes the message the receiver desired. We use the notation $\hat{b}$ rather than b in the formula 2 to denote the effect of channel noise. The overall process can be expressed in Fig. 1.

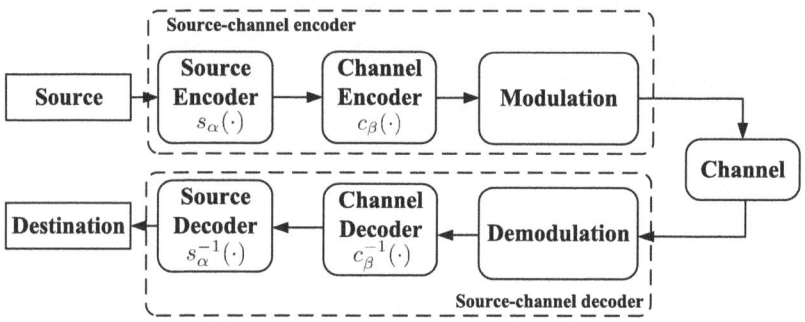

Fig. 1. Traditional digital communication block diagram. Source will pass through source encoder, channel encoder and modulator to generate channel sample.

In the deep learning based image wireless transmission, the architecture of our designed system is made up of two parts namely encoder and decoder, which respectively equals the $\mathbf{c}_\beta(\mathbf{s}_\alpha(\cdot))$and the $\mathbf{s}_\alpha^{-1}(\mathbf{c}_\beta^{-1}(\cdot))$ in the formula 1 and formula 2. In the deep learning based communication system, the encoder and decoder is usually implemented using the deep learning neural network. Here in our work, we use the classic and practical CNN as the backbone. The encoder captures deep features embedded in the input image, namely $\mathbf{f} = \mathbf{E}(I)$, where I denotes the input image with a shape of $\mathbf{I} \in \mathbb{R}^{h \times w \times 3}$. The notation $\mathbf{E}$ denotes the encoder and the notation $\mathbf{f}$ denotes the output feature which has a shape $\mathbf{f} \in \mathbb{R}^{h' \times w' \times n}$. The total length of the vector $\mathbf{f}$ is $2k$. The $2k$ units in the $\mathbf{f}$ will be combined in groups of two to form the final channel sample $z \in \mathbb{C}^k$.

The output feature tensor will be passed through the channel as $\hat{z} = \mathbf{C}(z)$. The $\mathbf{C}(\cdot)$ refers to the communication channel. We rewrite the noising progress as $\hat{z} = z + n$ considering the AWGN channel used in our design, where $n \sim \mathcal{CN}(0, \sigma^2 \mathbf{I}_{k \times k})$ is a complex Gaussian vector with covariance matrix $\mathbf{I}_{k \times k}$ as a $k \times k$ identity matrix [9].

At the receiver end, the receiver takes the received tensor $\hat{z}$ and input it to the decoder side to restore the original image as $\bar{\mathbf{I}} = \mathbf{D}(\hat{z})$ which the $\mathbf{D}(\cdot)$ refers to the decoder deployed on the receiver side. The entire transmission process can be written as:

$$\bar{I} = \mathbf{D}(\mathbf{C}(\mathbf{E}(I))) \tag{3}$$

The optimal parameters of the model can be get through optimizing the loss function through gradient descent while the optimization progress is written as:

$$\theta_{model} = \arg\min_{\theta} \mathcal{L}(I, \mathbf{D}(\mathbf{C}(\mathbf{E}(I)))) \tag{4}$$

We select the MSE loss to evaluate the distortion between the two images which is written as:

$$MSE = \frac{1}{NM} \sum_{i=1}^{N} \sum_{j=1}^{M} \|(a_{ij} - b_{ij})\|^2 \tag{5}$$

We assume that both transmitter and receiver can estimate the channel noise power σ^2 and define SNR as:

$$SNR = 10 \log_{10}(\frac{P}{\sigma^2}) dB \tag{6}$$

Without loss of generality, we set the P as $P = 1$. For fair comparison, we define the *bandwidth compression ratio* as:

$$\gamma = \frac{k}{H \times W \times C} \tag{7}$$

To better evaluate the performance of the proposed scheme, We set the power constraint as $\frac{1}{k}\mathbb{E}[\hat{z}^*\hat{z}] \leq P$. The final output tensor is reshaped to form a tensor with the shape as $z \in 1 \times 1 \times 2k$. The real numbers of the output tensor is passed through a normalization layer to force the output tensor to satisfy the constraint of power following the equation $\hat{z} = \sqrt{kP}\frac{z}{\sqrt{z^*z}}$ in which the z^* denotes the conjugate transpose of z. The output of the normalization layer is combined into k complex value channel input samples and forms the encoded signal representation, which is transmitted over the channel.

3   Attention JSCC Method

In this section, we will give a brief introduction on the deep learning based joint source channel coding used in our system. Our system employs the typical encoder decoder architecture which can be deployed separately as deploying the encoder in the edge devices such as cell phones and deploying the decoder on the server end.

3.1   Encoder and Decoder

In this section, we provide an overview of the AttenJSCC system used in our system, depicted in Fig. 2. The architecture comprises an encoder that compresses the input image into a feature vector for transmission and a decoder that reconstructs the image from this feature vector. The encoder consists of four main components: the encoding block, encoding Res-block, the Enhanced Attention Feature (EAF) module, and the ECA attention block, with the decoder featuring symmetrical counterparts.

The encoding block includes a 2D convolution layer, generalized divisive normalization (GDN) [10] and a PReLU activation function, with the latter chosen for its adaptability to noised data due to a learnable parameter α when $x \leq 0$. The encoding Res-block [11], designed to mitigate degradation in deep learning, comprises two convolution layers. The input tensor is first padded to proper size and then normalized using a GDN layer and activated via PReLU. The subsequent layer repeats this process, excluding the final PReLU activation. An optional dropout layer is incorporated to prevent overfit. The ECA attention mechanism [12], known for its simplicity and effectiveness, has been used in multiple networks. The ECA attention mechanism pools the input tensor along the channel dimension to form a factor vector, which is then convoluted to scale the input tensor in the channel dimension. The scaled tensor is residual connected to the input tensor to form the encoding Res-block output tensor.

This tensor then enters the proposed EAF module which adjusts channel weights to enhance features and reduce noise impact through an attention mechanism. Received tensor will be flattened to add restore the height and width dimension. In the decoder, the Transposed Conv2D and the inverse GDN effectively reverse the encoding process. The rest parts in the decoding module remains symmetric as the encoder.

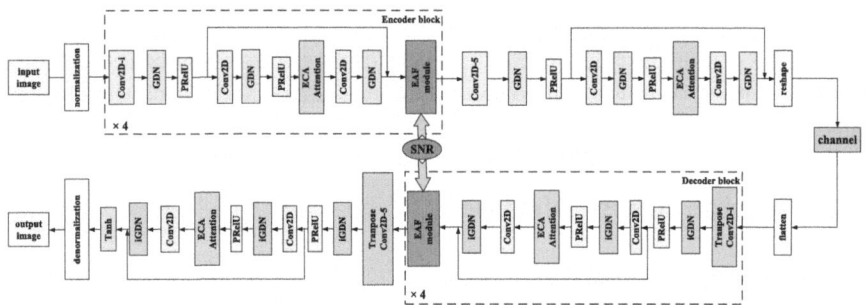

Fig. 2. Proposed model overview. We stack the Conv2D PReLU function, Res-block, GDN normalization and EAF module together as the encoder block, the final block doesn't include EAF module. '-i' denotes the i-th module and correspond to the parameter in the following section.

3.2 Enhanced Attention Feature Module

In this section, we introduce the Enhanced Attention Feature (EAF) Module used in our architecture. Previous approaches [13] used an Attention Feature (AF) module [14] that concatenated the SNR and feature vector to output a reweighed feature vector, aiming to mitigate noise effects. However, we suppose that a separation in the reweighting process, allowing the network to distinctly enhance image features and diminish noise effects. To better restore the original image, the weights of core feature maps should be amplified first and the amplified feature vector should be recalibrated with SNR afterwards.

Figure 3 depicts the EAF module's structure. It starts with global average pooling across the channel dimension of the input tensor to derive a factor tensor that reflects the weight of features across different channels. This tensor undergoes transformation through a linear layer and a PReLU function [15], repeated twice to refine the feature weighting factor. Subsequently, this factor tensor is merged(concatenated) with an SNR value to form an SNR factor vector, which is processed through another linear layer and a Sigmoid function to produce the final scaling weights. These weights are then applied element wise multiplication to the original tensor to produce the scaled tensor, effectively adjusting the image data in response to varying SNR levels. The performance of our design is evaluated in the following section.

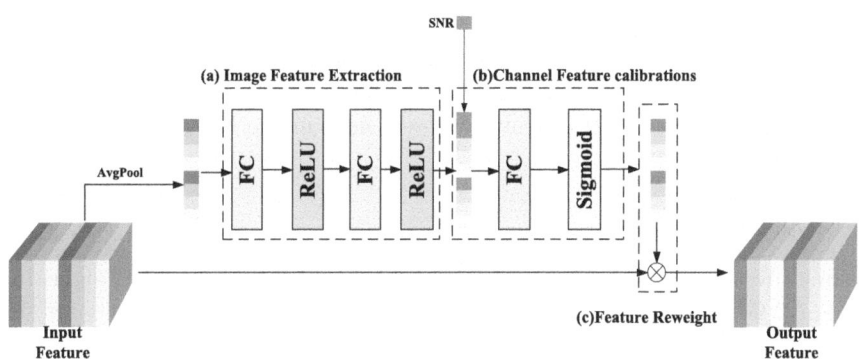

Fig. 3. Proposed **E**nhanced **A**ttention **F**eature Module. EAF module contains three parts: (a) Image Feature Extraction, (b) Channel Feature Calibrations, (c) Feature Reweight.

4 Implementation and Performance Evaluation

4.1 Experiment Setup

We conducted multiple experiments to evaluate our proposed model's effectiveness using the CIFAR-10 dataset, which contains 60,000 32×32 training images. We split the dataset into training and test sets at a $5 : 1$ ratio. The initial learning rate was set at 10^{-3} and was reduced by 0.1 every 400 epochs, with training capped at 2000 epochs. We incorporated early stopping to halt training if the validation loss did not decrease by at least 0.00005 over 50 epochs. The training used a mini batch size of 64, and performance evaluation involved transmitting each image 50 times to counteract channel randomness.

Table 1. Encoder and Decoder parameters

Operation	Parameters	Operation	Parameters
conv2D-1	$9 \times 9 \times 256 \times 2 \times 4$	transconv2D-1	$5 \times 5 \times 256 \times 1 \times 2$
conv2D-2	$5 \times 5 \times 256 \times 2 \times 2$	transconv2D-2	$5 \times 5 \times 256 \times 1 \times 2$
conv2D-3	$5 \times 5 \times 256 \times 1 \times 2$	transconv2D-3	$5 \times 5 \times 256 \times 1 \times 2$
conv2D-4	$5 \times 5 \times 256 \times 1 \times 2$	transconv2D-4	$5 \times 5 \times 256 \times 2 \times 2$
conv2D-5	$5 \times 5 \times 256 \times 1 \times 2$	transconv2D-5	$8 \times 8 \times 3 \times 2 \times 2$

This setup was implemented in PyTorch, using the Adam optimizer [16] and MSE loss. Input images were normalized from $[0, 1]$ to $[-1, 1]$ by dividing by the maximum pixel value of 255 and normalization. The GDN and iGDN layers used a fixed reduction parameter of 16. The channel configuration was set as $[3, 256, 256, 256, 256, C]$, with the inverse configuration in the decoder. The C denotes the final output channel. The output channel will be set as 8 for the bandwidth ratio $\gamma = \frac{1}{12}$. The detailed parameters used in our design is listed in Table 1. The notation $K \times K \times F \times S \times P$ denotes a Conv2D/TransConv2D layer with F filters with kernel size $K \times K$ and stride S which pads the input tensor with P. For the 2D convolution layer used in the Res-block, we set the kernel size of the filter as 3.

4.2   Performance Evaluation

We first investigate the performance of our proposed deep AttenJSCC algorithm in the AWGN setting. We change the SNR used in the testing scenario and use PSNR [17] as the metric to evaluate the performance of the proposed scheme. Figure 4 illustrates the performance of our proposed scheme under different testing scenario while the compression is set to $\frac{1}{12}$. For low SNR regime, performance has surpassed some of the most powerful communication schemes in prior work. Our proposed scheme achieved an amazing performance and reached a PSNR of 22.97 dB when the channel situation is extremely limited (SNR = −2 dB, indicating that the power of noise has surpassed the power of signal). When the AttenJSCC is tested on 3dB, the performance is even on par with the some of the DL based methods trained on medium and high SNR region thus exhibiting stronger noise resistance capability. For high SNR regime, our work remains competitive as the results illustrate that our scheme outperforms prior work.

Figure 5 illustrates the performance of our proposed scheme under different testing scenario while the compression is set to $\frac{1}{6}$. Our work remains competitive under the whole SNR range. In challenging low SNR scenarios, performance

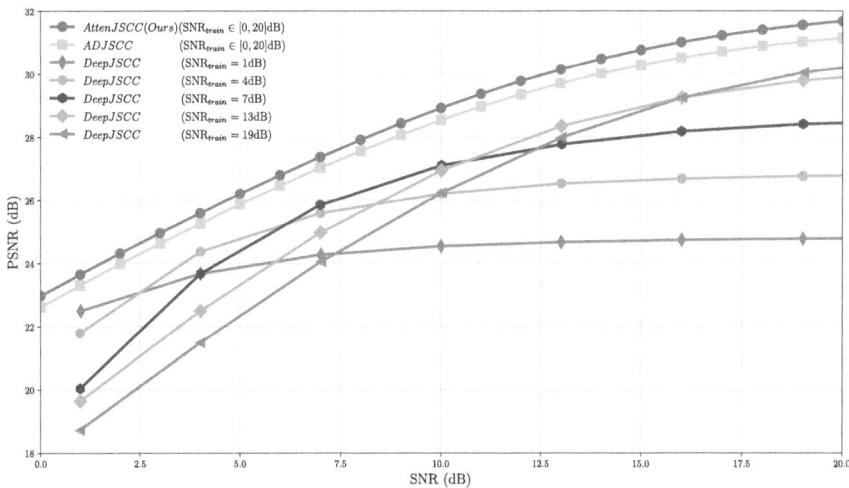

Fig. 4. Performance under different test SNR on CIFAR-10 test images while R = 1/12. The curve of AttenJSCC is trained under the uniform distribution of SNR from 0dB to 20 dB. Each curve of DeepJSCC is trained at a specific SNR.

of our work falls within a moderate range when compared to the DeepJSCC-f. However, we want to emphasize that our work has more advantages and is easier to implement. First, our work is trained on a target SNR range rather on specific target SNR value such that the edge devices only need to store one set of parameters rather than multiple sets. Second, our work is made up of simple encoder decoder architecture rather than complicated architecture with feedback. When compared with ADJSCC, the performance on higher SNR regime generally resides within a moderate spectrum. Our architecture demonstrates stronger image recovery capabilities in low SNR environments thus we believe that it may be prone to overfitting in high SNR regions. Such performance degradation can be seen as reasonable tradeoff for the performance improve under low SNR.

Also, to test our architecture's performance on larger images, we implemented extensive experiments on Kodak [18] images, which has 24 high quality images with 768 × 512 resolutions and is frequently used as a standard dataset for evaluating image compression performance. The performance is compared with DeepJSCC under different scenarios and the result is shown in Fig. 6. We trained our model on COCO2017 dataset [19] until convergence. COCO2017 is a high quality and high resolution image dataset with elaborate notations and contains

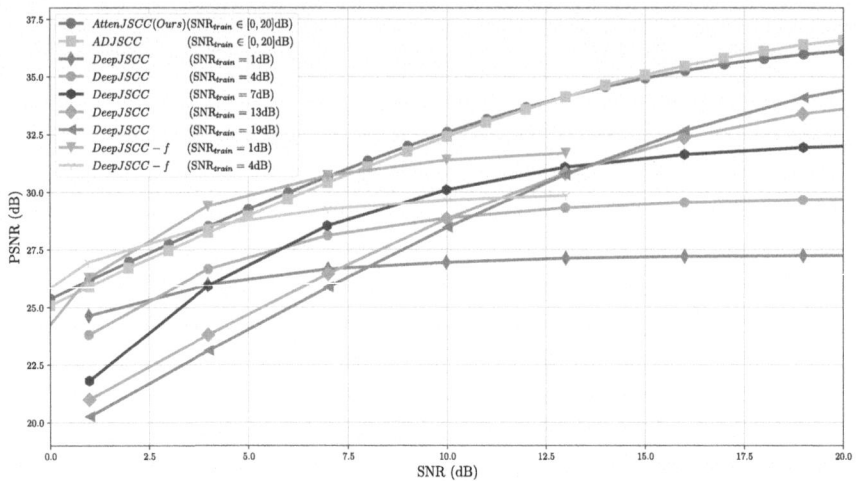

Fig. 5. Performance under different test SNR on CIFAR-10 test images while R =1/6.

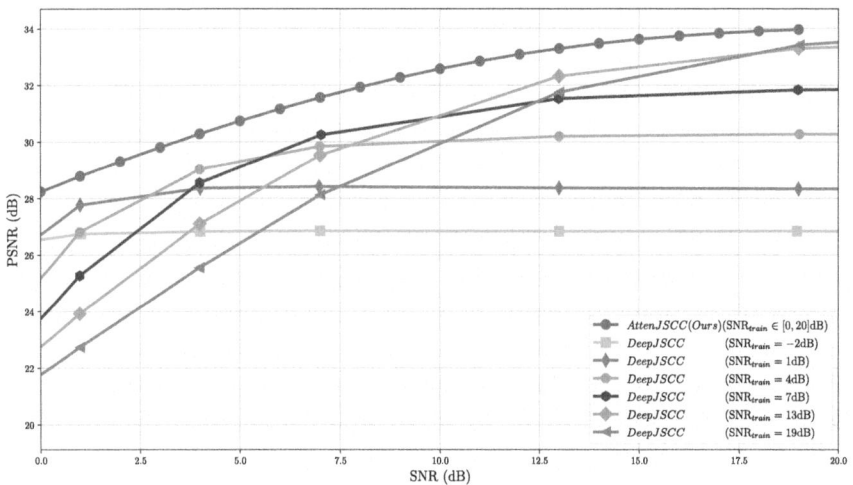

Fig. 6. Performance under different test SNR on Kodak images while R =1/12.

complicated scenarios rather than simple objects which is harder to restore. During evaluation, each image in Kodak dataset is transmitted 30 times to diminish the randomness of channel noise. Figure 6 illustrates that the performance of proposed system is competitive even on larger and complicated images.

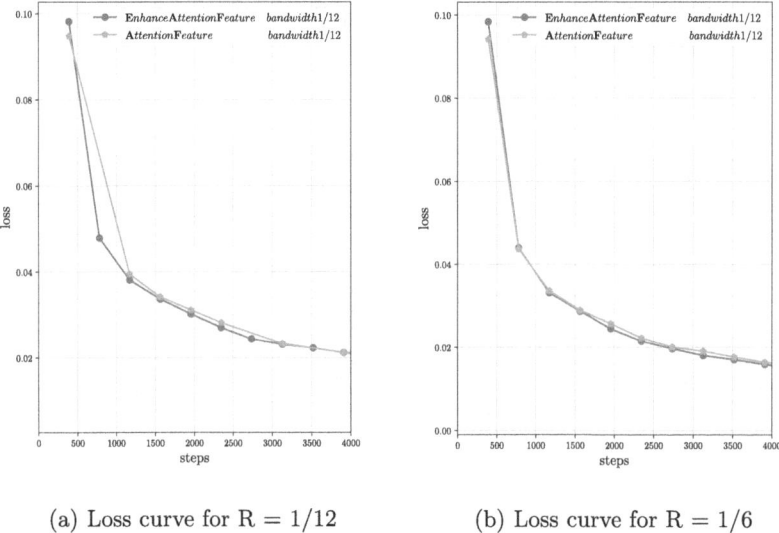

(a) Loss curve for R = 1/12   (b) Loss curve for R = 1/6

Fig. 7. Loss curve for different setup. The rest of the network remains same while using different Attention Feature module.

To compare the effectiveness of our proposed enhanced attention feature module, we show the loss curves of two different setups in Fig. 7 which illustrates the loss curve of two different setups. The only difference in the two experiment setup is the attention feature module. We can tell from the loss curve that the proposed module helps to converge to a better solution point faster. Such performance comparison shows that our proposed EAF module captures the inner feature of the image better and thus amplify the weight of core features before interacting with the channel SNR.

5 Conclusion

In this paper, we have proposed a novel deep attention joint source channel coding named AttenJSCC architecture for transmitting images over wireless channels. In this architecture, both the encoder and decoder are designed as complementary convolutional neural networks and are trained jointly to minimize the MSE of the reconstructed images. We implemented relative experiments thus demonstrates validity of proposed EAF module. Also, we evaluated the performance of this AttenJSCC approach against some of the most powerful and famous previous works on both small datasets with single objects and large datasets with complicated scenarios. Our extensive numerical simulations demonstrate that AttenJSCC significantly outperforms particularly in environments with low SNR condition.

Acknowledgment. This research was funded by National Key R&D Program of China (2022YFC3801100) and Heilongjiang Province Key R&D Program (2022ZX01A31).

References

1. Said, D.: A survey on information communication technologies in modern demand-side management for smart grids: Challenges, solutions, and opportunities. IEEE Eng. Manage. Rev. **51**(1), 76–107 (2023)
2. Zhou, R., Tian, C., Liu, T.: Exactly tight information-theoretic generalization error bound for the quadratic Gaussian problem. IEEE J. Selected Areas Inform. Theory **5**, 94–104 (2024). https://doi.org/10.1109/JSAIT.2024.3380598
3. Yang, M., Bian, C., Kim, H.S.: Deep joint source channel coding for wireless image transmission with ofdm. In: ICC 2021 - IEEE International Conference on Communications, pp. 1–6 (2021)
4. Kurka, D.B., Gündüz, D.: Bandwidth-agile image transmission with deep joint source-channel coding. IEEE Trans. Wireless Commun. **20**(12), 8081–8095 (2021)
5. Xuan, Z., Narayanan, K.: Analog joint source-channel coding for gaussian sources over awgn channels with deep learning. In: 2020 International Conference on Signal Processing and Communications (SPCOM), pp. 1–5. IEEE (2020)
6. Bourtsoulatze, E., Burth Kurka, D., Gunduz, D.: Deep joint source-channel coding for wireless image transmission. IEEE Trans. Cogn. Commun. Network. **5**(3), 567–579 (2019). https://doi.org/10.1109/TCCN.2019.2919300
7. Kurka, D.B., Gündüz, D.: Deepjscc-f: Deep joint source-channel coding of images with feedback. IEEE J. Select. Areas Inform. Theory **1**(1), 178–193 (2020)
8. Tung, T.Y., Kurka, D.B., Jankowski, M., Gündüz, D.: Deepjscc-q: Channel input constrained deep joint source-channel coding. In: ICC 2022-IEEE International Conference on Communications, pp. 3880–3885. IEEE (2022)
9. Dai, J., et al.: Nonlinear transform source-channel coding for semantic communications. IEEE J. Sel. Areas Commun. **40**(8), 2300–2316 (2022)
10. Ballé, J., Laparra, V., Simoncelli, E.P.: End-to-end optimized image compression. In: International Conference on Learning Representations (2016)
11. He, K., Zhang, X., Ren, S., Sun, J.: Deep residual learning for image recognition. In: 2016 IEEE Conference on Computer Vision and Pattern Recognition (CVPR), pp. 770–778 (2016)
12. Wang, Q., Wu, B., Zhu, P., Li, P., Zuo, W., Hu, Q.: Eca-net: efficient channel attention for deep convolutional neural networks. In: 2020 IEEE/CVF Conference on Computer Vision and Pattern Recognition (CVPR), pp. 11531–11539 (2020)
13. Jialong, X., Ai, B., Chen, W., Yang, A., Sun, P., Rodrigues, M.: Wireless image transmission using deep source channel coding with attention modules. IEEE Trans. Circuits Syst. Video Technol. **32**(4), 2315–2328 (2021)
14. Hu, J., Shen, L., Sun, G.: Squeeze-and-excitation networks. In: 2018 IEEE/CVF Conference on Computer Vision and Pattern Recognition, pp. 7132–7141 (2018)
15. Crnjanski, J., Krstić, M., Totović, A., Pleros, N., Gvozdić, D.: Adaptive sigmoid-like and prelu activation functions for all-optical perceptron. Opt. Lett. **46**(9), 2003–2006 (2021)
16. Kingma, D.P., Ba, J.: Adam: Amethod for stochastic optimization
17. Sheikh, H.R., Sabir, M.F., Bovik, A.C.: A statistical evaluation of recent full reference image quality assessment algorithms. IEEE Trans. Image Process. **15**(11), 3440–3451 (2006)

18. Kiku, D., Monno, Y., Tanaka, M., Okutomi, M.: Residual interpolation for color image demosaicking. In: 2013 IEEE International Conference on Image Processing, pp. 2304–2308. IEEE (2013)
19. Lin, T.Y., et al.: Microsoft coco: common objects in context. In: Computer Vision–ECCV 2014: 13th European Conference, Zurich, Switzerland, September 6-12, 2014, Proceedings, Part V 13, pp. 740–755. Springer (2014). https://doi.org/10.1007/978-3-319-10602-1_48

Joint Signal Adaptive Modulation Recognition and Radio Frequency Fingerprinting Based on Multi-task Learning

Zhuo Li[1], Zhongqiu He[1], Congan Xu[2,3(✉)], Wei Zhang[4], Haoran Zha[1], Yu Wang[5], and Zeyu Tang[2,3]

[1] Harbin Engineering University, Harbin 150001, China
[2] Naval Aviation University, Yantai 26400, China
a9732707021z@163.com
[3] Advanced Technology Research institute, Beijing institute of Technology, Jinan 250300, China
[4] National Key Laboratory of Electromagnetic SpaceSecurity, Chengdu, Sichuan 610036, China
[5] Nanjing University of Posts and Telecommunications, 210003 NanJing, China

Abstract. Radio Frequency Fingerprinting Identification (RFFI) leverages inherent discrepancies in radiation source hardware, which are challenging to mimic and counterfeit. This attribute enhances the security of wireless networks and ensures the protection of data privacy, vital for secure communications. Inherent challenges such as channel fading and frequency drift affect radio signals. This paper explores the synergy between Automatic Modulation Recognition (AMR) and RFFI by employing a multi-label dataset to strategically influence the relationship between signal labels and individual radiation sources. We propose an advanced multi-gate mixture-of-experts convolutional neural network model, the MMOE-CNN-Transformer, which operates within a multi-task soft sharing framework. Our empirical results reveal that this model significantly enhances RFFI classification accuracy, particularly at a 0dB signal-to-noise ratio, outperforming traditional single-task learning (STL) approaches and surpassing the efficacy of hard sharing architectures, exemplified by the Shared-Bottom model. This study underscores the potential of integrating sophisticated neural network architectures in enhancing the robustness and precision of radio frequency identification systems.

Keywords: Radio frequency fingerprint · deep learning · automatic modulation recognition · multi-task learning

This work is supported by the National Natural Science Foundation of China (No: 62201172), the National Key Research and Development Program of China (2022YFE0136800). This work is also supported by Science and Technology on Electronic Information Control Laboratory.

H.-H. Chen and W. Meng (Eds.): WiSATS 2024, LNICST 605, pp. 324–337, 2025.
https://doi.org/10.1007/978-3-031-86196-3_28

1   Introduction

With the advancement of networking, informatization and intelligence, the number of radio equipment has surged, and electromagnetic spectrum resources have become more and more scarce. The ability of modulation methods and other parameters [1], especially in the field full of confrontation and games, has pushed the competition for the electromagnetic spectrum to a new height, and these factors have led to a more complex electromagnetic environment for radio equipment to work, more difficult to use and control the electromagnetic spectrum, and more severe challenges in maintaining the security of electromagnetic space. Radio frequency fingerprinting (RFF) is derived from the difference in the hardware of the radiation source, which is difficult to imitate and clone, which can enhance the security of wireless networks, protect data privacy [2] , improve the anti-spoofing capabilities in key civilian fields such as the Global Positioning System (GPS) and Automatic Dependent Dependent Broadcast (ADS-B) systems [3], and improve the capabilities of electronic intelligence detection and reconnaissance and situational awareness of the electromagnetic spectrum [4] It is one of the key technologies for maintaining national electromagnetic space security, and has broad application prospects in both civil and military fields. [5]Automatic Modulation Classification (AMR) is also an important means to monitor and manage spectrum resources [6].

Automatic Modulation Classification (AMR) [7–11] and Radio Frequency Fingerprinting (RFFI) [12–14] are two important technologies for wireless signal classification. AMR refers to the automatic identification of the modulation pattern of the signal after the signal reaches the receiver but before demodulation, which provides a basis for subsequent signal extraction and processing [15]. AMR is a novel technology in which the modulation class of a signal can be successfully identified by the signal receiver using AMR technology. In a non-cooperative communication scenario. Proper identification of the modulation type can help reduce communication overhead and help better identify unknown signals [16] .RFFI is based on Radio frequency fingerprinting (RFF) characteristics,these characteristics are caused by random hardware defects in the manufacturing process of wireless devices. These defects typically manifest as direct current (DC) bias, harmonic distortion, filter error, phase noise, I/Q gain imbalance, local oscillator leakage, nonlinearity, and quadrature offset [17,18] , and carrier frequency offset. These features can be extracted from component defects during the manufacturing process [19] to identify different emitter entities . Two technologies, Automatic Modulation Classification (AMR) and Radio Frequency Fingerprinting (RFFI), are of great interest in both the military and civilian sectors.

Deep learning methods have shown great advantages in the fields of image processing and text translation, unlike data such as images, radio signals do not have a visual form that can be intuitively understood, and a receiver is required to convert the RF signal into a complex baseband signal, which is often saved as in-phase/quadrature (I/Q) data. The size of I/Q data is generally $2 \times N$, the first dimension is 2, representing the isotropic component I and the orthogonal component Q, and the second dimension is N, representing the length of the sequence along the temporal direction. [20]At present, most emitter identification datasets contain only one modulation scheme [21–24]. Theoretically, even if the same device uses different modulation methods to send signals, it can extract fingerprint features, that is, it has a certain degree of robustness, and the performance will not be greatly reduced due to the change of modulation mode. Moreover, the individual radiation source is inadvertently modulated due to confounding factors, and the modulation recognition task extracts the modulation features, and the extracted intentional modulation feature theory can help the RFF filter the redundant features of non-confounding factors, thereby helping to extract the fingerprint features. Multi-task learning (MTL) [25] aims to improve model generalization by utilizing domain-specific information contained in the training signals of related tasks. In the era of deep learning, MTL translates into designing networks capable of learning shared representations from multitask-supervised signals. Compared to single-task situations, related tasks have the potential to improve performance if they share complementary information or act as regularizers for each other. For example, many radios can operate in transmitter signal modes with different modulation schemes and parameters.The two tasks, AMR and RFFI, can complement each other to improve their performance. The main contribution made by this article:

1. In this paper, a soft-shared multi-task network (MMOE-CNN-Transformer) is designed, which uses a multi-gate mixture-of-experts network (MMOE) to solve two tasks (AMR and RFFI) at the same time using a multi-label dataset, which is much better than the single-task learning baseline method, and when the performance of AMR task is not much different, it is better than the hard-sharing model.

2. The Transfomer encoder module is introduced, which combines the technologies of self-attention mechanism, global attention mechanism and residual connection, which can effectively encode the input sequence, transmit information between different positions, and capture the long-distance dependencies in the sequence at the head of each task, so as to help each task extract better features unique to each task outside the shared network.

2   Problem Formulation

From the receiver's point of view, the wireless signal can be represented in the presence of additive white Gaussian noise (AWGN):

$$s[h] = x[h] + n[h], 0 <= h <= H \tag{1}$$

where x[h] represents a wireless signal without any noise, n[h] represents additive Gaussian white noise, H is the number of sampling points, and h is the sampling index point.

In this paper, the dataset used includes eight modulated waveforms: BPSK, QPSK, 8PSK, 16PSK, 16QAM, 64QAM, 256QAM, and 1024QAM, which are modulated signals from six emitter transmitting devices. The datasets used are described in detail in Sect. 4.

For n learning tasks $\{T\}_{i=1}^{n}$,MTL is a learning paradigm in which n tasks share a part of the network for joint learning, so as to achieve the effect of knowledge transfer and sharing between tasks [26]. In this paper, an MTL scheme is adopted that is the soft parameter sharingcite [27] , and unlike the hard parameter sharing as shown in Fig. 1, networks with hard-parameter sharing completely share a backbone network to extract features, and each passes through the shared backbone network for single-head output. The soft shared network used in this paper is a multi-task learning network based on the Multi-Gate Hybrid Expert [28] (MMOE) structure, as shown in Fig. 2. The formulation of the joint AMR and RFFI tasks as MTL tasks can be expressed as:$T = \{\mathcal{O}_A, \mathcal{O}_R\}$,where $\mathcal{O}_A$ and $\mathcal{O}_R$ represent AMR and RFFI tasks, respectively. Let $X = \{x_j | 1 \leq j \leq K\}$ represent the training data, and $Y = \{(\mathbf{y}_j^A, \mathbf{y}_j^R) | 1 \leq j \leq K\}$ corresponding to the training target, where K is the number of samples. The AMR task and the RFFI task share the same training data $X \in \mathcal{X}, Y \in \mathcal{Y}$, in which each training data has two labels $\mathcal{Y}^A$ and $\mathcal{Y}^R$, representing the modulation type label and the RFF label, respectively. The multitasking definition is shown in Fig 1. The corresponding modulation type is obtained by the AMR task, which is denoted as $y_j^A = \{c_j \mid 1 \leq j \leq K\}$. RFFI task is denoted as $y_j^R = \{d_j \mid 1 \leq j \leq K\}$. Thus, the function $\mathcal{H}_{MTL} : \mathcal{X} \rightarrow \mathcal{Y}$ is formulated using a training dataset that maps the data space $\mathcal{X}$ to the corresponding target space $\mathcal{Y}$. The learning function $\mathcal{H}_{MTL}$ achieves both AMR and RFFI tasks to get the output of each task.

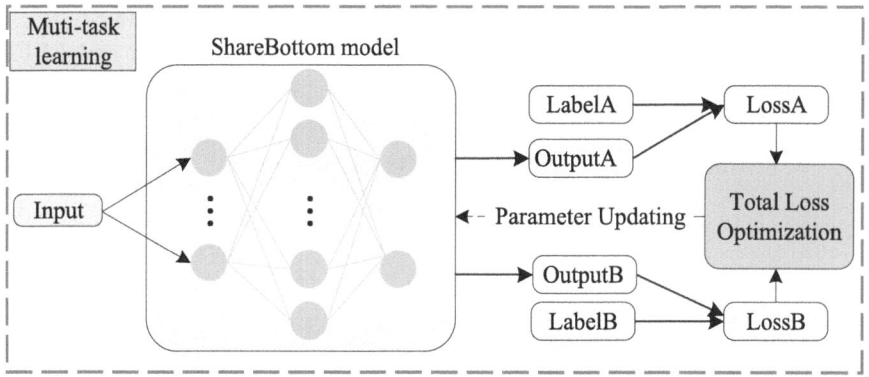

Fig. 1. Shared-Bottom model.

3   Method

This section introduces the MMOE-CNN-Transformer model, and the overall processing framework is shown in Fig 2. First, the overall framework is introduced, and then the two major modules in the framework, namely the shared

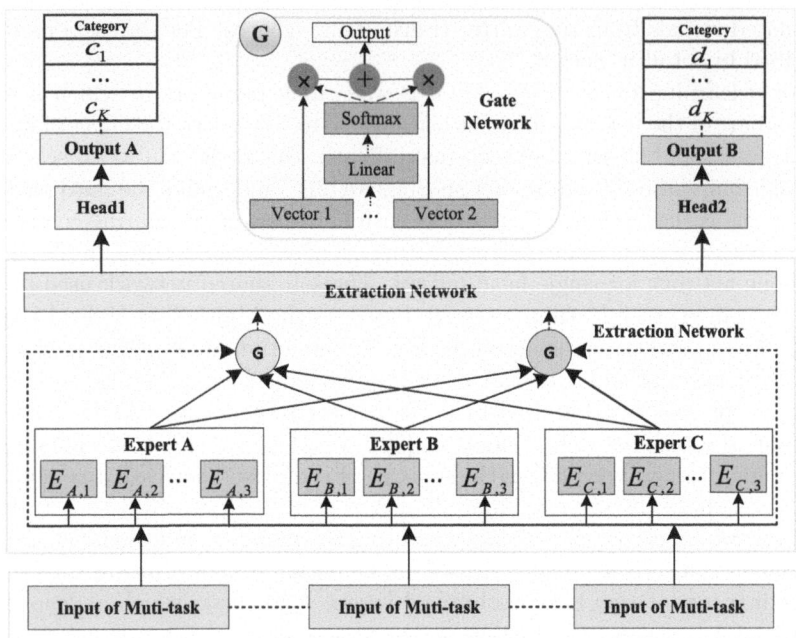

Fig. 2. Schematic diagram of an MMOE-CNN-Transformer for joint AMR and RFFI identification tasks. Three layers of shared experts extract shared features from the inputs, passing to the AMR and RFFI to implement the prediction classes.

layer module and the task-specific output module (i.e., AMRHead and RFFI-Head), are elaborated in detail.

3.1   A Framework of MMOE-CNN-Transformer

Let's say there are M tasks, the ShareBottom(SB) model ,the hard-shared model in multi-task , It can be expressed as a function f and a M tower network h_m, where m = 1, 2,...,M represents tasks. Each task in the SB network fully shares a special extraction network, and the multi-head output is performed at the end. Output of each task is $\mathcal{Y}_m$. For task m, SB net model can be represented as Eq. 2.

$$y_m = h^m(f(x)) \tag{2}$$

MMOE-CNN-Transformer network is based on the Multi-task Learning with Multi-gate Mixture-of-Exper (MMOE) model in soft sharing, which can better capture the differences between tasks without the need for more model parameters layer), each expert network is represented as. Add a separate gated network $g^m(x)$ for each task m. The weights of each expert network in task m are controlled by the training gated network, and then the characteristics extracted by each task in the shared expert network are obtained by weighting, and the whole process of extraction network can be expressed as Eq. 3 and Eq. 4.

$$g^m(x) = \text{softmax}(W_{gm}x) \tag{3}$$

$$f^m(x) = \sum_{i=1}^{n} g^m(x)_j f_j(x) \tag{4}$$

where $g^m(x)_j$ represents the probability that the m-th task corresponds to the j-th expert, and n represents the total number of tasks and $W_{gm} \in \mathbb{R}^{n \times c}$. n is the number of experts, and c is the feature dimension. Finally, each task passes through a specific head network to obtain its own output, as shown in Eq. 5.

$$y_m = h^m(f^m(x)) \tag{5}$$

3.2   Shared Experts and Head

As shown in Fig. 3, the share layers of the MMOE-CNN-Transformer model all use three identical nine-layer CNN expert networks as the shared feature pools, and adopt adaptive pooling and a Flatten layer in the last layer to perform weighted fusion with the gate network. Gate uses a full connectivity layer to connect to a network of three experts.

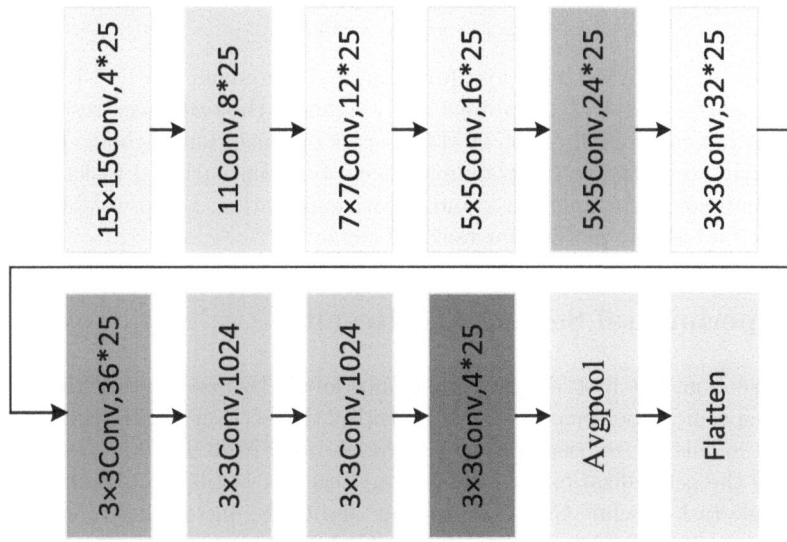

Fig. 3. Shared Expert layers

The two task Headers are classified and output by a Transformer module and a fully connected layer respectively. The Transformer module uses the attention mechanism to better extract the characteristics of AMR tasks and RFFI tasks. The self-attention mechanism allows the output of each position to take into account the information of all other positions in the input sequence, thus capturing global dependencies. In signal processing, this means that the model can take into account the characteristics of the entire signal at the same time, without being limited by the size of the local window. The Transformer Decoder module used is shown in Fig. 4.

In the training phase, during the training phase, the total loss is the linear sum of the two tasks. The overall loss function L_{mtl} is shown in Eq. 6.

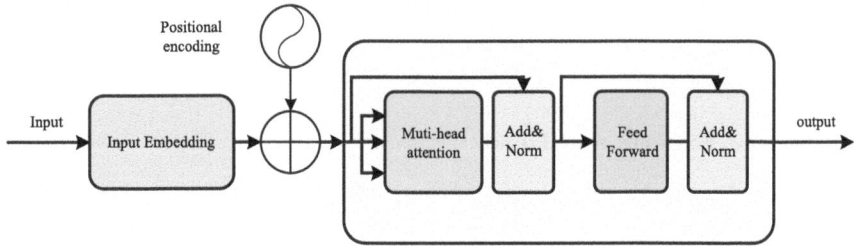

Fig. 4. Transformer Encoder.

$$L_{mtl} = w_R L_R + w_A L_A \qquad (6)$$

L_A represents the AMR task loss function, L_R represents the RFFI task loss function, $w_R L_R$ and $w_A L_A$ represent the weights of the two tasks, respectively. An important research direction of MTL is task optimization methods. For MTL particularly, we optimize the training process between balanced tasks to avoid being dominated by a single task and negative migration. Fixed-weight MTL is considered a baseline method for task balancing.

4   Experimental Setting and Results

In this section, we first describe the multi-label dataset used in this paper and the specific experimental setup. Secondly, this section verifies the network designed in this paper based on multi-task learning: MMOE-CNN-Transformer improves the generalization performance and accuracy of RFFI tasks compared with single-task baseline CNN-Transformer and CNN, and verifies that the network designed in this paper is better than CNN-Transformer and Share Bottom model, then the correlation fusion experiment was designed, and finally the influence for different task's weights on MTL was studied, and compared with other task balancing methods.

4.1   Dateset and Setting

The signal dataset used is from literature , and the acquisition device consists of a signal generator (VSG 60 A), a signal receiver (BB60C), a personal computer (PC), and six target power amplifiers (PA). The stable hardware characteristics of the transmitter, such as the amplitude, phase, and frequency distortion of the signal, can be reflected by the nonlinear distortion of the power amplifier. Therefore, nonlinear distortion of power amplifiers is often cited as the main cause of RFF. The center frequency of the signal sample in the dataset is 2.4 GHz, and the sampling rate is 10 Msample/s [28]. The size of the raw I/Q data is 17.8GB and includes a total of eight modulation schemes, i.e., BPSK, QPSK, 8 PSK, 16 PSK, 16 QAM, 64 QAM, 256 QAM, and 1024 QAM from 6 PAs. Table 1 shows the specific acquisition settings.

Table 1. Signal acquisition settings

numbers of devices	Setting
Data dimension	6
numbers of modulations	8
Center Frequency	2.4 GHz
Symbol rate	1 MHz
Sampling Frequency	2.4 GHz
Signal generator	VSG60A
Spectrum analyzer	BB60C

By adding noise to the original dataset in MATALAB software, the dataset with SNR in the range of 0,5,10,15,20 dB was obtained and normalized. The dimension of data is 6000×2. The experimental environment is based on Python 3.9, and the experimental setup is shown in Table 2.

Table 2. Experiment Setting

Data dimension	Setting
Data dimension	6000 × 2
Optimizer	Data6
Batch-size	128
Learning rate	0.1
Epoch	100
Sample size	36000
The proportion of the training, validation, and test sets	7:2:1
SNR	{0, 5, 10, 15, 20}dB

4.2   Multi-task Learning and Single-Task Learning

In this section, AMR and RFFI tasks are executed under the CNN baseline network and CNN-Transformer baseline network, respectively, and AMR and RFFI tasks are jointly executed using the hard-shared ShareBottom model in multi-tasking, and the accuracy of the above tasks is compared with that of the joint execution of AMR and RFFI tasks in MMOE-CNN-Transformer, and the superiority of the multi-task network designed in this paper is verified. The simulation results are shown in Table 3, where uniform represents the equal weight of the loss function of the two tasks, because in multi-task learning, each task is considered to be equally important, and the equal weight is taken as the baseline method. SB stands for Hard Sharing Model.

Table 3. MMOE-CNN-Transformer classification precision shared with single-task baseline methods and hard.

SNR	0dB	5dB	10dB	15dB	20dB
CNN-RFF	55.58%	80.19%	93.03%	98.17%	99.58%
CNN-AMR	99.94%	100%	100%	100%	100%
CNN-Transformer-RFF	62.97%	83.69%	95.58%	98.58%	99.19%
CNN-Transformer-AMR	99.92%	100%	100%	100%	100%
SB-CNN-Transformer-RFF(uniform)	73.86%	90.56%	97.25%	98.83%	99.14%
SB-CNN-Transformer-AMR(uniform)	99.86%	100%	100%	100	100%
MMOE-CNN-Transformer-RFF(ours) (uniform)	75.14%(↑19.56%)	90.89 %(↑10.7%)	97.47%(↑4.44%)	99.17%(↑1%)	99.67%(↑0.09%)
MMOE-CNN-Transformer-AMR(ours) (uniform)	100%	100%	100%	100%	100%

As can be seen from Table 3, MMOE-CNN-Transformer ensures that the AMR accuracy is close to 100% in the multi-label dataset used, and effectively reduces the error of RFFI. By combining the characteristics of RFFI and AMR, multi-task enables two identification tasks to share information to discover relationships and improve performance. The RFFI task is greatly improved, because the emitter individual produces unintentional modulation due to confounding factors, and the modulation recognition task extracts the modulation features, and the extracted intentional modulation feature theory can help the RFF filter the redundant features of non-confounding factors, so as to help better extract the fingerprint features. Two confusion matrices are also presented, as shown in Fig. 5, which are the confusion matrix for MMOE-CNN-Transformer pair of RFFI classification at 0dB and the confusion matrix for RFFI classification under CNN-Transformer single-task learning.

4.3   Ablation Experiments

The proposed MMOE-CNN-Transformer network consists of multiple CNN shared expert network layers and task layers, with the task-specific layer containing AMR and RFFI headers, both of which are composed of Transformer modules and fully connected classifiers for extracting individual features for each

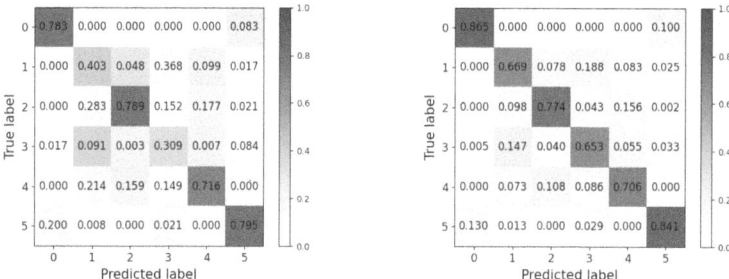

(a) Accuary of Confusion matrix is (b) Accuary of Confusion matrix is
62.07%   75.14%

Fig. 5. (a) Confusion matrix for RFFI classification at 0 dB MMOE-CNN-Transformer (b) Confusion matrix of RFFI classification under CNN-Transformer single-task learning

task. This section validates the contribution of different treatment steps by using different configurations for ablation studies.

1) Verify that the MTL is retained to a single task-specific header, so that the two tasks can share information, effectively improving the performance of the RFFI task, and these configurations are represented as single-head AMR and single-head RFFI; The two single-task structures are represented as MMOE-CNN-Transformer-A and MMOE-CNN-Transformer-R.

2) The header is configured without a Transformer (MMOE-CNN), MMOE-CNN-RFF represents the RFFI recognition accuracy and MMOE-CNN-AMR represents the AMR recognition accuracy in this configuration.

The performance of AMR and RFFI using different structures on the dataset is shown in Fig. 6, and it is particularly noted that in the multi-task architecture, the performance of AMR under the five signal-to-noise ratios is close to 100% under the three configurations, and the RFF performance decreases greatly at 0dB and 5dB under the MMOE-CNN configuration. Moreover, the multi-task method we designed is also much improved under the low signal-to-noise ratio compared with the MMOE-CNNTransformer-R configuration, which proves that multi-task knowledge sharing can help RFFI tasks extract features that are more difficult to extract from a single task to identify the correct individual. It can be seen from Fig. 6 that the RFFI task performance of our network is always the highest under the five signal-to-noise ratios, and the designed network effectively improves the recognition performance of RFFI tasks on the basis of ensuring that the modulation recognition does not decrease.Therefore, this paper chooses the DWA task balancing method to train the MMOE-CNN-Transformer network.

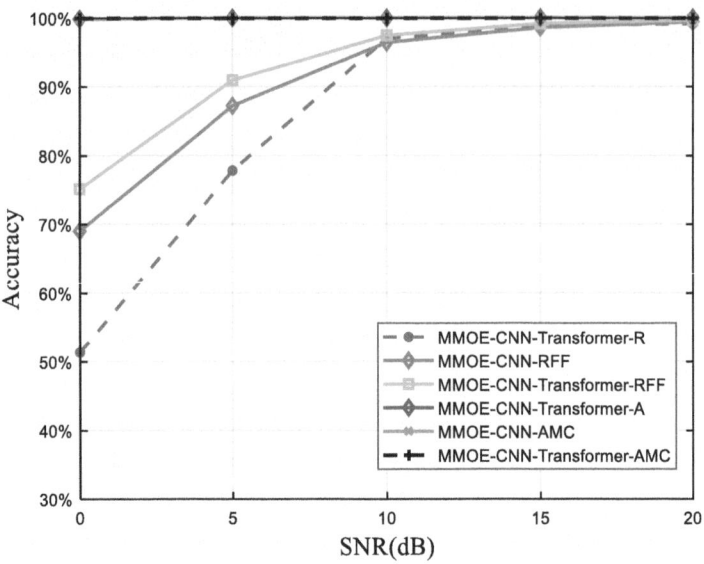

Fig. 6. Ablation experiments

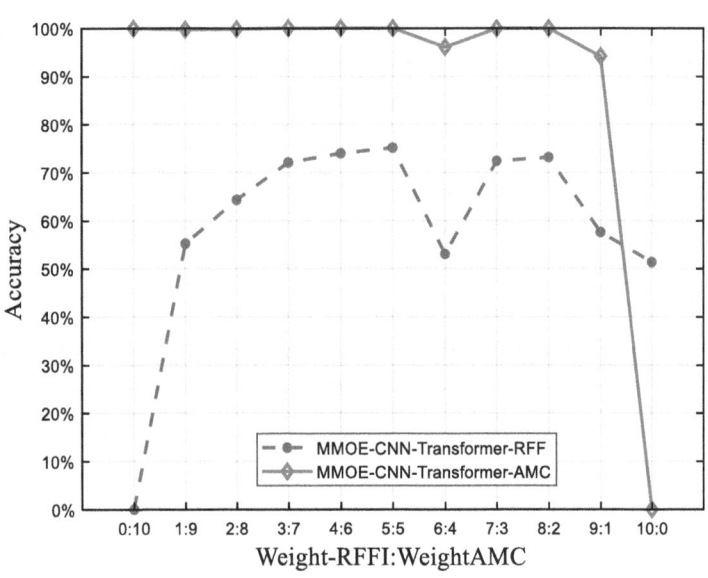

Fig. 7. Identification performance of RFFI and AMR tasks under different weights

4.4   Task Balance

In this section, the task balancing method in multi-task learning is studied, the unform represents the baseline method of task equal weight, the training process of MMOE-CNN-Transformer is optimized by using grid search, Dynamic Weight Average (DWA) [29], and uncertain [30] method, and decrease the weight distribution by using steps of 0.1 to set the weight ration of loss function of two signal recognition tasks, as shown in Fig. 7. It can be seen that when the weight ratio of RFFI and AMR is 1:1, the RFFI performance is improved to 75.14%, and the difference between the AMR recognition accuracy and other weight ratios is very small. Therefore, this weight is chosen as the best weight for grid search.

The specific results of different task balancing methods are shown in Table 4, in which the DWA method dynamically updates the weights to balance the training speed of the two methods. The accuracy of different task balancing methods for AMR tasks is almost the same, while the accuracy of the DWA method for RFFI tasks is the highest at 0, 5, 10, and 20 dB, and it is only 0.28% lower than that of the gridsearch method for RFFI tasks at 15 dB.

Table 4. Different task balancing methods identify effects

SNR	0 dB	5 dB	10 dB	15 dB	20 dB
MMOE-CNN-Transformer-RFF(uniform)	75.14%	90.89%	97.47%	99.17%	99.67%
MMOE-CNN-Transformer-AMR(uniform)	100%	100%	100%	100%	100%
MMOE-CNN-Transformer-RFF(grid)	75.14%	90.89%	97.47%	99.17%	99.67%
MMOE-CNN-Transformer-AMR(grid)	100%	100%	100%	100%	100%
MMOE-CNN-Transformer-RFF(uncertain)	74.28%	90.50%	97.22%	98.75%	99.17%
MMOE-CNN-Transformer–AMR(uncertain)	99.29%	100%	100%	100%	100%
MMOE-CNN-Transformer-RFF(DWA)	75.67%	90.97%	97.44%	98.89%	99.67%
MMOE-CNN-Transformer–AMR(DWA)	99.86%	100%	100%	100%	100%

5   Conclusion

In this paper, we design an MMOE-CNN-Transformer method to achieve two signal recognition tasks, i.e., AMR and RFFI. Experiments show that our method can access successfully better individual emitter recognition performance compared with single-task learning and hard-shared multi-task learning when the performance of AMR task is almost constant, especially in the case of low signal-to-noise ratio.The multi-task based method proposed by ge in this paper makes use of knowledge sharing among radiation source individuals with different modulation modes, so as to help better extract the characteristics of each radiation individual.

References

1. Zeyu, C.: 6G, LIFI and WIFI wireless systems: challenges, development and prospects. In: 2021 18th International Computer Conference on Wavelet Active Media Technology and Information Processing (ICCWAMTIP), pp. 322–325. IEEE (2021)

2. Restuccia, F., Melodia, T.: Deep learning at the physical layer: system challenges and applications to 5G and beyond. IEEE Commun. Mag. **58**(10), 58–64 (2020)
3. Kožović, D.V., Đurđević, D.Ž: Spoofing in aviation: security threats on GPS and ADS-B systems. Vojnotehnički glasnik/Mil. Tech. Courier **69**(2), 461–485 (2021)
4. Wong, L.J., Clark, W.H., Flowers, B., Buehrer, R.M., Headley, W.C., Michaels, A.J.: An RFML ecosystem: considerations for the application of deep learning to spectrum situational awareness. IEEE Open J. Commun. Soc. **2**, 2243–2264 (2021)
5. Soltanieh, N., Norouzi, Y., Yang, Y., Karmakar, N.C.: A review of radio frequency fingerprinting techniques. IEEE J. Radio Freq. Identif. **4**(3), 222–233 (2020)
6. Meng, F., Chen, P., Lenan, W., Wang, X.: Automatic modulation classification: a deep learning enabled approach. IEEE Trans. Veh. Technol. **67**(11), 10760–10772 (2018)
7. Lin, Y., Ya, T., Dou, Z.: An improved neural network pruning technology for automatic modulation classification in edge devices. IEEE Trans. Veh. Technol. **69**(5), 5703–5706 (2020)
8. Lin, Y., Ya, T., Dou, Z., Chen, L., Mao, S.: Contour stella image and deep learning for signal recognition in the physical layer. IEEE Trans. Cogn. Commun. Netw. **7**(1), 34–46 (2020)
9. Lin, Y., Wang, M., Zhou, X., Ding, G., Mao, S.: Dynamic spectrum interaction of UAV flight formation communication with priority: a deep reinforcement learning approach. IEEE Trans. Cogn. Commun. Netw. **6**(3), 892–903 (2020)
10. Lin, Y., Zhao, H., Ma, X., Ya, T., Wang, M.: Adversarial attacks in modulation recognition with convolutional neural networks. IEEE Trans. Reliab. **70**(1), 389–401 (2020)
11. Ya, T., Lin, Y., Hou, C., Mao, S.: Complex-valued networks for automatic modulation classification. IEEE Trans. Veh. Technol. **69**(9), 10085–10089 (2020)
12. Tu, Y., Lin, Y., Wang, J., Kim, J.U.: Semi-supervised learning with generative adversarial networks on digital signal modulation classification. Comput. Mater. Continua **55**(2) (2018)
13. Shen, G., Zhang, J., Marshall, A., Cavallaro, J.R.: Towards scalable and channel-robust radio frequency fingerprint identification for LoRa. IEEE Trans. Inf. Forensics Secur. **17**, 774–787 (2022)
14. Zha, H., et al.: LT-SEI: long-tailed specific emitter identification based on decoupled representation learning in low-resource scenarios. IEEE Trans. Intell. Transp. Syst. (2023)
15. Rehman, S.U., Sowerby, K.W., Alam, S., Ardekani, I.: Radio frequency fingerprinting and its challenges. In: 2014 IEEE Conference on Communications and Network Security, pp. 496–497. IEEE (2014)
16. Xing, Z., Gao, Y.: A modulation classification algorithm for multipath signals based on cepstrum. IEEE Trans. Instrum. Meas. **69**(7), 4742–4752 (2019)
17. Polak, A.C., Dolatshahi, S., Goeckel, D.L.: Identifying wireless users via transmitter imperfections. IEEE J. Sel. Areas Commun. **29**(7), 1469–1479 (2011)
18. Sun, J., Shi, W., Yang, Z., Yang, J., Gui, G.: Behavioral modeling and linearization of wideband RF power amplifiers using BiLSTM networks for 5G wireless systems. IEEE Trans. Veh. Technol. **68**(11), 10348–10356 (2019)
19. Feng, Z., Zha, H., Xu, C., He, Y., Lin, Y.: FCGCN: feature correlation graph convolution network for few-shot individual identification. IEEE Trans. Consum. Electron. (2023)

20. O'Shea, T.J., Corgan, J., Clancy, T.C.: Convolutional radio modulation recognition networks. In: Engineering Applications of Neural Networks: 17th International Conference, EANN 2016, Aberdeen, UK, September 2-5, 2016, Proceedings 17, pp. 213–226. Springer (2016)
21. Ya, T., et al.: Large-scale real-world radio signal recognition with deep learning. Chin. J. Aeronaut. **35**(9), 35–48 (2022)
22. Tang, P., Xu, Y., Ding, G., Jiao, Y., Song, Y., Wei, G.: Causal learning for robust specific emitter identification over unknown channel statistics. IEEE Trans. Inf. Forensics Secur. (2024)
23. Elmaghbub, A., Hamdaoui, B.: LoRa device fingerprinting in the wild: disclosing RF data-driven fingerprint sensitivity to deployment variability. IEEE Access **9**, 142893–142909 (2021)
24. Vandenhende, S., Georgoulis, S., Van Gansbeke, W., Proesmans, M., Dai, D., Van Gool, L.: Multi-task learning for dense prediction tasks: a survey. IEEE Trans. Pattern Anal. Mach. Intell. **44**(7), 3614–3633 (2021)
25. Crawshaw, M.: Multi-task learning with deep neural networks: a survey. arXiv preprint arXiv:2009.09796 (2020)
26. Ruder, S.: An overview of multi-task learning in deep neural networks. arXiv preprint arXiv:1706.05098 (2017)
27. Ma, J., Zhao, Z., Yi, X., Chen, J., Hong, L., Chi, E.H.: Modeling task relationships in multi-task learning with multi-gate mixture-of-experts. In: Proceedings of the 24th ACM SIGKDD International Conference on Knowledge Discovery & Data Mining, pp. 1930–1939 (2018)
28. Liu, H., Hao, C., Peng, Y., Wang, Y., Ohtsuki, T., Gui, G.: An effective radio frequency signal classification method based on multi-task learning mechanism. In: 2022 IEEE 96th Vehicular Technology Conference (VTC2022-Fall), pp. 1–5. IEEE (2022)
29. Liu, S., Johns, E., Davison, A.J.: End-to-end multi-task learning with attention. In: Proceedings of the IEEE/CVF Conference on Computer Vision and Pattern Recognition, pp. 1871–1880 (2019)
30. Kendall, A., Gal, Y., Cipolla, R.: Multi-task learning using uncertainty to weigh losses for scene geometry and semantics. In: Proceedings of the IEEE Conference on Computer Vision and Pattern Recognition, pp. 7482–7491 (2018)

Does LoRa Work for Vehicular Networks?

Wenwen Yang and Zijun Gong$^{(\boxtimes)}$

IoT Thrust, HKUST (Guangzhou), Guangzhou, China
wyang018@connect.hkust-gz.edu.cn, gongzijun@hkust-gz.edu.cn

Abstract. The low power wide area network (LPWAN) is the bone of the Internet of Things. As the most successful wireless access technique for LPWAN, LoRa modulation has been widely applied to low mobility or static use cases. But can we use LoRa for high mobility applications, such as outdoor assets or animal tracking? We will answer this question by investigating the possibility of using LoRa in vehicular networks. In LoRa modulation, both propagation delay and Doppler shift can potentially lead to symbol detection errors. Based on our analysis, these two channel parameters are playing very similar roles in deteriorating system performance, and a linear combination of them can be used to quantify how good/bad the channel is. A fundamental tradeoff between signal resilience to delay and Doppler spreads is unveiled, which sheds light on waveform design for LoRa modulation in doubly dispersive channels. This observation is verified through simulations.

Keywords: Chirp signal · LoRa modulation · Delay spread · Doppler spread

1 Introduction

In recent years, the rapid explosion of the Internet of Things (IoT) has revived the research interest in long range communication technologies. Unlike traditional cellular communications that primarily aim to improve spectral efficiency, energy efficiency and communication rate within small cells, IoT requires cost effective and wide area networks. The LoRa (Long Range) is one such technology designed specifically for low power and wide coverage, making it ideal for IoT devices [3].

The application of IoT is wide and diverse, encompassing various scenarios. Some IoT nodes are fixed indoors, and responsible for monitoring, collecting, and transmitting data. Other nodes may be mobile, potentially changing positions as people, vehicles, or other carriers move. The extent to which existing IoT wireless access technologies support node mobility has become a crucial question.

When signals are transmitted through wireless channels with multiple paths, different paths will experience different delays and Doppler shifts, i.e., delay spread and Doppler spread. Larger spreads lead to faster channel variation in time and frequency domains, and add challenges for reliable data detection. There are existing papers talking about the impacts of delay spread [4] and

H.-H. Chen and W. Meng (Eds.): WiSATS 2024, LNICST 605, pp. 338–345, 2025.
https://doi.org/10.1007/978-3-031-86196-3_29

Doppler spread [5] individually. But comprehensive performance evaluation of LoRa modulation in doubly dispersive channels is still missing.

This paper aims to investigate whether LoRa modulation works for vehicular networks, under large delay spread and Doppler spread simultaneously. We will use the symbol error rate (SER) as an evaluation metric [2]. In the following sections, we will first introduce the modulation and demodulation processes in the LoRa protocol. Subsequently, we will analyze the impacts of propagation delay and Doppler shift on the LoRa signals. Finally, we present simulation results to illustrate the system performance of LoRa under various delay and Doppler spread combinations.

2 LoRa Signal Model

2.1 Modulation

The LoRa modulation is a proprietary technique based on the spread spectrum communications technique, for increased communication range with reduced transmit power [1]. The signal spectrum is spread by modulating symbols on chirp signals, and the spreading factor SF is chosen from $\{7, \cdots, 12\}$. For a given spreading factor, there are totally $M = 2^{SF}$ possible symbols. Each symbol is modulated on a waveform of duration T_s, and the maximum instantaneous frequency is given by $B = M/T_s$, with $B \in \{125\,\text{kHz}, 250\,\text{kHz}, 500\,\text{kHz}\}$.

For a symbol $a \in \{0, 1, \cdots, M-1\}$, the instantaneous frequency starts at f_a and increases linearly at a rate of B/T_s until it reaches B. The instantaneous frequency will then be wrapped to 0 and continue to increase linearly at a rate of B/T_s. The instantaneous frequency of symbol a in a symbol duration can be written as

$$f_a(t) = \text{mod}\left(a\frac{B}{M} + \frac{B}{T_s}t, B\right). \tag{1}$$

Figure 1 illustrates the instantaneous frequency of the waveform corresponding to symbol a in the LoRa modulation. The instantaneous frequency reaches the maximum B at $t_a = T_s\left(1 - \frac{a}{M}\right)$. The instantaneous phase can be calculated by integrating the instantaneous frequency, given by

$$\phi_a(t) = 2\pi \int_0^{T_s} f_a(\tau)d\tau = \begin{cases} 2\pi\left(a\frac{B}{M}t + \frac{1}{2}\frac{B}{T_s}t^2\right), & 0 \leq t \leq t_a \\ 2\pi\left(a\frac{B}{M}t + \frac{1}{2}\frac{B}{T_s}t^2 - Bt\right), & t_a < t \leq T_s \end{cases}. \tag{2}$$

The waveform of the modulated signal can be expressed as

$$s_a(t) = e^{j2\pi\phi_a(t)} = \begin{cases} e^{j2\pi Bt\left(\frac{a}{M} + \frac{1}{2}\frac{t}{T_s}\right)}, & 0 \leq t \leq t_a \\ e^{j2\pi Bt\left(\frac{a}{M} + \frac{1}{2}\frac{t}{T_s} - 1\right)}, & t_a < t \leq T_s \end{cases}. \tag{3}$$

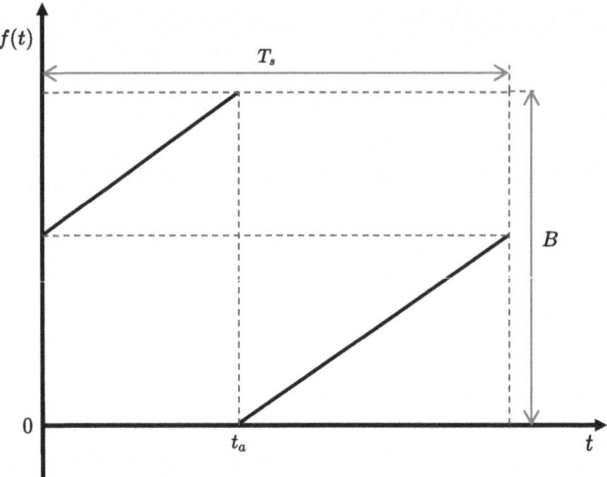

Fig. 1. LoRa signal representation.

2.2   Demodulation

As LoRa is a proprietary technology, its technical details have not been fully disclosed [6], and we don't know exactly how LoRa signals are demodulated in commercial LoRa chips. Nonetheless, many possible ways for demodulation can be found in the literature [7]. In this paper, we will focus on the maximum likelihood (MLE) detector.

For the additive white Gaussian noise channel, the received signal is

$$r(t) = s_a(t) + w(t), \tag{4}$$

where $w(t) \sim \mathcal{CN}(0, \sigma^2)$ is a zero mean complex white Gaussian noise. Then the received signal is correlated with the reference signal $s_0^*(t) = e^{-j2\pi \frac{1}{2} \frac{B}{T_s} t^2}$ to get the detection signal $d(t)$

$$d(t) = r(t)s_0^*(t) = \begin{cases} e^{j2\pi Bt\frac{a}{M}} + \tilde{w}(t), & 0 \le t \le t_a \\ e^{j2\pi Bt\left(\frac{a}{M}-1\right)} + \tilde{w}(t), & t_a < t \le T_s \end{cases}, \tag{5}$$

where $\tilde{w}(t) = w(t)s_0^*(t)$.

Then we can discretize the signal $d(t)$ with a sampling interval of $T = 1/B$, and the sampled sequence is

$$d[n] = d(nT) = e^{j2\pi a \frac{n}{M}} + \tilde{w}[n], \tag{6}$$

where $\tilde{w}[n] = \tilde{w}(nT)$. This is a discrete complex sinusoid contaminated by white noise, and our goal is to estimate a. This can be done by computing the discrete

Fourier transform (DFT) of $d[n]$ as

$$
\begin{aligned}
D[k] &= \sum_{n=0}^{M-1} d[n] e^{-j2\pi k \frac{n}{M}} \\
&= \frac{1 - e^{j2\pi(a-k)}}{1 - e^{j2\pi\left(\frac{a}{M} - \frac{k}{M}\right)}} + \tilde{W}[k] \\
&= M\delta(k-a) + \tilde{W}[k],
\end{aligned}
\tag{7}
$$

where $\tilde{W}[k] = \sum_{n=0}^{M-1} \tilde{w}[n] e^{-j2\pi k \frac{n}{M}}$ is the DFT of the noise and $\delta(\cdot)$ is a Dirac delta function, defined as

$$
\delta(t) = \begin{cases} 1, t = 0 \\ 0, t \neq 0 \end{cases}.
\tag{8}
$$

The symbol detection is then conducted by $\hat{a} = \arg\max_k |D[k]|$. The magnitude $|D[k]|$ is thus given by

$$
|D[k]| = \begin{cases} M + \tilde{W}[a], & k = a \\ \tilde{W}[k], & k \neq a \end{cases}.
\tag{9}
$$

As we can see, the LoRa modulation is reliable in ideal wireless channels, with no delay or Doppler spread. In the following section, we will investigate the impact of doubly dispersive channels on LoRa signals.

3   LoRa Signal in Doubly Dispersive Channels

In general, the delay and Doppler spread deform communication signals in very different ways. However, they will manifest themselves on LoRa signals with similar consequences. It turns out that the LoRa signals have limited capacities for distortion resilience, shared by both delay and Doppler spreads. We will first investigate the impacts of delay and Doppler shift on LoRa signals, and then consider them jointly.

3.1   Impact of Doppler Shift

When there is a relative velocity between the transmitter and the receiver, the received signal frequency will change, resulting in a Doppler shift. The received signal with Doppler shift ν is

$$
r_d(t) = e^{j2\pi\nu t} s_a(t) + w(t).
\tag{10}
$$

The instantaneous frequency of the signal will thus be changed by ν Hz, resulting in a vertical shift demonstrated in Fig. 2. A positive Doppler shift causes the signal to move upward, while a negative one leads to a downward shift. This shift will boost the possibility of incorrect decisions in symbol detection.

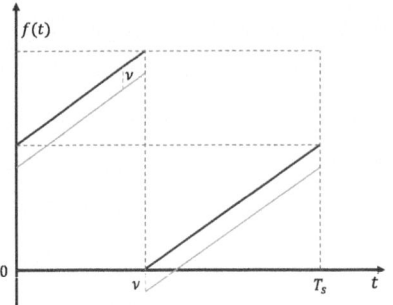

Fig. 2. Impact of Doppler shift.   **Fig. 3.** Impact of propagation delay.

The detection signal will also be shifted by ν Hz in this case, and the DFT of the sampled detection signal is given by

$$D_d[k] = e^{-j2\pi B\tau} \sum_{n=0}^{M-1} e^{-j2\pi \frac{n}{M}(k-(a+\nu T_s))} + \tilde{W}[k]. \tag{11}$$

When νT_s is exactly an integer, the peak of the spectrum will be identified as $k = a + \nu T_s$, leading to a symbol detection error. The distance between two symbols in the frequency domain is B/M, and a Doppler shift of $B/M/2$ will significantly deteriorate the system performance.

3.2   Impact of Propagation Delay

The received signal with a propagation delay τ is given as

$$r_p(t) = s_a(t - \tau) + w(t). \tag{12}$$

A propagation delay leads to a horizontal shift of the instantaneous frequency, depicted in Fig. 3, leading to an increased detection error rate.

The detection signal will also experience a delay of τ. We can then get the DFT of the sampled detection signal as

$$\begin{aligned} D_p[k] = e^{-j\theta_1} &\sum_{n=0}^{M-a+\lfloor B\tau \rfloor} e^{j2\pi \frac{n}{M}(a-B\tau-k)} \\ + e^{-j\theta_2} &\sum_{M-a+\lfloor B\tau \rfloor+1}^{M-1} e^{j2\pi \frac{n}{M}(a-B\tau-k)} + \tilde{W}[k], \end{aligned} \tag{13}$$

where $\theta_1 = 2\pi B\tau \left(\frac{a}{M} - \frac{\tau}{2T_s}\right)$ and $\theta_2 = 2\pi B\tau \left(\frac{a}{M} - \frac{\tau}{2T_s} - 1\right)$. Both θ_1 and θ_2 are the phase factors independent of n and we are only concerned with the magnitude of $|D_p[k]|$. So we can simplify the expression

$$|D_p[k]| = \left| \sum_{n=0}^{M-1} e^{-j2\pi \frac{n}{M}(k-(a-B\tau))} + \tilde{W}[k] \right|. \tag{14}$$

The propagation delay will cause a shift of the spectrum of the detection signal, leading to increased symbol detection error rate. Similar to the case of the Doppler shift, when $a - B\tau$ is an integer, the peak value is obtained at $k = a - B\tau$.

Interestingly, a propagation of τ will approximately lead to a peak shift of τB in the spectrum of detection signal. Recall that a Doppler shift of ν means a peak shift of νT_s in the spectrum shift. The delay and Doppler shift are actually playing very similar roles in deteriorating system performance.

3.3 Joint Impact of Delay and Doppler

Consider a doubly dispersive channel with L propagation paths, and the received signal will be

$$r(t) = A_0 s_a(t) + \sum_{l=1}^{L-1} A_l e^{-j2\pi\nu_l(t-\tau_l)} s_a(t - \tau_l) + w(t). \tag{15}$$

where A_l, ν_l and τ_l are the overall attenuation, propagation delay and Doppler shift in the l-th path.

After the correlation and sampling, we can get the DFT of the detection signal as

$$D[k] = MA_0\delta(k - a) + \sum_{l=1}^{L-1} \tilde{A}_l \sum_{n=0}^{M-1} e^{j2\pi\frac{n}{M}(a-B\tau_l-T_s\nu_l-k)} + \tilde{W}[k], \tag{16}$$

where $\tilde{A}_l = A_l e^{2\pi B\frac{\tau_l}{M}(a-B\tau_l/2-\nu_l T_s)}$. Clearly, Doppler shift and propagation delay lead to a peak shift of $\tau_l B + \nu_l T_s$. A larger shift means an increased possibility of symbol detection error rate. For two different combinations of delay and Doppler shift, i.e., (τ_1, ν_1) and (τ_2, ν_2), as long as $\tau_1 B + \nu_1 T_s = \tau_2 B + \nu_2 T_s$, the overall impact on system performance will be approximately the same. This is visually demonstrated in Fig. 4.

4 Simulation Results

In this section, we present the simulation results obtained using MATLAB to evaluate the performance of LoRa modulation under various conditions. Figure 5 illustrates the performance of different spreading factors under an AWGN channel. Figure 6 demonstrates the performance characteristics for a bandwidth of 125 kHz and a spreading factor of 8, where the combination of delay and Doppler shifts maintains a constant value of 0.35. It can be observed that the performance of the signal remains the same for different combinations of delay and Doppler, validating our previous assertion.

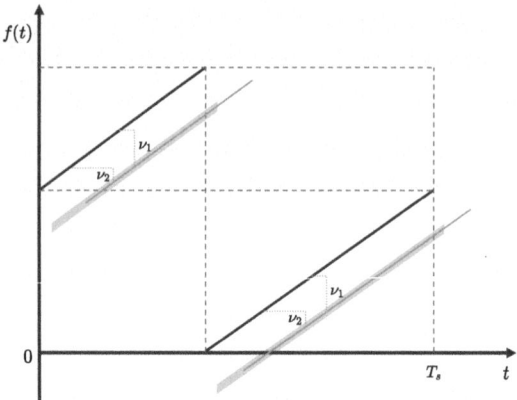

Fig. 4. Different groups of delay and Doppler.

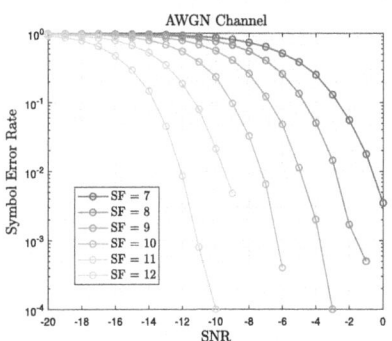

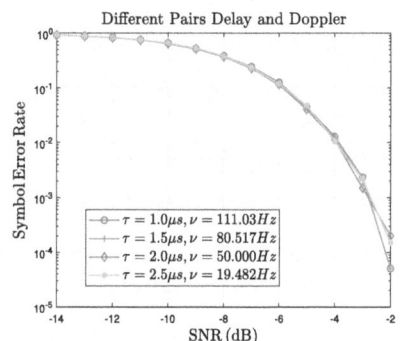

Fig. 5. Performance of different spreading factors under AWGN channel.

Fig. 6. Constant impact of different delay and Doppler.

5   Conclusion and Future Work

In this paper, we investigated the feasibility of LoRa modulation in vehicular networks, focusing on the impacts of propagation delay and Doppler shift. The primary goal was to assess whether LoRa could maintain reliable communication performance under typical vehicular conditions. We analyzed the effects of delay and Doppler separately. Our analysis shows that the impact of delay and Doppler on signal demodulation is similar. A metric is identified to quantify the overall impact of delay spread and Doppler spread, which is confirmed by our simulation results. In future work, we will consider adjust the modulation parameter like spreading factor and bandwidth in order to enhance the robustness and reliability of LoRa modulation in vehicular networks.

Acknowledgement. Z. Gong is the corresponding author. This work was supported in part by the National Natural Science Foundation of China (62201162); in part by the Guangzhou-HKUST(GZ) Joint Funding Scheme (2023A03J0132); in part by the Guangzhou Basic and Applied Basic Research Scheme (2024A04J4303); in part by the Guangdong Provincial Key Lab of Integrated Communication, Sensing and Computation for Ubiquitous Internet of Things (2023B1212010007); in part by Guangzhou Municipal Science and Technology Project (2023A03J0011).

References

1. Adelantado, F., Vilajosana, X., Tuset-Peiro, P., Martinez, B., Melia-Segui, J., Watteyne, T.: Understanding the limits of LoRaWAN. IEEE Commun. Mag. **55**(9), 34–40 (2017). https://doi.org/10.1109/MCOM.2017.1600613
2. Afisiadis, O., Cotting, M., Burg, A., Balatsoukas-Stimming, A.: On the error rate of the LoRa modulation with interference. IEEE Trans. Wireless Commun. **19**(2), 1292–1304 (2019)
3. Centenaro, M., Vangelista, L., Zanella, A., Zorzi, M.: Long-range communications in unlicensed bands: the rising stars in the IoT and smart city scenarios. IEEE Wirel. Commun. **23**(5), 60–67 (2016). https://doi.org/10.1109/MWC.2016.7721743
4. Demeslay, C., Rostaing, P., Gautier, R.: Theoretical performance of LoRa system in multipath and interference channels. IEEE Internet Things J. **9**(9), 6830–6843 (2021)
5. Petäjäjärvi, J., Mikhaylov, K., Pettissalo, M., Janhunen, J., Iinatti, J.: Performance of a low-power wide-area network based on LoRa technology: doppler robustness, scalability, and coverage. Int. J. Distrib. Sens. Netw. **13**(3), 1550147717699412 (2017)
6. Seller, O.B.A., Sornin, N.: Low power long range transmitter. U.S. Patent US9252834B2 (2016). assigned to Semtech Corporation. https://patents.google.com/patent/US20140219329A1/en
7. Vangelista, L.: Frequency shift chirp modulation: the LoRa modulation. IEEE Signal Process. Lett. **24**(12), 1818–1821 (2017)

On the Stability of Random Access
with Congestion Control

Yu Xu[1], Chen Cui[2], Zhenyong Wang[1,3(✉)], and Qing Guo[1]

[1] School of Electronics and Information Engineering, Harbin Institute of
Technology, Harbin 150001, China
{xu_yu,zywang,qguo}@hit.edu.cn

[2] National Engineering Research Center of Visual Technology, School of Computer
Science, Peking University, Beijing 100871, China
chencui@pku.edu.cn

[3] Songjiang Laboratory, Harbin Institute of Technology, Harbin 150001, China

Abstract. The random access protocol is a critical technique widely
used in various wireless networks. A significant challenge is analyzing
the stability of the random access system when a large number of users
transmit packets independently. Although the congestion control policy
can enhance the stability of the system, there is currently a lack of quantitative analysis on the stability of random access with congestion control. In this paper, we analyze the random access system with congestion
control and quantify its stability. Specifically, we consider a congestion
control scheme to enhance the stability of the random access system and
present the graphical analytical model. Based on this graphical model, we
qualitatively discuss the behavioral variations of the system as it works
and quantify its stability.

Keywords: Random access · Slotted ALOHA · Retransmission
policy · Congestion control · Stability analysis

1 Introduction

The random access protocol is a critical technique widely used in various wireless
networks. Among them, slotted ALOHA [1] enjoys high popularity. In slotted
ALOHA systems, users share a channel without coordination, which can lead
to signal collisions. Due to signal collisions resulting from two or more users
accessing the channel simultaneously, the peak throughput of a slotted ALOHA
system is limited to 0.37. Numerous studies focus on enhancing the throughput
performance of slotted ALOHA systems, which determines the allowable number of users accessing wireless networks. Based on slotted ALOHA, the study
in [2] proposes diversity slotted ALOHA (DSA) to enhance throughput performance, which only outperforms slotted ALOHA slightly at low normalized

This work was supported by the National Natural Science Foundation of China (No.
62301008) and the research project fund of Songjiang Laboratory (No. SL20230104).

H.-H. Chen and W. Meng (Eds.): WiSATS 2024, LNICST 605, pp. 346–360, 2025.
https://doi.org/10.1007/978-3-031-86196-3_30

loads. A breakthrough in random access is contention resolution diversity slotted ALOHA (CRDSA) [3], which combines diversity transmission with successive interference cancellation (SIC) to enhance throughput performance. Specifically, each user repeatedly transmits a packet over a medium access control (MAC) frame. The receiver attempts to decode the non-collision packets and subtracts the decoded packets from the slots in which their copies are located. Based on CRDSA, [4] introduces irregular repetition slotted ALOHA (IRSA). In contrast to CRDSA, where the packet repetition rate is the same for all users, in IRSA, the packet repetition rate is chosen according to an optimized probability distribution. Additionally, coded slotted ALOHA (CSA) is proposed in [5], where users utilize erasure-correcting codes on packet segments instead of directly repeating the packet, and then transmit the encoded packet segments in the shared channel. In [6], it is proven that the throughput of the SIC-based ALOHA scheme can be arbitrarily close to 1 in the asymptotic frame size setting, which is the upper bound on performance without considering the capture effect and multiple user detection techniques.

In addition to enhancing throughput performance, another crucial aspect of the research on random access is analyzing the stability of the system. In general random access research, it is commonly assumed that for a given channel traffic, an equilibrium point is reached where the average number of packet transmissions is equal to the average number of successful packet transmissions. However, when considering the number of previous unsuccessful retransmissions, the random access system becomes inherently unstable. Actually, the retransmission policy is a key element in ensuring the reliability of data transmission in most wireless networks [7]. Only a few studies concentrate on analyzing the stability of the random access system with a retransmission policy. [8,9] formulate the mathematical analytical model for the slotted ALOHA system with a retransmission policy and discuss its stability, respectively. Following this, [10,11] extend the analytical model and method presented in [8,9] to the CRDSA system, respectively. Furthermore, [12] investigates the stability of an asynchronous random access system by adopting the analytical model in [9]. On the other hand, to enhance the stability of the random access system, [13] proposes several congestion control schemes to prevent the system from becoming unstable, and [14] applies these congestion control schemes to the CRDSA system. However, the current research on the stability of random access with congestion control focuses on qualitatively discussing the behavioral variations of the system, especially in terms of throughput and delay performance. There is a lack of quantitative analysis on the stability of random access with congestion control, which is crucial for calculating the maximum allowable number of accessing users and measuring the performance improvement of the congestion control scheme.

To bridge this gap, in this paper, we analyze the random access system with congestion control and quantify its stability. We initially analyze the stability of several uncontrolled random access systems and discuss their limitations. Subsequently, we consider a congestion control scheme to enhance the stability of the system and present the graphical analytical model. Based on this graphical model, we qualitatively discuss the behavioral variations of the system as it works and quantify its stability.

The rest of this paper is organized as follows: In Sect. 2, we provide a brief review of the SIC-based ALOHA scheme. Section 3 analyzes the stability of several uncontrolled random access systems. In Sect. 4, a congestion control scheme and the corresponding graphical analytical model are presented. In Sect. 5, we analyze the stability of random access with congestion control qualitatively and quantitatively based on the graphical analytical model. This paper concludes in Sect. 6.

2   Review of SIC-Based ALOHA Scheme

In this section, we briefly review the SIC-based ALOHA scheme, which represents the current advanced random access schemes, and analyze its stability later. More details and relative performance analysis can be referred to [3,4]. When transmitting, we consider the time division multiple access (TDMA) scheme, where the transmission period is a TDMA frame, and each TDMA frame consists of n slots with the same duration. In each TDMA frame, the number of active users is denoted by m. Each active user attempts to transmit a packet and makes only one transmission, which means no retransmission occurs within the same TDMA frame. The packet duration is equal to the slot duration if guard time is neglected, and the packets keep slot synchronization. The normalized channel traffic G is defined as $G = m/n$ and represents the average number of packet transmissions per slot. The normalized throughput T is the average number of successful packet transmissions per slot.

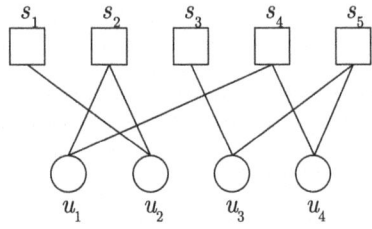

Fig. 1. The bipartite graph representation of a random access process within a TDMA frame, where $m = 4$, $n = 5$, and $l = 2$ for all users.

In the SIC-based ALOHA scheme, each user appends a pointer to the data payload to create a packet. When transmitting, each user creates l packet copies and transmits them over l slots selected randomly from the n slots within a TDMA frame, where l is a design parameter denoting the packet repetition rate. The pointer serves the function of indicating the slots where the other copies are located. For CRDSA, the packet repetition rate is the same for all users, while for IRSA, the packet repetition rate is determined according to an optimized probability distribution termed the degree distribution. According to [4], it is beneficial to represent the random access process within a TDMA frame using a bipartite graph. Figure 1 depicts the bipartite graph representation of an example random access process. The circular nodes are user nodes whose packets need recovery, while the square nodes are slot nodes indicating the received signals in corresponding slots. If user k transmits a packet copy in the jth slot, it creates an edge between u_k and s_j.

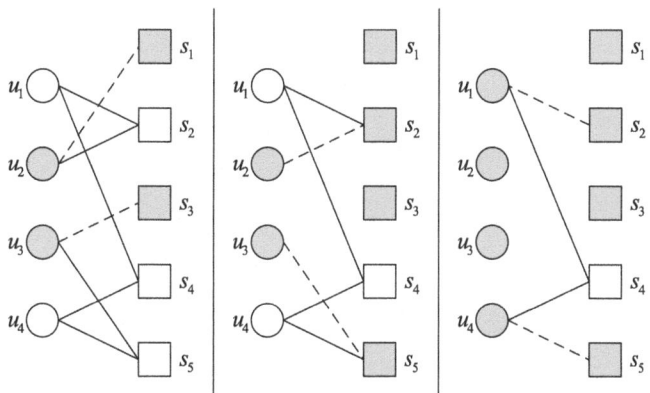

Fig. 2. The bipartite graph representation of the SIC decoding process.

Whenever a packet copy is detected and successfully decoded in a collision-free slot, the receiver reconstructs and subtracts the interference signal in the slots where the other copies are located according to the embedded pointer using the SIC decoding algorithm. As a result, the collision slots may be transformed into collision-free slots, allowing for successful decoding of packet copies from other users in these slots. The SIC decoding algorithm is performed iteratively until no collision-free slots remain. The bipartite graph representation of the SIC decoding process is shown in Fig. 2. Specifically, s_1 and s_3 are collision-free slots where the packet copies of u_2 and u_3 are detected and successfully decoded. The receiver reconstructs and subtracts the interference signals of u_2 and u_3 in s_2 and s_5, respectively. Consequently, s_2 and s_5 are converted into collision-free slots, and the packet copies of u_1 and u_4 can also be detected and successfully decoded.

Figure 3 presents a normalized throughput performance comparison for various random access schemes, where $n = 100$ and the degree distribution of IRSA is $\Lambda(x) = 0.5x^2 + 0.28x^3 + 0.22x^8$ [4]. As depicted in Fig. 3, all performance curves exhibit a trend of increasing and then decreasing as G increases. Hence, there exists a peak throughput for each random access scheme, denoted as T_p. As G increases, when T exceeds T_p, the larger the T_p, the more sharply T descends. However, in the following section, we will discuss that the system may actually

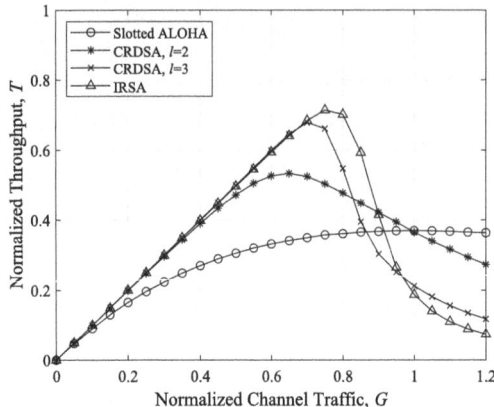

Fig. 3. Normalized throughput performance comparison for various random access schemes.

fail to achieve the theoretical peak throughput of the random access scheme when considering the previous unsuccessful retransmissions, which may lead to system congestion.

3 Stability Analysis for Uncontrolled Random Access Systems

In this section, we analyze the stability of several uncontrolled random access systems and discuss their limitations. Our analysis is based on a graphical representation of the random access process similar to that in [9,11]. However, we specifically focus on the traffic model involving an infinite population, which is closer to the real application scenario where a large number of users transmit packets independently, regardless of whether previous transmissions are still pending or not. Figure 4 depicts the graphical model for the uncontrolled random access system with a retransmission policy within a TDMA frame. Defining:

N_A^f: the number of newly arrived active users in the fth frame, which is a Poisson random variable with parameter λ, i.e., $N_A^f \sim Poisson(\lambda)$

N_B^f: the number of backlogged users whose packets were unsuccessfully received in the fth frame

$G_T^f = N_A^f/n$: the normalized channel traffic coming from the packet transmissions of the newly arrived active users in the fth frame

$G_B^f = N_B^{(f-1)}/n$: the normalized channel traffic coming from the packet retransmissions of the backlogged users in the fth frame

$G_{IN}^f = G_T^f + G_B^f$: the sum normalized channel traffic in the fth frame

$T^f = G_{IN}^f \left(1 - plr(G_{IN}^f, n)\right)$: the normalized throughput in the fth frame, where $plr(\cdot)$ is the packet loss rate of the random access scheme.

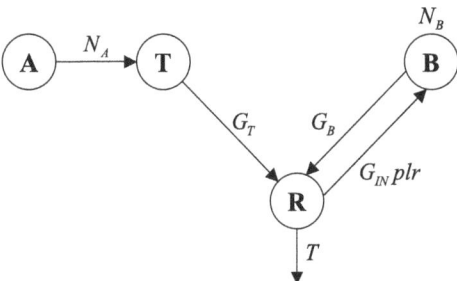

Fig. 4. Graphical model for the uncontrolled random access system with a retransmission policy.

When the random access system works in a stable state, we have

$$G_T = T = G_{IN} \cdot (1 - plr\,(G_{IN}, n)), \tag{1}$$

and

$$N_B = G_{IN} \cdot plr\,(G_{IN}, n) \cdot n, \tag{2}$$

where the superscript f is omitted, which means that in each frame, the newly offered channel traffic should be approximately equal to the throughput, and the number of backlogged users should remain constant dynamically. Equations (1) and (2) completely describe the equilibrium contour on the (G_T, N_B) plane, which is proposed in [9,11] to analyze the behavioral variations of the system. Since the number of newly arrived active users in each frame can be modeled as a Poisson random variable with parameter λ, the channel load line is defined as

$$G_T = \frac{\lambda}{n}, \tag{3}$$

which means that the newly offered channel traffic is constant and independent of the number of backlogged users.

Figure 5 depicts the equilibrium contours for various random access schemes and the channel load line, where $n = 100$, $\lambda = 45$, and the degree distribution of IRSA is set to $\Lambda(x) = 0.5x^2 + 0.28x^3 + 0.22x^8$. Here, we simply cite the conclusion regarding the relationship between the stability of the random access system and the equilibrium contour, and a more detailed analysis can be found in [9,11]. As can be seen from the figure, the channel load line and each equilibrium contour may have one, two, or no intersection points. If the number of intersection points is one or zero, the random access system is unstable, whereas if the number of intersection points is two, the random access system is locally stable. Specifically, we assume that there are two intersection points between the channel load line and an equilibrium contour, denoted as N_B^S and N_B^U, where $N_B^U > N_B^S$. When N_B, the number of backlogged users, satisfies $0 \le N_B < N_B^U$, it shows a tendency to converge to N_B^S as the system works, indicating that N_B^S

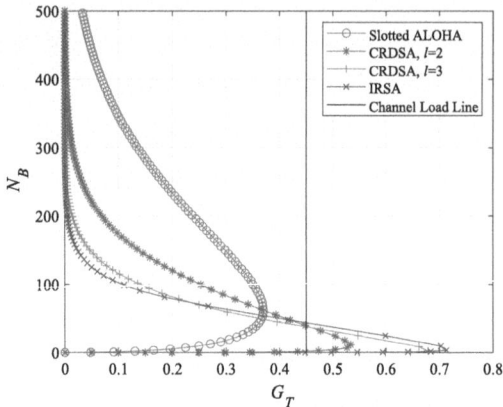

Fig. 5. Equilibrium contours for various random access schemes.

is a locally stable equilibrium point. Once $N_B \geq N_B^U$ due to statistical variations, N_B will increase to infinity as the system works, thus N_B^U is an unstable
equilibrium point. Consequently, the random access system is locally stable.

To illustrate the essence of system stability, Fig. 6 depicts the variation trends
of the normalized throughput and the number of backlogged users as the system
works in a stable state for IRSA, respectively, where $n = 100$, $\lambda = 55$, and the
degree distribution of IRSA is set to $\Lambda(x) = 0.5x^2 + 0.28x^3 + 0.22x^8$. As can be
seen from the figure, the average offered channel traffic is approximately equal to
the average throughput, and the number of backlogged users remains constant
in each frame dynamically, consistent with the previous description. Moreover,

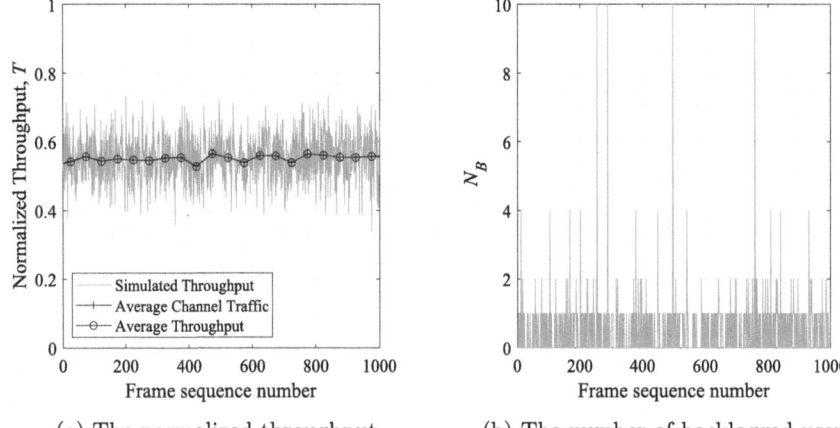

(a) The normalized throughput   (b) The number of backlogged users

Fig. 6. The variation trends of the performance metrics as the system works for IRSA
with $\lambda = 55$ (stable state).

the simulated throughput and the number of backlogged users in each frame fluctuate around a certain value as the system works, respectively. Theoretically, the values correspond to the locally stable equilibrium point N_B^S in Fig. 5.

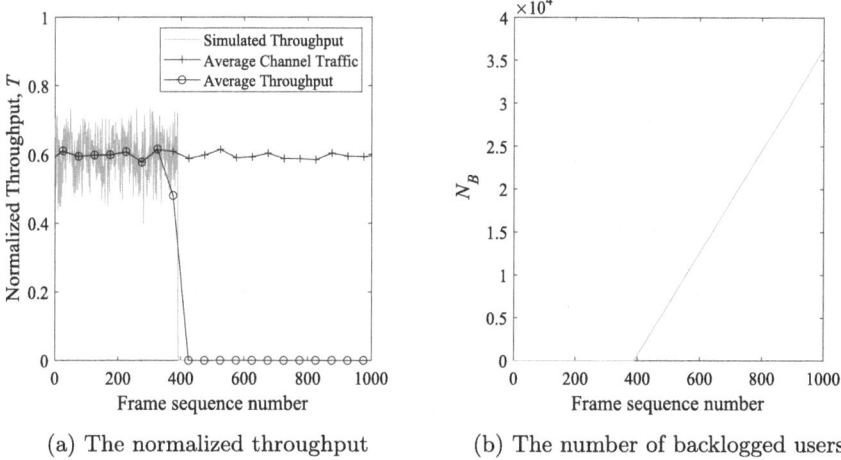

(a) The normalized throughput   (b) The number of backlogged users

Fig. 7. The variation trends of the performance metrics as the system works for IRSA with $\lambda = 60$ (unstable state).

For comparison, Fig. 7 presents the variation trends of the same performance metrics as the system works with $\lambda = 60$. However, what differs from Fig. 6 is that at a specific moment, the number of backlogged users, N_B, exceeds the unstable equilibrium point N_B^U due to statistical variations, leading to system congestion and thus nonfunctional. In this case, the throughput rapidly converges to zero, and the number of backlogged users increases infinitely as the system works. As discussed in the analysis of the simulation results shown in Fig. 3, if the offered channel traffic exceeds the threshold at which the system achieves peak throughput, the throughput will decrease sharply, resulting in a rapid increase in the number of backlogged users. The increase in the number of backlogged users, in turn, causes the offered channel traffic to exceed the threshold again, leading to a vicious cycle that results in system congestion.

It is obvious that the probability of the random access system becoming unstable increases as λ rises. To quantify stability, [9] proposes the concept of average first exit time (FET), defined as the average time that a random access system takes from startup to being in an unstable state. Apparently, the longer the average FET is taken, the more stable the random access system works. Figure 8 compares the average FET for various random access schemes, where $n = 100$. Combined with the simulation results shown in Fig. 3, it can be seen that the higher the peak throughput performance of the random access scheme, the greater its stability. Moreover, taking IRSA as an example, the maximum

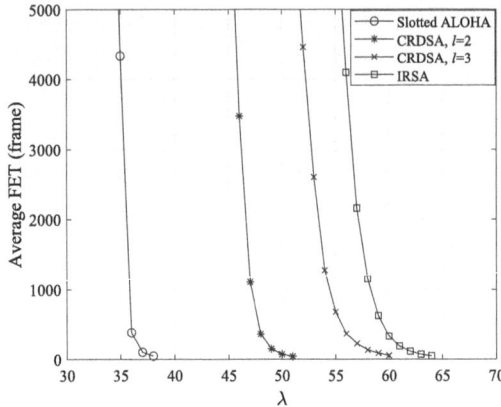

Fig. 8. Average FET for various random access schemes.

allowable average number of accessing users is $\lambda = 55$ to achieve the target average FET of 5000 frames. When λ exceeds this value, the stability of the random access system decreases rapidly. In this case, the achievable maximum normalized throughput of the system is approximately $T = 0.55$, which has a significant gap with the theoretical peak throughput of IRSA in Fig. 3. Consequently, to ensure system stability in light of previous unsuccessful retransmissions, it is essential to restrict the maximum average number of accessing users to a relatively lower value, thus preventing the system from achieving the theoretical peak throughput performance of the random access scheme.

4   The Congestion Control Scheme

In this section, we consider a congestion control scheme to enhance the stability of the random access system and present the corresponding graphical analytical model. The congestion control scheme operates by controlling the access probability for active users. Despite its simplicity, it has proven to be highly effective in practice. The random access process with congestion control is depicted in Fig. 9.

In Fig. 9, for a newly arrived active user with a packet to transmit, the first step is to determine whether the packet is permitted for transmission in the current frame according to the congestion control policy. Specifically, the receiver calculates the control factor, denoted as p_c, based on the estimation of the current number of active users, where $0 \leq p_c \leq 1$. Subsequently, the receiver broadcasts the calculated control factor to all active users over the downlink broadcast channel. Each active user independently generates a random number between 0 and 1 and compares it with the received control factor p_c. If the random number is smaller than p_c, the user is permitted to transmit the packet in the current frame; otherwise, the user needs to wait until the next frame to repeat the aforementioned process.

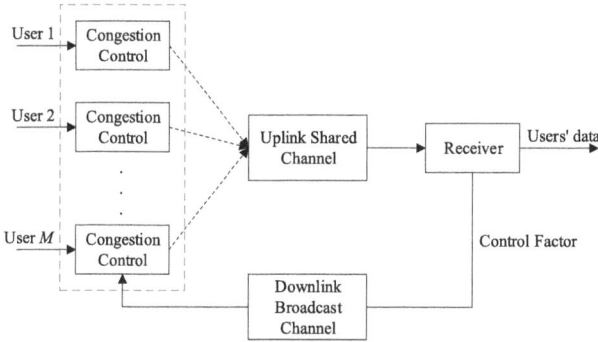

Fig. 9. The random access process with congestion control.

A critical point in designing the congestion control policy is the calculation of the control factor p_c. In the considered congestion control scheme, the control factor is calculated as

$$p_c = \min\left(1, \frac{G^* n}{\hat{M}}\right),\tag{4}$$

where G^* is the threshold of the offered channel traffic at which the system achieves peak throughput of the random access scheme, n is the number of slots contained in a TDMA frame, and $\hat{M}$ is the estimated number of active users in the current frame at the receiver. To simplify the analysis, we assume a perfect estimation of the number of active users at the receiver. It is designed so that when the offered channel traffic exceeds the corresponding threshold of the random access scheme, the expected average channel traffic is controlled to G^*.

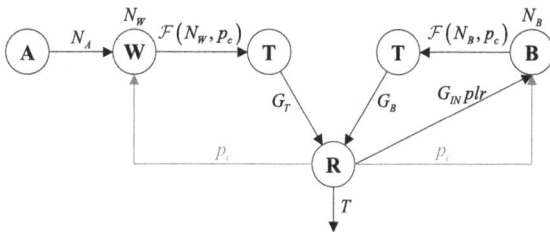

Fig. 10. Graphical model for the random access system with congestion control.

To analyze stability, Fig. 10 presents the graphical model for the random access system with congestion control, defining:

N_A^f: the number of newly arrived active users in the fth frame, which is a Poisson random variable with parameter λ, i.e., $N_A^f \sim Poisson(\lambda)$

$N_W^f = N_W^{(f-1)} - \mathcal{F}\left(N_W^{(f-1)}, p_c^{(f-1)}\right) + N_A^f$: the number of active users in a waiting state in the fth frame, each with a packet to transmit, including both the newly arrived active users and those who were previously prohibited from transmitting the packet due to the congestion control policy. $\mathcal{F}\left(N_W^f, p_c^f\right)$ denotes the number of active users in a waiting state permitted to transmit the packet in the fth frame

N_B^f: the number of backlogged users whose packets were unsuccessfully received in the fth frame and previous frames

p_c^f: the control factor in the fth frame, calculated by the receiver according to (4)

$G_T^f = \mathcal{F}\left(N_W^f, p_c^f\right)/n$: the normalized channel traffic coming from the packet transmissions by some of the active users in a waiting state in the fth frame

$G_B^f = \mathcal{F}\left(N_B^{(f-1)}, p_c^f\right)/n$: the normalized channel traffic coming from the packet retransmissions by some of the backlogged users in the fth frame

$G_{IN}^f = G_T^f + G_B^f$: the sum normalized channel traffic in the fth frame

$T^f = G_{IN}^f\left(1 - plr(G_{IN}^f, n)\right)$: the normalized throughput in the fth frame, where $plr(\cdot)$ is the packet loss rate of the random access scheme.

5   Simulation Results

In this section, we analyze the stability of the random access system with congestion control based on the graphical model in Fig. 10. Figure 11 presents the variation trends of the relevant performance metrics as the system works in a stable state for IRSA with congestion control, where $n = 100$, $\lambda = 65$, and the degree distribution of IRSA is set to $\Lambda(x) = 0.5x^2 + 0.28x^3 + 0.22x^8$. It can be seen that the variation trends in Fig. 11 exhibit some similarities with those in Fig. 6. Specifically, the average offered channel traffic is approximately equal to the average throughput. In contrast, the number of backlogged users fluctuates more sharply around a certain value compared to that in Fig. 6. As for the number of users in a waiting state, it varies dynamically but remains finite.

However, as λ continues to increase, the random access system with congestion control will eventually become unstable. To this end, Fig. 12 presents the variation trends of the same performance metrics as the system works for IRSA with congestion control in the case of $\lambda = 68$, which is the average number of accessing users that can lead to the system becoming unstable with high probability. In contrast to those shown in Fig. 7, when the average offered channel traffic is not equal to the average throughput due to statistical variations, indicating that the system becomes unstable, the throughput of the IRSA system with congestion control does not tend to 0, but instead fluctuates dynamically around a relatively lower value. However, since the average offered channel traffic exceeds the average throughput, both the number of backlogged users and the number of users in a waiting state grow infinitely, but the number of backlogged

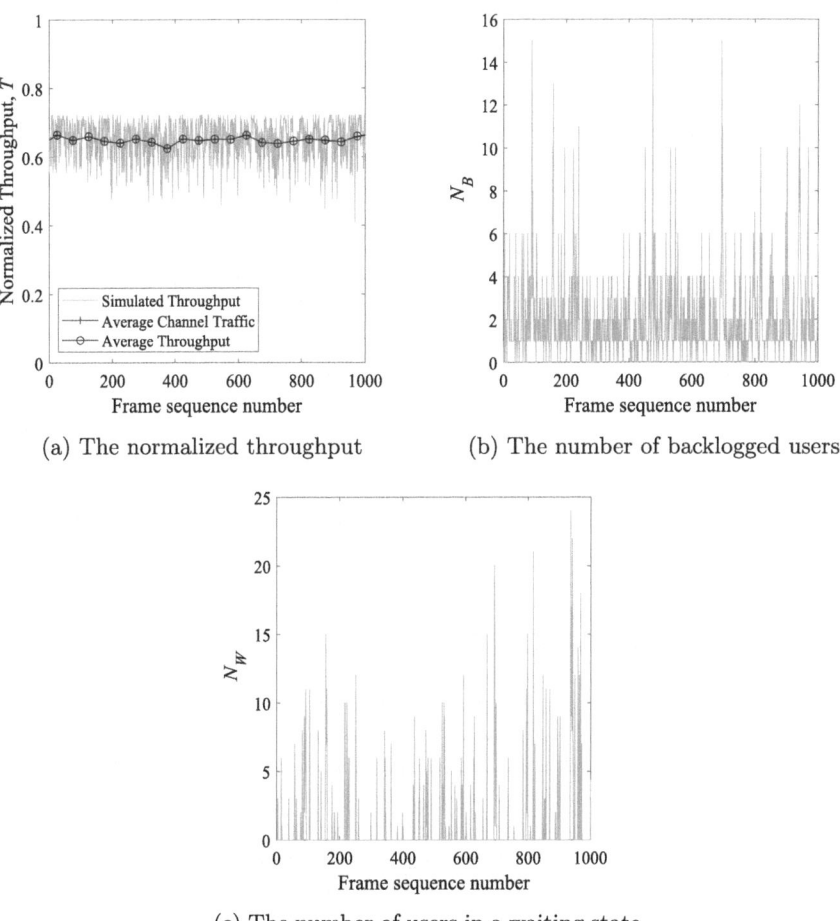

(a) The normalized throughput

(b) The number of backlogged users

(c) The number of users in a waiting state

Fig. 11. The variation trends of the performance metrics as the system works for IRSA with congestion control (stable state), $\lambda = 65$.

users increases much more slowly compared to that in the uncontrolled system shown in Fig. 7.

To measure the performance improvement of the congestion control scheme, it is essential to quantify the stability of a random access system with congestion control. However, the calculation algorithm for FET proposed in [9], which is based on calculating the probability that the number of backlogged users exceeds the unstable equilibrium point, can only be applied in the case of the uncontrolled random access system. According to the simulation results shown in Fig. 11 and Fig. 12, it can be seen that the number of users in a waiting state, N_W, reflects the state of the system more accurately since the variation of the number of backlogged users fluctuates sharply. Therefore, we can define a threshold for N_W, denoted as $\bar{N}_W$. Once N_W exceeds the defined threshold $\bar{N}_W$

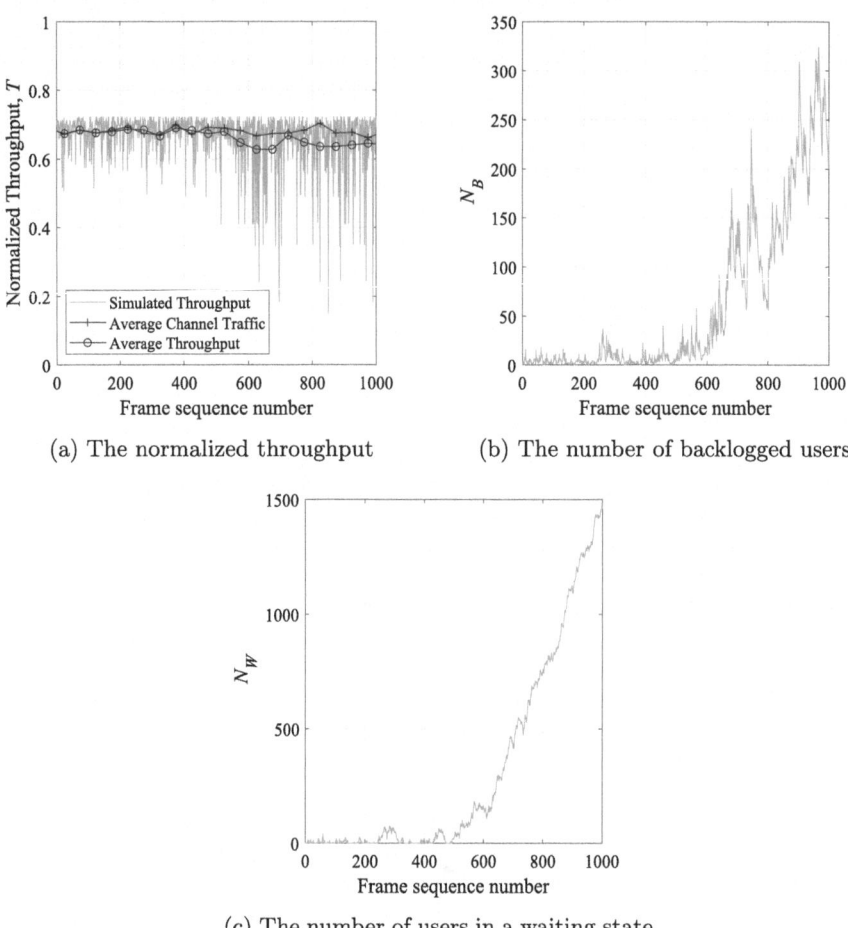

(a) The normalized throughput   (b) The number of backlogged users

(c) The number of users in a waiting state

Fig. 12. The variation trends of the performance metrics as the system works for IRSA with congestion control (unstable state), $\lambda = 68$.

as the system works, it signifies that the system is beginning to be in an unstable state. Based on this, Fig. 13 depicts the average FET for various random access schemes with and without congestion control (congestion control is denoted as "CC" in Fig. 13), where $n = 100$, $\bar{N}_W = 200$, and the degree distribution of IRSA is set to $\Lambda(x) = 0.5x^2 + 0.28x^3 + 0.22x^8$. As can be seen from the figure, to achieve the target of an average FET of 5000 frames in the uncontrolled random access system, the maximum allowable average number of accessing users is $\lambda = 45, 51$, and 55 for CRDSA with $l = 2$, CRDSA with $l = 3$, and IRSA, respectively. While for random access systems with congestion control, the maximum allowable average number of accessing users is increased to $\lambda = 51, 63$, and 66 for CRDSA with $l = 2$, CRDSA with $l = 3$, and IRSA, resulting in performance improvements of 13.3%, 23.5%, and 20%, respectively. It can be seen that the

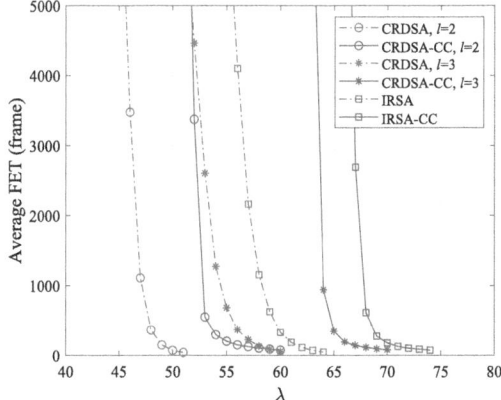

Fig. 13. Average FET for various random access schemes with and without congestion control.

congestion control scheme can notably enhance the stability of random access systems, thereby improving their throughput performance.

6   Conclusions

Quantifying the stability of random access with congestion control is crucial, especially when a large number of users transmit packets independently, for calculating the maximum allowable number of accessing users and measuring the performance improvement of the congestion control scheme. In this paper, we analyzed the stability of various uncontrolled random access systems and discussed their limitations. Based on this, we considered a congestion control scheme to enhance stability and presented the corresponding graphical analytical model. Finally, we qualitatively explored the behavioral variations of the system with congestion control as it works and quantified its stability through the graphical model.

References

1. Roberts, L.G.: ALOHA packet system with and without slots and capture. ACM SIGCOMM Comput. Commun. Rev. **5**(2), 28–42 (1975)
2. Choudhury, G., Rappaport, S.: Diversity ALOHA - A random access scheme for satellite communications. IEEE Trans. Commun. **31**(3), 450–457 (1983)
3. Casini, E., De Gaudenzi, R., Del Rio Herrero, O.: Contention resolution diversity slotted ALOHA (CRDSA): an enhanced random access scheme for satellite access packet networks. IEEE Trans. Wireless Commun. **6**(4), 1408–1419 (2007)
4. Liva, G.: Graph-based analysis and optimization of contention resolution diversity slotted ALOHA. IEEE Trans. Commun. **59**(2), 477–487 (2011)
5. Paolini, E., Liva, G., Chiani, M.: Coded slotted ALOHA: a graph-based method for uncoordinated multiple access. IEEE Trans. Inf. Theory **61**(12), 6815–6832 (2015)

6. Narayanan, K.R., Pfister, H.D.: Iterative collision resolution for slotted ALOHA: an optimal uncoordinated transmission policy. In: 2012 7th International Symposium on Turbo Codes and Iterative Information Processing (ISTC), pp. 136–139 (2012)

7. Ahmed, A., Al-Dweik, A., Iraqi, Y., Mukhtar, H., Naeem, M., Hossain, E.: Hybrid automatic repeat request (HARQ) in wireless communications systems and standards: a contemporary survey. IEEE Commun. Surv. Tutorials **23**(4), 2711–2752 (2021)

8. Carleial, A., Hellman, M.: Bistable behavior of ALOHA-type systems. IEEE Trans. Commun. **23**(4), 401–410 (1975)

9. Kleinrock, L., Lam, S.: Packet switching in a multiaccess broadcast channel: performance evaluation. IEEE Trans. Commun. **23**(4), 410–423 (1975)

10. Kissling, C.: On the stability of contention resolution diversity slotted ALOHA (CRDSA). In: 2011 IEEE Global Telecommunications Conference - GLOBECOM 2011, pp. 1–6 (2011)

11. Meloni, A., Murroni, M.: CRDSA, CRDSA++ and IRSA: stability and performance evaluation. In: 2012 6th Advanced Satellite Multimedia Systems Conference (ASMS) and 12th Signal Processing for Space Communications Workshop (SPSC), pp. 220–225 (2012)

12. Meloni, A., Murroni, M.: On the stability of asynchronous random access schemes. In: 2013 9th International Wireless Communications and Mobile Computing Conference (IWCMC), pp. 843–848 (2013)

13. Lam, S., Kleinrock, L.: Packet switching in a multiaccess broadcast channel: dynamic control procedures. IEEE Trans. Commun. **23**(9), 891–904 (1975)

14. Meloni, A., Murroni, M.: Random access in DVB-RCS2: design and dynamic control for congestion avoidance. IEEE Trans. Broadcast. **60**(1), 16–28 (2014)

Outage Performance Analysis of RIS Assisted RSMA Network with On-Off Control

Haiyan Huang[1][(✉)][ID], Dongjie Jiang[1][ID], Nina Zhang[2][ID], Linlin Liang[3][ID], and Hongyan Zhang[1][ID]

[1] Lanzhou Jiaotong University, Lanzhou, Gansu 730070, China
huanghaiyan@mail.lzjtu.cn
[2] Shaanxi General Staff of PAP, Xi'an 710054, Shaanxi, China
[3] Xidian University, Xi'an 710071, Shaanxi, China

Abstract. In order to make future wireless communication networks efficient in spectrum and energy, reconfigurable intelligent surface (RIS) has become a practical technology that can significantly improve the coverage and performance of wireless networks. In this paper, we discuss the application of RIS technology in Rate-Splitting Multiple Access (RSMA), where the base station (BS) sends superimposed signals to multiusers through RIS. To delve deeper into investigating the efficacy of RIS-aided RSMA networks, we adopt a On-Off control scheme and consider the system performance under imperfect successive interference cancellation (ipSIC) and perfect successive interference cancellation (pSIC) respectively. On this basis, we use ipSIC/pSIC to derive the outage probability expression of the kth user. Based on the outcome analysis, the diversity order of users exhibits a correlation with the quantity of reflective elements in the RIS and channel prioritization under pSIC conditions. In addition, increasing the quantity of RIS reflective units can make up for the decrease of system outage performance caused by residual interference, and further improve the outage performance of the system.

Keywords: Reconfigurable Intelligent Surface · Rate-Splitting Multiple Access · Imperfect SIC · On-Off Control

1 Introduction

As the field of wireless communication technology advances at a brisk pace, the urgency to amplify spectrum efficiency and augment network capacity has mounted considerably. [1]. To address this challenge, reconfigurable intelligent surfaces (RIS), a groundbreaking technology, have garnered significant attention due to their ability to intelligently manipulate the wireless propagation environment [2]. RIS, a two-dimensional structure comprised of numerous programmable

Supported by organization Lanzhou jiaotong University.

reflection units, possesses the ability to intelligently regulate the phase, amplitude, and polarization properties of wireless signals. This enables real-time adjustment of the RIS reflection mode, reducing signal attenuation and interference, thereby enhancing the spectrum efficiency and network capacity of the system. Furthermore, as a generalized multiple access (MA) technique, Rate-Splitting Multiple Access (RSMA) technology stands out in its proficiency in enhancing spectrum efficiency and user fairness, making it a promising contender for 6G wireless communication [3]. By splitting user messages and employing non-orthogonal transmission of both common messages and user-specific private messages [4], RSMA adeptly integrates two contrasting approaches to interference mitigation: comprehensively decoding disruptive signals and managing them as background noise, thereby bridging the gap between these seemingly opposed strategies.

In recent years, researchers have explored the combination of RIS assisted communication system and RSMA protocol. The author of [5] analyzed the outage probability of RIS assisted downlink NOMA systems. Taking into account the user's usage, the authors in [6] examined the discrete phase shift RIS reflection of RIS-assisted OMA or NOMA. When prioritizing users, a jointly optimization approach is employed to refine both the beamforming vector and the phase shift matrix, aiming to minimize the transmission power requirements, as demonstrated in [7]. Considering ipSIC in NOMA communication [8], the author analyzes the outage performance of the system. The authors of [9] designed a low-complexity joint optimization scheme for RIS assisted uplink RSMA systems, which significantly improves the maximum transmission delay. In [10], the RSMA system of RIS-aided cell-boundary and adjacent users is scrutinized, in which the outage performance expression is derived by considering the phase-shift-based switching technology. Yang [11] et al. considered the energy efficiency maximization of RIS-assisted RSMA communication by jointly optimizing RIS phase shift and BS beamforming.

It is noteworthy that while an outage analysis has been conducted for RIS-assisted NOMA systems in Reference [5], a comparable analysis for RSMA systems remains unresolved. In addition, the discrete phase shift of RIS-assisted NOMA and OMA systems is considered in [6], and the imperfect successive interference cancellation in NOMA systems is studied in [8]. The analysis of RSMA systems remains to be carried out. In [10] considers the RIS-integrated RSMA setup, but neglects to present the mathematical formalism for discrete phase modulation.

Drawing upon the aforementioned analysis, this paper delves into the RIS-assisted RSMA network. Considering the discrete phase modulation, user utilization rate and user ordering of RIS, the outage probability expression of the network is derived. The influence of imperfect continuous interference cancellation and discrete phase shift of RIS on the outage performance of the communication system is investigated.

2   System Model

According to the illustration in Fig. 1, the RIS-assisted RSMA communication model consists of three parts, including a base station (BS), RIS, and K end users. It is assumed that each of the BS and users is endowed with a single antenna, where BS sends signals to K end users through the use of RIS. RIS is furnished with N reflection units, which are controllable through software focused on communication functionality. The complex channel coefficients for teh BS-RIS link, as well as the RIS-users link, are expressed by h_i and g_{ik} respectively. Both h_i and g_{ik} follow the complex Gaussian distribution with the mean set to zero and the variance specified as σ^2 and are independent of each other. Given that the BS-users link is obstructed by tall buildings, resulting in a lack of direct interconnection, the communication channel between any two nodes within this environment is characterized by the Rayleigh fading model. The background noise of these wireless links is additive white Gaussian noise, with statistical properties including a mean of zero and a variance of N_0.

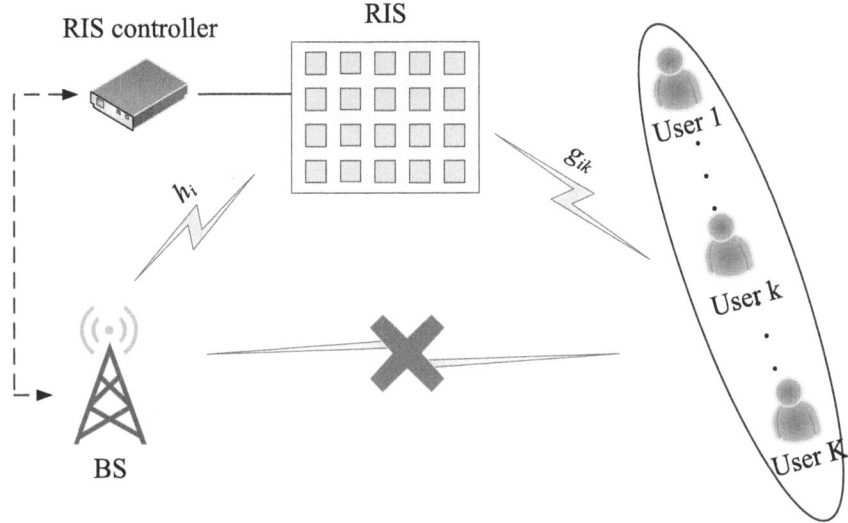

Fig. 1. RIS-assisted downlink RSMA network model.

The communication system assumes that the channel state information, the geographic coordinates of the BS, and the seamless feedback to the RIS can be implemented accurately. In order to facilitate the analysis, the effective cascade channel gain of the BS-RIS-user link is sorted: $\left|g_{i1}^H \Phi h_i\right|^2 \leq \cdots \leq \left|g_{ik}^H \Phi h_i\right|^2 \leq \cdots \leq \left|g_{ik}^H \Phi h_i\right|^2$, where $\Phi = diag\left(\beta e^{-j\theta_1}, ..., \beta e^{-j\theta_i}, ..., \beta e^{-j\theta_K}\right)$ represents the phase shift matrix of RIS, and $\beta \in [0,1]$ and $\theta_i \in [0, 2\pi)$ represent the fixed reflection amplitude and phase shift parameter of the k-th reflection unit of RIS, respectively. Without loss of generality, it is assumed that when the RIS is not within the frequency band, that is, the incident frequency does not fall within the designed unit's response band, the RIS is basically total reflection.

In the communication process, BS uses the RSMA protocol, and the superimposed signal sent to the end user includes a public message x_c and K mutually orthogonal private information x_k, $\{k \in 1, 2, \ldots, K\}$ represents K different users. As a result, the signal that receives at the k-th user after RIS reflection is:

$$y_k = \left(g_{ik}^H \Phi h_i\right) \left(\sqrt{\alpha_c P_B} x_c + \sum_{i=1}^{K} \sqrt{\alpha_i P_B} x_i\right) + w_k \tag{1}$$

where P_B is the transmission power of the BS, α_c and α_i are the rate splitting factors of the base station sending public information and private information respectively. In order to meet the user fairness, the rate splitting factors of the public information and the kth user satisfy the relationship $\alpha_c + \sum_{i=1}^{K} \alpha_i = 1$, and $\alpha_c \geq \alpha_1 \geq \cdots \geq \alpha_k \geq \cdots \geq \alpha_K$. x_c, x_i represent the public information sent and the private information of K users respectively, and $E\left\{x_c^2\right\} = E\left\{x_i^2\right\} = 1$. w_k are additive Gaussian white noise with mean value of 0 and variance N_0.

After receiving the superimposed signal sent by BS, user U_k first decodes the public message x_c, and then decodes his own private message x_k after deleting the public message x_c by SIC. When decoding x_c, all private messages will cause interference, and when x_k is decoded, the private information of other users will cause interference. Therefore, the signal to interference plus noise ratio (SINR) of U_k decoding public message and private messages can be expressed:

$$\Gamma_k^c = \frac{\alpha_c P_B \left|g_{ik}^H \Phi h_i\right|^2}{\sum_{i=1}^{K} \alpha_i P_B \left|g_{ik}^H \Phi h_i\right|^2 + N_0} \tag{2}$$

$$\Gamma_k^p = \frac{\alpha_k P_B \left|g_{ik}^H \Phi h_i\right|^2}{\sum_{\substack{i=1 \\ i \neq k}}^{K} \alpha_i P_B \left|g_{ik}^H \Phi h_i\right|^2 + \varpi P_B |h_{iru}|^2 + N_0} \tag{3}$$

where $\varpi \in [0, 1]$ is the imperfect successive interference cancellation coefficient, $\varpi = 0$ denotes ipSIC and $\varpi = 1$ denotes pSIC.

For the convenience of analysis, Assuming the residual interference arising from the implementation of ipSIC follows a Rayleigh fading model, and the corresponding complex channel parameter is represented by h_{iru}, which obeys the complex Gaussian distribution with mean 0 and variance σ_{iru}^2. In addition, in order to facilitate the next calculation, the probability density function(PDF) of $|h_{iru}|^2$ is:

$$f_{|h_{iru}|^2}(y) = \frac{1}{\sigma_{iru}^2} e^{\left(-\frac{y}{\sigma_{iru}^2}\right)} \tag{4}$$

3   On-Off Control Scheme

Considering that in the actual communication scenario, constantly changing the reflection elements of RIS to adjust and control the amplitude and phase of the signal is conducive to improving the performance of the network. However, this alternative requires precise design specifications, as well as an expensive hardware configuration, which will lead to the cost of RIS becoming higher. For the sake of convenient analysis and implementation, a low-cost implementation is to apply switch control to the RIS-RSMA network to realize the amplitude and phase shift level of the RIS-assisted RSMA network [12], that is, each diagonal element in the phase shift matrix Φ is either 0 (off) or 1 (on). Meanwhile, increasing the number of reflection units remains a scalable and cost-effective solution.

RIS has N reflection units. Suppose $N = LQ$, where L and Q are both integers. Let $\Psi = \frac{1}{\sqrt{Q}} I_L \otimes 1_Q$, where I_L is the unit matrix of $L \times L$, 1_Q is the 1-vector of $Q \times 1$, Ψ_l denotes the l column of Ψ, and for $l \neq p$, $\Psi_l^H \Psi_p = 0$, $\Psi_l^H \Psi_l = 1$. Using On-Off control, a random column of Ψ_l can be selected to maximize the SINR of user U_k decoding. (2) and (3) can be rewritten as:

$$\tilde{\gamma}_k^c = \max_{\Psi_l} \frac{\alpha_c P_B \left| \Psi_l^H D_k h_i \right|^2}{\sum\limits_{i=1}^{K} \alpha_i P_B \left| \Psi_l^H D_k h_i \right|^2 + N_0} \tag{5}$$

$$\tilde{\gamma}_k^p = \max_{\Psi_l} \frac{\alpha_k P_B \left| \Psi_l^H D_k h_i \right|^2}{\sum\limits_{\substack{i=1 \\ i \neq k}}^{K} \alpha_i P_B \left| \Psi_l^H D_k h_i \right|^2 + \varpi P_B |h_{iru}|^2 + N_0} \tag{6}$$

where D_k is a diagonal matrix whose diagonal elements are obtained by g_{ik}.

Theorem 1. *In order to simplify the analysis of the outage performance of the system, the cascade channel gain of the RIS aided link is expressed as $|Z|^2 = \left| \Psi_l^H D_k h_i \right|^2$ by using the On-Off control scheme. At this point, the cumulative distribution function(CDF) of $|Z|^2$ can be written as:*

$$F_{|Z|^2}(z) = \frac{K!}{(K-k)!(k-1)} \\ \times \sum_{b=0}^{K-k} \binom{K-k}{b} \frac{(-1)^b}{k+b} \left[1 - \frac{2}{\Gamma(Q)} \left(\frac{\sqrt{z}}{\sigma^2} \right)^Q K_Q \left(\frac{2\sqrt{z}}{\sigma^2} \right) \right]^{k+b} \tag{7}$$

Proof. According to [13], the PDF of the Rayleigh cascade channel $|Z|^2$ from BS to RIS to the user is:

$$f_{|Z|^2}(z) = \frac{2\sqrt{z}^{Q-1}}{\Gamma(Q) \sigma^{2(Q+1)}} \cdot K_{Q-1} \left(\frac{2\sqrt{z}}{\sigma^2} \right) \tag{8}$$

where $\Gamma(\cdot)$ denotes the Gamma function and $K_v(\cdot)$ denotes the second modified Bessel function of order v.

Based on the above assumptions, the effective cascade channel gain of the RIS auxiliary link using the switching control scheme is sorted to the user: $\left| \Psi_p^H D_1 g_{i1} \right|^2 \leq \cdots \leq \left| \Psi_p^H D_k g_{ik} \right|^2 \leq \cdots \leq \left| \Psi_p^H D_K g_{iK} \right|^2$. The CDF of the sorted effective cascade channel gain $F_{|Z|^2}(z)$ has a specific correlation with unordered channel gain [7,14]:

$$F_{|Z|^2}(z) = \frac{K!}{(K-k)!\,(k-1)} \sum_{b=0}^{K-k} \binom{K-k}{b} \times \frac{(-1)^b}{k+b} \left[\widehat{F}_{|Z|^2}(z)\right]^{k+b} \tag{9}$$

where $F_{|Z|^2}(z)$ is the cumulative distribution function of the unsorted cascaded channel gain.

From (7), the PDF of the unsorted concatenated channel is:

$$\widehat{f}_{|Z|^2}(z) = \frac{2\sqrt{z}^{Q-1}}{\Gamma(Q)\,\sigma^{2(Q+1)}} \cdot K_{Q-1}\left(\frac{2\sqrt{z}}{\sigma^2}\right) \tag{10}$$

By integrating the (9), the CDF of the unsorted cascaded channel is obtained:

$$\widehat{F}_{|Z|^2}(z) = \frac{2}{\Gamma(Q)\,\sigma^{2(Q+1)}} \int_0^z x^{\frac{Q-1}{2}} \cdot K_{Q-1}\left(\frac{2\sqrt{x}}{\sigma^2}\right) dx \tag{11}$$

Let $x = zy$, the Gauss-Laguerre quadrature formula is used for (10):

$$\widehat{F}_{|Z|^2}(z) = 1 - \frac{2}{\Gamma(Q)} \left(\frac{\sqrt{z}}{\sigma^2}\right)^Q K_Q\left(\frac{2\sqrt{z}}{\sigma^2}\right) \tag{12}$$

Finally, (11) is substituted into (8), and the CDF of the effective cascade channel after the RIS auxiliary link is sorted is obtained, and the proof is completed.

4   Outage Probability

In wireless communication, outage probability is an important performance metric to measure the reliability of communication links under certain conditions. The outage performance refers to the probability that the communication link is interrupted within a given period of time, which is contingent upon the mean SNR of the communication link, along with the specific model that characterizes its channel fading distribution

According to the principle of RSMA, there are two cases in the RIS-assisted RSMA communication network that may cause communication interruption: (1) U_k cannot successfully decode the public information x_c after BS sends the superimposed signal; (2) U_k successfully decodes public information x_c, but cannot successfully decode its own private information x_k. Therefore, the outage probability of user U_k is defined as:

$$\begin{aligned} OP &= \Pr\left(\widetilde{\Gamma}_k^c < \Gamma_{th_c}\right) + \Pr\left(\widetilde{\Gamma}_k^c > \Gamma_{th_c}, \widetilde{\Gamma}_k^p < \Gamma_{th_p}\right) \\ &= 1 - \Pr\left(\widetilde{\Gamma}_k^c > \Gamma_{th_c}, \widetilde{\Gamma}_k^p > \Gamma_{th_p}\right) \end{aligned} \tag{13}$$

where $\Gamma_{thc} = 2^{R_c} - 1$ and $\Gamma_{thp} = 2^{R_p} - 1$ are the threshold SINRs for the transmission of public and private messages, respectively, R_c and R_p are the target data rates at which they decode the messages, respectively. $\Pr(\cdot, \cdot)$ denotes the joint probability. By the concept of joint probability in [15], the outage probability of (12) can be further simplified as :

$$OP = F_{\tilde{\Gamma}_k^c}\left(\Gamma_{th_c}\right) + F_{\tilde{\Gamma}_k^p}\left(\Gamma_{th_p}\right) - F_{\tilde{\Gamma}_k^c, \tilde{\Gamma}_k^p}\left(\Gamma_{th_c}, \Gamma_{th_p}\right) \tag{14}$$

where $F_X(\cdot)$ is the cumulative distribution function of the variable X, and $F_{X,Y}(\cdot, \cdot)$ is the joint CDF of X and Y.

In the realm of wireless communication, attaining perfect SIC is often considered an idealized scenario. However, in practical communication settings, achieving such perfection becomes challenging due to various factors, including hardware limitations, channel estimation errors, and signal processing constraints. In the subsequent analysis, we provide outage probability expressions for both perfect SIC and imperfect SIC scenarios. Furthermore, in the following chapter, these two cases will be simulated and verified accordingly.

4.1 Imperfect SIC

Using the On-Off control scheme, and considering the existence of imperfect SIC to generate residual interference, (13) can be rewritten as:

$$OP = \prod_{l=1}^{L} F_{|Z|^2}\left(\tau_c\right) + \prod_{l=1}^{L} F_{|Z|^2}\left(\left(\varpi P_B |h_{iru}|^2 + N_0\right)\tau_p\right)$$
$$- \prod_{l=1}^{L} F_{|Z|^2}\left(\min\left\{\tau_c, \left(\varpi P_B |h_{iru}|^2 + N_0\right)\tau_p\right\}\right) \tag{15}$$

where $\tau_c = \dfrac{\Gamma_{th_c} N_0}{\left(\alpha_c - \sum\limits_{i=1}^{K} \alpha_i \Gamma_{th_c}\right) P_B}$, $\tau_p = \dfrac{\Gamma_{th_p}}{\left(\alpha_k - \Gamma_{th_p} \sum\limits_{\substack{i=1 \\ i \neq k}}^{K} \alpha_i\right) P_B}$

In order to facilitate analysis and implementation, assuming that the marginal and joint statistics of $\tilde{\Gamma}_k^c$ and $\tilde{\Gamma}_k^c$ are the same for all l [10], the outage probability of (14) can be further written as:

$$OP_{ipSIC} = \left[F_{|Z|^2}\left(\tau_c\right)\right]^L + \left[F_{|Z|^2}\left(\left(\varpi P_B |h_{iru}|^2 + N_0\right)\tau_p\right)\right]^L$$
$$- \left[F_{|Z|^2}\left(\min\left\{\tau_c, \left(\varpi P_B |h_{iru}|^2 + N_0\right)\tau_p\right\}\right)\right]^L \tag{16}$$

where,

$$F_{|Z|^2}\left(\tau_c\right) = \Pr\left(\frac{\alpha_c P_B |Z|^2}{\sum\limits_{i=1}^{K} \alpha_i P_B Z + N_0} \leq \Gamma_{th_c}\right) = \Pr\left(|Z|^2 \leq \tau_c\right)$$
$$= \frac{K!}{(K-k)!(k-1)} \sum_{b=0}^{K-k} \binom{K-k}{b} \times \frac{(-1)^b}{k+b}\left[1 - \frac{2}{\Gamma(Q)}\left(\frac{\sqrt{\tau_c}}{\sigma^2}\right)^Q K_Q\left(\frac{2\sqrt{\tau_c}}{\sigma^2}\right)\right]^{k+b} \tag{17}$$

Similarly,

$$
\begin{aligned}
&F_{|Z|^2}\left(\left(\varpi P_B|h_{iru}|^2 + N_0\right)\tau_p\right) \\
&= \int_0^\infty f_{|h_{iru}|^2}(y)F_{|Z|^2}\left((\varpi P_B y + N_0)\tau_p\right)dy \\
&= \int_0^\infty \frac{1}{2\sigma_{iru}^2}e^{\left(-\frac{y}{2\sigma_{iru}^2}\right)}\frac{K!}{(K-k)!(k-1)}\sum_{b=0}^{K-k}\binom{K-k}{b} \\
&\times \frac{(-1)^b}{k+b}\left[1 - \frac{2}{\Gamma(Q)}\left(\frac{\sqrt{(\varpi P_B y + N_0)\tau_p}}{\sigma^2}\right)^Q K_Q\left(\frac{2\sqrt{(\varpi P_B y + N_0)\tau_p}}{\sigma^2}\right)\right]^{k+b}dy \\
&\approx \frac{K!}{(K-k)!(k-1)}\sum_{a=1}^{A}\sum_{b=0}^{K-k}\binom{K-k}{b}\times\frac{(-1)^b W_a}{k+b} \\
&\times \left[1 - \frac{2}{\Gamma(Q)}\left(\frac{\sqrt{(2\varpi P_B \sigma_{iru}^2 \xi_a + N_0)\tau_p}}{\sigma^2}\right)^Q K_Q\left(\frac{2\sqrt{(2\varpi P_B \sigma_{iru}^2 \xi_a + N_0)\tau_p}}{\sigma^2}\right)\right]^{k+b}
\end{aligned}
\tag{18}
$$

where $W_a = \frac{(A!)^2 \xi_a}{[L_{A+1}(\xi_a)]^2}$ is the weight of Gauss-Laguerre quadrature formula, ξ_a is the zero point of Laguerre polynomial $L_A(\xi_a)$, $a = 1,2,3,\ldots A$, A is the complexity trade-off accuracy, and when $A \to \infty$, the above formula takes the equal sign.

In summary, by substituting (16), (17) into (15), formulations for the outage probability in the case of ipSIC is:

$$
OP_{ipSIC} = \begin{cases} [F_Z(\tau_c)]^L, & \left(\varpi P_B|h_{iru}|^2 + N_0\right)\tau_p < \tau_c \\ \left[F_Z\left(\left(\varpi P_B|h_{iru}|^2 + N_0\right)\tau_p\right)\right]^L, & \left(\varpi P_B|h_{iru}|^2 + N_0\right)\tau_p > \tau_c \end{cases}
\tag{19}
$$

4.2 Perfect SIC

Available with Sect. 4.1, ideally, the outage probability expression of the system to achieve perfect SIC is:

$$
\begin{aligned}
OP_{pSIC} &= [F_Z(\tau_c)]^L + [F_Z(\widehat{\tau}_p)]^L - [F_Z(\min\{\tau_c, \widehat{\tau}_p\})]^L \\
&= \begin{cases} [F_Z(\tau_c)]^L, & \widehat{\tau}_p < \tau_c \\ [F_Z(\widehat{\tau}_p)]^L, & \widehat{\tau}_p > \tau_c \end{cases}
\end{aligned}
\tag{20}
$$

where $\widehat{\tau}_p = N_0 \tau_p$,

$$
\begin{aligned}
F_Z(\widehat{\tau}_p) &= \Pr\left(\frac{\alpha_k P_B|Z|^2}{\sum_{\substack{i=1 \\ i\neq k}}^{K}\alpha_i P_B|Z|^2 + \varpi P_B|h_{iru}|^2 + N_0} \leq \Gamma_{th_p}\right) = \Pr\left(|Z|^2 \leq \widehat{\tau}_p\right) \\
&= \frac{K!}{(K-k)!(k-1)}\sum_{b=0}^{K-k}\binom{K-k}{b}\times\frac{(-1)^b}{k+b}\left[1 - \frac{2}{\Gamma(Q)}\left(\frac{\sqrt{\widehat{\tau}_p}}{\sigma^2}\right)^Q K_Q\left(\frac{2\sqrt{\widehat{\tau}_p}}{\sigma^2}\right)\right]^{k+b}
\end{aligned}
\tag{21}
$$

5   Performance Analysis

In this section, we delve deeper into the theoretical framework by conducting specific simulation experiments. These experiments aim to empirically validate the theoretical expressions and further examine the intricate impacts of two key factors: the number of reflection elements and the imperfect implementation of successive interference cancellation on the outage performance of the system. Set the complexity trade-off accuracy $A = 5$, BS transmission power $P_B = 10\,dB$.

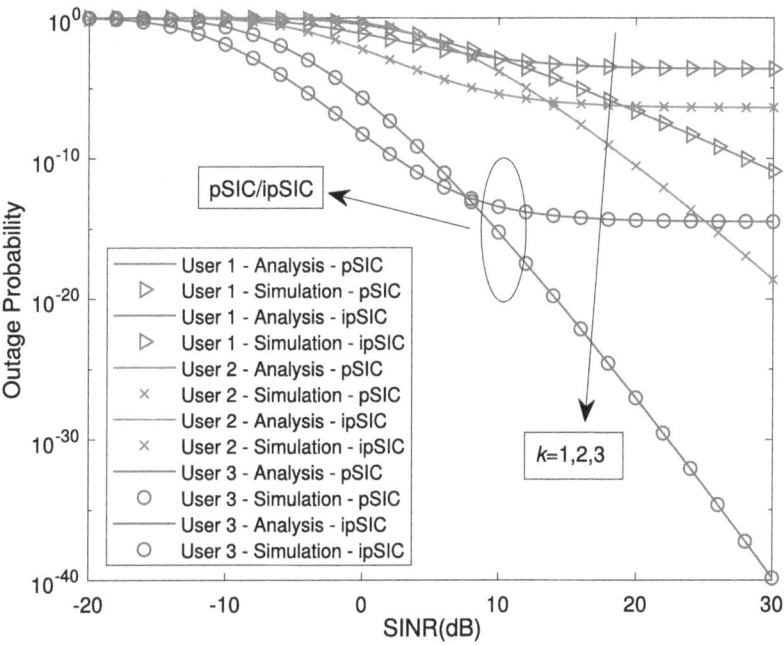

Fig. 2. Outage probability of various users vs the transmit SINR.

Figure 2 plot the relationship between the outage probability of users and the SINR in the instance of ipSIC and pSIC. Set $N = 5$, $K = 3$, $Q = 1$, the normalized power of residual interference $E\left\{|h_{iru}|^2\right\} = -10\,dB$, the rate splitting factor of public information and private information of each user are set to $\alpha_c = 0.4$, $\alpha_1 = 0.3$, $\alpha_2 = 0.2$, $\alpha_3 = 0.1$ respectively. The graph in Fig. 2 demonstrates that the outage probability simulation values of multi-user in two cases coincide with the theoretical analysis, which corroborates the precision of the theoretical expression. An increase in SINR corresponds to a decrease in the system's outage capability. Secondly, in the case of pSIC, the outage probability curve decreases more than that of ipSIC, indicating that the RIS-RSMA network with pSIC has better outage performance.

The relationship between the outage probability of the system and SINR is depicted in Fig. 3 for users located far from the BS, considering different numbers of elements in the RIS under ipSIC and pSIC scenarios. In the simulation, set $K = 3$, $k = 1$, $Q = 1$, $\alpha_c = 0.4$, $R_1 = 0.5$, $E\left\{|h_{iru}|^2\right\} = -10\,dB$. Take $N = 5, 10, 15$ respectively. Similarly, it can be observed from Fig. 3 that the simulation value of the outage performance of the system coincides perfectly with the theoretical value, and decreases with the increase of SINR. The results show that when RIS reflection units N is increased, the outage capacity of the system can be improved in both cases of ipSIC and pSIC.

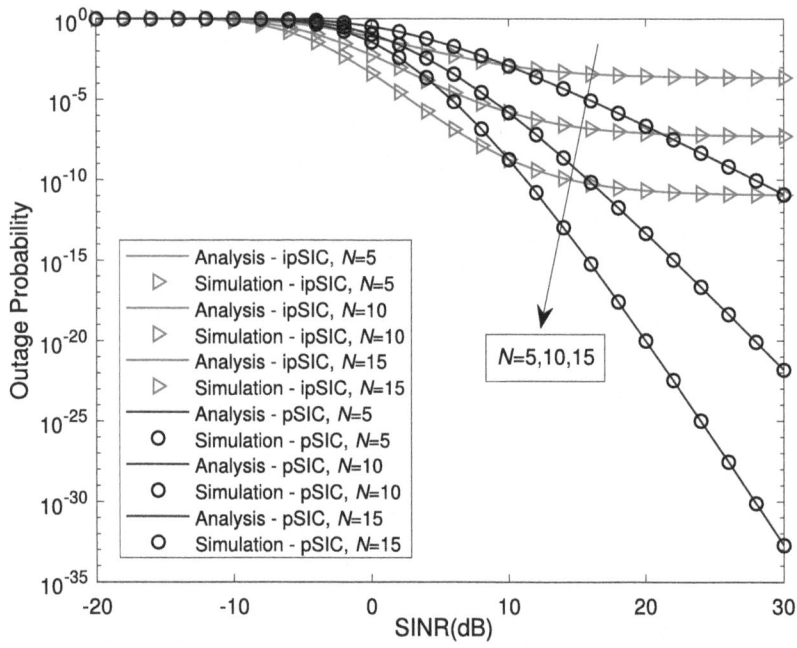

Fig. 3. Outage probability of various N vs the transmit SINR.

Figure 4 illustrates the connection between the outage probability of each user and the SINR of multiple users in the case of ipSIC and changing the residual interference size. In the simulation, we configure the parameters as follows: $N = 5$, $K = 3$, $Q = 1$, $\alpha_c = 0.4$. The rate splitting factor of three users is $\alpha_1 = 0.3$, $\alpha_2 = 0.2$, $\alpha_3 = 0.1$. The residual interference normalized power $E\left\{|h_{iru}|^2\right\} = -10, -8, -6\,dB$ is taken respectively.

As can be seen from Fig. 4, when considering the user sorting, the user ($k = 3$) closer to the BS has better outage performance than the user ($k = 1, 2$) farther away from the BS, which is owing to the fact that near users have a higher diversity order. Secondly, taking residual interference into account, as the SINR value of the RIS-RSMA network with ipSIC is large, the outage performance of the system tends to be constant, that is, the slope of the outage probability curve tends to be 0. At this time, the diversity order of the system is 0, as the residual interference power intensifies, the system's outage probability diminishes correspondingly. Consequently, it holds paramount importance to take into account the effect of ipSIC on the practical performance metrics of RIS-NOMA network deployments.

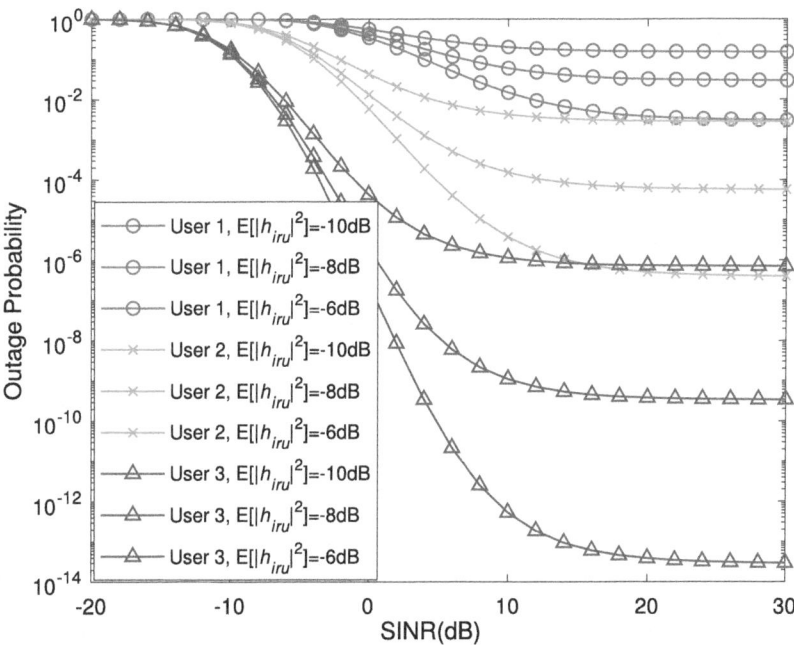

Fig. 4. Outage probability of various residual interference power vs the transmit SINR.

6   Conclusion

In many studies, the analysis of outage performance in the presence of residual interference in RIS-assisted RSMA communication systems is still insufficient, and most studies do not consider the effective cascaded channel gain for user ordering and the discrete phase shift parameter of RIS. In this paper, the existence of residual interference in the communication system is discussed in depth, and the communication scenario of RIS using On-Off control scheme is considered. Through performance analysis, it is indicated that the quantity of reflection units and residual interference of RIS make a marked difference to the overall communication performance. Although the residual interference has a certain impact on the system's performance, by increasing the number of RIS reflection elements, the system can obtain higher diversity gain, so as to effectively offset the influence of residual interference and further improve the outage probability of the system. In addition, another promising research direction in the future is to design a combined beamforming and power allocation strategy, which will significantly improve the performance of RIS-RSMA.

Funding. This work was supported by the Tianyou Youth Talent Lift Program of Lanzhou Jiaotong University; the National Natural Science Foundation of China under grant 61901201, 62001359; the Key Research and Development Project of Lanzhou Jiaotong University (ZDYF2304).

References

1. Liu, Y., et al.: Evolution of NOMA toward next generation multiple access (NGMA) for 6G. Journal **4**(40), 1037–1071 (2022)
2. Li, Z., Yuan, W., Li, B., Wu, J., You, C., Meng, F.: Reconfigurable-intelligent-surface-aided OTFS: transmission scheme and channel estimation. Journal **10**(22), 19518–19532 (2023)
3. Katwe, M., Singh, K., Clerckx, B., Li, C.-P.: Rate-splitting multiple access and dynamic user clustering for sum-rate maximization in multiple RISs-aided uplink mmWave system. Journal **70**(11), 7365–7383 (2022)
4. Mao, Y., Dizdar, O., Clerckx, B., Schober, R., Popovski, P., Poor, H.V.: Rate-splitting multiple access: fundamentals, survey, and future research trends. Journal **24**(4), 2073–2126 (2022)
5. Sadia, H., Abbas, Z.H., Hassan, A.K., Abbas,G.: Outage probability analysis of reconfigurable intelligent surface (RIS)-Enabled NOMA Network. In: 10th International Conference on Wireless Networks and Mobile Communications (WINCOM), pp. 1–6. Istanbul, Turkiye (2023)
6. Zheng, B., Wu, Q., Zhang, R.: Intelligent reflecting surface-assisted multiple access with user pairing: NOMA or OMA? Journal **24**(4), 753–757 (2020)
7. Fu, M., Zhou, Y., Shi, Y.: Intelligent reflecting surface for downlink non-orthogonal multiple access networks. In: IEEE Globecom Workshops (GC Wkshps), pp. 1–6. Waikoloa, HI, USA (2019)
8. Gu, J., Wang, M., Duan, W. Zhang, L., Zhang, H.: Imperfect SIC for NOMA communications under Nakagami-m fading: comparison of RIS and Relay. In: 20th International Conference on the Design of Reliable Communication Networks (DRCN), pp. 17–23. Montreal, QC, Canada (2024)
9. Hu, J., Liu, G., Ma, Z., Xiao, M., Fan, P.: Low-complexity resource allocation for uplink RSMA in future 6G wireless networks. Journal **13**(2), 565–569 (2024)
10. Bansal, A., Singh, K., Clerckx, B., Li, C.-P., Alouini, M.-S.: Rate-splitting multiple access for intelligent reflecting surface aided multi-user communications. Journal **70**(9), 9217–9229 (2021)
11. Yang, Z., Shi, J., Li, Z., Chen, M., Xu, W., Shikh-Bahaei, M.: Energy efficient rate splitting multiple access (RSMA) with reconfigurable intelligent surface. In: IEEE International Conference on Communications Workshops (ICC Workshops), pp. 1–6. Dublin, Ireland (2020)
12. Ding, Z., Vincent Poor, H.: A simple design of IRS-NOMA transmission. Journal **24**(5), 1119–1123 (2020)

13. Liu, H., Ding, H., Xiang, L., Yuan, J., Zheng, L.: Outage and BER performance analysis of cascade channel in relay networks. Journal **34**(8), 23–30 (2014)
14. Yue, X., Qin, Z., Liu, Y., Kang, S., Chen, Y.: A unified framework for non-orthogonal multiple access. Journal **66**(11), 5346–5359 (2018)
15. Papoulis, A., U. Pillai, S.: Probability, Random Variables, and Stochastic Processes. 4th edn. McGraw-Hill, New York, NY, USA (2002)

Author Index

© ICST Institute for Computer Sciences, Social Informatics and Telecommunications Engineering 2025
Published by Springer Nature Switzerland AG 2025. All Rights Reserved
H.-H. Chen and W. Meng (Eds.): WiSATS 2024, LNICST 605, pp. 375–377, 2025.
https://doi.org/10.1007/978-3-031-86196-3

The manufacturer's authorised representative in the EU is Springer
Nature Customer Service Centre GmbH, Europaplatz 3, 69115 Heidelberg,
Germany. If you have any concerns regarding our products, please
contact ProductSafety@springernature.com

Printed and bound by CPI Group (UK) Ltd, Croydon, CR0 4YY

29/04/2026

02099544-0012